CFA Institute®
CFA Program

AF886044

CORPORATE FINANCE AND EQUITY

CFA® Program Curriculum
2020 • LEVEL I • VOLUME 4

WILEY

ISBN 978-1-946442-79-6 (paper)
ISBN 978-1-950157-03-7 (ebk)

SKY839CEDFB-FA82-43EE-80F0-7C831DEA3174_091620

Please visit our website at
www.WileyGlobalFinance.com.

WILEY

FSC
www.fsc.org
MIX
Paper from responsible sources
FSC® C084269

CONTENTS

Equity Investments

How to Use the CFA Program Curriculum

Congratulations on your decision to enter the Chartered Financial Analyst (CFA®) Program. This exciting and rewarding program of study reflects your desire to become a serious investment professional. You are embarking on a program noted for its high ethical standards and the breadth of knowledge, skills, and abilities (competencies) it develops. Your commitment to the CFA Program should be educationally and professionally rewarding.

The credential you seek is respected around the world as a mark of accomplishment and dedication. Each level of the program represents a distinct achievement in professional development. Successful completion of the program is rewarded with membership in a prestigious global community of investment professionals. CFA charterholders are dedicated to life-long learning and maintaining currency with the ever-changing dynamics of a challenging profession. The CFA Program represents the first step toward a career-long commitment to professional education.

The CFA examination measures your mastery of the core knowledge, skills, and abilities required to succeed as an investment professional. These core competencies are the basis for the Candidate Body of Knowledge (CBOK™). The CBOK consists of four components:

- A broad outline that lists the major topic areas covered in the CFA Program (https://www.cfainstitute.org/programs/cfa/curriculum/cbok);
- Topic area weights that indicate the relative exam weightings of the top-level topic areas (https://www.cfainstitute.org/programs/cfa/curriculum/overview);
- Learning outcome statements (LOS) that advise candidates about the specific knowledge, skills, and abilities they should acquire from readings covering a topic area (LOS are provided in candidate study sessions and at the beginning of each reading); and
- The CFA Program curriculum that candidates receive upon examination registration.

Therefore, the key to your success on the CFA examinations is studying and understanding the CBOK. The following sections provide background on the CBOK, the organization of the curriculum, features of the curriculum, and tips for designing an effective personal study program.

BACKGROUND ON THE CBOK

The CFA Program is grounded in the practice of the investment profession. Beginning with the Global Body of Investment Knowledge (GBIK), CFA Institute performs a continuous practice analysis with investment professionals around the world to determine the competencies that are relevant to the profession. Regional expert panels and targeted surveys are conducted annually to verify and reinforce the continuous feedback about the GBIK. The practice analysis process ultimately defines the CBOK. The

CBOK reflects the competencies that are generally accepted and applied by investment professionals. These competencies are used in practice in a generalist context and are expected to be demonstrated by a recently qualified CFA charterholder.

The CFA Institute staff, in conjunction with the Education Advisory Committee and Curriculum Level Advisors, who consist of practicing CFA charterholders, designs the CFA Program curriculum in order to deliver the CBOK to candidates. The examinations, also written by CFA charterholders, are designed to allow you to demonstrate your mastery of the CBOK as set forth in the CFA Program curriculum. As you structure your personal study program, you should emphasize mastery of the CBOK and the practical application of that knowledge. For more information on the practice analysis, CBOK, and development of the CFA Program curriculum, please visit www.cfainstitute.org.

ORGANIZATION OF THE CURRICULUM

The Level I CFA Program curriculum is organized into 10 topic areas. Each topic area begins with a brief statement of the material and the depth of knowledge expected. It is then divided into one or more study sessions. These study sessions—19 sessions in the Level I curriculum—should form the basic structure of your reading and preparation. Each study session includes a statement of its structure and objective and is further divided into assigned readings. An outline illustrating the organization of these 19 study sessions can be found at the front of each volume of the curriculum.

The readings are commissioned by CFA Institute and written by content experts, including investment professionals and university professors. Each reading includes LOS and the core material to be studied, often a combination of text, exhibits, and in-text examples and questions. A reading typically ends with practice problems followed by solutions to these problems to help you understand and master the material. The LOS indicate what you should be able to accomplish after studying the material. The LOS, the core material, and the practice problems are dependent on each other, with the core material and the practice problems providing context for understanding the scope of the LOS and enabling you to apply a principle or concept in a variety of scenarios.

The entire readings, including the practice problems at the end of the readings, are the basis for all examination questions and are selected or developed specifically to teach the knowledge, skills, and abilities reflected in the CBOK.

You should use the LOS to guide and focus your study because each examination question is based on one or more LOS and the core material and practice problems associated with the LOS. As a candidate, you are responsible for the entirety of the required material in a study session.

We encourage you to review the information about the LOS on our website (www.cfainstitute.org/programs/cfa/curriculum/study-sessions), including the descriptions of LOS "command words" on the candidate resources page at www.cfainstitute.org.

FEATURES OF THE CURRICULUM

OPTIONAL SEGMENT

Required vs. Optional Segments You should read all of an assigned reading. In some cases, though, we have reprinted an entire publication and marked certain parts of the reading as "optional." The CFA examination is based only on the required segments, and the optional segments are included only when it is determined that they might help you to better understand the required segments (by seeing the required material in its full context). When an optional segment begins, you will see an icon and a dashed vertical bar in the outside margin that will continue until the optional segment ends, accompanied by another icon. *Unless the material is specifically marked as optional, you should assume it is required.* You should rely on the required segments and the reading-specific LOS in preparing for the examination.

END OPTIONAL SEGMENT

Practice Problems/Solutions *All practice problems at the end of the readings as well as their solutions are part of the curriculum and are required material for the examination.* In addition to the in-text examples and questions, these practice problems should help demonstrate practical applications and reinforce your understanding of the concepts presented. Some of these practice problems are adapted from past CFA examinations and/or may serve as a basis for examination questions.

Glossary For your convenience, each volume includes a comprehensive glossary. Throughout the curriculum, a **bolded** word in a reading denotes a term defined in the glossary.

Note that the digital curriculum that is included in your examination registration fee is searchable for key words, including glossary terms.

LOS Self-Check We have inserted checkboxes next to each LOS that you can use to track your progress in mastering the concepts in each reading.

Source Material The CFA Institute curriculum cites textbooks, journal articles, and other publications that provide additional context or information about topics covered in the readings. As a candidate, you are not responsible for familiarity with the original source materials cited in the curriculum.

Note that some readings may contain a web address or URL. The referenced sites were live at the time the reading was written or updated but may have been deactivated since then.

Some readings in the curriculum cite articles published in the *Financial Analysts Journal*®, which is the flagship publication of CFA Institute. Since its launch in 1945, the *Financial Analysts Journal* has established itself as the leading practitioner-oriented journal in the investment management community. Over the years, it has advanced the knowledge and understanding of the practice of investment management through the publication of peer-reviewed practitioner-relevant research from leading academics and practitioners. It has also featured thought-provoking opinion pieces that advance the common level of discourse within the investment management profession. Some of the most influential research in the area of investment management has appeared in the pages of the *Financial Analysts Journal*, and several Nobel laureates have contributed articles.

Candidates are not responsible for familiarity with *Financial Analysts Journal* articles that are cited in the curriculum. But, as your time and studies allow, we strongly encourage you to begin supplementing your understanding of key investment management issues by reading this practice-oriented publication. Candidates have full online access to the *Financial Analysts Journal* and associated resources. All you need is to log in on www.cfapubs.org using your candidate credentials.

Errata The curriculum development process is rigorous and includes multiple rounds of reviews by content experts. Despite our efforts to produce a curriculum that is free of errors, there are times when we must make corrections. Curriculum errata are periodically updated and posted on the candidate resources page at www.cfainstitute.org.

DESIGNING YOUR PERSONAL STUDY PROGRAM

Create a Schedule An orderly, systematic approach to examination preparation is critical. You should dedicate a consistent block of time every week to reading and studying. Complete all assigned readings and the associated problems and solutions in each study session. Review the LOS both before and after you study each reading to ensure that you have mastered the applicable content and can demonstrate the knowledge, skills, and abilities described by the LOS and the assigned reading. Use the LOS self-check to track your progress and highlight areas of weakness for later review.

Successful candidates report an average of more than 300 hours preparing for each examination. Your preparation time will vary based on your prior education and experience, and you will probably spend more time on some study sessions than on others. As the Level I curriculum includes 19 study sessions, a good plan is to devote 15–20 hours per week for 19 weeks to studying the material and use the final four to six weeks before the examination to review what you have learned and practice with practice questions and mock examinations. This recommendation, however, may underestimate the hours needed for appropriate examination preparation depending on your individual circumstances, relevant experience, and academic background. You will undoubtedly adjust your study time to conform to your own strengths and weaknesses and to your educational and professional background.

You should allow ample time for both in-depth study of all topic areas and additional concentration on those topic areas for which you feel the least prepared.

As part of the supplemental study tools that are included in your examination registration fee, you have access to a study planner to help you plan your study time. The study planner calculates your study progress and pace based on the time remaining until examination. For more information on the study planner and other supplemental study tools, please visit www.cfainstitute.org.

As you prepare for your examination, we will e-mail you important examination updates, testing policies, and study tips. Be sure to read these carefully.

CFA Institute Practice Questions Your examination registration fee includes digital access to hundreds of practice questions that are additional to the practice problems at the end of the readings. These practice questions are intended to help you assess your mastery of individual topic areas as you progress through your studies. After each practice question, you will be able to receive immediate feedback noting the correct responses and indicating the relevant assigned reading so you can identify areas of weakness for further study. For more information on the practice questions, please visit www.cfainstitute.org.

CFA Institute Mock Examinations Your examination registration fee also includes digital access to three-hour mock examinations that simulate the morning and afternoon sessions of the actual CFA examination. These mock examinations are intended to be taken after you complete your study of the full curriculum and take practice questions so you can test your understanding of the curriculum and your readiness for the examination. You will receive feedback at the end of the mock examination, noting the correct responses and indicating the relevant assigned readings so you can assess areas of weakness for further study during your review period. We recommend that you take mock examinations during the final stages of your preparation for the actual CFA examination. For more information on the mock examinations, please visit www.cfainstitute.org.

Preparatory Providers After you enroll in the CFA Program, you may receive numerous solicitations for preparatory courses and review materials. When considering a preparatory course, make sure the provider belongs to the CFA Institute Approved Prep Provider Program. Approved Prep Providers have committed to follow CFA Institute guidelines and high standards in their offerings and communications with candidates. For more information on the Approved Prep Providers, please visit www.cfainstitute.org/programs/cfa/exam/prep-providers.

Remember, however, that there are no shortcuts to success on the CFA examinations; reading and studying the CFA curriculum *is* the key to success on the examination. The CFA examinations reference only the CFA Institute assigned curriculum—no preparatory course or review course materials are consulted or referenced.

SUMMARY

Every question on the CFA examination is based on the content contained in the required readings and on one or more LOS. Frequently, an examination question is based on a specific example highlighted within a reading or on a specific practice problem and its solution. To make effective use of the CFA Program curriculum, please remember these key points:

1. All pages of the curriculum are required reading for the examination except for occasional sections marked as optional. You may read optional pages as background, but you will not be tested on them.
2. All questions, problems, and their solutions—found at the end of readings—are part of the curriculum and are required study material for the examination.
3. You should make appropriate use of the practice questions and mock examinations as well as other supplemental study tools and candidate resources available at www.cfainstitute.org.
4. Create a schedule and commit sufficient study time to cover the 19 study sessions, using the study planner. You should also plan to review the materials and take practice questions and mock examinations.
5. Some of the concepts in the study sessions may be superseded by updated rulings and/or pronouncements issued after a reading was published. Candidates are expected to be familiar with the overall analytical framework contained in the assigned readings. Candidates are not responsible for changes that occur after the material was written.

FEEDBACK

At CFA Institute, we are committed to delivering a comprehensive and rigorous curriculum for the development of competent, ethically grounded investment professionals. We rely on candidate and investment professional comments and feedback as we work to improve the curriculum, supplemental study tools, and candidate resources.

Please send any comments or feedback to info@cfainstitute.org. You can be assured that we will review your suggestions carefully. Ongoing improvements in the curriculum will help you prepare for success on the upcoming examinations and for a lifetime of learning as a serious investment professional.

Corporate Finance

STUDY SESSION

Study Session 10	Corporate Finance (1)
Study Session 11	Corporate Finance (2)

TOPIC LEVEL LEARNING OUTCOME

The candidate should be able to evaluate a company's corporate governance; to analyze a capital budgeting problem; to estimate a company's cost of capital; to evaluate a company's operating and financial leverage and its working capital management.

Some academic studies have shown that well governed companies may perform better in financial terms. Increasingly, investment approaches that consider environmental, social, and governance factors, known as ESG, are being adopted. In addition to good governance practices, management decisions regarding investment and financing also play a central role in corporate profitability and performance. To remain in business as a going concern and to increase shareholder value over time, management must consistently identify and invest in profitable long-term capital projects relative to cost of capital (financing) and make optimal use of leverage and working capital in day to day operations.

CORPORATE FINANCE

STUDY SESSION 10

Corporate Finance (1)

This study session provides an introduction to corporate governance and investing and financing decisions. An overview of corporate governance is presented along with a framework for understanding and analyzing corporate governance and stakeholder management. The growing impact of environmental and social considerations in investing is also highlighted. Capital budgeting and the assessment of capital investments are covered next. The session ends with practical techniques to estimate a company's or project's cost of capital.

READING ASSIGNMENTS

Reading 31	Introduction to Corporate Governance and Other ESG Considerations by Assem Safieddine, PhD, Young Lee, CFA, Donna F. Anderson, CFA, and Deborah Kidd, CFA
Reading 32	Capital Budgeting by John D. Stowe, PhD, CFA, and Jacques R. Gagné, FSA, CFA, CIPM
Reading 33	Cost of Capital by Yves Courtois, CMT, MRICS, CFA, Gene C. Lai, PhD, and Pamela Peterson Drake, PhD, CFA

READING

31

Introduction to Corporate Governance and Other ESG Considerations

by Assem Safieddine, PhD, Young Lee, CFA, Donna F. Anderson, CFA, and Deborah S. Kidd, CFA

Assem Safieddine, PhD, is at Suliman Olayan Business School, American University of Beirut (Lebanon). Young Lee, CFA, is at MacKay Shields LLC (USA) and MacKay Shields UK LLP (United Kingdom). Donna F. Anderson, CFA (USA). Deborah S. Kidd, CFA (USA).

LEARNING OUTCOMES

Mastery	*The candidate should be able to:*
☐	a. describe corporate governance;
☐	b. describe a company's stakeholder groups and compare interests of stakeholder groups;
☐	c. describe principal–agent and other relationships in corporate governance and the conflicts that may arise in these relationships;
☐	d. describe stakeholder management;
☐	e. describe mechanisms to manage stakeholder relationships and mitigate associated risks;
☐	f. describe functions and responsibilities of a company's board of directors and its committees;
☐	g. describe market and non-market factors that can affect stakeholder relationships and corporate governance;
☐	h. identify potential risks of poor corporate governance and stakeholder management and identify benefits from effective corporate governance and stakeholder management;
☐	i. describe factors relevant to the analysis of corporate governance and stakeholder management;
☐	j. describe environmental and social considerations in investment analysis;
☐	k. describe how environmental, social, and governance factors may be used in investment analysis.

1 INTRODUCTION

Weak corporate governance is a common thread found in many company failures. A lack of proper oversight by the board of directors, inadequate protection for minority shareholders, and incentives at companies that promote excessive risk taking are just a few of the examples that can be problematic for a company. Poor corporate governance practices resulted in several high-profile accounting scandals and corporate bankruptcies over the past several decades and have been cited as significantly contributing to the 2008–2009 global financial crisis.

In response to these company failures, regulations have been introduced to promote stronger governance practices and protect financial markets and investors. Academics, policy makers, and other groups have published numerous works discussing the benefits of good corporate governance and identifying core corporate governance principles believed to be essential to ensuring sound capital markets and the stability of the financial system.

The investment community has also demonstrated a greater appreciation for the importance of good corporate governance. The assessment of a company's corporate governance system, including consideration of conflicts of interest and transparency of operations, has increasingly become an essential factor in the investment decision-making process. Additionally, investors have become more attentive to environment and social issues related to a company's operations. Collectively, these areas often are referred to as environmental, social, and governance (**ESG**).

Section 2 of this reading provides an overview of corporate governance, including its underlying principles and theories. Section 3 discusses the various stakeholders of a company and conflicts of interest that exist among stakeholder groups. Section 4 describes stakeholder management, reflecting how companies manage their relationships with stakeholders. Section 5 focuses on the role of the board of directors and its committees as overseers of the company. Section 6 explores certain key factors that affect corporate governance. Section 7 highlights the risks and benefits that underlie a corporate governance structure. Section 8 provides an overview of corporate governance issues relevant for investment professionals. Finally, Section 9 discusses the growing effect of environmental and social considerations in the investment process.

2 CORPORATE GOVERNANCE OVERVIEW

Corporate governance can be defined as "the system of internal controls and procedures by which individual companies are managed. It provides a framework that defines the rights, roles and responsibilities of various groups . . . within an organization. At its core, corporate governance is the arrangement of checks, balances, and incentives a company needs in order to minimize and manage the conflicting interests between insiders and external shareowners."[1]

Corporate governance practices differ among countries and jurisdictions, and even within countries different corporate governance systems may co-exist. The corporate governance systems adopted in most of the world typically reflect the influences of either *shareholder theory* or *stakeholder theory* to a varying extent, as well as historical, cultural, legal, political, and other influences specific to a region.

1 CFA Institute Centre for Financial Market Integrity, *The Corporate Governance of Listed Companies: A Manual for Investors*, 2nd ed. (Charlottesville, VA: CFA Institute, 2009).

Shareholder theory takes the view that the most important responsibility of a company's managers is to maximize shareholder returns. Stakeholder theory broadens a company's focus beyond the interests of only its shareholders to its customers, suppliers, employees, and others who have an interest in the company. The approach to corporate governance in a given country typically places greater emphasis on one of the two theories but can also exhibit a combination of the two. Notwithstanding the system of corporate governance used, nearly all companies depend on contributions from a number of stakeholders for their long-term success. The company's strategy is set by the board of directors, which also oversees management; in turn, the company's strategy is executed by its managers; financial capital to fund the company's activities and operations is supplied by shareholders, creditors, and suppliers; human capital is provided by employees; and demand for goods and services comes from customers. Other stakeholders include governments and regulators, which seek to protect the interests and well-being of their citizens. Certain external forces, such as the legal environment and competition, affect the way a company operates and the relationships among its stakeholders.

Two reports issued during the 1990s, the Cadbury Report and the Principles of Corporate Governance, were particularly influential in shaping the global corporate governance landscape. In 1991, the Committee on the Financial Aspects of Corporate Governance was established in the United Kingdom by the Financial Reporting Council, the London Stock Exchange, and the accountancy profession to examine corporate governance. In the following year, the report of the committee—commonly referred to as the Cadbury Report, after its chairman—defined corporate governance simply as "the system by which companies are directed and controlled." The report focused on the responsibilities of a company's board of directors, shareholders, and auditors, with shareholders implicitly identified as the primary stakeholder. In 1999, the Organisation for Economic Co-operation and Development (OECD) produced the *Principles of Corporate Governance*, which expanded the scope of corporate governance to consider the interests of other stakeholders—notably employees, creditors, and suppliers. According to the OECD, "Corporate governance includes a set of relationships between a company's management, its board, its shareholders, and other stakeholders." The *Principles of Corporate Governance*, which was revised in 2004 and again in 2015, also discusses potential positive outcomes of good corporate governance practices (including financial market stability and economic growth) and includes standards and guidelines designed to evaluate and improve the corporate governance framework throughout the world.

There is evidence that some movement toward global convergence of corporate governance systems is underway. One trend is the increased acceptance and adoption of corporate governance regulations with similar principles from one jurisdiction to another. For example, a number of countries implemented regulations similar to those of the US Sarbanes–Oxley Act of 2002 (SOX) in response to corporate and accounting scandals of the early 2000s. Although these regulations are not identical, they share the same objective of improving internal controls and restoring investor confidence in financial disclosures. Another trend is initiatives by international agencies to build greater consensus on important corporate governance principles. The *Principles of Corporate Governance*, for example, has been ratified by more than 30 member countries, representing a broad range of corporate governance models. The *Principles of Corporate Governance* do not mandate, or even promote, the adoption of a single corporate governance regime; rather, the principles were designed to serve as a framework that can be adopted by any number of corporate governance systems.

EXAMPLE 1

Corporate Governance Overview

Which statement regarding corporate governance is *most* accurate?

A Most countries have similar corporate governance regulations.

B A single definition of corporate governance is widely accepted in practice.

C Both shareholder theory and stakeholder theory consider the needs of a company's shareholders.

Solution:

C is correct. Both shareholder and stakeholder theories consider the needs of shareholders, with the latter extending to a broader group of stakeholders. A is incorrect because corporate governance regulations differ across countries, although there is a trend toward convergence. B is incorrect because a universally accepted definition of corporate governance remains elusive.

3 COMPANY STAKEHOLDERS

A corporate governance system is likely to be influenced by several stakeholder groups. These groups do not necessarily share similar goals or needs; in fact, the interests of any one group may conflict with the interests of another group. The varying influences of these groups are important considerations for investment professionals when analyzing a corporate governance system. This section provides an overview of a corporation's primary stakeholder groups, followed by a discussion of principal–agent considerations and the conflicts that may arise among the groups.

3.1 Stakeholder Groups

The primary stakeholder groups of a corporation consist of shareholders, creditors, managers (or executives), other employees, board of directors, customers, suppliers, and governments/regulators (and, by extension, affected individuals and community groups). The interests of each of these groups are discussed in the following sections.

3.1.1 *Shareholders*

Shareholders own shares of stock in a corporation and are entitled to certain rights, such as the right to receive dividends and to vote on certain corporate issues.[2] In terms of capital structure, shareholders are the most junior class of capital providers; in case of a company bankruptcy, shareholders receive proceeds only after all creditors' claims are paid. Shareholder interests are, therefore, typically focused on growth in corporate profitability that maximizes the value of a company's equity.

As a company grows in size and its operations and structure become more complex, most individual shareholders have little involvement in the company's activities. Shareholders maintain control over the company through their power to elect the board of directors and vote for specified resolutions. The board of directors is expected to represent shareholders—protecting their interests, appointing senior management, providing strategic direction, and monitoring company and management performance.

2 https://themoderncorporation.wordpress.com/company-law-memo/

In publicly traded companies that have dispersed ownership, the voting power in general meetings is distributed among a large number of shareholders. But in some companies, a particular shareholder or block of shareholders may hold a percentage of shares that gives them sufficient voting power to control the election of the board of directors and to influence the approval or blockage of a company resolution; these shareholders are known as **controlling shareholders**. In contrast, non-controlling shareholders (**minority shareholders**) hold a much smaller proportion of a company's outstanding shares, resulting in a more limited ability to exercise control in voting activities.

3.1.2 *Creditors*

Creditors, most commonly bondholders and banks, are a company's lenders and the providers of debt financing. Creditors do not hold voting power (unlike common shareholders) and typically have limited influence over a company's operations. Creditors may protect themselves and exert some control over a company by using covenants, which restrict activities of the borrower. In return for capital provided, creditors expect to receive interest and principal payments. These payments are pre-determined from the terms of a debt contract and are typically not contingent on the company's performance. Creditors usually do not participate in a company's superior performance beyond receiving promised interest and principal payments. The company's ability to generate cash flows, mainly through its operations, is the primary source of payments for creditors. Consequently, creditors generally prefer stability in company operations and performance, which contrasts with the interests of shareholders, who generally are inclined to tolerate higher risks in return for higher return potential from strong company performance.

3.1.3 *Managers and Employees*

Senior executives and other high-level managers are normally compensated through salary, bonuses, equity-based remuneration (or compensation),[3] and certain perquisites. As a result, managers may be motivated to maximize the value of their total remuneration while also protecting their employment positions. Lower-level employees normally seek fair remuneration, good working conditions, access to promotions, career development opportunities, training and development, job security, and a safe and healthy work environment.

As with shareholders and creditors, managers and employees have a significant interest in the company's viability. Managers and employees tend to benefit if the company performs well and are among the most adversely affected stakeholders if a company's financial position weakens. Despite some similarities, the interests of managers and employees and other stakeholders can conflict. For example, a company may be presented with a takeover offer that is attractive to shareholders but would jeopardize the interests of managers in preserving their employment at the company.

3.1.4 *Board of Directors*

A company's board of directors is elected by shareholders to protect shareholders' interests, provide strategic direction, and monitor company and management performance. A board is typically structured as either *one-tier* or *two-tier*.

A one-tier structure consists of a single board of directors, composed of executive and non-executive directors. Executive (sometimes called "internal") directors are employees, typically senior managers, of the company. Non-executive (sometimes

3 The terms "remuneration" and "compensation" are typically interchangeable, with compensation generally used in North America and remuneration generally used outside North America. In this reading, unless specifically identified with North America, we primarily use "remuneration".

called "external") directors are not employees of the company. Countries in which one-tier boards are common include the United States, the United Kingdom, and India. A two-tier structure consists of two separate boards: (1) a *supervisory board*, which is primarily composed of non-executive directors, and (2) a *management (executive) board*, which is composed of executive directors. The supervisory board oversees the management board. Two-tier boards are common in such countries as Germany, the Netherlands, Finland, and China.

In this reading, unless specified otherwise, the term "board" refers to the single board of directors in a one-tier structure and the supervisory board in a two-tier structure. Directors, both internal and external, are typically experienced individuals who are focused on fulfilling their responsibilities toward shareholders and the company while maintaining a good reputation in the business community. Directors are also typically concerned with their exposure to liability for breach of duty. Directors can mitigate this exposure by exercising appropriate levels of control over the company's operations and its management. A company's board of directors is discussed in more detail in Section 5 of this reading.

3.1.5 *Customers*

Customers expect a company's products or services to satisfy their needs and provide appropriate benefits given the price paid, as well as to meet applicable standards of safety. Depending on the type of product or service and the duration of their relationship with the company, customers may desire ongoing support, product guarantees, and after-sale service. Companies are concerned with customer satisfaction given its potential correlation with sales revenues and profit. Compared with other stakeholder groups, customers tend to be less concerned with, and affected by, a company's financial performance. However, customers, particularly those with long-term relationships with the company, typically have an interest in a company's stability.

3.1.6 *Suppliers*

A company's suppliers have a primary interest in being paid as contracted or agreed on, and in a timely manner, for products or services delivered to the company. Suppliers often seek to build long-term relationships with companies for the benefit of both parties and aim for these relationships to be fair and transparent. Suppliers, like creditors, are concerned with a company's ability to generate sufficient cash flows to meet its financial obligations.

3.1.7 *Governments/Regulators*

Governments and regulators seek to protect the interests of the general public and ensure the well-being of their nations' economies. Because corporations have a significant effect on a nation's economic output, capital flows, employment, and social welfare, among other factors, regulators have an interest in ensuring that corporations behave in a manner that is consistent with applicable laws. As the collector of tax revenues, a government can also be considered one of the company's major stakeholders.

Stakeholders in Non-profit Organizations

The stakeholders of a non-profit organization tend to differ from those of for-profit companies. Non-profit organizations do not have shareholders. Their stakeholders most commonly include board directors or trustees, employees, regulators, society, patrons of the organization, donors, and volunteers. The stakeholders of non-profit organizations are generally focused on ensuring that the organization is serving the intended cause and that the donated funds are used as promised.

EXAMPLE 2

Stakeholder Groups

Which stakeholders would *most likely* realize the greatest benefit from a significant increase in the market value of the company?

A Creditors

B Customers

C Shareholders

Solution:

C is correct. Shareholders own shares of stock in the company, and their wealth is directly related to the market value of the company. A is incorrect because creditors are usually not entitled to any additional cash flows (beyond interest and debt repayment) if the company's value increases. B is incorrect because customers may have an interest in the company's stability and long-term viability but they do not benefit directly from an increase in a company's value.

3.2 Principal–Agent and Other Relationships in Corporate Governance

A **principal–agent relationship** (also known as an agency relationship) is created when a principal hires an agent to perform a particular task or service. The principal–agent relationship involves obligations, trust, and expectations of loyalty; the agent is expected to act in the best interests of the principal. In a company, agency theory stipulates that principal–agent relationships often lead to conflicts—for example, when managers do not act in the best interests of shareholders.[4] Examples of principal–agent relationships and potential conflicts between the principal and agent are discussed in the following sections. Conflicts among stakeholder groups are also discussed but do not involve principal–agent relationships.

3.2.1 *Shareholder and Manager/Director Relationships*

In shareholder-owned companies, shareholders typically grant directors and managers the responsibility to make most corporate decisions. According to traditional shareholder theory discussed earlier, the central duty of directors and managers is to act in the best interests of shareholders. In certain circumstances, managers may seek to maximize their personal benefits (e.g., remuneration and perquisites) to the detriment of shareholders' interests.

4 Agency theory considers the problems that can arise in a business relationship when one person delegates decision-making authority to another. The traditional view in the investment community is that directors and managers are agents of shareholders. More recently, however, many legal experts have argued that in several countries, corporations are separate "legal persons" and thus directors and managers are agents of the corporations rather than shareholders (or a subset of shareholders). See https://themoderncorporation.wordpress.com/company-law-memo.

Shareholder and manager (or shareholder and director) interests can also diverge with respect to risk tolerance. In some cases, shareholders with diversified investment portfolios may have a relatively high risk tolerance because the risk undertaken by a specific company can be diversified across the shareholders' investments. Managers and directors, however, are typically more risk averse in their corporate decision making so they can better protect their employment status. Such behavior may differ from the company's value creation objective. In addition, compared with shareholders, managers typically have greater access to information about the business and are more knowledgeable about its operations. Such "information asymmetry" (that is, unequal access to information) makes it easier for managers to make strategic decisions that are not necessarily in the best interest of shareholders and weakens the ability of shareholders to exercise control. Another conflict of interest might arise between shareholders and directors when the board is influenced by insiders. In this case, the ability of the board to properly perform its monitoring and control role may be hindered. Finally, a conflict between the two groups may occur if directors favor certain influential shareholders over other shareholders.

3.2.2 *Controlling and Minority Shareholder Relationships*

In companies in which a particular shareholder holds a controlling stake, conflicts of interest may arise among the controlling and minority shareholders. In such ownership structures, the opinions of minority shareholders are often outweighed or overshadowed by the influence of the controlling shareholders. Minority shareholders often have limited or no control over management and limited or no voice in director appointments or in major transactions that could have a direct effect on the value of their shares. For instance, in companies that adopt **straight voting** (that is, one vote for each share owned), controlling shareholders clearly wield the most influence in board of director elections, leaving minority shareholders with much less representation on the board.

The decisions made by controlling shareholders, or their board representatives, could also have an effect on corporate performance and, consequently, on minority shareholders' wealth. Takeover transactions are notable situations in which controlling shareholders typically have greater influence than do minority shareholders with regard to the consideration received and other deal terms. A historical example of note occurred in 2007 when Qtel, Qatar's largest telecommunications company, executed a deal with a consortium of the shareholders of Wataniya, Kuwait's telecommunications company, to acquire the consortium's shares in Wataniya (representing a 51% stake in the target). The consortium of Wataniya's shareholders sold their shares to Qtel at a premium of 48% on the stock price to the exclusion of minority shareholders.

Related-party transactions are another example for which controlling shareholders may place their interests ahead of minority shareholders' interests. Such a situation could occur when a controlling shareholder maintains a financial interest in a transaction between the company and a third party and that transaction conflicts with the company's best interests. Consider, for example, a controlling shareholder that arranges a deal between the company and a third-party supplier that is owned by the shareholder's spouse whereby the supplier provides the company with inventory at above market prices. Such a transaction would benefit the controlling shareholder and the spouse's interests but could harm the profitability of the company and the interests of minority shareholders.

Lastly, an equity structure with multiple share classes in which one class is non-voting or has limited voting rights creates a divergence between the ownership and control rights of different classes of shareholders. Under a multiple-class structure (traditionally called a *dual-class structure* when there are two share classes), the company's founders, executives, and other key insiders control the company by virtue of ownership of a share class with superior voting powers. The multiple-class structure enables controlling shareholders to mitigate dilution of their voting power when new shares are issued. Examples of companies that have adopted multiple-class stock structures are Alibaba and Facebook (each with two share classes), as well as Comcast and Google (each with three share classes).

3.2.3 *Manager and Board Relationships*

Given that a board of directors typically relies on management to operate the company, the board's monitoring role can be compromised in the event of limited information provided to the board. This conflict is particularly pronounced for non-executive directors who are typically not involved in the day-to-day operations of a company.

3.2.4 *Shareholder versus Creditor Interests*

Shareholders typically seek growth in corporate profitability because of the residual nature of equity returns. However, the pre-determined returns of debt obligations normally prevent creditors from receiving any cash flows beyond principal and interest payments, but do expose creditors to default risk in case of extremely poor corporate performance. From an investment perspective, shareholders would likely prefer riskier projects with a strong likelihood of higher return potential, whereas creditors would likely prefer stable performance and lower-risk activities. A divergence in risk tolerance regarding the company's investments thus exists between shareholders and creditors.

Creditors may also find their interests jeopardized when the company attempts to increase its borrowings to a level that would increase default risk. If the company's operations and investments fail to generate sufficient returns required to repay the increased interest and debt obligations, creditors will be increasingly exposed to default risk. The distribution of excessive dividends to shareholders might also conflict with creditors' interests if it impairs the company's ability to pay interest and principal.

3.2.5 *Other Stakeholder Conflicts*

In a corporation, interests can also conflict among other stakeholders. Some of these situations are as follows:

- *Conflict between customers and shareholders*: For example, a company decides to charge a high price for its products or reduces product safety features to reduce costs.
- *Conflict between customers and suppliers*: A company offers overly lenient credit terms to its customers, whereby the company's ability to repay suppliers on time may be affected.
- *Conflict between shareholders and governments or regulators*: Examples of such conflicts may include a company adopting accounting and reporting practices that reduce its tax burden, thus potentially benefiting shareholders, or a bank's shareholders preferring a lower equity capital base while regulators prefer a higher capital position. This last conflict is fairly common in the banking industry and has been increasingly in focus since the global financial crisis of 2008–2009.

EXAMPLE 3

Stakeholder Relationships

A controlling shareholder of XYZ Company owns 55% of XYZ's shares, and the remaining shares are spread among a large group of shareholders. In this situation, conflicts of interest are *most likely* to arise between:

A shareholders and regulators.

B the controlling shareholder and managers.

C the controlling shareholder and minority shareholders.

Solution:

C is correct. In this ownership structure, the controlling shareholder's power is likely more influential than that of minority shareholders. Thus, the controlling shareholder may be able to exploit its position to the detriment of the interests of the remaining shareholders. Choices A and B are incorrect because the ownership structure in and of itself is unlikely to create material conflicts between shareholders and regulators or shareholders and managers.

4 STAKEHOLDER MANAGEMENT

Because interests among stakeholder groups differ, companies often adopt mechanisms to more efficiently manage stakeholder relationships. **Stakeholder management** involves identifying, prioritizing, and understanding the interests of stakeholder groups, and, on that basis, managing the company's relationships with these groups.

4.1 Overview of Stakeholder Management

Effective communication and active engagement with the various stakeholders form the basis of stakeholder management. Although the practices underlying stakeholder management may vary, companies typically seek to balance the interests of their various stakeholders and thus limit the effect of conflicts.

To help balance these interests, corporate governance and stakeholder management frameworks reflect a legal, contractual, organizational, and governmental infrastructure that defines the rights, responsibilities, and powers of each group. The *legal infrastructure* defines the framework for rights established by law and the availability or ease of legal recourse for any violation of these rights. The *contractual infrastructure* is shaped by the contractual arrangements entered into by the company and its stakeholders that help define and secure the rights of both parties. The *organizational infrastructure* refers to internal systems, governance procedures, and practices adopted and controlled by the company in managing its stakeholder relationships. Lastly, the *governmental infrastructure* refers to regulations imposed on companies.

The corporate governance systems in such countries as France, Germany, and Japan focus on a broader range of stakeholders relative to the more shareholder-driven Anglo-American systems. Globally, there is a growing movement among regulators and practitioners to more effectively balance the interests of all stakeholders. For instance, the Companies Act 2006 in the United Kingdom introduced "enlightened shareholder value," which requires directors to consider the interests of all stakeholders—not just shareholders. Several regulators, such as those in the United Kingdom and Japan, have adopted stewardship codes that encourage more active engagement of institutional investors with companies.

EXAMPLE 4

Stakeholder Management

The component of stakeholder management in which a corporation has the *most* control is:

A legal infrastructure.

B contractual infrastructure.

C governmental infrastructure.

Solution:

B is correct. A corporation's contractual infrastructure refers to the contractual arrangements between the corporation and stakeholders. As such, the corporation has control over these arrangements. A is incorrect because the legal infrastructure is established by law, which is outside the corporation's own control. Similarly, C is incorrect because a corporation's governmental structure is largely imposed by regulators.

4.2 Mechanisms of Stakeholder Management

Stakeholder management and governance practices attempt to manage the interests of all stakeholders. As mentioned earlier, a prescribed or standard set of rights and practices does not exist across all companies, and the principles vary across countries and jurisdictions. Still, there are some common control elements and governance mechanisms among companies.

4.2.1 *General Meetings*

Corporate laws grant shareholders certain powers and controls. The participation of shareholders in general meetings, also known as general assemblies, and the exercise of their voting rights are among the most influential tools available. General meetings enable shareholders to participate in discussions and to vote on major corporate matters and transactions that are not delegated to the board of directors.

Companies are ordinarily required to hold an annual general meeting (AGM) within a certain period following the end of their fiscal year. The main purpose of those meetings is to present shareholders with the annual audited financial statements of the company, provide an overview of the company's performance and activities, and address shareholder questions. Shareholders also elect the directors at the AGM and, in some countries, may be required to approve the financial statements, discharge directors of their duties, appoint external auditors, or vote on the remuneration of the board and/or top management. Extraordinary general meetings can be called by the company or by shareholders throughout the year when significant resolutions requiring shareholder approval are proposed. These resolutions might relate to proposed material corporate changes, such as amendments to the company's bylaws or rights attached to a class of shares, mergers and acquisitions, or the sale of significant corporate assets or businesses.

All shareholders typically have the right to attend, speak at, and vote at general meetings. Regulations, particularly corporate laws, specify conditions for inviting shareholders to general meetings and circulating information to shareholders. These conditions vary across regulations but generally aim at ensuring the participation of a large number of shareholders in general meetings without imposing excessive restrictions on the ability of the company to hold a meeting. By engaging in general meetings, shareholders can exercise their voting rights on major corporate issues and better monitor the performance of the board and senior management. General meetings and the underlying voting procedures are among the most widely adopted practices by companies in mitigating agency problems and their associated risks.

Some resolutions, such as the approval of financial statements and the election of directors and auditors, are considered ordinary at general meetings because they require only a simple majority of votes to be passed. Decisions that are more material in nature may require a supermajority vote, such as two-thirds or 75% of votes, to be passed. Such special resolutions may include amendments to bylaws, voting on a merger or takeover transaction, or waiving pre-emptive rights. Depending on the ownership structure, supermajority requirements may make it harder for majority shareholders to influence corporate decisions at the expense of minority shareholders.

Proxy voting is a process that enables shareholders who are unable to attend a meeting to authorize another individual (for example, another shareholder or director) to vote on their behalf. Proxy voting is the most common form of investor participation in general meetings. Although most resolutions at most companies pass without controversy, sometimes minority shareholders attempt to strengthen their influence at companies via proxy voting. Several shareholders sometimes use this process to collectively vote their shares in favor of or in opposition to a certain resolution. **Cumulative voting** (as opposed to straight voting) enables each shareholder to accumulate and vote all his or her shares for a single candidate in an election involving more than one director. This voting process raises the likelihood that minority shareholders are represented by at least one director on the board, but it may not be compatible with majority voting standards for director elections in which share ownership is widely dispersed. In terms of worldwide practice, the existence of cumulative voting varies; for example, it is mandated in Spain but not allowed in several countries, such as Germany, Japan, Singapore, and Turkey.

Minority shareholders are often granted rights to protect their interests in acquisitions. For example, companies in European Union member states are required to adopt sell-out rights. These rights allow minority shareholders who have voted against a merger offer to force a bidder with more than 90% of the target's voting rights to buy their shares at a fair price upon the deal's approval.

EXAMPLE 5

General Meetings

Which of the statements about extraordinary general meetings (EGMs) of shareholders is true?

A The appointment of external auditors occurs during the EGM.

B A corporation provides an overview of corporate performance at the EGM.

C An amendment to a corporation's bylaws typically occurs during the EGM.

Solution:

C is correct. An amendment to corporate bylaws would normally take place during an EGM, which covers significant changes to a company, such as bylaw amendments. A and B are incorrect because the appointment of external auditors and a corporate performance overview would typically take place during the AGM.

4.2.2 *Board of Director Mechanisms*

In companies with complex ownership structures and operations, it is impractical for shareholders to be involved in strategy formulation and day-to-day activities. Shareholders thus elect a board of directors to provide broad oversight of the company. Shareholders monitor the board's performance through exercise of voting power and participation in general meetings. The board, in turn, appoints the top management of the company. The board is accountable primarily to shareholders and is responsible for the proper governance of the company; in this regard, the board is the link between shareholders and managers. The board guides managers on the company's strategic direction, oversees and monitors management's actions in implementing the strategy, and evaluates and rewards or disciplines management performance. The board also supervises the company's audit, control, and risk management functions and ensures the adoption of proper governance systems and compliance with all applicable laws and regulations. In Section 5 of this reading, we provide more detail regarding the functions and responsibilities of the board of directors and its committees.

4.2.3 *The Audit Function*

The audit function is an integral component of any governance structure. The function represents the systems, controls, and policies/procedures in place to examine the company's operations and financial records. Internal audits are conducted by an independent internal audit function or department. External auditors are independent from the company and conduct an annual audit of the company's financial records to provide reasonable and independent assurance of the accuracy of financial statements and their fair representation of the financial position of the company. External auditors are typically recommended by an audit committee (which we discuss later in the reading) for appointment by shareholders or, in some jurisdictions, by the board. The board of directors is generally required to receive and review the financial statements and auditors' reports and confirm their accuracy before they are presented to shareholders for approval at the AGM. Senior management of publicly traded companies is also required to review and provide assurance of the effectiveness of the internal control systems to the board of directors or to shareholders. Overall, a company's audit function limits insiders' discretion with regard to the use of company resources and to its financial reporting. The audit function is also designed to mitigate incidents of fraud or misstatements of accounting and financial information.

4.2.4 *Reporting and Transparency*

Shareholders have access to a range of financial and non-financial information concerning the company, typically through annual reports, proxy statements, disclosures on the company's website, the investor relations department, and other means of communication (e.g., social media). This information may relate to the company's operations, its strategic direction or objectives, audited financial statements, governance structure, ownership structure, remuneration policies, related-party transactions, and risk factors. Such information is essential for shareholders to

- reduce the extent of information asymmetry between shareholders and managers;
- assess the performance of the company and of its directors and managers;
- make informed decisions in valuing the company and deciding to purchase, sell, or transfer shares; and
- vote on key corporate matters or changes.

4.2.5 *Policies on Related-Party Transactions*

The development and implementation of policies for related-party transactions and other conflicts of interest is an increasingly common practice among companies. These policies establish the procedures for mitigating, managing, and disclosing such cases. Typically, directors and managers are required to disclose any actual or potential, or direct or indirect, conflict of interest they have with the company, as well as any material interests in a transaction that may affect the company. Often, these policies require such transactions or matters to be voted on by the board (or shareholders) excluding the director (or shareholder) holding the interest. The adoption of these policies and procedures aims at ensuring that related-party transactions are handled fairly and that they do not advance the interests of the related party at the expense of the interests of the company or other shareholders.

4.2.6 *Remuneration Policies*

Executive remuneration plans have gained significant attention in the investment world, with a primary goal of aligning the interests of managers with those of shareholders. For this purpose, incentive plans increasingly include a variable component—typically profit sharing, stocks, or stock options—that is contingent on corporate or stock price performance. However, the granting of stock-based remuneration does not serve its purpose if managers can improve their personal gains at the expense of the company while limiting their exposure to weak stock performance. As a result, companies are increasingly designing incentive plans that discourage either "short-termism" or excessive risk taking by managers. Some incentive plans include granting shares, rather than options, to managers and restricting their vesting or sale for several years or until retirement. A long-term incentive plan delays the payment of remuneration, either partially or in total, until company strategic objectives (typically performance targets) are met.

Regulators across the world are also increasingly focused on remuneration policies. In some cases, regulators require companies to base remuneration specifically on long-term performance measures. A number of regulators are requiring companies, including many in the financial industry, to adopt clawback provisions. These provisions allow a company to recover previously paid remuneration if certain events, such as financial restatements, misconduct, breach of the law, or risk management deficiencies, are uncovered.

4.2.7 *Say on Pay*

Given the role of remuneration plans in aligning the interests of executives with those of shareholders, regulators and companies are increasingly seeking shareholder views on pay. The concept of **say on pay** enables shareholders to vote on executive remuneration matters. Say on pay was first introduced in the United Kingdom in the early 2000s. In an early example of shareholder rejection, in 2003 the shareholders of GlaxoSmithKline rejected the company's remuneration report because of opposition to the proposed executive pay. This was the first such rejection by the shareholders of a large UK-based company. Shortly thereafter, the practice of say on pay spread to other parts of the world and was implemented in the United States as part of the Dodd–Frank Act in 2011. In 2018, there were a number of instances in which shareholders voted against remuneration reports. In the United Kingdom, for example, Inmarsat plc's remuneration report was rejected by 58% of voters over concerns that executive compensation was not aligned with company performance. In the United States, 52% of Walt Disney Co.'s shareholders voted against what they believed was an excessive executive compensation package.

The scope and effect of say on pay varies across countries and companies. Some countries, such as Canada, have a non-mandatory and advisory (non-binding) say on pay system in which shareholders signal, rather than impose, their views on proposed remuneration. In other countries, such as the United States, France, and South Africa, say on pay is mandatory but non-binding. In these countries, the board is required to enable shareholders to vote on remuneration plans or packages, but the board does not have to abide by the result of the vote. Conversely, countries in which shareholder votes on say on pay are binding include the Netherlands, the United Kingdom, and China.

Say on pay has been subject to criticism because of the fact that shareholders often have limited involvement in a company's strategy and operations. These opponents argue that the board is better suited to determine remuneration matters. Conversely, by allowing shareholders to express their views on remuneration-related matters, companies can limit the discretion of directors and managers in granting themselves excessive or inadequate remuneration. This approach could thus reduce a critical agency conflict in stakeholder management by better aligning the interests of principals and agents.

4.2.8 *Contractual Agreements with Creditors*

The rights of creditors are established by laws and according to contracts executed with the company. Laws vary by jurisdiction but commonly contain provisions to protect creditors' interests and provide legal recourse. One such provision is an **indenture**, which is a legal contract that describes the structure of a bond, the obligations of the issuer, and the rights of the bondholders. To limit creditors' risk during the term of a bond (or loan), debtholders may choose to impose **covenants** within indentures or contracts. Covenants are the terms and conditions of lending agreements, enabling creditors to specify the actions an issuer is obligated to perform or prohibited from performing. **Collaterals** are another tool often used by creditors to guarantee repayment, representing assets or financial guarantees that are above and beyond an issuer's promise to repay its obligations.

To further protect their rights, creditors usually require the company to provide periodic information (including financial statements) to ensure that covenants are not violated and thus potential default risk is not increased. Because it is usually impractical and costly for individual bondholders to fully scrutinize a bond issue, companies often hire a financial institution to act as a trustee and monitor the issue on behalf of a class of bondholders. In some countries, credit committees, particularly for unsecured bondholders, are established once a company files for bankruptcy. Such committees are expected to represent bondholders throughout the bankruptcy proceedings and protect bondholder interests in any restructuring or liquidation.

4.2.9 *Employee Laws and Contracts*

Employee rights are primarily secured through labor laws, which define the standards for employees' rights and responsibilities and cover such matters as labor hours, pension and retirement plans, hiring and firing, and vacation and leave. In most countries, employees have the right to create unions. Unions seek to influence certain matters affecting employees. In the European Union, companies meeting specific size and geographic criteria are required to establish European Works Councils that are composed of employees who meet with management at least annually. Although not a common practice in the United States and many other parts of the world, employees are sometimes represented on the board of directors—or supervisory boards—of companies meeting certain size or ownership criteria (e.g., in Germany, Austria, and Luxembourg). In Japan, the employee model stresses reaching a consensus between management and employees in decision making.

At the individual level, employment contracts specify an employee's various rights and responsibilities. Employment contracts typically do not cover every situation between employees and employers, and thus there is some area of discretion in the employment relationship. Human resources policies also help companies manage their relationships with employees. Effective human resources policies seek to attract and recruit high-quality employees while providing remuneration, training/development, and career growth to improve employee retention. Some companies have employee stock ownership plans (ESOPs) to help retain and motivate employees. As part of an ESOP, a company establishes a fund consisting of cash and/or company shares. The shares, which have designated vesting periods, are granted to employees.

Codes of ethics and business conduct also serve an important role in the relationship between employees and the company. Such codes establish the company's values and the standards of ethical and legal behavior that employees must follow. Companies typically assign a compliance or corporate governance officer (or a board committee) to implement these codes, receive violation reports, and resolve ethical matters.

By managing its relationships with its employees, a company seeks to comply with employees' rights and mitigate legal or reputational risks in violation of these rights. Employee relationship management also helps ensure that employees are fulfilling their responsibilities toward the company and are qualified and motivated to act in the company's best interests.

4.2.10 *Contractual Agreements with Customers and Suppliers*

Both customers and suppliers enter into contractual agreements with a company that specify the products and services underlying the relationship, the prices or fees and the payment terms, the rights and responsibilities of each party, the after-sale relationship, and any guarantees. Contracts also specify actions to be taken and recourse available if either party breaches the terms of the contract.

4.2.11 *Laws and Regulations*

As part of their public service roles, governments and regulatory authorities develop laws that companies must follow and monitor companies' compliance with these laws. Such laws may address or protect the rights of a specific group, such as consumers or the environment. Some industries or sectors whose services, products, or operations are more likely to endanger the public or specific stakeholders' interests are usually subject to a more rigorous regulatory framework. Examples of these industries are banks, food manufacturers, and health care companies.

Many regulatory authorities have also adopted corporate governance codes that consist of guiding principles for publicly traded companies. Publicly traded companies, in turn, are generally required to annually publish corporate governance reports describing their governance structure and explain any deviations from guiding principles. Companies normally seek to adopt internal governance and compliance procedures and adhere to the relevant financial reporting and transparency requirements imposed by regulators.

EXAMPLE 6

Stakeholder Relationships

Which of the following is **not** typically used to protect creditors' rights?

A Proxy voting

B Collateral to secure debt obligations

C The imposition of a covenant to limit a company's debt level

Solution:

A is correct. Proxy voting is a practice adopted by shareholders, not creditors. B and C are incorrect because both collateral and covenants are used by creditors to help mitigate the default risk of a company.

BOARD OF DIRECTORS AND COMMITTEES

5

As discussed earlier in the reading, the board of directors is a central component of a company's governance structure. The board serves as the link between shareholders and managers and acts as the shareholders' monitoring tool within the company. As the relevance of corporate governance has grown within the investment field, the responsibilities of the board of directors have also increased in importance.

5.1 Composition of the Board of Directors

The structure and composition of a board of directors vary by company and geography. There is no single or optimal structure, and the number of directors may differ depending on the company size, structure, and complexity of operations. Most corporate governance codes require that the board include a diverse mix of expertise, backgrounds, and competencies. Such qualifications may include specialized knowledge of the company's industry as well as experience in certain functions, such as strategy, finance/audit, risk management, human resources, or legal. Moreover, many companies seek age, gender, and racial diversity in board composition.

Boards with one-tier structures comprise a mix of executive and non-executive directors. Executive (or internal) directors are employed by the company and are typically members of senior management. Non-executive (or external) directors provide objective decision making, monitoring, and performance assessment. Additionally, non-executive directors can serve an important role in challenging management and using past expertise in strategy and board issues. An *independent director* is a specific type of non-executive director that does not have a material relationship with the company with regard to employment, ownership, or remuneration.

In two-tier structures, the supervisory and management boards are independent from each other. Regulators generally prohibit members of the management board from serving on the supervisory board or limit the number of individuals serving on both boards. Employee representatives are typically elected by the company's employees and could make up half of the supervisory board in large companies.

In many countries, the chief executive officer (CEO) and chairperson roles are increasingly separated. In the United States, many companies have historically had "CEO duality," in which the CEO also serves as chairperson of the board. Nevertheless, the percentage of companies separating the two roles, particularly in the United States, has increased considerably in recent years. The appointment of a lead independent director is an alternative that is sometimes practiced by boards of companies without CEO duality. The lead independent director generally has the authority to request and oversee meetings of all independent directors. Duality is not applicable in two-tier structures that prohibit the members of the management board from serving on the supervisory board. In these models, the chairperson of the supervisory board is typically external and the CEO usually chairs the management board.

Staggered Boards

The general practice for boards is that elections occur simultaneously and for specified terms (three years, for example). Some companies, however, have **staggered boards** whereby directors are typically divided into three classes that are elected separately in consecutive years—that is, one class every year. Because shareholders would need several years to replace a full board, this election process limits their ability to effect a major change of control at the company. This staggered board model was historically prevalent in the United States but has been generally replaced by regular board election terms. In contrast, the practice is common in Australia.

5.2 Functions and Responsibilities of the Board

As mentioned earlier, a company's board of directors is elected by shareholders to act on their behalf. In fulfilling their functions, directors have a responsibility to consider the interests of all stakeholders. The duties of directors are mandated by law in many countries but vary across jurisdictions. Two widely established elements of directors' responsibilities are the *duty of care* and the *duty of loyalty*. According to the OECD's *Principles of Corporate Governance*, duty of care "requires board members to act on a fully informed basis, in good faith, with due diligence and care." The OECD further notes that duty of loyalty "is the duty of the board member to act in the interest of the company and shareholders. The duty of loyalty should prevent individual board members from acting in their own interest, or the interest of another individual or group, at the expense of the company and all shareholders."

A board of directors does not typically engage in the company's day-to-day activities; rather, those activities are delegated to management. The board guides and approves the company's strategic direction, taking into consideration the company's risk profile. It delegates the implementation of the company's strategy to senior management, oversees the execution of the strategy, and establishes milestones to monitor the progress in reaching the objectives. The board also reviews corporate performance and determines relevant courses of action accordingly. In doing so, the board can monitor and evaluate management's performance and determine whether senior executive remuneration is aligned with the long-term interests of the company. The board is also responsible for selecting, appointing, and terminating the employment of senior managers (or the management board in case of a two-tier structure). One of the board's main responsibilities is to ensure leadership continuity though succession planning for the CEO and other key executives.

The board plays a central role in ensuring the effectiveness of the company's audit and control systems. It sets the overall structure of these systems and oversees their implementation, including oversight of the financial reporting practices and the review of the financial statements for fairness and accuracy. The board also oversees reports by internal audit, the audit committee, and the external auditors and proposes and follows up on remedial actions. The board has the ultimate responsibility to ensure that the company adopts and implements proper corporate governance principles and complies with all applicable internal and external laws and regulations, including ethical standards.

In addition, the board typically ensures that the company has an appropriate enterprise risk management system in place, whereby risks are identified, mitigated, assessed, and managed appropriately. The board monitors the effectiveness of these systems through regular reviews and reports received from both management and the company's risk function. The board also has the responsibility to review any proposals for corporate transactions or changes, such as major capital acquisitions, divestures, mergers, and acquisitions, before they are referred to shareholders for approval, if applicable.

5.3 Board of Directors Committees

A company's board of directors typically establishes committees that focus on specific functions. Such committees, in turn, provide recommendations that are reported to the board on a regular basis. Despite the delegation of responsibilities to committees, the overall board remains ultimately responsible to shareholders and is not discharged of its liabilities to shareholders. Although board committees may vary by organization, some of the most common committees are discussed in the following sections.

5.3.1 *Audit Committee*

The audit committee is perhaps the most common board committee among companies worldwide. The audit committee plays a key role in overseeing the audit and control systems at the company and ensuring their effectiveness. In this regard, the committee monitors the financial reporting process, including the application of accounting policies; ensures the integrity of financial statements; supervises the internal audit function and ensures its independence and competence; and presents an annual audit plan to the board and monitors its implementation by the internal audit function. The audit committee is also responsible for recommending the appointment of an independent external auditor and proposing the auditor's remuneration. Both internal and external auditors report their findings to the audit committee, which in turn proposes remedial action for highlighted issues or matters.

5.3.2 *Governance Committee*

The primary role of the governance (or corporate governance) committee is to ensure that the company adopts good corporate governance practices. In doing so, the committee develops and oversees the implementation of the corporate governance code, the charters of the board and its committees, and the company's code of ethics and conflict of interest policy. The governance committee reviews these policies on a regular basis to incorporate any regulatory requirements or relevant developments in the field. Most importantly, the committee monitors the implementation of the governance policies and standards as well as the compliance with the applicable laws and regulations throughout the company. Remedial actions are recommended if any flaws or breaches of laws or regulations are identified. In some companies, the governance committee may be responsible for overseeing an annual evaluation of the board to ensure that its structure and activities are aligned with the governance principles.

5.3.3 *Remuneration or Compensation Committee*

The remuneration (or compensation) committee of the board specializes in remuneration matters. This committee develops and proposes remuneration policies for the directors and key executives and presents them for approval by the board or by shareholders. The committee may also be involved in handling the contracts of managers and directors as well as in setting performance criteria and evaluating the performance of managers. The responsibilities of the remuneration committee may extend to establishing human resources policies for the company when remuneration matters are involved. In some companies, the remuneration committee also sets and oversees the implementation of employee benefit plans, including insurance, pension, severance benefits, and retirement plans (including monitoring investment performance of benefit plan funds).

5.3.4 *Nomination Committee*

The nomination committee identifies candidates who are qualified to serve as directors and recommends their nomination for election by shareholders. The committee also establishes the nomination procedures and policies, including the criteria for board directors, the search process, and the identification of qualified candidates for director positions. Director independence, including what constitutes an independent director, is also a function of the nomination committee. Through these roles, the nomination committee can help ensure that the board's composition is well balanced and aligned with the company's governance principles.

5.3.5 *Risk Committee*

The risk committee assists the board in determining the risk policy, profile, and appetite of the company. Accordingly, the committee oversees establishing enterprise risk management plans and monitors their implementation. It also supervises the risk management functions in the company, receives regular reports, and reports on its findings and recommendations to the board.

5.3.6 *Investment Committee*

The investment committee of the board reviews material investment opportunities proposed by management and considers their viability for the company. Such opportunities may include large projects, acquisitions, and expansion plans, as well as divestures or major asset disposals. The committee often challenges, when necessary, management assumptions underlying investment prospects, monitors the performance of investments, and reports its findings to the board. The committee also is typically responsible for establishing and revising the investment strategy and policies of the company.

The specific board committees discussed in previous sections are the most commonly used, although the composition and number of committees may vary depending on the jurisdiction or on company-specific factors (e.g., company size, industry, complexity of operations, or regulatory requirements). An audit committee, for instance, is a regulatory requirement in a large number of jurisdictions. For banks and other financial institutions, a risk committee is strongly recommended by some regulators and required by others. In Brazil, the Central Bank of Brazil requires financial institutions to establish a remuneration committee at the board level. Some companies choose to combine two or more committees into one—for example, a nomination and remuneration (or compensation) committee or an audit and risk committee. Companies may also find it valuable to establish committees with other specializations, such as a compliance committee, an ethics committee, a human resources committee, or a health/environmental/safety committee.

The composition of a board committee is normally aligned with its scope of responsibilities. For instance, many regulators request that executive (internal) directors do not rule on matters underlying conflicts of interest or on matters requiring an unbiased judgment (such as audit, remuneration, or related-party transaction matters). As such, a large number of rules, including those adopted by the London Stock Exchange and the New York Stock Exchange, require that the audit and the compensation committees be composed of independent directors only. Less stringent regulations, such as those of the Gulf Cooperation Council, require the audit committee to be composed of external (non-executive) directors, the majority of which should be independent (including the chairperson).

EXAMPLE 7

Responsibilities of Board Committees

A primary responsibility of a board's audit committee does **not** include the:

A proper application of accounting policies.

B adoption of proper corporate governance.

C recommendation of remuneration for the external auditor(s).

Solution:

B is correct. The adoption of proper corporate governance is the responsibility of a corporation's governance committee. Both A and C are incorrect because proper application of accounting policies and the remuneration of external auditors fall under the domain of the audit committee.

FACTORS AFFECTING STAKEHOLDER RELATIONSHIPS AND CORPORATE GOVERNANCE 6

This section explores ways in which certain factors, both market and non-market related, can affect stakeholder relationships and corporate governance. For this section, market factors include those that relate to capital markets whereas non-market factors do not.

6.1 Market Factors

This section focuses on shareholder engagement, shareholder activism, and competitive forces, all of which are influential market factors for a company. Shareholder engagement involves a company's interactions with its shareholders, whereas shareholder activism describes the efforts by shareholders to create a change within a corporation or modify a corporation's behavior. Meanwhile, competitive dynamics can help align managerial interests with those of its stakeholders.

6.1.1 *Shareholder Engagement*

The engagement of companies with shareholders—called **shareholder engagement**—has traditionally involved certain events, such as the annual shareholder meeting and analyst calls, the scope of which was limited to financial and strategic matters. There is a growing trend, however, for greater engagement between companies and their shareholders beyond these venues and topics. Companies have increasingly recognized the benefits that frequent, year-round engagement with shareholders can provide, such as building support against short-term activist investors, countering negative recommendations from proxy advisory firms, and receiving greater support for management's position.

6.1.2 *Shareholder Activism*

Shareholder activism refers to strategies used by shareholders to attempt to compel a company to act in a desired manner. Although shareholder activism can focus on a range of issues, including those involving social or political considerations, the primary motivation of activist shareholders is to increase shareholder value. Activist shareholders often pressure management through such tactics as initiating proxy battles (fights), proposing shareholder resolutions, and publicly raising awareness on issues of contention.

Shareholder activists may pursue additional tactics, such as shareholder derivative lawsuits, which are legal proceedings initiated by one or more shareholders against board directors, management, and/or controlling shareholders of the company. The theory behind this type of lawsuit is that the plaintiff shareholder is deemed to be acting on behalf of the company in place of its directors and officers who have failed to adequately act for the benefit of the company and its shareholders. In many countries, however, the law restricts shareholders from pursuing legal action via the court system—in some cases, by imposing thresholds that enable only shareholders with interests above a minimum amount to pursue legal actions or by denying legal action altogether.

Hedge funds are among the most predominant shareholder activists. Compared with most traditional institutional investors, the fee structure of hedge funds often provides a significant stake in the financial success of any activist campaign. Furthermore, unlike regulated investment entities that are typically subject to restrictions on their investments (e.g., limitations on leverage or ownership of distressed or illiquid securities), hedge funds are loosely regulated and can thus pursue a greater range of activist opportunities.

6.1.3 *Competition and Takeovers*

Metrics that measure a company's success, such as market share or earnings growth, provide information that is useful for shareholders to judge the performance of a company's management team or board of directors and compare such performance with that of competitors. Senior managers risk their employment status in the event of underperformance, and directors, in turn, can be voted out by shareholders.

The traditional view of the market for corporate control (often known as the takeover market) is one in which shareholders of a company hire and fire management to achieve better resource utilization. Corporate takeovers can be pursued in several different ways. One mechanism is the **proxy contest** (or proxy fight). In a proxy contest, shareholders are persuaded to vote for a group seeking a controlling position on a company's board of directors. Managerial teams can also be displaced through a **tender offer**, which involves shareholders selling their interests directly to the group seeking to gain control. A contest for corporate control may attract arbitrageurs and takeover specialists, who facilitate transfers of control by accumulating long positions from existing shareholders in the target company and later selling the positions to the highest bidder. Finally, a **hostile takeover** is an attempt by one entity to acquire a company without the consent of the company's management.

Preservation of their employment status serves as an incentive for board members and managers to focus on shareholder wealth maximization. This threat of removal, however, can also have negative implications for a company's corporate governance practices if the company chooses to adopt anti-takeover measures, such as a staggered board or a shareholder rights plan (also known as a poison pill) to reduce the likelihood of an unwanted takeover. Staggering director elections can dilute the value of shareholder voting rights by extending the term that each director serves and eliminating the ability of shareholders to replace the entire board at any given election. Shareholder rights plans enable shareholders to buy additional shares at a discount if another shareholder purchases a certain percentage of the company's shares. These plans are designed to increase the cost to any bidder seeking to take over a company.

EXAMPLE 8

Shareholder Activism

Which of the following is true of shareholder activism?

A Shareholder activists rarely include hedge funds.

B Regulators play a prominent role in shareholder activism.

C A primary goal of shareholder activism is to increase shareholder value.

Solution:

C is correct. Although the subject of shareholder activism may involve social and political issues, activist shareholders' primary motivation is to increase shareholder value. A is incorrect because hedge funds commonly serve as shareholder activists. B is incorrect because regulators play a prominent role in standard setting, not shareholder activism.

6.2 Non-market Factors

This section focuses on certain non-market factors, such as a company's legal environment, the role of the media, and the corporate governance industry, that can have an effect on stakeholder relationships and corporate governance.

6.2.1 *Legal Environment*

The legal environment in which a company operates can significantly influence the rights and remedies of stakeholders. Countries that have a common law system (such as the United Kingdom, the United States, India, and Canada) are generally considered to offer superior protection of the interests of shareholders and creditors relative to those that have adopted a civil law system (such as France, Germany, Italy, and Japan). The key difference between the two systems lies in the ability of a judge to create laws. In civil law systems, laws are created primarily through statutes and codes enacted by the legislature. The role of judges is generally limited to rigidly applying the statutes and codes to the specific case brought before the court. In contrast, in common law systems, laws are created both from statutes enacted by the legislature and by judges through judicial opinions. In common law systems, shareholders and creditors have the ability to appeal to a judge to rule against management actions and decisions that are not expressly forbidden by statute or code, whereas in civil law systems, this option is generally not possible.

Regardless of a country's legal system, creditors are generally more successful in seeking remedies in court to enforce their rights than shareholders are because shareholder disputes often involve complex legal theories, such as whether a manager or director breached a duty owed to shareholders. In contrast, disputes involving creditors, such as whether the terms of an indenture or other debt contract have been breached, are more straightforward and therefore are more easily determinable by a court.

6.2.2 *The Media*

The media can affect corporate governance and influence stakeholder relationships through its ability to spread information quickly and shape public opinion. As an example, negative media attention can adversely affect the reputation or public perception of a company or its managers and directors. Senior management's concern over reputational risk can thus reduce the cost of monitoring management activities by stakeholders. Media attention can motivate politicians and regulators to introduce corporate governance reforms or enforce laws that protect stakeholders and society at large. This influence was evident in the aftermath of the 2008–2009 financial crisis, when significant media attention was a factor in the adoption of new laws and regulations designed to address perceived deficiencies in corporate governance.

Social media has become a powerful tool that stakeholders have increasingly used to protect their interests or enhance their influence on corporate matters. Prior to the advent of social media, companies typically had an advantage in distributing information because of their considerable resources as well as relationships with traditional media organizations. Through social media, stakeholders can instantly broadcast information with little cost or effort and are better able to compete with company management in influencing public sentiment.

6.2.3 *The Corporate Governance Industry*

An important catalyst for the rise of the corporate governance industry occurred in 2003, when the Securities and Exchange Commission (SEC) required US-registered mutual funds to disclose their proxy voting records annually. The same rule also required US mutual funds to adopt policies and procedures designed to reasonably ensure that proxies would be voted in the best interests of their clients. In the years following the SEC's 2003 mutual fund rule, institutional investors have, to varying degrees, committed additional resources to monitor and vote proxies for the large number of companies in which they invest.

With the increased importance and relevance of corporate governance among investors, the demand for external corporate governance services has grown considerably. In particular, some institutional investors have retained outside experts to assist with corporate governance monitoring and proxy voting. In response to this demand, an industry that provides corporate governance services, including governance ratings and proxy advice, has developed. Because the corporate governance industry is relatively concentrated, these vendors have considerable influence in corporate governance practices, and in turn, corporations are generally compelled to pay attention to ratings and recommendations produced by the corporate governance industry.

7 CORPORATE GOVERNANCE AND STAKEHOLDER MANAGEMENT RISKS AND BENEFITS

As illustrated thus far, good corporate governance and stakeholder management can have a meaningfully positive effect on a company. A company will likely not meet the expectations of all stakeholders if one group is able to extract private benefits at the expense of another group. Depending on their nature and magnitude, unmanaged conflicts of interest and weak control over a company's operations may expose the company to various risks, such as legal, regulatory, reputational, or default risks. By adopting effective guidelines for managing the interests of stakeholder groups and instituting adequate levels of control, corporate governance can be reflected in better company relationships, superior levels of efficiency in operations, and improved financial performance.

7.1 Risks of Poor Governance and Stakeholder Management

Weaknesses in stakeholder management mechanisms or the adoption of poor governance structures can create various risks for a company and its stakeholders. A weak control environment can encourage misconduct and hinder the ability of the company to identify and manage risks.

7.1.1 *Weak Control Systems*

In a company with weak control systems or inefficient monitoring tools, such as poor audit procedures or insufficient scrutiny by the board, one stakeholder group may benefit at the expense of the company or other stakeholders. This could consequently have an adverse effect on the company's resources, performance, and value. The audit deficiencies at Enron, for instance, prevented the uncovering of the acts of fraud, erroneous accounting records, and other related issues that led to one of the largest corporate bankruptcies in US history.

7.1.2 *Ineffective Decision Making*

When the quality and quantity of information available to managers are superior to those available to the board or shareholders, in the absence of sufficient monitoring tools, managers have an opportunity to make decisions that benefit themselves relative to the company or shareholders. Without proper scrutiny, such practices might go unnoticed. Deficient decisions could include managing the company with a lower risk profile relative to shareholders' tolerance, thus avoiding investment opportunities that could create value for the company. Conversely, manager overconfidence may result in poor investment decisions without proper examination of their effect on the company or on shareholders' wealth.

Remuneration policies for management could also have significant implications for the company. Outsized remuneration packages for executives could have an adverse effect on shareholders' wealth, constitute a burden on corporate performance, and affect the interests of other stakeholders, such as employees, customers, or creditors. Remuneration policies that are not carefully designed may also encourage managers to seek immediate personal gains by taking excessive risks or focusing on creating short-term performance or stock price increases. Related-party transactions that underlie unfair terms for the company are another example of activities that are not aligned with the objective of value creation and that could be facilitated by a poor governance system.

7.1.3 *Legal, Regulatory, and Reputational Risks*

Compliance weaknesses in the implementation of regulatory requirements or lack of proper reporting practices may expose the company to legal, regulatory, or reputational risks. In such cases, the company may become subject to investigation by government or regulatory authorities for violation of applicable laws. A company could also be exposed to lawsuits filed by shareholders, employees, creditors, or other parties for breach of contractual agreements or company bylaws or for violation of stakeholders' legal rights. In today's markets, information flows rapidly. Improperly managed conflicts of interest or governance failures could bring reputational damage to the company, and its associated costs could be significant. Such risks are particularly acute for publicly listed companies subject to scrutiny by investors, analysts, and other market participants.

7.1.4 *Default and Bankruptcy Risks*

Poor corporate governance, including weak management of creditors' interests, can affect the company's financial position and may hinder its ability to honor its debt obligations. To the extent that the deterioration of corporate performance results in a debt default, the company may be exposed to bankruptcy risk if creditors choose to take legal action. The adverse consequences of corporate failures are not limited to the company's shareholders; they extend to other stakeholders, such as managers and employees and even society and the environment.

7.2 Benefits of Effective Governance and Stakeholder Management

The development of good governance practices can play a vital role in aligning the interests of managers and the board of directors with those of shareholders, while balancing the interests of the company's stakeholders. A good governance structure can be reflected in operational efficiency, improved control processes, better financial performance, and lower levels of risk.

7.2.1 *Operational Efficiency*

As part of a good governance structure, an organization clarifies the delegation of responsibilities and reporting lines across the company and ensures that all employees have a clear understanding of their respective duties. When balanced with adequate internal control mechanisms, the governance structure can ensure that corporate decisions and activities are properly monitored and controlled to mitigate risk and help improve the operational efficiency of the company.

7.2.2 *Improved Control*

Governance practices seek to institute more effective control exercised at all corporate levels, from shareholders to the board of directors and management. These practices can help identify and manage risk at early stages that can otherwise hinder corporate performance and/or damage reputation. Control can be enhanced by the proper functioning of a company's audit committee and the effectiveness of its audit systems. By adopting procedures for monitoring compliance with internal policies and external regulations and for reporting any violations, the company can better mitigate regulatory or legal risks and their associated costs. Additionally, the adoption of formal procedures with regard to conflicts of interest and related-party transactions allows the company to ensure fairness in its relationships with those parties.

7.2.3 *Better Operating and Financial Performance*

Good governance and stakeholder management can help a company improve its operating performance and reduce the costs associated with weak control systems. The costs of poor investments, legal proceedings against the company, and excessive perquisites are just a few examples that could be mitigated by well-functioning governance systems. Enhanced corporate governance could also allow the company to improve its decision-making process and respond faster to market factors. Proper remuneration policies are another governance tool that can motivate managers to make decisions with the objective of creating corporate value.

7.2.4 *Lower Default Risk and Cost of Debt*

Good corporate governance can lower business and investment risk. Governance arrangements that manage conflicts of interest with creditors, and that help protect creditor rights, can reduce a company's cost of debt and default risk. Default risk can also often be mitigated by proper functioning of audit systems, improved transparency (e.g., reporting of earnings), and the control of information asymmetries between the company and its capital providers. With regard to credit risk, corporate governance mechanisms have become increasingly relevant criteria among credit rating agencies when assessing a company's creditworthiness.

EXAMPLE 9

Benefits of Corporate Governance

Which of the following is **not** a benefit of an effective corporate governance structure?

- **A** Operating performance can be improved.
- **B** A corporation's cost of debt can be reduced.
- **C** Corporate decisions and activities require less control.

Solution:

C is correct. A benefit of an effective corporate governance system is to enable adequate scrutiny and control over operations. B is incorrect because an effective governance structure can reduce investors' perceived credit risk of a corporation, thus potentially lowering the corporation's cost of debt. A is incorrect because operating efficiency may indeed be a benefit of an effective corporate governance structure.

ANALYST CONSIDERATIONS IN CORPORATE GOVERNANCE AND STAKEHOLDER MANAGEMENT

8

In the past, analysts may have considered corporate governance and stakeholder management issues to be only peripherally related to traditional fundamental analysis. Generally, these issues were seen as obscure and unlikely to be material drivers of performance. Following a number of governance failures since the early 2000s, the global financial crisis, and the rise of shareholder activism around the world, there is little doubt that governance and stakeholder issues have become increasingly important topics for analysts.

Some key questions that analysts may consider when assessing a company's corporate governance or stakeholder management system are as follows:

- What is the company's ownership and voting structure among shareholders?
- Who represents shareholders on this company's board?
- What are the main drivers of the management team's remuneration and incentive structure?
- Who are the significant investors in the company?
- How robust are the shareholder rights at the company, including relative to peers?
- How effectively is the company managing long-term risks, such as securing access to necessary resources, managing human capital, exhibiting integrity and leadership, and strengthening the long-term sustainability of the enterprise?

A qualitative analysis of these issues—typically provided by a company's proxy statements, annual reports, and sustainability reports, if available—can provide important insights about the quality of management and sources of potential risk.

8.1 Economic Ownership and Voting Control

Generally speaking, corporations with publicly traded equity have a voting structure that involves one vote for each share. That is, any shareholder's voting power is equal to the percentage of the company's outstanding shares owned by that shareholder. When there are exceptions to this norm and economic ownership becomes separated from control, investors can face significant potential risks.

In a small number of markets, dual-class structures are allowed under the local regulatory framework or exchange rules, which is the most common way that voting power is decoupled from ownership. In these cases, common shares may be divided into two classes, one of which has superior voting rights to the other. A common arrangement is when a share class (for example, Class A) carries one vote per share and is publicly traded whereas another share class (for example, Class B) carries several votes per share and is held exclusively by company insiders or family members. This structure is used by Facebook, for example. In this way, the founders and/or insiders of a company may continue to control board elections, strategic decisions, and all other significant voting matters for a long period—even once their ownership level declines to less than 50% of the company's shares.

Another mechanism used to separate voting control from economic ownership is when one class of stock (held by insiders) elects a majority of the board; outside shareholders who hold a different share class would then be entitled to elect only a minority of the board. Technically, each share carries equal voting rights, but with this structure, the insiders retain substantial power over the affairs of the corporation because they control a majority of the board. Alibaba's partnership structure is one example of this type of control.

Proponents of dual share systems, such as those just mentioned, argue that the systems promote company stability and enable management to make long-term strategic investments, insulated from the short-term pressures of outside investors. Critics of these structures believe they create conflicts of interest between the providers of capital and the management of the business.

It is virtually impossible for outside investors to dismantle dual-class structures because of the inherent design of their unequal voting rights. Therefore, these structures can remain in place even through generational changes within a founding family. Investors with long time horizons may want to consider the motivations of the controlling stockholders, generational dynamics, succession planning, and the relationship between the board and management. In addition, there may be potential valuation implications because dual-class companies tend to trade at a discount to their peers.

8.2 Board of Directors Representation

In most markets, investors have access to basic biographical information about the non-executive members of corporate boards. Analysts can assess the available information to determine whether the experience and skill sets on the board match the current and future needs of the company.

In particular, questions regarding directors' independence, tenure, experience, and diversity may bring useful investment insights. For example, if the board has multiple directors engaging in related-party transactions with the company, investors may have cause for concern about any conflicts of interest that arise. The issue of board tenure can also be a useful tool for investors. Directors with long periods of service to a company clearly offer valuable experience and expertise, but if the board composition is dominated by such long-tenured members, it may have a negative effect on the board's diversity and adaptability.

An example in which board composition had a significant effect on company performance occurred at a European pharmaceutical company. At one point in its history, the company had become overleveraged and faced significant financial distress. In response, non-executive directors with banking and turnaround experience were added to the board. With the help of these directors, the company recovered. Seven years later, the most promising product in the company's pharmaceutical portfolio began to cause serious side effects in its patient population. The situation required both a meaningful understanding of the medical issues involved and a rapid response from the company. However, the board was still composed of directors with financial expertise rather than medical training. The company struggled with its response to the crisis, and its stock price fell sharply. This situation was one in which the board's composition had been ideal for a certain point in the company's history, but ultimately the directors failed to refresh the board's membership as the needs of the business changed.

8.3 Remuneration and Company Performance

The availability and quality of information about executive remuneration plans varies widely across markets. In those markets where such disclosures are available, analysts can assess the elements of the remuneration program to determine whether they support or conflict with the key drivers of performance for the company.

Generally speaking, current executive remuneration programs consist of a base salary, a short-term bonus usually delivered in the form of cash, and a multi-year incentive plan delivered in one or more forms of equity (options, time-vested shares, and/or performance-vested shares). Often, these short-term and long-term plans are contingent on achieving financial or operational objectives, and often these objectives are disclosed. In these situations, an analyst can assess whether the primary drivers of the remuneration plan are the same factors that, in the analyst's view, drive overall company results.

Assessment of the suitability of a remuneration plan for a particular company is a subjective exercise and is highly dependent on industry and geographic norms. But there are some warning signs that may warrant particular scrutiny:

- **Plans offering little alignment with shareholders.** As an example, if a plan offers only cash-based payouts and no equity, there may be a misalignment of incentives between executives and investors unless management already owns a significant stake in the company.
- **Plans exhibiting little variation in results over multiple years.** If an award is described as performance-based but still pays in full every year regardless of the company's results, investors may have concerns about the rigor of the performance hurdles underlying the awards.
- **Plans with excessive payouts relative to comparable companies with comparable performance.** Investors may want to understand the cause of the anomaly and whether it is a temporary issue or a result of flawed remuneration plan design.
- **Plans that may have specific strategic implications.** As an example, some remuneration plans contain payouts tied to specific milestones, such as regulatory approval of a product, completion of an acquisition, or achievement of specific cost reductions. In addition, some companies offer particularly high post-employment pay arrangements tied to the sale of the company, whereas

others offer no such arrangements. These factors are not necessarily negative features, but investors may want to understand whether the milestones driving the incentive plan align with the company's objectives.

- **Plans based on incentives from an earlier period in the company's life cycle.** A frequent example of such a plan relates to a company that has matured beyond its fast growth phase. The company's business may have matured, and competition may have limited the opportunity for market share gains. Investors may believe the company should become more focused on both returns and disciplined capital allocation. Even after the company communicates to the investor community a more returns-oriented strategy, the financial incentives in the remuneration plan may still be based purely on revenue growth. Investors may want to understand such potential misalignment of interests.

8.4 Investors in the Company

Examining the composition of investors in a company can be another source of useful insight for analysts. The behavior of these investors can result in both limitations and catalysts with regard to changes in the corporation. For example, cross-shareholdings are still prevalent in a number of markets. This situation occurs when a company, particularly a publicly listed one, holds a large, passive, minority stake in another company. Such holdings generally help to protect management from shareholder pressures because implicit in a cross-shareholding arrangement is the guarantee that the owner of the shares will support management on all voting issues. In effect, these shareholdings act as takeover defenses.

Similarly, the presence of a sizable affiliated stockholder (such as an individual, family trust, endowment, or private equity fund) can shield a company from the effects of voting by outside shareholders. As an example, a US consumer goods company has an affiliated charitable foundation that owns more than 20% of the outstanding shares. The company also has a provision in its corporate charter requiring that any changes to the charter must be approved by two-thirds of outstanding shares. As a result, it is virtually impossible for any measure to pass without the support of the foundation. The interests of the foundation thus conflict with the interests of the overall shareholder base. In effect, this single minority shareholder most likely holds the power to block the votes of the majority.

Analysts should note that market context is important in assessing the potential effects of affiliated stockholders. In certain countries, the presence of such shareholders is common, viewed by local market participants as a means of enhancing stability, strengthening the relationship between companies and their business partners, and fostering a long-term perspective by protecting the company against hostile takeover bids.

A final aspect of investor composition that has become increasingly relevant relates to activist shareholders, which we discussed earlier. The presence of activist shareholders can meaningfully and rapidly change the investment thesis for a company. Experienced activists, together with short-term-oriented investors who follow their activities, can create substantial turnover in a company's shareholder composition in a short amount of time. This is because an activist often serves as a catalyst for new strategic alternatives at a company and can attract new investors and/or arbitrageurs.

8.5 Strength of Shareholders' Rights

Within a framework of regional regulations and corporate governance codes, analysts may want to understand whether the shareholder rights of a particular company are strong, weak, or average compared with other companies. For example, if an analyst's viewpoint includes the possibility that a company will merge in the future, he or she may want to understand whether there are significant structural obstacles to transactions that are embedded in the company's charter or bylaws. Similarly, if the thesis involves an outside catalyst, such as an activist shareholder who will introduce change at the company and improve performance, the analyst must take a position on whether shareholders are sufficiently empowered to advance such a change. If it is impossible for shareholders to remove directors from the board or to convene special stockholder meetings, it will be difficult for external initiatives to be successful.

In a number of developed markets, including the United Kingdom, the Netherlands, and Japan, regulatory agencies or stock exchanges have adopted governance codes, which are standards of governance reflecting local investors' expectations with regard to disclosure, board composition, shareholder rights, and other related issues. Often, these governance codes are implemented on a "comply or explain" basis, which indicates that standards are voluntary in nature. However, any deviation from the code must be explained by the company in a public disclosure. If a company has elected to deviate from the locally accepted governance practice, the analyst may want to understand the reasoning behind the decision.

8.6 Managing Long-Term Risks

Analysts may uncover useful insights regarding how a company manages various issues, such as long-term environmental risks, management of human capital, transparency, and treatment of investors and other stakeholders. Of particular note, the academic evidence linking these and other management quality issues to share price performance remains mixed, in part because indicators of management quality are often correlated with each other and, therefore, difficult to isolate. However, poor stakeholder relations and inadequate management of long-term risks have indeed had an enormous negative effect on share value in certain instances. Therefore, analysts may consider the assessment of such issues to be a useful component of their overall risk assessment of the company.

One way to evaluate management quality issues is to assess whether the company demonstrates a persistent pattern of wrongdoings, fines, regulatory penalties, investigations, and the like. A notable example is Toshiba Corp., beginning in 2015 when an investigation revealed that company managers had manufactured nearly $2 billion in profits since 2008. Poor internal controls allowed the fraudulent accounting to remain undetected for seven years. Over the next several years, Toshiba experienced the massive write-down of its Westinghouse Electric Co. unit, clashes with its auditors, negative equity, and legal disputes. Toshiba's dividend was withdrawn, Westinghouse filed for bankruptcy protection, and the company was forced to sell its profitable semiconductor unit along with other business units. Ultimately, the company's shares were moved to the second section of Tokyo's stock exchange, triggering forced sales from funds that track the first section (Topix) or the Nikkei 250 indexes. Even in the absence of circumstances as extreme as these, poor management of stakeholder interests can have a significant effect on company operations, reputation, and valuation.

8.7 Summary of Analyst Considerations

The analysis of corporate governance, stakeholder management, and other non-financial (often termed "extra-financial") considerations is inherently a subjective exercise. Governance practices that may raise the risk profile of one company may be perfectly acceptable in a different context, depending on geographic norms, mitigating circumstances, or the investor's risk tolerance and investment thesis. In this section, we have provided a basic framework for investors interested in uncovering incremental insights about a company by analyzing its governance standards, practices, and risks.

EXAMPLE 10

Analyst Considerations

1 Which of the following *best* describes dual-class share structures?

A Dual-class share structures can be easily changed over time.

B Company insiders can maintain significant power over the organization.

C Conflicts of interest between management and stakeholder groups are less likely than with single share structures.

2 An investment analyst would likely be *most* concerned with an executive remuneration plan that:

A varies each year.

B is consistent with a company's competitors.

C is cash-based only, without an equity component.

3 Which of the following *best* describes activist shareholders? Activist shareholders:

A help stabilize a company's strategic direction.

B have little effect on the company's long-term investors.

C can alter the composition of a company's shareholder base.

Solution to 1:

B is correct. Under dual-class share systems, company founders or insiders may control board elections, strategic decisions, and other significant voting matters. A is incorrect because dual share systems are virtually impossible to dismantle once adopted. C is incorrect because conflicts of interest between management and stakeholders are more likely than with single share structures because of the potential control element under dual systems.

Solution to 2:

C is correct. If an executive remuneration plan offers cash only, the incentives between management and investors and other stakeholders may be misaligned. A is incorrect because a plan that varies over time would typically be of less concern to an analyst compared with one that did not change. B is incorrect because an analyst would likely be concerned if a company's executives were excessively compensated relative to competitors.

Solution to 3:

C is correct. The presence of activist shareholders can create substantial turnover in the company's shareholder composition. A is incorrect because the presence of activist shareholders can materially change a company's strategic direction. B is incorrect because long-term investors in a company need to consider how activist shareholders affect the company.

9 ESG CONSIDERATIONS FOR INVESTORS

The inclusion of governance factors in investment analysis has evolved considerably. Management and accountability structures are relatively transparent, and information regarding them is widely available. Also, the risks of poor corporate governance have long been understood by analysts and shareholders. In contrast, the practice of considering environmental and social factors, which collectively with governance form the commonly used acronym "ESG," has evolved more slowly. A large number of environmental and social issues exist, and identifying which factors are likely to affect company performance is not an easy task. Issues driving the inclusion of environmental and social information in the investment process include scarcity of natural resources, climate change, global economic and demographic trends, and societal evolution. Although ESG factors were once regarded as intangible or qualitative information, refinements in the identification and analysis of such factors, as well as increased corporate disclosures, have resulted in increasingly quantifiable information. Still, the process of reflecting quantitative ESG-related information and data in financial valuation is evolving.

9.1 ESG Terminology

Several ESG-related terms exist, and distinguishing among them can be challenging because of the lack of definitive terminology in the investment community. Among the most common—and broadest—terms are **sustainable investing** (SI) and **responsible investing** (RI). Both of these terms refer to identifying companies that, in an investor's view, efficiently manage their financial, environmental, and human capital resources to generate attractive long-term profitability; that is, the companies are deemed to have "sustainable" business models. Sustainable investing and responsible investing, along with the term **ESG investing**, generally refer to the consideration of ESG factors in the investment process.

Socially responsible investing (SRI) is a related term that tends to have multiple meanings, creating confusion among investors. Socially responsible investing has traditionally referred to the practice of excluding investments in companies or industries, such as weapons and defense, that deviate from an investor's beliefs. The term has evolved to include investment objectives that promote positive social attributes, often by investing in companies with favorable environmental or social profiles.

9.2 ESG Implementation Approaches

Implementation approaches to ESG range from *value*-based to *values*-based. The objective of a *value*-based approach is to mitigate risks and identify opportunities by analyzing ESG considerations in addition to traditional financial metrics. Conversely, the objective of a *values*-based approach is to express the moral or ethical beliefs of an investor. Between the value-based and values-based approaches lie a continuum of approaches that strives for value creation through values investing.

Specific ESG investment styles include negative screening, positive screening, **relative/best-in-class screening**, full integration, overlay/portfolio tilt, risk factor/risk premium investing, thematic investment, and engagement/active ownership. **Negative screening** is the exclusion of certain sectors, companies, or practices from a fund or portfolio on the basis of specific ESG criteria. Examples include excluding the fossil fuel extraction or production sector or excluding companies that deviate from accepted standards in areas such as human rights or environmental concerns. Many of these negative screens use a specific set of standards, such as the UN Global Compact's Ten Principles on human rights, labor, the environment, and corruption.

In contrast to negative screening, **positive screening** and relative/best-in-class approaches focus on investments with favorable ESG aspects. Positive screening, typically implemented through an ESG ranking or scoring approach, is the inclusion of certain sectors, companies, or practices in a fund or portfolio on the basis of specific ESG criteria. For example, positive screening may include seeking companies that promote employee rights, workplace well-being, and customer safety. Relative/

best-in-class screening is the investment in sectors, companies, or projects selected for ESG performance relative to industry peers. The relative/best-in-class approach does not exclude any industries but instead focuses on finding the best representation within each sector. This approach typically maintains sector weightings comparable to a relative benchmark index to avoid overweighting or underweighting risk exposures.

Full integration into individual stock valuation is the explicit inclusion of ESG factors into traditional financial analysis of individual stocks (e.g., as inputs into cash flow forecasts and/or cost-of-capital estimates). The focus of full integration is to identify risks and opportunities arising from ESG factors and to determine whether a company is properly managing its environmental, social, and governance resources in accordance with a sustainable business model.

Overlay/portfolio tilt is the use of certain investment strategies or products to change specific aggregate ESG characteristics of a fund or investment portfolio to a desired level (e.g., tilting an investment portfolio toward a desired carbon footprint). **Risk factor/risk premium investing** is the inclusion of ESG information in the analysis of systematic risks as, for example, in smart beta and factor investment strategies (similar to size, value, momentum, and growth strategies).

Thematic investment is investment in themes or assets specifically related to ESG factors, such as clean energy, green technology, or sustainable agriculture. This approach is often based on needs arising from economic or social trends. Two common ESG-related trends are increased demand for energy and water, as well as the availability of alternative sources of each. Global economic development has raised the demand for energy, whereas increased carbon emissions are believed to negatively affect the earth's climate. Similarly, rising global living standards and industrial needs have created a greater demand for water along with the need to prevent drought or increase access to clean drinking water in certain regions of the world.

Engagement/active ownership is the use of shareholder power to influence corporate behavior through direct corporate engagement (i.e., communicating with senior management and/or boards of companies), filing or co-filing shareholder proposals, and proxy voting that is directed by ESG guidelines. Engagement/active ownership seeks to achieve targeted social or environmental objectives along with measurable financial returns. Engagement/active ownership can be executed through various asset classes and investment vehicles and often through direct transactions, such as venture capital investing. Another example of engagement/active ownership relates to **green finance**. According to the Organisation for Economic Co-operation and Development (OECD), green finance relates to "achieving economic growth while reducing pollution and greenhouse gas emissions, minimising waste and improving efficiency in the use of natural resources."[5] As with other previously mentioned ESG terms, there are several definitions for green finance in practice. The primary investment vehicles used in green finance are **green bonds**, in which issuers earmark the proceeds towards environmental-related projects. Green bond issuance has grown significantly in recent years. According to the Climate Bond Initiative, total worldwide green bond issuance for 2017 totaled USD 163 billion, compared to USD 37 billion for 2014. The United States is the largest green bond market in the world, but China has quickly become the second-largest, accounting for 15% of global green bond issuance in 2017. China's first green bond was issued in July 2015 as the country has prioritized environmental projects to address air and water pollution issues resulting from its rapid growth.

5 http://www.oecd-ilibrary.org/environment/green-finance-and-investment_24090344

9.3 Catalysts for ESG Growth

ESG considerations have become increasingly relevant over the past several years after many investors suffered substantial losses from environmental disasters, social controversies, or governance deficiencies. In one notable example, the 2015 collapse of the Fundão tailings dam, constructed by Samarco Mineracao SA to restrain iron ore waste from mining, released more than 450,000 gallons of toxic water and sediment in Brazil's Doce river and nearby villages. The surrounding communities experienced the loss of more than a dozen lives and hundreds of homes as well as the destruction of their water supply and thousands of fish. Samarco was jointly owned by Vale SA and BHP Billiton Ltd and has since been shut down. Samarco paid millions of dollars in fines, and the three companies paid more than a billion dollars in clean-up costs. A number of executives from the three companies were charged with qualified homicide, and investors and local Brazilian governments filed tens of billions of dollars in lawsuits. The Brazilian government was also criticized for its lax oversight of mining companies because the region had suffered multiple dam failures in the decade prior to the Fundão disaster.

In addition to environmental issues, investors have become increasingly conscious of issues such as workplace, human rights, data privacy, and governance—and the costs associated with them. For example, lax cybersecurity measures at Equifax, Inc., led to a data breach and the theft of identity and financial data belonging to more than 140 million US citizens in 2017. Equifax has since incurred hundreds of millions of dollars in expenses resulting from the breach and has faced numerous lawsuits and investigations. An example of investor loss related to corporate governance occurred in 2015 at German automaker Volkswagen. Specifically, many investors believed that inadequate governance oversight at Volkswagen permitted more than 11 million of its diesel cars to pass emissions tests yet emit unlawful amounts of nitrogen oxide. Many investors attributed their losses to internal audit and compliance shortcomings, as well as a lack of independence in Volkswagen's board of directors. The company ultimately incurred several billion dollars of civil and criminal penalties.

Another investor development that has supported ESG growth is the adoption of more sophisticated views about sustainable growth and its effect on investment performance. To this end, some large institutional asset owners embrace the concept of being "universal owners." **Universal owners** are long-term investors, such as pension funds, that have significant assets invested in globally diversified portfolios. Given their size and scope, the investment portfolios of universal owners are linked to economic growth and unavoidably exposed to costs resulting from external factors, such as environmental damages. Because their funds' long-term performance and the interests of their beneficiaries are at stake, some universal owners strive to positively influence the way companies conduct business to minimize exposure to ESG-related costs. Institutions that adhere to the universal owner philosophy believe that sustainable global economic growth is essential to successful investment performance.

9.4 ESG Market Overview

Reflecting the growth of ESG-related information in the marketplace, the amount of global assets under management (AUM) dedicated to the consideration of ESG factors in portfolio selection and management has increased substantially. According to the Global Sustainable Investing Alliance (GSIA), a collaboration of organizations dedicated to advancing sustainable investing in the financial markets, nearly US$23 trillion of AUM were dedicated toward sustainable investment mandates as of year-end 2015. Europe (53%) and the United States (38%) accounted for the vast majority of these AUM. Determining the true size of the ESG investment universe is difficult, however, because managers and investors define and implement sustainable and ESG mandates in many different ways. There are often differences regarding which ESG factors should be considered—as well as how they are considered—in the investment process.

The increased interest in sustainable investing has led to increased corporate disclosures of ESG issues, as well as a growing number of companies that collect and analyze ESG data. In addition to the GSIA, several organizations have been formed to monitor and advance the mission of sustainable investing. For example, the Global Reporting Initiative (GRI), a non-profit organization formed in 1997, produces a sustainability reporting framework that measures and reports sustainability-related issues and performance. In 2006, the United Nations and a consortium of institutional investors launched the Principles of Responsible Investment (PRI) to support investors committed to including ESG issues into their investment decision-making and ownership practices. In 2011, the non-profit Sustainability Accounting Standards Board (SASB) was formed to develop sustainability accounting standards for companies when disclosing material ESG information. In addition to these key organizations, several others exist that promote the advancement of sustainable investing. To help educate investors, CFA Institute published "Environmental, Social, and Governance Issues in Investing: A Guide for Investment Professionals" in November 2015.[6]

9.5 ESG Factors in Investment Analysis

The materiality of ESG factors in investment analysis, particularly environmental and social factors, often differ meaningfully among sectors. An ESG factor is considered to be material when it is believed to have an impact on a company's long-term business model. For example, environmental factors such as emissions and water usage will likely be significant for utilities or mining companies, yet are relatively inconsequential for financial institutions.

Overall, environmental factors that are generally considered material in investment analysis include natural resource management, pollution prevention, water conservation, energy efficiency and reduced emissions, the existence of carbon assets, and adherence to environmental safety and regulatory standards. A specific concern among investors of energy companies is also the existence of "stranded assets," i.e., carbon-intensive assets that are at risk of no longer being economically viable because of changes in regulation or investor sentiment. Analysts may find it difficult to assess potentially significant financial risks of energy companies because of limited information on the existence of these companies' carbon assets, as well as the difficulty in determining political and regulatory risks. Material environmental effects can arise from strategic or operational decisions based on inadequate governance processes or errors in judgment. For example, oil spills, industrial waste contamination events, and local resource depletion can result from poor environmental standards, breaches in safety standards, or unsustainable business models. Such events can be costly in terms of regulatory fines, litigation, clean-up costs, reputational risk, and resource management.

Social factors considered in ESG implementation generally pertain to the management of the human capital of a business, including human rights and welfare concerns in the workplace; product development; and, in some cases, community impact. Staff turnover, worker training and safety, employee morale, ethics policies, employee diversity, and supply chain management can all affect a company's ability to sustain its competitive advantage. In addition, minimizing social risks can lower a company's costs (e.g., through higher employee productivity, lower employee turnover, and reduced litigation potential) and reduce its reputational risk.

---

6 https://www.cfapubs.org/doi/pdf/10.2469/ccb.v2015.n11.1

As mentioned earlier, governance factors have long been recognized in investment analysis. Many performance indicators can help evaluate risks arising from governance issues such as ownership structure, board independence and composition, and compensation. Although several governance factors may apply across industries and geographic regions, other factors are unique (such as systemic risk management for financial services companies).

One area of debate has been whether the consideration of ESG factors is consistent with fiduciary duty—particularly when overseeing and managing pension fund assets. Pension fund regulation regarding ESG considerations varies globally. In the United States, the Employee Retirement Income Security Act of 1974 (ERISA) sets the standards for the protection of private pension plan beneficiaries. A fiduciary must act solely in the interest of pension plan participants and beneficiaries. Accepting lower returns or assuming greater risk in a private pension plan to promote environmental, social, or public policy causes would violate fiduciary duty and is prohibited by ERISA. In a series of bulletins issued in October 2015, December 2016, and May 2018, the US Department of Labor (DOL) determined that certain ESG-related investment practices do not violate ERISA or fiduciary duty. These practices include the addition of the consideration of ESG factors in investment policy statements; the integration of ESG factors in the evaluation of an investment's risk or return; and the use of ESG considerations as determining factors, or "tie-breakers," when choosing among investments that have equivalent economic benefits for a pension plan.

EXAMPLE 11

ESG Implementation Methods

The ESG implementation method that is *most* associated with excluding certain sectors or companies is:

A thematic investing.

B negative screening.

C relative/best-in-class.

Solution:

B is correct. Negative screening entails excluding certain companies or sectors, such as fossil fuel extraction, from a portfolio. A is incorrect because thematic investing typically focuses on investing in companies within a specific sector or following a specific theme, such as energy efficiency or climate change, as opposed to merely excluding a set of companies or industries from a portfolio. Likewise, C is incorrect because relative/best-in-class focuses on companies that rank (or score) most favorably compared to their peers with regard to ESG factors.

SUMMARY

The investment community has increasingly recognized the importance of corporate governance, as well as environmental and social considerations. Although practices concerning corporate governance (and ESG overall) will undoubtedly continue to evolve, investment analysts who have a good understanding of these concepts can better appreciate the implications of ESG considerations in investment decision making. The core concepts covered in this reading are as follows:

- Corporate governance can be defined as a system of controls and procedures by which individual companies are managed.
- There are many systems of corporate governance, most reflecting the influences of either shareholder theory or stakeholder theory, or both. Current trends, however, point to increasing convergence.
- A corporation's governance system is influenced by several stakeholder groups, and the interests of the groups often diverge or conflict.
- The primary stakeholder groups of a corporation consist of shareholders, creditors, managers and employees, the board of directors, customers, suppliers, and government/regulators.
- A principal–agent relationship (or agency relationship) entails a principal hiring an agent to perform a particular task or service. In a corporate structure, such relationships often lead to conflicts among various stakeholders.
- Stakeholder management involves identifying, prioritizing, and understanding the interests of stakeholder groups and on that basis managing the company's relationships with stakeholders. The framework of corporate governance and stakeholder management reflects a legal, contractual, organizational, and governmental infrastructure.
- Mechanisms of stakeholder management may include general meetings, a board of directors, the audit function, company reporting and transparency, related-party transactions, remuneration policies (including say on pay), and other mechanisms to manage the company's relationship with its creditors, employees, customers, suppliers, and regulators.
- A board of directors is the central pillar of the governance structure, serves as the link between shareholders and managers, and acts as the shareholders' internal monitoring tool within the company.
- The structure and composition of a board of directors vary across countries and companies. The number of directors may vary, and the board typically includes a mix of expertise levels, backgrounds, and competencies.
- Executive (internal) directors are employed by the company and are typically members of senior management. Non-executive (external) directors have limited involvement in daily operations but serve an important oversight role.
- Two primary duties of a board of directors are duty of care and duty of loyalty.
- A company's board of directors typically has several committees that are responsible for specific functions and report to the board. Although the types of committees may vary across organization, the most common are the audit committee, governance committee, remuneration (compensation) committee, nomination committee, risk committee, and investment committee.
- Stakeholder relationships and corporate governance are continually shaped and influenced by a variety of market and non-market factors.
- Shareholder engagement by a company can provide benefits that include building support against short-term activist investors, countering negative recommendations from proxy advisory firms, and receiving greater support for management's position.
- Shareholder activism encompasses a range of strategies that may be used by shareholders when seeking to compel a company to act in a desired manner.

- From a corporation's perspective, risks of poor governance include weak control systems; ineffective decision making; and legal, regulatory, reputational, and default risk. Benefits include better operational efficiency, control, and operating and financial performance, as well as lower default risk (or cost of debt).
- Key analyst considerations in corporate governance and stakeholder management include economic ownership and voting control, board of directors representation, remuneration and company performance, investor composition, strength of shareholders' rights, and the management of long-term risks.
- Several terms—sometimes interchangeable—and investment approaches have evolved in relation to ESG: sustainable investing; responsible investing; ESG investing; and socially responsible investing.
- Specific ESG investment styles include:

ESG Investment Style	Description
Negative Screening	Excluding companies or sectors based on business activities or environmental or social concerns
Positive Screening	Including sectors or companies based on specific ESG criteria
Relative/best-in-class screening	Investing in sectors, companies, or projects based on ESG performance relative to industry peers
Full integration	Including ESG factors into the traditional financial analysis of individual stocks
Overlay/portfolio tilt	Using strategies or products to achieve certain ESG characteristics for a fund or portfolio
Risk factor/risk premium investing	Including ESG information in the analysis of systematic risks such as smart beta or factor investing
Thematic investment	Investing in themes or assets related to ESG factors
Engagement/active ownership	Using shareholder power to influence corporate behavior to achieve targeted ESG objectives along with financial returns

PRACTICE PROBLEMS

1 Corporate governance:

A complies with a set of global standards.

B is independent of both shareholder theory and stakeholder theory.

C seeks to minimize and manage conflicting interests between insiders and external shareholders.

2 Which group of company stakeholders would be *least* affected if the firm's financial position weakens?

A Suppliers

B Customers

C Managers and employees

3 Which of the following represents a principal–agent conflict between shareholders and management?

A Risk tolerance

B Multiple share classes

C Accounting and reporting practices

4 Which of the following issues discussed at a shareholders' general meeting would *most likely* require only a simple majority vote for approval?

A Voting on a merger

B Election of directors

C Amendments to bylaws

5 Which of the following statements regarding stakeholder management is *most* accurate?

A Company management ensures compliance with all applicable laws and regulations.

B Directors are excluded from voting on transactions in which they hold material interest.

C The use of variable incentive plans in executive remuneration is decreasing.

6 Which of the following represents a responsibility of a company's board of directors?

A Implementation of strategy

B Enterprise risk management

C Considering the interests of shareholders only

7 Which of the following statements about non-market factors in corporate governance is *most* accurate?

A Stakeholders can spread information quickly and shape public opinion.

B A civil law system offers better protection of shareholder interests than does a common law system.

C Vendors providing corporate governance services have limited influence on corporate governance practices.

8 Which of the following statements regarding corporate shareholders is *most* accurate?

A Cross-shareholdings help promote corporate mergers.

B Dual-class structures are used to align economic ownership with control.

C Affiliated shareholders can protect a company against hostile takeover bids.

9 Which of the following statements about environmental, social, and governance (ESG) in investment analysis is correct?

A ESG factors are strictly intangible in nature.

B ESG terminology is easily distinguishable among investors.

C Environmental and social factors have been adopted in investment analysis more slowly than governance factors.

10 Which of the following statements regarding ESG implementation methods is *most accurate*?

A Negative screening is the most commonly applied method.

B Thematic investing considers multiple factors.

C Relative/best-in-class screening excludes industries with unfavorable ESG aspects.

SOLUTIONS

1 C is correct. Corporate governance is the arrangement of checks, balances, and incentives a company needs to minimize and manage the conflicting interests between insiders and external shareholders.

2 B is correct. Compared with other stakeholder groups, customers tend to be less concerned with, and affected by, a company's financial performance.

3 A is correct. Shareholder and manager interests can diverge with respect to risk tolerance. In some cases, shareholders with diversified investment portfolios can have a fairly high risk tolerance because specific company risk can be diversified away. Managers are typically more risk averse in their corporate decision making to better protect their employment status.

4 B is correct. The election of directors is considered an ordinary resolution and, therefore, requires only a simple majority of votes to be passed.

5 B is correct. Often, policies on related-party transactions require that such transactions or matters be voted on by the board (or shareholders), excluding the director holding the interest.

6 B is correct. The board typically ensures that the company has an appropriate enterprise risk management system in place.

7 A is correct. Social media has become a powerful tool for stakeholders to instantly broadcast information with little cost or effort and to compete with company management in influencing public sentiment.

8 C is correct. The presence of a sizable affiliated stockholder (such as an individual, family trust, endowment, or private equity fund) can shield a company from the effects of voting by outside shareholders.

9 C is correct. The risks of poor corporate governance have long been understood by analysts and shareholders. In contrast, the practice of considering environmental and social factors has been slower to take hold.

10 A is correct. Negative screening, which refers to the practice of excluding certain sectors, companies, or practices that violate accepted standards in such areas as human rights or environmental concerns, is the most common ESG investment style.

READING

32

Capital Budgeting

by John D. Stowe, PhD, CFA, and Jacques R. Gagné, FSA, CFA, CIPM

John D. Stowe, PhD, CFA, is at Ohio University (USA). Jacques R. Gagné, FSA, CFA, CIPM, is at ENAP (Canada).

LEARNING OUTCOMES

Mastery	The candidate should be able to:
☐	a. describe the capital budgeting process and distinguish among the various categories of capital projects;
☐	b. describe the basic principles of capital budgeting;
☐	c. explain how the evaluation and selection of capital projects is affected by mutually exclusive projects, project sequencing, and capital rationing;
☐	d. calculate and interpret net present value (NPV), internal rate of return (IRR), payback period, discounted payback period, and profitability index (PI) of a single capital project;
☐	e. explain the NPV profile, compare the NPV and IRR methods when evaluating independent and mutually exclusive projects, and describe the problems associated with each of the evaluation methods;
☐	f. contrast the NPV decision rule to the IRR decision rule and identify problems associated with the IRR rule;
☐	g. describe expected relations among an investment's NPV, company value, and share price.

INTRODUCTION

1

Capital budgeting is the process that companies use for decision making on capital projects—those projects with a life of a year or more. This is a fundamental area of knowledge for financial analysts for many reasons.

- First, capital budgeting is very important for corporations. Capital projects, which make up the long-term asset portion of the balance sheet, can be so large that sound capital budgeting decisions ultimately decide the future of many corporations. Capital decisions cannot be reversed at a low cost, so mistakes are very costly. Indeed, the real capital investments of a company describe a company better than its working capital or capital structures, which are intangible and tend to be similar for many corporations.

- Second, the principles of capital budgeting have been adapted for many other corporate decisions, such as investments in working capital, leasing, mergers and acquisitions, and bond refunding.
- Third, the valuation principles used in capital budgeting are similar to the valuation principles used in security analysis and portfolio management. Many of the methods used by security analysts and portfolio managers are based on capital budgeting methods. Conversely, there have been innovations in security analysis and portfolio management that have also been adapted to capital budgeting.
- Finally, although analysts have a vantage point outside the company, their interest in valuation coincides with the capital budgeting focus of maximizing shareholder value. Because capital budgeting information is not ordinarily available outside the company, the analyst may attempt to estimate the process, within reason, at least for companies that are not too complex. Further, analysts may be able to appraise the quality of the company's capital budgeting process—for example, on the basis of whether the company has an accounting focus or an economic focus.

This reading is organized as follows: Section 2 presents the steps in a typical capital budgeting process. After introducing the basic principles of capital budgeting in Section 3, in Section 4 we discuss the criteria by which a decision to invest in a project may be made.

2 THE CAPITAL BUDGETING PROCESS

The specific capital budgeting procedures that a manager uses depend on the manager's level in the organization, the size and complexity of the project being evaluated, and the size of the organization. The typical steps in the capital budgeting process are as follows:

- Step One: Generating Ideas—Investment ideas can come from anywhere, from the top or the bottom of the organization, from any department or functional area, or from outside the company. Generating good investment ideas to consider is the most important step in the process.
- Step Two: Analyzing Individual Proposals—This step involves gathering the information to forecast cash flows for each project and then evaluating the project's profitability.
- Step Three: Planning the Capital Budget—The company must organize the profitable proposals into a coordinated whole that fits within the company's overall strategies, and it also must consider the projects' timing. Some projects that look good when considered in isolation may be undesirable strategically. Because of financial and real resource issues, the scheduling and prioritizing of projects is important.
- Step Four: Monitoring and Post-auditing—In a post-audit, actual results are compared to planned or predicted results, and any differences must be explained. For example, how do the revenues, expenses, and cash flows realized from an investment compare to the predictions? Post-auditing capital projects is important for several reasons. First, it helps monitor the forecasts and

analysis that underlie the capital budgeting process. Systematic errors, such as overly optimistic forecasts, become apparent. Second, it helps improve business operations. If sales or costs are out of line, it will focus attention on bringing performance closer to expectations if at all possible. Finally, monitoring and post-auditing recent capital investments will produce concrete ideas for future investments. Managers can decide to invest more heavily in profitable areas and scale down or cancel investments in areas that are disappointing.

Planning for capital investments can be very complex, often involving many persons inside and outside of the company. Information about marketing, science, engineering, regulation, taxation, finance, production, and behavioral issues must be systematically gathered and evaluated. The authority to make capital decisions depends on the size and complexity of the project. Lower-level managers may have discretion to make decisions that involve less than a given amount of money, or that do not exceed a given capital budget. Larger and more complex decisions are reserved for top management, and some are so significant that the company's board of directors ultimately has the decision-making authority.

Like everything else, capital budgeting is a cost–benefit exercise. At the margin, the benefits from the improved decision making should exceed the costs of the capital budgeting efforts.

Companies often put capital budgeting projects into some rough categories for analysis. One such classification would be as follows:

1 Replacement projects. These are among the easier capital budgeting decisions. If a piece of equipment breaks down or wears out, whether to replace it may not require careful analysis. If the expenditure is modest and if not investing has significant implications for production, operations, or sales, it would be a waste of resources to overanalyze the decision. Just make the replacement. Other replacement decisions involve replacing existing equipment with newer, more efficient equipment, or perhaps choosing one type of equipment over another. These replacement decisions are often amenable to very detailed analysis, and you might have a lot of confidence in the final decision.

2 Expansion projects. Instead of merely maintaining a company's existing business activities, expansion projects increase the size of the business. These expansion decisions may involve more uncertainties than replacement decisions, and these decisions will be more carefully considered.

3 New products and services. These investments expose the company to even more uncertainties than expansion projects. These decisions are more complex and will involve more people in the decision-making process.

4 Regulatory, safety, and environmental projects. These projects are frequently required by a governmental agency, an insurance company, or some other external party. They may generate no revenue and might not be undertaken by a company maximizing its own private interests. Often, the company will accept the required investment and continue to operate. Occasionally, however, the cost of the regulatory/safety/environmental project is sufficiently high that the company would do better to cease operating altogether or to shut down any part of the business that is related to the project.

5 Other. The projects above are all susceptible to capital budgeting analysis, and they can be accepted or rejected using the **net present value** (NPV) or some other criterion. Some projects escape such analysis. These are either pet projects of someone in the company (such as the CEO buying a new aircraft) or so risky that they are difficult to analyze by the usual methods (such as some research and development decisions).

3 BASIC PRINCIPLES OF CAPITAL BUDGETING

Capital budgeting has a rich history and sometimes employs some pretty sophisticated procedures. Fortunately, capital budgeting relies on just a few basic principles. Capital budgeting usually uses the following assumptions:

1 Decisions are based on cash flows. The decisions are not based on accounting concepts, such as net income. Furthermore, intangible costs and benefits are often ignored because, if they are real, they should result in cash flows at some other time.

2 Timing of cash flows is crucial. Analysts make an extraordinary effort to detail precisely when cash flows occur.

3 Cash flows are based on opportunity costs. What are the incremental cash flows that occur with an investment compared to what they would have been without the investment?

4 Cash flows are analyzed on an after-tax basis. Taxes must be fully reflected in all capital budgeting decisions.

5 Financing costs are ignored. This may seem unrealistic, but it is not. Most of the time, analysts want to know the after-tax operating cash flows that result from a capital investment. Then, these after-tax cash flows and the investment outlays are discounted at the "required rate of return" to find the net present value (NPV). Financing costs are reflected in the required rate of return. If we included financing costs in the cash flows and in the discount rate, we would be double-counting the financing costs. So even though a project may be financed with some combination of debt and equity, we ignore these costs, focusing on the operating cash flows and capturing the costs of debt (and other capital) in the discount rate.

6 Capital budgeting cash flows are not accounting net income. Accounting net income is reduced by noncash charges such as accounting depreciation. Furthermore, to reflect the cost of debt financing, interest expenses are also subtracted from accounting net income. (No subtraction is made for the cost of equity financing in arriving at accounting net income.) Accounting net income also differs from economic income, which is the cash inflow plus the change in the market value of the company. Economic income does not subtract the **cost of debt** financing, and it is based on the changes in the market value of the company, not changes in its book value (accounting depreciation).

In assumption 5 above, we referred to the rate used in discounting the cash flows as the "required rate of return." The required rate of return is the discount rate that investors should require given the riskiness of the project. This discount rate is frequently called the "opportunity cost of funds" or the "cost of capital." If the company can invest elsewhere and earn a return of *r*, or if the company can repay its sources of capital and save a cost of *r*, then *r* is the company's opportunity cost of funds. If the company cannot earn more than its opportunity cost of funds on an investment, it should not undertake that investment. Unless an investment earns more than the cost of funds from its suppliers of capital, the investment should not be undertaken. The cost-of-capital concept is discussed more extensively elsewhere. Regardless of what it is called, an economically sound discount rate is essential for making capital budgeting decisions.

Although the principles of capital budgeting are simple, they are easily confused in practice, leading to unfortunate decisions. Some important capital budgeting concepts that managers find very useful are given below.

- A **sunk cost** is one that has already been incurred. You cannot change a sunk cost. Today's decisions, on the other hand, should be based on current and future cash flows and should not be affected by prior, or sunk, costs.
- An **opportunity cost** is what a resource is worth in its next-best use. For example, if a company uses some idle property, what should it record as the investment outlay: the purchase price several years ago, the current market value, or nothing? If you replace an old machine with a new one, what is the opportunity cost? If you invest $10 million, what is the opportunity cost? The answers to these three questions are, respectively: the current market value, the cash flows the old machine would generate, and $10 million (which you could invest elsewhere).
- An **incremental cash flow** is the cash flow that is realized because of a decision: the cash flow *with* a decision minus the cash flow *without* that decision. If opportunity costs are correctly assessed, the incremental cash flows provide a sound basis for capital budgeting.
- An **externality** is the effect of an investment on other things besides the investment itself. Frequently, an investment affects the cash flows of other parts of the company, and these externalities can be positive or negative. If possible, these should be part of the investment decision. Sometimes externalities occur outside of the company. An investment might benefit (or harm) other companies or society at large, and yet the company is not compensated for these benefits (or charged for the costs). **Cannibalization** is one externality. Cannibalization occurs when an investment takes customers and sales away from another part of the company.
- **Conventional cash flows** versus **nonconventional cash flows**—A conventional cash flow pattern is one with an initial outflow followed by a series of inflows. In a nonconventional cash flow pattern, the initial outflow is not followed by inflows only, but the cash flows can flip from positive to negative again (or even change signs several times). An investment that involved outlays (negative cash flows) for the first couple of years that were then followed by positive cash flows would be considered to have a conventional pattern. If cash flows change signs once, the pattern is conventional. If cash flows change signs two or more times, the pattern is nonconventional.

Several types of project interactions make the incremental cash flow analysis challenging. The following are some of these interactions:

- **Independent projects** versus **mutually exclusive projects**—Independent projects are projects whose cash flows are independent of each other. Mutually exclusive projects compete directly with each other. For example, if Projects A and B are mutually exclusive, you can choose A or B, but you cannot choose both. Sometimes there are several mutually exclusive projects, and you can choose only one from the group.
- **Project sequencing**—Many projects are sequenced through time, so that investing in a project creates the option to invest in future projects. For example, you might invest in a project today and then in one year invest in a second

project if the financial results of the first project or new economic conditions are favorable. If the results of the first project or new economic conditions are not favorable, you do not invest in the second project.

- **Unlimited funds** versus **capital rationing**—An unlimited funds environment assumes that the company can raise the funds it wants for all profitable projects simply by paying the required rate of return. Capital rationing exists when the company has a fixed amount of funds to invest. If the company has more profitable projects than it has funds for, it must allocate the funds to achieve the maximum shareholder value subject to the funding constraints.

4 INVESTMENT DECISION CRITERIA

Analysts use several important criteria to evaluate capital investments. The two most comprehensive measures of whether a project is profitable or unprofitable are the net present value (NPV) and **internal rate of return** (IRR). In addition to these, we present four other criteria that are frequently used: the **payback period**, **discounted payback period**, **average accounting rate of return** (AAR), and **profitability index** (PI). An analyst must fully understand the economic logic behind each of these investment decision criteria as well as its strengths and limitations in practice.

4.1 Net Present Value

For a project with one investment outlay, made initially, the net present value (NPV) is the present value of the future after-tax cash flows minus the investment outlay, or

$$\text{NPV} = \sum_{t=1}^{n} \frac{\text{CF}_t}{(1+r)^t} - \text{Outlay} \quad (1)$$

where

CF_t = after-tax cash flow at time t

r = required rate of return for the investment

Outlay = investment cash flow at time zero

To illustrate the net present value criterion, we will take a look at a simple example. Assume that Gerhardt Corporation is considering an investment of €50 million in a capital project that will return after-tax cash flows of €16 million per year for the next four years plus another €20 million in Year 5. The required rate of return is 10 percent.

For the Gerhardt example, the NPV would be[1]

$$\text{NPV} = \frac{16}{1.10^1} + \frac{16}{1.10^2} + \frac{16}{1.10^3} + \frac{16}{1.10^4} + \frac{20}{1.10^5} - 50$$

$$\text{NPV} = 14.545 + 13.223 + 12.021 + 10.928 + 12.418 - 50$$

$$\text{NPV} = 63.136 - 50 = €13.136 \text{ million.}$$

1 Occasionally, you will notice some rounding errors in our examples. In this case, the present values of the cash flows, as rounded, add up to €63.135. Without rounding, they add up to €63.13627, or €63.136. We will usually report the more accurate result, the one that you would get from your calculator or computer without rounding intermediate results.

The investment has a total value, or present value of future cash flows, of €63.136 million. Since this investment can be acquired at a cost of €50 million, the investing company is giving up €50 million of its wealth in exchange for an investment worth €63.136 million. The investor's wealth increases by a net of €13.136 million.

Because the NPV is the amount by which the investor's wealth increases as a result of the investment, the decision rule for the NPV is as follows:

Invest if	NPV > 0
Do not invest if	NPV < 0

Positive NPV investments are wealth-increasing, whereas negative NPV investments are wealth-decreasing.

Many investments have cash flow patterns in which outflows may occur not only at time zero, but also at future dates. It is useful to consider the NPV to be the present value of all cash flows:

$$\text{NPV} = \text{CF}_0 + \frac{\text{CF}_1}{(1+r)^1} + \frac{\text{CF}_2}{(1+r)^2} + \cdots + \frac{\text{CF}_n}{(1+r)^n}, \text{ or}$$

$$\text{NPV} = \sum_{t=0}^{n} \frac{\text{CF}_t}{(1+r)^t} \tag{2}$$

In Equation 2, the investment outlay, CF_0, is simply a negative cash flow. Future cash flows can also be negative.

4.2 Internal Rate of Return

The internal rate of return (IRR) is one of the most frequently used concepts in capital budgeting and in security analysis. The IRR definition is one that all analysts know by heart. For a project with one investment outlay, made initially, the IRR is the discount rate that makes the present value of the future after-tax cash flows equal that investment outlay. Written out in equation form, the IRR solves this equation:

$$\sum_{t=1}^{n} \frac{\text{CF}_t}{(1+\text{IRR})^t} = \text{Outlay}$$

where IRR is the internal rate of return. The left-hand side of this equation is the present value of the project's future cash flows, which, discounted at the IRR, equals the investment outlay. This equation will also be seen rearranged as

$$\sum_{t=1}^{n} \frac{\text{CF}_t}{(1+\text{IRR})^t} - \text{Outlay} = 0 \tag{3}$$

In this form, Equation 3 looks like the NPV equation, Equation 1, except that the discount rate is the IRR instead of r (the required rate of return). Discounted at the IRR, the NPV is equal to zero.

In the Gerhardt Corporation example, we want to find a discount rate that makes the total present value of all cash flows, the NPV, equal zero. In equation form, the IRR is the discount rate that solves this equation:

$$-50 + \frac{16}{(1+\text{IRR})^1} + \frac{16}{(1+\text{IRR})^2} + \frac{16}{(1+\text{IRR})^3} + \frac{16}{(1+\text{IRR})^4} + \frac{20}{(1+\text{IRR})^5} = 0$$

Algebraically, this equation would be very difficult to solve. We normally resort to trial and error, systematically choosing various discount rates until we find one, the IRR, that satisfies the equation. We previously discounted these cash flows at 10 percent and found the NPV to be €13.136 million. Since the NPV is positive, the IRR is probably greater than 10 percent. If we use 20 percent as the discount rate, the NPV is −€0.543 million, so 20 percent is a little high. One might try several other discount rates until the NPV is equal to zero; this approach is illustrated in Exhibit 1.

Exhibit 1 Trial and Error Process for Finding IRR

Discount Rate (%)	NPV
10	13.136
20	−0.543
19	0.598
19.5	0.022
19.51	0.011
19.52	0.000

The IRR is 19.52 percent. Financial calculators and spreadsheet software have routines that calculate the IRR for us, so we do not have to go through this trial and error procedure ourselves. The IRR, computed more precisely, is 19.5197 percent.

The decision rule for the IRR is to invest if the IRR exceeds the required rate of return for a project:

Invest if	IRR > r
Do not invest if	IRR < r

The required rate of return is often termed the **hurdle rate**, the rate that a project's IRR must exceed for the project to be accepted. In the Gerhardt example, since the IRR of 19.52 percent exceeds the project's required rate of return of 10 percent, Gerhardt should invest.

Many investments have cash flow patterns in which the outlays occur at time zero and at future dates. Thus, it is common to define the IRR as the discount rate that makes the present values of all cash flows sum to zero:

$$\sum_{t=0}^{n} \frac{CF_t}{(1 + IRR)^t} = 0 \quad (4)$$

Equation 4 is a more general version of Equation 3.

4.3 Payback Period

The payback period is the number of years required to recover the original investment in a project. The payback is based on cash flows. For example, if you invest $10 million in a project, how long will it be until you recover the full original investment? Exhibit 2 below illustrates the calculation of the payback period by following an investment's cash flows and cumulative cash flows.

Exhibit 2 Payback Period Example

Year	0	1	2	3	4	5
Cash flow	−10,000	2,500	2,500	3,000	3,000	3,000
Cumulative cash flow	−10,000	−7,500	−5,000	−2,000	1,000	4,000

In the first year, the company recovers 2,500 of the original investment, with 7,500 still unrecovered. You can see that the company recoups its original investment between Year 3 and Year 4. After three years, 2,000 is still unrecovered. Since the Year 4 cash flow is 3,000, it would take two-thirds of the Year 4 cash flow to bring the cumulative cash flow to zero. So, the payback period is three years plus two-thirds of the Year 4 cash flow, or 3.67 years.

The drawbacks of the payback period are transparent. Since the cash flows are not discounted at the project's required rate of return, the payback period ignores the time value of money and the risk of the project. Additionally, the payback period ignores cash flows after the payback period is reached. In Exhibit 2 above, for example, the Year 5 cash flow is completely ignored in the payback computation!

Example 1 is designed to illustrate some of the implications of these drawbacks of the payback period.

EXAMPLE 1

Drawbacks of the Payback Period

The cash flows, payback periods, and NPVs for Projects A through F are given in Exhibit 3. For all of the projects, the required rate of return is 10 percent.

Exhibit 3 Examples of Drawbacks of the Payback Period

	Cash Flows					
Year	Project A	Project B	Project C	Project D	Project E	Project F
0	−1,000	−1,000	−1,000	−1,000	−1,000	−1,000
1	1,000	100	400	500	400	500
2		200	300	500	400	500
3		300	200	500	400	10,000
4		400	100		400	
5		500	500		400	
Payback period	1.0	4.0	4.0	2.0	2.5	2.0
NPV	-90.91	65.26	140.60	243.43	516.31	7,380.92

Comment on why the payback period provides misleading information about the following:

1 Project A.

2 Project B versus Project C.

3 Project D versus Project E.

4 Project D versus Project F.

Solution to 1:

Project A does indeed pay itself back in one year. However, this result is misleading because the investment is unprofitable, with a negative NPV.

Solution to 2:

Although Projects B and C have the same payback period and the same cash flow after the payback period, the payback period does not detect the fact that Project C's cash flows within the payback period occur earlier and result in a higher NPV.

Solution to 3:

Projects D and E illustrate a common situation. The project with the shorter payback period is the less profitable project. Project E has a longer payback and higher NPV.

Solution to 4:

Projects D and F illustrate an important flaw of the payback period—that the payback period ignores cash flows after the payback period is reached. In this case, Project F has a much larger cash flow in Year 3, but the payback period does not recognize its value.

The payback period has many drawbacks—it is a measure of payback and not a measure of profitability. By itself, the payback period would be a dangerous criterion for evaluating capital projects. Its simplicity, however, is an advantage. The payback period is very easy to calculate and to explain. The payback period may also be used as an indicator of project liquidity. A project with a two-year payback may be more liquid than another project with a longer payback.

Because it is not economically sound, the payback period has no decision rule like that of the NPV or IRR. If the payback period is being used (perhaps as a measure of liquidity), analysts should also use an NPV or IRR to ensure that their decisions also reflect the profitability of the projects being considered.

4.4 Discounted Payback Period

The discounted payback period is the number of years it takes for the cumulative discounted cash flows from a project to equal the original investment. The discounted payback period partially addresses the weaknesses of the payback period. Exhibit 4 gives an example of calculating the payback period and discounted payback period. The example assumes a discount rate of 10 percent.

Exhibit 4 Payback Period and Discounted Payback Period

Year	0	1	2	3	4	5
Cash flow (CF)	−5,000	1,500.00	1,500.00	1,500.00	1,500.00	1,500.00
Cumulative CF	−5,000	−3,500.00	−2,000.00	−500.00	1,000.00	2,500.00
Discounted CF	−5,000	1,363.64	1,239.67	1,126.97	1,024.52	931.38
Cumulative discounted CF	−5,000	−3,636.36	−2,396.69	−1,269.72	−245.20	686.18

The payback period is three years plus 500/1,500 = 1/3 of the fourth year's cash flow, or 3.33 years. The discounted payback period is between four and five years. The discounted payback period is four years plus 245.20/931.38 = 0.26 of the fifth year's discounted cash flow, or 4.26 years.

The discounted payback period relies on discounted cash flows, much as the NPV criterion does. If a project has a negative NPV, it will usually not have a discounted payback period since it never recovers the initial investment.

The discounted payback does account for the time value of money and risk within the discounted payback period, but it ignores cash flows after the discounted payback period is reached. This drawback has two consequences. First, the discounted payback period is not a good measure of profitability because it ignores these cash flows. Second, another idiosyncrasy of the discounted payback period comes from the possibility of negative cash flows after the discounted payback period is reached. It is possible for a project to have a negative NPV but to have a positive cumulative discounted cash flow in the middle of its life and, thus, a reasonable discounted payback period. The NPV and IRR, which consider all of a project's cash flows, do not suffer from this problem.

4.5 Average Accounting Rate of Return

The average accounting rate of return (AAR) can be defined as

$$\text{AAR} = \frac{\text{Average net income}}{\text{Average book value}}$$

To understand this measure of return, we will use a numerical example.

Assume a company invests $200,000 in a project that is depreciated straight-line over a five-year life to a zero salvage value. Sales revenues and cash operating expenses for each year are as shown in Exhibit 5. The exhibit also shows the annual income taxes (at a 40 percent tax rate) and the net income.

Exhibit 5 Net Income for Calculating an Average Accounting Rate of Return

	Year 1	Year 2	Year 3	Year 4	Year 5
Sales	$100,000	$150,000	$240,000	$130,000	$80,000
Cash expenses	50,000	70,000	120,000	60,000	50,000
Depreciation	40,000	40,000	40,000	40,000	40,000
Earnings before taxes	10,000	40,000	80,000	30,000	–10,000
Taxes (at 40 percent)	4,000	16,000	32,000	12,000	–4,000[a]
Net income	6,000	24,000	48,000	18,000	–6,000

[a] Negative taxes occur in Year 5 because the earnings before taxes of –$10,000 can be deducted against earnings on other projects, thus reducing the tax bill by $4,000.

For the five-year period, the average net income is $18,000. The initial book value is $200,000, declining by $40,000 per year until the final book value is $0. The average book value for this asset is ($200,000 – $0) / 2 = $100,000. The average accounting rate of return is

$$\text{AAR} = \frac{\text{Average net income}}{\text{Average book value}} = \frac{18{,}000}{100{,}000} = 18\%$$

The advantages of the AAR are that it is easy to understand and easy to calculate. The AAR has some important disadvantages, however. Unlike the other capital budgeting criteria discussed here, the AAR is based on accounting numbers and not based on cash flows. This is an important conceptual and practical limitation. The AAR also does not account for the time value of money, and there is no conceptually sound cutoff for the AAR that distinguishes between profitable and unprofitable investments. The AAR is frequently calculated in different ways, so the analyst should verify the formula behind any AAR numbers that are supplied by someone else. Analysts should know the AAR and its potential limitations in practice, but they should rely on more economically sound methods like the NPV and IRR.

4.6 Profitability Index

The profitability index (PI) is the present value of a project's future cash flows divided by the initial investment. It can be expressed as

$$\text{PI} = \frac{\text{PV of future cash flows}}{\text{Initial investment}} = 1 + \frac{\text{NPV}}{\text{Initial investment}} \tag{5}$$

You can see that the PI is closely related to the NPV. The PI is the *ratio* of the PV of future cash flows to the initial investment, whereas an NPV is the *difference* between the PV of future cash flows and the initial investment. Whenever the NPV is positive, the PI will be greater than 1.0; conversely, whenever the NPV is negative, the PI will be less than 1.0. The investment decision rule for the PI is as follows:

Invest if	$\text{PI} > 1.0$
Do not invest if	$\text{PI} < 1.0$

Because the PV of future cash flows equals the initial investment plus the NPV, the PI can also be expressed as 1.0 plus the ratio of the NPV to the initial investment, as shown in Equation 5 above. Example 2 illustrates the PI calculation.

EXAMPLE 2

Example of a PI Calculation

The Gerhardt Corporation investment (discussed earlier) had an outlay of €50 million, a present value of future cash flows of €63.136 million, and an NPV of €13.136 million. The profitability index is

$$\text{PI} = \frac{\text{PV of future cash flows}}{\text{Initial investment}} = \frac{63.136}{50.000} = 1.26$$

The PI can also be calculated as

$$\text{PI} = 1 + \frac{\text{NPV}}{\text{Initial investment}} = 1 + \frac{13.136}{50.000} = 1.26$$

Because the PI > 1.0, this is a profitable investment.

The PI indicates the value you are receiving in exchange for one unit of currency invested. Although the PI is used less frequently than the NPV and IRR, it is sometimes used as a guide in capital rationing. The PI is usually called the profitability index in corporations, but it is commonly referred to as a "benefit–cost ratio" in governmental and not-for-profit organizations.

4.7 NPV Profile

The NPV profile shows a project's NPV graphed as a function of various discount rates. Typically, the NPV is graphed vertically (on the y-axis), and the discount rates are graphed horizontally (on the x-axis). The NPV profile for the Gerhardt capital budgeting project is shown in Example 3.

EXAMPLE 3

NPV Profile

For the Gerhardt example, we have already calculated several NPVs for different discount rates. At 10 percent the NPV is €13.136 million; at 20 percent the NPV is –€0.543 million; and at 19.52 percent (the IRR), the NPV is zero. What is the NPV if the discount rate is 0 percent? The NPV discounted at 0 percent is €34 million, which is simply the sum of all of the undiscounted cash flows. Exhibit 6 and Exhibit 7 show the NPV profile for the Gerhardt example for discount rates between 0 percent and 30 percent.

Exhibit 6 Gerhardt NPV Profile

Discount Rate (%)	NPV (€ Millions)
0	34.000
5.00	22.406
10.00	13.136
15.00	5.623
19.52	0.000
20.00	–0.543
25.00	–5.661
30.00	–9.954

Exhibit 7 Gerhardt NPV Profile

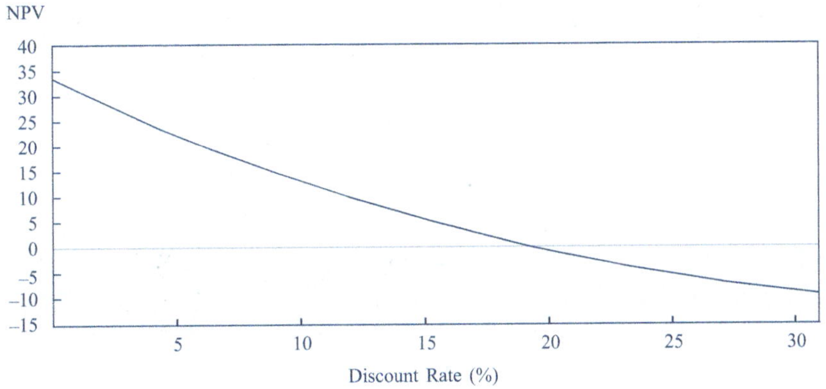

Three interesting points on this NPV profile are where the profile goes through the vertical axis (the NPV when the discount rate is zero), where the profile goes through the horizontal axis (where the discount rate is the IRR), and the NPV for the required rate of return (NPV is €13.136 million when the discount rate is the 10 percent required rate of return).

The NPV profile in Exhibit 7 is simple. The NPV declines at a decreasing rate as the discount rate increases. The profile is convex from the origin (convex from below). You will shortly see some examples in which the NPV profile is more complex.

4.8 Ranking Conflicts between NPV and IRR

For a single conventional project, the NPV and IRR will agree on whether to invest or to not invest. For independent, conventional projects, no conflict exists between the decision rules for the NPV and IRR. However, in the case of two mutually exclusive projects, the two criteria will sometimes disagree. For example, Project A might have a larger NPV than Project B, but Project B has a higher IRR than Project A. In this case, should you invest in Project A or in Project B?

Differing cash flow patterns can cause two projects to rank differently with the NPV and IRR. For example, suppose Project A has shorter-term payoffs than Project B. This situation is presented in Example 4.

EXAMPLE 4

Ranking Conflict Due to Differing Cash Flow Patterns

Projects A and B have similar outlays but different patterns of future cash flows. Project A realizes most of its cash payoffs earlier than Project B. The cash flows, as well as the NPV and IRR for the two projects, are shown in Exhibit 8. For both projects, the required rate of return is 10 percent.

Exhibit 8 Cash Flows, NPV, and IRR for Two Projects with Different Cash Flow Patterns

	Cash Flows						
Year	**0**	**1**	**2**	**3**	**4**	**NPV**	**IRR (%)**
Project A	−200	80	80	80	80	53.59	21.86
Project B	−200	0	0	0	400	73.21	18.92

If the two projects were not mutually exclusive, you would invest in both because they are both profitable. However, you can choose either A (which has the higher IRR) or B (which has the higher NPV).

Exhibit 9 and Exhibit 10 show the NPVs for Project A and Project B for various discount rates between 0 percent and 30 percent.

Exhibit 9 NPV Profiles for Two Projects with Different Cash Flow Patterns

Discount Rate (%)	NPV for Project A	NPV for Project B
0	120.00	200.00
5.00	83.68	129.08
10.00	53.59	73.21
15.00	28.40	28.70
15.09	27.98	27.98
18.92	11.41	0.00
20.00	7.10	−7.10
21.86	0.00	−18.62

Exhibit 9 (Continued)

Discount Rate (%)	NPV for Project A	NPV for Project B
25.00	−11.07	−36.16
30.00	−26.70	−59.95

Exhibit 10 NPV Profiles for Two Projects with Different Cash Flow Patterns

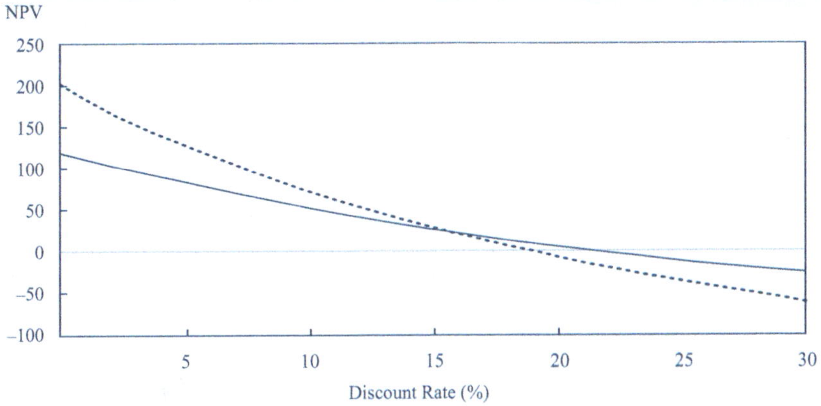

Project B (broken line) has the higher NPV for discount rates between 0 percent and 15.09 percent. Project A (solid line) has the higher NPV for discount rates exceeding 15.09 percent. The crossover point of 15.09 percent in Exhibit 10 corresponds to the discount rate at which both projects have the same NPV (of 27.98). Project B has the higher NPV below the crossover point, and Project A has the higher NPV above it.

Whenever the NPV and IRR rank two mutually exclusive projects differently, as they do in the example above, you should choose the project based on the NPV. Project B, with the higher NPV, is the better project because of the reinvestment assumption. Mathematically, whenever you discount a cash flow at a particular discount rate, you are implicitly assuming that you can reinvest a cash flow at that same discount rate.[2] In the NPV calculation, you use a discount rate of 10 percent for both projects. In the IRR calculation, you use a discount rate equal to the IRR of 21.86 percent for Project A and 18.92 percent for Project B.

Can you reinvest the cash inflows from the projects at 10 percent, or 21.86 percent, or 18.92 percent? When you assume the required rate of return is 10 percent, you are assuming an opportunity cost of 10 percent—that you can either find other projects that pay a 10 percent return or pay back your sources of capital that cost you 10 percent. The fact that you earned 21.86 percent in Project A or 18.92 percent in Project

2 For example, assume that you are receiving \$100 in one year discounted at 10 percent. The present value is \$100/\$1.10 = \$90.91. Instead of receiving the \$100 in one year, invest it for one additional year at 10 percent, and it grows to \$110. What is the present value of \$110 received in two years discounted at 10 percent? It is the same \$90.91. Because both future cash flows are worth the same, you are implicitly assuming that reinvesting the earlier cash flow at the discount rate of 10 percent has no effect on its value.

B does not mean that you can reinvest future cash flows at those rates. (In fact, if you can reinvest future cash flows at 21.86 percent or 18.92 percent, these should have been used as your required rate of return instead of 10 percent.) Because the NPV criterion uses the most realistic discount rate—the opportunity cost of funds—the NPV criterion should be used for evaluating mutually exclusive projects.

Another circumstance that frequently causes mutually exclusive projects to be ranked differently by NPV and IRR criteria is project scale—the sizes of the projects. Would you rather have a small project with a higher rate of return or a large project with a lower rate of return? Sometimes, the larger, low rate of return project has the better NPV. This case is developed in Example 5.

EXAMPLE 5

Ranking Conflicts due to Differing Project Scale

Project A has a much smaller outlay than Project B, although they have similar future cash flow patterns. The cash flows, as well as the NPVs and IRRs for the two projects, are shown in Exhibit 11. For both projects, the required rate of return is 10 percent.

Exhibit 11 Cash Flows, NPV, and IRR for Two Projects of Differing Scale

	Cash Flows						
Year	0	1	2	3	4	NPV	IRR (%)
Project A	−100	50	50	50	50	58.49	34.90
Project B	−400	170	170	170	170	138.88	25.21

If they were not mutually exclusive, you would invest in both projects because they are both profitable. However, you can choose either Project A (which has the higher IRR) or Project B (which has the higher NPV).

Exhibit 12 and Exhibit 13 show the NPVs for Project A and Project B for various discount rates between 0 percent and 30 percent.

Exhibit 12 NPV Profiles for Two Projects of Differing Scale

Discount Rate (%)	NPV for Project A	NPV for Project B
0	100.00	280.00
5.00	77.30	202.81
10.00	58.49	138.88
15.00	42.75	85.35
20.00	29.44	40.08
21.86	25.00	25.00
25.00	18.08	1.47
25.21	17.65	0.00
30.00	8.31	−31.74
34.90	0.00	−60.00
35.00	−0.15	−60.52

Exhibit 13 NPV Profiles for Two Projects of Differing Scale

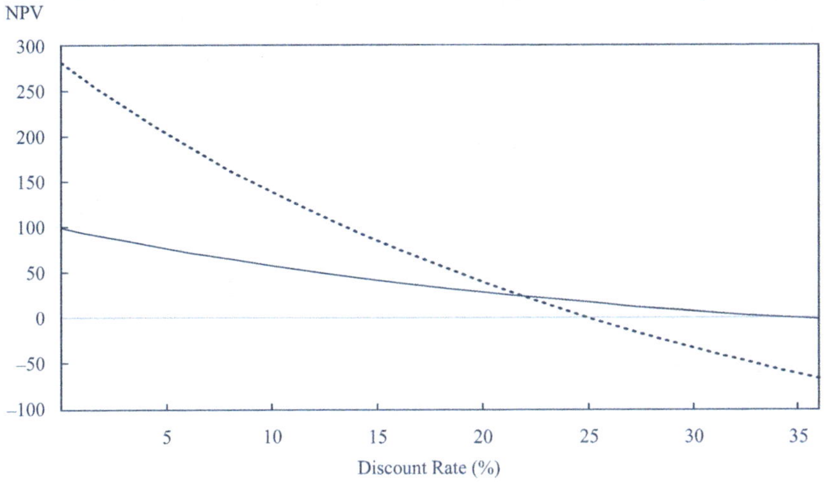

Project B (broken line) has the higher NPV for discount rates between 0 percent and 21.86 percent. Project A has the higher NPV for discount rates exceeding 21.86 percent. The crossover point of 21.86 percent in Exhibit 13 corresponds to the discount rate at which both projects have the same NPV (of 25.00). Below the crossover point, Project B has the higher NPV, and above it, Project A has the higher NPV. When cash flows are discounted at the 10 percent required rate of return, the choice is clear—Project B, the larger project, which has the superior NPV.

The good news is that the NPV and IRR criteria will usually indicate the same investment decision for a given project. They will usually both recommend acceptance or rejection of the project. When the choice is between two mutually exclusive projects and the NPV and IRR rank the two projects differently, the NPV criterion is strongly preferred. There are good reasons for this preference. The NPV shows the amount of gain, or wealth increase, as a currency amount. The NPV assumes reinvestment of cash flows at the required rate of return, while the IRR assumes reinvestment at the IRR. The reinvestment assumption of the NPV is the more economically realistic. The IRR does give you a rate of return, but the IRR could be for a small investment or for only a short period of time. As a practical matter, once a corporation has the data to calculate the NPV, it is fairly trivial to go ahead and calculate the IRR and other capital budgeting criteria. However, the most appropriate and theoretically sound criterion is the NPV.

4.9 The Multiple IRR Problem and the No IRR Problem

A problem that can arise with the IRR criterion is the "multiple IRR problem." We can illustrate this problem with the following nonconventional cash flow pattern:[3]

3 This example is adapted from Hirschleifer (1958).

Time	0	1	2
Cash flow	−1,000	5,000	−6,000

The IRR for these cash flows satisfies this equation:

$$-1{,}000 + \frac{5{,}000}{(1 + \text{IRR})^1} + \frac{-6{,}000}{(1 + \text{IRR})^2} = 0$$

It turns out that there are two values of IRR that satisfy the equation: IRR = 1 = 100% and IRR = 2 = 200%. To further understand this problem, consider the NPV profile for this investment, which is shown in Exhibit 14 and Exhibit 15.

As you can see in the NPV profile, the NPV is equal to zero at IRR = 100% and IRR = 200%. The NPV is negative for discount rates below 100 percent, positive between 100 percent and 200 percent, and then negative above 200 percent. The NPV reaches its highest value when the discount rate is 140 percent.

It is also possible to have an investment project with no IRR. The "no-IRR problem" occurs with this cash flow pattern:[4]

Time	0	1	2
Cash flow	100	−300	250

The IRR for these cash flows satisfies this equation:

$$100 + \frac{-300}{(1 + \text{IRR})^1} + \frac{250}{(1 + \text{IRR})^2} = 0$$

For these cash flows, no discount rate exists that results in a zero NPV. Does that mean this project is a bad investment? In this case, the project is actually a good investment. As Exhibit 16 and Exhibit 17 show, the NPV is positive for all discount rates. The lowest NPV, of 10, occurs for a discount rate of 66.67 percent, and the NPV is always greater than zero. Consequently, no IRR exists.

Exhibit 14 NPV Profile for a Multiple IRR Example

Discount Rate (%)	NPV
0	−2,000.00
25	−840.00
50	−333.33
75	−102.04
100	0.00
125	37.04
140	41.67
150	40.00
175	24.79
200	0.00
225	−29.59
250	−61.22
300	−125.00
350	−185.19
400	−240.00

4 This example is also adapted from Hirschleifer.

Exhibit 14 (Continued)

Discount Rate (%)	NPV
500	–333.33
1,000	–595.04
2,000	–775.51
3,000	–844.95
4,000	–881.62
10,000	–951.08
1,000,000	–999.50

Exhibit 15 NPV Profile for a Multiple IRR Example

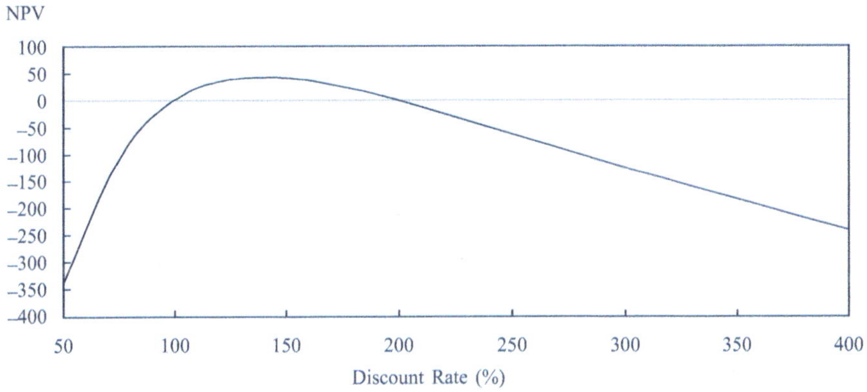

Exhibit 16 NPV Profile for a Project with No IRR

Discount Rate (%)	NPV
0	50.00
25	20.00
50	11.11
66.67	10.00
75	10.20
100	12.50
125	16.05
150	20.00
175	23.97
200	27.78
225	31.36
250	34.69
275	37.78
300	40.63
325	43.25

(continued)

Exhibit 16 (Continued)

Discount Rate (%)	NPV
350	45.68
375	47.92
400	50.00

Exhibit 17 NPV Profile for a Project with No IRR

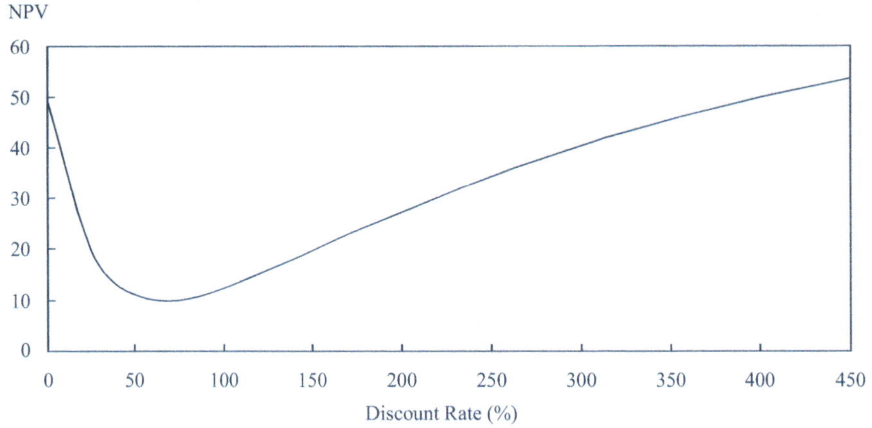

For conventional projects that have outlays followed by inflows—negative cash flows followed by positive cash flows—the multiple IRR problem cannot occur. However, for nonconventional projects, as in the example above, the multiple IRR problem can occur. The IRR equation is essentially an nth degree polynomial. An nth degree polynomial can have up to n solutions, although it will have no more real solutions than the number of cash flow sign changes. For example, a project with two sign changes could have zero, one, or two IRRs. Having two sign changes does not mean that you *will* have multiple IRRs; it just means that you *might*. Fortunately, most capital budgeting projects have only one IRR. Analysts should always be aware of the unusual cash flow patterns that can generate the multiple IRR problem.

4.10 Corporate Usage of Various Capital Budgeting Methods

Analysts need to know the basic logic of the various capital budgeting criteria as well as the practicalities involved in using them in real corporations. The usefulness of any analytical tool always depends on the specific application.

Although financial textbooks argue the superiority of the NPV and IRR techniques, corporations also use other capital budgeting techniques. In particular, payback period is widely used in some world markets.

These capital budgeting techniques are essential tools for corporate managers. Capital budgeting is also relevant to external analysts. Because a corporation's investing decisions ultimately determine the value of its financial obligations, the corporation's investing processes are vital. The NPV criterion is the criterion most directly related to stock prices. If a corporation invests in positive NPV projects, these should add to the wealth of its shareholders. Example 6 illustrates this scenario.

EXAMPLE 6

NPVs and Stock Prices

Freitag Corporation is investing €600 million in distribution facilities. The present value of the future after-tax cash flows is estimated to be €850 million. Freitag has 200 million outstanding shares with a current market price of €32.00 per share. This investment is new information, and it is independent of other expectations about the company. What should be the effect of the project on the value of the company and the stock price?

Solution:

The NPV of the project is €850 million – €600 million = €250 million. The total market value of the company prior to the investment is €32.00 × 200 million shares = €6,400 million. The value of the company should increase by €250 million to €6,650 million. The price per share should increase by the NPV per share, or €250 million/200 million shares = €1.25 per share. The share price should increase from €32.00 to €33.25.

The effect of a capital budgeting project's positive or negative NPV on share price is more complicated than Example 6 above, in which the value of the stock increased by the project's NPV. The value of a company is the value of its existing investments plus the net present values of all of its future investments. If an analyst learns of an investment, the impact of that investment on the stock price will depend on whether the investment's profitability is more or less than expected. For example, an analyst could learn of a positive NPV project, but if the project's profitability is less than expectations, this stock might drop in price on the news. Alternatively, news of a particular capital project might be considered as a signal about other capital projects underway or in the future. A project that by itself might add, say, €0.25 to the value of the stock might signal the existence of other profitable projects. News of this project might increase the stock price by far more than €0.25.

The integrity of a corporation's capital budgeting processes is important to analysts. Management's capital budgeting processes can demonstrate two things about the quality of management: the degree to which management embraces the goal of shareholder wealth maximization, and its effectiveness in pursuing that goal. Both of these factors are important to shareholders.

SUMMARY

Capital budgeting is the process that companies use for decision making on capital projects—those projects with a life of a year or more. This reading developed the principles behind the basic capital budgeting model, the cash flows that go into the model, and several extensions of the basic model.

- Capital budgeting supports the most critical investments for many corporations—their investments in long-term assets. The principles of capital budgeting have been applied to other corporate investing and financing decisions and to security analysis and portfolio management.
- The typical steps in the capital budgeting process are: 1) generating ideas, 2) analyzing individual proposals, 3) planning the capital budget, and 4) monitoring and post-auditing.

- Types of projects appropriate for the capital budgeting process can be categorized as: 1) replacement, 2) expansion, 3) new products and services, and 4) regulatory, safety and environmental.
- Capital budgeting decisions are based on incremental after-tax cash flows discounted at the opportunity cost of funds. Financing costs are ignored because both the cost of debt and the cost of other capital are captured in the discount rate.
- The net present value (NPV) is the present value of all after-tax cash flows, or

$$NPV = \sum_{t=0}^{n} \frac{CF_t}{(1+r)^t}$$

where the investment outlays are negative cash flows included in the CF_ts and where r is the required rate of return for the investment.

- The IRR is the discount rate that makes the present value of all future cash flows sum to zero. This equation can be solved for the IRR:

$$\sum_{t=0}^{n} \frac{CF_t}{(1+IRR)^t} = 0$$

- The payback period is the number of years required to recover the original investment in a project. The payback is based on cash flows.
- The discounted payback period is the number of years it takes for the cumulative discounted cash flows from a project to equal the original investment.
- The average accounting rate of return (AAR) can be defined as follows:

$$AAR = \frac{\text{Average net income}}{\text{Average book value}}$$

- The profitability index (PI) is the present value of a project's future cash flows divided by the initial investment:

$$PI = \frac{\text{PV of future cash flows}}{\text{Initial investment}} = 1 + \frac{\text{NPV}}{\text{Initial investment}}$$

- The capital budgeting decision rules are to invest if the NPV > 0, if the IRR > r, or if the PI > 1.0 There are no decision rules for the payback period, discounted payback period, and AAR because they are not always sound measures.
- The NPV profile is a graph that shows a project's NPV graphed as a function of various discount rates.
- For mutually exclusive projects that are ranked differently by the NPV and IRR, it is economically sound to choose the project with the higher NPV.
- The "multiple IRR problem" and the "no IRR problem" can arise for a project with nonconventional cash flows—cash flows that change signs more than once during the project's life.
- The fact that projects with positive NPVs theoretically increase the value of the company and the value of its stock could explain the popularity of NPV as an evaluation method.

PRACTICE PROBLEMS

1 The net present value (NPV) of an investment is equal to the sum of the expected cash flows discounted at the:

A internal rate of return.

B risk-free rate.

C opportunity cost of capital.

2 A $2.2 million investment will result in the cash flows shown below:

Year	Year-End Cash Flow (millions)
1	$1.3
2	$1.6
3	$1.9
4	$0.8

Using an 8% opportunity cost of capital, the project's net present value (NPV) is *closest* to:

A $2.47 million.

B $3.40 million.

C $4.67 million.

3 The internal rate of return (IRR) is *best* described as the:

A opportunity cost of capital.

B time-weighted rate of return.

C discount rate that makes the net present value equal to zero.

4 A three-year investment requires an initial outlay of £1,000. It is expected to provide three year-end cash flows of £200 plus a net salvage value of £700 at the end of three years. Its internal rate of return (IRR) is *closest* to:

A 10%.

B 11%.

C 20%.

5 Given the following cash flows for a capital project, calculate the NPV and IRR. The required rate of return is 8 percent.

Year	0	1	2	3	4	5
Cash flow	−50,000	15,000	15,000	20,000	10,000	5,000

	NPV	IRR
A	$1,905	10.9%
B	$1,905	26.0%
C	$3,379	10.9%

6 Given the following cash flows for a capital project, calculate its payback period and discounted payback period. The required rate of return is 8 percent.

Year	0	1	2	3	4	5
Cash flow	–50,000	15,000	15,000	20,000	10,000	5,000

The discounted payback period is:

A 0.16 years longer than the payback period.

B 0.51 years longer than the payback period.

C 1.01 years longer than the payback period.

7 An investment of $100 generates after-tax cash flows of $40 in Year 1, $80 in Year 2, and $120 in Year 3. The required rate of return is 20 percent. The net present value is *closest* to:

A $42.22.

B $58.33.

C $68.52.

8 An investment of $150,000 is expected to generate an after-tax cash flow of $100,000 in one year and another $120,000 in two years. The cost of capital is 10 percent. What is the internal rate of return?

A 28.39 percent.

B 28.59 percent.

C 28.79 percent.

9 Kim Corporation is considering an investment of 750 million won with expected after-tax cash inflows of 175 million won per year for seven years. The required rate of return is 10 percent. What is the project's:

	NPV?	IRR?
A	102 million won	14.0%
B	157 million won	23.3%
C	193 million won	10.0%

10 Kim Corporation is considering an investment of 750 million won with expected after-tax cash inflows of 175 million won per year for seven years. The required rate of return is 10 percent. Expressed in years, the project's payback period and discounted payback period, respectively, are *closest* to:

A 4.3 years and 5.4 years.

B 4.3 years and 5.9 years.

C 4.8 years and 6.3 years.

11 An investment of $20,000 will create a perpetual after-tax cash flow of $2,000. The required rate of return is 8 percent. What is the investment's profitability index?

A 1.08.

B 1.16.

C 1.25.

12 Hermann Corporation is considering an investment of €375 million with expected after-tax cash inflows of €115 million per year for seven years and an additional after-tax salvage value of €50 million in Year 7. The required rate of return is 10 percent. What is the investment's PI?

A 1.19.

B 1.33.

C 1.56.

13 Erin Chou is reviewing a profitable investment project that has a conventional cash flow pattern. If the cash flows for the project, initial outlay, and future after-tax cash flows all double, Chou would predict that the IRR would:

A increase and the NPV would increase.

B stay the same and the NPV would increase.

C stay the same and the NPV would stay the same.

14 Shirley Shea has evaluated an investment proposal and found that its payback period is one year, it has a negative NPV, and it has a positive IRR. Is this combination of results possible?

A Yes.

B No, because a project with a positive IRR has a positive NPV.

C No, because a project with such a rapid payback period has a positive NPV.

15 An investment has an outlay of 100 and after-tax cash flows of 40 annually for four years. A project enhancement increases the outlay by 15 and the annual after-tax cash flows by 5. As a result, the vertical intercept of the NPV profile of the enhanced project shifts:

A up and the horizontal intercept shifts left.

B up and the horizontal intercept shifts right.

C down and the horizontal intercept shifts left.

16 Projects 1 and 2 have similar outlays, although the patterns of future cash flows are different. The cash flows as well as the NPV and IRR for the two projects are shown below. For both projects, the required rate of return is 10 percent.

	Cash Flows						
Year	**0**	**1**	**2**	**3**	**4**	**NPV**	**IRR (%)**
Project 1	−50	20	20	20	20	13.40	21.86
Project 2	−50	0	0	0	100	18.30	18.92

The two projects are mutually exclusive. What is the appropriate investment decision?

A Invest in both projects.

B Invest in Project 1 because it has the higher IRR.

C Invest in Project 2 because it has the higher NPV.

17 Consider the two projects below. The cash flows as well as the NPV and IRR for the two projects are given. For both projects, the required rate of return is 10 percent.

	Cash Flows						
Year	**0**	**1**	**2**	**3**	**4**	**NPV**	**IRR (%)**
Project 1	−100	36	36	36	36	14.12	16.37
Project 2	−100	0	0	0	175	19.53	15.02

What discount rate would result in the same NPV for both projects?

A A rate between 0.00 percent and 10.00 percent.

B A rate between 10.00 percent and 15.02 percent.

C A rate between 15.02 percent and 16.37 percent.

18 Wilson Flannery is concerned that this project has multiple IRRs.

Year	0	1	2	3
Cash flows	–50	100	0	–50

How many discount rates produce a zero NPV for this project?

A One, a discount rate of 0 percent.

B Two, discount rates of 0 percent and 32 percent.

C Two, discount rates of 0 percent and 62 percent.

19 With regard to the net present value (NPV) profiles of two projects, the crossover rate is *best* described as the discount rate at which:

A two projects have the same NPV.

B two projects have the same internal rate of return.

C a project's NPV changes from positive to negative.

20 With regard to net present value (NPV) profiles, the point at which a profile crosses the vertical axis is *best* described as:

A the point at which two projects have the same NPV.

B the sum of the undiscounted cash flows from a project.

C a project's internal rate of return when the project's NPV is equal to zero.

21 With regard to net present value (NPV) profiles, the point at which a profile crosses the horizontal axis is *best* described as:

A the point at which two projects have the same NPV.

B the sum of the undiscounted cash flows from a project.

C a project's internal rate of return when the project's NPV is equal to zero.

22 With regard to capital budgeting, an appropriate estimate of the incremental cash flows from a project is *least likely* to include:

A externalities.

B interest costs.

C opportunity costs.

SOLUTIONS

1 C is correct. The NPV sums the project's expected cash flows (CF) discounted at the opportunity cost of capital. The NPV calculation is

$$\text{NPV} = \sum_{t=0}^{N} \frac{\text{CF}_t}{(1+r)^t}$$

where

CF_t = the expected net cash flow at time t
N = the investment's projected life
r = the discount rate or opportunity cost of capital

2 A is correct.

$$\text{The NPV} = -\$2.2 + \frac{\$1.3}{(1.08)} + \frac{\$1.6}{(1.08)^2} + \frac{\$1.9}{(1.08)^3} + \frac{\$0.8}{(1.08)^4} = \$2.47 \text{ million.}$$

3 C is correct. The internal rate of return is computed by identifying all cash flows and solving for the rate that makes the net present value of those cash flows equal to zero.

4 B is correct. IRR is determined by setting the net present value equal to zero for the cash flows shown in the table.

Year	Cash Flow (£)
0	–1,000
1	200
2	200
3	900

5 C is correct.

$$\text{NPV} = -50{,}000 + \frac{15{,}000}{1.08} + \frac{15{,}000}{1.08^2} + \frac{20{,}000}{1.08^3} + \frac{10{,}000}{1.08^4} + \frac{5{,}000}{1.08^5}$$

$$\text{NPV} = -50{,}000 + 13{,}888.89 + 12{,}860.08 + 15{,}876.64 + 7{,}350.30 + 3{,}402.92$$

$$\text{NPV} = -50{,}000 + 53{,}378.83 = 3{,}378.83$$

The IRR, found with a financial calculator, is 10.88 percent.

6 C is correct.

Year	0	1	2	3	4	5
Cash flow	–50,000	15,000	15,000	20,000	10,000	5,000
Cumulative cash flow	–50,000	–35,000	–20,000	0	10,000	15,000
Discounted cash flow	–50,000	13,888.89	12,860.08	15,876.64	7,350.30	3,402.92
Cumulative DCF	–50,000	–36,111.11	–23,251.03	–7,374.38	–24.09	3,378.83

As the exhibit shows, the cumulative cash flow offsets the initial investment in exactly three years. The payback period is 3.00 years. The discounted payback period is between four and five years. The discounted payback period is 4 years plus 24.09/3,402.92 = 0.007 of the fifth year cash flow, or 4.007 = 4.01 years. The discounted payback period is 4.01 – 3.00 = 1.01 years longer than the payback period.

7 B is correct.

$$\text{NPV} = \sum_{t=0}^{3} \frac{CF_t}{(1+r)^t} = -100 + \frac{40}{1.20} + \frac{80}{1.20^2} + \frac{120}{1.20^3} = \$58.33$$

8 C is correct. The IRR can be found using a financial calculator or with trial and error. Using trial and error, the total PV is equal to zero if the discount rate is 28.79 percent.

		Present Value			
Year	**Cash Flow**	**28.19%**	**28.39%**	**28.59%**	**28.79%**
0	−150,000	−150,000	−150,000	−150,000	−150,000
1	100,000	78,009	77,888	77,767	77,646
2	120,000	73,025	72,798	72,572	72,346
Total		1,034	686	338	−8

A more precise IRR of 28.7854 percent has a total PV closer to zero.

9 A is correct.

$$\text{The NPV} = -750 + \sum_{t=1}^{7} \frac{175}{1.10^t} = -750 + 851.97 = 101.97 \text{ million won.}$$

The IRR, found with a financial calculator, is 14.02 percent. (The PV is −750, N = 7, and PMT = 175.)

10 B is correct.

Year	**0**	**1**	**2**	**3**	**4**	**5**	**6**	**7**
Cash flow	−750	175	175	175	175	175	175	175
Cumulative cash flow	−750	−575	−400	−225	−50	125	300	475

The payback period is between four and five years. The payback period is four years plus 50/175 = 0.29 of the fifth year cash flow, or 4.29 years.

Year	**0**	**1**	**2**	**3**	**4**	**5**	**6**	**7**
Cash flow	−750	175	175	175	175	175	175	175
Discounted cash flow	−750	159.09	144.63	131.48	119.53	108.66	98.78	89.80
Cumulative DCF	−750	−590.91	−446.28	−314.80	−195.27	−86.61	12.17	101.97

The discounted payback period is between five and six years. The discounted payback period is five years plus 86.61/98.78 = 0.88 of the sixth year cash flow, or 5.88 years.

11 C is correct.

$$\text{The present value of future cash flows is PV} = \frac{2{,}000}{0.08} = 25{,}000$$

$$\text{The profitability index is PI} = \frac{\text{PV}}{\text{Investment}} = \frac{25{,}000}{20{,}000} = 1.25$$

12 C is correct.

$$PV = \sum_{t=1}^{7} \frac{115}{1.10^t} + \frac{50}{1.10^7} = 585.53 \text{ million euros}$$

$$PI = \frac{585.53}{375} = 1.56$$

13 B is correct. The IRR would stay the same because both the initial outlay and the after-tax cash flows double, so that the return on each dollar invested remains the same. All of the cash flows and their present values double. The difference between total present value of the future cash flows and the initial outlay (the NPV) also doubles.

14 A is correct. If the cumulative cash flow in one year equals the outlay and additional cash flows are not very large, this scenario is possible. For example, assume the outlay is 100, the cash flow in Year 1 is 100 and the cash flow in Year 2 is 5. The required return is 10 percent. This project would have a payback of 1.0 years, an NPV of −4.96, and an IRR of 4.77 percent.

15 A is correct. The vertical intercept changes from 60 to 65 (NPV when cost of capital is 0%), and the horizontal intercept (IRR, when NPV equals zero) changes from 21.86 percent to 20.68 percent.

16 C is correct. When valuing mutually exclusive projects, the decision should be made with the NPV method because this method uses the most realistic discount rate, namely the opportunity cost of funds. In this example, the reinvestment rate for the NPV method (here 10 percent) is more realistic than the reinvestment rate for the IRR method (here 21.86 percent or 18.92 percent).

17 B is correct. For these projects, a discount rate of 13.16 percent would yield the same NPV for both (an NPV of 6.73).

18 C is correct. Discount rates of 0 percent and approximately 61.8 percent both give a zero NPV.

Rate	0%	20%	40%	60%	61.8%	80%	100%
NPV	0.00	4.40	3.21	0.29	0.00	−3.02	−6.25

19 A is correct. The crossover rate is the discount rate at which the NPV profiles for two projects cross; it is the only point where the NPVs of the projects are the same.

20 B is correct. The vertical axis represents a discount rate of zero. The point where the profile crosses the vertical axis is simply the sum of the cash flows.

21 C is correct. The horizontal axis represents an NPV of zero. By definition, the project's IRR equals an NPV of zero.

22 B is correct. Costs to finance the project are taken into account when the cash flows are discounted at the appropriate cost of capital; including interest costs in the cash flows would result in double-counting the cost of debt.

READING

33

Cost of Capital

by Yves Courtois, CMT, MRICS, CFA, Gene C. Lai, PhD, and Pamela Peterson Drake, PhD, CFA

Yves Courtois, CMT, MRICS, CFA, is at KPMG (Luxembourg). Gene C. Lai, PhD, is at University of North Carolina at Charlotte (USA). Pamela Peterson Drake, PhD, CFA, is at James Madison University (USA).

LEARNING OUTCOMES

Mastery	*The candidate should be able to:*
☐	**a.** calculate and interpret the weighted average cost of capital (WACC) of a company;
☐	**b.** describe how taxes affect the cost of capital from different capital sources;
☐	**c.** describe the use of target capital structure in estimating WACC and how target capital structure weights may be determined;
☐	**d.** explain how the marginal cost of capital and the investment opportunity schedule are used to determine the optimal capital budget;
☐	**e.** explain the marginal cost of capital's role in determining the net present value of a project;
☐	**f.** calculate and interpret the cost of debt capital using the yield-to-maturity approach and the debt-rating approach;
☐	**g.** calculate and interpret the cost of noncallable, nonconvertible preferred stock;
☐	**h.** calculate and interpret the cost of equity capital using the capital asset pricing model approach, the dividend discount model approach, and the bond-yield-plus risk-premium approach;
☐	**i.** calculate and interpret the beta and cost of capital for a project;
☐	**j.** describe uses of country risk premiums in estimating the cost of equity;
☐	**k.** describe the marginal cost of capital schedule, explain why it may be upward-sloping with respect to additional capital, and calculate and interpret its break-points;
☐	**l.** explain and demonstrate the correct treatment of flotation costs.

1 INTRODUCTION

A company grows by making investments that are expected to increase revenues and profits. The company acquires the capital or funds necessary to make such investments by borrowing or using funds from owners. By applying this capital to investments with long-term benefits, the company is producing value today. But, how much value? The answer depends not only on the investments' expected future cash flows but also on the cost of the funds. Borrowing is not costless. Neither is using owners' funds.

The cost of this capital is an important ingredient in both investment decision making by the company's management and the valuation of the company by investors. If a company invests in projects that produce a return in excess of the cost of capital, the company has created value; in contrast, if the company invests in projects whose returns are less than the cost of capital, the company has actually destroyed value. Therefore, the estimation of the cost of capital is a central issue in corporate financial management. For the analyst seeking to evaluate a company's investment program and its competitive position, an accurate estimate of a company's cost of capital is important as well.

Cost of capital estimation is a challenging task. As we have already implied, the cost of capital is not observable but, rather, must be estimated. Arriving at a cost of capital estimate requires a host of assumptions and estimates. Another challenge is that the cost of capital that is appropriately applied to a specific investment depends on the characteristics of that investment: The riskier the investment's cash flows, the greater its cost of capital. In reality, a company must estimate project-specific costs of capital. What is often done, however, is to estimate the cost of capital for the company as a whole and then adjust this overall corporate cost of capital upward or downward to reflect the risk of the contemplated project relative to the company's average project.

This reading is organized as follows: In the next section, we introduce the cost of capital and its basic computation. Section 3 presents a selection of methods for estimating the costs of the various sources of capital. Section 4 discusses issues an analyst faces in using the cost of capital. A summary concludes the reading.

2 COST OF CAPITAL

The **cost of capital** is the rate of return that the suppliers of capital—bondholders and owners—require as compensation for their contribution of capital. Another way of looking at the cost of capital is that it is the opportunity cost of funds for the suppliers of capital: A potential supplier of capital will not voluntarily invest in a company unless its return meets or exceeds what the supplier could earn elsewhere in an investment of comparable risk.

A company typically has several alternatives for raising capital, including issuing equity, debt, and instruments that share characteristics of debt and equity. Each source selected becomes a component of the company's funding and has a cost (required rate of return) that may be called a **component cost of capital**. Because we are using the cost of capital in the evaluation of investment opportunities, we are dealing with a *marginal* cost—what it would cost to raise additional funds for the potential investment project. Therefore, the cost of capital that the investment analyst is concerned with is a marginal cost.

Let us focus on the cost of capital for the entire company (later we will address how to adjust that for specific projects). The cost of capital of a company is the required rate of return that investors demand for the average-risk investment of a company. The most common way to estimate this required rate of return is to calculate the marginal cost of each of the various sources of capital and then calculate a weighted average of these costs. This weighted average is referred to as the **weighted average cost of capital** (WACC). The WACC is also referred to as the marginal cost of capital (MCC) because it is the cost that a company incurs for additional capital. The weights in this weighted average are the proportions of the various sources of capital that the company uses to support its investment program. Taking the sources of capital to be common stock, preferred stock, and debt and allowing for the fact (explained further in section 2.1) that in some jurisdictions interest expense may be tax deductible, the expression for WACC is

$$\text{WACC} = w_d r_d (1 - t) + w_p r_p + w_e r_e \quad (1)$$

where

w_d = the proportion of debt that the company uses when it raises new funds
r_d = the before-tax marginal cost of debt
t = the company's marginal tax rate
w_p = the proportion of preferred stock the company uses when it raises new funds
r_p = the marginal cost of preferred stock
w_e = the proportion of equity that the company uses when it raises new funds
r_e = the marginal cost of equity

There are important points concerning the calculation of the WACC as shown in Equation 1 that the analyst must be familiar with. The next two sections address two key issues: taxes and the selection of weights.

2.1 Taxes and the Cost of Capital

The marginal cost of debt financing is the cost of debt after considering the allowable deduction for interest on debt based on the country's tax law. If interest cannot be deducted for tax purposes, the tax rate applied is zero so that the effective marginal cost of debt is equal to r_d in Equation 1. If interest can be deducted in full, the tax deductibility of debt reduces the effective marginal cost of debt to reflect the income shielded from taxation and the marginal cost of debt is $r_d(1 - t)$. For example, suppose a company pays €1 million in interest on its €10 million of debt. The cost of this debt is not €1 million because this interest expense reduces taxable income by €1 million, resulting in a lower tax. If the company has a marginal tax rate of 40 percent, this €1 million of interest costs the company (€1 million)(1 – 0.4) = €0.6 million because the interest reduces the company's tax bill by €0.4 million. In this case, the before-tax cost of debt is 10 percent, whereas the after-tax cost of debt is (€0.6 million)/(€10 million) = 6 percent, which can also be calculated as 10%(1 – 0.4).

In jurisdictions in which a tax deduction for a business's interest expense is allowed, for reasons related to the business's financial position (e.g., having positive income to offset with interest expense) and/or the terms of the tax law, the business may be in a situation in which additional interest expense is not tax deductible. If the above company with €10 million in debt were in that position, its effective marginal cost of debt would be 10 percent rather than 6 percent because any additional interest expense would not be deductible for tax purposes. In other words, if the limit on tax deductibility is reached, the marginal cost of debt is the cost of debt without any adjustment for a tax shield: using r_d^* to represent the effective marginal cost of debt, $r_d^* = r_d$.

EXAMPLE 1

Computing the Weighted Average Cost of Capital

Assume that ABC Corporation has the following capital structure: 30 percent debt, 10 percent preferred stock, and 60 percent equity. Also assume that interest expense is tax deductible. ABC Corporation wishes to maintain these proportions as it raises new funds. Its before-tax cost of debt is 8 percent, its cost of preferred stock is 10 percent, and its cost of equity is 15 percent. If the company's marginal tax rate is 40 percent, what is ABC's weighted average cost of capital?

Solution:

The weighted average cost of capital is

$$\text{WACC} = (0.3)(0.08)(1 - 0.40) + (0.1)(0.1) + (0.6)(0.15)$$
$$= 11.44 \text{ percent}$$

EXAMPLE 2

Incorporating the Effect of Taxes on the Costs of Capital

Jorge Ricard, a financial analyst, is estimating the costs of capital for the Zeale Corporation. In the process of this estimation, Ricard has estimated the before-tax costs of capital for Zeale's debt and equity as 4 percent and 6 percent, respectively. What are the after-tax costs of debt and equity if there is no limit to the tax deductibility of interest and Zeale's marginal tax rate is:

1 30 percent?

2 48 percent?

	Marginal Tax Rate	After-Tax Cost of Debt	After-Tax Cost of Equity
Solution to 1:	30 percent	0.04(1 – 0.30) = 2.80 percent	6 percent
Solution to 2:	48 percent	0.04(1 – 0.48) = 2.08 percent	6 percent

Note: There is no adjustment for taxes in the case of equity; the before-tax cost of equity is equal to the after-tax cost of equity.

2.2 Weights of the Weighted Average

How do we determine what weights to use? Ideally, we want to use the proportion of each source of capital that the company would use in the project or company. If we assume that a company has a target capital structure and raises capital consistent with this target, we should use this target capital structure. The **target capital structure** is the capital structure that a company is striving to obtain. If we know the company's target capital structure, then, of course, we should use this in our analysis. Someone outside the company, however, such as an analyst, typically does not know the target capital structure and must estimate it using one of several approaches:

1 Assume the company's current capital structure, at market value weights for the components, represents the company's target capital structure.

2 Examine trends in the company's capital structure or statements by management regarding capital structure policy to infer the target capital structure.

3 Use averages of comparable companies' capital structures as the target capital structure.

In the absence of knowledge of a company's target capital structure, we may take Method 1 as the baseline. Note that in applying Method 3, we use an unweighted, arithmetic average, as is often done for simplicity. An alternative is to calculate a weighted average, which would give more weight to larger companies.

Suppose we are using the company's current capital structure as a proxy for the target capital structure. In this case, we use the market value of the different capital sources in the calculation of these proportions. For example, if a company has the following market values for its capital

Bonds outstanding	$5 million
Preferred stock	1 million
Common stock	14 million
Total capital	$20 million

the weights that we apply would be

$w_d = 0.25$

$w_p = 0.05$

$w_e = 0.70$

Example 3 illustrates the estimation of weights. Note that a simple way of transforming a debt-to-equity ratio D/E into a weight—that is, D/(D + E)—is to divide D/E by 1 + D/E.

EXAMPLE 3

Estimating the Proportions of Capital

Fin Anziell is a financial analyst with Analytiker Firma. Anziell is in the process of estimating the cost of capital of Gewicht GmbH. The following information is provided:

Gewicht GmbH

Market value of debt	€50 million
Market value of equity	€60 million

Primary competitors and their capital structures (in millions):

Competitor	Market Value of Debt	Market Value of Equity
A	€25	€50
B	€101	€190
C	£40	£60

What are Gewicht's proportions of debt and equity that Anziell would use if estimating these proportions using the company's:

1 current capital structure?

2 competitors' capital structure?

3 Suppose Gewicht announces that a debt-to-equity ratio of 0.7 reflects its target capital structure. What weights should Anziell use in the cost of capital calculations?

Solution to 1:

Current capital structure

$$w_d = \frac{€50 \text{ million}}{€50 \text{ million} + €60 \text{ million}} = 0.4545$$

$$w_e = \frac{€60 \text{ million}}{€50 \text{ million} + €60 \text{ million}} = 0.5454$$

Solution to 2:

Competitors' capital structure:[1]

$$w_d = \frac{\left(\frac{€25}{€25 + €50}\right) + \left(\frac{€101}{€101 + €190}\right) + \left(\frac{£40}{£40 + £60}\right)}{3} = 0.3601$$

$$w_e = \frac{\left(\frac{€50}{€25 + €50}\right) + \left(\frac{€190}{€101 + €190}\right) + \left(\frac{£60}{£40 + £60}\right)}{3} = 0.6399$$

Solution to 3:

A debt-to-equity ratio of 0.7 represents a weight on debt of 0.7/1.7 = 0.4118 so that w_d = 0.4118 and w_e = 1 − 0.4118 = 0.5882. These would be the preferred weights to use in a cost of capital calculation.

2.3 Applying the Cost of Capital to Capital Budgeting and Security Valuation

With some insight now into the calculation of the cost of capital, let us continue to improve our understanding of the roles it plays in financial analysis. A chief use of the marginal cost of capital estimate is in capital-budgeting decision making. What role does the marginal cost of capital play in a company's investment program, and how do we adapt it when we need to evaluate a specific investment project?

A company's marginal cost of capital (MCC) may increase as additional capital is raised, whereas returns to a company's investment opportunities are generally believed to decrease as the company makes additional investments, as represented by the **investment opportunity schedule** (IOS).[2] We show this relation in Exhibit 1, graphing the upward-sloping marginal cost of capital schedule against the downward-sloping investment opportunity schedule. In the context of a company's investment decision, the optimal capital budget is that amount of capital raised and invested at which the marginal cost of capital is equal to the marginal return from investing. In other words, the optimal capital budget occurs when the marginal cost of capital intersects with the investment opportunity schedule as seen in Exhibit 1.

The relation between the MCC and the IOS provides a broad picture of the basic decision-making problem of a company. However, we are often interested in valuing an individual project or even a portion of a company, such as a division or product line. In these applications, we are interested in the cost of capital for the project, product, or division as opposed to the cost of capital for the company overall. The

1 These weights represent the arithmetic average of the three companies' debt proportion and equity proportion, respectively.

2 The investment opportunity schedule originates with Fisher's production opportunities [Irving Fisher, *The Theory of Interest* (New York: MacMillan Co.), 1930] and was adapted to capital budgeting by John Hirshleifer ["On the Theory of Optimal Investment Decision," *Journal of Political Economy*, Vol. 66, No. 4 (August 1958), pp. 329–352.]

cost of capital in these applications should reflect the riskiness of the future cash flows of the project, product, or division. For an average-risk project, the opportunity cost of capital is the company's WACC. If the systematic risk of the project is above or below average relative to the company's current portfolio of projects, an upward or downward adjustment, respectively, is made to the company's WACC. Companies may take an *ad hoc* or a systematic approach to making such adjustments. The discussion of a systematic approach is a somewhat advanced topic that we defer to Section 4.1.

Exhibit 1 Optimal Investment Decision

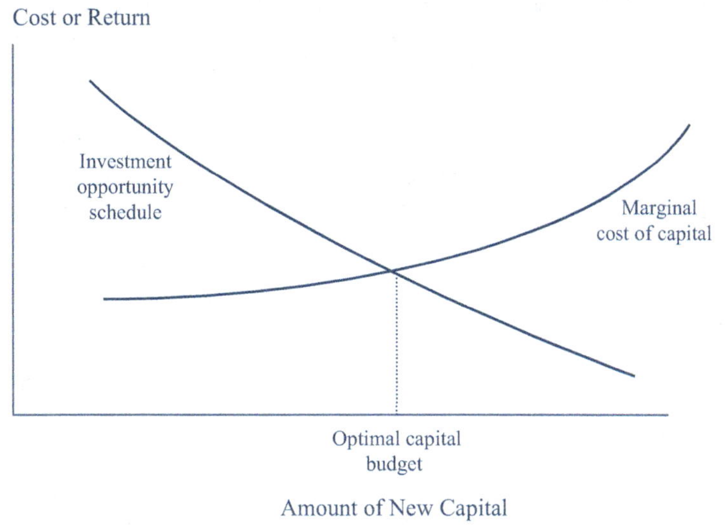

The WACC or MCC corresponding to the average risk of the company, adjusted appropriately for the risk of a given project, plays a role in capital-budgeting decision making based on the **net present value** (NPV) of that project. Recall from the reading on capital budgeting that the NPV is the present value of all the project cash flows. It is useful to think of it as the difference between the present value of the cash inflows, discounted at the opportunity cost of capital applicable to the specific project, and the present value of the cash outflows, discounted using that same opportunity cost of capital:

NPV = Present value of inflows − Present value of outflows

If an investment's NPV is positive, the company should undertake the project. If we choose to use the company's WACC in the calculation of the NPV of a project, we are assuming that the project:

- has the same risk as the average-risk project of the company, and
- will have a constant target capital structure throughout its useful life.[3]

These may not be realistic or appropriate assumptions and are potential drawbacks to using the company's WACC in valuing projects. However, alternative approaches are subject to drawbacks as well, and the approach outlined has wide acceptance.[4]

3 WACC is estimated using fixed proportions of equity and debt. The NPV method assumes a constant required rate of return, whereas a fluctuating capital structure would cause WACC to fluctuate. The importance of this issue is demonstrated by James A. Miles and John R. Ezzell, "The Weighted Average Cost of Capital, Perfect Capital Markets, and Project Life: A Clarification," *Journal of Financial and Quantitative Analysis*, Vol. 15, No. 3 (September 1980), pp. 719–730.

4 See the reading on capital budgeting for a discussion.

For the analyst, the second key use of the marginal cost of capital is in security valuation using any one of several discounted cash flow valuation models available.[5] For a particular valuation model, if these cash flows are cash flows to the company's suppliers of capital (that is, free cash flow to the firm), the analyst uses the weighted average cost of capital of the company in the valuation.[6] If these cash flows are strictly those belonging to the company's owners, such as the free cash flow to equity, or dividends, the analyst uses the cost of equity capital to find the present value of these flows.[7]

In the next section, we discuss how an analyst may approach the calculation of the component costs of capital, focusing on debt, preferred stock, and common equity.

3 COSTS OF THE DIFFERENT SOURCES OF CAPITAL

Each source of capital has a different cost because of the differences among the sources, such as seniority, contractual commitments, and potential value as a tax shield. We focus on the costs of three primary sources of capital: debt, preferred equity, and common equity.

3.1 Cost of Debt

The **cost of debt** is the cost of debt financing to a company when it issues a bond or takes out a bank loan. We discuss two methods to estimate the before-tax cost of debt, r_d: the yield-to-maturity approach and debt-rating approach.

3.1.1 *Yield-to-Maturity Approach*

The **yield to maturity** (YTM) is the annual return that an investor earns on a bond if the investor purchases the bond today and holds it until maturity. In other words, it is the yield, r_d, that equates the present value of the bond's promised payments to its market price:

$$P_0 = \frac{PMT_1}{\left(1+\frac{r_d}{2}\right)} + \ldots + \frac{PMT_n}{\left(1+\frac{r_d}{2}\right)^n} + \frac{FV}{\left(1+\frac{r_d}{2}\right)^n} = \left(\sum_{t=1}^{n} \frac{PMT_t}{\left(1+\frac{r_d}{2}\right)^t}\right) + \frac{FV}{\left(1+\frac{r_d}{2}\right)^n} \quad (2)$$

where

P_0 = the current market price of the bond

PMT_t = the interest payment in period t

r_d = the yield to maturity

n = the number of periods remaining to maturity

FV = the maturity value of the bond

5 Such models are discussed thoroughly at Level II of the CFA Program.

6 **Free cash flow to the firm (FCFF)** is the cash flow available to the company's suppliers of capital after all operating expenses (including taxes) have been paid and necessary investments in working capital (e.g., inventory) and fixed capital (e.g., plant and equipment) have been made.

7 **Free cash flow to equity (FCFE)** is the cash flow available to holders of the company's common equity after all operating expenses, interest, and principal payments have been paid and necessary investments in working capital and fixed capital have been made.

This valuation equation assumes the bond pays semi-annual interest and that any intermediate cash flows (in this case the interest prior to maturity) are reinvested at the rate $r_d/2$.[8]

Example 4 illustrates the calculation of the after-tax cost of debt.

EXAMPLE 4

Calculating the After-Tax Cost of Debt

Valence Industries issues a bond to finance a new project. It offers a 10-year, $1,000 face value, 5 percent semi-annual coupon bond. Upon issue, the bond sells at $1,025. What is Valence's before-tax cost of debt? If Valence's marginal tax rate is 35 percent, what is Valence's after-tax cost of debt?

Solution:

Given:

$$PV = \$1{,}025$$
$$FV = \$1{,}000$$
$$PMT = 5 \text{ percent of } 1{,}000 \div 2 = \$25$$
$$n = 10 \times 2 = 20$$
$$\$1{,}025 = \left(\sum_{t=1}^{20} \frac{\$25}{(1+i)^t}\right) + \frac{\$1{,}000}{(1+i)^{20}}$$

Use a financial calculator to solve for i, the six-month yield. Because i = 2.342 percent, the before-tax cost of debt is r_d = 2.342 percent × 2 = 4.684 percent, and Valence's after-tax cost of debt is $r_d\,(1 - t) = 0.04684\,(1 - 0.35) = 0.03045$ or 3.045 percent.

3.1.2 *Debt-Rating Approach*

When a reliable current market price for a company's debt is not available, the **debt-rating approach** can be used to estimate the before-tax cost of debt. Based on a company's debt rating, we estimate the before-tax cost of debt by using the yield on comparably rated bonds for maturities that closely match that of the company's existing debt.

Suppose a company's capital structure includes debt with an average maturity (or duration) of 10 years and the company's marginal tax rate is 35 percent. If the company's rating is AAA and the yield on debt with the same debt rating and similar maturity is 4 percent, the company's after-tax cost of debt is

$$r_d(1 - t) = 4 \text{ percent}(1 - 0.35) = 2.6 \text{ percent}$$

A consideration when using this approach is that debt ratings are ratings of the debt issue itself, with the issuer being only one of the considerations. Other factors, such as debt seniority and security, also affect ratings and yields, so care must be taken to consider the likely type of debt to be issued by the company in determining the comparable debt rating and yield. The debt-rating approach is a simple example of pricing on the basis of valuation-relevant characteristics, which in bond markets has been known as evaluated pricing or **matrix pricing**.

8 r_d is expressed as an annual rate and is divided by the number of payment periods per year. Because most corporate bonds pay semi-annual interest, we divided r_d by 2 in this calculation. The interest payment for each period thus corresponds with the bond's semi-annual coupon payment.

3.1.3 *Issues in Estimating the Cost of Debt*

3.1.3.1 Fixed-Rate Debt versus Floating-Rate Debt Up to now, we have assumed that the interest on debt is a fixed amount each period. We can observe market yields of the company's existing debt or market yields of debt of similar risk in estimating the before-tax cost of debt. However, the company may also issue floating-rate debt in which the interest rate adjusts periodically according to a prescribed index, such as the prime rate or Libor, over the life of the instrument.

Estimating the cost of a floating-rate security is difficult because the cost of this form of capital over the long term depends not only on the current yields but also on the future yields. The analyst may use the current term structure of interest rates and term structure theory to assign an average cost to such instruments.

3.1.3.2 Debt with Optionlike Features How should an analyst determine the cost of debt when the company used debt with optionlike features, such as call, conversion, or put provisions? Clearly, options affect the value of debt. For example, a callable bond would have a yield greater than a similar noncallable bond of the same issuer because bondholders want to be compensated for the call risk associated with the bond. In a similar manner, the put feature of a bond, which provides the investor with an option to sell the bond back to the issuer at a predetermined price, has the effect of lowering the yield on a bond below that of a similar nonputable bond.

If the company already has debt outstanding incorporating optionlike features that the analyst believes are representative of the future debt issuance of the company, the analyst may simply use the yield to maturity on such debt in estimating the cost of debt.

If the analyst believes that the company will add or remove option features in future debt issuance, the analyst can make market value adjustments to the current YTM to reflect the value of such additions and/or deletions. The technology for such adjustments is an advanced topic that is outside the scope of this reading.

3.1.3.3 Nonrated Debt If a company does not have any debt outstanding or if the yields on the company's existing debt are not available, the analyst may not always be able to use the yield on similarly rated debt securities. It may be the case that the company does not have rated bonds. Though researchers offer approaches for estimating a company's "synthetic" debt rating based on financial ratios, these methods are imprecise because debt ratings incorporate not only financial ratios but also information about the particular bond issue and the issuer that are not captured in financial ratios.

3.1.3.4 Leases A lease is a contractual obligation that can substitute for other forms of borrowing. This is true whether the lease is an **operating lease** or a **finance lease** (**capital lease**). If the company uses leasing as a source of capital, the cost of these leases should be included in the cost of capital. The cost of this form of borrowing is similar to that of the company's other long-term borrowing.

3.2 Cost of Preferred Stock

The **cost of preferred stock** is the cost that a company has committed to pay preferred stockholders as a preferred dividend when it issues preferred stock. In the case of nonconvertible, noncallable preferred stock that has a fixed dividend rate and no maturity date (**fixed rate perpetual preferred stock**), we can use the formula for the value of a preferred stock:

$$P_p = \frac{D_p}{r_p}$$

where

P_p = the current preferred stock price per share

D_p = the preferred stock dividend per share

r_p = the cost of preferred stock

We can rearrange this equation to solve for the cost of preferred stock:

$$r_p = \frac{D_p}{P_p} \tag{3}$$

Therefore, the cost of preferred stock is the preferred stock's dividend per share divided by the current preferred stock's price per share. Unlike interest on debt, the dividend on preferred stock is not tax-deductible by the company; therefore, there is no adjustment to the cost for taxes.[9]

A preferred stock may have a number of features that affect the yield and hence the cost of preferred stock. These features include a call option, cumulative dividends, participating dividends, adjustable-rate dividends, or convertibility into common stock. When estimating a yield based on current yields of the company's preferred stock, we must make appropriate adjustments for the effects of these features on the yield of an issue. For example, if the company has callable, convertible preferred stock outstanding, yet it is expected that the company will issue only noncallable, nonconvertible preferred stock in the future, we would have to either use the current yields on comparable companies' noncallable, nonconvertible preferred stock or estimate the yield on preferred equity using methods outside the scope of this reading.

EXAMPLE 5

Calculating the Cost of Preferred Equity

Consider a company that has one issue of preferred stock outstanding with a $3.75 cumulative preferred stock, for which there are 600,000 shares outstanding. If the price of this stock is $80, what is the estimate of its cost of preferred equity?

Solution:

Cost of preferred stock = $3.75/$80 = 4.6875 percent.

EXAMPLE 6

Choosing the Best Estimate of the Cost of Preferred Equity

Wim Vanistendael is finance director of De Gouden Tulip N.V., a leading Dutch flower producer and distributor. He has been asked by the CEO to calculate the cost of preferred equity and has recently obtained the following information:

- The issue price of preferred stock was €3.5 million and the preferred dividend is 5 percent.
- If the company issued new preferred stock today, the preferred coupon rate would be 6.5 percent.
- The company's marginal tax rate is 30.5 percent.

9 This is not to be confused, however, with the dividends-received deduction, which reduces the effective tax on intercorporate preferred dividends received.

What is the cost of preferred equity for De Gouden Tulip N.V.?

Solution:

If De Gouden Tulip were to issue new preferred stock today, the coupon rate would be close to 6.5 percent. The current terms thus prevail over the past terms when evaluating the actual cost of preferred stock. The cost of preferred stock for De Gouden Tulip is, therefore, 6.5 percent. Because preferred dividends offer no tax shield, there is no adjustment made based upon the marginal tax rate.

3.3 Cost of Common Equity

The cost of common equity, (r_e), usually referred to simply as the cost of equity, is the rate of return required by a company's common shareholders. A company may increase common equity through the reinvestment of earnings—that is, retained earnings—or through the issuance of new shares of stock.

As we discussed earlier, the estimation of the cost of equity is challenging because of the uncertain nature of the future cash flows in terms of the amount and timing. Commonly used approaches for estimating the cost of equity include the capital asset pricing model, the dividend discount model, and the bond yield plus risk premium method.

3.3.1 *Capital Asset Pricing Model Approach*

In the capital asset pricing model (CAPM) approach, we use the basic relationship from the capital asset pricing model theory that the expected return on a stock, $E(R_i)$, is the sum of the risk-free rate of interest, R_F, and a premium for bearing the stock's market risk, $\beta_i(R_M - R_F)$:

$$E(R_i) = R_F + \beta_i\left[E(R_M) - R_F\right] \tag{4}$$

where

β_i = the return sensitivity of stock i to changes in the market return

$E(R_M)$ = the expected return on the market

$E(R_M) - R_F$ = the expected market risk premium

A risk-free asset is defined here as an asset that has no default risk. A common proxy for the risk-free rate is the yield on a default-free government debt instrument. In general, the selection of the appropriate risk-free rate should be guided by the duration of projected cash flows. If we are evaluating a project with an estimated useful life of 10 years, we may want to use the rate on the 10-year Treasury bond.

EXAMPLE 7

Using the CAPM to Estimate the Cost of Equity

Valence Industries wants to know its cost of equity. Its CFO believes the risk-free rate is 5 percent, equity risk premium is 7 percent, and Valence's equity beta is 1.5. What is Valence's cost of equity using the CAPM approach?

Solution:

Cost of common stock = 5 percent + 1.5(7 percent) = 15.5 percent.

The expected market risk premium, or $E(R_M - R_F)$, is the premium that investors demand for investing in a market portfolio relative to the risk-free rate. When using the CAPM to estimate the cost of equity, in practice we typically estimate beta relative to an equity market index. In that case, the market premium estimate we are using is actually an estimate of the **equity risk premium** (ERP).

An alternative to the CAPM to accommodate risks that may not be captured by the market portfolio alone is a multifactor model that incorporates factors that may be other sources of **priced risk** (risk for which investors demand compensation for bearing), including macroeconomic factors and company-specific factors. In general

$$\begin{aligned} E(R_i) = R_F &+ \beta_{i1}(\text{Factor risk premium})_1 \\ &+ \beta_{i2}(\text{Factor risk premium})_2 + \ldots \\ &+ \beta_{ij}(\text{Factor risk premium})_j \end{aligned} \quad (5)$$

where

β_{ij} = stock i's sensitivity to changes in the jth factor

$(\text{Factor risk premium})_j$ = expected risk premium for the jth factor

The basic idea behind these multifactor models is that the CAPM beta may not capture all the risks, especially in a global context, which include inflation, business-cycle, interest rate, exchange rate, and default risks.[10,11]

There are several ways to estimate the equity risk premium, though there is no general agreement as to the best approach. The three we discuss are the historical equity risk premium approach, the dividend discount model approach, and the survey approach.

The **historical equity risk premium approach** is a well-established approach based on the assumption that the realized equity risk premium observed over a long period of time is a good indicator of the expected equity risk premium. This approach requires compiling historical data to find the average rate of return of a country's market portfolio and the average rate of return for the risk-free rate in that country. For example, an analyst might use the historical returns to the TOPIX Index to estimate the risk premium for Japanese equities. The exceptional bull market observed during the second half of the 1990s, and the bursting of the technology bubble that followed during the years 2000–2002, reminds us that the time period for such estimates should cover complete market cycles.

Elroy Dimson, Paul Marsh, and Mike Staunton conducted an analysis of the equity risk premiums observed in markets located in 21 countries, including the United States, over the period 1900–2017.[12] These researchers found that the annualized US equity risk premium relative to US Treasury bills was 5.6 percent (geometric mean) and 7.5 percent (arithmetic mean). They also found that the annualized US equity risk premium relative to bonds was 4.4 percent (geometric mean) and 6.5 percent

10 An example of the multi-factor model is the three-factor Fama and French model [Eugene Fama and Kenneth French, "The Cross-Section of Expected Stock Returns," *Journal of Finance*, Vol. 47, No. 2 (1992), pp. 427–465], which includes factors for the market, equity capitalization, and the ratio of book value of equity to the market value of equity.

11 These models are discussed in more detail by Robert F. Bruner, Robert M. Conroy, Wei Li, Elizabeth O'Halloran, and Miquel Palacios Lleras [*Investing in Emerging Markets*, AIMR Research Foundation monograph (August 2003)] and by Eugene F. Fama and Kenneth R. French, "The Capital Asset Pricing Model: Theory and Evidence," *Journal of Economic Perspectives*, Vol. 18, No. 3 (Summer 2004), pp. 3–24.

12 Credit Suisse Global Investment Returns Yearbook 2018, E. Dimson, P. Marsh, M. Staunton. February 2018.

(arithmetic mean).[13] Note that the arithmetic mean is greater than the geometric mean as a result of the significant volatility of the observed market rate of return and of the observed risk-free rate. Under the assumption of an unchanging distribution of returns through time, the arithmetic mean is the unbiased estimate of the expected single-period equity risk premium, but the geometric mean better reflects growth rate over multiple periods.[14] In Exhibit 2 we provide historical estimates of the equity risk premium for 20 developed markets from Dimson, Marsh, and Staunton's study.

Exhibit 2 Equity Risk Premiums Relative to Bonds (1900 to 2017)

	Mean	
	Geometric	**Arithmetic**
Australia	5.0%	6.6%
Belgium	2.2	4.3
Canada	3.5	5.1
Denmark	2.2	3.8
Finland	5.2	8.7
France	3.1	5.4
Germany	5.1	8.4
Ireland	2.7	4.7
Italy	3.2	6.5
Japan	5.1	9.1
Netherlands	3.3	5.6
New Zealand	4.0	5.6
Norway	2.5	5.4
Portugal	5.3	9.4
South Africa	5.3	7.1
Spain	1.8	3.8
Sweden	3.1	5.3
Switzerland	2.2	3.7
United Kingdom	3.7	5.0
United States	4.4	6.5
World	3.2	4.4

Note: Germany excludes 1922–23.
Source: Dimson, Marsh, and Staunton (2018).

13 Jeremy Siegel presents a longer time series of market returns, covering the period from 1802 through 2004, and observes an equity return of 6.82 percent and an equity risk premium in the range of 3.31 to 5.36 percent. See Jeremy J. Siegel, "Perspectives on the Equity Risk Premium," *Financial Analysts Journal*, Vol. 61, No. 6 (November/December 2005), pp. 61–73. The range depends on the method of calculation (compounded or arithmetic) and the benchmark (bonds or bills).

14 Aside from the method of averaging (geometric versus arithmetic), estimates of the historical equity risk premium differ depending on the assumed investment horizon (short versus intermediate versus long), whether conditional on some variable or unconditional, whether US or global markets are examined, the source of the data, the period observed, and whether nominal or real returns are estimated.

To illustrate the historical method as applied in the CAPM, suppose that we use the historical geometric mean for US equity of 4.4 percent to value Apple Computer as of early August 2018. According to Yahoo Finance, Apple had a beta of 1.14 at that time. Using a 10-year US Treasury bond yield of 3.0 percent to represent the risk-free rate, the estimate of the cost of equity for Apple Computer is 3.0 percent + 1.14(4.4 percent) = 8.016 percent.

The historical premium approach has several limitations. One limitation is that the level of risk of the stock index may change over time. Another is that the risk aversion of investors may change over time. And still another limitation is that the estimates are sensitive to the method of estimation and the historical period covered.

EXAMPLE 8

Estimating the Equity Risk Premium Using Historical Rates of Return

Suppose that the arithmetic average T-bond rate observed over the last 90 years is an unbiased estimator for the risk-free rate and is 4.88 percent. Likewise, suppose the arithmetic average of return on the market observed over the last 90 years is an unbiased estimator for the expected return for the market. The average rate of return of the market was 9.65 percent. Calculate the equity risk premium.

Solution:

$$\text{ERP} = \overline{R}_M - \overline{R}_F = 9.65 \text{ percent} - 4.88 \text{ percent} = 4.77 \text{ percent}$$

A second approach for estimating the equity risk premium is the **dividend discount model based approach** or implied risk premium approach, which is implemented using the Gordon growth model (also known as the constant-growth dividend discount model). For developed markets, corporate earnings often meet, at least approximately, the model's assumption of a long-run trend growth rate. We extract the premium by analyzing how the market prices an index. That is, we use the relationship between the value of an index and expected dividends, assuming a constant growth in dividends:

$$P_0 = \frac{D_1}{r_e - g}$$

where P_0 is the current market value of the equity market index, D_1 are the dividends expected next period on the index, r_e is the required rate of return on the market, and g is the expected growth rate of dividends. We solve for the required rate of return on the market as

$$r_e = \frac{D_1}{P_0} + g \qquad (6)$$

Therefore, the expected return on the market is the sum of the dividend yield and the growth rate in dividends. The equity risk premium thus is the difference between the expected return on the equity market and the risk-free rate.

Suppose the expected dividend yield on an equity index is 5 percent and the expected growth rate of dividends on the index is 2 percent. The expected return on the market according to the Gordon growth model is

$$E(R_m) = 5 \text{ percent} + 2 \text{ percent} = 7 \text{ percent}$$

A risk-free rate of interest of 3.8 percent implies an equity risk premium of 7 percent − 3.8 percent = 3.2 percent.

Another approach to estimate the equity risk premium is quite direct: Ask a panel of finance experts for their estimates and take the mean response. This is the **survey approach**. For example, survey of US CFOs in December 2017 found that the average expected US equity risk premium over the next 10 years was 4.42 percent and the median was 3.63 percent.[15]

Once we have an estimate of the equity risk premium, we fine-tune this estimate for the particular company or project by adjusting it for the specific systematic risk of the project. We adjust for the specific systematic risk by multiplying the market risk premium by beta to arrive at the company's or project's risk premium, which we then add to the risk-free rate to determine the cost of equity within the framework of the CAPM.[16]

3.3.2 *Dividend Discount Model Approach*

Earlier we used the Gordon growth model to develop an estimate of the equity risk premium for use in the CAPM. We can also use the Gordon growth model directly to obtain an estimate of the cost of equity. To review, the dividend discount model in general states that the intrinsic value of a share of stock is the present value of the share's expected future dividends:

$$V_0 = \sum_{t=1}^{\infty}\left(\frac{D_t}{(1+r_e)^t}\right) = \frac{D_1}{(1+r_e)} + \frac{D_2}{(1+r_e)^2} + \ldots$$

where

V_0 = the intrinsic value of a share

D_t = the share's dividend at the end of period t

r_e = the cost of equity

Based on Gordon's constant growth formulation, we assume dividends are expected to grow at a constant rate, g.[17] Therefore, if we assume that price reflects intrinsic value ($V_0 = P_0$), we can rewrite the valuation of the stock as

$$P_0 = \frac{D_1}{r_e - g}$$

We can then rewrite the above equation and estimate the cost of equity as we did for Equation 6 in Section 3.3.1:

$$r_e = \frac{D_1}{P_0} + g$$

Therefore, to estimate r_e, we need to estimate the dividend in the next period and the assumed constant dividend growth rate. The current stock price, P_0, is known, and the dividend of the next period, D_1, can be predicted if the company has a stable dividend policy. (The ratio D_1/P_0 may be called the forward annual dividend yield.) The challenge is estimating the growth rate.

There are at least two ways to estimate the growth rate. The first is to use a forecasted growth rate from a published source or vendor. A second is to use a relationship between the growth rate, the retention rate, and the return on equity. In this context,

---

15 John R. Graham and Campbell R. Harvey, "The Equity Risk Premium in 2018", working paper(March 27, 2018). Available at SSRN: https://ssrn.com/abstract=3151162 or http://dx.doi.org/10.2139/ssrn.3151162.

16 Some researchers argue that the equity risk premium should reflect a country risk premium. For example, a multinational company or project may have a higher cost of capital than a comparable domestic company because of political risk, foreign exchange risk, or higher agency costs. In most cases, this risk is unsystematic and hence does not affect the cost of capital estimate.

17 Myron J. Gordon, *The Investment, Financing, and Valuation of the Corporation*, Homewood, IL: Irwin, 1962.

this is often referred to as the **sustainable growth rate** and is interpretable as the rate of dividend (and earnings) growth that can be sustained over time for a given level of return on equity, keeping the capital structure constant and without issuing additional common stock. The relationship is given in Equation 7:

$$g = (1 - D/\text{EPS})\text{ROE} \tag{7}$$

where D/EPS represents the assumed stable dividend payout ratio and ROE is the historical return on equity. The term (1 – D/EPS) is the company's earnings retention rate.

Consider Apple Computer in early August 2018. Apple had an earnings retention rate of 76.31 percent, a forward annual dividend yield of 1.4 percent, and a trailing return on equity of approximately 12.22 percent. Suppose Apple's estimated average return on equity going forward is the same as the trailing return of 12.22. According to Equation 7, Apple's sustainable growth rate is 0.7631(12.22 percent) = 9.325 percent. The dividend discount model estimate of the cost of equity is, therefore, 9.325 percent + 1.4 percent = 10.725 percent.

3.3.3 *Bond Yield plus Risk Premium Approach*

The **bond yield plus risk premium approach** is based on the fundamental tenet in financial theory that the cost of capital of riskier cash flows is higher than that of less risky cash flows. In this approach, we sum the before-tax cost of debt, r_d, and a risk premium that captures the additional yield on a company's stock relative to its bonds. The estimate is, therefore,

$$r_e = r_d + \text{Risk premium} \tag{8}$$

The risk premium compensates for the additional risk of equity compared with debt.[18] Ideally, this risk premium is forward looking, representing the additional risk associated with the stock of the company as compared with the bonds of the same company. However, we often estimate this premium using historical spreads between bond yields and stock yields. In developed country markets, a typical risk premium added is in the range of 3 to 5 percent.

Looking again at Apple Computer, as of early August 2018, the yield to maturity of the Apple's 3.35s bonds maturing in 2027 was approximately 3.56 percent. Adding an arbitrary risk premium of 4.0 percent produces an estimate of the cost of equity of 3.56 + 4.0 = 7.56 percent. This estimate contrasts with the higher estimates of 9.042 percent under the CAPM approach, and 10.725 percent under the dividend discount model approach. Such disparities are not uncommon and reflect the difficulty of cost of equity estimation.

TOPICS IN COST OF CAPITAL ESTIMATION

4

When calculating a company's weighted average cost of capital (WACC), it is essential to understand the risk factors that have been considered in determining the risk-free rate, the equity risk premium, and beta to ensure a consistent calculation of WACC and avoid the double counting or omission of pertinent risk factors.

---

18 This risk premium is not to be confused with the equity risk premium. The equity risk premium is the difference between the cost of equity and the *risk-free rate of interest.* The risk premium in the bond yield plus risk premium approach is the difference between the cost of equity and the *company's cost of debt.*

4.1 Estimating Beta and Determining a Project Beta

When the analyst uses the CAPM to estimate the cost of equity, he or she must estimate beta. The estimation of beta presents many choices as well as challenges.

One common method of estimating the company's stock beta is to use a market model regression of the company's stock returns (R_i) against market returns (R_m) over T periods:[19]

$$R_{it} = \hat{a} + \hat{b}R_{mt} \qquad t = 1,2,\ldots T$$

where $\hat{a}$ is the estimated intercept and $\hat{b}$ is the estimated slope of the regression that is used as an estimate of beta. However, beta estimates are sensitive to the method of estimation and data used. Consider some of the issues:

- *Estimation period.* The estimated beta is sensitive to the length of the estimation period, with beta commonly estimated using data over two to nine years. Selection of the estimation period is a trade-off between data richness captured by longer estimation periods and company-specific changes that are better reflected with shorter estimation periods. In general, longer estimation periods are applied to companies with a long and stable operating history, and shorter estimation periods are used for companies that have undergone significant structural changes in the recent past (such as restructuring, recent acquisition, or divestiture) or changes in financial and operating leverage.
- *Periodicity of the return interval* (e.g., daily, weekly, or monthly). Researchers have observed smaller standard error in beta estimated using smaller return intervals, such as daily returns.[20]
- *Selection of an appropriate market index.* The choice of market index affects the estimate of beta.
- *Use of a smoothing technique.* Some analysts adjust historical betas to reflect the tendency of betas to revert to 1.[21] As an example, the expression $\beta_{i,\text{adj}} = 0.333 + 0.667\beta_i$ adjusts betas above and below 1.0 toward 1.0.
- *Adjustments for small-capitalization stocks.* Small-capitalization stocks have generally exhibited greater risks and greater returns than large-capitalization stocks over the long run. Roger Ibbotson, Paul Kaplan, and James Peterson argue that betas for small-capitalization companies be adjusted upward.[22]

Arriving at an estimated beta for publicly traded companies is generally not a problem because of the accessibility of stock return data, the ease of use of estimating beta using simple regression, and the availability of estimated betas on publicly traded companies from financial analysis vendors, such as Barra, Bloomberg, Thompson Financial's Datastream, Reuters, and Value Line. The challenge is to estimate a beta for a company that is not publicly traded or to estimate a beta for a project that is not the average or typical project of a publicly traded company. Estimating a beta in these cases requires proxying for the beta by using the information on the project or company combined with a beta of a publicly traded company.

---

19 This equation is commonly referred to as the *market model* and was first introduced by Michael C. Jensen in "The Performance of Mutual Funds in the Period 1945–1964," *Journal of Finance*, Vol. 23, No. 2 (1969), pp. 389–416.

20 Phillip R. Daves, Michael C. Ehrhardt, and Robert A. Kunkel, "Estimating Systematic Risk: The Choice of Return Interval and Estimation Period," *Journal of Financial and Strategic Decisions*, Vol. 13, No. 1 (Spring 2000), pp. 7–13.

21 Marshall Blume, "On the Assessment of Risk," *Journal of Finance*, Vol. 26, No. 1 (March 1971), pp. 1–10.

22 Roger G. Ibbotson, Paul D. Kaplan, and James D. Peterson, "Estimates of Small Stock Betas Are Much Too Low," *Journal of Portfolio Management* (Summer 1997), pp. 104–110.

The beta of a company or project is affected by the systematic components of business risk and by financial risk. Both of these factors affect the uncertainty of the cash flows of the company or project. The **business risk** of a company or project is the risk related to the uncertainty of revenues, referred to as **sales risk**, and to **operating risk**, which is the risk attributed to the company's operating cost structure. Sales risk is affected by the elasticity of the demand of the product, the cyclicality of the revenues, and the structure of competition in the industry. Operating risk is affected by the relative mix of fixed and variable operating costs: the greater the fixed operating costs, relative to variable operating costs, the greater the uncertainty of income and cash flows from operations.

Financial risk is the uncertainty of net income and net cash flows attributed to the use of financing that has a fixed cost, such as debt and leases. The greater the use of fixed-financing sources of capital, relative to variable sources, the greater the financial risk. In other words, a company that relies heavily on debt financing instead of equity financing is assuming a great deal of financial risk.

How does a financial analyst estimate a beta for a company or project that is not publicly traded? One common method is the **pure-play method**, which requires using a comparable publicly traded company's beta and adjusting it for financial leverage differences.

A **comparable company** is a company that has similar business risk. The reason it is referred to as the *pure-play* method is that one of the easiest ways of identifying a comparable for a project is to find a company in the same industry that is in that *single* line of business. For example, if the analyst is examining a project that involves drug stores, appropriate comparables in the United States may be Walgreens, CVS Corporation, and Rite Aid Corporation.

In estimating a beta in this way, the analyst must make adjustments to account for differing degrees of financial leverage. This requires a process of "unlevering" and "levering" the beta. The beta of the comparable is first "unlevered" by removing the effects of its financial leverage.[23] The unlevered beta is often referred to as the **asset beta** because it reflects the business risk of the assets. Once we determine the unlevered beta, we adjust it for the capital structure of the company or project that is the focus of our analysis. In other words, we "lever" the asset beta to arrive at an estimate of the equity beta for the project or company of interest.

For a given company, we can unlever its equity beta to estimate its asset beta. To do this, we must determine the relationship between a company's asset beta and its equity beta. Because the company's risk is shared between creditors and owners, we can represent the company's risk, β_{asset}, as the weighted average of the company's creditors' market risk, β_{debt}, and the market risk of the owners, β_{equity}:

$$\beta_{asset} = \beta_{debt} w_d + \beta_{equity} w_e$$

or

$$\beta_{asset} = \beta_{debt}\left(\frac{D}{D+E}\right) + \beta_{equity}\left(\frac{E}{D+E}\right)$$

where

E = market value of equity

D = market value of debt

w_d = proportion of debt = $D/(D + E)$

w_e = proportion of equity = $E/(D + E)$

23 The process of unlevering and levering a beta was developed by Robert S. Hamada ["The Effect of the Firm's Capital Structure on the Systematic Risk of Common Stocks," *Journal of Finance* (May 1972), pp. 435–452] and is based on the capital structure theories of Franco Modigliani and Merton Miller.

But interest on debt is deducted by the company to arrive at taxable income, so the claim that creditors have on the company's assets does not cost the company the full amount but, rather, the after-tax claim; the burden of debt financing is actually less due to interest deductibility. We can represent the asset beta of a company as the weighted average of the betas of debt and equity after considering the effects of the tax-deductibility of interest:

$$\beta_{asset} = \beta_{debt}\frac{(1-t)D}{(1-t)D+E} + \beta_{equity}\frac{E}{(1-t)D+E}$$

where t is the marginal tax rate.

We generally assume that a company's debt does not have market risk, so β_{debt} = 0. This means that the returns on debt do not vary with the returns on the market, which we generally assume to be true for most large companies. If $\beta_{debt} = 0$, then[24]

$$\beta_{asset} = \beta_{equity}\left[\frac{1}{1+\left((1-t)\frac{D}{E}\right)}\right] \tag{9}$$

Therefore, the market risk of a company's equity is affected by both the asset's market risk, β_{asset}, and a factor representing the nondiversifiable portion of the company's financial risk, $\left[1+\left((1-t)\frac{D}{E}\right)\right]$:

$$\beta_{equity} = \beta_{asset}\left[1+\left((1-t)\frac{D}{E}\right)\right] \tag{10}$$

Suppose a company has an equity beta of 1.5, a debt-to-equity ratio of 0.4, and a marginal tax rate of 30 percent. Using Equation 9, the company's asset beta is 1.1719:

$$\beta_{asset} = 1.5\left[\frac{1}{1+\left((1-0.3)(0.4)\right)}\right] = 1.5[0.7813] = 1.1719$$

In other words, if the company did not have any debt financing, its $\beta_{asset} = \beta_{equity}$ = 1.1719; however, the use of debt financing increases its β_{equity} from 1.1719 to 1.5. What would the company's equity beta be if the company's debt-to-equity ratio were 0.5 instead of 0.4? In this case, we apply Equation 10, using the debt-to-equity ratio of 0.5:

$$\beta_{equity} = 1.1719\left[1+\left((1-0.3)(0.5)\right)\right] = 1.5821$$

Therefore, the unlevering calculation produces a measure of market risk for the assets of the company—ignoring the company's capital structure. We use the levering calculation in Equation 10 to estimate the market risk of a company given a specific asset risk, marginal tax rate, and capital structure.

We can use the same unlevering and levering calculations to estimate the asset risk and equity risk for a project. We start with the equity beta of the comparable company, which is the levered beta, $\beta_{L,comparable}$, and then convert it into the equivalent asset beta for the unlevered company, $\beta_{U,comparable}$. Once we have the estimate of the unlevered beta, which is the company's asset risk, we then can use the project's capital structure and marginal tax rate to convert this asset beta into an equity beta for the project, $\beta_{L,project}$.

24 The first step is $\beta_{asset} = \beta_{equity}\left[\frac{E}{(1-t)D+E}\right]$, which we simplify to arrive at Equation 9.

Estimating a Beta Using the Pure-Play Method

Step 1: Select the comparable Determine comparable company or companies. These are companies with similar business risk.

↓

Step 2: Estimate comparable's beta Estimate the equity beta of the comparable company or companies.

↓

Step 3: Unlever the comparable's beta Unlever the beta of the comparable company or companies, removing the financial risk component of the equity beta, leaving the business risk component of the beta.

↓

Step 4: Lever the beta for the project's financial risk Lever the beta of the project by adjusting the asset beta for the financial risk of the project.

We begin by estimating the levered beta of the comparable company, $\beta_{L,comparable}$. Using the capital structure and tax rate of the levered company, we estimate the asset beta for the comparable company, $\beta_{U,comparable}$:

$$\beta_{U,comparable} = \frac{\beta_{L,comparable}}{\left[1 + \left(\left(1 - t_{comparable}\right)\frac{D_{comparable}}{E_{comparable}}\right)\right]} \tag{11}$$

We then consider the financial leverage of the project or company and calculate its equity risk, $\beta_{L,project}$:

$$\beta_{L,project} = \beta_{U,comparable}\left[1 + \left(\left(1 - t_{project}\right)\frac{D_{project}}{E_{project}}\right)\right] \tag{12}$$

To illustrate the use of these equations, suppose we want to evaluate a project that will be financed with debt and equity in a ratio of 0.4:1 [a debt-to-equity ratio of 0.4, corresponding to approximately 0.4/(0.4 + 1.0) = €0.286 for each euro of capital needed]. We find a comparable company operating in the same line of business as the project. The marginal tax rate for the company sponsoring the project and the comparable company is 35 percent. The comparable company has a beta of 1.2 and a debt-to-equity ratio of 0.125. The unlevered beta of the comparable is 1.1098:

$$\beta_{U,comparable} = \frac{1.2}{\left[1 + \left(\left(1 - 0.35\right)0.125\right)\right]} = 1.1098$$

The levered beta for the project is 1.3983:

$$\beta_{L,project} = 1.1098\left[1 + \left(\left(1 - 0.35\right)0.4\right)\right] = 1.3983$$

We then use the 1.3983 as the beta in our CAPM estimate of the component cost of equity for the project and, combined with the cost of debt in a weighted average, provide an estimate of the cost of capital for the project.[25]

---

25 In this example, the weights are $w_d = 0.4/1.4 = 0.2857$ and $w_e = 1/1.4 = 0.7143$.

EXAMPLE 9

Inferring an Asset Beta

Suppose that the beta of a publicly traded company's stock is 1.3 and that the market value of equity and debt are, respectively, C$540 million and C$720 million. If the marginal tax rate of this company is 40 percent, what is the asset beta of this company?

Solution:

$$\beta_U = \frac{1.3}{\left[1 + \left((1 - 0.4)\frac{720}{540}\right)\right]} = 0.72$$

EXAMPLE 10

Calculating a Beta Using the Pure-Play Method

Raymond Cordier is the business development manager of Aerotechnique S.A., a private Belgian subcontractor of aerospace parts. Although Aerotechnique is not listed on the Belgian stock exchange, Cordier needs to evaluate the levered beta for the company. He has access to the following information:

- The average levered and average unlevered betas for the group of comparable companies operating in different European countries are 1.6 and 1.0, respectively.
- Aerotechnique's debt-to-equity ratio, based on market values, is 1.4.
- Aerotechnique's corporate tax rate is 34 percent.

Solution:

The beta for Aerotechnique is estimated on the basis of the average unlevered beta extracted from the group of comparable companies. On that basis, and applying the financing structure of Aerotechnique, the estimated beta for Aerotechnique is

$$\beta_{\text{Aerotechnique}} = 1.0\left[1 + \left((1 - 0.34)(1.4)\right)\right] = 1.924$$

EXAMPLE 11

Estimating the Weighted Average Cost of Capital

Georg Schrempp is the CFO of Bayern Chemicals KgaA, a large German manufacturer of industrial, commercial, and consumer chemical products. Bayern Chemicals is privately owned, and its shares are not listed on an exchange. The CFO has appointed Markus Meier, CFA, of Crystal Clear Valuation Advisors, a third-party valuator, to perform a stand-alone valuation of Bayern Chemicals. Meier had access to the following information to calculate Bayern Chemicals' weighted average cost of capital:

- The nominal risk-free rate is represented by the yield on the long-term 10-year German bund, which at the valuation date was 4.5 percent.

- The average long-term historical equity risk premium in Germany is assumed at 5.7 percent.[26]
- Bayern Chemicals' corporate tax rate is 38 percent.
- Bayern Chemicals' target debt-to-equity ratio is 0.7. Bayern is operating at its target debt-to-equity ratio.
- Bayern Chemicals' cost of debt has an estimated spread of 225 basis points over the 10-year bund.
- Exhibit 3 supplies additional information on comparables for Bayern Chemicals.

Exhibit 3 Information on Comparables

Comparable Companies	Country	Tax Rate (%)	Market Capitalization in Millions	Net Debt in Millions	D/E	Beta
British Chemicals Ltd.	United Kingdom	30.0	4,500	6,000	1.33	1.45
Compagnie Petrochimique S.A.	France	30.3	9,300	8,700	0.94	0.75
Rotterdam Chemie N.V.	Netherlands	30.5	7,000	7,900	1.13	1.05
Average					1.13	1.08

Based only on the information given, calculate Bayern Chemicals' WACC.

Solution:

To calculate the cost of equity, the first step is to "unlever" the betas of the comparable companies and calculate an average for a company with business risk similar to the average of these companies:

Comparable Companies	Unlevered Beta
British Chemicals Ltd.	0.75
Compagnie Petrochimique S.A.	0.45
Rotterdam Chemie N.V.	0.59
Average*	0.60

* An analyst must apply judgment and experience to determine a representative average for the comparable companies. This example uses a simple average, but in some situations a weighted average based on some factor such as market capitalization may be more appropriate.

Levering the average unlevered beta for the peer group average, applying Bayern Chemicals' target debt-to-equity ratio and marginal tax rate, results in a beta of 0.86:

$$\beta_{\text{Bayern Chemical}} = 0.60\{1 + [(1 - 0.38)0.7]\} = 0.86$$

26 Dimson, Marsh, and Staunton, *op. cit.*

The cost of equity of Bayern Chemicals (r_e) can be calculated as follows:

$$r_e = 4.5 \text{ percent} + (0.86)(5.7 \text{ percent}) = 9.4 \text{ percent}$$

The weights for the cost of equity and cost of debt may be calculated as follows:

$$w_d = \frac{D/E}{\left(\frac{D}{E} + 1\right)} = \frac{0.7}{1.7} = 0.41$$

$$w_e = 1 - w_d = 1 - 0.41 = 0.59$$

The before-tax cost of debt of Bayern Chemicals (r_d) is 6.75 percent:

$$r_d = 4.5 \text{ percent} + 2.25 \text{ percent} = 6.75 \text{ percent}$$

As a result, Bayern Chemicals' WACC is 7.27 percent:

$$\begin{aligned} \text{WACC} &= [(0.41)(0.0675)(1 - 0.38)] + [(0.59)(0.094)] \\ &= 0.0726 \text{ or } 7.26 \text{ percent} \end{aligned}$$

4.2 Country Risk

The use of a stock's beta to capture the country risks of a project is well supported in empirical studies that examine developed nations. However, beta does not appear to adequately capture country risk for companies in developing nations.[27] A common approach for dealing with this problem is to adjust the cost of equity estimated using the CAPM by adding a country spread to the market risk premium.[28] The country spread is also referred to as a country risk premium.

Perhaps the simplest estimate of the country spread is the **sovereign yield spread**, which is the difference between the government bond yield in that country, denominated in the currency of a developed country, and the Treasury bond yield on a similar maturity bond in the developed country.[29] However, this approach may be too coarse for the purposes of risk premium estimation.

27 Campbell R. Harvey, "The International Cost of Capital and Risk Calculator," Duke University working paper (July 2001).

28 Adding the country spread to the market risk premium for a developing country and then multiplying this sum by the market risk of the project is making the assumption that the country risk premium varies according to market risk. An alternative method calculates the cost of equity as the sum of three terms: 1) the risk-free rate of interest, 2) the product of the beta and the developed market risk premium, and 3) the country risk premium. This latter method assumes that the country risk premium is the same, regardless of the project's market risk.

29 Jorge O. Mariscal and Rafaelina M. Lee, "The Valuation of Mexican Stocks: An Extension of the Capital Asset Pricing Model," New York: Goldman Sachs (1993).

Another approach is to calculate the country risk premium as the product of the sovereign yield spread and the ratio of the volatility of the developing country equity market to that of the sovereign bond market denominated in terms of the currency of a developed country:[30]

$$\begin{array}{l}\text{Country equity premium}\\ = \text{Sovereign yield spread}\end{array}\left[\frac{\begin{array}{c}\text{Annualized standard deviation}\\ \text{of equity index}\end{array}}{\begin{array}{c}\text{Annualized standard deviation of the}\\ \text{sovereign bond market in terms}\\ \text{of the developed market currency}\end{array}}\right] \quad (13)$$

The logic of this calculation is that the sovereign yield spread captures the general risk of the country, which is then adjusted for the volatility of the stock market relative to the bond market. This country risk premium is then used in addition to the equity premium estimated for a project in a developed country. Therefore, if the equity risk premium for a project in a developed country is 4.5 percent and the country risk premium is 3 percent, the total equity risk premium used in the CAPM estimation is 7.5 percent. If the appropriate beta is 1.2 and the risk-free rate of interest is 4 percent, the cost of equity is

Cost of equity = 0.04 + 1.2(0.045 + 0.03) = 0.13 or 13 percent

EXAMPLE 12

Estimating the Country Risk Premium

Miles Smyth, an analyst with the Global Company, is estimating a country risk premium to include in his estimate of the cost of equity capital for Global's investment in Aksarben, an emerging market country. Smyth has researched yields in Aksarben and observed that the Akserbenian government's 10-year bond is 6.2 percent. A similar maturity US Treasury bond has a yield of 3.0 percent. The annualized standard deviation of the Aksarben stock index during the most recent period was 40 percent. The annualized standard deviation of the Aksarben dollar-denominated 10-year government bond over the recent period was 28 percent.

What is the estimated country risk premium for Aksarben based on Smyth's research?

Solution:

$$\text{Country risk premium} = 0.032\left(\frac{0.40}{0.28}\right) = 0.32(1.4286) = 0.0457 \text{ or } 4.57 \text{ percent}$$

Still another approach is to use country credit ratings to estimate the expected rates of returns for countries that have credit ratings but no equity markets.[31] This method requires estimating reward to credit risk measures for a large sample of countries for which there are both credit ratings and equity markets and then applying this ratio to those countries without equity markets based on the country's credit rating.

30 Aswath Damodaran, "Estimating Equity Risk Premiums," New York University working paper (1999) and Aswath Damodaran, "Measuring Company Exposure to Country Risk: Theory and Practice," New York University working paper (September 2003).

31 Claude Erb, Campbell R. Harvey, and Tadas Viskanta, "Expected Returns and Volatility in 135 Countries," *Journal of Portfolio Management* (Spring 1996), pp. 46–58.

4.3 Marginal Cost of Capital Schedule

As we noted in Section 2.3, as a company raises more funds, the costs of the different sources of capital may change, resulting in a change in the weighted average cost of capital for different levels of financing. The result is the marginal cost of capital (MCC) schedule, which we often depict in graphical form as the weighted average cost of capital for different amounts of capital raised, as we showed earlier in Exhibit 1.[32]

Why would the cost of capital change as more capital is raised? One source of a difference in cost depending on the amount of capital raised is that a company may have existing debt with a bond covenant that restricts the company from issuing debt with similar seniority as existing debt. Or, a **debt incurrence test** may restrict a company's ability to incur additional debt at the same seniority based on one or more financial tests or conditions. For example, if a company issues senior debt such that any additional debt at that seniority violates the debt incurrence test of an existing bond covenant, the company may have to issue less senior debt or even equity, which would have a higher cost.

Another source of increasing marginal costs of capital is a deviation from the target capital structure. In the ideal, theoretical world, a company has a target capital structure and goes to the market each period and raises capital in these proportions. However, as a practical matter, companies do not necessarily tap the market in these ideal proportions because of considerations for economies of scale in raising new capital and market conditions. Because of such perceived economies of scale, companies tend to issue new securities such that in any given period, it may deviate from the proportions dictated by any target or optimal capital structure. In other words, these short-run deviations are due to the "lumpiness" of security issuance. As the company experiences deviations from the target capital structure, the marginal cost of capital may increase, reflecting these deviations.

The amount of capital at which the weighted average cost of capital changes—which means that the cost of one of the sources of capital changes—is referred to as a **break point**. The reality of raising capital is that the marginal cost of capital schedule is not as smooth as we depicted in Exhibit 1 but, rather, is a step-up cost schedule as shown in Exhibit 4.

32 Later in this section, we will discuss cases where a company's WACC may actually decrease as additional capital is raised. For example, if a company financed solely with common equity raises additional capital via debt, then the tax advantages provided by debt will result in a lower WACC under the new capital structure. For this discussion, we are assuming that the company is already operating at or near its optimum balance of debt versus equity.

Exhibit 4 Marginal Cost of Capital Schedule

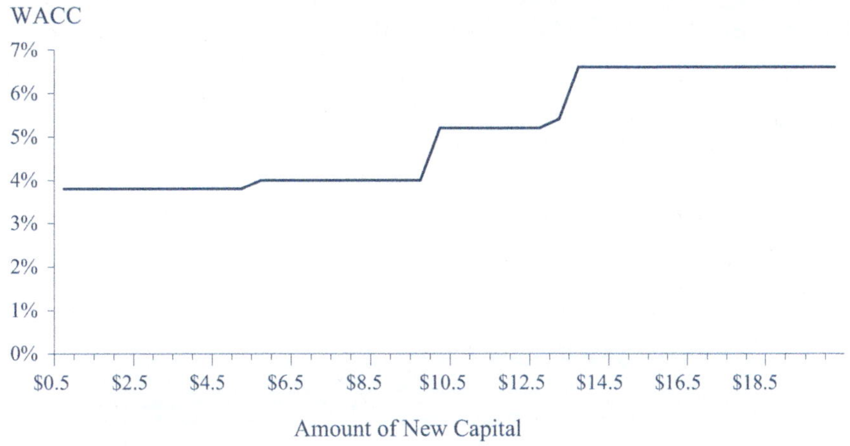

Consider the case of a company facing the costs of capital given in Exhibit 5.

Exhibit 5 Schedule of the Costs of Debt and Equity

Amount of New Debt (in Millions)	After-Tax Cost of Debt	Amount of New Equity (in Millions)	Cost of Equity
new debt ≤ €2	2.0 percent	new equity ≤ €6	5.0 percent
€2 < new debt ≤ €5	2.5 percent	€6 < new equity ≤ €8	7.0 percent
€5 < new debt	3.0 percent	€8 < new equity	9.0 percent

If the company raises capital according to its target capital structure proportions of 40 percent debt and 60 percent equity, this company faces a marginal cost of capital schedule that is upward sloping, with break points at €5 million, €10 million, €12.5 million, and €13.3 million, as depicted in Exhibit 4. These break points are determined from the amounts of capital at which the cost changes, calculated as

$$\text{Break point} = \frac{\text{Amount of capital at which the source's cost of capital changes}}{\text{Proportion of new capital raised from the source}} \quad (14)$$

For example, the first break point for debt financing is reached with €2 million/0.4 = €5 million of new capital raised. The first break point attributed to a change in equity cost occurs at €6 million/0.6 = €10 million. Example 13 illustrates a marginal cost of capital schedule with break points and also how the WACC figures in the choice of an optimal capital structure.

EXAMPLE 13

Marginal Cost of Capital Schedule

Alan Conlon is the CFO of Allied Canadian Breweries Ltd. He wants to determine the capital structure that will result in the lowest cost of capital for Allied. He has access to the following information:

- The minimum rate at which the company can borrow is the 12-month Libor rate plus a premium that varies with the debt-to-capital ratio [$D/(D + E)$] as given in Exhibit 6.

Exhibit 6 Spreads over Libor for Alternative Debt-to-Capital Ratios

$\frac{D}{D+E}$	Spread (bps)
Less than 0.40	200
0.40 to 0.49	300
0.50 to 0.59	400
0.60 to 0.69	600
0.70 to 0.79	800
0.80 to 0.89	1,000
0.90 or higher	1,200

- The current 12-month Libor is 2.8 percent.
- The market risk premium is 5 percent, and unleveraged beta is 0.9.
- The risk-free rate is 3 percent.
- The company's tax rate is 36 percent.

1 Determine the WACC for 10 percent intervals of the debt-to-capital ratio (i.e., 0.1, 0.2, etc.) based on the information given in Exhibit 6.

2 Recommend a target capital structure based on 10 percent intervals of the debt-to-capital ratio, recommend a target capital structure.

Solution to 1:

The WACC expressed as a function of the capital structure is shown in Exhibit 7.

Exhibit 7 WACC for Alternative Capital Structures

$\frac{D}{D+E}$	β	r_d (Percent)	r_e (Percent)	WACC (Percent)
0.1	0.96	4.8	7.82	7.35
0.2	1.04	4.8	8.22	7.19
0.3	1.15	4.8	8.73	7.04
0.4	1.28	5.8	9.42	7.14

Exhibit 7 (Continued)

$\frac{D}{D+E}$	β	r_d (Percent)	r_e (Percent)	WACC (Percent)
0.5	1.48	6.8	10.38	7.37
0.6	1.76	8.8	11.82	8.11
0.7	2.24	10.8	14.22	9.10
0.8	3.20	12.8	19.02	10.36
0.9	6.08	14.8	33.42	11.87

Solution to 2:

The optimal capital structure is 30 percent debt; based on 10 percent intervals of the debt-to-capital ratio, this will achieve the lowest possible cost of capital.

4.4 Flotation Costs

When a company raises new capital, it generally seeks the assistance of investment bankers. Investment bankers charge the company a fee based on the size and type of offering. This fee is referred to as the **flotation cost**. In the case of debt and preferred stock, we do not usually incorporate flotation costs in the estimated cost of capital because the amount of these costs is quite small, often less than 1 percent.[33]

However, with equity issuance, the flotation costs may be substantial, so we should consider these when estimating the cost of external equity capital. Average flotation costs for new equity have been estimated at 7.11% in the United States,[34] 1.65% in Germany,[35] 5.78% in the United Kingdom,[36] and 4.53% in Switzerland.[37] A large part of the differences in costs among these studies is likely attributed to the type of offering; cash underwritten offers, typical in the United States, are generally more expensive than rights offerings, which are common in Europe.

Should we incorporate flotation costs into the cost of capital? There are two views on this topic. One view, which you can find often in textbooks, is to incorporate the flotation costs into the cost of capital. The other view is that flotation costs should not be included in the cost of capital but, rather, incorporated into any valuation analysis as an additional cost of the project.

33 We can incorporate them for these sources by simply treating the flotation costs as an outlay, hence reducing proceeds from the source.

34 Inmoo Lee, Scott Lochhead, Jay R. Ritter, and Quanshui Zhao, "The Costs of Raising Capital," *Journal of Financial Research*, Vol. 19 (Spring, 1996), pp. 59–71.

35 Thomas Bühner and Christoph Kaserer, "External Financing Costs and Economies of Scale in Investment Banking: The Case of Seasoned Equity Offerings in Germany," *European Financial Management*, Vol. 9 (June 2002), pp. 249.

36 Seth Armitage, "The Direct Costs of UK Rights Issues and Open Offers, "*European Financial Management*, Vol. 6 (2000), pp. 57–68.

37 Christoph Kaserer and Fabian Steiner, "The Cost of Raising Capital—New Evidence from Seasoned Equity Offerings in Switzerland," Technische Universität München working paper (February 2004).

Consistent with the first view, we can specify flotation costs in monetary terms, as an amount per share or as a percentage of the share price. With flotation costs in monetary terms on a per share basis, F, the cost of external equity is

$$r_e = \left(\frac{D_1}{P_0 - F}\right) + g \tag{15}$$

As a percentage applied against the price per share, the cost of external equity is

$$r_e = \left(\frac{D_1}{P_0(1 - f)}\right) + g \tag{16}$$

where f is the flotation cost as a percentage of the issue price.

Suppose a company has a current dividend of \$2 per share, a current price of \$40 per share, and an expected growth rate of 5 percent. The cost of internally generated equity would be 10.25 percent:

$$r_e = \left(\frac{\$2(1 + 0.05)}{\$40}\right) + 0.05 = 0.0525 + 0.05 = 0.1025, \text{ or } 10.25 \text{ percent}$$

If the flotation costs are 4 percent of the issuance, the cost of externally generated equity would be slightly higher at 10.469 percent:

$$r_e = \left(\frac{\$2(1 + 0.05)}{\$40(1 - 0.04)}\right) + 0.05 = 0.05469 + 0.05 = 0.1047, \text{ or } 10.47 \text{ percent}$$

The problem with this approach is that the flotation costs are a cash flow at the initiation of the project and affect the value of any project by reducing the initial cash flow. Adjusting the cost of capital for flotation costs is incorrect because by doing so, we are adjusting the present value of the future cash flows by a fixed percentage—in the above example, a difference of 22 basis points, which does not necessarily equate to the present value of the flotation costs.[38]

The alternative and recommended approach is to make the adjustment to the cash flows in the valuation computation. For example, consider a project that requires a €60,000 initial cash outlay and is expected to produce cash flows of €10,000 each year for 10 years. Suppose the company's marginal tax rate is 40 percent and that the before-tax cost of debt is 5 percent. Furthermore, suppose that the company's dividend next period is €1, the current price of the stock is €20, and the expected growth rate is 5 percent so that the cost of equity using the dividend discount model is (€1/€20) + 0.05 = 0.10 or 10 percent. Assume the company will finance the project with 40 percent debt and 60 percent equity. Exhibit 8 summarizes the information on the component costs of capital.

Exhibit 8 After-Tax Costs of Debt and Equity

Source of Capital	Amount Raised (€)	Proportion	Marginal After-Tax Cost
Debt	24,000	0.40	0.05(1 − 0.4) = 0.03
Equity	36,000	0.60	0.10

38 This argument is made by John R. Ezzell and R. Burr Porter ["Flotation Costs and the Weighted Average Cost of Capital," *Journal of Financial and Quantitative Analysis*, Vol. 11, No. 3 (September 1976), pp. 403–413]. They argue that the correct treatment is to deduct flotation costs as part of the valuation as one of the initial-period cash flows.

The weighted average cost of capital is 7.2 percent calculated as 0.40(3 percent) + 0.60(10 percent). Ignoring flotation costs for the moment, the net present value (NPV) of this project is

NPV = €69,591 − €60,000 = €9,591

If the flotation costs are, say, 5 percent of the new equity capital, the flotation costs are €1,800. The net present value considering flotation costs is

NPV = €69,591 − €60,000 − €1,800 = €7,791

If flotation costs are not tax deductible, or €69,591 − €60,000 − €1,800(0.6) = €8,511, if flotation costs are tax deductible.

If, instead of considering the flotation costs as part of the cash flows, we adjust the cost of equity, the cost of capital is 7.3578 percent and the NPV is

NPV = €69,089 − €60,000 = €9,089

As you can see, we arrive at different assessments of value using these two methods.

So, if it is preferred to deduct the flotation costs as part of the net present value calculation, why do we see the adjustment in the cost of capital so often in textbooks? The first reason is that it is often difficult to identify particular financing associated with a project. Using the adjustment for the flotation costs in the cost of capital may be useful if specific project financing cannot be identified. Second, by adjusting the cost of capital for the flotation costs, it is easier to demonstrate how costs of financing a company change as a company exhausts internally generated equity (i.e., retained earnings) and switches to externally generated equity (i.e., a new stock issue).

4.5 What Do CFOs Do?

In this reading, we have introduced you to methods that may be used to estimate the cost of capital for a company or a project. What do companies actually use when making investment decisions? In a survey of a large number of US company CFOs, John Graham and Campbell Harvey asked about the methods that companies actually use.[39] Their survey revealed the following:

- The most popular method for estimating the cost of equity is the capital asset pricing model.
- Few companies use the dividend cash flow model to estimate a cost of equity.
- Publicly traded companies are more likely to use the capital asset pricing model than are private companies.
- In evaluating projects, the majority use a single company cost of capital, but a large portion apply some type of risk adjustment for individual projects.

The survey also reveals that the single-factor capital asset pricing model is the most popular method for estimating the cost of equity, though the next most popular methods, respectively, are average stock returns and multifactor return models. The lack of popularity of the dividend discount model indicates that this approach, which was once favored, has lost its following in practice.[40]

---

39 John Graham and Campbell Harvey, "How Do CFOs Make Capital Budgeting and Capital Structure Decisions," *Journal of Applied Corporate Finance*, Vol. 15, No. 1 (Spring 2002), pp. 8–23.

40 A survey published in 1982 by Lawrence Gitman and V. Mercurio ["Cost of Capital Techniques Used by Major US Firms: Survey and Analysis of Fortune's 1000," *Financial Management*, Vol. 14, No. 4 (Winter 1982), pp. 21–29] indicated that fewer than 30 percent used the CAPM model in the estimation of the cost of equity.

In a survey of publicly traded multinational European companies, Franck Bancel and Usha Mittoo provide evidence consistent with the Graham and Harvey survey.[41] They find that over 70 percent of companies use the CAPM to determine the cost of equity; this compares with the 73.5 percent of US companies that use the CAPM. In a survey of both publicly traded and private European companies, Dirk Brounen, Abe de Jong, and Kees Koedijk confirm the result of Graham and Harvey that larger companies are more likely to use the more sophisticated methods, such as CAPM, in estimating the cost of equity.[42] Brounen, Jong, and Koedijk find that the popularity of the use of CAPM is less for their sample (ranging from 34 percent to 55.6 percent, depending on the country) than for the other two surveys, which may reflect the inclusion of smaller, private companies in the latter sample.

We learn from the survey evidence that the CAPM is a popular method for estimating the cost of equity capital and that it is used less by smaller, private companies. This latter result is not surprising because of the difficulty in estimating systematic risk in cases in which the company's equity is not publicly traded.

SUMMARY

In this reading, we provided an overview of the techniques used to calculate the cost of capital for companies and projects. We examined the weighted average cost of capital, discussing the methods commonly used to estimate the component costs of capital and the weights applied to these components. The international dimension of the cost of capital, as well as key factors influencing the cost of capital, were also analyzed.

- The weighted average cost of capital is a weighted average of the after-tax marginal costs of each source of capital: $\text{WACC} = w_d r_d(1 - t) + w_p r_p + w_e r_e$
- An analyst uses the WACC in valuation. For example, the WACC is used to value a project using the net present value method:

  NPV = Present value of inflows – Present value of the outflows

- The before-tax cost of debt is generally estimated by means of one of the two methods: yield to maturity or bond rating.
- The yield-to-maturity method of estimating the before-tax cost of debt uses the familiar bond valuation equation. Assuming semi-annual coupon payments, the equation is

$$P_0 = \frac{PMT_1}{\left(1+\frac{r_d}{2}\right)} + \ldots + \frac{PMT_n}{\left(1+\frac{r_d}{2}\right)^n} + \frac{FV}{\left(1+\frac{r_d}{2}\right)^n} = \left(\sum_{t=1}^{n}\frac{PMT_t}{\left(1+\frac{r_d}{2}\right)^t}\right) + \frac{FV}{\left(1+\frac{r_d}{2}\right)^n}$$

  We solve for the six-month yield ($r_d/2$) and then annualize it to arrive at the before-tax cost of debt, r_d.

41 Franck Bancel and Usha Mittoo, "The Determinants of Capital Structure Choice: A Survey of European Firms," *Financial Management*, Vol. 44, No. 4 (Winter 2004).

42 Dirk Brounen, Abe de Jong, and Kees Koedijk, "Corporate Finance in Europe: Confronting Theory with Practice," *Financial Management*, Vol. 44, No. 4 (Winter 2004).

- Because interest payments are generally tax-deductible, the after-tax cost is the true, effective cost of debt to the company. If a current yield or bond rating is not available, such as in the case of a private company without rated debt or a project, the estimate of the cost of debt becomes more challenging.
- The cost of preferred stock is the preferred stock dividend divided by the current preferred stock price:

$$r_p = \frac{D_p}{P_p}$$

- The cost of equity is the rate of return required by a company's common stockholders. We estimate this cost using the CAPM (or its variants) or the dividend discount method.
- The CAPM is the approach most commonly used to calculate the cost of common stock. The three components needed to calculate the cost of common stock are the risk-free rate, the equity risk premium, and beta:

$$E(R_i) = R_F + \beta_i\left[E(R_M) - R_F\right]$$

- When estimating the cost of equity capital using the CAPM when we do not have publicly traded equity, we may be able to use the pure-play method in which we estimate the unlevered beta for a company with similar business risk, β_U,

$$\beta_{U,\text{comparable}} = \frac{\beta_{L,\text{comparable}}}{\left[1 + \left(\left(1 - t_{\text{comparable}}\right)\frac{D_{\text{comparable}}}{E_{\text{comparable}}}\right)\right]}$$

and then lever this beta to reflect the financial risk of the project or company:

$$\beta_{L,\text{project}} = \beta_{U,\text{comparable}}\left[1 + \left(\left(1 - t_{\text{project}}\right)\frac{D_{\text{project}}}{E_{\text{project}}}\right)\right]$$

- It is often the case that country and foreign exchange risk are diversified so that we can use the estimated β in the CAPM analysis. However, in the case in which these risks cannot be diversified away, we can adjust our measure of systematic risk by a country equity premium to reflect this nondiversified risk:

$$\text{Country equity premium} = \text{Sovereign yield spread}\left[\frac{\begin{array}{c}\text{Annualized standard deviation}\\ \text{of equity index}\end{array}}{\begin{array}{c}\text{Annualized standard deviation of the}\\ \text{sovereign bond market in terms}\\ \text{of the developed market currency}\end{array}}\right]$$

- The dividend discount model approach is an alternative approach to calculating the cost of equity, whereby the cost of equity is estimated as follows:

$$r_e = \frac{D_1}{P_0} + g$$

- We can estimate the growth rate in the dividend discount model by using published forecasts of analysts or by estimating the sustainable growth rate:

$$g = (1 - D/\text{EPS})\text{ROE}$$

- In estimating the cost of equity, an alternative to the CAPM and dividend discount approaches is the bond yield plus risk premium approach. In this approach, we estimate the before-tax cost of debt and add a risk premium that reflects the additional risk associated with the company's equity.
- The marginal cost of capital schedule is a graph plotting the new funds raised by a company on the x-axis and the cost of capital on the y-axis. The cost of capital is level to the point at which one of the costs of capital changes, such as when the company bumps up against a debt covenant, requiring it to use another form of capital. We calculate a break point using information on when the different sources' costs change and the proportions that the company uses when it raises additional capital:

$$\text{Break point} = \frac{\text{Amount of capital at which the source's cost of capital changes}}{\text{Proportion of new capital raised from the source}}$$

- Flotation costs are costs incurred in the process of raising additional capital. The preferred method of including these costs in the analysis is as an initial cash flow in the valuation analysis.
- Survey evidence tells us that the CAPM method is the most popular method used by companies in estimating the cost of equity. The CAPM is more popular with larger, publicly traded companies, which is understandable considering the additional analyses and assumptions required in estimating systematic risk for a private company or project.

PRACTICE PROBLEMS

1 The cost of equity is equal to the:

A expected market return.

B rate of return required by stockholders.

C cost of retained earnings plus dividends.

2 Which of the following statements is correct?

A The appropriate tax rate to use in the adjustment of the before-tax cost of debt to determine the after-tax cost of debt is the average tax rate because interest is deductible against the company's entire taxable income.

B For a given company, the after-tax cost of debt is generally less than both the cost of preferred equity and the cost of common equity.

C For a given company, the investment opportunity schedule is upward sloping because as a company invests more in capital projects, the returns from investing increase.

3 Using the dividend discount model, what is the cost of equity capital for Zeller Mining if the company will pay a dividend of C$2.30 next year, has a payout ratio of 30 percent, a return on equity (ROE) of 15 percent, and a stock price of C$45?

A 9.61 percent.

B 10.50 percent.

C 15.61 percent.

4 Dot.Com has determined that it could issue $1,000 face value bonds with an 8 percent coupon paid semi-annually and a five-year maturity at $900 per bond. If Dot.Com's marginal tax rate is 38 percent, its after-tax cost of debt is *closest* to:

A 6.2 percent.

B 6.4 percent.

C 6.6 percent.

5 The cost of debt can be determined using the yield-to-maturity and the bond rating approaches. If the bond rating approach is used, the:

A coupon is the yield.

B yield is based on the interest coverage ratio.

C company is rated and the rating can be used to assess the credit default spread of the company's debt.

6 Morgan Insurance Ltd. issued a fixed-rate perpetual preferred stock three years ago and placed it privately with institutional investors. The stock was issued at $25 per share with a $1.75 dividend. If the company were to issue preferred stock today, the yield would be 6.5 percent. The stock's current value is:

A $25.00.

B $26.92.

C $37.31.

7 A financial analyst at Buckco Ltd. wants to compute the company's weighted average cost of capital (WACC) using the dividend discount model. The analyst has gathered the following data:

Before-tax cost of new debt	8 percent
Tax rate	40 percent
Target debt-to-equity ratio	0.8033
Stock price	$30
Next year's dividend	$1.50
Estimated growth rate	7 percent

Buckco's WACC is *closest* to:

A 8 percent.

B 9 percent.

C 12 percent.

8 The Gearing Company has an after-tax cost of debt capital of 4 percent, a cost of preferred stock of 8 percent, a cost of equity capital of 10 percent, and a weighted average cost of capital of 7 percent. Gearing intends to maintain its current capital structure as it raises additional capital. In making its capital-budgeting decisions for the average-risk project, the relevant cost of capital is:

A 4 percent.

B 7 percent.

C 8 percent.

9 Fran McClure of Alba Advisers is estimating the cost of capital of Frontier Corporation as part of her valuation analysis of Frontier. McClure will be using this estimate, along with projected cash flows from Frontier's new projects, to estimate the effect of these new projects on the value of Frontier. McClure has gathered the following information on Frontier Corporation:

	Current Year ($)	Forecasted for Next Year ($)
Book value of debt	50	50
Market value of debt	62	63
Book value of shareholders' equity	55	58
Market value of shareholders' equity	210	220

The weights that McClure should apply in estimating Frontier's cost of capital for debt and equity are, respectively:

A $w_d = 0.200$; $w_e = 0.800$.

B $w_d = 0.185$; $w_e = 0.815$.

C $w_d = 0.223$; $w_e = 0.777$.

10 Wang Securities had a long-term stable debt-to-equity ratio of 0.65. Recent bank borrowing for expansion into South America raised the ratio to 0.75. The increased leverage has what effect on the asset beta and equity beta of the company?

A The asset beta and the equity beta will both rise.

B The asset beta will remain the same and the equity beta will rise.

C The asset beta will remain the same and the equity beta will decline.

11 Brandon Wiene is a financial analyst covering the beverage industry. He is evaluating the impact of DEF Beverage's new product line of flavored waters. DEF currently has a debt-to-equity ratio of 0.6. The new product line would be financed with $50 million of debt and $100 million of equity. In estimating the valuation impact of this new product line on DEF's value, Wiene has estimated the equity beta and asset beta of comparable companies. In calculating the equity beta for the product line, Wiene is intending to use DEF's existing capital structure when converting the asset beta into a project beta. Which of the following statements is correct?

A Using DEF's debt-to-equity ratio of 0.6 is appropriate in calculating the new product line's equity beta.

B Using DEF's debt-to-equity ratio of 0.6 is not appropriate, but rather the debt-to-equity ratio of the new product, 0.5, is appropriate to use in calculating the new product line's equity beta.

C Wiene should use the new debt-to-equity ratio of DEF that would result from the additional \$50 million debt and \$100 million equity in calculating the new product line's equity beta.

12 Happy Resorts Company currently has 1.2 million common shares of stock outstanding and the stock has a beta of 2.2. It also has \$10 million face value of bonds that have five years remaining to maturity and 8 percent coupon with semi-annual payments, and are priced to yield 13.65 percent. If Happy issues up to \$2.5 million of new bonds, the bonds will be priced at par and have a yield of 13.65 percent; if it issues bonds beyond \$2.5 million, the expected yield on the entire issuance will be 16 percent. Happy has learned that it can issue new common stock at \$10 a share. The current risk-free rate of interest is 3 percent and the expected market return is 10 percent. Happy's marginal tax rate is 30 percent. If Happy raises \$7.5 million of new capital while maintaining the same debt-to-equity ratio, its weighted average cost of capital is *closest* to:

A 14.5 percent.

B 15.5 percent.

C 16.5 percent.

The following information relates to Questions 13–18[1]

Jurgen Knudsen has been hired to provide industry expertise to Henrik Sandell, CFA, an analyst for a pension plan managing a global large-cap fund internally. Sandell is concerned about one of the fund's larger holdings, auto parts manufacturer Kruspa AB. Kruspa currently operates in 80 countries, with the previous year's global revenues at €5.6 billion. Recently, Kruspa's CFO announced plans for expansion into Trutan, a country with a developing economy. Sandell worries that this expansion will change the company's risk profile and wonders if he should recommend a sale of the position.

Sandell provides Knudsen with the basic information. Kruspa's global annual free cash flow to the firm is €500 million and earnings are €400 million. Sandell estimates that cash flow will level off at a 2 percent rate of growth. Sandell also estimates that Kruspa's after-tax free cash flow to the firm on the Trutan project for next three years is, respectively, €48 million, €52 million, and €54.4 million. Kruspa recently announced a dividend of €4.00 per share of stock. For the initial analysis, Sandell requests that Knudsen ignore possible currency fluctuations. He expects the Trutanese plant to sell only to customers within Trutan for the first three years. Knudsen is asked to evaluate Kruspa's planned financing of the required €100 million with a €80 million public offering of 10-year debt in Sweden and the remainder with an equity offering.

1 The Level I exam uses only independent questions. This minicase is intended as a learning exercise.

Additional information:	
Equity risk premium, Sweden	4.82 percent
Risk-free rate of interest, Sweden	4.25 percent
Industry debt-to-equity ratio	0.3
Market value of Kruspa's debt	€900 million
Market value of Kruspa's equity	€2.4 billion
Kruspa's equity beta	1.3
Kruspa's before-tax cost of debt	9.25 percent
Trutan credit A2 country risk premium	1.88 percent
Corporate tax rate	37.5 percent
Interest payments each year	Level

13 Using the capital asset pricing model, Kruspa's cost of equity capital for its typical project is *closest* to:

A 7.62 percent.

B 10.52 percent.

C 12.40 percent.

14 Sandell is interested in the weighted average cost of capital of Kruspa AB prior to its investing in the Trutan project. This weighted average cost of capital (WACC) is *closest* to:

A 7.65 percent.

B 9.23 percent.

C 10.17 percent.

15 In his estimation of the project's cost of capital, Sandell would like to use the asset beta of Kruspa as a base in his calculations. The estimated asset beta of Kruspa prior to the Trutan project is *closest* to:

A 1.053.

B 1.110.

C 1.327.

16 Sandell is performing a sensitivity analysis of the effect of the new project on the company's cost of capital. If the Trutan project has the same asset risk as Kruspa, the estimated project beta for the Trutan project, if it is financed 80 percent with debt, is *closest* to:

A 1.300.

B 2.635.

C 3.686.

17 As part of the sensitivity analysis of the effect of the new project on the company's cost of capital, Sandell is estimating the cost of equity of the Trutan project considering that the Trutan project requires a country equity premium to capture the risk of the project. The cost of equity for the project in this case is *closest* to:

A 10.52 percent.

B 19.91 percent.

C 28.95 percent.

18 In his report, Sandell would like to discuss the sensitivity of the project's net present value to the estimation of the cost of equity. The Trutan project's net present value calculated using the equity beta without and with the country risk premium are, respectively:

A €26 million and €24 million.

B €28 million and €25 million.

C €30 million and €27 million.

The following information relates to Questions 19–22[2]

Boris Duarte, CFA, covers initial public offerings for Zellweger Analytics, an independent research firm specializing in global small-cap equities. He has been asked to evaluate the upcoming new issue of TagOn, a US-based business intelligence software company. The industry has grown at 26 percent per year for the previous three years. Large companies dominate the market, but sizable "pure-play" companies such as Relevant, Ltd., ABJ, Inc., and Opus Software Pvt. Ltd also compete. Each of these competitors is domiciled in a different country, but they all have shares of stock that trade on the US NASDAQ. The debt ratio of the industry has risen slightly in recent years.

Company	Sales in Millions ($)	Market Value Equity in Millions ($)	Market Value Debt in Millions ($)	Equity Beta	Tax Rate	Share Price ($)
Relevant Ltd.	752	3,800	0.0	1.702	23 percent	42
ABJ, Inc.	843	2,150	6.5	2.800	23 percent	24
Opus Software Pvt. Ltd.	211	972	13.0	3.400	23 percent	13

Duarte uses the information from the preliminary prospectus for TagOn's initial offering. The company intends to issue 1 million new shares. In his conversation with the investment bankers for the deal, he concludes the offering price will be between $7 and $12. The current capital structure of TagOn consists of a $2.4 million five-year non-callable bond issue and 1 million common shares. Other information that Duarte has gathered:

Currently outstanding bonds	$2.4 million five-year bonds, coupon of 12.5 percent, with a market value of $2.156 million
Risk-free rate of interest	5.25 percent
Estimated equity risk premium	7 percent
Tax rate	23 percent

19 The asset betas for Relevant, ABJ, and Opus, respectively, are:

A 1.70, 2.52, and 2.73.

B 1.70, 2.79, and 3.37.

C 1.70, 2.81, and 3.44.

---

2 The Level I exam uses only independent questions. This minicase is intended as a learning exercise.

20 The average asset beta for the pure players in this industry, Relevant, ABJ, and Opus, weighted by market value of equity is *closest* to:

A 1.67.

B 1.97.

C 2.27.

21 Using the capital asset pricing model, the cost of equity capital for a company in this industry with a debt-to-equity ratio of 0.01, asset beta of 2.27, and a marginal tax rate of 23 percent is *closest* to:

A 17 percent.

B 21 percent.

C 24 percent.

22 The marginal cost of capital for TagOn, based on an average asset beta of 2.27 for the industry and assuming that new stock can be issued at $8 per share, is *closest* to:

A 20.5 percent.

B 21.0 percent.

C 21.5 percent.

---

23 Two years ago, a company issued $20 million in long-term bonds at par value with a coupon rate of 9 percent. The company has decided to issue an additional $20 million in bonds and expects the new issue to be priced at par value with a coupon rate of 7 percent. The company has no other debt outstanding and has a tax rate of 40 percent. To compute the company's weighted average cost of capital, the appropriate after-tax cost of debt is *closest* to:

A 4.2%.

B 4.8%.

C 5.4%.

24 An analyst gathered the following information about a company and the market:

Current market price per share of common stock	$28.00
Most recent dividend per share paid on common stock (D_0)	$2.00
Expected dividend payout rate	40%
Expected return on equity (ROE)	15%
Beta for the common stock	1.3
Expected rate of return on the market portfolio	13%
Risk-free rate of return	4%

Using the discounted cash flow (DCF) approach, the cost of retained earnings for the company is *closest* to:

A 15.7%.

B 16.1%.

C 16.8%.

25 An analyst gathered the following information about a company and the market:

Current market price per share of common stock	\$28.00
Most recent dividend per share paid on common stock (D_0)	\$2.00
Expected dividend payout rate	40%
Expected return on equity (ROE)	15%
Beta for the common stock	1.3
Expected rate of return on the market portfolio	13%
Risk-free rate of return	4%

Using the Capital Asset Pricing Model (CAPM) approach, the cost of retained earnings for the company is *closest* to:

A 13.6%.

B 15.7%.

C 16.1%.

26 An analyst gathered the following information about a private company and its publicly traded competitor:

Comparable Companies	Tax Rate (%)	Debt/Equity	Equity Beta
Private company	30.0	1.00	N.A.
Public company	35.0	0.90	1.75

Using the pure-play method, the estimated equity beta for the private company is *closest* to:

A 1.029.

B 1.104.

C 1.877.

27 An analyst gathered the following information about the capital markets in the United States and in Paragon, a developing country.

Selected Market Information (%)	
Yield on US 10-year Treasury bond	4.5
Yield on Paragon 10-year government bond	10.5
Annualized standard deviation of Paragon stock index	35.0
Annualized standard deviation of Paragon dollar-denominated government bond	25.0

Based on the analyst's data, the estimated country equity premium for Paragon is *closest* to:

A 4.29%.

B 6.00%.

C 8.40%.

SOLUTIONS

1 B is correct. The cost of equity is defined as the rate of return required by stockholders.

2 B is correct. Debt is generally less costly than preferred or common stock. The cost of debt is further reduced if interest expense is tax deductible.

3 C is correct. First calculate the growth rate using the sustainable growth calculation, and then calculate the cost of equity using the rearranged dividend discount model:

g = (1 – Dividend payout ratio)(Return on equity) = (1 – 0.30)(15%) = 10.5%

$r_e = (D_1/P_0) + g$ = (\$2.30/\$45) + 10.50% = 15.61%

4 C is correct. FV = \$1,000; PMT = \$40; N = 10; PV = \$900

Solve for i. The six-month yield, i, is 5.3149%

YTM = 5.3149% × 2 = 10.62985%

$r_d(1 - t)$ = 10.62985%(1 – 0.38) = 6.5905%

5 C is correct. The bond rating approach depends on knowledge of the company's rating and can be compared with yields on bonds in the public market.

6 B is correct. The company can issue preferred stock at 6.5%.

P_p = \$1.75/0.065 = \$26.92

7 B is correct.

Cost of equity = $D_1/P_0 + g$ = \$1.50/\$30 + 7% = 5% + 7% = 12%

$D/(D + E)$ = 0.8033/1.8033 = 0.445

WACC = [(0.445) (0.08)(1 – 0.4)] + [(0.555)(0.12)] = 8.8%

8 B is correct. The weighted average cost of capital, using weights derived from the current capital structure, is the best estimate of the cost of capital for the average-risk project of a company.

9 C is correct.

w_d = \$63/(\$220 + 63) = 0.223

w_e = \$220/(\$220 + 63) = 0.777

10 B is correct. Asset risk does not change with a higher debt-to-equity ratio. Equity risk rises with higher debt.

11 B is correct. The debt-to-equity ratio of the new product should be used when making the adjustment from the asset beta, derived from the comparables, to the equity beta of the new product.

12 B is correct.

Capital structure:

Market value of debt: FV = \$10,000,000, PMT = \$400,000, N = 10,

I/YR = 6.825%. Solving for PV gives the answer \$7,999,688.

Market value of equity: 1.2 million shares outstanding at \$10 = \$12,000,000

Market value of debt	$7,999,688	40%
Market value of equity	12,000,000	60%
Total capital	$19,999,688	100%

To raise $7.5 million of new capital while maintaining the same capital structure, the company would issue $7.5 million × 40% = $3.0 million in bonds, which results in a before-tax rate of 16 percent.

$r_d(1 - t) = 0.16(1 - 0.3) = 0.112$ or 11.2%

$r_e = 0.03 + 2.2\ (0.10 - 0.03) = 0.184$ or 18.4%

WACC = [0.40(0.112)] + [0.6(0.184)] = 0.0448 + 0.1104 = 0.1552 or 15.52%

13 B is correct.

$r_e = 0.0425 + (1.3)(0.0482) = 0.1052$ or 10.52%

14 B is correct.

WACC = [(€900/€3300) .0925 (1 − 0.375)] + [(€2400/€3300)(0.1052)]
= 0.0923 or 9.23%

15 A is correct.

Asset beta = Unlevered beta = 1.3/(1 + [(1−0.375)(€900/€2400)] = 1.053

16 C is correct.

Project beta = 1.053 {1 + [(1 − 0.375)(€80/€20)]} = 1.053 {3.5} = 3.686

17 C is correct.

$r_e = 0.0425 + 3.686(0.0482 + 0.0188) = 0.2895$ or 28.95%

18 C is correct.

Cost of equity without the country risk premium:

$r_e = 0.0425 + 3.686\ (0.0482) = 0.2202$ or 22.02%

Cost of equity with the country risk premium:

$r_e = 0.0425 + 3.686\ (0.0482 + 0.0188) = 0.2895$ or 28.95%

Weighted average cost of capital without the country risk premium:

WACC = [0.80 (0.0925) (1 − 0.375)] + [0.20 (0.2202)] = 0.04625 + 0.04404
= 0.09038 or 9.03 percent

Weighted average cost of capital with the country risk premium:

WACC = [0.80 (0.0925) (1 − 0.375)] + [0.20 (0.2895)] = 0.04625 + 0.0579
= 0.1042 or 10.42 percent

NPV without the country risk premium:

$$\begin{aligned} \text{NPV} &= \frac{€48 \text{ million}}{(1 + 0.0903)^1} + \frac{€52 \text{ million}}{(1 + 0.0903)^2} + \frac{€54.4 \text{ million}}{(1 + 0.0903)^3} - €100 \text{ million} \\ &= €44.03 \text{ million} + 43.74 \text{ million} + 41.97 \text{ million} - €100 \text{ million} \\ &= €29.74 \text{ million} \end{aligned}$$

NPV with the country risk premium:

$$\text{NPV} = \frac{€48 \text{ million}}{(1+0.1042)^1} + \frac{€52 \text{ million}}{(1+0.1042)^2} + \frac{€54.4 \text{ million}}{(1+0.1042)^3} - €100 \text{ million}$$

$$= €43.47 \text{ million} + 42.65 \text{ million} + 40.41 \text{ million} - €100 \text{ million}$$

$$= €26.53 \text{ million}$$

19 B is correct.

Asset betas: $\beta_{equity}/[1 + (1 - t)(D/E)]$

Relevant = 1.702/[1 + (0.77)(0)] = 1.702

ABJ = 2.8/[1 + (0.77)(0.003)] = 2.7918

Opus = 3.4/1 + [(0.77)(0.013)] = 3.3663

20 C is correct.

Weights are determined based on relative market values:

Pure-Play	Market Value of Equity in Millions	Proportion of Total
Relevant	$3,800	0.5490
ABJ	2,150	0.3106
Opus	972	0.1404
Total	$6,922	1.0000

Weighted average beta (0.5490)(1.702) + (0.3106)(2.7918) + (0.1404)(3.3572) = 2.27.

21 B is correct.

Asset beta = 2.27

Levered beta = 2.27 {1 + [(1 − 0.23)(0.01)]} = 2.2875

Cost of equity capital = 0.0525 + (2.2875)(0.07) = 0.2126 or 21.26%

22 C is correct.

For debt: FV = 2,400,000; PV = 2,156,000; n = 10; PMT = 150,000

Solve for i. i = 0.07748. YTM = 15.5%

Before-tax cost of debt = 15.5%

Market value of equity = 1 million shares outstanding + 1 million newly issued shares = 2 million shares at $8 = $16 million

Total market capitalization = $2.156 million + $16 million = $18.156 million

Levered beta = 2.27 {1 + [(1 − 0.23)(2.156/16)]} = 2.27 (1.1038) = 2.5055

Cost of equity = 0.0525 + 2.5055 (0.07) = 0.2279 or 22.79%

Debt weight = $2.156/$18.156 = 0.1187

Equity weight = $16/$18.156 = 0.8813

TagOn's MCC = [(0.1187)(0.155)(1 − 0.23)] + [(0.8813)(0.2279)]
= 0.01417 + 0.20083
= 0.2150 or 21.50%

23 A is correct. The relevant cost is the marginal cost of debt. The before-tax marginal cost of debt can be estimated by the yield to maturity on a comparable outstanding. After adjusting for tax, the after-tax cost is 7(1 – 0.4) = 7(0.6) = 4.2%.

24 C is correct. The expected return is the sum of the expected dividend yield plus expected growth. The expected growth is (1 – 0.4)15% = 9%. The expected dividend yield is \$2.18/\$28 = 7.8%. The sum is 16.8%.

25 B is correct. Using the CAPM approach, 4% + 1.3(9%) = 15.7%.

26 C is correct. Inferring the asset beta for the public company: unlevered beta = 1.75/[1 + (1 – 0.35) (0.90)] = 1.104. Relevering to reflect the target debt ratio of the private firm: levered beta = 1.104 × [1 + (1 – 0.30) (1.00)] = 1.877.

27 C is correct. The country equity premium can be estimated as the sovereign yield spread times the volatility of the country's stock market relative to its bond market. Paragon's equity premium is (10.5% – 4.5%) × (35%/25%) = 6% × 1.4 = 8.40%.

CORPORATE FINANCE

STUDY SESSION

11

Corporate Finance (2)

This study session covers how companies make use of leverage and manage their working capital to meet short-term operational needs. The various types of leverage (operating, financial, total), measures of leverage, and how leverage affects a company's earnings and financial ratios are examined. A discussion then follows on the different types of working capital and the management issues associated with each. The session concludes with techniques for assessing the effectiveness of working capital management.

READING ASSIGNMENTS

Reading 34	Measures of Leverage by Pamela Peterson Drake, PhD, CFA, Raj Aggarwal, PhD, CFA, Cynthia Harrington, CFA, and Adam Kobor, PhD, CFA
Reading 35	Working Capital Management by Edgar A. Norton, Jr., PhD, CFA, Kenneth L. Parkinson, MBA, CCM, and Pamela Peterson Drake, PhD, CFA

READING

34

Measures of Leverage

by Pamela Peterson Drake, PhD, CFA, Raj Aggarwal, PhD, CFA, Cynthia Harrington, CFA, and Adam Kobor, PhD, CFA

Pamela Peterson Drake, PhD, CFA, is at James Madison University (USA). Raj Aggarwal, PhD, CFA (USA). Cynthia Harrington, CFA, is at teamyou.co (USA). Adam Kobor, PhD, CFA, is at New York University (USA).

LEARNING OUTCOMES

Mastery	*The candidate should be able to:*
☐	a. define and explain leverage, business risk, sales risk, operating risk, and financial risk and classify a risk;
☐	b. calculate and interpret the degree of operating leverage, the degree of financial leverage, and the degree of total leverage;
☐	c. analyze the effect of financial leverage on a company's net income and return on equity;
☐	d. calculate the breakeven quantity of sales and determine the company's net income at various sales levels;
☐	e. calculate and interpret the operating breakeven quantity of sales.

INTRODUCTION

1

This reading presents elementary topics in leverage. **Leverage** is the use of fixed costs in a company's cost structure. Fixed costs that are operating costs (such as depreciation or rent) create operating leverage. Fixed costs that are financial costs (such as interest expense) create financial leverage.

Analysts refer to the use of fixed costs as leverage because fixed costs act as a fulcrum for the company's earnings. Leverage can magnify earnings both up and down. The profits of highly leveraged companies might soar with small upturns in revenue. But the reverse is also true: Small downturns in revenue may lead to losses.

Analysts need to understand a company's use of leverage for three main reasons. First, the degree of leverage is an important component in assessing a company's risk and return characteristics. Second, analysts may be able to discern information about a company's business and future prospects from management's decisions about the use of operating and financial leverage. Knowing how to interpret these signals also helps the analyst evaluate the quality of management's decisions. Third, the valuation of a company requires forecasting future cash flows and assessing the risk associated with those cash flows. Understanding a company's use of leverage should help in forecasting cash flows and in selecting an appropriate discount rate for finding their present value.

The reading is organized as follows: Section 2 introduces leverage and defines important terms. Section 3 illustrates and discusses measures of operating leverage and financial leverage, which combine to define a measure of total leverage that gauges the sensitivity of net income to a given percent change in units sold. This section also covers breakeven points in using leverage and corporate reorganization (a possible consequence of using leverage inappropriately). A summary and practice problems conclude this reading.

2 LEVERAGE

Leverage increases the volatility of a company's earnings and cash flows and increases the risk of lending to or owning a company. Additionally, the valuation of a company and its equity is affected by the degree of leverage: The greater a company's leverage, the greater its risk and, hence, the greater the discount rate that should be applied in its valuation. Further, highly leveraged (levered) companies have a greater chance of incurring significant losses during downturns, thus accelerating conditions that lead to financial distress and bankruptcy.

Consider the simple example of two companies, Impulse Robotics, Inc., and Malvey Aerospace, Inc. These companies have the following performance for the period of study:[1]

Exhibit 1 Impulse Robotics and Malvey Aerospace

	Impulse Robotics	Malvey Aerospace
Revenues	$1,000,000	$1,000,000
Operating costs	700,000	750,000
Operating income	$300,000	$250,000
Financing expense	100,000	50,000
Net income	$200,000	$200,000

These companies have the same net income, but are they identical in terms of operating and financial characteristics? Would we appraise these two companies at the same value? Not necessarily.

The risk associated with future earnings and cash flows of a company are affected by the company's cost structure. The **cost structure** of a company is the mix of variable and fixed costs. **Variable costs** fluctuate with the level of production and sales. Some examples of variable costs are the cost of goods purchased for resale, costs of materials or supplies, shipping charges, delivery charges, wages for hourly employees, sales commissions, and sales or production bonuses. **Fixed costs** are expenses that are the same regardless of the production and sales of the company. These costs include depreciation, rent, interest on debt, insurance, and wages for salaried employees.

1 We are ignoring taxes for this example, but when taxes are included, the general conclusions remain the same.

Suppose that the cost structures of the companies differ in the manner shown in Exhibit 2.

Exhibit 2 Impulse Robotics and Malvey Aerospace

	Impulse Robotics	Malvey Aerospace
Number of units produced and sold	100,000	100,000
Sales price per unit	$10	$10
Variable cost per unit	$2	$6
Fixed operating cost	$500,000	$150,000
Fixed financing expense	$100,000	$50,000

The risk associated with these companies is different, although, as we saw in Exhibit 1, they have the same net income. They have different operating and financing cost structures, resulting in differing volatility of net income.

For example, if the number of units produced and sold is different from 100,000, the net income of the two companies diverges. If 50,000 units are produced and sold, Impulse Robotics has a loss of $200,000 and Malvey Aerospace has $0 earnings. If, on the other hand, the number of units produced and sold is 200,000, Impulse Robotics earns $1 million whereas Malvey Aerospace earns $600,000. In other words, the variability in net income is greater for Impulse Robotics, which has higher fixed costs in terms of both fixed operating costs and fixed financing costs.

Impulse Robotics' cost structure results in more leverage than that of Malvey Aerospace. We can see this effect when we plot the net income of each company against the number of units produced and sold, as in Exhibit 3. The greater leverage of Impulse Robotics is reflected in the greater slope of the line representing net income. This means that as the number of units sold changes, Impulse Robotics experiences a greater change in net income than does Malvey Aerospace for the same change in units sold.

Exhibit 3 Net Income for Different Numbers of Units Produced and Sold

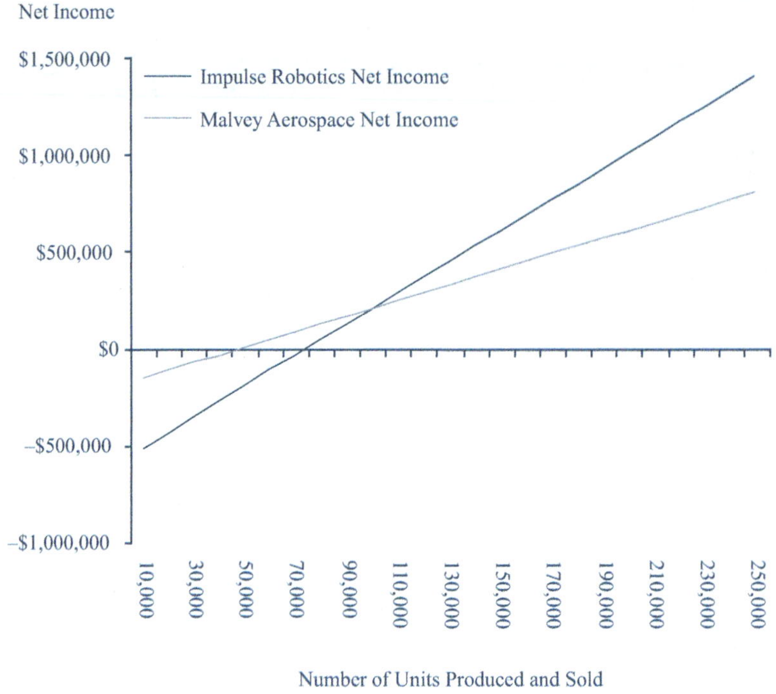

Companies that have more fixed costs relative to variable costs in their cost structures have greater variation in net income as revenues fluctuate and, hence, more risk.

3 BUSINESS RISK AND FINANCIAL RISK

Risk arises from both the operating and financing activities of a company. In the following, we address how that happens and the measures available to the analyst to gauge the risk in each case.

3.1 Business Risk and Its Components

Business risk is the risk associated with operating earnings. Operating earnings are risky because total revenues are risky, as are the costs of producing revenues. Revenues are affected by a large number of factors, including economic conditions, industry dynamics (including the actions of competitors), government regulation, and demographics. Therefore, prices of the company's goods or services or the quantity of sales may be different from what is expected. We refer to the uncertainty with respect to the price and quantity of goods and services as **sales risk**.

Operating risk is the risk attributed to the operating cost structure, in particular the use of fixed costs in operations. The greater the fixed operating costs relative to variable operating costs, the greater the operating risk. Business risk is therefore the combination of sales risk and operating risk. Companies that operate in the same line of business generally have similar business risk.

3.2 Sales Risk

Consider Impulse Robotics once again. Suppose that the forecasted number of units produced and sold in the next period is 100,000 but that the standard deviation of the number of units sold is 20,000. And suppose the price that the units sell for is expected to be $10 per unit but the standard deviation is $2. Contrast this situation with that of a company named Tolley Aerospace, Inc., which has the same cost structure but a standard deviation of units sold of 40,000 and a price standard deviation of $4.

If we assume, for simplicity's sake, that the fixed operating costs are known with certainty and that the units sold and price per unit follow a normal distribution, we can see the impact of the different risks on the operating income of the two companies through a simulation; the results are shown in Exhibit 4. Here, we see the differing distributions of operating income that result from the distributions of units sold and price per unit. So, even if the companies have the same cost structure, differing *sales risk* affects the potential variability of the company's profitability. In our example, Tolley Aerospace has a wider distribution of likely outcomes in terms of operating profit. This greater volatility in operating earnings means that Tolley Aerospace has more sales risk than Impulse Robotics.

Exhibit 4 Operating Income Simulations for Impulse Robotics and Tolley Aerospace

Panel A: Impulse Robotics

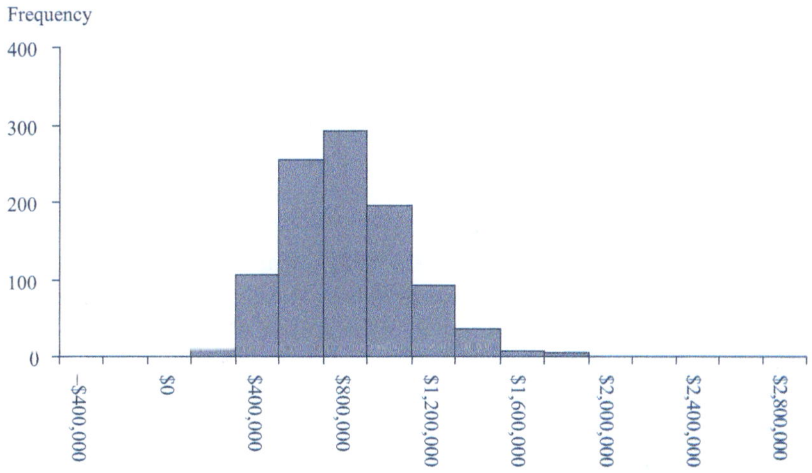

(continued)

Exhibit 4 (Continued)

Panel B: Tolley Aerospace

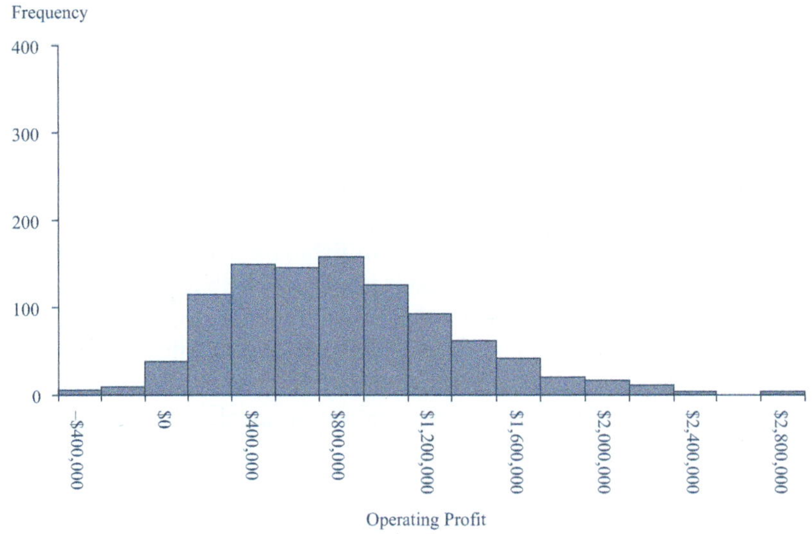

3.3 Operating Risk

The greater the fixed component of costs, the more difficult it is for a company to adjust its operating costs to changes in sales. The mixture of fixed and variable costs depends largely on the type of business. Even within the same line of business, companies can vary their fixed and variable costs to some degree. We refer to the risk arising from the mix of fixed and variable costs as **operating risk**. The greater the fixed operating costs relative to variable operating costs, the greater the operating risk.

Next, we look at how operating risk affects the variability of cash flows. A concept taught in microeconomics is **elasticity**, which is simply a measure of the sensitivity of changes in one item to changes in another. We can apply this concept to examine how sensitive a company's operating income is to changes in demand, as measured by unit sales. We will calculate the operating income elasticity, which we refer to as the **degree of operating leverage** (DOL). DOL is a quantitative measure of operating risk as it was defined earlier.

The degree of operating leverage is the ratio of the percentage change in operating income to the percentage change in units sold. We will simplify things and assume that the company sells all that it produces in the same period. Then,

$$\text{DOL} = \frac{\text{Percentage change in operating income}}{\text{Percentage change in units sold}} \tag{1}$$

For example, if DOL at a given level of unit sales is 2.0, a 5 percent increase in unit sales from that level would be expected to result in a (2.0)(5%) = 10 percent increase in operating income. As illustrated later in relation to Exhibit 6, a company's DOL is dependent on the level of unit sales being considered.

Returning to Impulse Robotics, the price per unit is \$10, the variable cost per unit is \$2, and the total fixed operating costs are \$500,000. If Impulse Robotics' output changes from 100,000 units to 110,000 units—an increase of 10 percent in the number of units sold—operating income changes from \$300,000 to \$380,000:[2]

Exhibit 5 Operating Leverage of Impulse Robotics

Item	Selling 100,000 Units	Selling 110,000 Units	Percentage Change
Revenues	\$1,000,000	\$1,100,000	+10.00
Less variable costs	200,000	220,000	+10.00
Less fixed costs	500,000	500,000	0.00
Operating income	\$300,000	\$380,000	+26.67

Operating income increases by 26.67 percent when units sold increases by 10 percent. What if the number of units *decreases* by 10 percent, from 100,000 to 90,000? Operating income is \$220,000, representing a *decline* of 26.67 percent.

What is happening is that for a 1 percent change in units sold, the operating income changes by 2.67 times that percentage, in the same direction. If units sold increases by 10 percent, operating income increases by 26.7 percent; if units sold decreased by 20 percent, operating income would decrease by 53.3 percent.

We can represent the degree of operating leverage as given in Equation 1 in terms of the basic elements of the price per unit, variable cost per unit, number of units sold, and fixed operating costs. Operating income is revenue minus total operating costs (with variable and fixed cost components):

$$\begin{aligned}\begin{pmatrix}\text{Operating}\\ \text{income}\end{pmatrix} &= \left[\begin{pmatrix}\text{Price}\\ \text{per unit}\end{pmatrix}\begin{pmatrix}\text{Number of}\\ \text{units sold}\end{pmatrix}\right]\\ &\quad - \left[\begin{pmatrix}\text{Variable cost}\\ \text{per unit}\end{pmatrix}\begin{pmatrix}\text{Number of}\\ \text{units sold}\end{pmatrix}\right] - \begin{bmatrix}\text{Fixed operating}\\ \text{costs}\end{bmatrix}\end{aligned}$$

or

$$\begin{matrix}\text{Operating}\\ \text{income}\end{matrix} = \underbrace{\begin{pmatrix}\text{Number of}\\ \text{units sold}\end{pmatrix}\left[\begin{pmatrix}\text{Price}\\ \text{per unit}\end{pmatrix} - \begin{pmatrix}\text{Variable cost}\\ \text{per unit}\end{pmatrix}\right]}_{\text{Contribution margin}} - \begin{bmatrix}\text{Fixed operating}\\ \text{costs}\end{bmatrix}$$

The **per unit contribution margin** is the amount that each unit sold contributes to covering fixed costs—that is, the difference between the price per unit and the variable cost per unit. That difference multiplied by the quantity sold is the **contribution margin**, which equals revenue minus variable costs.

2 We provide the variable and fixed operating costs for our sample companies used in this reading to illustrate the leverage and breakeven concepts. In reality, however, the financial analyst does not have these breakdowns but rather is faced with interpreting reported account values that often combine variable and fixed costs and costs for different product lines.

How much does operating income change when the number of units sold changes? Fixed costs do not change; therefore, operating income changes by the contribution margin. The percentage change in operating income for a given change in units sold simplifies to

$$\text{DOL} = \frac{Q(P-V)}{Q(P-V)-F} \quad (2)$$

where Q is the number of units, P is the price per unit, V is the variable operating cost per unit, and F is the fixed operating cost. Therefore, $P - V$ is the per unit contribution margin and $Q(P - V)$ is the contribution margin.

Applying the formula for DOL using the data for Impulse Robotics, we can calculate the sensitivity to change in units sold from 100,000 units:

$$\begin{array}{c}\text{DOL@} \\ 100{,}000\,\text{units}\end{array} = \frac{100{,}000(\$10-\$2)}{100{,}000(\$10-\$2)-\$500{,}000} = 2.67$$

A DOL of 2.67 means that a 1 percent change in units sold results in a 1% × 2.67 = 2.67% change in operating income; a DOL of 5 means that a 1 percent change in units sold results in a 5 percent change in operating income, and so on.

Why do we specify that the DOL is at a particular quantity sold (in this case, 100,000 units)? Because the DOL is different at different numbers of units produced and sold. For example, at 200,000 units,

$$\begin{array}{c}\text{DOL @} \\ 200{,}000\,\text{units}\end{array} = \frac{200{,}000(\$10-\$2)}{200{,}000(\$10-\$2)-\$500{,}000} = 1.45$$

We can see the sensitivity of the DOL for different numbers of units produced and sold in Exhibit 6. When operating profit is negative, the DOL is negative. At positions just below and just above the point where operating income is \$0, operating income is at its most sensitive on a percentage basis to changes in units produced and sold. At the point at which operating income is \$0 (at 62,500 units produced and sold in this example), the DOL is undefined because the denominator in the DOL calculation is \$0. After this point, the DOL gradually declines as more units are produced and sold.

Exhibit 6 Impulse Robotics' Degree of Operating Leverage for Different Number of Units Produced and Sold

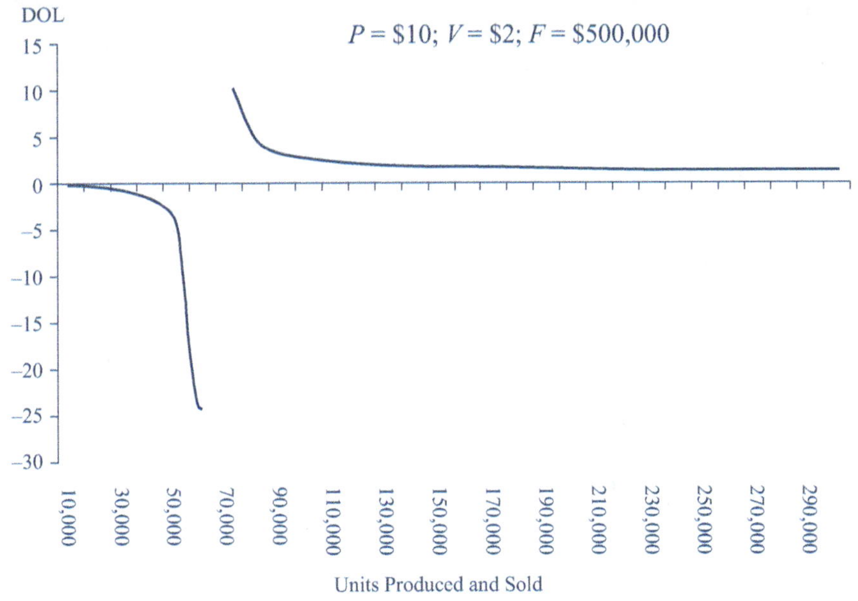

We will now look at a similar situation in which the company has shifted some of the operating costs away from fixed costs and into variable costs. Malvey Aerospace has a unit sales price of \$10, a variable cost of \$6 a unit, and \$150,000 in fixed costs. A change in units sold from 100,000 to 110,000 (a 10 percent change) changes operating profit from \$250,000 to \$290,000, or 16 percent. The DOL in this case is 1.6:

$$\begin{matrix}\text{DOL @} \\ \text{100,000 units}\end{matrix} = \frac{100{,}000(\$10 - \$6)}{100{,}000(\$10 - \$6) - \$150{,}000} = 1.6$$

and the change in operating income is 16 percent:

$$\begin{matrix}\text{Percentage change} \\ \text{in operating income}\end{matrix} = (\text{DOL})\begin{pmatrix}\text{Percentage change} \\ \text{in units sold}\end{pmatrix} = (1.6)(10\%) = 16\%$$

We can see the difference in leverage in the case of Impulse Robotics and Malvey Aerospace companies in Exhibit 7. In Panel A, we see that Impulse Robotics has higher operating income than Malvey Aerospace when both companies produce and sell more than 87,500 units, but lower operating income than Malvey when both companies produce and sell less than 87,500 units.[3]

Exhibit 7 Profitability and the DOL for Impulse Robotics and Malvey Aerospace

Impulse Robotics: P = \$10; V = \$2; F = \$500,000
Malvey Aerospace: P = \$10; V = \$6; F = \$150,000

(continued)

3 We can calculate the number of units that produce the same operating income for these two companies by equating the operating incomes and solving for the number of units. Let X be the number of units. The X at which Malvey Aerospace and Impulse Robotics generate the same operating income is the X that solves the following: $10X - 2X - 500{,}000 = 10X - 6X - 150{,}000$; that is, $X = 87{,}500$.

Exhibit 7 (Continued)

Panel A: Operating Income and Number of Units Produced and Sold

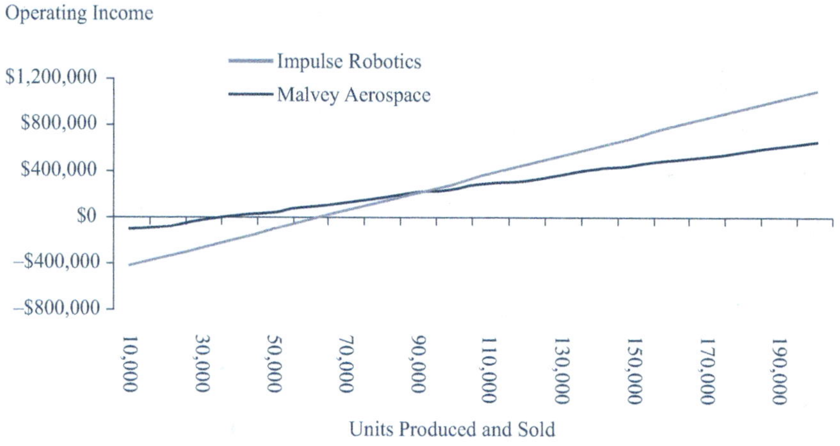

Panel B: Degree of Operating Leverage (DOL)

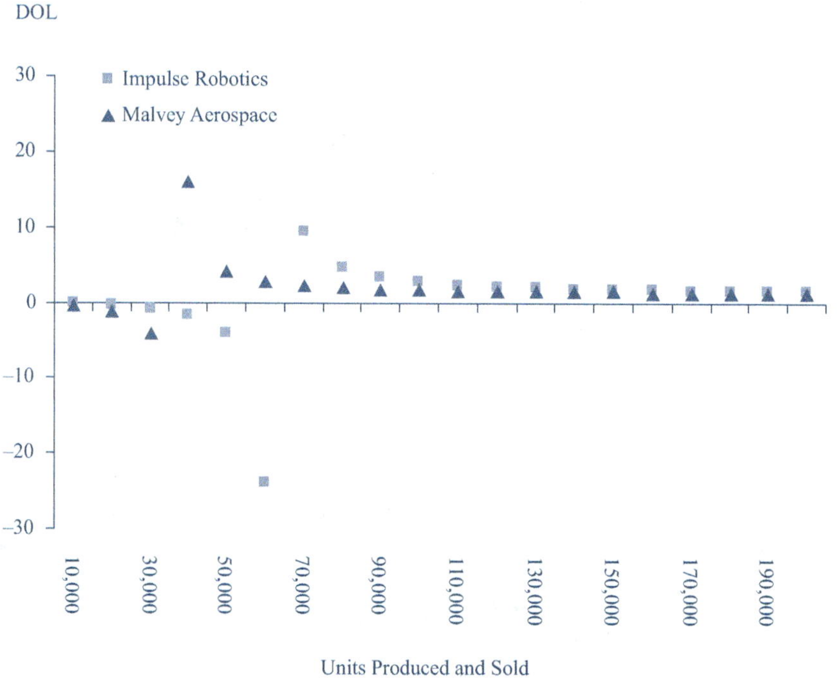

This example confirms what we saw earlier in our reasoning of fixed and variable costs: The greater the use of fixed, relative to variable, operating costs, the more sensitive operating income is to changes in units sold and, therefore, the more operating risk. Impulse Robotics has more operating risk because it has more operating leverage. However, as Panel B of Exhibit 7 shows, the degrees of operating leverage are similar for the two companies for larger numbers of units produced and sold.

Both sales risk and operating risk influence a company's business risk. And both sales risk and operating risk are determined in large part by the type of business the company is in. But management has more opportunity to manage and control operating risk than sales risk.

Suppose a company is deciding which equipment to buy to produce a particular product. The sales risk is the same no matter what equipment is chosen to produce the product. But the available equipment may differ in terms of the fixed and variable operating costs of producing the product. Financial analysts need to consider how the operating cost structure of a company affects the company's risk.

EXAMPLE 1

Calculating the Degree of Operating Leverage

Arnaud Kenigswald is analyzing the potential impact of an improving economy on earnings at Global Auto, one of the world's largest car manufacturers. Global is headquartered in Berlin. Global Auto manufactures passenger cars and produces revenues of €168 billion. Kenigswald projects that sales will improve by 10 percent due to increased demand for cars. He wants to see how Global's earnings might respond given that level of increase in sales. He first looks at the degree of leverage at Global, starting with operating leverage.

Global sold 6 million passenger cars in 2017. The average price per car was €28,000, fixed costs associated with passenger car production total €15 billion per year, and variable costs per car are €20,500. What is the degree of operating leverage of Global Auto?

Solution:

$$\text{DOL @ 6 million units} = \frac{6\text{ million }(€28{,}000 - €20{,}500)}{6\text{ million }(€28{,}000 - €20{,}500) - €15\text{ billion}} = 1.5$$

Operating income is [6 million × (€28,000 – €20,500)] – €15 billion = €30 billion

For a 10 percent increase in cars sold, operating income increases by 1.50 × 10% = 15.0%.

Industries that tend to have high operating leverage are those that invest up front to produce a product but spend relatively little on making and distributing it. Software developers and pharmaceutical companies fit this description. Alternatively, retailers have low operating leverage because much of the cost of goods sold is variable.

Because most companies produce more than one product, the ratio of variable to fixed costs is difficult to obtain. We can get an idea of the operating leverage of a company by looking at changes in operating income in relation to changes in sales for the entire company. This relation can be estimated by regressing changes in operating income (the variable to be explained) on changes in sales (the explanatory variable) over a recent time period.[4] Although this approach does not provide a precise measure of operating risk, it can help provide a general idea of the amount of operating leverage present. For example, compare the relation between operating earnings and revenues for Delta Air Lines, a transportation company, and Wal-Mart Stores, a discount retailer, as shown in Exhibit 8. Note that the slope of the least-squares regression line is greater for Delta Air Lines (with a slope coefficient of 0.1702) than for Wal-Mart (with a slope coefficient of 0.0493). (A visual comparison of slopes should not be relied upon because the scales of the x- and y-axes are different in diagrams for the

4 A least-squares regression is a procedure for finding the best-fitting line (called the least squares regression line) through a set of data points by minimizing the squared deviations from the line.

two regressions.) We can see that operating earnings are more sensitive to changes in revenues for the higher-operating-leveraged Delta Air Lines as compared to the lower-operating-leveraged Wal-Mart Stores.

Exhibit 8 Relation between Operating Earnings and Revenues

Panel A: Delta Airlines Operating Earnings and Revenues, 1990–2017

Estimated regression: Operating earnings = –$2,249 + 0.1702 Revenues
R^2 = 64.73%

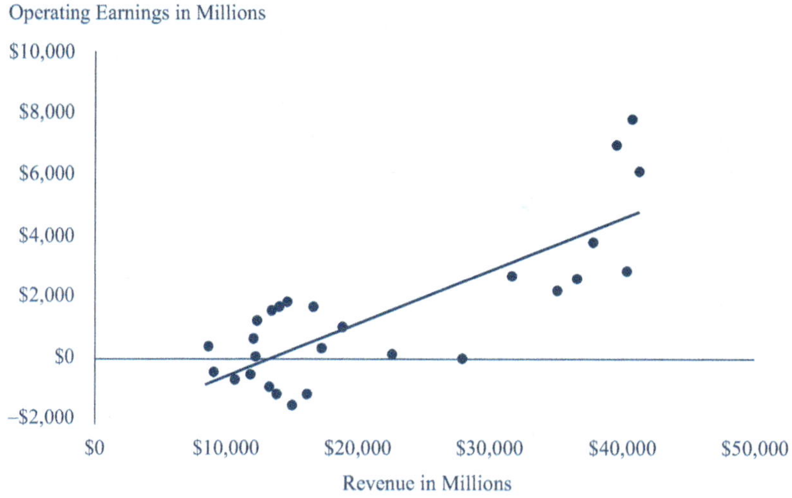

Panel B: Wal-Mart Stores Operating Earnings and Revenues, 1990–2017

Estimated regression: Operating earnings = $253.16 + 0.0493 Revenues
R^2 = 94.89%

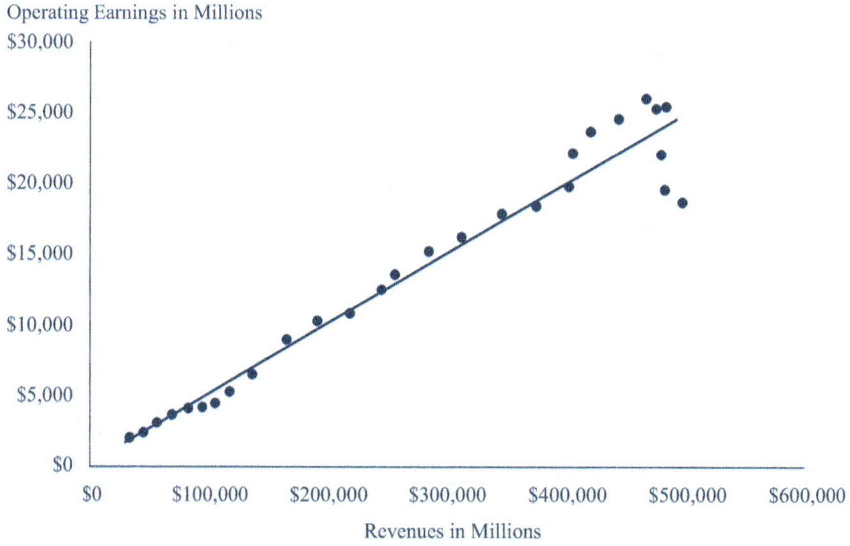

Sources: Delta Air Lines 10-K filings and Wal-Mart Stores 10-K filings, various years.

3.4 Financial Risk

We can expand on the concept of risk to accommodate the perspective of owning a security. A security represents a claim on the income and assets of a business; therefore, the risk of the security goes beyond the variability of operating earnings to include how the cash flows from those earnings are distributed among the claimants—the creditors and owners of the business. The risk of a security is therefore affected by both business risk and financial risk.

Financial risk is the risk associated with how a company finances its operations. If a company finances with debt, it is legally obligated to pay the amounts that make up its debts when due. By taking on fixed obligations, such as debt and long-term leases, the company increases its financial risk. If a company finances its business with common equity, generated either from operations (retained earnings) or from issuing new common shares, it does not incur fixed obligations. The more fixed-cost financial obligations (e.g., debt) incurred by the company, the greater its financial risk.

We can quantify this risk in the same way we did for operating risk, looking at the sensitivity of the cash flows available to owners when operating income changes. This sensitivity, which we refer to as the **degree of financial leverage** (DFL), is

$$\text{DFL} = \frac{\text{Percentage change in net income}}{\text{Percentage change in operating income}} \quad (3)$$

For example, if DFL at a given level of operating income is 1.1, a 5 percent increase in operating income would be expected to result in a (1.1)(5%) = 5.5 percent increase in net income. A company's DFL is dependent on the level of operating income being considered.

Net income is equal to operating income, less interest and taxes.[5] If operating income changes, how does net income change? Consider Impulse Robotics. Suppose the interest payments are $100,000 and, for simplicity, the tax rate is 0 percent: If operating income changes from $300,000 to $360,000, net income changes from $200,000 to $260,000:

Exhibit 9 Financial Risk of Impulse Robotics (1)

	Operating Income of $300,000	Operating Income of $360,000	Percentage Change
Operating income	$300,000	$360,000	+20
Less interest	100,000	100,000	0
Net income	$200,000	$260,000	+30

A 20 percent increase in operating income increases net income by $60,000, or 30 percent. What if the fixed financial costs are $150,000? A 20 percent change in operating income results in a 40 percent change in the net income, from $150,000 to $210,000:

5 More complex entities than we have been using for our examples may also need to account for other income (losses) and extraordinary income (losses) together with operating income as the basis for earnings before interest and taxes.

Exhibit 10 Financial Risk of Impulse Robotics (2)

	Operating Income of $300,000	Operating Income of $360,000	Percentage Change
Operating income	$300,000	$360,000	+20
Less interest	150,000	150,000	0
Net income	$150,000	$210,000	+40

Using more debt financing, which results in higher fixed costs, increases the sensitivity of net income to changes in operating income. We can represent the sensitivity of net income to a change in operating income, continuing the notation from before and including the fixed financial cost, C, and the tax rate, t, as

$$\text{DFL} = \frac{\left[Q(P-V)-F\right](1-t)}{\left[Q(P-V)-F-C\right](1-t)} = \frac{\left[Q(P-V)-F\right]}{\left[Q(P-V)-F-C\right]} \tag{4}$$

As you can see in Equation 4, the factor that adjusts for taxes, $(1 - t)$, cancels out of the equation. In other words, the DFL is not affected by the tax rate.

In the case in which operating income is $300,000 and fixed financing costs are $100,000, the degree of financial leverage is

$$\begin{array}{c}\text{DFL @}\\ \text{\$300,000 operating income}\end{array} = \frac{\$300{,}000}{\$300{,}000 - \$100{,}000} = 1.5$$

If, instead, fixed financial costs are $150,000, the DFL is equal to 2.0:

$$\begin{array}{c}\text{DFL @}\\ \text{\$300,000 operating income}\end{array} = \frac{\$300{,}000}{\$300{,}000 - \$150{,}000} = 2.0$$

Again, we need to qualify our degree of leverage by the level of operating income because DFL is different at different levels of operating income.

The greater the use of financing sources that require fixed obligations, such as interest, the greater the sensitivity of net income to changes in operating income.

EXAMPLE 2

Calculating the Degree of Financial Leverage

Global Auto also employs debt financing. If Global can borrow at 8 percent, the interest cost is €18 billion. What is the degree of financial leverage of Global Auto if 6 million cars are produced and sold?

Solution:

At 6 million cars produced and sold, operating income = €30 billion. Therefore:

$$\begin{array}{c}\text{DFL @}\\ \text{€30 billion operating income}\end{array} = \frac{\text{€30 billion}}{\text{€30 billion} - \text{€18 billion}} = 2.5$$

For every 1 percent change in operating income, net income changes 2.5 percent due to financial leverage.

Unlike operating leverage, the degree of financial leverage is most often a choice by the company's management. Whereas operating costs are very similar among companies in the same industry, competitors may decide on differing capital structures.

Companies with relatively high ratios of tangible assets to total assets may be able to use higher degrees of financial leverage than companies with relatively low ratios because the claim on the tangible assets that lenders would have in the event of a default may make lenders more confident in extending larger amounts of credit. In general, businesses with plants, land, and equipment that can be used to collateralize borrowings and businesses whose revenues have below-average business cycle sensitivity may be able to use more financial leverage than businesses without such assets and with relatively high business cycle sensitivity.

Using financial leverage generally increases the variability of return on equity (net income divided by shareholders' equity). In addition, its use by a profitable company may increase the level of return on equity. Example 3 illustrates both effects.

EXAMPLE 3

The Leveraging Role of Debt

Consider the Capital Company, which is expected to generate $1,500,000 in revenues and $500,000 in operating earnings next year. Currently, the Capital Company does not use debt financing and has assets of $2,000,000.

Suppose Capital were to change its capital structure, buying back $1,000,000 of stock and issuing $1,000,000 in debt. If we assume that interest on debt is 5 percent and income is taxed at a rate of 30 percent, what is the effect of debt financing on Capital's net income and return on equity if operating earnings may vary as much as 40 percent from expected earnings?

Exhibit 11 Return on Equity of Capital Company

No Debt (Shareholders' Equity = $2 million)	Expected Operating Earnings, Less 40%	Expected Operating Earnings	Expected Operating Earnings, Plus 40%
Earnings before interest and taxes	$300,000	$500,000	$700,000
Interest expense	0	0	0
Earnings before taxes	$300,000	$500,000	$700,000
Taxes	90,000	150,000	210,000
Net income	$210,000	$350,000	$490,000
Return on equity[1]	10.5%	17.5%	24.5%

Debt to Total Assets = 50%; (Shareholders' Equity = $1 million)	Expected Operating Earnings, Less 40%	Expected Operating Earnings	Expected Operating Earnings, Plus 40%
Earnings before interest and taxes	$300,000	$500,000	$700,000
Interest expense	50,000	50,000	50,000
Earnings before taxes	$250,000	$450,000	$650,000
Taxes	75,000	135,000	195,000

(continued)

Exhibit 11 (Continued)

Debt to Total Assets = 50%; (Shareholders' Equity = $1 million)	Expected Operating Earnings, Less 40%	Expected Operating Earnings	Expected Operating Earnings, Plus 40%
Net income	$175,000	$315,000	$455,000
Return on equity	17.5%	31.5%	45.5%

[1] Recall that ROE is calculated as net income/shareholders' equity.

Depicting a broader array of capital structures and operating earnings, ranging from an operating loss of $500,000 to operating earnings of $2,000,000, Exhibit 12 shows the effect of leverage on the return on equity for Capital Company:

Exhibit 12 Return on Equity of Capital Company for Different Levels of Operating Earnings and Different Financing Choices

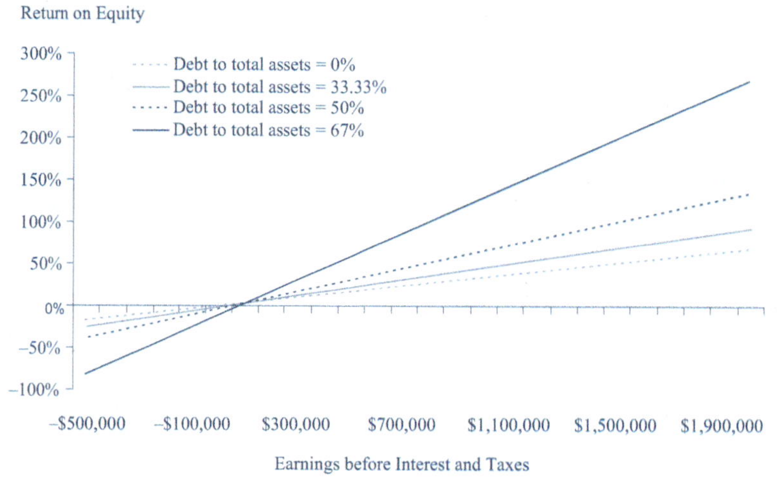

Business is generally an uncertain venture. Changes in the macroeconomic and competitive environments that influence sales and profitability are typically difficult to discern and forecast. The larger the proportion of debt in the financing mix of a business, the greater is the chance that it will face default. Similarly, the greater the proportion of debt in the capital structure, the more earnings are magnified upward in improving economic times. The bottom line? Financial leverage tends to increase the risk of ownership for shareholders.

3.5 Total Leverage

The degree of operating leverage gives us an idea of the sensitivity of operating income to changes in revenues. And the degree of financial leverage gives us an idea of the sensitivity of net income to changes in operating income. But often we are concerned about the combined effect of both operating leverage and financial leverage. Owners are concerned about the combined effect because both factors contribute to the risk associated with their future cash flows. And financial managers, making decisions intended to maximize owners' wealth, need to be concerned with how investment decisions (which affect the operating cost structure) and financing decisions (which affect the capital structure) affect lenders' and owners' risk.

Look back at the example of Impulse Robotics. The sensitivity of owners' cash flow to a given change in units sold is affected by both operating and financial leverage. Consider using 100,000 units as the base number produced and sold. A 10 percent increase in units sold results in a 27 percent increase in operating income and a 40 percent increase in net income; a like decrease in units sold results in a similar decrease in operating income and net income.

Exhibit 13 Total Leverage of Impulse Robotics

	Units Produced and Sold:		
	90,000	**100,000**	**110,000**
Revenues	$900,000	$1,000,000	$1,100,000
Less variable costs	180,000	200,000	220,000
Less fixed costs	500,000	500,000	500,000
Operating income	$220,000	$300,000	$380,000
Less interest	100,000	100,000	100,000
Net income	$120,000	$200,000	$280,000
Relative to 100,000 units produced and sold			
Percentage change in units sold	−10%		+10%
Percentage change in operating profit	−27%		+27%
Percentage change in net income	−40%		+40%

Combining a company's degree of operating leverage with its degree of financial leverage results in the **degree of total leverage** (DTL), a measure of the sensitivity of net income to changes in the number of units produced and sold. We again make the simplifying assumption that a company sells all that it produces in the same period:

$$\text{DTL} = \frac{\text{Percentage change in net income}}{\text{Percentage change in the number of units sold}} \tag{5}$$

or

$$\begin{aligned}\text{DTL} &= \underbrace{\frac{Q(P-V)}{Q(P-V)-F}}_{\text{DOL}} \times \underbrace{\frac{[Q(P-V)-F]}{[Q(P-V)-F-C]}}_{\text{DFL}} \\ &= \frac{Q(P-V)}{Q(P-V)-F-C}\end{aligned} \tag{6}$$

Suppose

Number of units sold	=	Q	=	100,000
Price per unit	=	P	=	$10
Variable cost per unit	=	V	=	$2
Fixed operating cost	=	F	=	$500,000
Fixed financing cost	=	C	=	$100,000

Then,

$$\text{DTL} = \frac{100{,}000(\$10 - \$2)}{100{,}000(\$10 - \$2) - \$500{,}000 - \$100{,}000} = 4.0$$

which we could also have determined by multiplying the DOL, 2.67, by the DFL, 1.5. This means that a 1 percent increase in units sold will result in a 4 percent increase in net income; a 50 percent increase in units produced and sold results in a 200 percent increase in net income; a 5 percent decline in units sold results in a 20 percent decline in income to owners; and so on.

Because the DOL is relative to the base number of units produced and sold and the DFL is relative to the base level of operating earnings, DTL is different depending on the number of units produced and sold. We can see the DOL, DFL, and DTL for Impulse Robotics for different numbers of units produced and sold, beginning at the number of units for which the degrees are positive, in Exhibit 14.

Exhibit 14 DOL, DFL, and DTL for Different Numbers of Units Produced and Sold

P = \$10, V = \$2, F = \$500,000, C = \$100,000

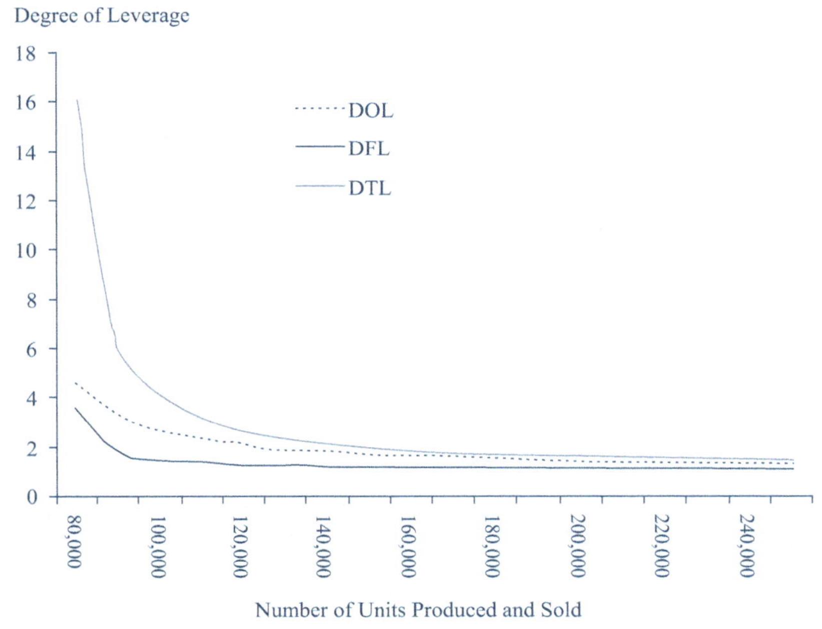

In the case of operating leverage, the fixed operating costs act as a fulcrum. The greater the proportion of operating costs that are fixed, the more sensitive operating income is to changes in sales. In the case of financial leverage, the fixed financial costs, such as interest, act as a fulcrum. The greater the proportion of financing with fixed cost sources, such as debt, the more sensitive cash flows available to owners are to changes in operating income. Combining the effects of both types of leverage, we see that fixed operating and financial costs together increase the sensitivity of earnings to owners.

EXAMPLE 4

Calculating the Degree of Total Leverage

Continuing from Examples 1 and 2, Global Auto's total leverage is

$$\begin{matrix}\text{DTL @} \\ \text{6 million units}\end{matrix} = \begin{matrix}\text{DOL @} \\ \text{6 million units}\end{matrix} \times \begin{matrix}\text{DFL @} \\ \text{€30 billion}\end{matrix}$$

$$\begin{matrix}\text{DTL @} \\ \text{6 million units}\end{matrix} = \frac{\text{6 million}(\text{€}28{,}000 - \text{€}20{,}500)}{\left[\text{6 million}(\text{€}28{,}000 - \text{€}20{,}500) - \text{€15 billion}\right] - \text{€18 billion}}$$

$$= \frac{\text{€45 billion}}{\text{€12 billion}} = 3.75$$

$$\begin{matrix}\text{DTL @} \\ \text{6 million units}\end{matrix} = 1.5 \times 2.5 = 3.75$$

Given Global Auto's operating and financial leverage, a 1 percent change in unit sales changes net income by 3.75 percent.

3.6 Breakeven Points and Operating Breakeven Points

Looking back at Exhibit 3, we see that there is a number of units at which the company goes from being unprofitable to being profitable—that is, the number of units at which the net income is zero. This number is referred to as the breakeven point. The **breakeven point**, Q_{BE}, is the number of units produced and sold at which the company's net income is zero—the point at which revenues are equal to costs.

Plotting revenues and total costs against the number of units produced and sold, as in Exhibit 15, indicates that the breakeven is at 75,000 units. At this number of units produced and sold, revenues are equal to costs and, hence, profit is zero.

Exhibit 15 Impulse Robotics Breakeven

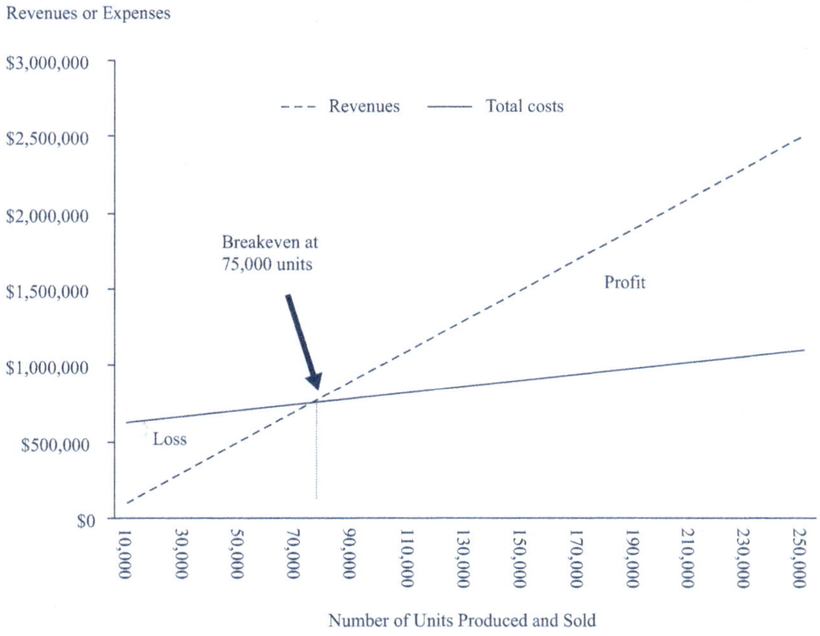

We can calculate this breakeven point for Impulse Robotics and Malvey Aerospace. Consider that net income is zero when the revenues are equal to the expenses. We can represent this equality of revenues and costs (summing variable operating costs, fixed operating costs, and fixed financing costs) by the following equation:

$$PQ = VQ + F + C$$

where

P = the price per unit
Q = the number of units produced and sold
V = the variable cost per unit
F = the fixed operating costs
C = the fixed financial cost

Therefore,

$$PQ_{BE} = VQ_{BE} + F + C$$

and the breakeven number of units, Q_{BE}, is[6]

$$Q_{BE} = \frac{F + C}{P - V} \tag{7}$$

In the case of Impulse Robotics and Malvey Aerospace, Impulse Robotics has a higher breakeven point. Using numbers taken from Exhibit 2:

$$\text{Impulse Robotics: } Q_{BE} = \frac{\$500{,}000 + \$100{,}000}{\$10 - \$2} = 75{,}000 \text{ units}$$

$$\text{Malvey Aerospace: } Q_{BE} = \frac{\$150{,}000 + \$50{,}000}{\$10 - \$6} = 50{,}000 \text{ units}$$

This means that Impulse Robotics must produce and sell more units to achieve a profit. So, while the higher-leveraged Impulse Robotics has a greater breakeven point relative to Malvey Aerospace, the profit that Impulse Robotics generates beyond this breakeven point is greater than that of Malvey Aerospace. Therefore, leverage has its rewards in terms of potentially greater profit, but it also increases risk.

In addition to the breakeven point specified in terms of net income, Q_{BE}, we can also specify the breakeven point in terms of operating profit, which we refer to as the **operating breakeven** point, Q_{OBE}. Revenues at the operating breakeven point are set equal to operating costs at the operating breakeven point to solve for the operating breakeven number of units, Q_{OBE}. The expression shows Q_{OBE} as equal to fixed operating costs divided by the difference between price per unit and variable cost per unit:

$$PQ_{OBE} = VQ_{OBE} + F$$

$$Q_{OBE} = \frac{F}{P - V}$$

For the two companies in our example, Impulse Robotics and Malvey Aerospace, the operating breakevens are 62,500 and 37,500 units, respectively:

$$\text{Impulse Robotics: } Q_{OBE} = \frac{\$500{,}000}{\$10 - \$2} = 62{,}500 \text{ units}$$

$$\text{Malvey Aerospace: } Q_{OBE} = \frac{\$150{,}000}{\$10 - \$6} = 37{,}500 \text{ units}$$

Impulse Robotics has a higher operating breakeven point in terms of the number of units produced and sold.

6 You will notice that we did not consider taxes in our calculation of the breakeven point. This is because at the point of breakeven, taxable income is zero.

EXAMPLE 5

Calculating Operating Breakeven and Breakeven Points

Continuing with his analysis, Kenigswald considers the effect of a possible downturn on Global Auto's earnings. He divides the fixed operating costs of €15 billion by the per unit contribution margin:

$$Q_{OBE} = \frac{€15\text{ billion}}{€28{,}000 - €20{,}500} = 2\text{ million cars}$$

The operating breakeven for Global is 2,000,000 cars, or €56 billion in revenues. We calculate the breakeven point by dividing fixed operating costs, plus interest costs, by the contribution margin:

$$Q_{BE} = \frac{€15\text{ billion} + €18\text{ billion}}{€28{,}000 - €20{,}500} = 4{,}400{,}000$$

Considering the degree of total leverage, Global's breakeven is 4.4 million cars, or revenues of €123.2 billion.

We can verify these calculations by constructing an income statement for the breakeven sales (in € billions):

	2,000,000 Cars	4,400,000 Cars
Revenues (= $P \times Q$)	€56.0	€123.2
Variable operating costs (= $V \times Q$)	41.0	90.2
Fixed operating costs (F)	15.0	15.0
Operating income	**€0**	€18.0
Fixed financial costs (C)	18.0	18.0
Net income	–€18.0	**€0**

As business expands or contracts beyond or below breakeven points, fixed costs do not change. The breakeven points for companies with low operating and financial leverage are less important than those for companies with high leverage. Companies with greater total leverage must generate more revenue to cover fixed operating and financing costs. The farther unit sales are from the breakeven point for high-leverage companies, the greater the magnifying effect of this leverage.

3.7 The Risks of Creditors and Owners

As we discussed earlier, business risk refers to the effect of economic conditions as well as the level of operating leverage. Uncertainty about demand, output prices, and costs are among the many factors that affect business risk. When conditions change for any of these factors, companies with higher business risk experience more volatile earnings. Financial risk is the additional risk that results from the use of debt and preferred stock. The degree of financial risk grows with greater use of debt. Who bears this risk?

The risk for providers of equity and debt capital differs because of the relative rights and responsibilities associated with the use of borrowed money in a business. Lenders have a prior claim on assets relative to shareholders, so they have greater security. In return for lending money to a business, lenders require the payment of interest and principal when due. These contractual payments to lenders must be made regardless of the profitability of the business. A business must satisfy these claims in a timely fashion or face the pain of bankruptcy should it default. In return for their higher priority in claims, lenders get predefined yet limited returns.

In contrast, equity providers claim whatever is left over after all expenses, including debt service, have been paid. So, unlike the fixed and known commitments to the lenders, what is left over for the owners may be a great deal or may be nothing. In exchange for this risk, providers of equity capital exercise the decision-making power over the business, including the right to hire, guide, and if necessary, fire managers. In public companies, ownership rights are usually exercised through an elected board of directors. They undertake the decisions over what portion of the business's earnings should be paid out as dividends for common shareholders.

Legal codes in most countries provide for these rights, as well as conditions for companies to file for bankruptcy (with reference to businesses, often called insolvency). A number of bankruptcy codes provide in some form for two categories of bankruptcies. One form provides for a temporary protection from creditors so that a viable business may reorganize. In the United States, the US Bankruptcy Code sets the terms for the form of negotiated **reorganization** of a company's capital structure that allows it to remain a going concern in Chapter 11.[7] For businesses that are not viable, the second form of bankruptcy process allows for the orderly satisfaction of the creditors' claims. In the United States, this form of bankruptcy is referred to as **liquidation**.[8] Whereas both types of bankruptcy lead to major dislocations in the rights and privileges of owners, lenders, employees, and managers, it is in this latter category of bankruptcy that the original business ceases to exist.

The difference between a company that reorganizes and emerges from bankruptcy and one that is liquidated is often the difference between operating and financial leverage. Companies with high operating leverage have less flexibility in making changes, and bankruptcy protection does little to help reduce operating costs. Companies with high financial leverage use bankruptcy laws and protection to change their capital structure and, once the restructuring is complete, can emerge as ongoing concerns.

EXAMPLE 6

Dow Corning: In and Out of Chapter 11 Bankruptcy

Dow Corning, a leading silicone producer, was a joint venture of Dow Chemical and Corning Inc. Dow Chemical filed for bankruptcy protection using Chapter 11 in 1995 as a result of the lawsuits related to silicone implants. The company was profitable at the time of filing, with more than $500 million in net income in 1994, but the potential liability from lawsuits, initially estimated around $2 billion, was significant when compared to its $4 billion in total assets. In 2004, Dow Corning emerged from bankruptcy, and in 2016 Dow Chemical completed the acquisition of 100 percent of Dow Corning, which currently operates as a wholly owned subsidiary of Dow Chemical Company.

7 US Code, Title 11—Bankruptcy, Chapter 11—Reorganization. Companies filing for bankruptcy under this code are referred to as having filed for Chapter 11 bankruptcy.
8 US Code, Title 11—Bankruptcy, Chapter 7—Liquidation.

EXAMPLE 7

Retailers Do Not Deliver

Traditional brick-and-mortar retail stores have been challenged with competition from online retailers. Whereas some retailers successfully added online access, others have struggled to compete effectively. A number of US retail stores filed for bankruptcy protection in 2017 and 2018, including Radio Shack, Nine West, Toys R Us, Brookstone, Payless, and hhgregg. Though some of these retailers were "reborn" online (e.g., hhgregg.com), others liquidated (e.g., Toys R Us), and many are closing stores and working closely with creditors to stave off liquidation.

Whereas the ability to file for bankruptcy is important to the economy, the goal of most investors is to avoid ownership of companies that are heading toward this extreme step, as well as to be able to evaluate opportunities among companies already in bankruptcy. Under both Chapter 7 and Chapter 11, providers of equity capital generally lose all value during the bankruptcy. On the other hand, debtholders typically receive at least a portion of their capital, but the payments of principal and interest are delayed during the period of bankruptcy protection.

SUMMARY

In this reading, we have reviewed the fundamentals of business risk, financial risk, and measures of leverage.

- Leverage is the use of fixed costs in a company's cost structure. Business risk is the risk associated with operating earnings and reflects both sales risk (uncertainty with respect to the price and quantity of sales) and operating risk (the risk related to the use of fixed costs in operations). Financial risk is the risk associated with how a company finances its operations (i.e., the split between equity and debt financing of the business).
- The degree of operating leverage (DOL) is the ratio of the percentage change in operating income to the percentage change in units sold. We can use the following formula to measure the degree of operating leverage:

$$\text{DOL} = \frac{Q(P-V)}{Q(P-V)-F}$$

- The degree of financial leverage (DFL) is the percentage change in net income for a one percent change in operating income. We can use the following formula to measure the degree of financial leverage:

$$\text{DFL} = \frac{\left[Q(P-V)-F\right](1-t)}{\left[Q(P-V)-F-C\right](1-t)} = \frac{\left[Q(P-V)-F\right]}{\left[Q(P-V)-F-C\right]}$$

- The degree of total leverage (DTL) is a measure of the sensitivity of net income to changes in unit sales, which is equivalent to DTL = DOL × DFL.
- The breakeven point, Q_{BE}, is the number of units produced and sold at which the company's net income is zero, which we calculate as

$$Q_{\text{BE}} = \frac{F+C}{P-V}$$

- The operating breakeven point, Q_{OBE}, is the number of units produced and sold at which the company's operating income is zero, which we calculate as

$$Q_{OBE} = \frac{F}{P - V}$$

PRACTICE PROBLEMS

1 If two companies have identical unit sales volume and operating risk, they are *most likely* to also have identical:

A sales risk.

B business risk.

C sensitivity of operating earnings to changes in the number of units produced and sold.

2 Degree of operating leverage is *best* described as a measure of the sensitivity of:

A net earnings to changes in sales.

B fixed operating costs to changes in variable costs.

C operating earnings to changes in the number of units produced and sold.

3 The Fulcrum Company produces decorative swivel platforms for home televisions. If Fulcrum produces 40 million units, it estimates that it can sell them for $100 each. Variable production costs are $65 per unit and fixed production costs are $1.05 billion. Which of the following statements is *most accurate*? Holding all else constant, the Fulcrum Company would:

A generate positive operating income if unit sales were 25 million.

B have less operating leverage if fixed production costs were 10 percent greater than $1.05 billion.

C generate 20 percent more operating income if unit sales were 5 percent greater than 40 million.

4 The business risk of a particular company is *most accurately* measured by the company's:

A debt-to-equity ratio.

B efficiency in using assets to generate sales.

C operating leverage and level of uncertainty about demand, output prices, and competition.

5 Consider two companies that operate in the same line of business and have the same degree of operating leverage: the Basic Company and the Grundlegend Company. The Basic Company and the Grundlegend Company have, respectively, no debt and 50 percent debt in their capital structure. Which of the following statements is *most accurate*? Compared to the Basic Company, the Grundlegend Company has:

A a lower sensitivity of net income to changes in unit sales.

B the same sensitivity of operating income to changes in unit sales.

C the same sensitivity of net income to changes in operating income.

6 Myundia Motors now sells 1 million units at ¥3,529 per unit. Fixed operating costs are ¥1,290 million and variable operating costs are ¥1,500 per unit. If the company pays ¥410 million in interest, the levels of sales at the operating breakeven and breakeven points are, respectively:

A ¥1,500,000,000 and ¥2,257,612,900.

B ¥2,243,671,760 and ¥2,956,776,737.

C ¥2,975,148,800 and ¥3,529,000,000.

7 Juan Alavanca is evaluating the risk of two companies in the machinery industry: The Gearing Company and Hebelkraft, Inc. Alavanca used the latest fiscal year's financial statements and interviews with managers of the respective companies to gather the following information:

	The Gearing Company	Hebelkraft, Inc.
Number of units produced and sold	1 million	1.5 million
Sales price per unit	$200	$200
Variable cost per unit	$120	$100
Fixed operating cost	$40 million	$90 million
Fixed financing expense	$20 million	$20 million

Based on this information, the breakeven points for The Gearing Company and Hebelkraft, Inc. are:

A 0.75 million and 1.1 million units, respectively.

B 1 million and 1.5 million units, respectively.

C 1.5 million and 0.75 million units, respectively.

The following information relates to Questions 8–16

Mary Benn, CFA, is a financial analyst for Twin Fields Investments, located in Storrs, Connecticut, USA. She has been asked by her supervisor, Bill Cho, to examine two small Japanese cell phone component manufacturers: 4G, Inc. and Qphone Corp. Cho indicates that his clients are most interested in the use of leverage by 4G and Qphone. Benn states, "I will have to specifically analyze each company's respective business risk, sales risk, operating risk, and financial risk." "Fine, I'll check back with you shortly," Cho, answers.

Benn begins her analysis by examining the sales prospects of the two firms. The results of her sales analysis appear in Exhibit 1. She also expects very little price variability for these cell phones. She next gathers more data on these two companies to assist her analysis of their operating and financial risk.

When Cho inquires as to her progress Benn responds, "I have calculated Qphone's degree of operating leverage (DOL) and degree of financial leverage (DFL) at Qphone's 2009 level of unit sales. I have also calculated Qphone's breakeven level for unit sales. I will have 4G's leverage results shortly."

Cho responds, "Good, I will call a meeting of some potential investors for tomorrow. Please help me explain these concepts to them, and the differences in use of leverage by these two companies. In preparation for the meeting, I have a number of questions":

- "You mentioned business risk; what is included in that?"
- "How would you classify the risk due to the varying mix of variable and fixed costs?"
- "Could you conduct an analysis and tell me how the two companies will fare relative to each other in terms of net income if their unit sales increased by 10 percent above their 2009 unit sales levels?"
- "Finally, what would be an accurate verbal description of the degree of total leverage?"

The relevant data for analysis of 4G is contained in Exhibit 2, and Benn's analysis of the Qphone data appears in Exhibit 3:

Exhibit 1 Benn's Unit Sales Estimates for 4G, Inc. and Qphone Corp.

Company	2009 Unit Sales	Standard Deviation of Unit Sales	2010 Expected Unit Sales Growth Rate (%)
4G, Inc.	1,000,000	25,000	15
Qphone Corp.	1,500,000	10,000	15

Exhibit 2 Sales, Cost, and Expense Data for 4G, Inc. (At Unit Sales of 1,000,000)

Number of units produced and sold	1,000,000
Sales price per unit	¥108
Variable cost per unit	¥72
Fixed operating cost	¥22,500,000
Fixed financing expense	¥9,000,000

Exhibit 3 Benn's Analysis of Qphone (At Unit Sales of 1,500,000)

Degree of operating leverage	1.40
Degree of financial leverage	1.15
Breakeven quantity (units)	571,429

8 Based on Benn's analysis, 4G's sales risk relative to Qphone's is *most likely* to be:

A lower.

B equal.

C higher.

9 What is the *most appropriate* response to Cho's question regarding the components of business risk?

A Sales risk and financial risk.

B Operating risk and sales risk.

C Financial risk and operating risk.

10 The *most appropriate* response to Cho's question regarding the classification of risk arising from the mixture of variable and fixed costs is:

A sales risk.

B financial risk.

C operating risk.

11 Based on the information in Exhibit 2, the degree of operating leverage (DOL) of 4G, Inc., at unit sales of 1,000,000, is *closest* to:

A 1.60.

B 2.67.

C 3.20.

12 Based on the information in Exhibit 2, 4G, Inc.'s degree of financial leverage (DFL), at unit sales of 1,000,000, is *closest* to:

A 1.33.

B 2.67.

C 3.00.

13 Based on the information in Exhibit 1 and Exhibit 3, Qphone's expected percentage change in operating income for 2010 is *closest* to:

A 17.25%.

B 21.00%.

C 24.30%.

14 4G's breakeven quantity of unit sales is *closest* to:

A 437,500 units.

B 625,000 units.

C 875,000 units.

15 In response to Cho's question regarding an increase in unit sales above 2009 unit sales levels, it is *most likely* that 4G's net income will increase at:

A a slower rate than Qphone's.

B the same rate as Qphone's.

C a faster rate than Qphone's.

16 The *most appropriate* response to Cho's question regarding a description of the degree of total leverage is that degree of total leverage is:

A the percentage change in net income divided by the percentage change in units sold.

B the percentage change in operating income divided by the percentage change in units sold.

C the percentage change in net income divided by the percentage change in operating income.

SOLUTIONS

1 C is correct. The companies' degree of operating leverage should be the same, consistent with C. Sales risk refers to the uncertainty of the number of units produced and sold and the price at which units are sold. Business risk is the joint effect of sales risk and operating risk.

2 C is correct. The degree of operating leverage is the elasticity of operating earnings with respect to the number of units produced and sold. As an elasticity, the degree of operating leverage measures the sensitivity of operating earnings to a change in the number of units produced and sold.

3 C is correct. Because DOL is 4, if unit sales increase by 5 percent, Fulcrum's operating earnings are expected to increase by 4 × 5% = 20%. The calculation for DOL is:

$$\text{DOL} = \frac{(40\text{ million})(\$100 - \$65)}{\left[(40\text{ million})(\$100 - \$65)\right] - \$1.05\text{ billion}}$$

$$= \frac{\$1.400\text{ billion}}{\$1.400\text{ billion} - \$1.05\text{ billion}} = \frac{\$1.4}{\$0.35} = 4$$

4 C is correct. Business risk reflects operating leverage and factors that affect sales (such as those given).

5 B is correct. Grundlegend's degree of operating leverage is the same as Basic Company's, whereas Grundlegend's degree of total leverage and degree of financial leverage are higher.

6 B is correct.

$$\text{Operating breakeven units} = \frac{¥1{,}290\text{ million}}{(¥3{,}529 - ¥1{,}500)} = 635{,}781.173\text{ units}$$

$$\text{Operating breakeven sales} = ¥3{,}529 \times 635{,}781.173\text{ units} = ¥2{,}243{,}671{,}760$$

or

$$\text{Operating breakeven sales} = \frac{¥1{,}290\text{ million}}{1 - (¥1{,}500/¥3{,}529)} = ¥2{,}243{,}671{,}760$$

$$\text{Total breakeven} = \frac{¥1{,}290\text{ million} + ¥410\text{ million}}{(¥3{,}529 - ¥1{,}500)} = \frac{¥1{,}700\text{ million}}{¥2{,}029}$$

$$= 837{,}851.1582\text{ units}$$

$$\text{Breakeven sales} = ¥3{,}529 \times 837{,}851.1582\text{ units} = ¥2{,}956{,}776{,}737$$

or

$$\text{Breakeven sales} = \frac{¥1{,}700\text{ million}}{1 - (¥1{,}500/¥3{,}529)} = ¥2{,}956{,}776{,}737$$

7 A is correct. For The Gearing Company,

$$Q_{\text{BE}} = \frac{F + C}{P - V} = \frac{\$40\text{ million} + \$20\text{ million}}{\$200 - \$120} = 750{,}000$$

For Hebelkraft, Inc.,

$$Q_{\text{BE}} = \frac{F + C}{P - V} = \frac{\$90\text{ million} + \$20\text{ million}}{\$200 - \$100} = 1{,}100{,}000$$

8 C is correct. Sales risk is defined as uncertainty with respect to the price or quantity of goods and services sold. 4G has a higher standard deviation of unit sales than Qphone; in addition, 4G's standard deviation of unit sales stated as a fraction of its level of unit sales, at 25,000/1,000,000 = 0.025, is greater than the comparable ratio for Qphone, 10,000/1,500,000 = 0.0067.

9 B is correct. Business risk is associated with operating earnings. Operating earnings are affected by sales risk (uncertainty with respect to price and quantity), and operating risk (the operating cost structure and the level of fixed costs).

10 C is correct. Operating risk refers to the risk arising from the mix of fixed and variable costs.

11 B is correct. $\text{DOL} = \dfrac{Q(P - V)}{Q(P - V) - F}$

$$\begin{array}{c}\text{DOL @}\\ \text{1,000,000 units}\end{array} = \frac{1{,}000{,}000(¥108 - ¥72)}{1{,}000{,}000(¥108 - ¥72) - ¥22{,}500{,}000} = 2.67$$

12 C is correct. Degree of financial leverage is

$$\text{DFL} = \frac{\left[Q(P - V) - F\right]}{\left[Q(P - V) - F - C\right]}$$

$$= \frac{1{,}000{,}000(¥108 - ¥72) - ¥22{,}500{,}000}{1{,}000{,}000(¥108 - ¥72) - ¥22{,}500{,}000 - ¥9{,}000{,}000} = 3.00$$

13 B is correct. The degree of operating leverage of Qphone is 1.4. The percentage change in operating income is equal to the DOL times the percentage change in units sold, therefore:

$$\begin{array}{c}\text{Percentage change}\\ \text{in operating income}\end{array} = (\text{DOL})\begin{pmatrix}\text{Percentage change}\\ \text{in units sold}\end{pmatrix} = (1.4)(15\%) = 21\%$$

14 C is correct. The breakeven quantity is computed

$$Q_{\text{BE}} = \frac{F + C}{P - V} = \frac{(¥22{,}500{,}000 + ¥9{,}000{,}000)}{(¥108 - ¥72)} = 875{,}000$$

15 C is correct. 4G, Inc.'s degree of total leverage can be shown to equal 8, whereas Qphone Corp.'s degree of total leverage is only DOL × DFL = 1.4 × 1.15 = 1.61. Therefore, a 10 percent increase in unit sales will mean an 80 percent increase in net income for 4G, but only a 16.1 percent increase in net income for Qphone Corp. The calculation for 4G, Inc.'s DTL is

$$\text{DTL} = \frac{Q(P - V)}{Q(P - V) - F - C}$$

$$= \frac{1{,}000{,}000(¥108 - ¥72)}{1{,}000{,}000(¥108 - ¥72) - ¥22{,}500{,}000 - ¥9{,}000{,}000} = 8.00$$

16 A is correct. Degree of total leverage is defined as the percentage change in net income divided by the percentage change in units sold.

READING

35

Working Capital Management

by Edgar A. Norton, Jr., PhD, CFA, Kenneth L. Parkinson, MBA, CCM, and Pamela Peterson Drake, PhD, CFA

Edgar A. Norton, Jr., PhD, CFA, is at Illinois State University (USA). Kenneth L. Parkinson, MBA, CCM, is at Treasury Information Services, LLC (USA). Pamela Peterson Drake, PhD, CFA, is at James Madison University (USA).

LEARNING OUTCOMES

Mastery	*The candidate should be able to:*
☐	a. describe primary and secondary sources of liquidity and factors that influence a company's liquidity position;
☐	b. compare a company's liquidity measures with those of peer companies;
☐	c. evaluate working capital effectiveness of a company based on its operating and cash conversion cycles and compare the company's effectiveness with that of peer companies;
☐	d. describe how different types of cash flows affect a company's net daily cash position;
☐	e. calculate and interpret comparable yields on various securities, compare portfolio returns against a standard benchmark, and evaluate a company's short-term investment policy guidelines;
☐	f. evaluate a company's management of accounts receivable, inventory, and accounts payable over time and compared to peer companies;
☐	g. evaluate the choices of short-term funding available to a company and recommend a financing method.

INTRODUCTION

1

The focus of this reading is on the short-term aspects of corporate finance activities collectively referred to as **working capital management**. The goal of effective working capital management is to ensure that a company has adequate ready access to the funds necessary for day-to-day operating expenses, while at the same time making sure that the company's assets are invested in the most productive way. Achieving this goal requires a balancing of concerns. Insufficient access to cash could ultimately lead to severe restructuring of a company by selling off assets, reorganization via bankruptcy proceedings, or final liquidation of the company. On the other hand, excessive investment in cash and liquid assets may not be the best use of company resources.

Effective working capital management encompasses several aspects of short-term finance: maintaining adequate levels of cash, converting short-term assets (i.e., accounts receivable and inventory) into cash, and controlling outgoing payments to vendors, employees, and others. To do this successfully, companies invest short-term funds in working capital portfolios of short-dated, highly liquid securities, or they maintain credit reserves in the form of bank lines of credit or access to financing by issuing commercial paper or other money market instruments.

Working capital management is a broad-based function. Effective execution requires managing and coordinating several tasks within the company, including managing short-term investments, granting credit to customers and collecting on this credit, managing inventory, and managing payables. Effective working capital management also requires reliable cash forecasts, as well as current and accurate information on transactions and bank balances.

Both internal and external factors influence working capital needs; we summarize them in Exhibit 1.

Exhibit 1 Internal and External Factors That Affect Working Capital Needs

Internal Factors	External Factors
■ Company size and growth rates	■ Banking services
■ Organizational structure	■ Interest rates
■ Sophistication of working capital management	■ New technologies and new products
■ Borrowing and investing positions/activities/capacities	■ The economy
	■ Competitors

The scope of working capital management includes transactions, relations, analyses, and focus:

- Transactions include payments for trade, financing, and investment.
- Relations with financial institutions and trading partners must be maintained to ensure that the transactions work effectively.
- Analyses of working capital management activities are required so that appropriate strategies can be formulated and implemented.
- Focus requires that organizations of all sizes today must have a global viewpoint with strong emphasis on liquidity.

In this reading, we examine the different types of working capital and the management issues associated with each. We also look at methods of evaluating the effectiveness of working capital management.

2 MANAGING AND MEASURING LIQUIDITY

Liquidity is the extent to which a company is able to meet its short-term obligations using assets that can be readily transformed into cash. When we evaluate the liquidity of an asset, we focus on two dimensions: the type of asset and the speed at which the asset can be converted to cash, either by sale or financing. Unlike many aspects of corporate finance, corporate liquidity management does not involve a great deal of theory or generally accepted principles. For companies that have the luxury of large excesses of cash, liquidity is typically taken for granted, and the focus is on putting the excess liquidity to its most productive use. On the other hand, when a company faces tighter financial situations, it is important to have effective liquidity management to ensure solvency. Unfortunately, this recognition comes too late for some companies, with bankruptcy and possible liquidation representing the company's final choice.

2.1 Defining Liquidity Management

Liquidity management refers to the ability of an organization to generate cash when and where it is needed. Liquidity refers to the resources available for an entity to tap into cash balances and to convert other assets or extend other liabilities into cash for use in keeping the entity solvent (i.e., being able to pay bills and continue in operation). For the most part, we associate liquidity with short-term assets and liabilities, yet longer-term assets can be converted into cash to provide liquidity. In addition, longer-term liabilities can also be renegotiated to reduce the drain on cash, thereby providing liquidity by preserving the limited supply of cash. Of course, the last two methods may come at a price as they tend to reduce the company's overall financial strength.

The challenges of managing liquidity include developing, implementing, and maintaining a liquidity policy. To do this effectively, a company must manage all of its key sources of liquidity efficiently. These key sources may vary from company to company, but they generally include the primary sources of liquidity, such as cash balances, and secondary sources of liquidity, such as selling assets.

2.1.1 *Primary Sources of Liquidity*

Primary sources of liquidity represent the most readily accessible resources available. They may be held as cash or as near-cash securities. Primary sources include:

- Ready cash balances, which is cash available in bank accounts, resulting from payment collections, investment income, liquidation of near-cash securities (i.e., those with maturities of less than 90 days), and other cash flows.
- Short-term funds, which may include items such as trade credit, bank lines of credit, and short-term investment portfolios.
- Cash flow management, which is the company's effectiveness in its cash management system and practices, and the degree of decentralization of the collections or payments processes. The more decentralized the system of collections, for example, the more likely the company will be to have cash tied up in the system and not available for use.

These sources represent liquidity that is typical for most companies. They represent funds that are readily accessible at relatively low cost.

2.1.2 *Secondary Sources of Liquidity*

The main difference between the primary and secondary sources of liquidity is that using a primary source is not likely to affect the normal operations of the company, whereas using a secondary source may result in a change in the company's financial and operating positions. Secondary sources include:

- negotiating debt contracts, relieving pressures from high interest payments or principal repayments;

- liquidating assets, which depends on the degree to which short-term and/or long-term assets can be liquidated and converted into cash without substantial loss in value; and
- filing for bankruptcy protection and reorganization.

Use of secondary sources may signal a company's deteriorating financial health and provide liquidity at a high price—the cost of giving up a company asset to produce emergency cash. The last source, reorganization through bankruptcy, may also be considered a liquidity tool because a company under bankruptcy protection that generates operating cash will be liquid and generally able to continue business operations until a restructuring has been devised and approved.

2.1.3 *Drags and Pulls on Liquidity*

Cash flow transactions—that is, cash receipts and disbursements—have significant effects on a company's liquidity position. We refer to these effects as drags and pulls on liquidity. A **drag on liquidity** is when receipts lag, creating pressure from the decreased available funds; a **pull on liquidity** is when disbursements are paid too quickly or trade credit availability is limited, requiring companies to expend funds before they receive funds from sales that could cover the liability.

Major drags on receipts involve pressures from credit management and deterioration in other assets and include:

- *Uncollected receivables.* The longer these are outstanding, the greater the risk that they will not be collected at all. They are indicated by the large number of days of receivables and high levels of bad debt expenses. Just as the drags on receipts may cause increased pressures on working capital, pulls on outgoing payments may have similar effects.
- *Obsolete inventory.* If inventory stands unused for long periods, it may be an indication that it is no longer usable. Slow inventory turnover ratios can also indicate obsolete inventory. Once identified, obsolete inventory should be attended to as soon as possible in order to minimize storage and other costs.
- *Tight credit.* When economic conditions make capital scarcer, short-term debt becomes more expensive to arrange and use. Attempting to smooth out peak borrowings can help blunt the impact of tight credit as can improving the company's collections.

In many cases, drags may be alleviated by stricter enforcement of credit and collection practices.[1]

However, managing the cash outflows may be as important as managing the inflows. If suppliers and other vendors who offer credit terms perceive a weakened financial position or are unfamiliar with a company, they may restrict payment terms so much that the company's liquidity reserves are stretched thin. Major pulls on payments include:

- *Making payments early.* By paying vendors, employees, or others before the due dates, companies forgo the use of funds. Effective payment management means not making early payments. Payables managers typically hold payments until they can be made by the due date.

1 In a survey of CFOs, companies have become more efficient in working capital management, with US companies in 2005 reducing their investment in working capital by 2.5 percent from 2004 levels and European companies reducing their investment by 3.3 percent (REL 2005 CFO Survey, www.relconsult.com).

- *Reduced credit limits.* If a company has a history of making late payments, suppliers may cut the amount of credit they will allow to be outstanding at any time, which can squeeze the company's liquidity. Some companies try to extend payment periods as long as possible, disregarding the possible impact of reduced credit limits.
- *Limits on short-term lines of credit.* If a company's bank reduces the line of credit it offers the company, a liquidity squeeze may result. Credit line restrictions may be government-mandated, market-related, or simply company-specific. Many companies try to avert this situation by establishing credit lines far in excess of what they are likely to need. This "over-banking" approach is often commonplace in emerging economies or even in more-developed countries where the banking system is not sound and the economy is shaky.
- *Low liquidity positions.* Many companies face chronic liquidity shortages, often because of their particular industry or from their weaker financial position. The major remedy for this situation is, of course, to improve the company's financial position, or else the company will be heavily affected by interest rates and credit availability. Most companies facing this situation have to deal with secured borrowing to obtain any working capital funds. Therefore, it is important for these companies to identify assets that can be used to help support the company's short-term borrowing activities.

It is critical that these drags and pulls be identified as soon as possible, often when they have not yet happened or have just arisen.

2.2 Measuring Liquidity

Liquidity contributes to a company's credit-worthiness. **Credit-worthiness** is the perceived ability of the borrower to pay what is owed on the borrowing in a timely manner and represents the ability of a company to withstand adverse impacts on its cash flows. Credit-worthiness allows the company to obtain lower borrowing costs and better terms for trade credit and contributes to the company's investment flexibility, enabling it to exploit profitable opportunities.

The less liquid the company, the greater the risk it will suffer financial distress or, in the extreme case, insolvency or bankruptcy. Because debt obligations are paid with cash, the company's cash flows ultimately determine solvency. The immediate source of funds for paying bills is cash on hand, proceeds from the sale of marketable securities, or the collection of accounts receivable. Additional liquidity also comes from inventory that can be sold and thus converted into cash either directly through cash sales or indirectly through credit sales (i.e., accounts receivable).

There is, however, some point at which a company may have too much invested in low- and non-earning assets. Cash, marketable securities, accounts receivable, and inventory represent a company's liquidity. However, these investments are low earning relative to the long-term, capital investment opportunities that companies may have available.

Various financial ratios can be used to assess a company's liquidity as well as its management of assets over time. Here we will look at some of these ratios in a little more detail.

We calculate **liquidity ratios** to measure a company's ability to meet short-term obligations to creditors as they mature or come due. This form of liquidity analysis focuses on the relationship between current assets and current liabilities and the rapidity with which receivables and inventory can be converted into cash during normal business operations.

In short-term financial management, a great deal of emphasis is placed on the levels of and changes in current assets and liabilities. The two most common measurements are the current ratio and the quick ratio. The **current ratio** is the ratio of current assets to current liabilities:

$$\text{Current ratio} = \frac{\text{Current assets}}{\text{Current liabilities}}$$

The **quick ratio** (also known as the **acid-test ratio**) is the ratio of the quick assets to current liabilities. **Quick assets** are those assets that can be most readily converted to cash. In most situations, the least liquid of the current assets is inventory. Hence, we typically exclude inventory when calculating the quick ratio:

$$\text{Quick ratio} = \frac{\text{Cash} + \text{Short-term marketable investments} + \text{Receivables}}{\text{Current liabilities}}$$

The greater the current ratio or the quick ratio (that is, the greater the potential ability to cover current liabilities), the higher a company's liquidity. Whether a given current or quick ratio is good or bad, however, depends on a number of factors, including the trend in these ratios, the comparability of these ratios with competitors, and the available opportunities in more-profitable, long-lived, capital investments.

In addition to looking at the relations among these balance sheet accounts, we can also form ratios that measure how well key current assets are managed over time. The key ratios for asset management are turnover ratios. For example, the **accounts receivable turnover** is the ratio of sales on credit to the average balance in accounts receivable:[2]

$$\text{Accounts receivable turnover} = \frac{\text{Credit sales}}{\text{Average receivables}}$$

This ratio is a measure of how many times, on average, accounts receivable are created by credit sales and collected on during the fiscal period. As another example, the **inventory turnover** is the ratio of the cost of goods sold to the balance in inventory:

$$\text{Inventory turnover} = \frac{\text{Cost of goods sold}}{\text{Average inventory}}$$

This ratio is a measure of how many times, on average, inventory is created or acquired and sold during the fiscal period.

Another perspective on the activity within the current accounts is to estimate the number of days of the current asset or liability that are on hand. For example, the **number of days of receivables**, also referred to as the **day's sales outstanding** and **days in receivables**, gives us an idea of the management of the extension and collection of credit to customers:

$$\text{Number of days of receivables} = \frac{\text{Average accounts receivable}}{\text{Average day's sales on credit}} = \frac{\text{Average accounts receivable}}{\text{Sales on credit}/365}$$

2 You will notice that we use credit sales instead of total revenue; the difference lies in the context. Within the context of working capital management, the corporate financial analyst would have access to details regarding the company's credit versus cash sales. For some companies, sales may be for cash or be some combination of cash sales and credit sales. For the analyst who is looking at the company without benefit of internal information regarding how much of sales is in the form of credit sales, an approximation is generally used based on industry norms for credit practices.

For example, if this number of days is 35.5, this tells us that it takes, on average, 35.5 days to collect on the credit accounts. Whether this is good or bad depends on credit terms that are offered to customers and the relation between sales and the extension of credit, which is often dictated by industry customs and competitive pressures.

The **number of days of inventory** gives us an indication of how well the inventory acquisition, process, and distribution is managed:

$$\text{Number of days of inventory} = \frac{\text{Average inventory}}{\text{Average day's cost of goods sold}} = \frac{\text{Average inventory}}{\text{Cost of goods sold}/365}$$

The number of days of inventory, also known as the average inventory period, day's sales in ending inventory, and the inventory holding period, is the length of time, on average, that the inventory remains within the company during the fiscal period. We expect variation in the number of days of inventory among industries because of differences in the production cycle of different types of inventory. For example, we expect a grocery store to have a lower number of days of inventory than, say, an aircraft manufacturer.

We can also look at the disbursement side of cash flows with the **number of days of payables**, which provides a measure of how long it takes the company to pay its own suppliers:

$$\text{Number of days of payables} = \frac{\text{Average accounts payable}}{\text{Average day's purchases}} = \frac{\text{Average accounts payable}}{\text{Purchases}/365}$$

The number of days of payables is also referred to as the day's payables outstanding and the average days payable. Purchases are not an item on published financial statements, so if you are evaluating a company's payables, you can estimate the purchases by using what you know about the company's cost of goods sold and beginning and ending balances in inventory.[3]

Each of these turnover ratios and numbers of days helps tell a story of how the company is managing its liquid assets. Like all ratios, the numbers themselves do not indicate much, but when we put these together with trends, information on the company's profitability, and information about competitors, we develop a good understanding of a company's performance.[4]

Some of the major applications of this type of analysis include performance evaluation, monitoring, credit-worthiness, and financial projections. But ratios are useful only when they can be compared. The comparison should be done in two ways—comparisons over time for the same company and over time for the company compared with its peer group. Peer groups can include competitors from the same industries as the company as well as other companies with comparable size and financial situations.

Consider Wal-Mart Stores, Inc. We can see the change in the current ratio and quick ratio over the fiscal years 1990 through 2017 in Exhibit 2, Panel A. Here, we see that the current ratio has declined, yet the quick ratio has increased slightly. We can see what is driving these trends in Panel B of this exhibit. One driver is the efficiency in the management of inventory, which results in holding on to inventory fewer days, as indicated by the downward trend in the number of days of inventory. Putting it in

3 We know that Beginning inventory + Purchases − Cost of goods sold = Ending inventory. Therefore, if we know the inventory balances (from the balance sheet) and the cost of goods sold (from the income statement), we can determine the purchases: Purchases = Cost of goods sold + Ending inventory − Beginning inventory.

4 For example, if we see a small number of days of inventory, it could mean that the company is managing its production very efficiently or it could mean that the company is at significant risk of a shortage of inventory. We don't know more until we look at what is needed or usual for companies in the industry, trends in turnover for the company, and the company's profitability in relation to the number of days of inventory.

perspective, this trend may be because of, in part, the product shift when Wal-Mart Stores increased its presence in the grocery line of business. Another driver is the increasing number of days of payables, which means that company is taking longer to pay what it owes suppliers.

Exhibit 2 Liquidity Analysis of Wal-Mart Stores

Panel A: Current and Quick Ratios, 1990–2017

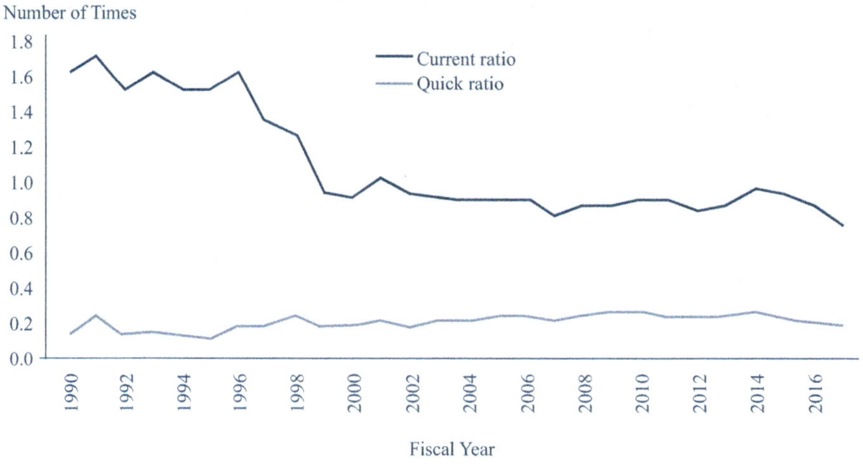

Panel B: Number of Days of Inventory and Number of Days of Payables, 1990–2017

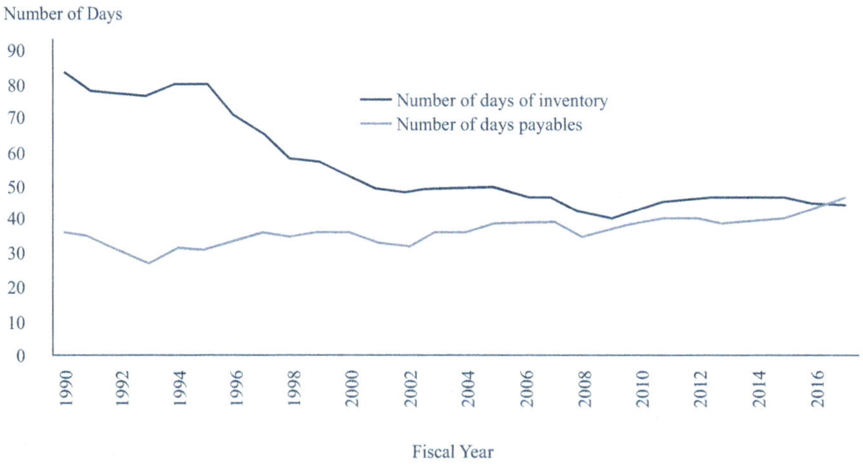

Source: Wal-Mart Stores, Inc., 10-K filings, various years.

Comparing Wal-Mart with Target Inc. and Kohl's in the 2017 fiscal year, as shown in Exhibit 3, we see some differences among these three competitors. These differences may be explained, in part, by the different product mixes (e.g., Wal-Mart has more sales from grocery lines than the others), as well as different inventory management systems and different inventory suppliers. The different need for liquidity may also be explained, in part, by the different operating cycles of the companies.

Exhibit 3 Liquidity Ratios among Discount Retailers

	Company		
Ratio for 2017 Fiscal Year	**Wal-Mart**	**Target**	**Kohl's**
Current ratio	0.76	0.9	2.0
Quick ratio	0.20	0.3	0.7
Number of days of inventory	44.04	61.8	106.2
Number of days of payables	46.27	61.5	38.9

Source: Company 10-K filings with Securities and Exchange Commission for fiscal year 2017.

EXAMPLE 1

Measuring Liquidity

Given the following ratios, how well has the company been managing its liquidity?

	Current Fiscal Year		Average for the Previous Five Fiscal Years	
Ratio	**Company**	**Industry**	**Company**	**Industry**
Current ratio	1.9	2.5	1.1	2.3
Quick ratio	0.7	1.0	0.4	0.9
Number of days of receivables	39.0	34.0	44.0	32.5
Number of days of inventory	41.0	30.3	45.0	27.4
Number of days of payables	34.3	36.0	29.4	35.5

Solution:

The ratios should be compared in two ways—over time (there would typically be an examination of the trend over time) and a comparison with the trend in the industry. In all ratios shown here, the current year shows improvement over the previous years in terms of increased liquidity. In each case, however, the company remains behind the industry average in terms of liquidity. A brief snapshot such as this example could be the starting point to initiate or encourage more improvements with the goal of reaching or beating the industry standards.

We can combine the number of days of inventory, number of days of receivables, and number of days of payables to get a sense of the company's operating cycle and net operating cycle. The **operating cycle** is a measure of the time needed to convert raw materials into cash from a sale. It consists of the number of days of inventory and the number of days of receivables:

$$\text{Operating cycle} = \begin{matrix}\text{Number of days} \\ \text{of inventory}\end{matrix} + \begin{matrix}\text{Number of days} \\ \text{of receivables}\end{matrix}$$

The operating cycle does not take everything into account, however, because the available cash flow is increased by deferring payment to suppliers. This deferral is considered in the **net operating cycle**, also called the **cash conversion cycle**. The net operating cycle is a measure of the time from paying suppliers for materials to collecting cash from the subsequent sale of goods produced from these supplies. It consists of the operating cycle minus the number of days of payables:

$$\text{Net operating cycle} = \begin{matrix}\text{Number of days}\\ \text{of inventory}\end{matrix} + \begin{matrix}\text{Number of days}\\ \text{of receivables}\end{matrix} - \begin{matrix}\text{Number of days}\\ \text{of payables}\end{matrix}$$

In general, the shorter these cycles the greater a company's cash-generating ability and the less its need for liquid assets or outside finance. For many companies, the cash conversion cycle represents a period of time that requires financing—that is, the company offsets some of the financing need by deferring payments through payables terms, but the remainder must be financed.

3 MANAGING THE CASH POSITION

Although the mix or magnitude of data items may change from day to day, the goal is the same: ensuring that the net cash position is not negative. Ideally, the company's daily cash inflows and outflows would be equal, but this is rarely the case. Without the reliability of matching these flows, companies must take other steps to ensure that the flows net out each day. Most companies try to avoid negative balances because the cost of garnering daily funds by issuing debt or by drawing on bank overdraft facilities is very costly, although the cost of maintaining a small short-term investment portfolio, in terms of an opportunity cost, is regarded as an acceptable cost of doing business.

In addition, it is difficult to borrow the exact amount needed, so many companies borrow a little extra to be safe and invest any small excesses overnight at lower rates than if they could invest them earlier or in securities with higher rates. To manage the cash position effectively, the treasury function, which is usually responsible for this activity, must gather information from various sources at all times during the day, making decisions based on the latest information.

Several critical factors help determine how a company can establish an efficient cash flow system. In most cases, the central treasury function may not be able to dictate how the company collects from customers or pays its vendors. What it can do, however, is use the best services and techniques associated with the company's payment configuration.

As an example of a typical cycle of cash management information that occurs daily, consider the process outlined in Exhibit 4. This hypothetical schedule shows how important it is to have an efficient, smooth-flowing information system that can meet the time requirements.

Exhibit 4 An Example of the Daily Cycle of Cash Management

Information from bank reporting systems is gathered and analyzed. *Morning*

↓

The cash manager receives information from company sources.

↓

The cash manager receives updates from the company's bank(s) on current-day transactions.

↓

The cash management staff is arranging short-term investments and/or loans, as necessary, through broker–dealers from their banks or investment banks.

Exhibit 4 (Continued)

↓	
The cash management staff makes funds transfers.	*Midday*
↓	
The cash movements for the day are completed or are scheduled for completion, and the company's cash position is finalized.	
↓	
Necessary paperwork for all transactions is completed. Also, the running cash worksheet is updated and set for the next business day.	*Close of the business day*

3.1 Forecasting Short-Term Cash Flows

Forecasting cash flows is necessary to allow effective management of working capital accounts. For cash forecasting to be effective, it has to be relatively precise. However, a forecast that is precise may not be *accurate*. There are many factors that are outside of the company's control, such as the general economy, unexpected raw material shortages, and changing interest rates. The uncertainty in forecasting encourages companies to maintain some minimum level of cash on hand as a buffer.

3.1.1 *Minimum Cash Balances*

Most companies want a cash buffer as protection from unexpected cash needs or to provide the financial flexibility to take advantage of attractive opportunities, such as procuring raw material inventory at a discount. This buffer is often expressed as a minimum desired cash balance. The size of this buffer depends on several influences, including the variation in the levels of the company's cash inflows and outflows, the company's ability to access other liquidity sources, and the company's ability to access borrowing facilities with little lead time.

3.1.2 *Identifying Typical Cash Flows*

Having an accurate forecast can help a financial manager make better use of the company's financial history. Many product lines, especially those that are not in high-growth stages but rather are in steadier, mature stages, will have similar cash flows from year to year or season to season. If an extensive database has been established, it will be possible to draw reasonable projections for the current period or longer.

Even in cases of heavy growth through mergers and acquisitions, companies should try to transfer the acquired company's cash flow history to be used as a starting point for consolidating the new operation into the rest of the company. The cash manager must identify cash flow elements to build a reliable forecast. These elements are not difficult to identify in general terms, but it is much harder to define them more specifically to be able to collect data regularly.

The cash elements that comprise a total forecast vary from company to company. However, it is good practice to identify the elements that pertain to any one individual company. Exhibit 5 shows typical elements arranged as inflows and outflows. It may be more useful to try to arrange the elements in this manner—i.e., show matching elements by the direction of their flow (in or out). In most cases, a company's data elements can be arranged this way to facilitate data gathering, reviewing variances, and presenting final reports to management and other cash users or providers.

Exhibit 5 Examples of Cash Inflows and Outflows

Inflows	Outflows
■ Receipts from operations, broken down by operating unit, departments, etc.	■ Payables and payroll disbursements, broken down by operating unit, departments, etc.
■ Funds transfers from subsidiaries, joint ventures, third parties	■ Funds transfers to subsidiaries
■ Maturing investments	■ Investments made
■ Debt proceeds (short and long term)	■ Debt repayments
■ Other income items (interest, etc.)	■ Interest and dividend payments
■ Tax refunds	■ Tax payments

These elements should reflect real cash flows, excluding such items as depreciation or accruals that are paid at a later date (these should be included when they are to be paid).

3.1.3 *Cash Forecasting Systems*

Cash forecasting should be structured as a system in order to be effective, and to do this, several aspects of the forecast must be considered. We provide some examples of these aspects in Exhibit 6, which highlights each aspect for three different forecast horizons. In some cases, one aspect may be more important than others. For instance, if daily cash is being handled fairly easily, it may be more critical to spend time and resources to ensure that the medium-term forecasting part of the overall system is functioning at the highest levels of reliability. In addition, some factors, such as format or time horizon, should not be changed arbitrarily because change may affect their accuracy and reliability levels.

Exhibit 6 Examples of Cash Forecasting Aspects over Different Forecast Horizons

	Short Term	Medium Term	Long Term
Data frequency	Daily/weekly for 4–6 weeks	Monthly for one year	Annually for 3–5 years
Format	Receipts and disbursements	Receipts and disbursements	Projected financial statements
Techniques	Simple projections	Projection models and averages	Statistical models
Accuracy	Very high	Moderate	Lowest
Reliability	Very high	Fairly high	Not as high
Uses	Daily cash management	Planning financial transactions	Long-range financial position

3.2 Monitoring Cash Uses and Levels

Another facet of cash forecasting is monitoring and control. Managing the cash position essentially means keeping a "running score" on daily cash flows. Monitoring daily cash flows is a key aspect of a company's cash forecasting system in that the financial manager in charge of managing the cash position must know the company's cash balance in the bank on virtually a real-time basis. However, it really is not *forecasting* as such, because most of the transactions are actually known; the challenge lies in the collection of this known information in time to do something with that information. For example, receiving information about a deposit too late to transfer the funds renders the information valueless.

To receive the appropriate information on a timely basis, information should be gathered from principal users and providers of cash, supplemented by short-term cash projections in days or even throughout the current day. The minimum level of cash available is estimated in advance, adjusted for known funds transfers, seasonality, or other factors, and is used as a **target balance** figure for each bank. Note that most companies use one major bank as their lead bank (or concentration bank) and control the balances for the bank through one main concentration account, with the target balance applied to the main account. For larger companies, more than one concentration bank is possible, but managing the cash positions in multiple concentration banks quickly makes the system complex and requires an efficient information processing system.

For most companies, it is necessary to manage a cash position with the assistance of short-term investments and borrowings. These short-term liquidity sources help counter the excesses and deficits that typically occur in a company's cash flow. The short-term investments are usually kept in a portfolio that is very liquid, with short maturities. In this way, funds are available whenever they are needed, but the company gives up the extra yield that might have been earned if the investments were made for longer periods of time or with securities with less liquidity. Short-term borrowing is for very short periods of time, but a borrower may find more economies in borrowing for regular periods, such as thirty days, to reduce the number of transactions and associated paperwork. Also, by extending the borrowing period, companies can usually obtain better rates and availabilities of funds than if they continually borrow very short maturities.

Many companies face predictable peaks and valleys in their business throughout the year. For instance, manufacturers of consumer electronics products achieve the bulk of their sales during the holiday shopping season (from late November through the end of the year), which means that they have build-up of products that are shipped well before they receive payment. Thus, they have to finance this inventory roll-out before they receive any cash. During this period, they are likely to use up most or all of the temporary excess funds they set aside or to tap into the credit lines they arranged for this purpose. When sales roll in during the busy shopping season, they use the proceeds to pay down the borrowing and then invest any excess.

Other influencing factors on a company's cash needs may be associated with non-operating activities, such as major capital expenditure programs, mergers and acquisitions, sales or disposition of company assets, and the timing of long-term financial transactions, such as bond issues, private placements of debt or equity, and equity issues.

Predicting the peak need caused by seasonality or other non-operating activities is important if the company is going to have to borrow funds to cover the need. If a company sets aside too much, it will incur excess costs that are unjustified. If it sets aside too little, it will have to pay a penalty to raise funds quickly. Either case is a costly error. A reliable forecast can help avoid this situation.

INVESTING SHORT-TERM FUNDS 4

Short-term investments represent a temporary store of funds that are not necessarily needed in a company's daily transactions. If a substantial portion of a company's working capital portfolio is not needed for short-term transactions, it should be separated from a working capital portfolio and placed in a longer-term portfolio. Such longer-term portfolios are often handled by another area or are handled by an outside money manager under the company's supervision. In this way, the risks, maturities, and portfolio management of longer-term portfolios can be managed independently of the working capital portfolio.

Short-term working capital portfolios consist of securities that are highly liquid, less risky, and shorter in maturity than other types of investment portfolios. Thus, a company's working capital portfolio may consist of short-term debt securities, such as short-term US government securities and short-term bank and corporate obligations. This type of portfolio changes almost constantly, as cash is needed or more excess cash is available for investments.

4.1 Short-Term Investment Instruments

We describe examples of the major instruments for short-term investments in Exhibit 7. The relative amounts of each security can vary from one company to another, depending on the company's risk tolerance and how quickly the invested funds will be needed.

Exhibit 7 Examples of Short-Term Investment Instruments

Instruments	Typical Maturities	Features	Risks
US Treasury Bills (T-bills)	13, 26, and 52 weeks	■ Obligations of US government (guaranteed), issued at a discount ■ Active secondary market ■ Lowest rates for traded securities	Virtually no risk
Federal agency securities	5–30 days	■ Obligations of US federal agencies (e.g., Fannie Mae, Federal Home Loan Board) issued as interest-bearing ■ Slightly higher yields than T-bills	Slight liquidity risk; insignificant credit risk
Bank certificates of deposit (CDs)	14–365 days	■ Bank obligations, issued interest-bearing in $100,000 increments ■ "Yankee" CDs offer slightly higher yields	Credit and liquidity risk (depending on bank's credit)
Banker's acceptances (BAs)	30–180 days	■ Bank obligations for trade transactions (usually foreign), issued at a discount ■ Investor protected by underlying company and trade flow itself ■ Small secondary market	Credit and liquidity risk (depending on bank's credit)
Eurodollar time deposits	1–180 days	■ Time deposit with bank off-shore (outside United States, such as Bahamas) ■ Can be CD or straight time deposit (TD) ■ Interest-bearing investment ■ Small secondary market for CDs, but not TDs	Credit risk (depending on bank) Very high liquidity risk for TDs
Bank sweep services	1 day	■ Service offered by banks that essentially provides interest on checking account balance (usually over a minimum level) ■ Large number of sweeps are for overnight	Credit and liquidity risk (depending on bank)
Repurchase agreements (Repos)	1 day +	■ Sale of securities with the agreement of the dealer (seller) to buy them back at a future time ■ Typically over-collateralized at 102 percent ■ Often done for very short maturities (< 1 week)	Credit and liquidity risk (depending on dealer)

Exhibit 7 (Continued)

Instruments	Typical Maturities	Features	Risks
Commercial paper (CP)	1–270 days	■ Unsecured obligations of corporations and financial institutions, issued at discount ■ Secondary market for large issuers ■ CP issuers obtain short-term credit ratings	Credit and liquidity risk (depending on credit rating)
Mutual funds and money market mutual funds	Varies	■ Money market mutual funds commonly used by smaller businesses ■ Low yields but high liquidity for money market funds; mutual fund liquidity dependent on underlying securities in fund ■ Can be linked with bank sweep arrangement	Credit and liquidity risk (depending on fund manager)
Tax-advantaged securities	7, 28, 35, 49, and 90 days	■ Preferred stock in many forms, including adjustable rate preferred stocks (ARPs), auction rate preferred stocks (AURPs), and convertible adjustable preferred stocks (CAPs) ■ Dutch auction often used to set rate ■ Offer higher yields	Credit and liquidity risk (depending on issuer's credit)

4.1.1 *Computing Yields on Short-Term Investments*

Some securities, such as T-bills and banker's acceptances, are issued at a discount. Thus, the investor invests less than the face value of the security and receives the face value back at maturity. For instance, a $1 million security that pays 5 percent in interest with one month remaining to maturity would be purchased at:

$$\text{Purchase price} = \$1{,}000{,}000 - \left[(0.05)(1/12)(\$1{,}000{,}000)\right] = \$995{,}833.33$$

$$\text{Proceeds (face value)} = \$1{,}000{,}000$$

The difference between the purchase price and the face value, $4,166.67, is the **discount interest**.

Interest-bearing securities differ from discounted securities in that the investor pays the face amount and receives back that same face amount plus the interest on the security. For example, a 5 percent, 30-day, $1 million security would return $1 million face value plus interest earned:

$$\text{Purchase price (face value)} = \$1{,}000{,}000$$

$$\text{Proceeds} = \$1{,}000{,}000 + \left[(0.05)(1/12)(\$1{,}000{,}000)\right] = \$1{,}004{,}166.67$$

Rates on securities may be quoted as nominal rates or as yields. A **nominal rate** is a rate of interest based on the security's face value. In the previous two examples, the nominal rate in each instance was 5 percent. A **yield**, on the other hand, is the actual return on the investment if it is held to maturity. For example, if you buy the discount security for $995,833.33 and hold it for one month until it matures for $1 million, your yield on this investment is

$$\text{Yield} = \left(\frac{\$1{,}000{,}000 - 995{,}833.33}{995{,}833.33}\right)(12) = (0.004184)(12) = 5.0209\%$$

where the second factor, 12, annualizes the monthly yield of 0.4184 percent. The factor that is used to annualize the yield depends on the type of security and the traditions for quoting yields. For example, the **money market yield** is typically annualized using the ratio of 360 to the number of days to maturity:

$$\text{Money market yield} = \left(\frac{\text{Face value} - \text{Purchase price}}{\text{Purchase price}}\right)\left(\frac{360}{\text{Number of days to maturity}}\right)$$

On the other hand, the **bond equivalent yield** is typically annualized using the ratio of 365 to the number of days to maturity:

$$\text{Bond equivalent yield} = \left(\frac{\text{Face value} - \text{Purchase price}}{\text{Purchase price}}\right)\left(\frac{365}{\text{Number of days to maturity}}\right)$$

One source of confusion is that the yield on US T-bills may be quoted on the basis of the discount basis or the bond equivalent basis (also referred to as the investment yield basis). The yield on a T-bill using the discount basis is calculated using the face value as the basis for the yield and then using a 360-day year:

$$\text{Discount-basis yield} = \left(\frac{\text{Face value} - \text{Purchase price}}{\text{Face value}}\right)\left(\frac{360}{\text{Number of days to maturity}}\right)$$

Although the relevant yield for investment decision purposes is the bond equivalent yield, it is important to understand the discount basis because it is often quoted in the context of these securities.

EXAMPLE 2

Computing Investment Yields

For a 91-day $100,000 US T-bill sold at a discounted rate of 2.10 percent, calculate the following:

1 Money market yield.

2 Bond equivalent yield.

$$\begin{aligned}\text{Purchase price} &= \$100{,}000 - \left[(0.021)(91/360)(\$100{,}000)\right] \\ &= \$99{,}469.17\end{aligned}$$

The discount is therefore $100,000 – 99,469.17 = 530.83.

Solution to 1:

Money market yield = [530.83/99,469.17] × [360/91] = 2.11 percent

Solution to 2:

Bond equivalent yield = [530.83/99,469.17] × [365/91] = 2.14 percent

4.1.2 *Investment Risks*

Investors face several types of risks. We list a number of these in Exhibit 8. In this exhibit, we list the types of risk—credit, market, liquidity, and foreign exchange—and the attributes and safety measures associated with each type. The attributes describe the conditions that contribute to the type of risk, and the safety measures describe the steps that investors usually take to prevent losses from the risk. With the exception of foreign exchange risk, the key safety measures taken are to shift to "safety" (i.e., government securities, such as US T-bills) or to shorten maturities so that securities will mature quicker, allowing an investor to shift funds to a safer type of security.

Exhibit 8 Types of Investment Risks and Safety Measures

Type of Risk	Key Attributes	Safety Measures
Credit (or default)	■ Issuer may default ■ Issuer could be adversely affected by economy, market ■ Little secondary market	■ Minimize amount ■ Keep maturities short ■ Watch for "questionable" names ■ Emphasize government securities
Market (or interest rate)	■ Price or rate changes may adversely affect return ■ There is no market to sell the maturity to, or there is only a small secondary market	■ Keep maturities short ■ Keep portfolio diverse in terms of maturity, issuers
Liquidity	■ Security is difficult or impossible to (re)sell ■ Security must be held to maturity and cannot be liquidated until then	■ Stick with government securities ■ Look for good secondary market ■ Keep maturities short
Foreign exchange	■ Adverse general market movement against your currency	■ Hedge regularly ■ Keep most in your currency and domestic market (avoid foreign exchange)

4.2 Strategies

Short-term investment strategies are fairly simple because the securities in a working capital portfolio are limited in type and are much shorter in maturity than a longer-term portfolio. Most short-term investors seek "reasonable" returns and do not want to take on substantial risk. Short-term investment strategies can be grouped into two types: passive and active. A **passive strategy** is characterized by one or two decision rules for making daily investments, whereas an **active strategy** involves constant monitoring and may involve matching, mismatching, or laddering strategies.

Passive strategies are less aggressive than active ones and place top priority on safety and liquidity. Yet, passive strategies do not have to offer poor returns, especially if companies have reliable cash forecasts. Often, companies with good cash forecasts can combine a passive strategy with an active matching strategy to enhance the yield of a working capital portfolio without taking on substantially greater risks.

The major problem associated with passive strategies is complacency, which can cause the company to roll over the portfolio mechanically, with little attention paid to yields and more focus on simply reinvesting funds as they mature. Passive strategies must be monitored, and the yield from investment portfolios should be benchmarked regularly against a suitable standard, such as a T-bill with comparable maturity.

Active strategies require more daily involvement and possibly a wider choice of investments. Although investments are rolled over with an active strategy, just as they are with a passive strategy, this type of strategy calls for more shopping around, better forecasts, and a more flexible investment policy/guideline.

Active strategies can include intentional matching or mismatching the timing of cash outflows with investment maturities. A **matching strategy** is the more conservative of the two and uses many of the same investment types as are used with passive strategies. A **mismatching strategy** is riskier and requires very accurate and reliable cash forecasts. These strategies usually use securities that are more liquid, such as T-bills, so that securities can be liquidated if adverse market conditions arise. Mismatching strategies may also be accomplished using derivatives, which may pose additional risks to a company unaccustomed to buying and selling derivatives.

A **laddering strategy** is another form of active strategy, which entails scheduling maturities on a systematic basis within the investment portfolio such that investments are spread out equally over the term of the ladder. A laddering strategy falls somewhere between a matching and a passive strategy. Laddering strategies have been used effectively in managing longer-term investment portfolios, but laddering also should be an effective short-term strategy.

Managing a working capital portfolio involves handling and safeguarding assets of the company. Accordingly, companies with investment portfolios should have a formal, written policy/guideline that protects the company and the investment managers. Investment policy/guidelines should not be very lengthy, especially because they must be understood by the company's investment managers and communicated to the company's investment dealers.

Although the investment policy/guideline should be customized for an individual company, the basic structure of such a policy is provided in Exhibit 9.

Exhibit 9 Sample Format of an Investment Policy

Purpose	List and explain the reasons that the portfolio exists and also describe the general attributes of the portfolio, such as a summary of the strategy that will be used and the general types of securities that are acceptable investments.
Authorities	Identify the executives who oversee the portfolio managers who make the investments that compose the portfolio and the outside managers that could be used and how they would be managed. Also describe procedures that must be performed if the policy is not followed.
Limitations and/or restrictions	Describe, in general terms, the types of investments that should be considered for inclusion in the portfolio. The list should not consist of specific securities; it should describe the general *types* of securities, such as commercial paper, US T-bills, or bank CDs. In this manner, the policy retains more flexibility than if specific issuers or securities are listed. In the latter case, the policy would require change every time an issuer was no longer issuing any securities. This section should also include any restrictions as to the relative amount of each security that is allowable in the overall portfolio. This section may also include procedures when a maximum has been exceeded or must be exceeded under special circumstances, such as when the portfolio is temporarily inflated prior to using the funds for an acquisition or other long-term use.

Exhibit 9 (Continued)

Quality	May be in a separate section or may be included with the previous one. Investments with working capital funds must be safe, so many companies include credit standards for potential investments in their policy statements. Reference may be made to long-term ratings or, more frequently, to short-term credit ratings. The ratings cited are usually those from the major rating agencies: Standard & Poor's and Moody's.
Other items	Other items are sometimes included in a policy/guideline, such as statements that require the portfolio to be included in the financial audit or that regular reports will be generated by the investment manager. Some companies also define the types of securities that are "eligible," but this does not seem necessary if the policy is well written.

EXAMPLE 3

Evaluating an Investment Policy

A sample investment policy is shown below. Review the client's investment policy, considering the basic investment policy structure shown in Exhibit 9. The average portfolio size is $100 million, with no significant peaks or valleys throughout the year. After reviewing the policy, answer the following questions:

1 Is the policy an effective one?

2 What shortcomings or potential problem areas, if any, does it have?

3 How would you change this policy, if at all?

Working Capital Portfolio Investment Policy/Guidelines

- Purpose: This is a working capital portfolio with emphasis on safety and liquidity. We will sacrifice return for either of these two goals.
- Authorities: The treasurer, with agreement from the CFO, will be in charge of managing short-term investments. Authority and control to execute can be delegated by the treasurer or CFO to another treasury manager if documented.
- Maximum maturity: Securities may not be made for longer than three (3) years.
- Types/amounts of investments permitted: no more than 10 percent of the portfolio or $50 million with any issuer, subject to the credit limitation that any eligible issuer must be rated A-1, P-1 by a nationally recognized statistical rating organization (NRSRO), such as S&P Global Ratings and Moody's Investors Service, Inc.
- Collateral for any repurchase agreements must maintain a market value of at least 102 percent of the value of the repurchase agreement, and any collateral must be highly marketable and easily priced.
- All investments must be held in safekeeping by XYZ Bank.
- The investment manager can execute exception transactions but must document them in writing.

Solution to 1:

The policy is fairly effective because it provides simple, understandable rules. It calls for credit quality, limits the possible position with any single issuer, and calls for safekeeping. It also has an exception procedure that is straightforward.

Solution to 2:

The credit ratings may be too restrictive. Many investment securities may not be rated by NRSROs. Also, the 10 percent limitation apparently is to be applied to all securities. However, most investment managers do not consider securities issued by governmental agencies or the government itself to be so risky that a limitation needs to be applied.

Solution to 3:

The words "or equivalent" should be added to the credit quality of the types of investments. Also, there should be no limitation to highly rated governmental securities, such as US Treasury-bills and the equivalent from the major developed countries. A credit rating reference could be applied to determine eligible governmental securities.

4.3 Evaluating Short-Term Funds Management

Tracking tools can range from simple spreadsheets to more expensive treasury workstations. If both portfolios are not too large or diversified, a spreadsheet may be sufficient to be able to compare effective yields and borrowing costs on an ongoing basis and to generate periodic performance reports.

Investment returns should be expressed as bond equivalent yields, to allow comparability among investment alternatives. In addition, the overall portfolio return should be weighted according to the currency size of the investment. We provide an abbreviated example of a portfolio report in Exhibit 10. The report provides the weighted average returns of the different investments. The yields are all calculated on a bond equivalent yield basis.

Exhibit 10 Short-Term Investment Portfolio Report

Security/Loan	Dealer/Bank	€ Amt (000)	Weight (%)	Yield (%)	Maturity
US T-bills	ABC Bank	23,575	39.8	3.50	90 days
Finco CP	XYZ Co.	20,084	33.9	4.65	45 days
Megabank CD	Megabank	15,560	26.3	5.05	30 days
Weighted average yield from investments				**4.30**	
Short-term benchmark rate[a]				**4.25**	

[a] Benchmark rate = independent source, such as synthetic portfolio maintained independently or rate provided by third party, such as a money manager or other empirical source (e.g., a financial institution, trade association, or central bank).

MANAGING ACCOUNTS RECEIVABLE

5

Credit accounts vary by type of customer and the industry, and granting credit involves a tradeoff between increasing sales and uncollectible accounts. There are three primary activities in accounts receivable management: granting credit and processing transactions, monitoring credit balances, and measuring performance of the credit function.

Processing accounts receivable transactions requires recording credit sales to create a record and posting customer payments—or at least monitoring the posting—to the accounts receivable account by applying the payment against the customer's outstanding credit balance. Monitoring the outstanding accounts receivable requires a regular reporting of outstanding receivable balances and notifying the collection managers of past due situations. Monitoring is an ongoing activity. Measuring the performance of the credit functions entails preparing and distributing key performance measurement reports, including an accounts receivable aging schedule and day's sales outstanding reports.

Essentially, the accounts receivable management function is a go-between for the credit manager, treasury manager, and accounting manager. This role is an important one because it can slow up the recording of payments, which may, in turn, prevent customers from purchasing more of the company's products or, worse yet, could prevent the treasury manager from depositing the check and converting the check to available funds.

The accounts receivable management function is also considered to be a derivative activity from credit granting because it helps in providing information needed by the credit management function. It depends on the source of the sale for its records, on the credit manager for additional information on the status of the accounts receivable record, and possibly on the treasury manager to establish an efficient system of getting the payment information to the accounts receivable manager for cash application (e.g., from a bank lockbox).

The goals for the accounts receivable management system include the following:

- efficient processing and maintaining accurate, up-to-date records that are available to credit managers and other interested parties as soon as possible after payments have been received;
- control of accounts receivable and ensuring that accounts receivable records are current and that no unauthorized entry into the accounts receivable file has occurred;
- collection on accounts and coordination with the treasury management function;
- coordination and notification with the credit managers frequently; and
- preparation of regular performance measurement reports.

Companies may achieve scale economies by centralizing the accounts receivable function by using a captive finance subsidiary.[5] A **captive finance subsidiary** is a wholly owned subsidiary of the company that is established to provide financing of the sales of the parent company.

5 As pointed out by Shehzad L. Mian and Clifford W. Smith ["Accounts Receivable Management Policy: Theory and Evidence," *Journal of Finance*, vol. 47, no. 1 (March 1992) pp. 169–200], companies that have highly variable accounts receivable (for example, from seasonality) may find the use of a captive finance subsidiary attractive because it may allow the subsidiary's debt indentures to differ from those of the parent company.

One of the challenges in accounts receivable management is monitoring receivables and collecting on accounts. Many companies resort to outsourcing the accounts receivable function, primarily to increase the collection on accounts, provide credit evaluation services, and to apply the most recent technology. Also, some companies may invest in credit insurance, which reduces the risk of bad debts and shifts some of the evaluation of credit-worthiness to the insurer.

5.1 Key Elements of the Trade Credit Granting Process

Credit management is an integral part of the collection process. It sets the framework for sales in that it can restrict sales by rejecting credit or expand it by loosening acceptance criteria. It also links the collection and cash application processes and has a profound effect on the method of collection as well. In addition, credit management techniques incorporate fundamental financial analysis methods in setting credit policy, granting credit, and managing existing credit customers.

A weak, ineffective credit management function may enhance sales, but many of those sales may become bad debts. On the other hand, a strong, active credit management function can work in tandem with sales and marketing on one side and accounting and treasury on the other. To establish an effective credit management function a company must have a well-conceived strategy customized to the company's needs and reflecting the company's goals.

Credit management policies are usually established as a set of basic guidelines to be used by credit managers. A company's credit policy sets the boundaries for the credit management function. It lays out procedures as part of the policy and offers guidance for each typical situation. The policy shows the steps in the granting process and provides decision rules for specific situations. The policy can also influence the sales level by making it easy or difficult for customers to buy on credit.

Customers may start out with one type of credit account that is restrictive, such as cash on delivery, and may eventually demonstrate that they are regular payers and can be given open book credit accounts.

The major types of credit accounts include the following:

- open book, which is the most common for company to company;
- documentary, with or without lines of credit, most common for cross-border transactions;
- installment credit, with regular timed payments; and
- revolving credit.

The types of credit terms offered vary by type of customer, the relative financial strength of the customer, and the type of credit terms the competition is offering. The different forms of terms of credit other than cash, which generally implies 7 to 10 days, include the following:

- **Ordinary terms**. Terms are set forth in a standard format—*net t* or d/t_1 *net* t_2, where t in the first example refers to the length of time a customer has to pay the invoice before becoming past due. In the second example, t_1 is the time period for taking discounts, and t_2 is the same as t in the first example. For example, *net 60* means that the full amount of the invoice is due in 60 days. Most trade credit customers will take the full 60 days. Terms of *1/10 net 30* mean that the customer can take a 1 percent discount if the invoice is paid within 10 days or else pay the full amount of the invoice by 30 days from the invoice date.

- **Cash before delivery (CBD)** terms require that the amount of the invoice must be paid in advance before delivery will be scheduled. Checks must clear before any shipment is made.
- **Cash on delivery (COD)** terms require that payment must be made (usually in the form of a bank check) when the product is delivered; otherwise, no delivery will be made.
- **Bill-to-bill**. These terms require that each prior bill must be paid before new shipments are possible.
- **Monthly billing**. These terms require payment monthly. They have a different format; for example, *2/10th Prox net 30th* means that the customer can take a 2 percent discount if it pays within the first 10 days of the next month or else it must pay the full amount of the invoice by the 30th day of the next month.

Credit managers may evaluate customers' credit-worthiness using a credit scoring model. A **credit scoring model** is a statistical model used to classify borrowers according to credit-worthiness. These models were first designed for assisting in making consumer credit decisions. Major credit card issuers needed a tool they could use to make mass credit decisions. It was also used for small business loans after many larger banks discovered that their costs of reviewing and deciding whether to grant loans were such that they could not efficiently make loans of the smaller sizes required by smaller businesses. To overcome this problem, they adopted credit scoring models.

Credit scoring models offer an opportunity for a company to make fast decisions on the basis of simple data, not requiring a great deal of paperwork. The scoring models give greater weight to such factors as:

- ready cash (e.g., high checking account balances);
- organization type, with corporations rated higher than sole proprietorships or partnership; and
- being current in supplier payments, as indicated by financial services such as Dun & Bradstreet.

The models penalize the potential borrower for:

- prior late payment behavior or defaults: payment patterns are habitual;
- heavy use of personal credit cards: no reserves or reduced reserves available;
- previous *personal* bankruptcy or tax liens: carries over from person to company; and
- high-risk categories: food services, hospitality industries.

Credit scoring can also be used to predict late payers.

5.2 Managing Customers' Receipts

Cash collections systems are a function of the types of customers a company has and the methods of payment that the customers use. For instance, if a company's sales are made at retail locations, it cannot take advantage of the benefits offered by bank lockbox services. Instead, it must deal with organizing and controlling local deposits and concentrating these deposits efficiently and economically. On the other hand, if a company manufactures and sells products to other businesses, it can use a bank lockbox services to expedite processing and clearing of check payments.

We illustrate a typical network for a company with both electronic and check payments in Exhibit 11. Checks from one type of customer are directed to a bank lockbox, while electronic payments from another type of customer are transmitted via **electronic funds transfer (EFT)** through one of the available networks, such as the **Automated Clearing House (ACH)** system or the **Giro system**. The ACH system is an electronic payment network available to businesses, individuals, and financial institutions in the United States, US Territories, and Canada. The Giro systems are postal-based systems in Europe and elsewhere.

Exhibit 11 Cash Collections and Concentration

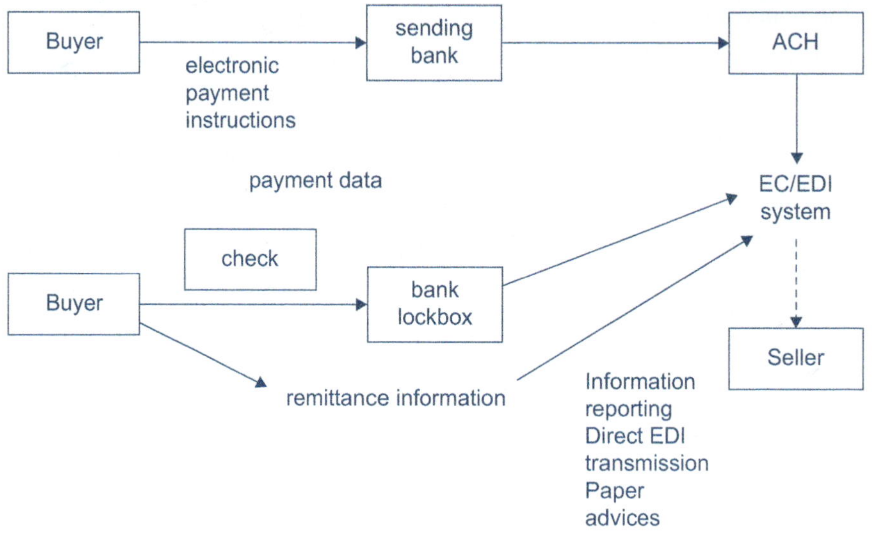

In most cases, the best practice for collections involves the establishment of a system that accelerates payments as well as their information content, such as the customer's name and identification number and which invoices are being paid. From the collecting company's point of view, the way to achieve this best practice is to establish an electronic collection network. This can apply to either retail or wholesale companies.

Retail payments can be made by credit/debit cards or electronic checks, which are converted to electronic debits or digitized images, or by direct debit. These payments clear electronically and can be facilitated through **point of sale (POS)** systems, which are systems that capture the transaction data at the physical location in which the sale is made. A **direct debit program** is an arrangement whereby the customer authorizes a debit to a demand account and is used by companies—such as utilities, telecommunications service providers, cable companies, insurance companies, and credit card companies—to collect routine payments for services.

If payments cannot be converted to electronic payments, the next best practice is to use a bank lockbox service. A **lockbox system** is coordinated with the banking institution in which customer payments are mailed to a post office box and the banking institution retrieves and deposits these payments several times a day, enabling the company to have use of the fund sooner than in a centralized system in which customer payments are sent to the company. An acceptable bank lockbox arrangement is one in which the checks deposited today are available tomorrow or the next business day. This one-day availability lays the groundwork for best practices in cash concentration.

A good performance measure for check deposits is a calculated **float factor**. The **float** in this context is the amount of money that is in transit between payments made by customers and the funds that are usable by the company. We compute the float factor by dividing the average daily deposit into the average daily float:[6]

$$\text{Float factor} = \frac{\text{Average daily float}}{\text{Average daily deposit}}$$

$$= \frac{\text{Average daily float}}{\text{Total amount of checks deposited/Number of days}}$$

This calculation gives the average number of days it took deposited checks to clear. If the float factor is very small (e.g., less than 1.0), it is probably worthwhile to investigate further to determine whether same-day wire transfers from the depository account are warranted, assuming the depository account is with a bank other than the company's lead bank. The float factor only measures how long it takes for checks to clear, not how long it takes to receive the checks, deposit them, and then have them clear. However, it is still very useful and can be computed easily for any depository accounts.

EXAMPLE 4

Calculating Float Factors

Given the following data, compute a float factor for this company bank account.

Total deposits for the month:	$3,360,900
Number of days in month:	30 days
Average daily float:	$154,040

Solution:

Average daily deposit = ($3,360,900)/30 = $112,030

Float factor = Average daily float/Average daily deposit
= $154,040/$112,030 = 1.375 days

Therefore, it takes, on average, 1.375 days for checks to clear the bank.

Cash concentration involves two major activities: consolidating deposits and moving funds between company accounts or to outside points. The best practice for cash concentration may be different for consolidating deposits than for moving funds, depending on the timing required and the availability of the funds being transferred.

For bank lockbox concentration, assuming that the checks clear in one business day (on average), the concentration technique of choice is the electronic funds transfer method. In this method, bank lockbox personnel call in the deposit via a reporting service or directly to the concentration bank. The concentration bank creates an electronic funds transfer debit that clears overnight, giving the company available funds in its concentration account. This system can be set up to run with or without intervention by the company's cash manager. In most cases, the best practice does not involve any intervention.

6 We determine the average daily float from an analysis of cash accounts.

Electronic funds transfers offer distinct advantages to companies that use them for concentration of funds. First, they are substantially cheaper than the alternative, the wire transfer. In addition, they are reliable in that the transfer can be made part of a routine that can be performed daily without exception. Even small payments that would not be economical to transfer out by wire can be transferred economically by electronic funds transfer.

5.3 Evaluating Accounts Receivable Management

There are numerous ways of measuring accounts receivable performance. Most of them deal with how effectively outstanding accounts receivable items can be converted into cash. Measures can be derived from general financial reports as well as more detailed internal financial records.

Many measures, such as number of days of receivables, can be calculated easily from financial statements. The standard number of days of receivables evaluates the total receivables outstanding but does not consider the age distribution within this outstanding balance.

5.3.1 *Accounts Receivable Aging Schedule*

One key report that accounts receivable managers should use is the **aging schedule**, which is a breakdown of the accounts into categories of days outstanding. We provide an example of an aging schedule in Exhibit 12, Panel A. As you can see in this example, the report shows the total sales and receivables for each reporting period (typically 30 days). It is handier to convert the aging schedule to percentages, as we show in this exhibit. Note that in the exhibit, it is easy to spot a change in April's aging: Accounts receivable have not been collected and converted to cash as rapidly as in previous months. In this case, the April change should be scrutinized. For example, the extension of credit terms may have been increased as part of a special program. This change could also signal a change in payments by the company's customers.

Exhibit 12 An Accounts Receivable Aging Schedule

Panel A: The Aging Schedule

($ Millions)	January	February	March	April
Sales	530	450	560	680
Total accounts receivable	600	560	650	720
Current (1–30 days old)	330	290	360	280
1–30 days past due	90	120	160	250
31–60 days past due	80	60	60	110
61–90 days past due	70	50	40	50
>90 days past due	30	40	30	30

Aging Expressed as Percent	January	February	March	April
Current (1–30 days old)	55.0	51.8	55.4	38.9
1–30 days past due	15.0	21.4	24.6	34.7
31–60 days past due	13.3	10.7	9.2	15.3
61–90 days past due	11.7	8.9	6.2	6.9
>90 days past due	5.0	7.1	4.6	4.2

Exhibit 12 (Continued)

Panel B: Calculation of the Weighted Average Collection Period

	March			April		
Aging Group	Collection Days[a]	Weight[b] (%)	Weighted Days[c]	Collection Days	Weight (%)	Weighted Days
Current (1–30 days)	20	55.4	11.1	29	38.9	11.3
31–60 days	48	24.6	11.8	55	34.7	19.1
61–90 days	80	9.2	7.4	88	15.3	13.5
91–120 days	110	6.2	6.8	115	6.9	7.9
121+ days	130	4.6	6.0	145	4.2	6.1
Weighted average collection days[d]			43.0			57.9

[a] The average days for collecting receivables in each grouping.
[b] The weighting from the aging schedule.
[c] This figure, expressed in days, is the product of the previous two columns.
[d] The sum of each grouping's product equals the overall days.

5.3.2 *The Number of Days of Receivables*

The number of days of receivables gives us the overall picture of accounts receivable collection. We can compare the number of days with the credit policy to give us an idea of how well the company is collecting on its accounts, relative to the terms that it grants credit. But we can take this a step further by calculating a weighted average of the collection period, or weighted average day's sales outstanding. By focusing on the time it takes to collect receivables, the weighted average collection period is a good measure of how long it is taking to collect from the company's customers regardless of the sales level or the changes in sales.

The calculation of the weighted average collection period requires data on the number of days it takes to collect accounts of each age grouping. For example, we could group receivables in regular increments, such as 30-day periods, and then weight the collection period in each group by the monetary amount of accounts in the group.

Using the data provided in Exhibit 12, Panel A, it is possible to compute number of days of receivables for March and April, as shown in Panel B of this exhibit. As you can see in this example, we can get a better idea of why the number of days of receivables changed from one month to the next. The weighted average collection days increased from March to April, primarily because of the large representation in receivable accounts in the 31–60 and 61–90 day ranges, which made up only 24.6 percent + 9.2 percent = 33.8 percent of accounts in March, but 50 percent of accounts in April.

The primary drawback to this measure is that it requires more information than number of days of receivables, and this information is not readily available, especially for comparisons among companies.

6 MANAGING INVENTORY

The primary goal for an inventory system is to maintain the level of inventory so that production management and sales management can make and sell the company's products without more than necessary invested in this asset. Like cash and accounts receivable management, inventory management involves balancing: having sufficient inventory, but not too much.

Inventory is a current asset that is created by purchasing, paid by accounts payable, and funded by the treasury. The investment in inventory does not produce cash until it is sold or otherwise disposed of. Excessive levels of inventory can possibly overstate the value of inventory because the more that is on hand, the greater the potential for obsolete inventory, which can be sold off, but at a discount. Shortages of inventory result in lost sales.

The amount of inventory that a company holds or feels it has to hold creates a financial requirement for the company. If the company's product lines are more diverse or if its production processes are more involved in using inventory to make final products and then store the products, the company may have a significant financial investment in inventory.

The investment in inventory has been quite staggering for many companies, which has caused them to look for new inventory management techniques. New techniques in inventory control, aided by improved technology, have enabled substantial reduction of the inventory levels a company must maintain and still be able to make products and have them available for sale as needed. For instance, newer just-in-time approaches to inventory management have lowered required inventory balances and cemented major trading partner relationships.

The motives for holding inventory, which dictate how much inventory will be held and, in turn, how much working capital will be tied up in inventory, are very similar to the need for holding cash. The major motives include the transactions motive, the precautionary motives, and the speculative motive.

The **transactions motive** reflects the need for inventory as part of the routine production–sales cycle. Inventory need is equal to the planned manufacturing activity, and the approach to inventory will be dictated by the manufacturing plan.

Precautionary stocks also may be desirable to avoid any **stock-out losses**, which are profits lost from not having sufficient inventory on hand to satisfy demand. Managing inventory well means keeping extra inventory, especially if it could become obsolete quickly, at a minimum. To do this, a company must have a reliable forecast and a flexible inventory approach. In addition, many companies that do not have a reliable forecast maintain a reserve as a precaution for shortfalls in the plan. Of course, how much stock is determined by the lead time for additional inventory purchases, the length of time it takes to deliver final products to the market, and how much can be spent on extra inventory.

In certain industries, managers may acquire inventory for speculative reasons, such as ensuring the availability and pricing of inventory. Inventory managers working together with purchasing managers can benefit from out-of-the-ordinary purchases. For instance, if a publisher is certain that paper costs will be increasing for the next year, it can buy more paper in the current year and store it for future use. This decision assumes that the storage costs are not greater than the savings.

Companies usually attempt to strike a balance in managing their inventory levels. Overinvestment can result in liquidity squeezes or related problems with an increase in debt without an increase in cash. Overinvestment can also lead to the misuse of facilities as more storage is required for the built-up inventory. Having large amounts of inventory on hand can result in losses from shrinkage, spoilage, and so on. Finally, overinvestment can reduce the company's competitiveness as it may not be able to match pricing because of its large inventory costs.

On the other hand, underinvestment in inventory can create problems from losing customers who could not purchase a product, or gaining their ill-will from long delays in delivery. Plant shutdowns and expensive special runs can also be costly. Finally, a risk with underinvestment is the company's inability to avoid price increases by suppliers.

6.1 Approaches to Managing Levels of Inventory

To control inventory costs, a company should adopt the appropriate approach for its inventory. The two basic approaches are the economic order quantity and just-in-time.

Many companies use the classical approach, **economic order quantity–reorder point (EOQ–ROP)**, at least for some portion of their inventory. This method is based on expected demand and the predictability of demand, and it requires determining the level of inventory at which new inventory is ordered. This ordering point is determined based on the costs of ordering and carrying inventory, such that the total cost associated with inventory is minimized. The demand and lead times determine the inventory level. For EOQ–ROP to work well, there must be a reliable short-term forecast. Often, a company may use EOQ–ROP for smaller items that have low unit costs.

Use of the EOQ–ROP method may involve safety stocks and anticipation stocks. A **safety stock** is a level of inventory beyond anticipated needs that provides a cushion in the event that it takes longer to replenish inventory than expected or in the case of greater than expected demand. A company may consider the number of days of inventory on hand and the lead time in replenishing stock in determining the appropriate level of the safety stock. An **anticipation stock** is inventory in excess of that needed for anticipated demand, which may fluctuate with the company's sales or production seasonality. We illustrate the EOQ–ROP method in Exhibit 13.

Exhibit 13 EOQ–ROP Inventory Method

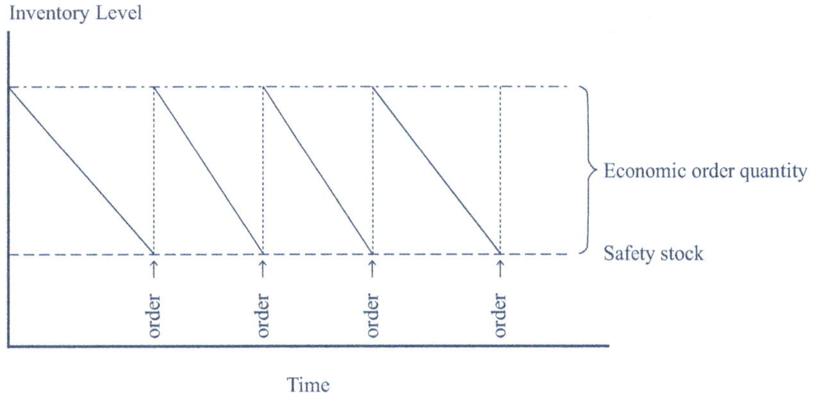

The **just-in-time (JIT) method** is a system that minimizes in-process inventory stocks—raw materials and in production—by evaluating the entire system of the delivery of materials and production. Materials are ordered, for example, at a point at which current stocks of material reach a reorder point, a point determined primarily by historical demand. Materials or **manufacturing resource planning (MRP)** systems incorporate production planning into inventory management. The analysis of production and materials needed for production are incorporated into an analysis that provides both a materials acquisition schedule and a production schedule. Combining the JIT and MRP methods can provide a broader base for integrating inventory into the company's supply chain management and effectively reduce inventory levels.[7]

In most instances, companies will have several types of inventory that can be managed effectively using one or more of these approaches. Obviously, a company should select the method that allows the most cost-beneficial investment in inventory.

6.2 Inventory Costs

There are several component costs of inventory. Some components represent opportunity costs, whereas others may be real costs. The component costs include:

- *Ordering.* Procurement or replenishment costs, both of which may be fixed or variable. These costs depend on the number of orders placed. Examples: freight, labor and handling, paperwork, machine setup.
- *Carrying.* Financing and holding costs, which are opportunity or real costs. These costs depend on average inventory levels and the type of goods. Examples: storage, capital costs, obsolescence, insurance, and taxes.
- *Stock-out.* Opportunity or real costs, which are affected by level of inventory, item mix, processing time versus term of sale. These costs might vary greatly depending on how they are estimated. Examples: lost sales, back-order costs, substitution costs.
- *Policy.* Costs of gathering data and general operating costs, which may be real costs or "soft" costs. These costs depend on inventory mix and complexity. Examples: data processing, labor charges, overtime, training.

6.3 Evaluating Inventory Management

The most common way to measure the company's investment in inventory and evaluate its inventory management is to compute the inventory turnover ratio and the number of days of inventory. The inventory turnover is a rough measure, but it is simple to calculate and compare with other standards or past history. Inventory turnover will vary among industries, as you can see in Exhibit 14, which provides a calculated inventory turnover and number of days of inventory for various industries.

Further, the inventory turnover may differ among companies within an industry because of different product mixes. For example, in fiscal year 2017, Wal-Mart Stores had an inventory turnover of 8.3 times compared with Target's 5.9 times. This difference may be because of Wal-Mart's greater foothold in the higher turnover grocery business, as compared with Target.

Although the analysis of trends is important, care should be taken when interpreting changes. For example, a decrease in the inventory turnover may mean that more inventory is on hand and is not moving through manufacturing and being sold. On the other hand, a decrease in inventory turnover may indicate a change in the company's product mix, or it may mean that the company is reducing its risk of inventory stock-outs.

7 Some companies have integrated cash management and inventory management. For example, the moment a customer orders and pays for a computer with Dell Corporation, the production process begins. This efficiency results in a negative operating cycle; that is, Dell Corporation is collecting on accounts as it invests in the inventory production. Because it uses trade credit for its supplies, it has little need for working capital.

Exhibit 14 Inventory Turnover and Number of Days of Inventory for US Corporations in Different Industries, 2013

Industry	Inventory Turnover (Times)	Number of Days of Inventory
Apparel manufacturing	3.8	96.9
Chemical manufacturing	4.9	74.8
Electronics and appliances stores	6.8	53.3
Food manufacturing	8.4	43.6
Food, beverage, and liquor stores	17.3	21.0
Machinery manufacturing	4.6	79.7
Mining	7.4	49.2
Motor vehicle dealers and parts dealers	4.2	86.7
Telecommunications	25.7	14.2
Transportation equipment manufacturing	6.4	56.8

Source: Statistics of Income, 2013, Corporation Returns with Net Income, Table 7, www.irs.gov.

EXAMPLE 5

Financial Impact of Inventory Methods

If a company's inventory turnover is 6.1 times (annually) and the industry average number of days of inventory is 52 days, how does the company compare with the industry average?

Solution:

Convert the turnover ratio to a number of days of inventory:

$$\begin{aligned}\text{Number of days of inventory} &= 365/\text{Inventory turnover}\\ &= 365/6.1 = 59.84 \text{ days}\end{aligned}$$

Comparing this answer with the industry average, 52.0 days, it appears that the company's inventory turnover is slower than the industry average.

MANAGING ACCOUNTS PAYABLE

7

Accounts payable are amounts due suppliers of goods and services that have not been paid. They arise from **trade credit**, which is a spontaneous form of credit in which a purchaser of the goods or service is, effectively, financing its purchase by delaying the date on which payment is made. Trade credit may involve a delay of payment, with a discount for early payment. The terms of the latter form of credit are generally stated in the discount form: A discount from the purchase price is allowed if payment is received within a specified number of days; otherwise the full amount is due by a specified date. For example, the terms "2/10, net 30" indicate that a 2 percent discount is available if the account is paid within 10 days; otherwise the full amount is due by the 30th day. The terms will differ among industries, influenced by tradition within the industry, terms of competitors, and current interest rates.

A key working capital link is the purchasing–inventory–payables process. This process is concerned with the procurement of goods—finished or not—that become the company's items for sale. Handled efficiently, the process minimizes excess funds "in the pipeline." Handled inefficiently, the process can create a severe drain on a company's liquidity, tying up funds and reducing the company's financial reserves.

Inefficiencies may arise in managing purchasing, inventory, and payables. Each area has to be organized and efficiently linked with the other areas. Purchasing can often influence how payments are to be made and the terms of credit. Here again, purchasing management needs to be kept informed as to the types of payment mechanisms the company can handle to avoid agreeing with suppliers to make payments in a medium that the company does not yet support.

The effective management of accounts payable is an important working capital management activity because inefficient payables management may result in opportunity costs from payments made too early, lost opportunities to take advantage of trade discounts, and failure to use the benefits of technologies offered by e-commerce and other web-based activities.

Accounts payable is the final step in the procurement cycle because it combines the paperwork, approvals, and disbursements of funds. An effective accounts payable function helps integrate the components of the cycle and does not require the uneconomical outlay of the company's funds until the outlay is due.

A company may not believe that it needs a formal guideline or policy to manage the function well. However, there must be some method to ensure that payables practices are organized, consistent, and cost-effective. For example, if payables management is decentralized and more than one operating entity deals with the same supplier, the credit terms offered to each entity should be the same unless there are special circumstances, such as volume constraints, that warrant different terms. To handle payables effectively, a company needs rules to ensure that company assets are not being depleted unnecessarily.

There are several factors that a company should consider as guidelines for effectively managing its accounts payable, including:

- *Financial organization's centralization.* The degree to which the company's core financial function is centralized or decentralized affects how tightly payables can be controlled.
- *Number, size, and location of vendors.* The composition of the company's supply chain and how dependent the company is on its trading partners (and vice versa) determines how sophisticated a payables system it needs.
- *Trade credit and cost of borrowing or alternative cost.* The importance of credit to the company and its ability to evaluate trade credit opportunities, such as trade discounts, encourages standardized payables procedures and enhanced information management throughout the company.
- *Control of disbursement float.* Many companies still pay suppliers by check and create **disbursement float**—the amount of time between check issuance and a check's clearing back against the company's account. This float has value to many companies because it allows them to use their funds longer than if they had to fund their checking account on the day the checks were mailed.
- *Inventory management.* Newer inventory control techniques, such as MRP and JIT, increase the number of payments that must be processed by accounts payable. Many older systems cannot accommodate this extra volume, so newer management techniques and systems are required.
- *E-commerce and electronic data interchange (EDI).* Global developments to use the internet and other direct connections between customer and supplier are revolutionizing the supply chain for many companies. Because payments

for many of these activities should be considered as part of the overall process, many companies have determined that paying electronically offers a more efficient, cost-effective alternative to checks, which only are more valuable when the disbursement float value is large and interest rates (which provide value to float) are also high.

Stretching payables, also known as pushing on payables when it stretches beyond the due date, is sometimes done by corporate cash managers and other financial managers.[8] Stretching payables is taking advantage of vendor grace periods. The evaluation of payables stretching opportunities is fairly straightforward. The number of additional days that payments can be extended or stretched is determined and valued by applying the company's opportunity cost for the additional days times the amount of the payable.

For example, if a payable that averaged \$100,000 can be stretched for an additional seven days, the company gains an additional seven days' use of the funds. This opportunity can be valued by multiplying the amount, \$100,000, by the company's opportunity cost for short-term funds. For example, if the company's estimated cost for short-term funds is 8 percent annually (0.02191 percent daily), then the value of stretching a \$100,000 payment for seven days is \$153.42. The values for each opportunity (throughout a year's activity) can be valued in this way to determine the overall benefit, which can then be weighed against the costs (both financial and nonfinancial ones).

There are basically two countering forces: paying too early is costly unless the company can take advantage of discounts, and paying late affects the company's perceived credit-worthiness.

7.1 The Economics of Taking a Trade Discount

One key activity that companies should review from time to time is the evaluation of trade discounts. Trade discounts should be evaluated using the formula shown below, which computes the implicit rate (of return) that is represented by the trade discount offer; that is, it is the equivalent return to the customer of an alternative investment.

The implicit rate is calculated as follows:

$$\text{Cost of trade credit} = \left(1 + \frac{\text{Discount}}{1 - \text{Discount}}\right)^{\left(365 \Big/ \begin{array}{c}\text{Number of days}\\ \text{beyond discount period}\end{array}\right)} - 1$$

The cost of funds during the discount period is 0 percent, so it is beneficial for the customer to pay close to the end of the discount period. Once the discount period ends, the cost of the credit to the customer jumps up and then declines as the net day is approached. For example, if the terms are 2/10, net 30, which means that there is a 2 percent discount for paying within 10 days and the net amount is due by the 30th day, the cost of trade credit is 109 percent if the credit is paid on the 20th day, but it is only 44.6 percent if paid on the 30th day.

If the customer's cost of funds or short-term investment rate is less than the calculated rate, the discount offers a better return or incremental return over the company's short-term borrowing rate.

8 Keep in mind that stretching payments beyond their due dates might be considered unethical and may draw retaliation from suppliers in the form of tighter credit terms in the future.

EXAMPLE 6

Evaluating Trade Discounts

Compute the cost of trade credit if terms are 1/10, net 30 and the account is paid on:

- the 20th day, and
- the 30th day.

Solution:

$$\text{Cost of trade credit if paid on day 20} = \left(1 + \frac{0.01}{1 - 0.01}\right)^{(365/10)} - 1$$
$$= 44.32 \text{ percent}$$

$$\text{Cost of trade credit if paid on day 30} = \left(1 + \frac{0.01}{1 - 0.01}\right)^{(365/20)} - 1$$
$$= 20.13 \text{ percent}$$

As you can see, the cost of the credit is much lower when the company pays on the net day than any day prior to the net day. Once the discount period is passed, waiting until the net day to pay will result in a lower cost of credit.

7.2 Managing Cash Disbursements

Handling cash disbursements effectively is a common goal for most companies. To accomplish this, companies use best practices that include the ability to delay funding bank accounts until the day checks clear, to erect safeguards against check fraud, to pay electronically when it is cost-effective to do so, and to manage bank charges for disbursement services. Best practices in cash disbursements, like check collections, depend on the nature of the payments—i.e., whether they are made electronically or by check.

Banks offer controlled disbursement services to optimize the funding of checks on the same day they clear against the company's account. When combined with a positive pay service, which provides a filter against check fraud, this method provides the best practice in handling paper-based (check) disbursements.

7.3 Evaluating Accounts Payable Management

The number of days of payables, which is also referred to as the average age of payables, is a useful measure in evaluating a company's credit extension and collection.

If the accounts payable balance from the company's balance sheet is €450 million and the amount of purchases is €4,100 million, the number of days of payables is

$$\text{Number of days of payables} = \frac{\text{Accounts payable}}{\text{Average day's purchases}} = \frac{450}{4100/365}$$
$$= 40.06 \text{ days}$$

Comparing the number of days of payables with the credit terms under which credit was granted to the company is important; paying sooner than necessary is costly in terms of the cost of credit, and paying later than the net day is costly in terms of relations with suppliers.

In some cases, treasurers will manage the company's payables closely, comparing the number of days of payables with the number of days of inventory because in some industries these two numbers of days are similar to one another.

MANAGING SHORT-TERM FINANCING

8

An overall short-term financial strategy should focus on ensuring that the company maintains a sound liquidity position. It should also reflect the degree of risk the company believes can be managed without affecting the company's stability. It is common to consider short-term financial strategies as applying mostly to investments. However, they should include other financial activities as well. In many cases, a company will only be an investor or borrower, but it is common for large multinational corporations to have both short-term investments and short-term borrowing.

A short-term policy should include guidelines for managing investment, borrowing, foreign exchange, and risk management activities and should encompass all the company's operations, including foreign subsidiaries and other domestic subsidiaries that are self-financing. These guidelines accomplish several things.

Too often companies do not explore their options sufficiently, and as a result, they do not take advantage of cost savings that some forms of borrowing offer. This lack of awareness usually indicates that a company's treasurer may not be familiar with the common forms of short-term borrowing and has not factored them into an effective borrowing strategy.

8.1 Sources of Short-Term Financing

The main types of short-term borrowing alternatives that borrowers should consider include bank sources as well as money market sources. The main types of bank short-term borrowing include uncommitted and committed bank lines of credit and revolving credit agreements ("revolvers"). The latter two types can be unsecured or secured, depending on the company's financial strength and the general credit situation, which may vary from country to country. Two of these types—uncommitted lines and revolvers—are more common in the United States, whereas regular lines are more common in other parts of the world. We provide examples of several types of short-term borrowing options in Exhibit 15, with bank sources in Panel A of this exhibit and nonbank sources in Panel B. In this exhibit, we provide the primary features for each type of borrowing, including the typical users, source(s) for the alternative, the base rate for computing interest, type of compensation required, and any other comments.

Exhibit 15 Short-Term Financing Instruments

Panel A: Bank Sources

Source/Type	Users	Rate Base	Compensation	Other
Uncommitted line	Large corporations		None	Mainly in United States; limited reliability
Regular line	All sizes	Prime (US) or base rate (other countries), money market, Libor +	Commitment fee	Common everywhere

(continued)

Exhibit 15 (Continued)

Source/Type	Users	Rate Base	Compensation	Other
Overdraft line	All sizes		Commitment fee	Mainly outside United States
Revolving credit agreement	Larger corporations		Commitment fee+ extra fees	Most reliable (primarily in United States)
Collateralized loan	Small, weak borrowers	Base +	Collateral	Common everywhere
Discounted receivables	Large companies	Varies	Extra fees	More overseas, but some in United States
Banker's acceptances	International companies	Spread over commercial paper	None	Small volume
Factoring	Smaller	Prime + +	Service fees	Special industries

Panel B: Nonbank Sources

Source/Type	Users	Rate Base	Compensation	Other
Nonbank finance companies	Small, weak borrowers	Prime + + +	Service fees	Less reliable
Commercial paper	Largest corporations	Money market sets rate	Backup line of credit, commissions +	Lowest rates for short-term funds

Uncommitted lines of credit are, as the name suggests, the least reliable form of bank borrowing. A bank may offer an uncommitted line of credit for an extended period of time, but it reserves the right to refuse to honor any request for use of the line. In other words, an uncommitted line is very unstable and is only as good as the bank's desire to offer it. Therefore, companies should not rely very much on uncommitted lines. In fact, banks will not "officially" acknowledge that an uncommitted line is usable, which means that uncommitted lines cannot be shown as a financial reserve in a footnote to the company's financial statements. The primary attraction of uncommitted lines is that they do not require any compensation other than interest.

Committed lines of credit are the form of bank line of credit that most companies refer to as regular lines of credit. They are more reliable than uncommitted because of the bank's formal commitment, which can be verified through an acknowledgment letter as part of the annual financial audit and can be footnoted in the company's annual report. These lines of credit are in effect for 364 days (one day short of a full year). This effectively makes sure that they are short-term liabilities, usually classified as notes payable or the equivalent, on the financial statements.

Regular lines are unsecured and are pre-payable without any penalties. The borrowing rate is a negotiated item. The most common interest rates negotiated are borrowing at the bank's prime rate or at a money market rate plus a spread. The most common money market rate is an offshore rate—the **London interbank offered rate (Libor)**, which is a Eurodollar rate—plus a spread. The spread varies depending on the borrower's credit-worthiness. Regular lines, unlike uncommitted lines, require compensation, usually in the form of a commitment fee. The fee is typically a fractional percent (e.g., ½ percent) of the full amount or the unused amount of the line, depending on bank–company negotiations.

Revolving credit agreements, which are often referred to as revolvers, are the most reliable form of short-term bank borrowing facilities. They have formal legal agreements that define the aspects of the agreement. These agreements are similar to regular lines with respect to borrowing rates, compensation, and being unsecured. Revolvers differ in that they are in effect for multiple years (e.g., 3–5 years) and may have optional medium-term loan features. In addition, they are often done for much larger amounts than a regular line, and these larger amounts are spread out among more than one bank.

For companies with weak financial positions, such as those facing financial distress or that have deteriorated profitability, and many smaller companies that do not have sufficient capital, banks or other lenders (see nonbank sources in Exhibit 15) require that the company (or individual for much smaller companies) provide collateral in the form of an asset, such as a fixed asset that the company owns or high-quality receivables and inventory. These assets are pledged against the loans, and banks or other lenders file a lien against them with the state in which the loan is made. This lien becomes part of the borrower's financial record and is shown on its credit report.

8.2 Short-Term Borrowing Approaches

Given the various forms of short-term borrowing, it is essential that a borrower have a planned strategy before getting stuck in an uneconomical situation. Many borrowing companies spend too little time establishing a sound strategy for their short-term borrowing beyond making sure that they are able to borrow at all, from any source.

The major objectives of a short-term borrowing strategy include the following:

- Ensuring that there is sufficient capacity to handle peak cash needs.
- Maintaining sufficient sources of credit to be able to fund ongoing cash needs.
- Ensuring that rates obtained are cost-effective and do not substantially exceed market averages.

In addition, there are several factors that borrowers should consider as part of their short-term borrowing strategies, including the following:

- *Size and credit-worthiness.* There is no doubt that the size of the borrower dictates the options available. Larger companies can take advantage of economies of scale to access commercial paper, banker's acceptances, and so on. The size of the borrower often reflects a manufacturing company's need for short-term financing. The size of lender is also an important criterion, as larger banks have higher house or legal lending limits. Credit-worthiness of the borrower will determine the rate, compensation, or even whether the loan will be made at all.
- *Sufficient access.* Borrowers should diversify to have adequate alternatives and not be too reliant on one lender or form of lending if the amount of their lending is very large. Even so, it is typical for borrowers to use one alternative primarily, but often with more than one provider. Borrowers should be ready to go to other sources and know how to. Borrowers should not stay too long with just one source or with lowest rates. Many borrowers are usually prepared to trade off rates (somewhat) for certainty.
- *Flexibility of borrowing options.* Flexibility means the ability to manage maturities efficiently; that is, there should not be any "big" days, when significant amounts of loans mature. To do this successfully, borrowers need active maturity management, awareness of the market conditions (e.g., knowing when the market or certain maturities should be avoided), and the ability to prepay loans when unexpected cash receipts happen.

Borrowing strategies, like investment strategies, can be either passive or active. Passive strategies usually involve minimal activity with one source or type of borrowing and with little (if any) planning. This "take what you can get" strategy is often reactive in responding to immediate needs or "panic attacks." Passive strategies are characterized by steady, often routine rollovers of borrowings for the same amount of funds each time, without much comparison shopping. Passive strategies may also arise when borrowing is restricted, such as instances where borrowers are limited to one or two lenders by agreement (e.g., in a secured loan arrangement).

Active strategies are usually more flexible, reflecting planning, reliable forecasting, and seeking the best deal. With active strategies, borrowers are more in control and do not fall into the rollover "trap" that is possible with passive strategies.

Many active strategies are matching strategies. Matching borrowing strategies function in a manner similar to matching investment strategies—loans are scheduled to mature when large cash receipts are expected. These receipts can pay back the loan, so the company does not have to invest the funds at potentially lower rates than the borrowing cost, thereby creating unnecessary costs.

8.3 Asset-Based Loans

Many companies that do not have the credit quality sufficient to qualify for unsecured bank loans may borrow from financial institutions by arranging for a secured loan, where the loan is secured using assets of the company. These secured loans are often referred to as **asset-based loans**. Often the assets used in short-term secured loans are the current assets of receivables and inventory. Unlike the collateral that may be used in longer-term borrowing, asset-based loans secured by accounts receivable and inventory present a challenge for the lender because the cash flows from accounts receivable depend on the amount and timing of collections and are influenced by the business risk of the company and its customers.

Lenders of these short-term asset-based loans are protected by the existence of the collateral and by provisions in the law that may provide them with a blanket lien on current and future assets of the company. The downside of a blanket lien is that even if the asset-based loan was secured by, say, accounts receivable, the lender may have a legal interest in other assets of the company until the loan is repaid.

Besides using working capital as the security for a loan, a company can use other means to generate cash flow from these working capital accounts. For example, a company can use its accounts receivable to generate cash flow through the **assignment of accounts receivable**, which is the use of these receivables as collateral for a loan, or a company can **factor** its accounts receivable, which is selling the receivables to the factor. In an assignment arrangement, the company remains responsible for the collection of the accounts, whereas in a factoring arrangement the company is shifting the credit granting and collection process to the factor. The cost of this credit depends on the credit quality of the accounts and the costs of collection.

Like accounts receivables, inventory may be a source of cash flow through the use of the inventory as collateral, with different types of arrangements possible:

- An **inventory blanket lien**, in which the lender has a claim on some or all of the company's inventory, but the company can sell the inventory in the ordinary course of business.
- A **trust receipt arrangement**, in which the lender requires the company to certify that the goods are segregated and held in trust, with proceeds of any sale remitted to the lender immediately.
- A **warehouse receipt arrangement** is similar to the trust receipt arrangement, but there is a third party (i.e., a warehouse company) that supervises the inventory.

The cost of asset-based loans security by inventory depends on the length of time it takes to sell the goods.

8.4 Computing the Costs of Borrowing

In carrying out a sound short-term borrowing strategy, one of the key decisions is selecting the most cost-effective form of short-term loan. However, this selection is often not a simple task, because each of the major forms has to be adjusted to be on a common basis for comparability. The fundamental rule is to compute the total cost of the form of borrowing and divide that number by the total amount of loan you received (i.e., net proceeds), adjusted for any discounting or compensating balances.

For example, in the case of a line of credit that requires a commitment fee,[9] the cost of the line of credit is

$$\text{Cost} = \frac{\text{Interest} + \text{Commitment fee}}{\text{Loan amount}}$$

On the other hand, if the interest rate is stated as "all inclusive" such that the amount borrowed includes the interest, as may be the case in a banker's acceptance, the interest is compared with the net proceeds when determining the cost:

$$\text{Cost} = \frac{\text{Interest}}{\text{Net proceeds}} = \frac{\text{Interest}}{\text{Loan amount} - \text{Interest}}$$

If there are dealer's fees and other fees, the expenses beyond the interest must be considered when determining the cost. For example, if a borrowing involves a dealer's fee and a backup fee and is quoted as all inclusive, the cost is

$$\text{Cost} = \frac{\text{Interest} + \text{Dealer's commission} + \text{Backup costs}}{\text{Loan amount} - \text{Interest}}$$

The key is to compare the interest and fees paid with the net proceeds of the loan. If the loan is for a period less than a year, then we annualize accordingly.

EXAMPLE 7

Computing the Effective Cost of Short-Term Borrowing Alternatives

You are asked to select one of the following choices as the best offer for borrowing $5,000,000 for one month:

1 Drawing down on a line of credit at 2.5 percent with a 1/2 percent commitment fee on the full amount. **Note:** One-twelfth of the cost of the commitment fee (which gives an option to borrow any time during the year) is allocated to the first month.

2 A banker's acceptance at 2.55 percent, an all-inclusive rate.

3 Commercial paper at 2.15 percent with a dealer's commission of 1/8 percent and a backup line cost of 1/4 percent, both of which would be assessed on the $5 million of commercial paper issued.

9 A commitment fee is a fee paid to the lender in return for the legal commitment to lend funds in the future.

Solution:

Line of credit cost:

$$\text{Line cost} = \frac{\text{Interest + Commitment fee}}{\text{Usable loan amount}} \times 12$$

$$= \frac{(0.025 \times \$5{,}000{,}000 \times 1/12) + (0.005 \times \$5{,}000{,}000 \times 1/12)}{\$5{,}000{,}000} \times 12$$

$$= \frac{\$10{,}416.67 + 2{,}083.33}{\$5{,}000{,}000} \times 12 = 0.03 \text{ or 3 percent}$$

Banker's acceptance cost:

$$\text{BA cost} = \frac{\text{Interest}}{\text{Net proceeds}} \times 12$$

$$= \frac{0.0255 \times \$5{,}000{,}000 \times 1/12}{\$5{,}000{,}000 - (0.0255 \times \$5{,}000{,}000 \times 1/12)} \times 12$$

$$= \frac{\$10{,}625}{\$4{,}989{,}375} \times 12 = 0.0256 \text{ or 2.56 percent}$$

Commercial paper cost (quoted as nominal rate at a discount):

$$\text{CP cost} = \frac{\text{Interest + Dealer's commissions + Backup costs}}{\text{Net proceeds}} \times 12$$

$$= \frac{(0.0215 \times \$5{,}000{,}000 \times 1/12) + (0.00125 \times \$5{,}000{,}000 \times 1/12) + (0.0025 \times \$5{,}000{,}000 \times 1/12)}{\$5{,}000{,}000 - (0.0215 \times \$5{,}000{,}000 \times 1/12)} \times 12$$

$$= \frac{\$8{,}958.33 + 520.83 + 1{,}041.67}{\$5{,}000{,}000 - 8{,}958.33} \times 12 = \frac{\$10{,}520.83}{\$4{,}991{,}041.67} \times 12 = 0.0253 \text{ or 2.53 percent}$$

We have simplified this cost analysis by assuming a loan for one month, using a factor of 1/12 to determine the interest and a factor of 12 to annualize. For specific arrangements for which the cost is determined using a 365-day or 360-day year, the appropriate adjustment would be required.

As the results show, the commercial paper alternative comes out with the lowest effective cost, and the line of credit has the highest effective cost. The commitment fee that was payable on the full line added more additional costs than the additional fees and discounting effects added in the other two options.

Line cost	3.00 percent
Banker's acceptance cost	2.56 percent
Commercial paper cost	2.53 percent

SUMMARY

In this reading, we considered a key aspect of financial management: the management of a company's working capital. This aspect of finance is a critical one in that it ensures, if done effectively, that the company will stay solvent and remain in business. If done improperly, the results can be disastrous for the company.

Working capital management covers a wide range of activities, most of which are focused on or involve the company's cash levels. Competing uses for the company's cash, which is often a scarce resource, create the need for an efficient method of handling the short-term financing of company activities.

Major points that were covered in this reading:

- Understanding how to evaluate a company's liquidity position.
- Calculating and interpreting operating and cash conversion cycles.
- Evaluating overall working capital effectiveness of a company and comparing it with other peer companies.
- Identifying the components of a cash forecast to be able to prepare a short-term (i.e., up to one year) cash forecast.
- Understanding the common types of short-term investments, and computing comparable yields on securities.
- Measuring the performance of a company's accounts receivable function.
- Measuring the financial performance of a company's inventory management function.
- Measuring the performance of a company's accounts payable function.
- Evaluating the short-term financing choices available to a company and recommending a financing method.

Working capital management is an integral part of the financial management of a company because many short-term activities have effects on long-term financial decisions. Having an effective short-term financial strategy, for example, allows a company to plan ahead with the confidence that its short-term concerns are being handled properly. Perhaps unlike other areas of finance, short-term finance has more qualitative features, making each company's case somewhat different from another's. This unique nature, combined with the short time frame associated with this aspect of finance, makes short-term finance a dynamic, challenging activity.

PRACTICE PROBLEMS

1 Suppose a company has a current ratio of 2.5 times and a quick ratio of 1.5 times. If the company's current liabilities are €100 million, the amount of inventory is *closest* to:

A €50 million.

B €100 million.

C €150 million.

2 Given the following financial statement data, calculate the operating cycle for this company.

	In Millions ($)
Credit sales	25,000
Cost of goods sold	20,000
Accounts receivable	2,500
Inventory—Beginning balance	2,000
Inventory—Ending balance	2,300
Accounts payable	1,700

The operating cycle for this company is *closest* to:

A 42.0 days.

B 47.9 days.

C 75.7 days.

3 Given the following financial statement data, calculate the net operating cycle for this company.

	In Millions ($)
Credit sales	40,000
Cost of goods sold	30,000
Accounts receivable	3,000
Inventory—Beginning balance	1,500
Inventory—Ending balance	2,000
Accounts payable	4,000

The net operating cycle of this company is *closest* to:

A 0.80 days.

B 24.3 days.

C 51.7 days.

4 The bond equivalent yield for a 182-day US Treasury bill that has a price of $9,725 per $10,000 face value is *closest* to:

A 5.44%.

B 5.53%.

C 5.67%.

5 A company increasing its credit terms for customers from 1/10, net 30 to 1/10, net 60 will *most likely* experience:

A an increase in cash on hand.

B a higher level of uncollectible accounts.

C an increase in the average collection period.

6 Suppose a company uses trade credit with the terms of 2/10, net 50. If the company pays its account on the 50th day, the effective borrowing cost of skipping the discount on day 10 is *closest* to:

A 14.9%.

B 15.0%.

C 20.2%.

7 William Jones is evaluating three possible means of borrowing $1 million for one month:

- Drawing down on a line of credit at 7.2 percent with a 1/2 percent commitment fee on the full amount with no compensating balances.
- A banker's acceptance at 7.1 percent, an all-inclusive rate.
- Commercial paper at 6.9 percent with a dealer's commission of 1/4 percent and a backup line cost of 1/3 percent, both of which would be assessed on the $1 million of commercial paper issued.

Which of these forms of borrowing results in the lowest cost of credit?

A Line of credit.

B Banker's acceptance.

C Commercial paper.

The following information relates to Questions 8–12

Mary Gonzales is evaluating companies in the office supply industry and has compiled the following information:

	20X1		20X2	
Company	**Credit Sales ($)**	**Average Receivables Balance ($)**	**Credit Sales ($)**	**Average Receivables Balance ($)**
A	5.0 million	1.0 million	6.0 million	1.2 million
B	3.0 million	1.2 million	4.0 million	1.5 million
C	2.5 million	0.8 million	3.0 million	1.0 million
D	0.5 million	0.1 million	0.6 million	0.2 million
Industry	25.0 million	5.0 million	28.0 million	5.4 million

8 Which of the companies had the highest number of days of receivables for the year 20X1?

A Company A.

B Company B.

C Company C.

9 Which of the companies has the lowest accounts receivable turnover in the year 20X2?

A Company A.

B Company B.

C Company D.

10 The industry average receivables collection period:

A increased from 20X1 to 20X2.

B decreased from 20X1 to 20X2.

C did not change from 20X1 to 20X2.

11 Which of the companies reduced the average time it took to collect on accounts receivable from 20X1 to 20X2?

A Company B.

B Company C.

C Company D.

12 Mary determined that Company A had an operating cycle of 100 days in 20X2, whereas Company D had an operating cycle of 145 days for the same fiscal year. This means that:

A Company D's inventory turnover is less than that of Company A.

B Company D's inventory turnover is greater than that of Company A.

C Company D's cash conversion cycle is shorter than that of Company A.

SOLUTIONS

1 B is correct.

Current ratio = Current assets/Current Liabilities = Current assets/ €100 million = 2.5

Therefore, current assets = €250 million

Quick ratio = (Current assets − Inventory)/ Current Liabilities = (€250 million − Inventory)/€100 million = 1.5

Therefore, Inventory = **€100 million**

2 C is correct.

Number of days of inventory = [($2,300 + $2,000)/2]/($20,000/365) = 39.238 days

Number of days of receivables = $2,500/($25,000/365) = 36.5 days

Operating cycle = 39.238 + 36.5 days = **75.738 days**

Note: The net operating cycle is 45.2 days.

Purchases = $20,000 + $2,300 − $2,000 = $20,300

Number of days of payables = $1,700/($20,300/365) = 30.567 days

The net operating cycle is 75.738 − 30.567 = 45.171 days

3 A is correct.

Number of days of inventory = [($2,000 + $1,500)/2]/($30,000/365) = 21.292 days

Number of days of receivables = $3,000/($40,000/365) = 27.375 days

Operating cycle = 21.292 + 27.375 days = 48.667 days

Purchases = $30,000 + $2,000 − $1,500 = $30,500

Number of days of payables = $4,000/($30,500/365) = 47.869 days

The net operating cycle is 48.667 − 47.869 = **0.798 days**

4 C is correct.

Bond equivalent yield = [($10,000 − 9,725)/$9,725] × (365/182) = **5.671 percent**

5 C is correct. A higher level of uncollectible accounts may occur, but a longer average collection period will certainly occur.

6 C is correct.

$$\text{Cost} = \left(1 + \frac{0.02}{0.98}\right)^{365/40} - 1 = 20.24 \text{ percent}$$

7 B is correct.

$$\text{Line cost} = \frac{\text{Interest} + \text{Commitment fee}}{\text{Net Proceed}} \times 12$$
$$= \frac{(0.072 \times \$1{,}000{,}000 \times 1/12) + (0.005 \times \$1{,}000{,}000 \times 1/12)}{\$1{,}000{,}000} \times 12$$
$$= \frac{\$6{,}000 + 416.67}{\$1{,}000{,}000} \times 12 = 0.077 \text{ or } 7.7 \text{ percent}$$

$$\text{Banker's acceptance cost} = \frac{\text{Interest}}{\text{Net Proceed}} \times 12$$
$$= \frac{(0.071 \times \$1{,}000{,}000 \times 1/12)}{\$1{,}000{,}000 - (0.071 \times \$1{,}000{,}000 \times 1/12)} \times 12$$
$$= \frac{\$5{,}916.67}{\$994{,}083.33} \times 12 = 0.0714 \text{ or } 7.14 \text{ percent}$$

$$\text{Commercial paper cost} = \frac{\text{Interest} + \text{Dealer's commission} + \text{Backup costs}}{\text{Net proceed}} \times 12$$
$$= \frac{(0.069 \times \$1{,}000{,}000 \times 1/12) + (0.0025 \times \$1{,}000{,}000 \times 1/12) + (0.003333 \times \$1{,}000{,}000 \times 1/12)}{\$1{,}000{,}000 - (0.069 \times \$1{,}000{,}000 \times 1/12)} \times 12$$
$$= \frac{\$5{,}750 + 208.33 + 277.78}{\$1{,}000{,}000 - 5{,}750} \times 12 = 0.0753 \text{ or } 7.53 \text{ percent}$$

8 B is correct.

Company A: \$1.0 million/(\$5.0 million/365) = 73.0 days

Company B: \$1.2 million/(\$3.0 million/365) = 146.0 days

Company C: \$0.8 million/(\$2.5 million/365) = 116.8 days

Company D: \$0.1 million/(\$0.5 million/365) = 73.0 days

9 B is correct.

Company A: \$6.0 million/\$1.2 million = 5.00

Company B: \$4.0 million/\$1.5 million = 2.67

Company C: \$3.0 million/\$1.0 million = 3.00

Company D: \$0.6 million/\$0.2 million = 3.00

10 B is correct.

20X1: 73 days

20X2: 70.393

Note: If the number of days decreased from 20X1 to 20X2, the receivable turnover increased.

11 A is correct.

Company B increased its accounts receivable (A/R) turnover and reduced its number of days of receivables between 20X1 and 20X2.

Company	20X1		20X2	
	A/R Turnover	Number of Days of Receivables	A/R Turnover	Number of Days of Receivables
A	5.000	73.000	5.000	73.000
B	2.500	146.000	2.667	136.875
C	3.125	116.800	3.000	121.667
D	5.000	73.000	3.000	121.667

12 B is correct.

Company A number of days of inventory = 100 – 73 = 27 days

Company D number of days of inventory = 145 – 121.67 = 23.33 days

Company A's turnover = 365/27 = 13.5 times

Company D's inventory turnover = 365/23.3 = 15.6 times

Equity Investments

STUDY SESSIONS

Study Session 12	Equity Investments (1)
Study Session 13	Equity Investments (2)

TOPIC LEVEL LEARNING OUTCOME

The candidate should be able to describe characteristics of equity investments, security markets, and indexes. The candidate should also be able to analyze industries, companies, and equity securities and to describe and demonstrate the use of basic equity valuation models.

Global equities are an important asset class for meeting longer term growth and diversification objectives. Global equities also represent a substantial share of capital markets that has been expanding in breadth and depth as developing economies come to market for equity capital. As developed and emerging economies continue to open their markets to investment, their activity is expected to significantly change the composition of world equity markets.

EQUITY INVESTMENTS

STUDY SESSION

12

Equity Investments (1)

This study session provides a structural overview of financial markets and their operating characteristics. Overview markets include equities, fixed income, derivatives, and alternative investments. Various asset types, market participants, and how assets trade within these markets and ecosystems are described. Coverage of these core asset classes continues in subsequent Level I study sessions, laying the foundation for further study in Levels II and III. The study session then turns to the calculation, construction, and use of security market indexes. A discussion of market efficiency and the degree to which market prices may reflect available information concludes the session.

READING ASSIGNMENTS

Reading 36	Market Organization and Structure by Larry Harris, PhD, CFA
Reading 37	Security Market Indexes by Paul D. Kaplan, PhD, CFA, and Dorothy C. Kelly, CFA
Reading 38	Market Efficiency by Sean Cleary, PhD, CFA, Howard J. Atkinson, CIMA, ICD.D, CFA, and Pamela Peterson Drake, PhD, CFA

READING

36

Market Organization and Structure

by Larry Harris, PhD, CFA

Larry Harris, PhD, CFA, is at the USC Marshall School of Business (USA).

LEARNING OUTCOMES

Mastery	*The candidate should be able to:*
☐	a. explain the main functions of the financial system;
☐	b. describe classifications of assets and markets;
☐	c. describe the major types of securities, currencies, contracts, commodities, and real assets that trade in organized markets, including their distinguishing characteristics and major subtypes;
☐	d. describe types of financial intermediaries and services that they provide;
☐	e. compare positions an investor can take in an asset;
☐	f. calculate and interpret the leverage ratio, the rate of return on a margin transaction, and the security price at which the investor would receive a margin call;
☐	g. compare execution, validity, and clearing instructions;
☐	h. compare market orders with limit orders;
☐	i. define primary and secondary markets and explain how secondary markets support primary markets;
☐	j. describe how securities, contracts, and currencies are traded in quote-driven, order-driven, and brokered markets;
☐	k. describe characteristics of a well-functioning financial system;
☐	l. describe objectives of market regulation.

1

INTRODUCTION

Financial analysts gather and process information to make investment decisions, including those related to buying and selling assets. Generally, the decisions involve trading securities, currencies, contracts, commodities, and real assets such as real estate. Consider several examples:

- Fixed income analysts evaluate issuer credit-worthiness and macroeconomic prospects to determine which bonds and notes to buy or sell to preserve capital while obtaining a fair rate of return.
- Stock analysts study corporate values to determine which stocks to buy or sell to maximize the value of their stock portfolios.
- Corporate treasurers analyze exchange rates, interest rates, and credit conditions to determine which currencies to trade and which notes to buy or sell to have funds available in a needed currency.
- Risk managers work for producers or users of commodities to calculate how many commodity futures contracts to buy or sell to manage inventory risks.

Financial analysts must understand the characteristics of the markets in which their decisions will be executed. This reading, by examining those markets from the analyst's perspective, provides that understanding.

This reading is organized as follows. Section 2 examines the functions of the financial system. Section 3 introduces assets that investors, information-motivated traders, and risk managers use to advance their financial objectives and presents ways practitioners classify these assets into markets. These assets include such financial instruments as securities, currencies, and some contracts; certain commodities; and real assets. Financial analysts must know the distinctive characteristics of these trading assets.

Section 4 is an overview of financial intermediaries (entities that facilitate the functioning of the financial system). Section 5 discusses the positions that can be obtained while trading assets. You will learn about the benefits and risks of long and short positions, how these positions can be financed, and how the financing affects their risks. Section 6 discusses how market participants order trades and how markets process those orders. These processes must be understood to achieve trading objectives while controlling transaction costs.

Section 7 focuses on describing primary markets. Section 8 describes the structures of secondary markets in securities. Sections 9 and 10 close the reading with discussions of the characteristics of a well-functioning financial system and of how regulation helps make financial markets function better. A summary reviews the reading's major ideas and points, and practice problems conclude.

2

THE FUNCTIONS OF THE FINANCIAL SYSTEM

The financial system includes markets and various financial intermediaries that help transfer financial assets, real assets, and financial risks in various forms from one entity to another, from one place to another, and from one point in time to another. These transfers take place whenever someone exchanges one asset or financial contract for another. The assets and contracts that people (people act on behalf of themselves, companies, charities, governments, etc., so the term "people" has a broad definition in this reading) trade include notes, bonds, stocks, exchange-traded funds, currencies, forward contracts, futures contracts, option contracts, swap contracts, and certain commodities. When the buyer and seller voluntarily arrange their trades, as is usually the case, the buyer and the seller both expect to be better off.

People use the financial system for six main purposes:

1. to save money for the future;
2. to borrow money for current use;
3. to raise equity capital;
4. to manage risks;
5. to exchange assets for immediate and future deliveries; and
6. to trade on information.

The main functions of the financial system are to facilitate:

1. the achievement of the purposes for which people use the financial system;
2. the discovery of the rates of return that equate aggregate savings with aggregate borrowings; and
3. the allocation of capital to the best uses.

These functions are extremely important to economic welfare. In a well-functioning financial system, transaction costs are low, analysts can value savings and investments, and scarce capital resources are used well.

Sections 2.1 through 2.3 expand on these three functions. The six subsections of Section 2.1 cover the six main purposes for which people use the financial system and how the financial system facilitates the achievement of those purposes. Sections 2.2 and 2.3 discuss determining rates of return and capital allocation efficiency, respectively.

2.1 Helping People Achieve Their Purposes in Using the Financial System

People often arrange transactions to achieve more than one purpose when using the financial system. For example, an investor who buys the stock of an oil producer may do so to move her wealth from the present to the future, to hedge the risk that she will have to pay more for energy in the future, and to exploit insightful research that she conducted that suggests the company's stock is undervalued in the marketplace. If the investment proves to be successful, she will have saved money for the future, managed her energy risk exposure, and obtained a return on her research.

The separate discussions of each of the six main uses of the financial system by people will help you better identify the reasons why people trade. Your ability to identify the various uses of the financial system will help you avoid confusion that often leads to poor financial decisions. The financial intermediaries that are mentioned in these discussions are explained further in Section 4.

2.1.1 *Saving*

People often have money that they choose not to spend now and that they want available in the future. For example, workers who save for their retirements need to move some of their current earnings into the future. When they retire, they will use their savings to replace the wages that they will no longer be earning. Similarly, companies save money from their sales revenue so that they can pay vendors when their bills come due, repay debt, or acquire assets (for example, other companies or machinery) in the future.

To move money from the present to the future, savers buy notes, certificates of deposit, bonds, stocks, mutual funds, or real assets such as real estate. These alternatives generally provide a better expected rate of return than simply storing money.

Savers then sell these assets in the future to fund their future expenditures. When savers commit money to earn a financial return, they commonly are called investors. They invest when they purchase assets, and they divest when they sell them.

Investors require a fair rate of return while their money is invested. The required fair rate of return compensates them for the use of their money and for the risk that they may lose money if the investment fails or if inflation reduces the real value of their investments.

The financial system facilitates savings when institutions create investment vehicles, such as bank deposits, notes, stocks, and mutual funds, that investors can acquire and sell without paying substantial transaction costs. When these instruments are fairly priced and easy to trade, investors will use them to save more.

2.1.2 *Borrowing*

People, companies, and governments often want to spend money now that they do not have. They can obtain money to fund projects that they wish to undertake now by borrowing it. Companies can also obtain funds by selling ownership or equity interests (covered in Section 2.1.3). Banks and other investors provide those requiring funds with money because they expect to be repaid with interest or because they expect to be compensated with future disbursements, such as dividends and capital gains, as the ownership interest appreciates in value.

People may borrow to pay for such items as vacations, homes, cars, or education. They generally borrow through mortgages and personal loans, or by using credit cards. People typically repay these loans with money they earn later.

Companies often require money to fund current operations or to engage in new capital projects. They may borrow the needed funds in a variety of ways, such as arranging a loan or a line of credit with a bank, or selling fixed income securities to investors. Companies typically repay their borrowing with income generated in the future. In addition to borrowing, companies may raise funds by selling ownership interests.

Governments may borrow money to pay salaries and other expenses, to fund projects, to provide welfare benefits to their citizens and residents, and to subsidize various activities. Governments borrow by selling bills, notes, or bonds. Governments repay their debt using future revenues from taxes and in some instances from the projects funded by these debts.

Borrowers can borrow from lenders only if the lenders believe that they will be repaid. If the lenders believe, however, that repayment in full with interest may not occur, they will demand higher rates of interest to cover their expected losses and to compensate them for the discomfit they experience wondering whether they will lose their money. To lower the costs of borrowing, borrowers often pledge assets as collateral for their loans. The assets pledged as collateral often include those that will be purchased by the proceeds of the loan. If the borrowers do not repay their loans, the lenders can sell the collateral and use the proceeds to settle the loans.

Lenders often will not loan to borrowers who intend to invest in risky projects, especially if the borrowers cannot pledge other collateral. Investors may still be willing to supply capital for these risky projects if they believe that the projects will likely produce valuable future cash flows. Rather than lending money, however, they will contribute capital in exchange for equity in the projects.

The financial system facilitates borrowing. Lenders aggregate from savers the funds that borrowers require. Borrowers must convince lenders that they can repay their loans, and that, in the event they cannot, lenders can recover most of the funds lent. Credit bureaus, credit rating agencies, and governments promote borrowing; credit bureaus and credit rating agencies do so by collecting and disseminating information that lenders need to analyze credit prospects and governments do so by establishing bankruptcy codes and courts that define and enforce the rights of borrowers and lenders. When the transaction costs of loans (i.e., the costs of arranging, monitoring, and collecting them) are low, borrowers can borrow more to fund current expenditures with credible promises to return the money in the future.

2.1.3 *Raising Equity Capital*

Companies often raise money for projects by selling (issuing) ownership interests (e.g., corporate common stock or partnership interests). Although these equity instruments legally represent ownership in companies rather than loans to the companies, selling equity to raise capital is simply another mechanism for moving money from the future to the present. When shareholders or partners contribute capital to a company, the company obtains money in the present in exchange for equity instruments that will be entitled to distributions in the future. Although the repayment of the money is not scheduled as it would be for loans, equity instruments also represent potential claims on money in the future.

The financial system facilitates raising equity capital. Investment banks help companies issue equities, analysts value the securities that companies sell, and regulatory reporting requirements and accounting standards attempt to ensure the production of meaningful financial disclosures. The financial system helps promote capital formation by producing the financial information needed to determine fair prices for equity. Liquid markets help companies raise capital. In these markets, shareholders can easily divest their equities as desired. When investors can easily value and trade equities, they are more willing to fund reasonable projects that companies wish to undertake.

EXAMPLE 1

Financing Capital Projects

As a chief financial officer (CFO) of a large industrial firm, you need to raise cash within a few months to pay for a project to expand existing and acquire new manufacturing facilities. What are the primary options available to you?

Solution:

Your primary options are to borrow the funds or to raise the funds by selling ownership interests. If the company borrows the funds, you may have the company pledge some or all of the project as collateral to reduce the cost of borrowing.

2.1.4 *Managing Risks*

Many people, companies, and governments face financial risks that concern them. These risks include default risk and the risk of changes in interest rates, exchange rates, raw material prices, and sale prices, among many other risks. These risks are often managed by trading contracts that serve as hedges for the risks.

For example, a farmer and a food processor both face risks related to the price of grain. The farmer fears that prices will be lower than expected when his grain is ready for sale whereas the food processor fears that prices will be higher than expected when she has to buy grain in the future. They both can eliminate their exposures to these risks if they enter into a binding forward contract for the farmer to sell a specified quantity of grain to the food processor at a future date at a mutually agreed upon price. By entering into a forward contract that sets the future trade price, they both eliminate their exposure to changing grain prices.

In general, hedgers trade to offset or insure against risks that concern them. In addition to forward contracts, they may use futures contracts, option contracts, or insurance contracts to transfer risk to other entities more willing to bear the risks (these contracts will be covered in Section 3.4). Often the hedger and the other entity face exactly the opposite risks, so the transfer makes both more secure, as in the grain example.

The financial system facilitates risk management when liquid markets exist in which risk managers can trade instruments that are correlated (or inversely correlated) with the risks that concern them without incurring substantial transaction costs. Investment banks, exchanges, and insurance companies devote substantial resources to designing such contracts and to ensuring that they will trade in liquid markets. When such markets exist, people are better able to manage the risks that they face and often are more willing to undertake risky activities that they expect will be profitable.

2.1.5 *Exchanging Assets for Immediate Delivery (Spot Market Trading)*

People and companies often trade one asset for another that they rate more highly or, equivalently, that is more useful to them. They may trade one currency for another currency, or money for a needed commodity or right. Following are some examples that illustrate these trades:

- Volkswagen pays its German workers in euros, but the company receives dollars when it sells cars in the United States. To convert money from dollars to euros, Volkswagen trades in the foreign exchange markets.
- A Mexican investor who is worried about the prospects for peso inflation or a potential devaluation of the peso may buy gold in the spot gold market. (This transaction may hedge against the risk of devaluation of the peso because the value of gold may increase with inflation.)
- A plastic producer must buy carbon credits to emit carbon dioxide when burning fuel to comply with environmental regulations. The carbon credit is a legal right that the producer must have to engage in activities that emit carbon dioxide.

In each of these cases, the trades are considered spot market trades because the instruments trade for immediate delivery. The financial system facilitates these exchanges when liquid spot markets exist in which people can arrange and settle trades without substantial transaction costs.

2.1.6 *Information-Motivated Trading*

Information-motivated traders trade to profit from information that they believe allows them to predict future prices. Like all other traders, they hope to buy at low prices and sell at higher prices. Unlike pure investors, however, they expect to earn a return on their information in addition to the normal return expected for bearing risk through time.

Active investment managers are information-motivated traders who collect and analyze information to identify securities, contracts, and other assets that their analyses indicate are under- or overvalued. They then buy those that they consider undervalued and sell those that they consider overvalued. If successful, they obtain a greater return than the unconditional return that would be expected for bearing the risk in their positions. The return that they expect to obtain is a conditional return earned on the basis of the information in their analyses. Practitioners often call this process active portfolio management.

Note that the distinction between pure investors and information-motivated traders depends on their motives for trading and not on the risks that they take or their expected holding periods. Investors trade to move wealth from the present to the future whereas information-motivated traders trade to profit from superior information about future values. When trading to move wealth forward, the time period may be short or long. For example, a bank treasurer may only need to move money overnight and might use money market instruments trading in an interbank funds market to accomplish that. A pension fund, however, may need to move money 30 years forward and might do that by using shares trading in a stock market. Both are investors although their expected holding periods and the risks in the instruments that they trade are vastly different.

In contrast, information-motivated traders trade because their information-based analyses suggest to them that prices of various instruments will increase or decrease in the future at a rate faster than others without their information or analytical models would expect. After establishing their positions, they hope that prices will change quickly in their favor so that they can close their positions, realize their profits, and redeploy their capital. These price changes may occur almost instantaneously, or they may take years to occur if information about the mispricing is difficult to obtain or understand.

The two categories of traders are not mutually exclusive. Investors also are often information-motivated traders. Many investors who want to move wealth forward through time collect and analyze information to select securities that will allow them to obtain conditional returns that are greater than the unconditional returns expected for securities in their asset classes. If they have rational reasons to expect that their efforts will indeed produce superior returns, they are information-motivated traders. If they consistently fail to produce such returns, their efforts will be futile, and they would have been better off simply buying and holding well-diversified portfolios.

EXAMPLE 2

Investing versus Information-Motivated Trading

The head of a large labor union with a pension fund asks you, a pension consultant, to distinguish between investing and information-motivated trading. You are expected to provide an explanation that addresses the financial problems that she faces. How would you respond?

Solution:

The object of investing for the pension fund is to move the union's pension assets from the present to the future when they will be needed to pay the union's retired pensioners. The pension fund managers will typically do this by buying stocks, bonds, and perhaps other assets. The pension fund managers expect to receive a fair rate of return on the pension fund's assets without paying excessive transaction costs and management fees. The return should compensate the fund for the risks that it bears and for the time that other people are using the fund's money.

The object of information-motivated trading is to earn a return in excess of the fair rate of return. Information-motivated traders analyze information that they collect with the hope that their analyses will allow them to predict better than others where prices will be in the future. They then buy assets that they think will produce excess returns and sell those that they think will underperform. Active investment managers are information-motivated traders.

The characteristic that most distinguishes investors from information-motivated traders is the return that they expect. Although both types of traders hope to obtain extraordinary returns, investors rationally expect to receive only fair returns during the periods of their investments. In contrast, information-motivated traders expect to make returns in excess of required fair rates of return. Of course, not all investing or information-motivated trading is successful (in other words, the actual returns may not equal or exceed the expected returns).

The financial system facilitates information-motivated trading when liquid markets allow active managers to trade without significant transaction costs. Accounting standards and reporting requirements that produce meaningful financial disclosures reduce the costs of being well informed, but do not necessarily help informed traders profit because they often compete with each other. The most profitable well-informed traders are often those that have the most unique insights into future values.

2.1.7 *Summary*

People use the financial system for many purposes, the most important of which are saving, borrowing, raising equity capital, managing risk, exchanging assets in spot markets, and information-motivated trading. The financial system best facilitates these uses when people can trade instruments that interest them in liquid markets, when institutions provide financial services at low cost, when information about assets and about credit risks is readily available, and when regulation helps ensure that everyone faithfully honors their contracts.

2.2 Determining Rates of Return

Saving, borrowing, and selling equity are all means of moving money through time. Savers move money from the present to the future whereas borrowers and equity issuers move money from the future to the present.

Because time machines do not exist, money can travel forward in time only if an equal amount of money is travelling in the other direction. This equality always occurs because borrowers and equity sellers create the securities in which savers invest. For example, the bond sold by a company that needs to move money from the future to the present is the same bond bought by a saver who needs to move money from the present to the future.

The aggregate amount of money that savers will move from the present to the future is related to the expected rate of return on their investments. If the expected return is high, they will forgo current consumption and move more money to the future. Similarly, the aggregate amount of money that borrowers and equity sellers will move from the future to the present depends on the costs of borrowing funds or of giving up ownership. These costs can be expressed as the rate of return that borrowers and equity sellers are expected to deliver in exchange for obtaining current funds. It is the same rate that savers expect to receive when delivering current funds. If this rate is low, borrowers and equity sellers will want to move more money to the present from the future. In other words, they will want to raise more funds.

Because the total money saved must equal the total money borrowed and received in exchange for equity, the expected rate of return depends on the aggregate supply of funds through savings and the aggregate demand for funds. If the rate is too high, savers will want to move more money to the future than borrowers and equity issuers will want to move to the present. The expected rate will have to be lower to discourage the savers and to encourage the borrowers and equity issuers. Conversely, if the rate is too low, savers will want to move less money forward than borrowers and equity issuers will want to move to the present. The expected rate will have to be higher to encourage the savers and to discourage the borrowers and equity issuers. Between rates too high and too low, an expected rate of return exists, in theory, in which the aggregate supply of funds for investing (supply of funds saved) and the aggregate demand for funds through borrowing and equity issuing are equal.

Economists call this rate the equilibrium interest rate. It is the price for moving money through time. Determining this rate is one of the most important functions of the financial system. The equilibrium interest rate is the only interest rate that would exist if all securities were equally risky, had equal terms, and were equally liquid. In fact, the required rates of return for securities vary by their risk characteristics, terms, and liquidity. For a given issuer, investors generally require higher rates of return for equity than for debt, for long-term securities than for short-term securities, and for illiquid securities than for liquid ones. Financial analysts recognize that all required rates of return depend on a common equilibrium interest rate plus adjustments for risk.

EXAMPLE 3

Interest Rates

For a presentation to private wealth clients by your firm's chief economist, you are asked to prepare the audience by explaining the most fundamental facts concerning the role of interest rates in the economy. You agree. What main points should you try to convey?

Solution:

Savers have money now that they will want to use in the future. Borrowers want to use money now that they do not have, but they expect that they will have money in the future. Borrowers are loaned money by savers and promise to repay it in the future.

The interest rate is the return that lenders, the savers, expect to receive from borrowers for allowing borrowers to use the savers' money. The interest rate is the price of using money.

Interest rates depend on the total amount of money that people want to borrow and the total amount of money that people are willing to lend. Interest rates are high when, in aggregate, people value having money now substantially more than they value having money in the future. In contrast, if many people with money want to use it in the future and few people presently need more money than they have, interest rates will be low.

2.3 Capital Allocation Efficiency

Primary capital markets (primary markets) are the markets in which companies and governments raise capital (funds). Companies may raise funds by borrowing money or by issuing equity. Governments may raise funds by borrowing money.

Economies are said to be **allocationally efficient** when their financial systems allocate capital (funds) to those uses that are most productive. Although companies may be interested in getting funding for many potential projects, not all projects are worth funding. One of the most important functions of the financial system is to ensure that only the best projects obtain scarce capital funds; the funds available from savers should be allocated to the most productive uses.

In market-based economies, savers determine, directly or indirectly, which projects obtain capital. Savers determine capital allocations directly by choosing which securities they will invest in. Savers determine capital allocations indirectly by giving funds to financial intermediaries that then invest the funds. Because investors fear the loss of their money, they will lend at lower interest rates to borrowers with the best credit prospects or the best collateral, and they will lend at higher rates to other borrowers with less secure prospects. Similarly, they will buy only those equities that they believe have the best prospects relative to their prices and risks.

To avoid losses, investors carefully study the prospects of the various investment opportunities available to them. The decisions that they make tend to be well informed, which helps ensure that capital is allocated efficiently. The fear of losses by investors and by those raising funds to invest in projects ensures that only the best projects tend to be funded. The process works best when investors are well informed about the prospects of the various projects.

In general, investors will fund an equity project if they expect that the value of the project is greater than its cost, and they will not fund projects otherwise. If the investor expectations are accurate, only projects that should be undertaken will be funded and all such projects will be funded. Accurate market information thus leads to efficient capital allocation.

EXAMPLE 4

Primary Market Capital Allocation

How can poor information about the value of a project result in poor capital allocation decisions?

Solution:

Projects should be undertaken only if their value is greater than their cost. If investors have poor information and overestimate the value of a project in which its true value is less than its cost, a wealth-diminishing project may be undertaken. Alternatively, if investors have poor information and underestimate the value of a project in which its true value is greater than its cost, a wealth-enhancing project may not be undertaken.

3 ASSETS AND CONTRACTS

People, companies, and governments use many different assets and contracts to further their financial goals and to manage their risks. The most common assets include financial assets (such as bank deposits, certificates of deposit, loans, mortgages, corporate and government bonds and notes, common and preferred stocks, real estate investment trusts, master limited partnership interests, pooled investment products, and exchange-traded funds), currencies, certain commodities (such as gold and oil), and real assets (such as real estate). The most common contracts are option, futures, forward, swap, and insurance contracts. People, companies, and governments use these assets and contracts to raise funds, to invest, to profit from information-motivated trading, to hedge risks, and/or to transfer money from one form to another.

3.1 Classifications of Assets and Markets

Practitioners often classify assets and the markets in which they trade by various common characteristics to facilitate communications with their clients, with each other, and with regulators.

The most actively traded assets are securities, currencies, contracts, and commodities. In addition, real assets are traded. Securities generally include debt instruments, equities, and shares in pooled investment vehicles. **Currencies** are monies issued by national monetary authorities. Contracts are agreements to exchange securities, currencies, commodities or other contracts in the future. Commodities include precious metals, energy products, industrial metals, and agricultural products. Real assets are tangible properties such as real estate, airplanes, or machinery. Securities, currencies, and contracts are classified as financial assets whereas commodities and real assets are classified as physical assets.

Securities are further classified as debt or equity. Debt instruments (also called fixed-income instruments) are promises to repay borrowed money. Equities represent ownership in companies. Pooled investment vehicle shares represent ownership of an undivided interest in an investment portfolio. The portfolio may include securities, currencies, contracts, commodities, or real assets. Pooled investment vehicles, such as exchange-traded funds, which exclusively own shares in other companies, generally are also considered equities.

Securities are also classified by whether they are public or private securities. Public securities are those registered to trade in public markets, such as on exchanges or through dealers. In most jurisdictions, issuers must meet stringent minimum regulatory standards, including reporting and corporate governance standards, to issue publicly traded securities.

Private securities are all other securities. Often, only specially qualified investors can purchase private equities and private debt instruments. Investors may purchase them directly from the issuer or indirectly through an investment vehicle specifically formed to hold such securities. Issuers often issue private securities when they find public reporting standards too burdensome or when they do not want to conform to the regulatory standards associated with public equity. Venture capital is private equity that investors supply to companies when or shortly after they are founded. Private securities generally are illiquid. In contrast, many public securities trade in liquid markets in which sellers can easily find buyers for their securities.

Contracts are derivative contracts if their values depend on the prices of other underlying assets. Derivative contracts may be classified as physical or financial depending on whether the underlying instruments are physical products or financial securities. Equity derivatives are contracts whose values depend on equities or indexes of equities. Fixed-income derivatives are contracts whose values depend on debt securities or indexes of debt securities.

Practitioners classify markets by whether the markets trade instruments for immediate delivery or for future delivery. Markets that trade contracts that call for delivery in the future are forward or futures markets. Those that trade for immediate delivery are called **spot markets** to distinguish them from forward markets that trade contracts on the same underlying instruments. Options markets trade contracts that deliver in the future, but delivery takes place only if the holders of the options choose to exercise them.

When issuers sell securities to investors, practitioners say that they trade in the **primary market**. When investors sell those securities to others, they trade in the **secondary market**. In the primary market, funds flow to the issuer of the security from the purchaser. In the secondary market, funds flow between traders.

Practitioners classify financial markets as money markets or capital markets. **Money markets** trade debt instruments maturing in one year or less. The most common such instruments are repurchase agreements (defined in Section 3.2.1), negotiable certificates of deposit, government bills, and commercial paper. In contrast, **capital markets** trade instruments of longer duration, such as bonds and equities, whose values depend on the credit-worthiness of the issuers and on payments of interest or dividends that will be made in the future and may be uncertain. Corporations generally finance their operations in the capital markets, but some also finance a portion of their operations by issuing short-term securities, such as commercial paper.

Finally, practitioners distinguish between **traditional investment markets** and **alternative investment markets**. Traditional investments include all publicly traded debts and equities and shares in pooled investment vehicles that hold publicly traded debts and/or equities. Alternative investments include **hedge funds**, private equities (including venture capital), commodities, real estate securities and real estate properties, securitized debts, operating leases, machinery, collectibles, and precious gems. Because these investments are often hard to trade and hard to value, they may sometimes trade at substantial deviations from their intrinsic values. The discounts compensate investors for the research that they must do to value these assets and for their inability to easily sell the assets if they need to liquidate a portion of their portfolios.

The remainder of this section describes the most common assets and contracts that people, companies, and governments trade.

EXAMPLE 5

Asset and Market Classification

The investment policy of a mutual fund only permits the fund to invest in public equities traded in secondary markets. Would the fund be able to purchase:

1 Common stock of a company that trades on a large stock exchange?
2 Common stock of a public company that trades only through dealers?
3 A government bond?
4 A single stock futures contract?
5 Common stock sold for the first time by a properly registered public company?
6 Shares in a privately held bank with €10 billion of capital?

Solution to 1:

Yes. Common stock is equity. Those common stocks that trade on large exchanges invariably are public equities that trade in secondary markets.

Solution to 2:

Yes. Dealer markets are secondary markets and the security is a public equity.

Solution to 3:

No. Although government bonds are public securities, they are not equities. They are debt securities.

Solution to 4:

No. Although the underlying instruments for single stock futures are invariably public equities, single stock futures are derivative contracts, not equities.

Solution to 5:

No. The fund would not be able to buy these shares because a purchase from the issuer would be in the primary market. The fund would have to wait until it could buy the shares from someone other than the issuer.

Solution to 6:

No. These shares are private equities, not public equities. The public prominence of the company does not make its securities public securities unless they have been properly registered as public securities.

3.2 Securities

People, companies, and governments sell securities to raise money. Securities include bonds, notes, commercial paper, mortgages, common stocks, preferred stocks, warrants, mutual fund shares, unit trusts, and depository receipts. These can be classified broadly as fixed-income instruments, equities, and shares in pooled investment vehicles. Note that the legal definition of a security varies by country and may or may not coincide with the usage here. Securities that are sold to the public or that can be resold to the public are called issues. Companies and governments are the most common issuers.

3.2.1 *Fixed Income*

Fixed-income instruments contractually include predetermined payment schedules that usually include interest and principal payments. Fixed-income instruments generally are promises to repay borrowed money but may include other instruments with payment schedules, such as settlements of legal cases or prizes from lotteries. The payment amounts may be pre-specified or they may vary according to a fixed formula that depends on the future values of an interest rate or a commodity price. Bonds, notes, bills, certificates of deposit, commercial paper, repurchase agreements, loan agreements, and mortgages are examples of promises to repay money in the future. People, companies, and governments create fixed-income instruments when they borrow money.

Corporations and governments issue bonds and notes. Fixed-income securities with shorter maturities are called "notes," those with longer maturities are called "bonds." The cutoff is usually at 10 years. In practice, however, the terms are generally used interchangeably. Both become short-term instruments when the remaining time until maturity is short, usually taken to be one year or less.

Some corporations issue convertible bonds, which are typically convertible into stock, usually at the option of the holder after some period. If stock prices are high so that conversion is likely, convertibles are valued like stock. Conversely, if stock prices are low so that conversion is unlikely, convertibles are valued like bonds.

Bills, certificates of deposit, and commercial paper are respectively issued by governments, banks, and corporations. They usually mature within a year of being issued; certificates of deposit sometimes have longer initial maturities.

Repurchase agreements (repos) are short-term lending instruments. The term can be as short as overnight. A borrower seeking funds will sell an instrument—typically a high-quality bond—to a lender with an agreement to repurchase it later at a slightly higher price based on an agreed upon interest rate.

Practitioners distinguish between short-term, intermediate-term, and long-term fixed-income securities. No general consensus exists about the definition of short-term, intermediate-term, and long-term. Instruments that mature in less than one to two years are considered short-term instruments whereas those that mature in more than five to ten years are considered long-term instruments. In the middle are intermediate-term instruments.

Instruments trading in money markets are called money market instruments. Such instruments are traded debt instruments maturing in one year or less. Money market funds and corporations seeking a return on their short-term cash balances typically hold money market instruments.

3.2.2 *Equities*

Equities represent ownership rights in companies. These include common and preferred shares. Common shareholders own residual rights to the assets of the company. They have the right to receive any dividends declared by the boards of directors, and in the event of liquidation, any assets remaining after all other claims are paid. Acting through the boards of directors that they elect, common shareholders usually can select the managers who run the corporations.

Preferred shares are equities that have preferred rights (relative to common shares) to the cash flows and assets of the company. Preferred shareholders generally have the right to receive a specific dividend on a regular basis. If the preferred share is a cumulative preferred equity, the company must pay the preferred shareholders any previously omitted dividends before it can pay dividends to the common shareholders.

Preferred shareholders also have higher claims to assets relative to common shareholders in the event of corporate liquidation. For valuation purposes, financial analysts generally treat preferred stocks as fixed-income securities when the issuers will clearly be able to pay their promised dividends in the foreseeable future.

Warrants are securities issued by a corporation that allow the warrant holders to buy a security issued by that corporation, if they so desire, usually at any time before the warrants expire or, if not, upon expiration. The security that warrant holders can buy usually is the issuer's common stock, in which case the warrants are considered equities because the warrant holders can obtain equity in the company by exercising their warrants. The warrant **exercise price** is the price that the warrant holder must pay to buy the security.

EXAMPLE 6

Securities

What factors distinguish fixed-income securities from equities?

Solution:

Fixed-income securities generate income on a regular schedule. They derive their value from the promise to pay a scheduled cash flow. The most common fixed-income securities are promises made by people, companies, and governments to repay loans.

Equities represent residual ownership in companies after all other claims—including any fixed-income liabilities of the company—have been satisfied. For corporations, the claims of preferred equities typically have priority over the claims of common equities. Common equities have the residual ownership in corporations.

3.2.3 *Pooled Investments*

Pooled investment vehicles are mutual funds, trusts, depositories, and hedge funds, that issue securities that represent shared ownership in the assets that these entities hold. The securities created by mutual funds, trusts, depositories, and hedge fund are respectively called *shares*, *units*, *depository receipts*, and *limited partnership interests* but practitioners often use these terms interchangeably. People invest in pooled investment vehicles to benefit from the investment management services of their managers and from diversification opportunities that are not readily available to them on an individual basis.

Mutual funds are investment vehicles that pool money from many investors for investment in a portfolio of securities. They are often legally organized as investment trusts or as corporate investment companies. Pooled investment vehicles may be open-ended or closed-ended. Open-ended funds issue new shares and redeem existing shares on demand, usually on a daily basis. The price at which a fund redeems and sells the fund's shares is based on the net asset value of the fund's portfolio, which is the difference between the fund's assets and liabilities, expressed on a per share basis. Investors generally buy and sell open-ended mutual funds by trading with the mutual fund.

In contrast, closed-end funds issue shares in primary market offerings that the fund or its investment bankers arrange. Once issued, investors cannot sell their shares of the fund back to the fund by demanding redemption. Instead, investors in closed-end funds must sell their shares to other investors in the secondary market. The secondary market prices of closed-end funds may differ—sometimes quite significantly—from their net asset values. Closed-end funds generally trade at a discount to their net asset values. The discount reflects the expenses of running the fund and sometimes investor concerns about the quality of the management. Closed-end funds may also trade at a discount or a premium to net asset value when investors believe that the portfolio securities are overvalued or undervalued. Many financial analysts thus believe that discounts and premiums on closed-end funds measure market sentiment.

Exchange-traded funds (ETFs) and exchange-traded notes (ETNs) are open-ended funds that investors can trade among themselves in secondary markets. The prices at which ETFs trade rarely differ much from net asset values because a class of investors, known as authorized participants (APs), has the option of trading directly with the ETF. If the market price of an equity ETF is sufficiently below its net asset value, APs will buy shares in the secondary market at market price and redeem shares at net asset value with the fund. Conversely, if the price of an ETF is sufficiently above its net asset value, APs will buy shares from the fund at net asset value and sell shares in the secondary market at market price. As a result, the market price and net asset values of ETFs tend to converge.

Many ETFs permit only in-kind deposits and redemptions. Buyers who buy directly from such a fund pay for their shares with a portfolio of securities rather than with cash. Similarly, sellers receive a portfolio of securities. The transaction portfolio generally is very similar—often essentially identical—to the portfolio held by the fund. Practitioners sometimes call such funds "depositories" because they issue depository receipts for the portfolios that traders deposit with them. The traders then trade the receipts in the secondary market. Some warehouses holding industrial materials and precious metals also issue tradable warehouse receipts.

Asset-backed securities are securities whose values and income payments are derived from a pool of assets, such as mortgage bonds, credit card debt, or car loans. These securities typically pass interest and principal payments received from the pool of assets through to their holders on a monthly basis. These payments may depend on formulas that give some classes of securities—called tranches—backed by the pool more value than other classes.

Hedge funds are investment funds that generally organize as limited partnerships. The hedge fund managers are the general partners. The limited partners are qualified investors who are wealthy enough and well informed enough to tolerate and accept substantial losses, should they occur. The regulatory requirements to participate in a hedge fund and the regulatory restrictions on hedge funds vary by jurisdiction. Most hedge funds follow only one investment strategy, but no single investment strategy characterizes hedge funds as a group. Hedge funds exist that follow almost every imaginable strategy ranging from long–short arbitrage in the stock markets to direct investments in exotic alternative assets.

The primary distinguishing characteristic of hedge funds is their management compensation scheme. Almost all funds pay their managers with an annual fee that is proportional to their assets and with an additional performance fee that depends on the wealth that the funds generate for their shareholders. A secondary distinguishing characteristic of many hedge funds is the use of leverage to increase risk exposure and to hopefully increase returns.

3.3 Currencies

Currencies are monies issued by national monetary authorities. Approximately 180 currencies are currently in use throughout the world. Some of these currencies are regarded as reserve currencies. Reserve currencies are currencies that national central banks and other monetary authorities hold in significant quantities. The primary reserve currencies are the US dollar and the euro. Secondary reserve currencies include the British pound, the Japanese yen, and the Swiss franc.

Currencies trade in foreign exchange markets. In spot currency transactions, one currency is immediately or almost immediately exchanged for another. The rate of exchange is called the spot exchange rate. Traders typically negotiate institutional trades in multiples of large quantities, such as US$1 million or ¥100 million. Institutional trades generally settle in two business days.

Retail currency trades most commonly take place through commercial banks when their customers exchange currencies at a location of the bank, use ATM machines when travelling to withdraw a different currency than the currency in which their bank accounts are denominated, or use credit cards to buy items priced in different currencies. Retail currency trades also take place at airport kiosks, at store front currency exchanges, or on the street.

3.4 Contracts

A contract is an agreement among traders to do something in the future. Contracts include forward, futures, swap, option, and insurance contracts. The values of most contracts depend on the value of an **underlying** asset. The underlying asset may be a commodity, a security, an index representing the values of other instruments, a currency pair or basket, or other contracts.

Contracts provide for some physical or cash settlement in the future. In a physically settled contract, settlement occurs when the parties to the contract physically exchange some item, such as avocados, pork bellies, or gold bars. Physical settlement also includes the delivery of such financial instruments as bonds, equities, or futures contracts even though the delivery is electronic. In contrast, cash settled contracts settle through cash payments. The amount of the payment depends on formulas specified in the contracts.

Financial analysts classify contracts by whether they are physical or financial based on the nature of the underlying asset. If the underlying asset is a physical product, the contract is a physical; otherwise, the contract is a financial. Examples of assets classified as physical include contracts for the delivery of petroleum, lumber, and gold. Examples of assets classified as financial include option contracts, and contracts on interest rates, stock indexes, currencies, and credit default swaps.

Contracts that call for immediate delivery are called spot contracts, and they trade in spot markets. Immediate delivery generally is three days or less, but depends on each market. All other contracts involve what practitioners call futurity. They derive their values from events that will take place in the future.

EXAMPLE 7

Contracts for Difference

Contracts for difference (CFD) allow people to speculate on price changes for an underlying asset, such as a common stock or an index. Dealers generally sell CFDs to their clients. When the clients sell the CFDs back to their dealer, they receive any appreciation in the underlying asset's price between the time of purchase and sale (open and close) of the contract. If the underlying asset's price drops over this interval, the client pays the dealer the difference.

1 Are contracts for difference derivative contracts?

2 Are contracts for difference based on copper prices cash settled or physically settled?

Solution to 1:

Contracts for difference are derivative contracts because their values are derived from changes in the prices of the underlying asset on which they are based.

Solution to 2:

All contracts for difference are cash settled contracts regardless of the underlying asset on which they are based because they settle in cash and not in the underlying asset.

3.4.1 *Forward Contracts*

A **forward contract** is an agreement to trade the underlying asset in the future at a price agreed upon today. For example, a contract for the sale of wheat after the harvest is a forward contract. People often use forward contracts to reduce risk. Before planting wheat, farmers like to know the price at which they will sell their crop. Similarly, before committing to sell flour to bakers in the future, millers like to know the prices that they will pay for wheat. The farmer and the miller both reduce their operating risks by agreeing to trade wheat forward.

Practitioners call such traders hedgers because they use their contractual commitments to hedge their risks. If the price of wheat falls, the wheat farmer's crop will drop in value on the spot market but he has a contract to sell wheat in the future at a higher fixed price. The forward contract has become more valuable to the farmer. Conversely, if the price of wheat rises, the miller's future obligation to sell flour will become more burdensome because of the high price he would have to pay for wheat on the spot market, but the miller has a contract to buy wheat at a lower fixed price. The forward contract has become more valuable to the miller. In both cases, fluctuations in the spot price are hedged by the forward contract. The forward contract offsets the operating risks that the hedgers face.

Consider a simple example of hedging. An avocado farmer in Mexico expects to harvest 15,000 kilograms of avocados and that the price at harvest will be 60 pesos per kilogram. That price, however, could fluctuate significantly before the harvest. If the price of avocados drops to 50 pesos, the farmer would lose 10 pesos per kilogram (60 pesos – 50 pesos) relative to his expectations, or a total of 150,000 pesos. Now, suppose that the farmer can sell avocados forward to Del Rey Avocado at 58 pesos for delivery at the harvest. If the farmer sells 15,000 kilograms forward, and the price of avocados drops to 50 pesos, the farmer would still be able to sell his avocados for 58 pesos, and thus would not suffer from the drop in the price of avocados below this level.

EXAMPLE 8

Hedging Gold Production

A Zimbabwean gold producer invests in a mine expansion project on the expectation that gold prices will remain at or above $1,200 USD per ounce when the new project starts producing ore.

1 What risks does the gold producer face with respect to the price of gold?

2 How might the gold producer hedge its gold price risk?

Solution to 1:

The gold producer faces the risk that the price of gold could fall below $1,200 USD before it can sell its new production. If so, the investment in the expansion project will be less profitable than expected, and may even generate losses for the mine.

Solution to 2:

The gold producer could hedge the gold price risk by selling gold forward, hopefully at a price near $1,200 USD. Even if the price of gold falls, the gold producer would get paid the contract price.

Forward contracts are very common, but two problems limit their usefulness for many market participants. The first problem is counterparty risk. **Counterparty risk** is the risk that the other party to a contract will fail to honor the terms of the contract. Concerns about counterparty risk ensure that generally only parties who have long-standing relationships with each other execute forward contracts. Trustworthiness is critical when prices are volatile because, after a large price change, one side or the other may prefer not to settle the contract.

The second problem is liquidity. Trading out of a forward contract is very difficult because it can only be done with the consent of the other party. The liquidity problem ensures that forward contracts tend to be executed only among participants for whom delivery is economically efficient and quite certain at the time of contracting so that both parties will want to arrange for delivery.

The counterparty risk problem and the liquidity problem often make it difficult for market participants to obtain the hedging benefits associated with forward contracting. Fortunately, futures contracts have been developed to mitigate these problems.

3.4.2 *Futures Contracts*

A **futures contract** is a standardized forward contract for which a clearinghouse guarantees the performance of all traders. The buyer of a futures contract is the side that will take physical delivery or its cash equivalent. The seller of a futures contract is the side that is liable for the delivery or its cash equivalent. A **clearinghouse** is an organization that ensures that no trader is harmed if another trader fails to honor the contract. In effect, the clearinghouse acts as the buyer for every seller and as the seller for every buyer. Buyers and sellers, therefore, can trade futures without worrying whether their counterparties are creditworthy. Because futures contracts are standardized, a buyer can eliminate his obligation to buy by selling his contract to anyone. A seller similarly can eliminate her obligation to deliver by buying a contact from anyone. In either case, the clearinghouse will release the trader from all future obligations if his or her long and short positions exactly offset each other.

To protect against defaults, futures clearinghouses require that all participants post with the clearinghouse an amount of money known as **initial margin** when they enter a contract. The clearinghouse then settles the margin accounts on a daily basis. All participants who have lost on their contracts that day will have the amount of their losses deducted from their margin by the clearinghouse. The clearinghouse similarly increases margins for all participants who gained on that day. Participants whose margins drop below the required **maintenance margin** must replenish their accounts. If a participant does not provide sufficient additional margin when required, the participant's broker will immediately trade to offset the participant's position. These **variation margin** payments ensure that the liabilities associated with futures contracts do not grow large.

EXAMPLE 9

Futures Margin

NYMEX's Light Sweet Crude Oil futures contract specifies the delivery of 1,000 barrels of West Texas Intermediate Crude Oil when the contract finally settles. A broker requires that its clients post an initial overnight margin of $7,763 per contract and an overnight maintenance margin of $5,750 per contract. A client buys ten contracts at $75 per barrel through this broker. On the next day, the contract settles for $72 per barrel. How much additional margin will the client have to provide to his broker?

Solution:

The client lost three dollars per barrel (he is the side committed to take delivery or its cash equivalent at $75 per barrel). This results in a $3,000 loss on each of his 10 contracts, and a total loss of $30,000. His initial margin of $77,630 is reduced by $30,000 leaving $47,630 in his margin account. Because his account has dropped below the maintenance margin requirement of $57,500, the client will get a margin call. The client must provide an additional $30,000 = $77,630 – $47,630 to replenish his margin account; the account is replenished to the amount of the initial margin. The client will only receive another margin call if his account drops to below $57,500 again.

Futures contracts have vastly improved the efficiency of forward contracting markets. Traders can trade standardized futures contracts with anyone without worrying about counterparty risk, and they can close their positions by arranging offsetting trades. Hedgers for whom the terms of the standard contract are not ideal generally still use the futures markets because the contracts embody most of the price risk that concerns them. They simply offset (close out) their futures positions, at the same time they enter spot contracts on which they make or take ultimate delivery.

EXAMPLE 10

Forward and Futures Contracts

What feature most distinguishes futures contracts from forward contracts?

Solution:

A futures contract is a standardized forward contract for which a clearinghouse guarantees the performance of all buyers and sellers. The clearinghouse reduces the counterparty risk problem. The clearinghouse allows a buyer who has bought a contract from one person and sold the same contract to another person to net out the two obligations so that she is no longer liable for either side of the contract; the positions are closed. The ability to trade futures contracts provides liquidity in futures contracts compared with forward contracts.

3.4.3 *Swap Contracts*

A **swap contract** is an agreement to exchange payments of periodic cash flows that depend on future asset prices or interest rates. For example, in a typical **interest rate swap**, at periodic intervals, one party makes fixed cash payments to the counterparty in exchange for variable cash payments from the counterparty. The variable payments are based on a pre-specified variable interest rate such as the London Interbank Offered

Rate (Libor). This swap effectively exchanges fixed interest payments for variable interest payments. Because the variable rate is set in the future, the cash flows for this contract are uncertain when the parties enter the contract.

Investment managers often enter interest rate swaps when they own a fixed long-term income stream that they want to convert to a cash flow that varies with current short-term interest rates, or vice versa. The conversion may allow them to substantially reduce the total interest rate risk to which they are exposed. Hedgers often use swap contracts to manage risks.

In a **commodity swap**, one party typically makes fixed payments in exchange for payments that depend on future prices of a commodity such as oil. In a **currency swap**, the parties exchange payments denominated in different currencies. The payments may be fixed, or they may vary depending on future interest rates in the two countries. In an **equity swap**, the parties exchange fixed cash payments for payments that depend on the returns to a stock or a stock index.

EXAMPLE 11

Swap and Forward Contracts

What feature most distinguishes a swap contract from a cash-settled forward contract?

Solution:

Both contracts provide for the exchange of cash payments in the future. A forward contract only has a single cash payment at the end that depends on an underlying price or index at the end. In contrast, a swap contract has several scheduled periodic payments, each of which depends on an underlying price or index at the time of the payment.

3.4.4 *Option Contracts*

An **option contract** allows the holder (the purchaser) of the **option** to buy or sell, depending on the type of option, an underlying instrument at a specified price at or before a specified date in the future. Those that do buy or sell are said to **exercise** their contracts. An option to buy is a **call option**, and an option to sell is a **put** option. The specified price is called the strike price (exercise price). If the holders can exercise their contracts only when they mature, they are **European-style** contracts. If they can exercise the contracts earlier, they are **American-style** contracts. Many exchanges list standardized option contracts on individual stocks, stock indexes, futures contracts, currencies, swaps, and precious metals. Institutions also trade many customized option contracts with dealers in the over-the-counter derivative market.

Option holders generally will exercise call options if the strike price is below the market price of the underlying instrument, in which case, they will be able to buy at a lower price than the market price. Similarly, they will exercise put options if the strike price is above the underlying instrument price so that they sell at a higher price than the market price. Otherwise, option holders allow their options to expire as worthless.

The price that traders pay for an option is the option premium. Options can be quite expensive because, unlike forward and futures contracts, they do not impose any liability on the holder. The premium compensates the sellers of options—called option writers—for giving the call option holders the right to potentially buy below market prices and put option holders the right to potentially sell above market prices. Because the writers must trade if the holders exercise their options, option contracts may impose substantial liabilities on the writers.

EXAMPLE 12

Option and Forward Contracts

What feature most distinguishes option contracts from forward contracts?

Solution:

The holder of an option contract has the right, but not the obligation, to buy (for a call option) or sell (for a put option) the underlying instrument at some time in the future. The writer of an option contract must trade the underlying instrument if the holder exercises the option.

In contrast, the two parties to a forward contract must trade the underlying instrument (or its equivalent value for a cash-settled contract) at some time in the future if either party wants to settle the contract.

3.4.5 *Other Contracts*

Insurance contracts pay their beneficiaries a cash benefit if some event occurs. Life, liability, and automobile insurance are examples of insurance contracts sold to retail clients. People generally use insurance contracts to compensate for losses that they will experience if bad things happen unexpectedly. Insurance contracts allow them to hedge risks that they face.

Credit default swaps (CDS) are insurance contracts that promise payment of principal in the event that a company defaults on its bonds. Bondholders use credit default swaps to convert risky bonds into more secure investments. Other creditors of the company may also buy them to hedge against the risk they will not be paid if the company goes bankrupt.

Well-informed traders who believe that a corporation will default on its bonds may buy credit default swaps written on the corporation's bonds if the swap prices are sufficiently low. If they are correct, the traders will profit if the payoff to the swap is more than the cost of buying and maintaining the swap position.

People sometimes also buy insurance contracts as investments, especially in jurisdictions where payouts from insurance contracts are not subject to as much taxation as are payouts to other investment vehicles. They may buy these contracts directly from insurance companies, or they may buy already issued contracts from their owners. For example, the life settlements market trades life insurance contracts that people sell to investors when they need cash.

3.5 Commodities

Commodities include precious metals, energy products, industrial metals, agricultural products, and carbon credits. Spot commodity markets trade commodities for immediate delivery whereas the forward and futures markets trade commodities for future delivery. Managers seeking positions in commodities can acquire them directly by trading in the spot markets or indirectly by trading forward and futures contracts.

The producers and processors of industrial metals and agricultural products are the primary users of the spot commodity markets because they generally are best able to take and make delivery and to store physical products. They undertake these activities in the normal course of operating their businesses. Their ability to handle physical products and the information that they gather operating businesses also gives them substantial advantages as information-motivated traders in these markets. Many producers employ financial analysts to help them analyze commodity market conditions so that they can best manage their inventories to hedge their operational risks and to speculate on future price changes.

Commodities also interest information-motivated traders and investment managers because they can use them as hedges against risks that they hold in their portfolios or as vehicles to speculate on future price changes. Most such traders take positions in the futures markets because they usually do not have facilities to handle most physical products nor can they easily obtain them. They also cannot easily cope with the normal variation in qualities that characterizes many commodities. Information-motivated traders and investment managers also prefer to trade in futures markets because most futures markets are more liquid than their associated spot markets and forward markets. The liquidity allows them to easily close their positions before delivery so that they can avoid handling physical products.

Some information-motivated traders and investment managers, however, trade in the spot commodity markets, especially when they can easily contract for low-cost storage. Commodities for which delivery and storage costs are lowest are nonperishable products for which the ratio of value to weight is high and variation in quality is low. These generally include precious metals, industrial diamonds, such high-value industrial metals as copper, aluminum, and mercury, and carbon credits.

3.6 Real Assets

Real assets include such tangible properties as real estate, airplanes, machinery, or lumber stands. These assets normally are held by operating companies, such as real estate developers, airplane leasing companies, manufacturers, or loggers. Many institutional investment managers, however, have been adding real assets to their portfolios as direct investments (involving direct ownership of the real assets) and indirect investments (involving indirect ownership, for example, purchase of securities of companies that invest in real assets or real estate investment trusts). Investments in real assets are attractive to them because of the income and tax benefits that they often generate, and because changes in their values may have a low correlation with other investments that the managers hold.

Direct investments in real assets generally require substantial management to ensure that the assets are maintained and used efficiently. Investment managers investing in such assets must either hire personnel to manage them or hire outside management companies. Either way, management of real assets is quite costly.

Real assets are unique properties in the sense that no two assets are alike. An example of a unique property is a real estate parcel. No two parcels are the same because, if nothing else, they are located in different places. Real assets generally differ in their conditions, remaining useful lives, locations, and suitability for various purposes. These differences are very important to the people who use them, so the market for a given real asset may be very limited. Thus, real assets tend to trade in very illiquid markets.

The heterogeneity of real assets, their illiquidity, and the substantial costs of managing them are all factors that complicate the valuation of real assets and generally make them unsuitable for most investment portfolios. These same problems, however, often cause real assets to be misvalued in the market, so astute information-motivated traders may occasionally identify significantly undervalued assets. The benefits from purchasing such assets, however, are often offset by the substantial costs of searching for them and by the substantial costs of managing them.

Many financial intermediaries create entities, such as real estate investment trusts (REITs) and master limited partnerships (MLPs), to securitize real assets and to facilitate indirect investment in real assets. The financial intermediaries manage the assets and pass through the net benefits after management costs to the investors who hold these securities. Because these securities are much more homogenous and divisible than the real assets that they represent, they tend to trade in much more liquid markets. Thus, they are much more suitable as investments than the real assets themselves.

Of course, investors seeking exposure to real assets can also buy shares in corporations that hold and operate real assets. Although almost all corporations hold and operate real assets, many specialize in assets that particularly interest investors seeking exposure to specific real asset classes. For example, investors interested in owning aircraft can buy an aircraft leasing company such as Waha Capital (Abu Dhabi Securities Exchange) and Aircastle Limited (NYSE).

EXAMPLE 13

Assets and Contracts

Consider the following assets and contracts:

Bank deposits	Hedge funds
Certificates of deposit	Master limited partnership interests
Common stocks	Mortgages
Corporate bonds	Mutual funds
Currencies	Stock option contracts
Exchange-traded funds	Preferred stocks
Lumber forward contracts	Real estate parcels
Crude oil futures contracts	Interest rate swaps
Gold	Treasury notes

1 Which of these represent ownership in corporations?

2 Which of these are debt instruments?

3 Which of these are created by traders rather than by issuers?

4 Which of these are pooled investment vehicles?

5 Which of these are real assets?

6 Which of these would a home builder most likely use to hedge construction costs?

7 Which of these would a corporation trade when moving cash balances among various countries?

Solution to 1:

Common and preferred stocks represent ownership in corporations.

Solution to 2:

Bank deposits, certificates of deposit, corporate bonds, mortgages, and Treasury notes are all debt instruments. They respectively represent loans made to banks, corporations, mortgagees (typically real estate owners), and the Treasury.

Solution to 3:

Lumber forward contracts, crude oil futures contracts, stock option contracts, and interest rate swaps are created when the seller sells them to a buyer.

Solution to 4:

Exchange-traded funds, hedge funds, and mutual funds are pooled investment vehicles. They represent shared ownership in a portfolio of other assets.

Solution to 5:

Real estate parcels are real assets.

Solution to 6:

A builder would buy lumber forward contracts to lock in the price of lumber needed to build homes.

Solution to 7:

Corporations often trade currencies when moving cash from one country to another.

4 FINANCIAL INTERMEDIARIES

Financial intermediaries help entities achieve their financial goals. These intermediaries include commercial, mortgage, and investment banks; credit unions, credit card companies, and various other finance corporations; brokers and exchanges; dealers and arbitrageurs; clearinghouses and depositories; mutual funds and hedge funds; and insurance companies. The services and products that financial intermediaries provide allow their clients to solve the financial problems that they face more efficiently than they could do so by themselves. Financial intermediaries are essential to well-functioning financial systems.

Financial intermediaries are called intermediaries because the services and products that they provide help connect buyers to sellers in various ways. Whether the connections are easy to identify or involve complex financial structures, financial intermediaries stand between one or more buyers and one or more sellers and help them transfer capital and risk between them. Financial intermediaries' activities allow buyers and sellers to benefit from trading, often without any knowledge of the other.

This section introduces the main financial intermediaries that provide services and products in well-developed financial markets. The discussion starts with those intermediaries whose services most obviously connect buyers to sellers and then proceeds to those intermediaries whose services create more subtle connections. Because many financial intermediaries provide many different types of services, some are mentioned more than once. The section concludes with a general characterization of the various ways in which financial intermediaries add value to the financial system.

4.1 Brokers, Exchanges, and Alternative Trading Systems

Brokers are agents who fill orders for their clients. They do not trade with their clients. Instead, they search for traders who are willing to take the other side of their clients' orders. Individual brokers may work for large brokerage firms, the brokerage arm of banks, or at exchanges. Some brokers match clients to clients personally. Others use specialized computer systems to identify potential trades and help their clients fill their orders. Brokers help their clients trade by reducing the costs of finding counterparties for their trades.

Block brokers provide brokerage service to large traders. Large orders are hard to fill because finding a counterparty willing to do a large trade is often quite difficult. A large buy order generally will trade at a premium to the current market price, and a large sell order generally will trade at a discount to the current market price. These price concessions encourage other traders to trade with the large traders. They also make large traders reluctant, however, to expose their orders to the public before their trades are arranged because they do not want to move the market. Block brokers, therefore, carefully manage the exposure of the orders entrusted to them, which makes filling them difficult.

Investment banks provide advice to their mostly corporate clients and help them arrange transactions such as initial and seasoned securities offerings. Their corporate finance divisions help corporations finance their business by issuing securities, such as common and preferred shares, notes, and bonds. Another function of corporate finance divisions is to help companies identify and acquire other companies (i.e., in mergers and acquisitions).

Exchanges provide places where traders can meet to arrange their trades. Historically, brokers and dealers met on an exchange floor to negotiate trades. Increasingly, exchanges arrange trades for traders based on orders that brokers and dealers submit to them. Such exchanges essentially act as brokers. The distinction between exchanges and brokers has become quite blurred. Exchanges and brokers that use electronic order matching systems to arrange trades among their clients are functionally indistinguishable in this respect. Examples of exchanges include the NYSE, Eurex, Frankfurt Stock Exchange, the Chicago Mercantile Exchange, the Tokyo Stock Exchange, and the Singapore Exchange.

Exchanges are easily distinguished from brokers by their regulatory operations. Most exchanges regulate their members' behavior when trading on the exchange, and sometimes away from the exchange.

Many securities exchanges regulate the issuers that list their securities on the exchange. These regulations generally require timely financial disclosure. Financial analysts use this information to value the securities traded at the exchange. Without such disclosure, valuing securities could be very difficult and market prices might not reflect the fundamental values of the securities. In such situations, well-informed participants may profit from less-informed participants. To avoid such losses, the less-informed participants may withdraw from the market, which can greatly increase corporate costs of capital.

Some exchanges also prohibit issuers from creating capital structures that would concentrate voting rights in the hands of a few owners who do not own a commensurate share of the equity. These regulations attempt to ensure that corporations are run for the benefit of all shareholders and not to promote the interests of controlling shareholders who do not have significant economic stakes in the company.

Exchanges derive their regulatory authority from their national or regional governments, or through the voluntary agreements of their members and issuers to subject themselves to the exchange regulations. In most countries, government regulators oversee the exchange rules and the regulatory operations. Most countries also impose financial disclosure standards on public issuers. Examples of government regulatory bodies include the Japanese Financial Services Agency, the British Financial Conduct Authority, the German Federal Financial Supervisory Authority (BaFin), the US Securities and Exchange Commission, the Ontario Securities Commission, and the Argentine National Securities Commission (CNV).

Alternative trading systems (ATSs), also known as **electronic communications networks** (ECNs) or **multilateral trading facilities** (MTFs) are trading venues that function like exchanges but that do not exercise regulatory authority over their subscribers except with respect to the conduct of their trading in their trading systems. Some ATSs operate electronic trading systems that are otherwise indistinguishable from the trading systems operated by exchanges. Others operate innovative trading systems that suggest trades to their customers based on information that their customers share with them or that they obtain through research into their customers' preferences. Many ATSs are known as **dark pools** because they do not display the orders that their clients send to them. Large investment managers especially like these systems because market prices often move to their disadvantage when other traders know about their large orders. ATSs may be owned and operated by broker–dealers, exchanges, banks, or by companies organized solely for this purpose, many of which may be owned by a consortia of brokers–dealers and banks. Examples of ATSs include

MATCHNow (Canada), BATS (United States), POSIT (United States), Liquidnet (United States), Baxter-FX (Ireland), and Turquoise (Europe). Many of these ATSs provide services in many markets besides the ones in which they are domiciled.

4.2 Dealers

Dealers fill their clients' orders by trading with them. When their clients want to sell securities or contracts, dealers buy the instruments for their own accounts. If their clients want to buy securities, dealers sell securities that they own or have borrowed. After completing a transaction, dealers hope to reverse the transaction by trading with another client on the other side of the market. When they are successful, they effectively connect a buyer who arrived at one point in time with a seller who arrived at another point in time.

The service that dealers provide is liquidity. **Liquidity** is the ability to buy or sell with low transactions costs when you want to trade. By allowing their clients to trade when they want to trade, dealers provide liquidity to them. In over-the-counter markets, dealers offer liquidity when their clients ask them to trade with them. In exchange markets, dealers offer liquidity to anyone who is willing to trade at the prices that the dealers offer at the exchange. Dealers profit when they can buy at prices that on average are lower than the prices at which they sell.

Dealers may organize their operations within proprietary trading houses, investment banks, and hedge funds, or as sole proprietorships. Some dealers are traditional dealers in the sense that individuals make trading decisions. Others use computerized trading to make all trading decisions. Examples of companies with large dealing operations include Deutsche Bank (Germany), RBC Capital Markets (Canada), Nomura Securities (Japan), Timber Hill (United States), Goldman Sachs (United States), and IG Group (United Kingdom). Almost all investment banks have large dealing operations.

Most dealers also broker orders, and many brokers deal to their customers. Accordingly, practitioners often use the term **broker–dealer** to refer to dealers and brokers. Broker–dealers have a conflict of interest with respect to how they fill their customers' orders. When acting as a broker, they must seek the best price for their customers' orders. When acting as dealers, however, they profit most when they sell to their customers at high prices or buy from their customers at low prices. The problem is most serious when the customer allows the broker–dealer to decide whether to trade the order with another trader or to fill it as a dealer. Consequently, when trading with a broker–dealer, some customers specify how they want their orders filled. They may also trade only with pure agency brokers who do not also deal.

Primary dealers are dealers with whom central banks trade when conducting monetary policy. They buy bills, notes, and bonds when the central banks sell them to decrease the money supply. The dealers then sell these instruments to their clients. Similarly, when the central banks want to increase the money supply, the primary dealers buy these instruments from their clients and sell them to the central banks.

EXAMPLE 14

Brokers and Dealers

What characteristic *most likely* distinguishes brokers from dealers?

Solution:

Brokers are agents that arrange trades on behalf of their clients. They do not trade with their clients. In contrast, dealers are proprietary traders who trade with their clients.

4.3 Securitizers

Banks and investment companies create new financial products when they buy and repackage securities or other assets. For example, mortgage banks commonly originate hundreds or thousands of residential mortgages by lending money to homeowners. They then place the mortgages in a pool and sell shares of the pool to investors as mortgage pass-through securities, which are also known as mortgage-backed securities. All payments of principal and interest are passed through to the investors each month, after deducting the costs of servicing the mortgages. Investors who purchase these pass-through securities obtain securities that in aggregate have the same net cash flows and associated risks as the pool of mortgages.

The process of buying assets, placing them in a pool, and then selling securities that represent ownership of the pool is called securitization.

Mortgage-backed securities have the advantage that default losses and early repayments are much more predictable for a diversified portfolio of mortgages than they are for individual mortgages. They are also attractive to investors who cannot efficiently service mortgages but wish to invest in mortgages. By securitizing mortgage pools, the mortgage banks allow investors who are not large enough to buy hundreds of mortgages to obtain the benefits of diversification and economies of scale in loan servicing.

Securitization greatly improves liquidity in the mortgage markets because it allows investors in the pass-through securities to buy mortgages indirectly that they otherwise would not buy. Because the financial risks associated with mortgage-backed securities (debt securities with specified claims on the cash flows of a portfolio of mortgages) are much more predictable than those of individual mortgages, mortgage-backed securities are easier to price and thus easier to sell when investors need to raise cash. These characteristics make the market for mortgage-backed securities much more liquid than the market for individual mortgages. Because investors value liquidity—the ability to sell when they want to—they will pay more for securitized mortgages than for individual mortgages. The homeowners benefit because higher mortgage prices imply lower interest rates.

The mortgage bank is a financial intermediary because it connects investors who want to buy mortgages to homeowners who want to borrow money. The homeowners sell mortgages to the bank when the bank lends them money.

Some mortgage banks form mortgage pools from mortgages that they buy from other banks that originate the loans. These mortgage banks are also financial intermediaries because they connect sellers of mortgages to buyers of mortgage-backed securities. Although the sellers of the mortgages are the originating lenders and not the borrowers, the benefits of creating liquid mortgage-backed securities ultimately flow back to the borrowers.

The creation of the pass-through securities generally takes place on the accounts of the mortgage bank. The bank buys mortgages and sells pass-through securities whose values depend on the mortgage pool. The mortgages appear on the bank's accounts as assets and the mortgage-backed securities appear as liabilities.

In many securitizations, the financial intermediary avoids placing the assets and liabilities on its balance sheet by setting up a special corporation or trust that buys the assets and issues the securities. That corporation or trust is called a **special purpose vehicle** (SPV) or alternatively a **special purpose entity** (SPE). Conducting a securitization through a special purpose vehicle is advantageous to investors because their interests in the asset pool are better protected in an SPV than they would be on the balance sheet of the financial intermediary if the financial intermediary were to go bankrupt.

Financial intermediaries securitize many assets. Besides mortgages, banks securitize car loans, credit card receivables, bank loans, and airplane leases, to name just a few assets. As a class, these securities are called asset-backed securities.

When financial intermediaries securitize assets, they often create several classes of securities, called tranches, that have different rights to the cash flows from the asset pool. The tranches are structured so that some produce more predictable cash flows than do others. The senior tranches have first rights to the cash flow from the asset pool. Because the overall risk of a given asset pool cannot be changed, the more junior tranches bear a disproportionate share of the risk of the pool. Practitioners often call the most junior tranche toxic waste because it is so risky. The complexity associated with slicing asset pools into tranches can make the resulting securities difficult to value. Mistakes in valuing these securities contributed to the financial crisis that started in 2007.

Investment companies also create pass-through securities based on investment pools. For example, an exchange-traded fund is an asset-backed security that represents ownership in the securities and contracts held by the fund. The shareholders benefit from the securitization because they can buy or sell an entire portfolio in a single transaction. Because the transaction cost savings are quite substantial, exchange-traded funds often trade in very liquid markets. The investment companies (and sometimes the arbitrageurs) that create exchange-traded funds are financial intermediaries because they connect the buyers of the funds to the sellers of the assets that make up the fund portfolios.

More generally, the creators of all pooled investment vehicles are financial intermediaries that transform portfolios of securities and contracts into securities that represent undivided ownership of the portfolios. The investors in these funds thus indirectly invest in the securities held by the fund. They benefit from the expertise of the investment manager and from obtaining a portfolio that may be more diversified than one they might otherwise be able to hold.

4.4 Depository Institutions and Other Financial Corporations

Depository institutions include commercial banks, savings and loan banks, credit unions, and similar institutions that raise funds from depositors and other investors and lend it to borrowers. The banks give their depositors interest and transaction services, such as check writing and check cashing, in exchange for using their money. They may also raise funds by selling bonds or equity in the bank.

These banks are financial intermediaries because they transfer funds from their depositors and investors to their borrowers. The depositors and investors benefit because they obtain a return (in interest, transaction services, dividends, or capital appreciation) on their funds without having to contract with the borrowers and manage their loans. The borrowers benefit because they obtain the funds that they need without having to search for investors who will trust them to repay their loans.

Many other financial corporations provide credit services. For example, acceptance corporations, discount corporations, payday advance corporations, and factors provide credit to borrowers by lending them money secured by such assets as consumer loans, machinery, future paychecks, or accounts receivables. They finance these loans by selling commercial paper, bonds, and shares to investors. These corporations are intermediaries because they connect investors to borrowers. The investors obtain investments secured by a diversified portfolio of loans while the borrowers obtain funds without having to search for investors.

Brokers also act as financial intermediaries when they lend funds to clients who want to buy securities on margin. They generally obtain the funds from other clients who deposit them in their accounts. Brokers who provide these services to hedge funds and other similar institutions are called prime brokers.

Banks, financial corporations, and brokers can only raise money from depositors and other lenders because their equity owners retain residual interests in the performance of the loans that they make. If the borrowers default, the depositors and other lenders have priority claims over the equity owners. If insufficient money is collected from the borrowers, shareholders' equity is used to pay their depositors and other lenders. The risk of losing capital focuses the equity owners' and management's attention so that credit is not offered foolishly.

Because the ability of these companies to cover their credit losses is limited by the capital that their owners invest in them, the depositors and other investors who lend them money pay close attention to how much money the owners have at risk. For example, if a finance corporation is poorly capitalized, its shareholders will lose little if its clients default on the loans that the finance corporation makes to them. In that case, the finance corporation will have little incentive to lend only to creditworthy borrowers and to effectively manage collection on those loans once they have been made. Worse, it may even choose to lend to borrowers with poor credit because the interest rates that they can charge such borrowers are higher. Until those loans default, the higher income will make the corporation appear to be more profitable than it actually is. Depositors and other investors are aware of these problems and generally pay close attention to them. Accordingly, poorly capitalized financial institutions cannot easily borrow money to finance their operations at favorable rates.

Depository banks and financial corporations are similar to securitized asset pools that issue pass-through securities. Their depositors and investors own securities that ultimately are backed by an asset pool consisting of their loan portfolios. The depositors generally hold the most senior tranche, followed by the other creditors. The shareholders hold the most junior tranche. In the event of bankruptcy, they are paid only if everyone else is paid.

EXAMPLE 15

Commercial Banks

What services do commercial banks provide that make them financial intermediaries?

Solution:

Commercial banks collect deposits from investors and lend them to borrowers. They are intermediaries because they connect lenders to borrowers. Commercial banks also provide transaction services that make it easier for the banks' depository customers to pay bills and collect funds from their own customers.

4.5 Insurance Companies

Insurance companies help people and companies offset risks that concern them. They do this by creating insurance contracts (policies) that provide a payment in the event that some loss occurs. The insured buy these contracts to hedge against potential losses. Common examples of insurance contracts include auto, fire, life, liability, medical, theft, and disaster insurance contracts.

Credit default swaps are also insurance contracts, but historically they have not been subject to the same reserve requirements that most governments apply to more traditional insurance contracts. They may be sold by insurance companies or by other financial entities, such as investment banks or hedge funds.

Insurance contracts transfer risk from those who buy the contracts to those who sell them. Although insurance companies occasionally broker trades between the insured and the insurer, they more commonly provide the insurance themselves. In that case, the insurance company's owners and creditors become the indirect insurers of the risks that the insurance company assumes. Insurance companies also often transfer risks that they do not wish to bear by buying reinsurance policies from reinsurers.

Insurers are financial intermediaries because they connect the buyers of their insurance contracts with investors, creditors, and reinsurers who are willing to bear the insured risks. The buyers benefit because they can easily obtain the risk transfers that they seek without searching for entities that would be willing to assume those risks.

The owners, creditors, and reinsurers of the insurance company benefit because the company allows them to sell their tolerance for risk easily without having to manage the insurance contracts. Instead, the company manages the relationships with the insured—primarily collections and claims—and hopefully controls the various problems—fraud, moral hazard, and adverse selection—that often plague insurance markets. Fraud occurs when people deliberately cause or falsely report losses to collect on insurance. Moral hazard occurs when people are less careful about avoiding insured losses than they would be if they were not insured so that losses occur more often than they would otherwise. Adverse selection occurs when only those who are most at risk buy insurance so that insured losses tend to be greater than average.

Everyone benefits because insurance companies hold large diversified portfolios of policies. Loss rates for well-diversified portfolios of insurance contracts are much more predictable than for single contracts. For such contracts as auto insurance in which losses are almost uncorrelated across policies, diversification ensures that the financial performance of a large portfolio of contracts will be quite predictable and so holding the portfolio will not be very risky. The insured benefit because they do not have to pay the insurers much to compensate them for bearing risk (the expected loss is quite predictable so the risk is relatively low). Instead, their insurance premiums primarily reflect the expected loss rate in the portfolio plus the costs of running and financing the company.

4.6 Arbitrageurs

Arbitrageurs trade when they can identify opportunities to buy and sell identical or essentially similar instruments at different prices in different markets. They profit when they can buy in one market for less than they sell in another market. Arbitrageurs are financial intermediaries because they connect buyers in one market to sellers in another market.

The purest form of arbitrage involves buying and selling the same instrument in two different markets. Arbitrageurs who do such trades sell to buyers in one market and buy from sellers in the other market. They provide liquidity to the markets because they make it easier for buyers and sellers to trade when and where they want to trade.

Because dealers and arbitrageurs both provide liquidity to other traders, they compete with each other. The dealers connect buyers and sellers who arrive in the same market at different times whereas the arbitrageurs connect buyers and sellers who arrive at the same time in different markets. In practice, traders who profit from offering liquidity rarely are purely dealers or purely arbitrageurs. Instead, most traders attempt to identify and exploit every opportunity they can to manage their inventories profitably.

If information about prices is readily available to market participants, pure arbitrages involving the same instrument will be quite rare. Traders who are well informed about market conditions usually route their orders to the market offering the best price so that arbitrageurs will have few opportunities to match traders across markets when they want to trade the exact same instrument.

Arbitrageurs often trade securities or contracts whose values depend on the same underlying factors. For example, dealers in equity option contracts often sell call options in the contract market and buy the underlying shares in the stock market. Because the values of the call options and of the underlying shares are closely correlated (the value of the call increases with the value of the shares), the long stock position hedges the risk in the short call position so that the dealer's net position is not too risky.

Similar to the pure arbitrage that involves the same instrument in different markets, these arbitrage trades connect buyers in one market to sellers in another market. In this case, however, the buyers and sellers are interested in different instruments whose values are closely related. In the example, the buyer is interested in buying a call options contract, the value of which is a nonlinear function of the value of the underlying stock; the seller is interested in selling the underlying stock.

Options dealers buy stock and sell calls when calls are overpriced relative to the underlying stocks. They use complicated financial models to value options in relation to underlying stock values, and they use financial engineering techniques to control the risk of their portfolios. Successful arbitrageurs must know valuation relations well and they must manage the risk in their portfolios well to trade profitably. They profit by buying the relatively undervalued instrument and selling the relatively overvalued instrument.

Buying a risk in one form and selling it another form involves a process called replication. Arbitrageurs use various trading strategies to replicate the returns to securities and contracts. If they can substantially replicate those returns, they can use the replication trading strategy to offset the risk of buying or selling the actual securities and contracts. The combined effect of their trading is to transform risk from one form to another. This process allows them to create or eliminate contracts in response to the excess demand for, and supply of, contracts.

For example, when traders want to buy more call contracts than are presently available, they push the call contract prices up so that calls become overvalued relative to the underlying stock. The arbitrageurs replicate calls by using a particular financial engineering strategy to buy the underlying stock, and then create the desired call option contracts by selling them short. In contrast, if more calls have been created than traders want to hold, call prices will fall so that calls become undervalued relative to the underlying stock. The arbitrageurs will trade stocks and contracts to absorb the excess contracts. Arbitrageurs who use these strategies are financial intermediaries because they connect buyers and sellers who want to trade the same underlying risks but in different forms.

EXAMPLE 16

Dealers and Arbitrageurs

With respect to providing liquidity to market participants, what characteristics most clearly distinguish dealers from arbitrageurs?

Solution:

Dealers provide liquidity to buyers and sellers who arrive at the same market at different times. They move liquidity through time. Arbitrageurs provide liquidity to buyers and sellers who arrive at different markets at the same time. They move liquidity across markets.

4.7 Settlement and Custodial Services

In addition to connecting buyers to sellers through a variety of direct and indirect means, financial intermediaries also help their customers settle their trades and ensure that the resulting positions are not stolen or pledged more than once as collateral.

Clearinghouses arrange for final settlement of trades. In futures markets, they guarantee contract performance. In other markets, they may act only as escrow agents, transferring money from the buyer to the seller while transferring securities from the seller to the buyer.

The members of a clearinghouse are the only traders for whom the clearinghouse will settle trades. To ensure that their members settle the trades that they present to the clearinghouse, clearinghouses require that their members have adequate capital and post-performance bonds (margins). Clearinghouses also limit the aggregate net (buy minus sell) quantities that their members can settle.

Brokers and dealers who are not members of the clearinghouse must arrange to have a clearinghouse member settle their trades. To ensure that the non-member brokers and dealers can settle their trades, clearinghouse members require that their customers (the non-member brokers and dealers) have adequate capital and post-margins. They also limit the aggregate net quantities that their customers can settle and they monitor their customers' trading to ensure that they do not arrange trades that they cannot settle.

Brokers and dealers similarly monitor the trades made by their retail and institutional customers, and regulate their customers to ensure that they do not arrange trades that they cannot settle.

This hierarchical system of responsibility generally ensures that traders settle their trades. The brokers and dealers guarantee settlement of the trades they arrange for their retail and institutional customers. The clearinghouse members guarantee settlement of the trades that their customers present to them, and clearinghouses guarantee settlement of all trades presented to them by their members. If a clearinghouse member fails to settle a trade, the clearinghouse settles the trade using its own capital or capital drafted from the other members.

Reliable settlement of all trades is extremely important to a well-functioning financial system because it allows strangers to confidently contract with each other without worrying too much about **counterparty risk**, the risk that their counterparties will not settle their trades. A secure clearinghouse system thus greatly increases liquidity because it greatly increases the number of counterparties with whom a trader can safely arrange a trade.

In many national markets, clearinghouses clear all securities trades so that traders can trade securities through any exchange, broker, alternative trading system, or dealer. These clearinghouse systems promote competition among these exchange service providers.

In contrast, most futures exchanges have their own clearinghouses. These clearinghouses usually will not accept trades arranged away from their exchanges so that a competing exchange cannot trade another exchange's contracts. Competing exchanges may create similar contracts, but moving traders from one established market to a new market is extraordinarily difficult because traders prefer to trade where other traders trade.

Depositories or custodians hold securities on behalf of their clients. These services, which are often offered by banks, help prevent the loss of securities through fraud, oversight, or natural disaster. Broker–dealers also often hold securities on behalf of their customers so that the customers do not have to hold the securities in certificate form. To avoid problems with lost certificates, securities increasingly are issued only in electronic form.

EXAMPLE 17

Financial Intermediaries

As a relatively new member of the business community, you decide it would be advantageous to join the local lunch club to network with businessmen. Upon learning that you are a financial analyst, club members soon enlist you to give a lunch speech. During the question and answer session afterwards, a member of the audience asks, "I keep reading in the newspaper about the need to regulate 'financial intermediaries', but really don't understand exactly what they are. Can you tell me?" How do you answer?

Solution:

Financial intermediaries are companies that help their clients achieve their financial goals. They are called intermediaries because, in some way or another, they stand between two or more people who would like to trade with each other, but for various reasons find it difficult to do so directly. The intermediary arranges the trade for them, or more often, trades with both sides.

For example, a commercial bank is an intermediary that connects investors with money to borrowers who need money. The investors buy certificates of deposit from the bank, buy bonds or stock issued by the bank, or simply are depositors in the bank. The borrowers borrow this money from the bank when they arrange loans. Without the bank's intermediation, the investors would have to find trustworthy borrowers themselves, which would be difficult, and the borrowers would have to find trusting lenders, which would also be difficult.

Similarly, an insurance company is an intermediary because it connects customers who want to insure risks with investors who are willing to bear those risks. The investors own shares or bonds issued by the insurance company, or they have sold reinsurance contracts to the insurance company. The insured benefit because they can more easily buy a policy from an insurance company than they can find counterparties who would be willing to bear their risks. The investors benefit because the insurance company creates a diversified portfolio of risks by selling insurance to thousands or millions of customers. Diversification ensures that the net risk borne by the insurance company and its investors will be predictable and thus financially manageable.

In both cases, the financial intermediary also manages the relationships with its customers and investors so that neither side has to worry about the credit-worthiness or trust-worthiness of its counterparties. For example, the bank manages credit quality and collections on its loans and the insurance company manages risk exposure and collections on its policies. These services benefit both sides by reducing the costs of connecting investors to borrowers or of insured to insurers.

These are only two examples of financial intermediation. Many others involve firms engaged in brokerage, dealing, arbitrage, securitization, investment management, and the clearing and settlement of trades. In all cases, the financial intermediary stands between a buyer and a seller, offering them services that allow them to better achieve their financial goals in a cost effective and efficient manner.

4.8 Summary

By facilitating transactions among buyers and sellers, financial intermediaries provide services essential to a well-functioning financial system. They facilitate transactions the following ways:

1. Brokers, exchanges, and various alternative trading systems match buyers and sellers interested in trading the same instrument at the same place and time. These financial intermediaries specialize in discovering and organizing information about who wants to trade.
2. Dealers and arbitrageurs connect buyers to sellers interested in trading the same instrument but who are not present at the same place and time. Dealers connect buyers to sellers who are present at the same place but at different times whereas arbitrageurs connect buyers to sellers who are present at the same time but in different places. These financial intermediaries trade for their own accounts when providing these services. Dealers buy or sell with one client and hope to do the offsetting transaction later with another client. Arbitrageurs buy from a seller in one market while simultaneously selling to a buyer in another market.
3. Many financial intermediaries create new instruments that depend on the cash flows and associated financial risks of other instruments. The intermediaries provide these services when they securitize assets, manage investment funds, operate banks and other finance corporations that offer investments to investors and loans to borrowers, and operate insurance companies that pool risks. The instruments that they create generally are more attractive to their clients than the instruments on which they are based. The new instruments also may be differentiated to appeal to diverse clienteles. Their efforts connect buyers of one or more instruments to sellers of other instruments, all of which in aggregate provide the same cash flows and risk exposures. Financial intermediaries thus effectively arrange trades among traders who otherwise would not trade with each other.
4. Arbitrageurs who conduct arbitrage among securities and contracts whose values depend on common factors convert risk from one form to another. Their trading connects buyers and sellers who want to trade similar risks expressed in different forms.
5. Banks, clearinghouses, and depositories provide services that ensure traders settle their trades and that the resulting positions are not stolen or pledged more than once as collateral.

5 POSITIONS

People generally solve their financial and risk management problems by taking positions in various assets or contracts. A **position** in an asset is the quantity of the instrument that an entity owns or owes. A portfolio consists of a set of positions.

People have **long positions** when they own assets or contracts. Examples of long positions include ownership of stocks, bonds, currencies, contracts, commodities, or real assets. Long positions benefit from an appreciation in the prices of the assets or contracts owned.

People have **short positions** when they have sold assets that they do not own, or when they write and sell contracts. Short positions benefit from a decrease in the prices of the assets or contracts sold. Short sellers profit by selling at high prices and repurchasing at lower prices. Information-motivated traders sell assets and contracts short positions when they believe that prices will fall.

Hedgers also often sell instruments short. They short securities and contracts when the financial risks inherent in the instruments are positively correlated with the risks to which they are exposed. For example, to hedge the risk associated with holding copper inventories, a wire manufacturer would sell short copper futures. If the price of copper falls, the manufacturer will lose on his copper inventories but gain on his short futures position. (If the risk in an instrument is inversely correlated with a risk to which hedgers are exposed, the hedgers will hedge with long positions.)

Contracts have long sides and short sides. The long side of a forward or futures contract is the side that will take physical delivery or its cash equivalent. The short side of such contracts is the side that is liable for the delivery. The long side of a futures contract increases in value when the value of the underlying asset increases in value.

The identification of the two sides can be confusing for option contracts. The long side of an option contract is the side that holds the right to exercise the option. The short side is the side that must satisfy the obligation. Practitioners say that that the long side *holds* the option and the short side *writes* the option, so the long side is the holder and the short side is the writer. The put contracts are the source of the potential confusion. The put contract holder has the right to sell the underlying to the writer. The holder will benefit if the price of the underlying falls, in which case the price of the put contract will rise. The holder is long the put contract and has an indirect short position in the underlying instrument. Analysts call the indirect short position short exposure to the underlying. The put contract holders have long exposure to their option contract and short exposure to the underlying instrument.

Exhibit 1 Option Positions and Their Associated Underlying Risk Exposures

Type of Option	Option Position	Exposure to Underlying Risk
Call	Long	Long
Call	Short	Short
Put	Long	Short
Put	Short	Long

The identification of the long side in a swap contract is often arbitrary because swap contracts call for the exchange of contractually determined cash flows rather than for the purchase (or the cash equivalent) of some underlying instrument. In general, the side that benefits from an increase in the quoted price is the long side.

The identification of the long side in currency contracts also may be confusing. In this case, the confusion stems from symmetry in the contracts. The buyer of one currency is the seller of the other currency, and vice versa for the seller. Thus, a long forward position in one currency is a short forward position in the other currency. When practitioners describe a position, they generally will say, "I'm long the dollar against the yen," which means they have bought dollars and sold yen.

5.1 Short Positions

Short sellers create short positions in contracts by selling contracts that they do not own. In a sense, they become the issuers of the contract when they create the liabilities associated with their contracts. This analogy will also help you better understand risk when you study corporate finance: Corporations create short positions in their bonds when they issue bonds in exchange for cash. Although bonds are generally considered to be securities, they are also contracts between the issuer and the bondholder.

Short sellers create short positions in securities by borrowing securities from security lenders who are long holders. The short sellers then sell the borrowed securities to other traders. Short sellers close their positions by repurchasing the securities and returning them to the security lenders. If the securities drop in value, the short sellers profit because they repurchase the securities at lower prices than the prices at which they sold the securities. If the securities rise in value, they will lose. Short sellers who buy to close their positions are said to cover their positions.

The potential gains in a long position generally are unbounded. For example, the stock prices of such highly successful companies as Yahoo! have increased more than 50-fold since they were first publicly traded. The potential losses on long positions, however, are limited to no more than 100 percent—a complete loss—for long positions without any associated liabilities.

In contrast, the potential gains on a short position are limited to no more than 100 percent whereas the potential losses are unbounded. The unbounded potential losses on short positions make short positions very risky in volatile instruments. As an extreme example of this, if you had shorted 100 shares of Yahoo! in July 1996 at $20 and kept the position open for four years, you would have lost $148,000 on your $2,000 initial short position. During this period, Yahoo! rose 75-fold to $1,500 on a split-adjusted equivalent basis.

Although security lenders generally believe that they are long the securities that they lend, in fact, they do not actually own the securities during the periods of their loans. Instead, they own promises made by the short sellers to return the securities. These promises are memorialized in security lending agreements. These agreements specify that the short sellers will pay the long sellers all dividends or interest that they otherwise would have received had they not lent their securities. These payments are called payments-in-lieu of dividends (or of interest), and they may have different tax treatments than actual dividends and interest. The security lending agreements also protect the lenders in the event of a stock split.

To secure the security loans, lenders require that the short seller leave the proceeds of the short sale on deposit with them as collateral for the stock loan. They invest the collateral in short-term securities, and they rebate the interest to the short sellers at rates called short rebate rates. The short rebate rates are determined in the market and generally are available only to institutional short-sellers and some large retail traders. If a security is hard to borrow, the rebate rate may be very small or even negative. Such securities are said to be "on special". Most security lending agreements require various margin payments to keep the credit risk among the parties from growing when prices change.

Securities lenders lend their securities because the short rebate rates they pay on the collateral are lower than the interest rates they receive from investing the collateral. The difference is because of the implicit loan fees that they receive from the borrowers for borrowing the stock. The difference also compensates lenders for risks that the lenders take when investing the collateral and for the risk that the borrowers will default if prices rise significantly.

EXAMPLE 18

Short Positions in Securities and Contracts

How is the process of short selling shares of Siemens different from that of short selling a Siemens equity call option contract?

Solution:

To short sell shares of Siemens, the seller (or his broker) must borrow the shares from a long holder so that he can deliver them to the buyer. To short sell a Siemens equity call option contract, the seller simply creates the contract when he sells it to the buyer.

5.2 Leveraged Positions

In many markets, traders can buy securities by borrowing some of the purchase price. They usually borrow the money from their brokers. The borrowed money is called the **margin loan**, and they are said to buy on margin. The interest rate that the buyers pay for their margin loan is called the **call money rate**. The call money rate is above the government bill rate and is negotiable. Large buyers generally obtain more favorable rates than do retail buyers. For institutional-size buyers, the call money rate is quite low because the loans are generally well secured by securities held as collateral by the lender.

Trader's equity is that portion of the security price that the buyer must supply. Traders who buy securities on margin are subject to minimum margin requirements. The **initial margin requirement** is the minimum fraction of the purchase price that must be trader's equity. This requirement may be set by the government, the exchange, or the exchange clearinghouse. For example, in the United States, the Federal Reserve Board sets the initial margin requirement through Regulation T. In Hong Kong SAR, the Securities and Futures Commission sets the margin requirements. In all markets, brokers often require more equity than the government-required minimum from their clients when lending to them.

Many markets allow brokers to lend their clients more money if the brokers use risk models to measure and control the overall risk of their clients' portfolios. This system is called portfolio margining.

Buying securities on margin can greatly increase the potential gains or losses for a given amount of equity in a position because the trader can buy more securities on margin than he could otherwise. The buyer thus earns greater profits when prices rise and suffers greater losses when prices fall. The relation between risk and borrowing is called **financial leverage** (often simply called leverage). Traders leverage their positions when they borrow to buy more securities. A highly leveraged position is large relative to the equity that supports it.

The leverage ratio is the ratio of the value of the position to the value of the equity investment in it. The leverage ratio indicates how many times larger a position is than the equity that supports it. The maximum leverage ratio associated with a position financed by the minimum margin requirement is one divided by the minimum margin requirement. If the requirement is 40 percent, then the maximum leverage ratio is 2.5 = 100% position ÷ 40% equity.

The leverage ratio indicates how much more risky a leveraged position is relative to an unleveraged position. For example, if a stock bought on 40 percent margin rises 10 percent, the buyer will experience a 25 percent (2.5 × 10%) return on the equity investment in her leveraged position. But if the stock falls by 10 percent, the return on the equity investment will be –25 percent (before the interest on the margin loan and before payment of commissions).

Financial analysts must be able to compute the total return to the equity investment in a leveraged position. The total return depends on the price change of the purchased security, the dividends or interest paid by the security, the interest paid on the margin loan, and the commissions paid to buy and sell the security. The following example illustrates the computation of the total return to a leveraged purchase of stock that pays a dividend.

EXAMPLE 19

Computing Total Return to a Leveraged Stock Purchase

A buyer buys stock on margin and holds the position for exactly one year, during which time the stock pays a dividend. For simplicity, assume that the interest on the loan and the dividend are both paid at the end of the year.

Purchase price	$20/share
Sale price	$15/share
Shares purchased	1,000
Leverage ratio	2.5
Call money rate	5%
Dividend	$0.10/share
Commission	$0.01/share

1 What is the total return on this investment?

2 Why is the loss greater than the 25 percent decrease in the market price?

Solution to 1:

To find the return on this investment, first determine the initial equity and then determine the equity remaining after the sale. The total purchase price is $20,000. The leverage ratio of 2.5 indicates that the buyer's equity financed 40 percent = (1 ÷ 2.5) of the purchase price. Thus, the equity investment is $8,000 = 40% of $20,000. The $12,000 remainder is borrowed. The actual investment is slightly higher because the buyer must pay a commission of $10 = $0.01/share × 1,000 shares to buy the stock. The total initial investment is $8,010.

At the end of the year, the stock price has declined by $5/share. The buyer lost $5,000 = $5/share × 1,000 shares as a result of the price change. In addition, the buyer has to pay interest at 5 percent on the $12,000 loan, or $600. The buyer also receives a dividend of $0.10/share, or $100. The trader's equity remaining after the sale is computed from the initial equity investment as follows:

Initial investment	$8,010
Purchase commission	–10
Trading gains/losses	–5,000
Margin interest paid	–600
Dividends received	100
Sales commission paid	–10
Remaining equity	$2,490

or

Proceeds on sale	$15,000
Payoff loan	–12,000

Margin interest paid	–600
Dividends received	100
Sales commission paid	–10
Remaining equity	$2,490

so that the return on the initial investment of \$8,010 is (2,490 – 8,010)/8,010 = –68.9%.

Solution to 2:

The realized loss is substantially greater than the stock price return of (\$15 – \$20)/\$20 = –25%. Most of the difference is because of the leverage with the remainder primarily the result of the interest paid on the loan. Based on the leverage alone and ignoring the other cash flows, we would expect that the return on the equity would be –62.5% = 2.5 leverage times the –25% stock price return.

In the above example, if the stock dropped more than the buyer's original 40 percent margin (ignoring commissions, interest, and dividends), the trader's equity would have become negative. In that case, the investor would owe his broker more than the stock is worth. Brokers often lose money in such situations if the buyer does not repay the loan out of other funds.

To prevent such losses, brokers require that margin buyers always have a minimum amount of equity in their positions. This minimum is called the **maintenance margin requirement**. It is usually 25 percent of the current value of the position, but it may be higher or lower depending on the volatility of the instrument and the policies of the broker.

If the value of the equity falls below the maintenance margin requirement, the buyer will receive a **margin call**, or request for additional equity. If the buyer does not deposit additional equity with the broker in a timely manner, the broker will close the position to prevent further losses and thereby secure repayment of the margin loan.

When you buy securities on margin, you must know the price at which you will receive a margin call if prices drop. The answer to this question depends on your initial equity and on the maintenance margin requirement.

EXAMPLE 20

Margin Call Price

A trader buys stock on margin posting 40 percent of the initial stock price of \$20 as equity. The maintenance margin requirement for the position is 25 percent. Below what price will a margin call occur?

Solution:

The trader's initial equity is 40 percent of the initial stock price of \$20, or \$8 per share. Subsequent changes in equity per share are equal to the share price change so that equity per share is equal to \$8 + (P – 20) where P is the current share price. The margin call takes place when equity drops below the 25 percent maintenance margin requirement. The price below which a margin call will take place is the solution to the following equation:

$$\frac{\text{Equity/share}}{\text{Price/share}} = \frac{\$8 + P - 20}{P} = 25\%$$

which occurs at P = 16. When the price drops below \$16, the equity will be under \$4/share, which is less than 25 percent of the price.

Traders who sell securities short are also subject to margin requirements because they have borrowed securities. Initially, the trader's equity supporting the short position must be at least equal to the margin requirement times the initial value of the short position. If prices rise, equity will be lost. At some point, the short seller will have to contribute additional equity to meet the maintenance margin requirement. Otherwise, the broker will buy the security back to cover the short position to prevent further losses and thereby secure repayment of the stock loan.

6 ORDERS

Buyers and sellers communicate with the brokers, exchanges, and dealers that arrange their trades by issuing **orders**. All orders specify what instrument to trade, how much to trade, and whether to buy or sell. Most orders also have other instructions attached to them. These additional instructions may include execution instructions, validity instructions, and clearing instructions. **Execution instructions** indicate how to fill the order, **validity instructions** indicate when the order may be filled, and **clearing instructions** indicate how to arrange the final settlement of the trade.

In this section, we introduce various order instructions and explain how traders use them to achieve their objectives. We discuss execution mechanisms—how exchanges, brokers and dealers fill orders—in the next section. To understand the concepts in this section, however, you need to know a little about order execution mechanisms.

In most markets, dealers and various other proprietary traders often are willing to buy from, or sell to, other traders seeking to sell or buy. The prices at which they are willing to buy are called **bid** prices and those at which they are willing to sell are called **ask** prices, or sometimes **offer** prices. The ask prices are invariably higher than the bid prices.

The traders who are willing to trade at various prices may also indicate the quantities that they will trade at those prices. These quantities are called **bid sizes** and **ask sizes** depending on whether they are attached to bids or offers.

Practitioners say that the traders who offer to trade make a market. Those who trade with them take the market.

The highest bid in the market is the **best bid**, and the lowest ask in the market is the **best offer**. The difference between the best bid and the best offer is the **market bid–ask spread**. When traders ask, "What's the market?" they want to know the best bid and ask prices and their associated sizes. Bid–ask spreads are an implicit cost of trading. Markets with small bid–ask spreads are markets in which the costs of trading are small, at least for the sizes quoted. Dealers often quote both bid and ask prices, and in that case, practitioners say that they quote a two-sided market. The market spread is never more than any dealer spread.

6.1 Execution Instructions

Market and limit orders convey the most common execution instructions. A **market order** instructs the broker or exchange to obtain the best price immediately available when filling the order. A **limit order** conveys almost the same instruction: Obtain the best price immediately available, but in no event accept a price higher than a specified limit price when buying or accept a price lower than a specified limit price when selling.

Many people mistakenly believe that limit orders specify the prices at which the orders will trade. Although limit orders do often trade at their limit prices, remember that the first instruction is to obtain the best price available. If better prices are available than the limit price, brokers and exchanges should obtain those prices for their clients.

Market orders generally execute immediately if other traders are willing to take the other side of the trade. The main drawback with market orders is that they can be expensive to execute, especially when the order is placed in a market for a thinly traded security, or more generally, when the order is large relative to the normal trading activity in the market. In that case, a market buy order may fill at a high price, or a market sell order may fill at a low price if no traders are willing to trade at better prices. High purchase prices and low sale prices represent price concessions given to other traders to encourage them to take the other side of the trade. Because the sizes of price concessions can be difficult to predict, and because prices often change between when a trader submits an order and when the order finally fills, the execution prices for market orders are often uncertain.

Buyers and sellers who are concerned about the possibility of trading at unacceptable prices add limit price instructions to their orders. The main problem with limit orders is that they may not execute. Limit orders do not execute if the limit price on a buy order is too low, or if the limit price on a sell order is too high. For example, if an investment manager submits a limit order to buy at the limit price of 20 (buy limit 20) and nobody is willing to sell at or below 20, the order will not trade. If prices never drop to 20, the manager will never buy. If the price subsequently rises, the manager will have lost the opportunity to profit from the price rise.

Whether traders use market orders or limit orders when trying to arrange trades depends on their concerns about price, trading quickly, and failing to trade. On average, limit orders trade at better prices than do market orders, but they often do not trade. Traders generally regret when their limit orders fail to trade because they usually would have profited if they had traded. Limit buy orders do not fill when prices are rising, and limit sell orders do not fill when prices are falling. In both cases, traders would be better off if their orders had filled.

The probability that a limit order will execute depends on where the order is placed relative to market prices. An aggressively priced order is more likely to trade than is a less aggressively priced order. A limit buy order is aggressively priced when the limit price is high relative to the market bid and ask prices. If the limit price is placed above the best offer, the buy order generally will partially or completely fill at the best offer price, depending on the size available at the best offer. Such limit orders are called **marketable limit orders** because at least part of the order can trade immediately. A limit buy order with a very high price relative to the market is essentially a market order.

If the buy order is placed above the best bid but below the best offer, traders say the order makes a new market because it becomes the new best bid. Such orders generally will not immediately trade, but they may attract sellers who are interested in trading. A buy order placed at the best bid is said to make market. It may have to wait until all other buy orders at that price trade first. Finally, a buy order placed below the best bid is **behind the market**. It will not execute unless market prices drop. Traders call limit orders that are waiting to trade **standing limit orders**.

Sell limit orders are aggressively priced if the limit price is low relative to market prices. The limit price of a marketable sell limit order is below the best bid. A limit sell order placed between the best bid and the best offer makes a new market on the sell side, one placed at the best offer makes market, and one placed above the best offer is behind the market.

Exhibit 2 presents a simplified **limit order book** in which orders are presented ranked by their limit prices for a hypothetical market. The market is "26 bid, offered at 28" because the best bid is 26 and the best offer (ask) is 28.

Exhibit 2 Terms Traders Use to Describe Standing Limit Orders

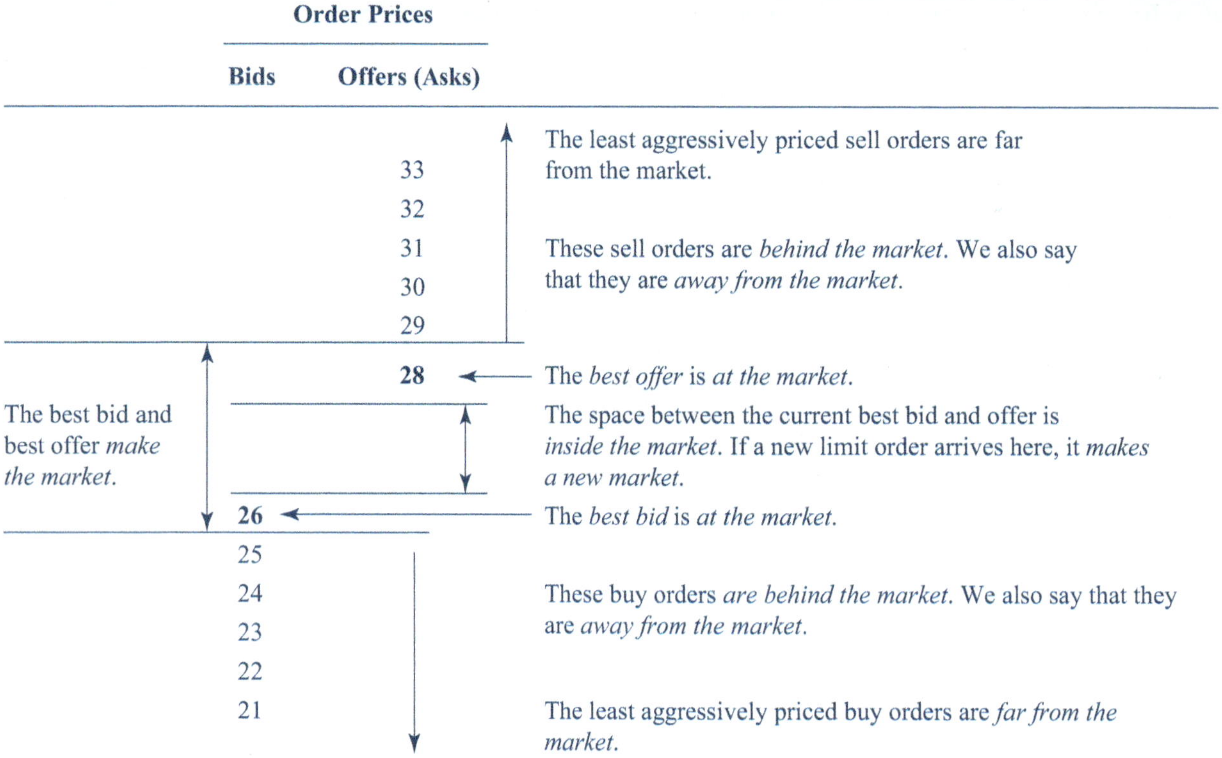

Source: Trading and Exchanges.
Harris, Larry. 2003. *Trading and Exchanges: Market Microstructure for Practitioners.* New York: Oxford University Press.

EXAMPLE 21

Making and Taking

1 What is the difference between making a market and taking a market?
2 What order types are most likely associated with making a market and taking a market?

Solution to 1:

A trader makes a market when the trader offers to trade. A trader takes a market when the trader accepts an offer to trade.

Solution to 2:

Traders place standing limit orders to give other traders opportunities to trade. Standing limit orders thus make markets. In contrast, traders use market orders or marketable limit orders to take offers to trade. These marketable orders take the market.

A trade-off exists between how aggressively priced an order is and the ultimate trade price. Although aggressively priced orders fill faster and with more certainty then do less aggressively priced limit orders, the prices at which they execute are inferior.

Buyers seeking to trade quickly must pay higher prices to increase the probability of trading quickly. Similarly, sellers seeking to trade quickly must accept lower prices to increase the probability of trading quickly.

Some order execution instructions specify conditions on size. For example, **all-or-nothing (AON) orders** can only trade if their entire sizes can be traded. Traders can similarly specify minimum fill sizes. This specification is common when settlement costs depend on the number of trades made to fill an order and not on the aggregate size of the order.

Exposure instructions indicate whether, how, and perhaps to whom orders should be exposed. **Hidden orders** are exposed only to the brokers or exchanges that receive them. These agencies cannot disclose hidden orders to other traders until they can fill them. Traders use hidden orders when they are afraid that other traders might behave strategically if they knew that a large order was in the market. Traders can discover hidden size only by submitting orders that will trade with that size. Thus, traders can only learn about hidden size after they have committed to trading with it.

Traders also often indicate a specific **display size** for their orders. Brokers and exchanges then expose only the display size for these orders. Any additional size is hidden from the public but can be filled if a suitably large order arrives. Traders sometimes call such orders **iceberg orders** because most of the order is hidden. Traders specify display sizes when they do not want to display their full sizes, but still want other traders to know that someone is willing to trade at the displayed price. Traders on the opposite side who wish to trade additional size at that price can discover the hidden size only if they trade the displayed size, at which point the broker or exchange will display any remaining size up to the display size. They also can discover the hidden size by submitting large orders that will trade with that size.

EXAMPLE 22

Market versus Limit and Hidden versus Displayed Orders

You are the buy-side trader for a very clever investment manager. The manager has hired a commercial satellite firm to take regular pictures of the parking lots in which new car dealers store their inventories. It has also hired some part-time workers to count the cars on the lots. With this information and some econometric analyses, the manager can predict weekly new car sale announcements more accurately than can most analysts. The manager typically makes a quarter percent each week on this strategy. Once a week, a day before the announcements are made, the manager gives you large orders to buy or sell car manufacturers based on his insights into their dealers' sales. What primary issues should you consider when deciding whether to:

1 use market or limit orders to fill his orders?

2 display the orders or hide them?

Solution to 1:

The manager's information is quite perishable. If his orders are not filled before the weekly sales are reported to the public, the manager will lose the opportunity to profit from the information as prices immediately adjust to the news. The manager, therefore, needs to get the orders filled quickly. This consideration suggests that the orders should be submitted as market orders. If submitted as limit orders, the orders might not execute and the firm would lose the opportunity to profit.

Large market orders, however, can be very expensive to execute, especially if few people are willing to trade significant size on the other side of the market. Because transaction costs can easily exceed the expected quarter percent return, you should submit limit orders to limit the execution prices that you are willing to accept. It is better to fail to trade than to trade at losing prices.

Solution to 2:

Your large orders could easily move the market if many people were aware of them, and even more so if others were aware that you are trading on behalf of a successful information-motivated trader. You thus should consider submitting hidden orders. The disadvantage of hidden orders is that they do not let people know that they can trade the other side if they want to.

6.2 Validity Instructions

Validity instructions indicate when an order may be filled. The most common validity instruction is the **day order**. A day order is good for the day on which it is submitted. If it has not been filled by the close of business, the order expires unfilled.

Good-till-cancelled orders (GTC) are just that. In practice, most brokers limit how long they will manage an order to ensure that they do not fill orders that their clients have forgotten. Such brokers may limit their GTC orders to a few months.

Immediate or cancel orders (IOC) are good only upon receipt by the broker or exchange. If they cannot be filled in part or in whole, they cancel immediately. In some markets these orders are also known as **fill or kill** orders. When searching for hidden liquidity, electronic algorithmic trading systems often submit thousands of these IOC orders for every order that they fill.

Good-on-close orders can only be filled at the close of trading. These orders often are market orders, so traders call them **market-on-close** orders. Traders often use on-close orders when they want to trade at the same prices that will be published as the closing prices of the day. Mutual funds often like to trade at such prices because they value their portfolios at closing prices. Many traders also use **good-on-open** orders.

6.2.1 *Stop Orders*

A **stop order** is an order in which a trader has specified a stop price condition. The stop order may not be filled until the stop price condition has satisfied. For a sell order, the stop price condition suspends execution of the order until a trade occurs at or below the stop price. After that trade, the stop condition is satisfied and the order becomes valid for execution, subject to all other execution instructions attached to it. If the market price subsequently rises above the sell order's stop price before the order trades, the order remains valid. Similarly, a buy order with a stop condition becomes valid only after a price rises above the specified stop price.

Traders often call stop orders **stop-loss orders** because many traders use them with the hope of stopping losses on positions that they have established. For example, a trader who has bought stock at 40 may want to sell the stock if the price falls below 30. In that case, the trader might submit a "GTC, stop 30, market sell" order. If the price falls to or below 30, the market order becomes valid and it should immediately execute at the best price then available in the market. That price may be substantially lower than 30 if the market is falling quickly. The stop-loss order thus does not guarantee a stop to losses at the stop price. If potential sellers are worried about trading at too low of a price, they can attach stop instructions to limit orders instead of market orders. In this example, if the trader is unwilling to sell below 25, the trader would submit a "GTC, stop 30, limit 25 sell" order.

If a trader wants to guarantee that he can sell at 30, the trader would buy a put option contract struck at 30. The purchase price of the option would include a premium for the insurance that the trader is buying. Option contracts can be viewed as limit orders for which execution is guaranteed at the strike price. A trader similarly might use a stop-buy order or a call option to limit losses on a short position.

A portfolio manager might use a stop-buy order when the manager believes that a security is undervalued but is unwilling to trade without market confirmation. For example, suppose that a stock currently trades for 50 RMB and a manager believes that it should be worth 100 RMB. Further, the manager believes that the stock will much more likely be worth 100 RMB if other traders are willing to buy it above 65 RMB. To best take advantage of this information, the manager would consider issuing a "GTC, stop 65 RMB, limit 100 RMB buy" order. Note that if the manager relies too much on the market when making this trading decision, however, he may violate CFA Standard of Professional Conduct V.A.2, which requires that all investment actions have a reasonable and adequate basis supported by appropriate research and investigation.

Because stop-sell orders become valid when prices are falling and stop-buy orders become valid when prices are rising, traders using stop orders contribute to market momentum as their sell orders push prices down further and their buy orders push prices up. Execution prices for stop orders thus are often quite poor.

EXAMPLE 23

Limit and Stop Instructions

In what ways do limit and stop instructions differ?

Solution:

Although both limit and stop instructions specify prices, the role that these prices play in the arrangement of a trade are completely different. A limit price places a limit on what trade prices will be acceptable to the trader. A buyer will accept prices only at or lower than the limit price whereas a seller will accept prices only at or above the limit price.

In contrast, a stop price indicates when an order can be filled. A buy order can only be filled once the market has traded at a price at or above the stop price. A sell order can only be filled once the market has traded at a price at or below the stop price.

Both order instructions may delay or prevent the execution of an order. A buy limit order will not execute until someone is willing to sell at or below the limit price. Similarly, a sell limit order will not execute until someone is willing to buy at or above the limit sell price. In contrast, a stop-buy order will not execute if the market price never rises to the stop price. Similarly, a stop-sell order will not execute if the market price never falls to the stop price.

6.3 Clearing Instructions

Clearing instructions tell brokers and exchanges how to arrange final settlement of trades. Traders generally do not attach these instructions to each order—instead they provide them as standing instructions. These instructions indicate what entity is responsible for clearing and settling the trade. For retail trades, that entity is the customer's broker. For institutional trades, that entity may be a custodian or another broker. When a client uses one broker to arrange trades and another broker to settle trades, traders say that the first broker gives up the trade to the other broker, who is often known as the prime broker. Institutional traders provide these instructions so they can obtain specialized execution services from different brokers while maintaining a single account for custodial services and other prime brokerage services, such as margin loans.

An important clearing instruction that must appear on security sale orders is an indication of whether the sale is a long sale or a short sale. In either case, the broker representing the sell order must ensure that the trader can deliver securities for settlement. For a long sale, the broker must confirm that the securities held are available for delivery. For a short sale, the broker must either borrow the security on behalf of the client or confirm that the client can borrow the security.

7 PRIMARY SECURITY MARKETS

When issuers first sell their securities to investors, practitioners say that the trades take place in the **primary markets**. An issuer makes an **initial public offering** (IPO)—sometimes called a placing—of a security issue when it sells the security to the public for the first time. A seasoned security is a security that an issuer has already issued. If the issuer wants to sell additional units of a previously issued security, it makes a **seasoned offering** (sometimes called a secondary offering). Both types of offerings occur in the **primary market** where issuers sell their securities to investors. Later, if investors trade these securities among themselves, they trade in **secondary markets**. This section discusses primary markets and the procedures that issuers use to offer their securities to the public.

7.1 Public Offerings

Corporations generally contract with an investment bank to help them sell their securities to the public. The investment bank then lines up subscribers who will buy the security. Investment bankers call this process **book building**. In London, the book builder is called the book runner. The bank tries to build a book of orders to which they can sell the offering. Investment banks often support their book building by providing investment information and opinion about the issuer to their clients and to the public. Before the offering, the issuer generally makes a very detailed disclosure of its business, of the risks inherent in it, and of the uses to which the new funds will be placed.

When time is of the essence, issuers in Europe may issue securities through an **accelerated book build**, in which the investment bank arranges the offering in only one or two days. Such sales often occur at discounted prices.

The first public offering of common stock in a company consists of newly issued shares to be sold by the company. It may also include shares that the founders and other early investors in the company seek to sell. The initial public offering provides these investors with a means of liquidating their investments.

In an **underwritten offering**—the most common type of offering—the investment bank guarantees the sale of the issue at an offering price that it negotiates with the issuer. If the issue is undersubscribed, the bank will buy whatever securities it cannot sell at the offering price. In the case of an IPO, the underwriter usually also promises to make a market in the security for about a month to ensure that the secondary market will be liquid and to provide price support, if necessary. For large issues, a syndicate of investment banks and broker–dealers helps the **lead underwriter** build the book. The issuer usually pays an underwriting fee of about 7 percent for these various services. The underwriting fee is a placement cost of the offering.

In a **best effort offering**, the investment bank acts only as broker. If the offering is undersubscribed, the issuer will not sell as much as it hoped to sell.

For both types of offerings, the issuer and the bank usually jointly set the offering price following a negotiation. If they set a price that buyers consider too high, the offering will be undersubscribed, and they will fail to sell the entire issue. If they set the price too low, the offering will be oversubscribed, in which case the securities are often allocated to preferred clients or on a pro-rata basis.

(Note that CFA Standard of Professional Conduct III.B—fair dealing—requires that the allocation be based on a written policy disclosed to clients and suggests that the securities be offered on a pro-rata basis among all clients who have comparable relationships with their broker–dealers.)

Investment banks have a conflict of interest with respect to the offering price in underwritten offerings. As agents for the issuers, they generally are supposed to select the offering price that will raise the most money. But as underwriters, they have strong incentives to choose a low price. If the price is low, the banks can allocate valuable shares to benefit their clients and thereby indirectly benefit the banks. If the price is too high, the underwriters will have to buy overvalued shares in the offering and perhaps also during the following month if they must support the price in the secondary market, which directly costs the banks. These considerations tend to lower initial offering prices so that prices in the secondary market often rise immediately following an IPO. They are less important in a seasoned offering because trading in the secondary market helps identify the proper price for the offering.

First time issuers generally accept lower offering prices because they and many others believe that an undersubscribed IPO conveys very unfavorable information to the market about the company's prospects at a time when it is most vulnerable to public opinion about its prospects. They fear that an undersubscribed initial public offering will make it substantially harder to raise additional capital in subsequent seasoned offerings.

EXAMPLE 24

The Healthybots Initial Public Offering

Healthybots is a health care company that treats diseases using artificial intelligence–based solutions. Healthybots raised approximately £265 million gross through an initial public offering of 103,142,466 ordinary shares at £2.57 per ordinary share. After the initial public offering, Healthybots had 213,333,333 ordinary shares issued and outstanding.

Healthybots received gross proceeds of approximately £34.3 million and net proceeds of £31.8 million. The ordinary shares that were sold to the public represented approximately 48 percent of Healthybots' total issued ordinary shares.

The shares commenced trading at 8:00 a.m. on the AIM market of the London Stock Exchange, where Healthybots opened at £2.74, traded 37 million shares between £2.68 and £2.74, and closed at £2.73.

1 Approximately how many new shares were issued by the company and how many shares were sold by the company's founders? What fraction of their holdings in the company did the founders sell?

2 Approximately what return did the subscribers who participated in the IPO make on the first day it traded?

3 Approximately how much did Healthybots pay in placement costs as a percentage of the new funds raised?

Solution to 1:

Healthybots received gross proceeds of £34.3 million at £2.57 per share, so the company issued and sold 13,346,304 shares (= £34.3 million/£2.57 per share). The total placement was for 103,142,466 shares, so the founders sold 89,796,162 shares (= 103,142,466 shares − 13,346,304 shares). Because approximately 200 million shares (= 213.3 million shares − 13.3 million shares) were outstanding before the placement, the founders sold approximately 45 percent (= 90 million shares/200 million shares) of the company.

Solution to 2:

The subscribers bought the stock for £2.57 per share, and it closed at £2.73. The first day return thus was $6.2\% = \frac{2.73 - 2.57}{2.57} \times 100$.

Solution to 3:

Healthybots obtained gross proceeds of £34.3 million but only raised net proceeds of £31.8 million. The £2.5 million difference was the total cost of the placement to the firm, which is 7.9 percent of net proceeds, or new funds raised (£2.5 million/£31.8 million).

7.2 Private Placements and Other Primary Market Transactions

Corporations sometimes issue their securities in private placements. In a **private placement**, corporations sell securities directly to a small group of qualified investors, usually with the assistance of an investment bank. Qualified investors have sufficient knowledge and experience to recognize the risks that they assume, and sufficient wealth to assume those risks responsibly. Most countries allow corporations to do private placements without nearly as much public disclosure as is required for public offerings. Private placements, therefore, may be cheaper than public offerings, but the buyers generally require higher returns (lower purchase prices) because they cannot subsequently trade the securities in an organized secondary market.

Corporations sometimes sell new issues of seasoned securities directly to the public on a piecemeal basis via a shelf registration. In a **shelf registration**, the corporation makes all public disclosures that it would for a regular offering, but it does not sell the shares in a single transaction. Instead, it sells the shares directly into the secondary market over time, generally when it needs additional capital. Shelf registrations provide corporations with flexibility in the timing of their capital transactions, and they can alleviate the downward price pressures often associated with large secondary offerings.

Many corporations may also issue shares via dividend reinvestment plans (DRPs or DRIPs, for short) that allow their shareholders to reinvest their dividends in newly issued shares of the corporation (in particular, DRPs specify that the corporation issue new shares for the plan rather than purchase them on the open market). These plans sometimes also allow existing shareholders and other investors to buy additional stock at a slight discount to current prices.

Finally, corporations can issue new stock via a rights offering. In a rights offering, the corporation distributes rights to buy stock at a fixed price to existing shareholders in proportion to their holdings. Because the rights need not be exercised, they are options. The exercise price, however, is set below the current market price of the stock so that buying stock with the rights is immediately profitable. Consequently, shareholders will experience dilution in the value of their existing shares. They can offset the dilution loss by exercising their rights or by selling the rights to others who will exercise them. Shareholders generally do not like rights offerings because they must provide additional capital (or sell their rights) to avoid losses through dilution. Financial analysts recognize that these securities, although called rights, are actually short-term stock warrants and value them accordingly.

The national governments of financially strong countries generally issue their bonds, notes, and bills in public auctions organized by a government agency (usually associated with the finance ministry). They may also sell them directly to dealers.

Smaller and less financially secure national governments and most regional governments often contract with investment banks to help them sell and distribute their securities. The laws of many governments, however, require that they auction their securities.

EXAMPLE 25

Private and Public Placements

In what ways do private placements differ from public placements?

Solution:

Issuers make private placements to a limited number of investors that generally are financially sophisticated and well informed about risk. The investors generally have some relationship to the issuer. Issuers make public placements when they sell securities to the general public. Public placements generally require substantially more financial disclosure than do private placements.

7.3 Importance of Secondary Markets to Primary Markets

Corporations and governments can raise money in the primary markets at lower cost when their securities will trade in liquid secondary markets. In a **liquid market**, traders can buy or sell with low transaction costs and small price concessions when they want to trade. Buyers value liquidity because they may need to sell their securities to meet liquidity needs. Investors thus will pay more for securities that they can easily sell than for those that they cannot easily sell. Higher prices translate into lower costs of capital for the issuers.

SECONDARY SECURITY MARKET AND CONTRACT MARKET STRUCTURES

8

Trading is the successful outcome to a bilateral search in which buyers look for sellers and sellers look for buyers. Many market structures have developed to reduce the costs of this search. Markets are liquid when the costs of finding a suitable counterparty to a trade are low.

Trading in securities and contracts takes place in a variety of market structures. The structures differ by when trades can be arranged, who arranges the trades, how they do so, and how traders learn about possible trading opportunities and executed trades. This section introduces the various market structures used to trade securities and contracts. We first consider trading sessions, then execution mechanisms, and finally market information systems.

8.1 Trading Sessions

Markets are organized as call markets or as continuous trading markets. In a **call market**, trades can be arranged only when the market is called at a particular time and place. In contrast in a **continuous trading market**, trades can be arranged and executed anytime the market is open.

Buyers can easily find sellers and vice versa in call markets because all traders interested in trading (or orders representing their interests) are present at the same time and place. Call markets thus have the potential to be very liquid when they are called. But they are completely illiquid between trading sessions. In contrast, traders can arrange and execute their trades at any time in continuous trading markets, but doing so can be difficult if the buyers and sellers (or their orders) are not both present at the same time.

Most call markets use single price auctions to match buyers to sellers. In these auctions, the market constructs order books representing all buy orders and all seller orders. The market then chooses a single trade price that will maximize the total volume of trade. The order books are supply and demand schedules, and the point at which they cross determines the trade price.

Call markets usually are organized just once a day, but some markets organize calls at more frequent intervals.

Many continuous trading markets start their trading with a call market auction. During a pre-opening period, traders submit their orders for the market call. At the opening, any possible trades are arranged and then trading continues in the continuous trading session. Some continuous trading markets also close their trading with a call. In these markets, traders who are only interested in trading in the closing call submit market- or limit-on-close orders.

EXAMPLE 26

Call Markets and Continuous Trading Markets

1 What is the main advantage of a call market compared with a continuous trading market?

2 What is the main advantage of a continuous trading market compared with a call market?

Solution to 1:

By gathering all traders to the same place at the same time, a call market makes it easier for buyers to find sellers and vice versa. In contrast, if buyers and sellers (or their orders) are not present at the same time in a continuous market, they cannot trade.

Solution to 2:

In a continuous trading market, a willing buyer and seller can trade at any time the market is open. In contrast, in a call market trading can take place only when the market is called.

8.2 Execution Mechanisms

The three main types of market structures are quote-driven markets (sometimes called price-driven or dealer markets), order-driven markets, and brokered markets. In **quote-driven markets**, customers trade with dealers. In **order-driven markets**, an order matching system run by an exchange, a broker, or an alternative trading system uses rules to arrange trades based on the orders that traders submit. Most exchanges and ECNs organize order-driven markets. In **brokered markets**, brokers arrange trades between their customers. Brokered markets are common for transactions of unique instruments, such as real estate properties, intellectual properties, or large blocks of securities. Many trading systems use more than one type of market structure.

8.2.1 *Quote-Driven Markets*

Worldwide, most trading, other than in stocks, takes place in quote-driven markets. Almost all bonds and currencies and most spot commodities trade in quote-driven markets. Traders call them quote-driven (or price-driven or dealer) because customers trade at the prices quoted by dealers. Depending on the instrument traded, the dealers work for commercial banks, for investment banks, for broker–dealers, or for proprietary trading houses.

Quote-driven markets also often are called over-the-counter (OTC) markets because securities used to be literally traded over the dealer's counter in the dealer's office. Now, most trades in OTC markets are conducted over proprietary computer communications networks, by telephone, or sometimes over instant messaging systems.

8.2.2 *Order-Driven Markets*

Order-driven markets arrange trades using rules to match buy orders to sell orders. The orders may be submitted by customers or by dealers. Almost all exchanges use order-driven trading systems, and every automated trading system is an order-driven system.

Because rules match buyers to sellers, traders often trade with complete strangers. Order-driven markets thus must have procedures to ensure that buyers and sellers perform on their trade contracts. Otherwise, dishonest traders would enter contracts that they would not settle if a change in market conditions made settlement unprofitable.

Two sets of rules characterize order-driven market mechanisms: Order matching rules and trade pricing rules. The order matching rules match buy orders to sell orders. The trade pricing rules determine the prices at which the matched trades take place.

8.2.2.1 Order Matching Rules Order-driven trading systems match buyers to sellers using rules that rank the buy orders and the sell orders based on price, and often along with other secondary criteria. The systems then match the highest-ranking buy order with the highest-ranking sell order. If the buyer is willing to pay at least as much as the seller is willing to receive, the system will arrange a trade for the minimum of the buy and sell quantities. The remaining size, if any, is then matched with the next order on the other side and the process continues until no further trades can be arranged.

The **order precedence hierarchy** determines which orders go first. The first rule is **price priority**: The highest priced buy orders and the lowest priced sell orders go first. They are the most aggressively priced orders. **Secondary precedence rules** determine how to rank orders at the same price. Most trading systems use time precedence to rank orders at the same price. The first order to arrive has precedence over other orders. In trading systems that permit hidden and partially hidden orders, displayed quantities at a given price generally have precedence over the undisplayed quantities. So the complete precedence hierarchy is given by price priority, display precedence at a given price, and finally time precedence among all orders with the same display status at a given price. These rules give traders incentives to improve price, display their orders, and arrive early if they want to trade quickly. These incentives increase market liquidity.

8.2.2.2 Trade Pricing Rules After the orders are matched, the trading system then uses its trade pricing rule to determine the trade price. The three rules that various order-driven markets use to price their trades are the uniform pricing rule, the discriminatory pricing rule, and the derivative pricing rule.

Call markets commonly use the uniform pricing rule. Under this rule, all trades execute at the same price. The market chooses the price that maximizes the total quantity traded.

Continuous trading markets use the **discriminatory pricing rule**. Under this rule, the limit price of the order or quote that first arrived—the standing order—determines the trade price. This rule allows a large arriving trader to discriminate among standing limit orders by filling the most aggressively priced orders first at their limit prices and then filling less aggressively priced orders at their less favorable (from the point of view of the arriving trader) limit prices. If trading systems did not use this pricing rule, large traders would break their orders into pieces to price discriminate on their own.

EXAMPLE 27

Filling a Large Order in a Continuous Trading Market

Before the arrival of a large order, the Tokyo Stock Exchange has the following limit orders standing on its book:

Buyer	Bid Size	Limit Price(¥)	Offer Size	Seller
Takumi	15	100.1		
Hiroto	8	100.2		
Shou	10	100.3		
		100.4	4	Hina
		100.5	6	Sakura
		100.6	12	Miku

Tsubasa submits a day order to buy 15 contracts, limit ¥100.5. With whom does he trade, what is his average trade price, and what does the limit order book look like afterward?

Solution:

Tsubasa's buy order first fills with the most aggressively priced sell order, which is Hina's order for four contracts. A trade takes place at ¥100.4 for four contracts, Hina's order fills completely, and Tsubasa still has 11 more contracts remaining.

The next most aggressively priced sell order is Sakura's order for six contracts. A second trade takes place at ¥100.5 for six contracts, Sakura's order fills completely, and Tsubasa still has five more contracts remaining.

The next most aggressively priced sell order is Miku's order at ¥100.6. No further trade is possible, however, because her limit sell price is above Tsubasa's limit buy price. Tsubasa's average trade price is ¥100.46 $= \frac{4 \times ¥100.4 + 6 \times ¥100.5}{4 + 6}$.

Because Tsubasa issued a day order, the remainder of his order is placed on the book on the buy side at ¥100.5. The following orders are then on the book:

Buyer	Bid Size	Limit Price (¥)	Offer Size	Seller
Takumi	15	100.1		
Hiroto	8	100.2		
Shou	10	100.3		

Buyer	Bid Size	Limit Price (¥)	Offer Size	Seller
		100.4		
Tsubasa	5	100.5		
		100.6	12	Miku

If Tsubasa had issued an immediate-or-cancel order, the remaining five contracts would have been cancelled.

Crossing networks use the derivative pricing rule. **Crossing networks** are trading systems that match buyers and sellers who are willing to trade at prices obtained from other markets. Most systems cross their trades at the midpoint of the best bid and ask quotes published by the exchange at which the security primarily trades. This pricing rule is called a **derivative pricing rule** because the price is derived from another market. In particular, the price does not depend on the orders submitted to the crossing network. Some crossing networks are organized as call markets and others as continuously trading markets. The most important crossing market is the equity trading system POSIT.

8.2.3 *Brokered Markets*

The third execution mechanism is the **brokered market**, in which brokers arrange trades among their clients. Brokers organize markets for instruments for which finding a buyer or a seller willing to trade is difficult because the instruments are unique and thus of interest only to a limited number of people or institutions. These instruments generally are also infrequently traded and expensive to carry in inventory. Examples of such instruments include very large blocks of stock, real estate properties, fine art masterpieces, intellectual properties, operating companies, liquor licenses, and taxi medallions. Because dealers generally are unable or unwilling to hold these assets in their inventories, they will not make markets in them. Organizing order-driven markets for these instruments is not sensible because too few traders would submit orders to them.

Successful brokers in these markets try to know everyone who might now or in the future be willing to trade. They spend most of their time on the telephone and in meetings building their networks.

EXAMPLE 28

Quote-Driven, Order-Driven, and Brokered Markets

What are the primary advantages of quote-driven, order-driven, and brokered markets?

Solution:

In a quote-driven market, dealers generally are available to supply liquidity. In an order-driven market, traders can supply liquidity to each other. In a brokered market, brokers help find traders who are willing to trade when dealers would not be willing to make markets and when traders would not be willing to post orders.

8.3 Market Information Systems

Markets vary in the type and quantity of data that they disseminate to the public. Traders say that a market is pre-trade transparent if the market publishes real-time data about quotes and orders. Markets are post-trade transparent if the market publishes trade prices and sizes soon after trades occur.

Buy-side traders value transparency because it allows them to better manage their trading, understand market values, and estimate their prospective and actual transaction costs. In contrast, dealers prefer to trade in opaque markets because, as frequent traders, they have an information advantage over those who know less than they do. Bid–ask spreads tend to be wider and transaction costs tend to be higher in opaque markets because finding the best available price is harder for traders in such markets.

9 WELL-FUNCTIONING FINANCIAL SYSTEMS

The financial system allows traders to solve financing and risk management problems. In a well-functioning financial system:

- investors can easily move money from the present to the future while obtaining a fair rate of return for the risks that they bear;
- borrowers can easily obtain funds that they need to undertake current projects if they can credibly promise to repay the funds in the future;
- hedgers can easily trade away or offset the risks that concern them; and
- traders can easily trade currencies for other currencies or commodities that they need.

If the assets or contracts needed to solve these problems are available to trade, the financial system has **complete markets**. If the costs of arranging these trades are low, the financial system is **operationally efficient**. If the prices of the assets and contracts reflect all available information related to fundamental values, the financial system is informationally efficient.

Well-functioning financial systems are characterized by:

- the existence of well-developed markets that trade instruments that help people solve their financial problems (complete markets);
- liquid markets in which the costs of trading—commissions, bid–ask spreads, and order price impacts—are low (operationally efficient markets);
- timely financial disclosures by corporations and governments that allow market participants to estimate the fundamental values of securities (support **informationally efficient markets**); and
- prices that reflect fundamental values so that prices vary primarily in response to changes in fundamental values and not to demands for liquidity made by uninformed traders (informationally efficient markets).

Such complete and operationally efficient markets are produced by financial intermediaries who:

- organize exchanges, brokerages, and alternative trading systems that match buyers to sellers;
- provide liquidity on demand to traders;
- securitize assets to produce investment instruments that are attractive to investors and thereby lower the costs of funds for borrowers;

- run banks that match investors to borrowers by taking deposits and making loans;
- run insurance companies that pool uncorrelated risks;
- provide investment advisory services that help investors manage and grow their assets at low cost;
- organize clearinghouses that ensure everyone settles their trades and contracts; and
- organize depositories that ensure nobody loses their assets.

The benefits of a well-functioning financial system are huge. In such systems, investors who need to move money to the future can easily connect with entrepreneurs who need money now to develop new products and services. Similarly, producers who would otherwise avoid valuable projects because they are too risky can easily transfer those risks to others who can better bear them. Most importantly, these transactions generally can take place among strangers so that the benefits from trading can be derived from an enormous number of potential matches.

In contrast, economies that have poorly functioning financial systems have great difficulties allocating capital among the many companies who could use it. Financial transactions tend to be limited to arrangements within families when people cannot easily find trustworthy counterparties who will honor their contracts. In such economies, capital is allocated inefficiently, risks are not easily shared, and production is inefficient.

An extraordinarily important byproduct of an operationally efficient financial system is the production of informationally efficient prices. Prices are informationally efficient when they reflect all available information about fundamental values. Informative prices are crucially important to the welfare of an economy because they help ensure that resources go where they are most valuable. Economies that use resources where they are most valuable are allocationally efficient. Economies that do not use resources where they are most valuable waste their resources and consequently often are quite poor.

Well-informed traders make prices informationally efficient. When they buy assets and contracts that they think are undervalued, they tend to push the assets' prices up. Similarly, when they sell assets and contracts that they think are overvalued, they tend to push the assets' prices down. The effect of their trading thus causes prices to reflect their information about values.

How accurately prices reflect fundamental information depends on the costs of obtaining fundamental information and on the liquidity available to well-informed traders. Accounting standards and reporting requirements that produce meaningful and timely financial disclosures reduce the costs of obtaining fundamental information and thereby allow analysts to form more accurate estimates of fundamental values. Liquid markets allow well-informed traders to fill their orders at low cost. If filling orders is very costly, informed trading may not be profitable. In that case, information-motivated traders will not commit resources to collect and analyze data and they will not trade. Without their research and their associated trading, prices would be less informative.

EXAMPLE 29

Well-Functioning Financial Systems

As a financial analyst specializing in emerging market equities, you understand that a well-functioning financial system contributes to the economic prosperity of a country. You are asked to start covering a new small market country. What factors will you consider when characterizing the quality of its financial markets?

Solution:

In general, you will consider whether:

- the country has markets that allow its companies and residents to finance projects, save for the future, and exchange risk;
- the costs of trading in those markets is low; and
- prices reflect fundamental values.

You may specifically check to see whether:

- fixed income and stock markets allow borrowers to easily obtain capital from investors;
- corporations disclose financial and operating data on a timely basis in conformity to widely respected reporting standards, such as IFRS;
- forward, futures, and options markets trade instruments that companies need to hedge their risks;
- dealers and arbitrageurs allow traders to trade when they want to;
- bid–ask spreads are small;
- trades and contracts invariably settle as expected;
- investment managers provide high-quality management services for reasonable fees;
- banks and other financing companies are well capitalized and thus able to help investors provide capital to borrowers;
- securitized assets are available and represent reasonable credit risks;
- insurance companies are well capitalized and thus able to help those exposed to risks insure against them; and
- price volatility appears consistent with changes in fundamental values.

10 MARKET REGULATION

Government agencies and practitioner organizations regulate many markets and the financial intermediaries that participate in them. The regulators generally seek to promote fair and orderly markets in which traders can trade at prices that accurately reflect fundamental values without incurring excessive transaction costs. This section identifies the problems that financial regulators hope to solve and the objectives of their regulations.

Regrettably, some people will steal from each other if given a chance, especially if the probability of detection is low or if the penalty for being caught is low. The number of ways that people can steal or misappropriate wealth generally increases with the complexity of their relationships and with asymmetries in their knowledge. Because financial markets tend to be complex, and because customers are often much less sophisticated than the professionals that serve them, the potential for losses through various frauds can be unacceptably high in unregulated markets.

Regulators thus ensure that systems are in place to protect customers from fraud. In principle, the customers themselves would demand such systems as a condition of doing business. When customers are unsophisticated or poorly informed, however, they may not know how to protect themselves. When the costs of learning are large—as they often are in complex financial markets—having regulators look out for the public interest can be economically efficient.

More customer money is probably lost in financial markets through negligence than through outright fraud. Most customers in financial markets use various agents to help them solve problems that they do not understand well. These agents include securities brokers, financial advisers, investment managers, and insurance agents. Because customers generally do not have much information about market conditions, they find it extremely difficult to measure the added value they obtain from their agents. This problem is especially challenging when performance has a strong random component. In that case, determining whether agents are skilled or lucky is very difficult. Moreover, if the agent is a good salesman, the customer may not critically evaluate their agent's performance. These conditions, which characterize most financial markets, ensure that customers cannot easily determine whether their agents are working faithfully for them. They tend to lose if their agents are unqualified or lazy, or if they unconsciously favor themselves and their friends over their clients, as is natural for even the most honest people.

Regulators help solve these agency problems by setting minimum standards of competence for agents and by defining and enforcing minimum standards of practice. CFA Institute provides significant standard setting leadership in the areas of investment management and investment performance reporting through its Chartered Financial Analyst Program, in which you are studying, and its Global Investment Performance Standards. In principle, regulation would not be necessary if customers could identify competent agents and effectively measure their performance. In the financial markets, doing so is very difficult.

Regulators often act to level the playing field for market participants. For example, in many jurisdictions, insider trading in securities is illegal. The rule prevents corporate insiders and others with access to corporate information from trading on material information that has not been released to the public. The purpose of the rule is to reduce the profits that insiders could extract from the markets. These profits would come from other traders who would lose when they trade with well-informed insiders. Because traders tend to withdraw from markets when they lose, rules against insider trading help keep markets liquid. They also keep corporate insiders from hoarding information.

Many situations arise in financial markets in which common standards benefit everyone involved. For example, having all companies report financial results on a common basis allows financial analysts to easily compare companies. Accordingly, the International Accounting Standards Board (IASB) and the US-based Financial Accounting Standards Board (FASB), among many others, promulgate common financial standards to which all companies must report. The benefits of having common reporting standards has led to a very successful and continuing effort to converge all accounting standards to a single worldwide standard. Without such regulations, investors might eventually refuse to invest in companies that do not report to a common standard, but such market-based discipline is a very slow regulator of behavior, and it would have little effect on companies that do not need to raise new capital.

Regulators generally require that financial firms maintain minimum levels of capital. These capital requirements serve two purposes. First, they ensure that the companies will be able to honor their contractual commitments when unexpected market movements or poor decisions cause them to lose money. Second, they ensure that the owners of financial firms have substantial interest in the decisions that they make. Without a substantial financial interest in the decisions that they make, companies often take too many risks and exercise poor judgment about extending credit to others. When such companies fail, they impose significant costs on others. Minimum capital requirements reduce the probability that financial firms will fail and they reduce the disruptions associated with those failures that do occur. In principle, a firm's customers and counterparties could require minimum capital levels as a condition of doing business with the firm, but they have more difficulty enforcing their contracts than do governments who can imprison people.

Regulators similarly regulate insurance companies and pension funds that make long-term promises to their clients. Such entities need to maintain adequate reserves to ensure that they can fund their liabilities. Unfortunately, their managers have a tendency to underestimate these reserves if they will not be around when the liabilities come due. Again, in principle, policyholders and employees could regulate the behavior of their insurance funds and their employers by refusing to contract with them if they do not promise to adequately fund their liabilities. In practice, however, the sophistication, information, and time necessary to write and enforce contracts that control these problems are beyond the reach of most people. The government thus is a sensible regulator of such problems.

Many regulators are self-regulating organizations (SROs) that regulate their members. Exchanges, clearinghouses, and dealer trade organizations are examples of self-regulating organizations. In some cases, the members of these organizations voluntarily subject themselves to the SRO's regulations to promote the common good. In other cases, governments delegate regulatory and enforcement authorities to SROs, usually subject to the supervision of a government agency, such as a national securities and exchange authority. Exchanges, dealer associations, and clearing agencies often regulate their members with these delegated powers.

By setting high standards of behavior, SROs help their members obtain the confidence of their customers. They also reduce the chance that members of the SRO will incur losses when dealing with other members of the SRO.

When regulators fail to solve the problems discussed here, the financial system does not function well. People who lose money stop saving and borrowers with good ideas cannot fund their projects. Similarly, hedgers withdraw from markets when the costs of hedging are high. Without the ability to hedge, producers become reluctant to specialize because specialization generally increases risk. Because specialization also decreases costs, however, production becomes less efficient as producers chose safer technologies. Economies that cannot solve the regulatory problems described in this section tend to operate less efficiently than do better regulated economies, and they tend to be less wealthy.

To summarize, the objectives of market regulation are to:

1 control fraud;

2 control agency problems;

3 promote fairness;

4 set mutually beneficial standards;

5 prevent undercapitalized financial firms from exploiting their investors by making excessively risky investments; and

6 ensure that long-term liabilities are funded.

Regulation is necessary because regulating certain behaviors through market-based mechanisms is too costly for people who are unsophisticated and uninformed. Effectively regulated markets allow people to better achieve their financial goals.

EXAMPLE 30

Bankrupt Traders

You are the chief executive officer of a brokerage that is a member of a clearinghouse. A trader who clears through your firm is bankrupt at midday, but you do not yet know it even though your clearing agreement with him explicitly requires that he immediately report significant losses. The trader knows that if he takes a large position, prices might move in his favor so that he will no longer be bankrupt. The trader attempts to do so and succeeds. You find out about this later in the evening.

1 Why does the clearinghouse regulate its members?

2 What should you do about the trader?

3 Why would the clearinghouse allow you to keep his trading profits?

Solution to 1:

The clearinghouse regulates its members to ensure that no member imposes costs on another member by failing to settle a trade.

Solution to 2:

You should immediately end your clearing relationship with the trader and confiscate his trading profits. The trader was trading with your firm's capital after he became bankrupt. Had he lost, your firm would have borne the loss.

Solution to 3:

If the clearinghouse did not permit you to keep his trading profits, other traders similarly situated might attempt the same strategy.

SUMMARY

This reading introduces how the financial system operates and explains how well-functioning financial systems lead to wealthy economies. Financial analysts need to understand how the financial system works because their analyses often lead to trading decisions.

The financial system consists of markets and the financial intermediaries that operate in them. These institutions allow buyers to connect with sellers. They may trade directly with each other when they trade the same instrument or they only may trade indirectly when a financial intermediary connects the buyer to the seller through transactions with each that appear on the intermediary's balance sheet. The buyer and seller may exchange instruments, cash flows, or risks.

The following points, among others, were made in this reading:

- The financial system consists of mechanisms that allow strangers to contract with each other to move money through time, to hedge risks, and to exchange assets that they value less for those that they value more.
- Investors move money from the present to the future when they save. They expect a normal rate of return for bearing risk through time. Borrowers move money from the future to the present to fund current projects and

expenditures. Hedgers trade to reduce their exposure to risks they prefer not to take. Information-motivated traders are active investment managers who try to identify under- and overvalued instruments.

- Securities are first sold in primary markets by their issuers. They then trade in secondary markets.
- People invest in pooled investment vehicles to benefit from the investment management services of their managers.
- Forward contracts allow buyers and sellers to arrange for future sales at predetermined prices. Futures contracts are forward contracts guaranteed by clearinghouses. The guarantee ensures that strangers are willing to trade with each other and that traders can offset their positions by trading with anybody. These features of futures contract markets make them highly attractive to hedgers and information-motivated traders.
- Many financial intermediaries connect buyers to sellers in a given instrument, acting directly as brokers and exchanges or indirectly as dealers and arbitrageurs.
- Financial intermediaries create instruments when they conduct arbitrage, securitize assets, borrow to lend, manage investment funds, or pool insurance contracts. These activities all transform cash flows and risks from one form to another. Their services allow buyers and sellers to connect with each other through instruments that meet their specific needs.
- Financial markets work best when strangers can contract with each other without worrying about whether their counterparts are able and willing to honor their contract. Clearinghouses, variation margins, maintenance margins, and settlement guarantees made by creditworthy brokers on behalf of their clients help manage credit risk and ultimately allow strangers to contract with each other.
- Information-motivated traders short sell when they expect that prices will fall. Hedgers short sell to reduce the risks of a long position in a related contract or commodity.
- Margin loans allow people to buy more securities than their equity would otherwise permit them to buy. The larger positions expose them to more risk so that gains and losses for a given amount of equity will be larger. The leverage ratio is the value of a position divided by the value of the equity supporting it. The returns to the equity in a position are equal to the leverage ratio times the returns to the unleveraged position.
- To protect against credit losses, brokers demand maintenance margin payments from their customers who have borrowed cash or securities when adverse price changes cause their customer's equity to drop below the maintenance margin ratio. Brokers close positions for customers who do not satisfy these margin calls.
- Orders are instructions to trade. They always specify instrument, side (buy or sell), and quantity. They usually also provide several other instructions.
- Market orders tend to fill quickly but often at inferior prices. Limit orders generally fill at better prices if they fill, but they may not fill. Traders choose order submission strategies on the basis of how quickly they want to trade, the prices they are willing to accept, and the consequences of failing to trade.
- Stop instructions are attached to other orders to delay efforts to fill them until the stop condition is satisfied. Although stop orders are often used to stop losses, they are not always effective.

- Issuers sell their securities using underwritten public offerings, best efforts public offerings, private placements, shelf registrations, dividend reinvestment programs, and rights offerings. Investment banks have a conflict of interests when setting the initial offering price in an IPO.
- Well-functioning secondary markets are essential to raising capital in the primary markets because investors value the ability to sell their securities if they no longer want to hold them or if they need to disinvest to raise cash. If they cannot trade their securities in a liquid market, they will not pay as much for them.
- Matching buyers and sellers in call markets is easy because the traders (or their orders) come together at the same time and place.
- Dealers provide liquidity in quote-driven markets. Public traders as well as dealers provide liquidity in order-driven markets.
- Order-driven markets arrange trades by ranking orders using precedence rules. The rules generally ensure that traders who provide the best prices, display the most size, and arrive early trade first. Continuous order-driven markets price orders using the discriminatory pricing rule. Under this rule, standing limit orders determine trade prices.
- Brokers help people trade unique instruments or positions for which finding a buyer or a seller is difficult.
- Transaction costs are lower in transparent markets than in opaque markets because traders can more easily determine market value and more easily manage their trading in transparent markets.
- A well-functioning financial system allows people to trade instruments that best solve their wealth and risk management problems with low transaction costs. Complete and liquid markets characterize a well-functioning financial system. Complete markets are markets in which the instruments needed to solve investment and risk management problems are available to trade. Liquid markets are markets in which traders can trade when they want to trade at low cost.
- The financial system is operationally efficient when its markets are liquid. Liquid markets lower the costs of raising capital.
- A well-functioning financial system promotes wealth by ensuring that capital allocation decisions are well made. A well-functioning financial system also promotes wealth by allowing people to share the risks associated with valuable products that would otherwise not be undertaken.
- Prices are informationally efficient when they reflect all available information about fundamental values. Information-motivated traders make prices informationally efficient. Prices will be most informative in liquid markets because information-motivated traders will not invest in information and research if establishing positions based on their analyses is too costly.
- Regulators generally seek to promote fair and orderly markets in which traders can trade at prices that accurately reflect fundamental values without incurring excessive transaction costs. Governmental agencies and self-regulating organizations of practitioners provide regulatory services that attempt to make markets safer and more efficient.
- Mandated financial disclosure programs for the issuers of publicly traded securities ensure that information necessary to estimate security values is available to financial analysts on a consistent basis.

PRACTICE PROBLEMS

1 Akihiko Takabe has designed a sophisticated forecasting model, which predicts the movements in the overall stock market, in the hope of earning a return in excess of a fair return for the risk involved. He uses the predictions of the model to decide whether to buy, hold, or sell the shares of an index fund that aims to replicate the movements of the stock market. Takabe would *best* be characterized as a(n):

A hedger.

B investor.

C information-motivated trader.

2 James Beach is young and has substantial wealth. A significant proportion of his stock portfolio consists of emerging market stocks that offer relatively high expected returns at the cost of relatively high risk. Beach believes that investment in emerging market stocks is appropriate for him given his ability and willingness to take risk. Which of the following labels *most appropriately* describes Beach?

A Hedger.

B Investor.

C Information-motivated trader.

3 Lisa Smith owns a manufacturing company in the United States. Her company has sold goods to a customer in Brazil and will be paid in Brazilian real (BRL) in three months. Smith is concerned about the possibility of the BRL depreciating more than expected against the US dollar (USD). Therefore, she is planning to sell three-month futures contracts on the BRL. The seller of such contracts generally gains when the BRL depreciates against the USD. If Smith were to sell these future contracts, she would *most appropriately* be described as a(n):

A hedger.

B investor.

C information-motivated trader.

4 Which of the following is *not* a function of the financial system?

A To regulate arbitrageurs' profits (excess returns).

B To help the economy achieve allocational efficiency.

C To facilitate borrowing by businesses to fund current operations.

5 An investor primarily invests in stocks of publicly traded companies. The investor wants to increase the diversification of his portfolio. A friend has recommended investing in real estate properties. The purchase of real estate would *best* be characterized as a transaction in the:

A derivative investment market.

B traditional investment market.

C alternative investment market.

6 A hedge fund holds its excess cash in 90-day commercial paper and negotiable certificates of deposit. The cash management policy of the hedge fund is *best described* as using:

A capital market instruments.

B money market instruments.

C intermediate-term debt instruments.

7 An oil and gas exploration and production company announces that it is offering 30 million shares to the public at $45.50 each. This transaction is *most likely* a sale in the:

A futures market.

B primary market.

C secondary market.

8 Consider a mutual fund that invests primarily in fixed-income securities that have been determined to be appropriate given the fund's investment goal. Which of the following is *least likely* to be a part of this fund?

A Warrants.

B Commercial paper.

C Repurchase agreements.

9 A friend has asked you to explain the differences between open-end and closed-end funds. Which of the following will you *most likely* include in your explanation?

A Closed-end funds are unavailable to new investors.

B When investors sell the shares of an open-end fund, they can receive a discount or a premium to the fund's net asset value.

C When selling shares, investors in an open-end fund sell the shares back to the fund whereas investors in a closed-end fund sell the shares to others in the secondary market.

10 The usefulness of a forward contract is limited by some problems. Which of the following is *most likely* one of those problems?

A Once you have entered into a forward contract, it is difficult to exit from the contract.

B Entering into a forward contract requires the long party to deposit an initial amount with the short party.

C If the price of the underlying asset moves adversely from the perspective of the long party, periodic payments must be made to the short party.

11 Tony Harris is planning to start trading in commodities. He has heard about the use of futures contracts on commodities and is learning more about them. Which of the following is Harris *least likely* to find associated with a futures contract?

A Existence of counterparty risk.

B Standardized contractual terms.

C Payment of an initial margin to enter into a contract.

12 A German company that exports machinery is expecting to receive $10 million in three months. The firm converts all its foreign currency receipts into euros. The chief financial officer of the company wishes to lock in a minimum fixed rate for converting the $10 million to euro but also wants to keep the flexibility to use the future spot rate if it is favorable. What hedging transaction is *most likely* to achieve this objective?

A Selling dollars forward.

B Buying put options on the dollar.

C Selling futures contracts on dollars.

13 A book publisher requires substantial quantities of paper. The publisher and a paper producer have entered into an agreement for the publisher to buy and the producer to supply a given quantity of paper four months later at a price agreed upon today. This agreement is a:

A futures contract.

B forward contract.

C commodity swap.

14 The Standard & Poor's Depositary Receipts (SPDRs) is an investment that tracks the S&P 500 stock market index. Purchases and sales of SPDRs during an average trading day are *best* described as:

A primary market transactions in a pooled investment.

B secondary market transactions in a pooled investment.

C secondary market transactions in an actively managed investment.

15 The Standard & Poor's Depositary Receipts (SPDRs) is an exchange-traded fund in the United States that is designed to track the S&P 500 stock market index. The latest price of a share of SPDRs is \$290. A trader has just bought call options on shares of SPDRs for a premium of \$3 per share. The call options expire in six months and have an exercise price of \$305 per share. On the expiration date, the trader will exercise the call options (ignore any transaction costs) if and only if the shares of SPDRs are trading:

A below \$305 per share.

B above \$305 per share.

C above \$308 per share.

16 Which of the following statements about exchange-traded funds is *most correct*?

A Exchange-traded funds are not backed by any assets.

B The investment companies that create exchange-traded funds are financial intermediaries.

C The transaction costs of trading shares of exchange-traded funds are substantially greater than the combined costs of trading the underlying assets of the fund.

17 Jason Schmidt works for a hedge fund and he specializes in finding profit opportunities that are the result of inefficiencies in the market for convertible bonds—bonds that can be converted into a predetermined amount of a company's common stock. Schmidt tries to find convertibles that are priced inefficiently relative to the underlying stock. The trading strategy involves the simultaneous purchase of the convertible bond and the short sale of the underlying common stock. The above process could best be described as:

A hedging.

B arbitrage.

C securitization.

18 Pierre-Louis Robert just purchased a call option on shares of the Michelin Group. A few days ago he wrote a put option on Michelin shares. The call and put options have the same exercise price, expiration date, and number of shares underlying. Considering both positions, Robert's exposure to the risk of the stock of the Michelin Group is:

A long.

B short.

C neutral.

19 An online brokerage firm has set the minimum margin requirement at 55 percent. What is the maximum leverage ratio associated with a position financed by this minimum margin requirement?

A 1.55.

B 1.82.

C 2.22.

20 A trader has purchased 200 shares of a non-dividend-paying firm on margin at a price of $50 per share. The leverage ratio is 2.5. Six months later, the trader sells these shares at $60 per share. Ignoring the interest paid on the borrowed amount and the transaction costs, what was the return to the trader during the six-month period?

A 20 percent.

B 33.33 percent.

C 50 percent.

21 Jason Williams purchased 500 shares of a company at $32 per share. The stock was bought on 75 percent margin. One month later, Williams had to pay interest on the amount borrowed at a rate of 2 percent per month. At that time, Williams received a dividend of $0.50 per share. Immediately after that he sold the shares at $28 per share. He paid commissions of $10 on the purchase and $10 on the sale of the stock. What was the rate of return on this investment for the one-month period?

A –12.5 percent.

B –15.4 percent.

C –50.1 percent.

22 Caroline Rogers believes the price of Gamma Corp. stock will go down in the near future. She has decided to sell short 200 shares of Gamma Corp. at the current market price of €47. The initial margin requirement is 40 percent. Which of the following is an appropriate statement regarding the margin requirement that Rogers is subject to on this short sale?

A She will need to contribute €3,760 as margin.

B She will need to contribute €5,640 as margin.

C She will only need to leave the proceeds from the short sale as deposit and does not need to contribute any additional funds.

23 The current price of a stock is $25 per share. You have $10,000 to invest. You borrow an additional $10,000 from your broker and invest $20,000 in the stock. If the maintenance margin is 30 percent, at what price will a margin call first occur?

A $9.62.

B $17.86.

C $19.71.

24 You have placed a sell market-on-open order—a market order that would automatically be submitted at the market's open tomorrow and would fill at the market price. Your instruction, to sell the shares at the market open, is a(n):

A execution instruction.

B validity instruction.

C clearing instruction.

25 A market has the following limit orders standing on its book for a particular stock. The bid and ask sizes are number of shares in hundreds.

Bid Size	Limit Price (€)	Offer Size
5	9.73	
12	9.81	
4	9.84	
6	9.95	
	10.02	5
	10.10	12
	10.14	8

What is the market?

A 9.73 bid, offered at 10.14.

B 9.81 bid, offered at 10.10.

C 9.95 bid, offered at 10.02.

26 Consider the following limit order book for a stock. The bid and ask sizes are number of shares in hundreds.

Bid Size	Limit Price (¥)	Offer Size
3	122.80	
8	123.00	
4	123.35	
	123.80	7
	124.10	6
	124.50	7

A new buy limit order is placed for 300 shares at ¥123.40. This limit order is said to:

A take the market.

B make the market.

C make a new market.

27 Currently, the market in a stock is "$54.62 bid, offered at $54.71." A new sell limit order is placed at $54.62. This limit order is said to:

A take the market.

B make the market.

C make a new market.

28 Jim White has sold short 100 shares of Super Stores at a price of $42 per share. He has also simultaneously placed a "good-till-cancelled, stop 50, limit 55 buy" order. Assume that if the stop condition specified by White is satisfied and the order becomes valid, it will get executed. Excluding transaction costs, what is the maximum possible loss that White can have?

A $800.

B $1,300.

C Unlimited.

29 You own shares of a company that are currently trading at $30 a share. Your technical analysis of the shares indicates a support level of $27.50. That is, if the price of the shares is going down, it is more likely to stay above this level rather than fall below it. If the price does fall below this level, however, you believe that the price may continue to decline. You have no immediate intent to sell the shares but are concerned about the possibility of a huge loss if the share price declines below the support level. Which of the following types of orders could you place to most appropriately address your concern?

A Short sell order.

B Good-till-cancelled stop sell order.

C Good-till-cancelled stop buy order.

30 In an underwritten offering, the risk that the entire issue may not be sold to the public at the stipulated offering price is borne by the:

A issuer.

B investment bank.

C buyers of the part of the issue that is sold.

31 A British company listed on AIM (formerly the Alternative Investment Market) of the London Stock Exchange announced the sale of 6,686,665 shares to a small group of qualified investors at £0.025 per share. Which of the following *best describes* this sale?

A Shelf registration.

B Private placement.

C Initial public offering.

32 A German publicly traded company, to raise new capital, gave its existing shareholders the opportunity to subscribe for new shares. The existing shareholders could purchase two new shares at a subscription price of €4.58 per share for every 15 shares held. This is an example of a(n):

A rights offering.

B private placement.

C initial public offering.

33 Consider an order-driven system that allows hidden orders. The following four sell orders on a particular stock are currently in the system's limit order book. Based on the commonly used order precedence hierarchy, which of these orders will have precedence over others?

Order	Time of Arrival (HH:MM:SS)	Limit Price (€)	Special Instruction (If any)
I	9:52:01	20.33	
II	9:52:08	20.29	Hidden order
III	9:53:04	20.29	
IV	9:53:49	20.29	

A Order I (time of arrival of 9:52:01).

B Order II (time of arrival of 9:52:08).

C Order III (time of arrival of 9:53:04).

34 Zhenhu Li has submitted an immediate-or-cancel buy order for 500 shares of a company at a limit price of CNY 74.25. There are two sell limit orders standing in that stock's order book at that time. One is for 300 shares at a limit price of CNY 74.30 and the other is for 400 shares at a limit price of CNY 74.35. How many shares in Li's order would get cancelled?

A None (the order would remain open but unfilled).

B 200 (300 shares would get filled).

C 500 (there would be no fill).

35 A market has the following limit orders standing on its book for a particular stock:

Buyer	Bid Size (Number of Shares)	Limit Price (£)	Offer Size (Number of Shares)	Seller
Keith	1,000	19.70		
Paul	200	19.84		
Ann	400	19.89		
Mary	300	20.02		
		20.03	800	Jack
		20.11	1,100	Margaret
		20.16	400	Jeff

Ian submits a day order to sell 1,000 shares, limit £19.83. Assuming that no more buy orders are submitted on that day after Ian submits his order, what would be Ian's average trade price?

A £19.70.

B £19.92.

C £20.05.

36 A financial analyst is examining whether a country's financial market is well functioning. She finds that the transaction costs in this market are low and trading volumes are high. She concludes that the market is quite liquid. In such a market:

A traders will find it hard to make use of their information.

B traders will find it easy to trade and their trading will make the market less informationally efficient.

C traders will find it easy to trade and their trading will make the market more informationally efficient.

37 The government of a country whose financial markets are in an early stage of development has hired you as a consultant on financial market regulation. Your first task is to prepare a list of the objectives of market regulation. Which of the following is *least likely* to be included in this list of objectives?

A Minimize agency problems in the financial markets.

B Ensure that financial markets are fair and orderly.

C Ensure that investors in the stock market achieve a rate of return that is at least equal to the risk-free rate of return.

SOLUTIONS

1 C is correct. Takabe is best characterized as an information-motivated trader. Takabe believes that his model provides him superior information about the movements in the stock market and his motive for trading is to profit from this information.

2 B is correct. Beach is an investor. He is simply investing in risky assets consistent with his level of risk aversion. Beach is not hedging any existing risk or using information to identify and trade mispriced securities. Therefore, he is not a hedger or an information-motivated trader.

3 A is correct. Smith is a hedger. The short position on the BRL futures contract offsets the BRL long position in three months. She is hedging the risk of the BRL depreciating against the USD. If the BRL depreciates, the value of the cash inflow goes down in USD terms but there is a gain on the futures contracts.

4 A is correct. Regulation of arbitrageurs' profits is not a function of the financial system. The financial system facilitates the allocation of capital to the best uses and the purposes for which people use the financial system, including borrowing money.

5 C is correct. The purchase of real estate properties is a transaction in the alternative investment market.

6 B is correct. The 90-day commercial paper and negotiable certificates of deposit are money market instruments.

7 B is correct. This transaction is a sale in the primary market. It is a sale of shares from the issuer to the investor and funds flow to the issuer of the security from the purchaser.

8 A is correct. Warrants are least likely to be part of the fund. Warrant holders have the right to buy the issuer's common stock. Thus, warrants are typically classified as equity and are least likely to be a part of a fixed-income mutual fund. Commercial paper and repurchase agreements are short-term fixed-income securities.

9 C is correct. When investors want to sell their shares, investors of an open-end fund sell the shares back to the fund whereas investors of a closed-end fund sell the shares to others in the secondary market. Closed-end funds are available to new investors but they must purchase shares in the fund in the secondary market. The shares of a closed-end fund trade at a premium or discount to net asset value.

10 A is correct. Once you have entered into a forward contract, it is difficult to exit from the contract. As opposed to a futures contract, trading out of a forward contract is quite difficult. There is no exchange of cash at the origination of a forward contract. There is no exchange on a forward contract until the maturity of the contract.

11 A is correct. Harris is least likely to find counterparty risk associated with a futures contract. There is limited counterparty risk in a futures contract because the clearinghouse is on the other side of every contract.

12 B is correct. Buying a put option on the dollar will ensure a minimum exchange rate but does not have to be exercised if the exchange rate moves in a favorable direction. Forward and futures contracts would lock in a fixed rate but would not allow for the possibility to profit in case the value of the dollar three months later in the spot market turns out to be greater than the value in the forward or futures contract.

13 B is correct. The agreement between the publisher and the paper supplier to respectively buy and supply paper in the future at a price agreed upon today is a forward contract.

14 B is correct. SPDRs trade in the secondary market and are a pooled investment vehicle.

15 B is correct. The holder of the call option will exercise the call options if the price is above the exercise price of $305 per share. Note that if the stock price is above $305 but less than $308, the option would be exercised even though the net result for the option buyer after considering the premium is a loss. For example, if the stock price is $307, the option buyer would exercise the option to make $2 = $307 – $305 per share, resulting in a loss of $1 = $3 – $2 after considering the premium. It is better to exercise and have a loss of only $1, however, rather than not exercise and lose the entire $3 premium.

16 B is correct. The investment companies that create exchange-traded funds (ETFs) are financial intermediaries. ETFs are securities that represent ownership in the assets held by the fund. The transaction costs of trading shares of ETFs are substantially lower than the combined costs of trading the underlying assets of the ETF.

17 B is correct. The process can best be described as arbitrage because it involves buying and selling instruments, whose values are closely related, at different prices in different markets.

18 A is correct. Robert's exposure to the risk of the stock of the Michelin Group is long. The exposure as a result of the long call position is long. The exposure as a result of the short put position is also long. Therefore, the combined exposure is long.

19 B is correct. The maximum leverage ratio is 1.82 = 100% position ÷ 55% equity. The maximum leverage ratio associated with a position financed by the minimum margin requirement is one divided by the minimum margin requirement.

20 C is correct. The return is 50 percent. If the position had been unleveraged, the return would be 20% = (60 – 50)/50. Because of leverage, the return is 50% = 2.5 × 20%.

Another way to look at this problem is that the equity contributed by the trader (the minimum margin requirement) is 40% = 100% ÷ 2.5. The trader contributed $20 = 40% of $50 per share. The gain is $10 per share, resulting in a return of 50% = 10/20.

21 B is correct. The return is –15.4 percent.

Total cost of the purchase = $16,000 = 500 × $32

Equity invested = $12,000 = 0.75 × $16,000

Amount borrowed = $4,000 = 16,000 – 12,000

Interest paid at month end = $80 = 0.02 × $4,000

Dividend received at month end = $250 = 500 × $0.50

Proceeds on stock sale = $14,000 = 500 × $28

Total commissions paid = $20 = $10 + $10

Net gain/loss = –$1,850 = –16,000 – 80 + 250 + 14,000 – 20

Initial investment including commission on purchase = $12,010

Return = –15.4% = –$1,850/$12,010

22 A is correct. She will need to contribute €3,760 as margin. In view of the possibility of a loss, if the stock price goes up, she will need to contribute €3,760 = 40% of €9,400 as the initial margin. Rogers will need to leave the proceeds from the short sale (€9,400 = 200 × €47) on deposit.

23 B is correct. A margin call will first occur at a price of $17.86. Because you have contributed half and borrowed the remaining half, your initial equity is 50 percent of the initial stock price, or $12.50 = 0.50 × $25. If *P* is the subsequent price, your equity would change by an amount equal to the change in price. So, your equity at price *P* would be 12.50 + (*P* – 25). A margin call will occur when the percentage margin drops to 30 percent. So, the price at which a margin call will occur is the solution to the following equation.

$$\frac{\text{Equity/Share}}{\text{Price/Share}} = \frac{12.50 + P - 25}{P} = 30\%$$

The solution is *P* = $17.86.

24 B is correct. An instruction regarding when to fill an order is considered a validity instruction.

25 C is correct. The market is 9.95 bid, offered at 10.02. The best bid is at €9.95 and the best offer is €10.02.

26 C is correct. This order is said to make a new market. The new buy order is at ¥123.40, which is better than the current best bid of ¥123.35. Therefore, the buy order is making a new market. Had the new order been at ¥123.35, it would be said to make the market. Because the new buy limit order is at a price less than the best offer of ¥123.80, it will not immediately execute and is not taking the market.

27 A is correct. This order is said to take the market. The new sell order is at $54.62, which is at the current best bid. Therefore, the new sell order will immediately trade with the current best bid and is taking the market.

28 B is correct. The maximum possible loss is $1,300. If the stock price crosses $50, the stop buy order will become valid and will get executed at a maximum limit price of $55. The maximum loss per share is $13 = $55 – $42, or $1,300 for 100 shares.

29 B is correct. The most appropriate order is a good-till-cancelled stop sell order. This order will be acted on if the stock price declines below a specified price (in this case, $27.50). This order is sometimes referred to as a good-till-cancelled stop loss sell order. You are generally bullish about the stock, as indicated by no immediate intent to sell, and would expect a loss on short selling the stock. A stop buy order is placed to buy a stock when the stock is going up.

30 B is correct. The investment bank bears the risk that the issue may be undersubscribed at the offering price. If the entire issue is not sold, the investment bank underwriting the issue will buy the unsold securities at the offering price.

31 B is correct. This sale is a private placement. As the company is already publicly traded, the share sale is clearly not an initial public offering. The sale also does not involve a shelf registration because the company is not selling shares to the public on a piecemeal basis.

32 A is correct. This offering is a rights offering. The company is distributing rights to buy stock at a fixed price to existing shareholders in proportion to their holdings.

33 C is correct. Order III (time of arrival of 9:53:04) has precedence. In the order precedence hierarchy, the first rule is price priority. Based on this rule, sell orders II, III, and IV get precedence over order I. The next rule is display precedence at a given price. Because order II is a hidden order, orders III and IV get precedence. Finally, order III gets precedence over order IV based on time priority at same price and same display status.

34 C is correct. The order for 500 shares would get cancelled; there would be no fill. Li is willing to buy at CNY 74.25 or less but the minimum offer price in the book is CNY 74.30; therefore, no part of the order would be filled. Because Li's order is immediate-or-cancel, it would be cancelled.

35 B is correct. Ian's average trade price is:

$$£19.92 = \frac{300 \times £20.02 + 400 \times £19.89 + 200 \times £19.84}{300 + 400 + 200}$$

Ian's sell order first fills with the most aggressively priced buy order, which is Mary's order for 300 shares at £20.02. Ian still has 700 shares for sale. The next most aggressively priced buy order is Ann's order for 400 shares at £19.89. This order is filled. Ian still has 300 shares for sale. The next most aggressively priced buy order is Paul's order for 200 shares at £19.84. A third trade takes place. Ian still has 100 shares for sale.

The next buy order is Keith's order for 1,000 shares at £19.70. However, this price is below Ian's limit price of £19.83. Therefore, no more trade is possible.

36 C is correct. In such a market, well-informed traders will find it easy to trade and their trading will make the market more informationally efficient. In a liquid market, it is easier for informed traders to fill their orders. Their trading will cause prices to incorporate their information and the prices will be more in line with the fundamental values.

37 C is correct. Ensure that investors in the stock market achieve a rate of return that is at least equal to the risk-free rate of return is least likely to be included as an objective of market regulation. Stocks are risky investments and there would be occasions when a stock market investment would not only have a return less than the risk-free rate but also a negative return. Minimizing agency costs and ensuring that financial markets are fair and orderly are objectives of market regulation.

READING

37

Security Market Indexes

by Paul D. Kaplan, PhD, CFA, and Dorothy C. Kelly, CFA

Paul D. Kaplan, PhD, CFA, is at Morningstar Research, Inc. (Canada). Dorothy C. Kelly, CFA, is at McIntire School of Commerce, University of Virginia (USA).

LEARNING OUTCOMES

Mastery	*The candidate should be able to:*
☐	**a.** describe a security market index;
☐	**b.** calculate and interpret the value, price return, and total return of an index;
☐	**c.** describe the choices and issues in index construction and management;
☐	**d.** compare the different weighting methods used in index construction;
☐	**e.** calculate and analyze the value and return of an index given its weighting method;
☐	**f.** describe rebalancing and reconstitution of an index;
☐	**g.** describe uses of security market indexes;
☐	**h.** describe types of equity indexes;
☐	**i.** describe types of fixed-income indexes;
☐	**j.** describe indexes representing alternative investments;
☐	**k.** compare types of security market indexes.

INTRODUCTION

1

Investors gather and analyze vast amounts of information about security markets on a continual basis. Because this work can be both time consuming and data intensive, investors often use a single measure that consolidates this information and reflects the performance of an entire security market.

Security market indexes were first introduced as a simple measure to reflect the performance of the US stock market. Since then, security market indexes have evolved into important multi-purpose tools that help investors track the performance of various security markets, estimate risk, and evaluate the performance of investment managers. They also form the basis for new investment products.

in·dex, *noun* (*pl.* **in·dex·es** *or* **in·di·ces**) Latin *indic-, index,* from *indicare* to indicate: an indicator, sign, or measure of something.

ORIGIN OF MARKET INDEXES

Investors had access to regularly published data on individual security prices in London as early as 1698, but nearly 200 years passed before they had access to a simple indicator to reflect security market information. To give readers a sense of how the US stock market in general performed on a given day, publishers Charles H. Dow and Edward D. Jones introduced the Dow Jones Average, the world's first security market index, in 1884. The index, which appeared in *The Customers' Afternoon Letter*, consisted of the stocks of nine railroads and two industrial companies. It eventually became the Dow Jones Transportation Average. Convinced that industrial companies, rather than railroads, would be "the great speculative market" of the future, Dow and Jones introduced a second index in May 1896—the Dow Jones Industrial Average (DJIA). It had an initial value of 40.94 and consisted of 12 stocks from major US industries. Today, investors can choose from among thousands of indexes to measure and monitor different security markets and asset classes.

This reading is organized as follows. Section 2 defines a security market index and explains how to calculate the price return and total return of an index for a single period and over multiple periods. Section 3 describes how indexes are constructed and managed. Section 4 discusses the use of market indexes. Sections 5, 6, and 7 discuss various types of indexes, and the final section summarizes the reading. Practice problems follow the conclusions and summary.

2 INDEX DEFINITION AND CALCULATIONS OF VALUE AND RETURNS

A **security market index** represents a given security market, market segment, or asset class. Most indexes are constructed as portfolios of marketable securities.

The value of an index is calculated on a regular basis using either the actual or estimated market prices of the individual securities, known as **constituent securities**, within the index. For each security market index, investors may encounter two versions of the same index (i.e., an index with identical constituent securities and weights): one version based on price return and one version based on total return. As the name suggests, a **price return index**, also known as a **price index**, reflects *only* the prices of the constituent securities within the index. A **total return index**, in contrast, reflects not only the prices of the constituent securities but also the reinvestment of all income received since inception.

At inception, the values of the price and total return versions of an index are equal. As time passes, however, the value of the total return index, which includes the reinvestment of all dividends and/or interest received, will exceed the value of the price return index by an increasing amount. A look at how the values of each version are calculated over multiple periods illustrates why.

The value of a price return index is calculated as:

$$V_{PRI} = \frac{\sum_{i=1}^{N} n_i P_i}{D} \quad (1)$$

where

V_{PRI} = the value of the price return index
n_i = the number of units of constituent security i held in the index portfolio
N = the number of constituent securities in the index
P_i = the unit price of constituent security i
D = the value of the divisor

The **divisor** is a number initially chosen at inception. It is frequently chosen so that the price index has a convenient initial value, such as 1,000. The index provider then adjusts the value of the divisor as necessary to avoid changes in the index value that are unrelated to changes in the prices of its constituent securities. For example, when changing index constituents, the index provider may adjust the divisor so that the value of the index with the new constituents equals the value of the index prior to the changes.

Index return calculations, like calculations of investment portfolio returns, may measure price return or total return. **Price return** measures only price appreciation or percentage change in price. **Total return** measures price appreciation plus interest, dividends, and other distributions.

2.1 Calculation of Single-Period Returns

For a security market index, price return can be calculated in two ways: either the percentage change in value of the price return index, or the weighted average of price returns of the constituent securities. The price return of an index can be expressed as:

$$\text{PR}_I = \frac{V_{PRI1} - V_{PRI0}}{V_{PRI0}} \quad (2)$$

where

PR_I = the price return of the index portfolio (as a decimal number, i.e., 12 percent is 0.12)
V_{PRI1} = the value of the price return index at the end of the period
V_{PRI0} = the value of the price return index at the beginning of the period

Similarly, the price return of each constituent security can be expressed as:

$$\text{PR}_i = \frac{P_{i1} - P_{i0}}{P_{i0}} \quad (3)$$

where

PR_i = the price return of constituent security i (as a decimal number)
P_{i1} = the price of constituent security i at the end of the period
P_{i0} = the price of constituent security i at the beginning of the period

Because the price return of the index equals the weighted average of price returns of the individual securities, we can write:

$$PR_I = \sum_{i=1}^{N} w_i PR_i = \sum_{i=1}^{N} w_i \left(\frac{P_{i1} - P_{i0}}{P_{i0}} \right) \tag{4}$$

where:

PR_I = the price return of index portfolio (as a decimal number)

PR_i = the price return of constituent security i (as a decimal number)

N = the number of individual securities in the index

w_i = the weight of security i (the fraction of the index portfolio allocated to security i)

P_{i1} = the price of constituent security i at the end of the period

P_{i0} = the price of constituent security i at the beginning of the period

Equation 4 can be rewritten simply as:

$$PR_I = w_1 PR_1 + w_2 PR_2 + \ldots + w_N PR_N \tag{5}$$

where

PR_I = the price return of index portfolio (as a decimal number)

PR_i = the price return of constituent security i (as a decimal number)

w_i = the weight of security i (the fraction of the index portfolio allocated to security i)

N = the number of securities in the index

Total return measures price appreciation plus interest, dividends, and other distributions. Thus, the **total return** of an index is the price appreciation, or change in the value of the price return index, plus income (dividends and/or interest) over the period, expressed as a percentage of the beginning value of the price return index. The total return of an index can be expressed as:

$$TR_I = \frac{V_{PRI1} - V_{PRI0} + Inc_I}{V_{PRI0}} \tag{6}$$

where

TR_I = the total return of the index portfolio (as a decimal number)

V_{PRI1} = the value of the price return index at the end of the period

V_{PRI0} = the value of the price return index at the beginning of the period

Inc_I = the total income (dividends and/or interest) from all securities in the index held over the period

The total return of an index can also be calculated as the weighted average of total returns of the constituent securities. The total return of each constituent security in the index is calculated as:

$$TR_i = \frac{P_{1i} - P_{0i} + Inc_i}{P_{0i}} \tag{7}$$

where

TR_i = the total return of constituent security i (as a decimal number)

P_{1i} = the price of constituent security i at the end of the period

P_{0i} = the price of constituent security i at the beginning of the period

Inc_i = the total income (dividends and/or interest) from security i over the period

Because the total return of an index can be calculated as the weighted average of total returns of the constituent securities, we can express total return as:

$$TR_I = \sum_{i=1}^{N} w_i TR_i = \sum_{i=1}^{N} w_i \left(\frac{P_{1i} - P_{0i} + Inc_i}{P_{0i}} \right) \tag{8}$$

Equation 8 can be rewritten simply as

$$TR_I = w_1 TR_1 + w_2 TR_2 + \ldots + w_N TR_N \tag{9}$$

where

TR_I = the total return of the index portfolio (as a decimal number)
TR_i = the total return of constituent security i (as a decimal number)
w_i = the weight of security i (the fraction of the index portfolio allocated to security i)
N = the number of securities in the index

2.2 Calculation of Index Values over Multiple Time Periods

The calculation of index values over multiple time periods requires geometrically linking the series of index returns. With a series of price returns for an index, we can calculate the value of the price return index with the following equation:

$$V_{PRIT} = V_{PRI0}(1 + PR_{I1})(1 + PR_{I2})\ldots(1 + PR_{IT}) \tag{10}$$

where

V_{PRI0} = the value of the price return index at inception
V_{PRIT} = the value of the price return index at time t
PR_{IT} = the price return (as a decimal number) on the index over period t, t = 1, 2, …, T

For an index with an inception value set to 1,000 and price returns of 5 percent and 3 percent for Periods 1 and 2 respectively, the values of the price return index would be calculated as follows:

Period	Return (%)	Calculation	Ending Value
0		1,000(1.00)	1,000.00
1	5.00	1,000(1.05)	1,050.00
2	3.00	1,000(1.05)(1.03)	1,081.50

Similarly, the series of total returns for an index is used to calculate the value of the total return index with the following equation:

$$V_{TRIT} = V_{TRI0}(1 + TR_{I1})(1 + TR_{I2})\ldots(1 + TR_{IT}) \tag{11}$$

where

V_{TRI0} = the value of the index at inception
V_{TRIT} = the value of the total return index at time t
TR_{IT} = the total return (as a decimal number) on the index over period t, t = 1, 2, …, T

Suppose that the same index yields an additional 1.5 percent return from income in Period 1 and an additional 2.0 percent return from income in Period 2, bringing the total returns for Periods 1 and 2, respectively, to 6.5 percent and 5 percent. The values of the total return index would be calculated as follows:

Period	Return (%)	Calculation	Ending Value
0		1,000(1.00)	1,000.00
1	6.50	1,000(1.065)	1,065.00
2	5.00	1,000(1.065)(1.05)	1,118.25

As illustrated above, as time passes, the value of the total return index, which includes the reinvestment of all dividends and/or interest received, exceeds the value of the price return index by an increasing amount.

3 INDEX CONSTRUCTION AND MANAGEMENT

Constructing and managing a security market index is similar to constructing and managing a portfolio of securities. Index providers must decide the following:

1 Which target market should the index represent?
2 Which securities should be selected from that target market?
3 How much weight should be allocated to each security in the index?
4 When should the index be rebalanced?
5 When should the security selection and weighting decision be re-examined?

3.1 Target Market and Security Selection

The first decision in index construction is identifying the target market, market segment, or asset class that the index is intended to represent. The target market may be defined very broadly or narrowly. It may be based on asset class (e.g., equities, fixed income, real estate, commodities, hedge funds); geographic region (e.g., Japan, South Africa, Latin America, Europe); the exchange on which the securities are traded (e.g., Shanghai, Toronto, Tokyo), and/or other characteristics (e.g., economic sector, company size, investment style, duration, or credit quality).

The target market determines the investment universe and the securities available for inclusion in the index. Once the investment universe is identified, the number of securities and the specific securities to include in the index must be determined. The constituent securities could be nearly all those in the target market or a representative sample of the target market. Some equity indexes, such as the S&P 500 Index and the FTSE 100, fix the number of securities included in the index and indicate this number in the name of the index. Other indexes allow the number of securities to vary to reflect changes in the target market or to maintain a certain percentage of the target market. For example, the Tokyo Stock Price Index (TOPIX) represents and includes all of the largest stocks, known as the First Section, listed on the Tokyo Stock Exchange. To be included in the First Section—and thus the TOPIX—stocks must meet certain criteria, such as the number of shares outstanding, the number of shareholders, and market capitalization. Stocks that no longer meet the criteria are removed from the First Section and also the TOPIX. Objective or mechanical rules determine the constituent securities of most, but not all, indexes. The S&P Bombay Stock Exchange Sensitive Index, also called the S&P BSE SENSEX and the S&P 500, for example, use a selection committee and more subjective decision-making rules to determine constituent securities.

3.2 Index Weighting

The weighting decision determines how much of each security to include in the index and has a substantial impact on an index's value. Index providers use a number of methods to weight the constituent securities in an index. Indexes can be price weighted, equal weighted, market-capitalization weighted, or fundamentally weighted. Each weighting method has its advantages and disadvantages.

3.2.1 *Price Weighting*

The simplest method to weight an index and the one used by Charles Dow to construct the Dow Jones Industrial Average is **price weighting**. In price weighting, the weight on each constituent security is determined by dividing its price by the sum of all the prices of the constituent securities. The weight is calculated using the following formula:

$$w_i^P = \frac{P_i}{\sum_{i=1}^{N} P_i} \quad (12)$$

Exhibit 1 illustrates the values, weights, and single-period returns following inception of a price-weighted equity index with five constituent securities. The value of the price-weighted index is determined by dividing the sum of the security values (101.50) by the divisor, which is typically set at inception to equal the initial number of securities in the index. Thus, in our example, the divisor is 5 and the initial value of the index is calculated as 101.50 ÷ 5 = 20.30.

As illustrated in this exhibit, Security A, which has the highest price, also has the highest weighting and thus will have the greatest impact on the return of the index. Note how both the price return and the total return of the index are calculated on the basis of the corresponding returns on the constituent securities.

A property unique to price-weighted indexes is that a stock split on one constituent security changes the weights on all the securities in the index.[1] To prevent the stock split and the resulting new weights from changing the value of the index, the index provider must adjust the value of the divisor as illustrated in Exhibit 2. Given a 2-for-1 split in Security A, the divisor is adjusted by dividing the sum of the constituent prices *after* the split (77.50) by the value of the index *before* the split (21.00). This adjustment results in changing the divisor from 5 to 3.69 so that the index value is maintained at 21.00.

The primary advantage of price weighting is its simplicity. The main disadvantage of price weighting is that it results in arbitrary weights for each security. In particular, a stock split in any one security causes arbitrary changes in the weights of all the constituents' securities.

Exhibit 2 Impact of 2-for-1 Split in Security A

Security	Price before Split	Weight before Split (%)	Price after Split	Weight after Split (%)
A	55.00	52.38	27.50	35.48
B	22.00	20.95	22.00	28.39
C	8.00	7.62	8.00	10.32
D	14.00	13.33	14.00	18.07

(continued)

1 A stock split is an increase in the number of shares outstanding and a proportionate decrease in the price per share such that the total market value of equity, as well as investors' proportionate ownership in the company, does not change.

Exhibit 1 Example of a Price-Weighted Equity Index

Security	Shares in Index	BOP Price	Value (Shares × BOP Price)	BOP Weight (%)	EOP Price	Dividends Per Share	Value (Shares × EOP Price)	Total Dividends	Price Return (%)	Total Return (%)	BOP Weight × Price Return (%)	BOP Weight × Total Return (%)	EOP Weight (%)
A	1	50.00	50.00	49.26	55.00	0.75	55.00	0.75	10.00	11.50	4.93	5.66	52.38
B	1	25.00	25.00	24.63	22.00	0.10	22.00	0.10	−12.00	−11.60	−2.96	−2.86	20.95
C	1	12.50	12.50	12.32	8.00	0.00	8.00	0.00	−36.00	−36.00	−4.43	−4.43	7.62
D	1	10.00	10.00	9.85	14.00	0.05	14.00	0.05	40.00	40.50	3.94	3.99	13.33
E	1	4.00	4.00	3.94	6.00	0.00	6.00	0.00	50.00	50.00	1.97	1.97	5.72
Total			**101.50**	**100.00**			**105.00**	**0.90**			**3.45**	**4.33**	**100.00**
Index Value			**20.30**				**21.00**	**0.18**	**3.45**	**4.33**			

Divisor = 5

BOP = Beginning of period

EOP = End of period

Type of Index	BOP Value	Return (%)	EOP Value
Price Return	20.30	3.45	21.00
Total Return	20.30	4.33	21.18

Exhibit 2 (Continued)

Security	Price before Split	Weight before Split (%)	Price after Split	Weight after Split (%)
E	6.00	5.72	6.00	7.74
Total	105.00	100.00	77.50	100.00
Divisor	5.00		3.69	
Index Value	21.00		21.00	

3.2.2 *Equal Weighting*

Another simple index weighting method is **equal weighting**. This method assigns an equal weight to each constituent security at inception. The weights are calculated as:

$$w_i^E = \frac{1}{N} \tag{13}$$

where

w_i = fraction of the portfolio that is allocated to security i or weight of security i

N = number of securities in the index

To construct an equal-weighted index from the five securities in Exhibit 1, the index provider allocates one-fifth (20 percent) of the value of the index (at the beginning of the period) to each security. Dividing the value allocated to each security by each security's individual share price determines the number of shares of each security to include in the index. Unlike a price-weighted index, where the weights are arbitrarily determined by the market prices, the weights in an equal-weighted index are arbitrarily assigned by the index provider.

Exhibit 3 illustrates the values, weights, and single-period returns following inception of an equal-weighted index with the same constituent securities as those in Exhibit 1. This example assumes a beginning index portfolio value of 10,000 (i.e., an investment of 2,000 in each security). To set the initial value of the index to 1,000, the divisor is set to 10 (10,000 ÷ 10 = 1,000).

Exhibits 1 and 3 demonstrate how different weighting methods result in different returns. The 10.4 percent price return of the equal-weighted index shown in Exhibit 3 differs significantly from the 3.45 percent price return of the price-weighted index in Exhibit 1.

Like price weighting, the primary advantage of equal weighting is its simplicity. Equal weighting, however, has a number of disadvantages. First, securities that constitute the largest fraction of the target market value are underrepresented, and securities that constitute a small fraction of the target market value are overrepresented. Second, after the index is constructed and the prices of constituent securities change, the index is no longer equally weighted. Therefore, maintaining equal weights requires frequent adjustments (rebalancing) to the index.

3.2.3 *Market-Capitalization Weighting*

In **market-capitalization weighting**, or value weighting, the weight on each constituent security is determined by dividing its market capitalization by the total market capitalization (the sum of the market capitalization) of all the securities in the index. Market capitalization or value is calculated by multiplying the number of shares outstanding by the market price per share.

Exhibit 3 Example of an Equal-Weighted Equity Index

Security	Shares in Index	BOP Price	Value (Shares × BOP Price)	Weight (%)	EOP Price	Dividends Per Share	Value (Shares × EOP Price)	Total Dividends	Price Return (%)	Total Return (%)	Weight × Price Return (%)	Weight × Total Return (%)	EOP Weight (%)
A	40	50.00	2,000	20.00	55.00	0.75	2,200	30	10.00	11.50	2.00	2.30	19.93
B	80	25.00	2,000	20.00	22.00	0.10	1,760	8	−12.00	−11.60	−2.40	−2.32	15.94
C	160	12.50	2,000	20.00	8.00	0.00	1,280	0	−36.00	−36.00	−7.20	−7.20	11.60
D	200	10.00	2,000	20.00	14.00	0.05	2,800	10	40.00	40.50	8.00	8.10	25.36
E	500	4.00	2,000	20.00	6.00	0.00	3,000	0	50.00	50.00	10.00	10.00	27.17
Total			**10,000**	**100.00**			**11,040**	**48**			**10.40**	**10.88**	**100.00**
Index Value			**1,000**				**1,104**	**4.80**	**10.40**	**10.88**			

Divisor = 10

BOP = Beginning of period

EOP = End of period

Type of Index	BOP Value	Return (%)	EOP Value
Price Return	1,000.00	10.40	1,104.00
Total Return	1,000.00	10.88	1,108.80

The market-capitalization weight of security i is:

$$w_i^M = \frac{Q_i P_i}{\sum_{j=1}^{N} Q_j P_j} \quad (14)$$

where

w_i = fraction of the portfolio that is allocated to security i or weight of security i

Q_i = number of shares outstanding of security i

P_i = share price of security i

N = number of securities in the index

Exhibit 4 illustrates the values, weights, and single-period returns following inception of a market-capitalization-weighted index for the same five-security market. Security A, with 3,000 shares outstanding and a price of 50 per share, has a market capitalization of 150,000 or 26.29 percent (150,000/570,500) of the entire index portfolio. The resulting index weights in the exhibit reflect the relative value of each security as measured by its market capitalization.

As shown in Exhibits 1, 3, and 4, the weighting method affects the index's returns. The price and total returns of the market-capitalization index in Exhibit 4 (1.49 percent and 2.13 percent, respectively) differ significantly from those of the price-weighted (3.45 percent and 4.33 percent, respectively) and equal-weighted (10.40 percent and 10.88 percent respectively) indexes. To understand the source and magnitude of the difference, compare the weights and returns of each security under each of the weighting methods. The weight of Security A, for example, ranges from 49.26 percent in the price-weighted index to 20 percent in the equal-weighted index. With a price return of 10 percent, Security A contributes 4.93 percent to the price return of the price-weighted index, 2.00 percent to the price return of the equal-weighted index, and 2.63 percent to the price return of the market-capitalization-weighted index. With a total return of 11.50 percent, Security A contributes 5.66 percent to the total return of the price-weighted index, 2.30 percent to the total return of the equal-weighted index, and 3.02 percent to the total return of the market-capitalization-weighted index.

3.2.3.1 Float-Adjusted Market-Capitalization Weighting In **float-adjusted market-capitalization weighting**, the weight on each constituent security is determined by adjusting its market capitalization for its **market float**. Typically, market float is the number of shares of the constituent security that are available to the investing public. For companies that are closely held, only a portion of the shares outstanding are available to the investing public (the rest are held by a small group of controlling investors). In addition to excluding shares held by controlling shareholders, most float-adjusted market-capitalization-weighted indexes also exclude shares held by other corporations and governments. Some providers of indexes that are designed to represent the investment opportunities of global investors further reduce the number of shares included in the index by excluding shares that are not available to foreigner investors. The index providers may refer to these indexes as "free-float-adjusted market-capitalization-weighted indexes."

Float-adjusted market-capitalization-weighted indexes reflect the shares available for public trading by multiplying the market price per share by the number of shares available to the investing public (i.e., the float-adjusted market capitalization) rather than the total number of shares outstanding (total market capitalization). Currently, most market-capitalization-weighted indexes are float adjusted. Therefore, unless otherwise indicated, for the remainder of this reading, "market-capitalization" weighting refers to float-adjusted market-capitalization weighting.

Exhibit 4 Example of a Market-Capitalization-Weighted Equity Index

Stock	Shares Out-standing	BOP Price	BOP Market Cap	BOP Weight (%)	EOP Price	Dividends Per Share	EOP Market Cap	Total Dividends	Price Return (%)	Total Return (%)	BOP Weight × Price Return (%)	BOP Weight × Total Return (%)	EOP Weight (%)
A	3,000	50.00	150,000	26.29	55.00	0.75	165,000	2,250	10.00	11.50	2.63	3.02	28.50
B	10,000	25.00	250,000	43.82	22.00	0.10	220,000	1,000	−12.00	−11.60	−5.26	−5.08	38.00
C	5,000	12.50	62,500	10.96	8.00	0.00	40,000	0	−36.00	−36.00	−3.95	−3.95	6.91
D	8,000	10.00	80,000	14.02	14.00	0.05	112,000	400	40.00	40.50	5.61	5.68	19.34
E	7,000	4.00	28,000	4.91	6.00	0.00	42,000	0	50.00	50.00	2.46	2.46	7.25
Total			**570,500**	**100.00**			**579,000**	**3,650**			**1.49**	**2.13**	**100.00**
Index Value			**1,000**				**1,014.90**	**6.40**	**1.49**	**2.13**			

Divisor = 570.50

BOP = Beginning of period

EOP = End of period

Type of Index	BOP Value	Return (%)	EOP Value
Price Return	1,000.00	1.49	1,014.90
Total Return	1,000.00	2.13	1,021.30

The float-adjusted market-capitalization weight of security i is calculated as:

$$w_i^M = \frac{f_i Q_i P_i}{\sum_{j=1}^{N} f_j Q_j P_j} \tag{15}$$

where

f_i = fraction of shares outstanding in the market float

w_i = fraction of the portfolio that is allocated to security i or weight of security i

Q_i = number of shares outstanding of security i

P_i = share price of security i

N = number of securities in the index

Exhibit 5 illustrates the values, weights, and single-period returns following inception of a float-adjusted market-capitalization-weighted equity index using the same five securities as before. The low percentage of shares of Security D in the market float compared with the number of shares outstanding indicates that the security is closely held.

The primary advantage of market-capitalization weighting (including float adjusted) is that constituent securities are held in proportion to their value in the target market. The primary disadvantage is that constituent securities whose prices have risen the most (or fallen the most) have a greater (or lower) weight in the index (i.e., as a security's price rises relative to other securities in the index, its weight increases; and as its price decreases in value relative to other securities in the index, its weight decreases). This weighting method leads to overweighting stocks that have risen in price (and may be overvalued) and underweighting stocks that have declined in price (and may be undervalued). The effect of this weighting method is similar to a momentum investment strategy in that over time, the securities that have risen in price the most will have the largest weights in the index.

3.2.4 *Fundamental Weighting*

Fundamental weighting attempts to address the disadvantages of market-capitalization weighting by using measures of a company's size that are independent of its security price to determine the weight on each constituent security. These measures include book value, cash flow, revenues, earnings, dividends, and number of employees.

Some fundamental indexes use a single measure, such as total dividends, to weight the constituent securities, whereas others combine the weights from several measures to form a composite value that is used for weighting.

Letting F_i denote a given fundamental size measure of company i, the fundamental weight on security i is:

$$w_i^F = \frac{F_i}{\sum_{j=1}^{N} F_j} \tag{16}$$

Relative to a market-capitalization-weighted index, a fundamental index with weights based on such an item as earnings will result in greater weights on constituent securities with earnings yields (earnings divided by price) that are higher than the earnings yield of the overall market-weighted portfolio. Similarly, stocks with earnings yields less than the yield on the overall market-weighted portfolio will have lower weights. For example, suppose there are two stocks in an index. Stock A has a market capitalization of €200 million, Stock B has a market capitalization of €800 million, and their aggregate market capitalization is €1 billion (€1,000 million). Both companies

Exhibit 5 Example of Float-Adjusted Market-Capitalization-Weighted Equity Index

Stock	Shares Out-standing	% Shares in Market Float	Shares in Index	BOP Price	BOP Float-Adjusted Market Cap	BOP Weight (%)	EOP Price	Dividends Per Share	Ending Float-Adjusted Market Cap	Total Dividends	Price Return (%)	Total Return (%)	BOP Weight × Price Return (%)	BOP Weight × Total Return (%)	EOP Weight (%)
A	3,000	100	3,000	50.00	150,000	35.40	55.00	0.75	165,000	2,250	10.00	11.50	3.54	4.07	39.61
B	10,000	70	7,000	25.00	175,000	41.31	22.00	0.10	154,000	700	−12.00	−11.60	−4.96	−4.79	36.97
C	5,000	90	4,500	12.50	56,250	13.28	8.00	0.00	36,000	0	−36.00	−36.00	−4.78	−4.78	8.64
D	8,000	25	2,000	10.00	20,000	4.72	14.00	0.05	28,000	100	40.00	40.50	1.89	1.91	6.72
E	7,000	80	5,600	4.00	22,400	5.29	6.00	0.00	33,600	0	50.00	50.00	2.65	2.65	8.06
Total					**423,650**	**100.00**			**416,600**	**3,050**			**−1.66**	**−0.94**	**100.00**
Index Value					**1,000**				**983.36**	**7.20**	**−1.66**	**−0.94**			

Divisor = 423.65

BOP = Beginning of period

EOP = End of period

Type of Index	Initial Value	Return (%)	Ending Value
Price Return	1,000.00	−1.66	983.36
Total Return	1,000.00	−0.94	990.56

have earnings of €20 million and aggregate earnings of €40 million. Thus, Stock A has an earnings yield of 10 percent (20/200) and Stock B has an earnings yield of 2.5 percent (20/800). The earnings weight of Stock A is 50 percent (20/40), which is higher than its market-capitalization weight of 20 percent (200/1,000). The earnings weight of Stock B is 50 percent (20/40), which is less than its market-capitalization weight of 80 percent (800/1,000). Relative to the market-cap-weighted index, the earnings-weighted index over-weights the high-yield Stock A and under-weights the low-yield Stock B.

The most important property of fundamental weighting is that it leads to indexes that have a "value" tilt. That is, a fundamentally weighted index has ratios of book value, earnings, dividends, etc. to market value that are higher than its market-capitalization-weighted counterpart. Also, in contrast to the momentum "effect" of market-capitalization-weighted indexes, fundamentally weighted indexes generally will have a contrarian "effect" in that the portfolio weights will shift away from securities that have increased in relative value and toward securities that have fallen in relative value whenever the portfolio is rebalanced.

3.3 Index Management: Rebalancing and Reconstitution

So far, we have discussed index construction. Index management entails the two remaining questions:

- When should the index be rebalanced?
- When should the security selection and weighting decisions be re-examined?

3.3.1 *Rebalancing*

Rebalancing refers to adjusting the weights of the constituent securities in the index. To maintain the weight of each security consistent with the index's weighting method, the index provider rebalances the index by adjusting the weights of the constituent securities on a regularly scheduled basis (rebalancing dates)—usually quarterly. Rebalancing is necessary because the weights of the constituent securities change as their market prices change. Note, for example, that the weights of the securities in the equal-weighted index (Exhibit 3) at the end of the period are no longer equal (i.e., 20 percent):

Security A	19.93%
Security B	15.94
Security C	11.60
Security D	25.36
Security E	27.17

In rebalancing the index, the weights of Securities D and E (which had the highest returns) would be decreased and the weights of Securities A, B, and C (which had the lowest returns) would be increased. Thus, rebalancing creates turnover within an index.

Price-weighted indexes are not rebalanced because the weight of each constituent security is determined by its price. For market-capitalization-weighted indexes, rebalancing is less of a concern because the indexes largely rebalance themselves. In our market-capitalization index, for example, the weight of Security C automatically declined from 10.96 percent to 6.91 percent, reflecting the 36 percent decline in its market price. Market-capitalization weights are only adjusted to reflect mergers, acquisitions, liquidations, and other corporate actions between rebalancing dates.

3.3.2 *Reconstitution*

Reconstitution is the process of changing the constituent securities in an index. It is similar to a portfolio manager deciding to change the securities in his or her portfolio. Reconstitution is part of the rebalancing cycle. The reconstitution date is the date on which index providers review the constituent securities, re-apply the initial criteria for inclusion in the index, and select which securities to retain, remove, or add. Constituent securities that no longer meet the criteria are replaced with securities that do meet the criteria. Once the revised list of constituent securities is determined, the weighting method is re-applied. Indexes are reconstituted to reflect changes in the target market (bankruptcies, de-listings, mergers, acquisitions, etc.) and/or to reflect the judgment of the selection committee.

Reconstitution creates turnover in a number of different ways, particularly for market-capitalization-weighted indexes. When one security is removed and another is added, the index provider has to change the weights of the other securities in order to maintain the market-capitalization weighting of the index.

The frequency of reconstitution is a major issue for widely used indexes and their constituent securities. The Russell 2000 Index, for example, reconstitutes annually. It is used as a benchmark by numerous investment funds, and each year, prior to the index's reconstitution, the managers of these funds buy stocks they think will be added to the index—driving those stocks' prices up—and sell stocks they think will be deleted from the index—driving those stocks' prices down. Exhibit 6 illustrates a historical example of the potential impact of these decisions. Beginning in late April 2009, some managers began acquiring and bidding up the price of Uranium Energy Corporation (UEC) because they believed that it would be included in the reconstituted Russell 2000 Index. On 12 June, Russell listed UEC as a preliminary addition to the Russell 2000 Index and the Russell 3000 Index.[2] By that time, the stock value had increased by more than 300 percent. Investors continued to bid up the stock price in the weeks following the announcement, and the stock closed on the reconstitution date of 30 June at USD2.90, up nearly 400 percent for the quarter.

---

2 According to the press release, final membership in the index would be published after market close on Friday, 26 June.

Exhibit 6 Three-Month Performance of Uranium Energy Corporation and NASDAQ April through June 2009

Source: Yahoo! Finance and Capital IQ.

USES OF MARKET INDEXES

4

Indexes were initially created to give a sense of how a particular security market performed on a given day. With the development of modern financial theory, their uses in investment management have expanded significantly. Some of the major uses of indexes include:

- gauges of market sentiment;
- proxies for measuring and modeling returns, systematic risk, and risk-adjusted performance;
- proxies for asset classes in asset allocation models;
- benchmarks for actively managed portfolios; and
- model portfolios for such investment products as index funds and exchange-traded funds (ETFs).

Investors using security market indexes must be familiar with how various indexes are constructed in order to select the index or indexes most appropriate for their needs.

4.1 Gauges of Market Sentiment

The original purpose of stock market indexes was to provide a gauge of investor confidence or market sentiment. As indicators of the collective opinion of market participants, indexes reflect investor attitudes and behavior. The Dow Jones Industrial Average has a long history, is frequently quoted in the media, and remains a popular gauge of market sentiment. It may not accurately reflect the overall attitude of investors or the "market," however, because the index consists of only 30 of the thousands of US stocks traded each day.

4.2 Proxies for Measuring and Modeling Returns, Systematic Risk, and Risk-Adjusted Performance

The capital asset pricing model (CAPM) defines beta as the systematic risk of a security with respect to the entire market. The market portfolio in the CAPM consists of all risky securities. To represent the performance of the market portfolio, investors use a broad index. For example, the Tokyo Price Index (TOPIX) and the S&P 500 often serve as proxies for the market portfolio in Japan and the United States, respectively, and are used for measuring and modeling systematic risk and market returns.

Security market indexes also serve as market proxies when measuring risk-adjusted performance. The beta of an actively managed portfolio allows investors to form a passive alternative with the same level of systematic risk. For example, if the beta of an actively managed portfolio of global stocks is 0.95 with respect to the MSCI World Index, investors can create a passive portfolio with the same systematic risk by investing 95 percent of their portfolio in a MSCI World Index fund and holding the remaining 5 percent in cash. Alpha, the difference between the return of the actively managed portfolio and the return of the passive portfolio, is a measure of risk-adjusted return or investment performance. Alpha can be the result of manager skill (or lack thereof), transaction costs, and fees.

4.3 Proxies for Asset Classes in Asset Allocation Models

Because indexes exhibit the risk and return profiles of select groups of securities, they play a critical role as proxies for asset classes in asset allocation models. They provide the historical data used to model the risks and returns of different asset classes.

4.4 Benchmarks for Actively Managed Portfolios

Investors often use indexes as benchmarks to evaluate the performance of active portfolio managers. The index selected as the benchmark should reflect the investment strategy used by the manager. For example, an active manager investing in global small-capitalization stocks should be evaluated using a benchmark index, such as the FTSE Global Small Cap Index, which includes approximately 4,400 liquid small-capitalization stocks across 47 countries as of August 2018.

The choice of an index to use as a benchmark is important because an inappropriate index could lead to incorrect conclusions regarding an active manager's investment performance. Suppose that the small-cap manager underperformed the small-cap index but outperformed a broad equity market index. If investors use the broad market index as a benchmark, they might conclude that the small-cap manager is earning his or her fees and should be retained or given additional assets to invest. Using the small-cap index as a benchmark might lead to a very different conclusion.

4.5 Model Portfolios for Investment Products

Indexes also serve as the basis for the development of new investment products. Using indexes as benchmarks for actively managed portfolios has led some investors to conclude that they should invest in the benchmarks instead. Based on the CAPM's conclusion that investors should hold the market portfolio, broad market index funds have been developed to function as proxies for the market portfolio.

Investment management firms initially developed and managed index portfolios for institutional investors. Eventually, mutual fund companies introduced index funds for individual investors. Subsequently, investment management firms introduced exchange-traded funds, which are managed the same way as index mutual funds but trade like stocks.

The first ETFs were based on existing indexes. As the popularity of ETFs increased, index providers created new indexes for the specific purpose of forming ETFs, leading to the creation of numerous narrowly defined indexes with corresponding ETFs. The VanEck Vectors Vietnam ETF, for example, allows investors to invest in the equity market of Vietnam.

The choice of indexes to meet the needs of investors is extensive. Index providers are constantly looking for opportunities to develop indexes to meet the needs of investors.

EQUITY INDEXES 5

A wide variety of equity indexes exist, including broad market, multi-market, sector, and style indexes.

5.1 Broad Market Indexes

A broad equity market index, as its name suggests, represents an entire given equity market and typically includes securities representing more than 90 percent of the selected market. For example, the Shanghai Stock Exchange Composite Index (SSE) is a market-capitalization-weighted index of all shares that trade on the Shanghai Stock Exchange. In the United States, the Wilshire 5000 Total Market Index is a market-capitalization-weighted index that includes all US equities with readily available prices and is designed to represent the entire US equity market.[3] The Russell 3000, consisting of the largest 3,000 stocks by market capitalization, represents approximately 98 percent of the US equity market.

5.2 Multi-Market Indexes

Multi-market indexes usually comprise indexes from different countries and regions and are designed to represent multiple security markets. Multi-market indexes may represent multiple national markets, geographic regions, economic development groups, and, in some cases, the entire world. World indexes are of importance to investors who take a global approach to equity investing without any particular bias toward a particular country or region. A number of index providers publish families of multi-market equity indexes.

MSCI offers a number of multi-market indexes. As shown in Exhibit 7, MSCI classifies countries and regions along two dimensions: level of economic development and geographic region. Developmental groups, which MSCI refers to as market classifications, include developed markets, emerging markets, and frontier markets. The geographic regions are largely divided by longitudinal lines of the globe: the Americas, Europe with Africa, and Asia with the Pacific. MSCI provides country- and region-specific indexes for each of the developed and emerging markets within its

3 Despite its name, the Wilshire 5000 has no constraint on the number of securities that can be included. It included approximately 5,000 securities at inception.

multi-market indexes. MSCI periodically reviews the classifications of markets in its indexes for movement from frontier markets to emerging markets and from emerging markets to developed markets and reconstitutes the indexes accordingly.

Exhibit 7 MSCI Global Investable Market Indexes (as of October 2018)

Developed Markets

Americas	Europe and Middle East	Pacific
Canada, United States	Austria, Belgium, Denmark, Finland, France, Germany, Ireland, Israel, Italy, Netherlands, Norway, Portugal, Spain, Sweden, Switzerland, United Kingdom	Australia, Hong Kong SAR, Japan, New Zealand, Singapore

Emerging Markets

Americas	Europe, Middle East, Africa	Asia
Brazil, Chile, Colombia, Mexico, Peru	Czech Republic, Egypt, Greece, Hungary, Poland, Qatar, Russia, South Africa, Turkey, United Arab Emirates	Chinese mainland, India, Indonesia, South Korea, Malaysia, Pakistan, Philippines, Taiwan region, Thailand

Frontier Markets

Americas	Europe & CIS	Africa	Middle East	Asia
Argentina	Croatia, Estonia, Lithuania, Kazakhstan, Romania, Serbia, Slovenia	Kenya, Mauritius, Morocco, Nigeria, Tunisia, WAEMU[1]	Bahrain, Jordan, Kuwait, Lebanon, Oman	Bangladesh, Sri Lanka, Vietnam

MSCI Standalone Market Indexes[2]

Europe, Middle East, and Africa	Americas	Europe and CIS	Africa	Middle East
Saudi Arabia	Jamaica, Panama,[3] Trinidad & Tobago	Bosnia Herzegovina, Bulgaria, Ukraine	Botswana, Ghana, Zimbabwe	Palestine

[1] The West African Economic and Monetary Union (WAEMU) consists of the following countries: Benin, Burkina Faso, Ivory Coast, Guinea-Bissau, Mali, Niger, Senegal, and Togo. Currently the MSCI WAEMU Indexes include securities classified in Senegal, Ivory Coast, and Burkina Faso.

[2] The MSCI Standalone Market Indexes are not included in the MSCI Emerging Markets Index or MSCI Frontier Markets Index. However, these indexes use either the Emerging Markets or the Frontier Markets methodological criteria concerning size and liquidity.

[3] MSCI Panama Index has been launched as a Standalone Market Index.

Source: adapted from MSCI (https://www.msci.com/en/market-cap-weighted-indexes), October 2018.

5.2.1 *Fundamental Weighting in Multi-Market Indexes*

Some index providers weight the securities within each country/region by market capitalization and then weight each country/region in the overall index in proportion to its relative GDP, effectively creating fundamental weighting in multi-market indexes. GDP-weighted indexes were some of the first fundamentally weighted indexes created. Introduced in 1987 by MSCI to address the 60 percent weight of Japanese equities in the market-capitalization-weighted MSCI EAFE Index at the time, GDP-weighted indexes reduced the allocation to Japanese equities by half.[4]

4 Steven A. Schoenfeld, *Active Index Investing* (Hoboken, NJ: John Wiley & Sons, 2004):220.

5.3 Sector Indexes

Sector indexes represent and track different economic sectors—such as consumer goods, energy, finance, health care, and technology—on either a national, regional, or global basis. Because different sectors of the economy behave differently over the course of the business cycle, some investors may seek to overweight or underweight their exposure to particular sectors.

Sector indexes are organized as families; each index within the family represents an economic sector. Typically, the aggregation of a sector index family is equivalent to a broad market index. Economic sector classification can be applied on a global, regional, or country-specific basis, but no universally agreed upon sector classification method exists.

Sector indexes play an important role in performance analysis because they provide a means to determine whether a portfolio manager is more successful at stock selection or sector allocation. Sector indexes also serve as model portfolios for sector-specific ETFs and other investment products.

5.4 Style Indexes

Style indexes represent groups of securities classified according to market capitalization, value, growth, or a combination of these characteristics. They are intended to reflect the investing styles of certain investors, such as the growth investor, value investor, and small-cap investor.

5.4.1 *Market Capitalization*

Market-capitalization indexes represent securities categorized according to the major capitalization categories: large cap, midcap, and small cap. With no universal definition of these categories, the indexes differ on the distinctions between large cap and midcap and between midcap and small cap, as well as the minimum market-capitalization size required to be included in a small-cap index. Classification into categories can be based on absolute market capitalization (e.g., below €100 million) or relative market capitalization (e.g., the smallest 2,500 stocks).

5.4.2 *Value/Growth Classification*

Some indexes represent categories of stocks based on their classifications as either value or growth stocks. Different index providers use different factors and valuation ratios (low price-to-book ratios, low price-to-earnings ratios, high dividend yields, etc.) to distinguish between value and growth equities.

5.4.3 *Market Capitalization and Value/Growth Classification*

Combining the three market-capitalization groups with value and growth classifications results in six basic style index categories:

- Large-Cap Value
- Mid-Cap Value
- Small-Cap Value
- Large-Cap Growth
- Mid-Cap Growth
- Small-Cap Growth

Because indexes use different size and valuation classifications, the constituents of indexes designed to represent a given style, such as small-cap value, may differ—sometimes substantially.

Because valuation ratios and market capitalizations change over time, stocks frequently migrate from one style index category to another on reconstitution dates. As a result, style indexes generally have much higher turnover than do broad market indexes.

6 FIXED-INCOME INDEXES

A wide variety of fixed-income indexes exists, but the nature of the fixed-income markets and fixed-income securities leads to some very important challenges to fixed-income index construction and replication. These challenges are the number of securities in the fixed-income universe, the availability of pricing data, and the liquidity of the securities.

6.1 Construction

The fixed-income universe includes securities issued by governments, government agencies, and corporations. Each of these entities may issue a variety of fixed-income securities with different characteristics. As a result, the number of fixed-income securities is many times larger than the number of equity securities. To represent a specific fixed-income market or segment, indexes may include thousands of different securities. Over time, these fixed-income securities mature, and issuers offer new securities to meet their financing needs, leading to turnover in fixed-income indexes.

Another challenge in index construction is that fixed-income markets are predominantly dealer markets. This means that firms (dealers) are assigned to specific securities and are responsible for creating liquid markets for those securities by purchasing and selling them from their inventory. In addition, many securities do not trade frequently and, as a result, are relatively illiquid. As a result, index providers must contact dealers to obtain current prices on constituent securities to update the index or they must estimate the prices of constituent securities using the prices of traded fixed-income securities with similar characteristics.

These challenges can result in indexes with dissimilar numbers of bonds representing the same markets. The large number of fixed-income securities—combined with the lack of liquidity of some securities—has made it more costly and difficult, compared with equity indexes, for investors to replicate fixed-income indexes and duplicate their performance.

6.2 Types of Fixed-Income Indexes

The wide variety of fixed-income securities, ranging from zero-coupon bonds to bonds with embedded options (i.e., callable or putable bonds), results in a number of different types of fixed-income indexes. Similar to equities, fixed-income securities can be categorized according to the issuer's economic sector, the issuer's geographic region, or the economic development of the issuer's geographic region. Fixed-income securities can also be classified along the following dimensions:

- type of issuer (government, government agency, corporation);
- type of financing (general obligation, collateralized);
- currency of payments;
- maturity;
- credit quality (investment grade, high yield, credit agency ratings); and
- absence or presence of inflation protection.

Fixed-income indexes are based on these various dimensions and can be categorized as follows:

- aggregate or broad market indexes;
- market sector indexes;
- style indexes;

- economic sector indexes; and
- specialized indexes such as high-yield, inflation-linked, and emerging market indexes.

The first fixed-income index created, the Bloomberg Barclays US Aggregate Bond Index (formerly the Barclays Capital Aggregate Bond Index), is an example of a single-country aggregate index. Designed to represent the broad market of US fixed-income securities, it comprises approximately 8,000 securities, including US Treasury, government-related, corporate, mortgage-backed, asset-backed, and commercial mortgage-backed securities.

Aggregate indexes can be subdivided by market sector (government, government agency, collateralized, corporate); style (maturity, credit quality); economic sector, or some other characteristic to create more narrowly defined indexes. A common distinction reflected in indexes is between investment grade (e.g., those with a Standard & Poor's credit rating of BBB– or better) and high-yield securities. Investment-grade indexes are typically further subdivided by maturity (i.e., short, intermediate, or long) and by credit rating (e.g., AAA, BBB, etc.).[5] The wide variety of fixed-income indexes reflects the partitioning of fixed-income securities on the basis of a variety of dimensions.

Exhibit 8 illustrates how the major types of fixed-income indexes can be organized on the basis of various dimensions.

Exhibit 8 Dimensions of Fixed-Income Indexes

Market	Global			
	Regional			
	Country or currency zone			
Type	Corporate	Collateralized *Securitized* *Mortgage-backed*	Government agency	Government
Maturity	For example, 1–3, 3–5, 5–7, 7–10, 10+ years; short-term, medium-term, or long-term			
Credit quality	For example, AAA, AA, A, BBB, etc.; Aaa, Aa, A, Baa, etc.; investment grade, high yield			

All aggregate indexes include a variety of market sectors and credit ratings. The breakdown of the Bloomberg Barclays Global Aggregate Bond Index by market sectors and by credit rating is shown in Exhibit 9 and Exhibit 10, respectively.

5 Credit ratings are discussed in depth in the Level I CFA Program reading "Fundamentals of Credit Analysis."

Exhibit 9 Market Sector Breakdown of the Bloomberg Barclays Global Aggregate Bond Index

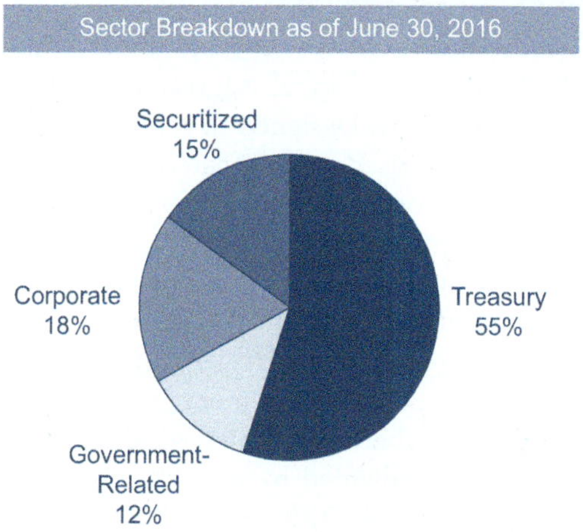

Source: Bloomberg Barclays Indices, Global Aggregate Index Factsheet, August 24, 2016. https://data.bloomberglp.com/indices/sites/2/2016/08/Factsheet-Global-Aggregate.pdf.

Exhibit 10 Credit Breakdown of the Bloomberg Barclays Global Aggregate Bond Index

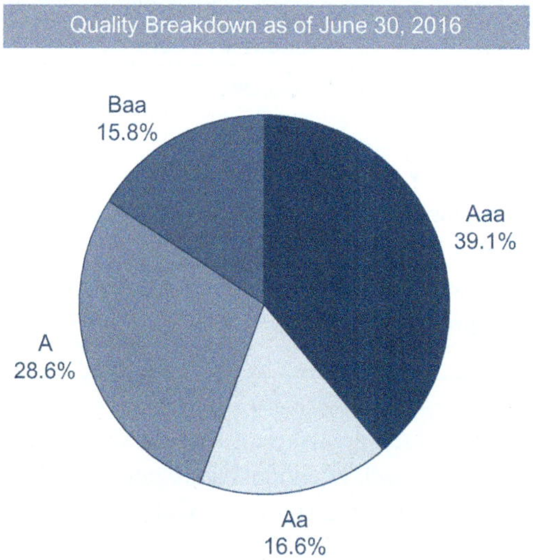

Source: Bloomberg Barclays Indices, Global Aggregate Index Factsheet, August 24, 2016. https://data.bloomberglp.com/indices/sites/2/2016/08/Factsheet-Global-Aggregate.pdf.

INDEXES FOR ALTERNATIVE INVESTMENTS

7

Many investors seek to lower the risk or enhance the performance of their portfolios by investing in assets classes other than equities and fixed income. Interest in alternative assets and investment strategies has led to the creation of indexes designed to represent broad classes of alternative investments. Three of the most widely followed alternative investment classes are commodities, real estate, and hedge funds.

7.1 Commodity Indexes

Commodity indexes consist of futures contracts on one or more commodities, such as agricultural products (rice, wheat, sugar), livestock (cattle, hogs), precious and common metals (gold, silver, copper), and energy commodities (crude oil, natural gas).

Although some commodity indexes may include the same commodities, the returns of these indexes may differ because each index may use a different weighting method. Because commodity indexes do not have an obvious weighting mechanism, such as market capitalization, commodity index providers create their own weighting methods. Some indexes, such as the Thomson Reuters/Core Commodity CRB Index (TR/CC CRB Index), formerly known as the Commodity Research Bureau (CRB) Index, contain a fixed number of commodities that are weighted equally. The S&P GSCI uses a combination of liquidity measures and world production values in its weighting scheme and allocates more weight to commodities that have risen in price. Other indexes have fixed weights that are determined by a committee.

The different weighting methods can also lead to large differences in exposure to specific commodities. The S&P GSCI in 2018, for example, weights the energy-sector approximately 50% higher and the agriculture sector 40% lower than the CRB Index. These differences result in indexes with very different risk and return profiles. Unlike commodity indexes, broad equity and fixed-income indexes that target the same markets share similar risk and return profiles.

The performance of commodity indexes can also be quite different from their underlying commodities because the indexes consist of futures contracts on the commodities rather than the actual commodities. Index returns are affected by factors other than changes in the prices of the underlying commodities because futures contracts must be continually "rolled over" (i.e., replacing a contract nearing expiration with a new contract). Commodity index returns reflect the risk-free interest rate, the changes in future prices, and the roll yield. Therefore, a commodity index return can be quite different from the return based on changes in the prices of the underlying commodities.

7.2 Real Estate Investment Trust Indexes

Real estate indexes represent not only the market for real estate securities but also the market for real estate—a highly illiquid market and asset class with infrequent transactions and pricing information. Real estate indexes can be categorized as appraisal indexes, repeat sales indexes, and real estate investment trust (REIT) indexes.

REIT indexes consist of shares of publicly traded REITs. REITS are public or private corporations organized specifically to invest in real estate, either through ownership of properties or investment in mortgages. Shares of public REITs are traded on the world's various stock exchanges and are a popular choice for investing in commercial real estate properties. Because REIT indexes are based on publicly traded REITs with continuous market pricing, the value of REIT indexes is calculated continuously.

The FTSE EPRA/NAREIT global family of REIT indexes shown in Exhibit 11 seeks to represent trends in real estate stocks worldwide and includes representation from the European Public Real Estate Association (EPRA) and the National Association of Real Estate Investment Trusts (NAREIT).

Exhibit 11 The FTSE EPRA/NAREIT Global REIT Index Family

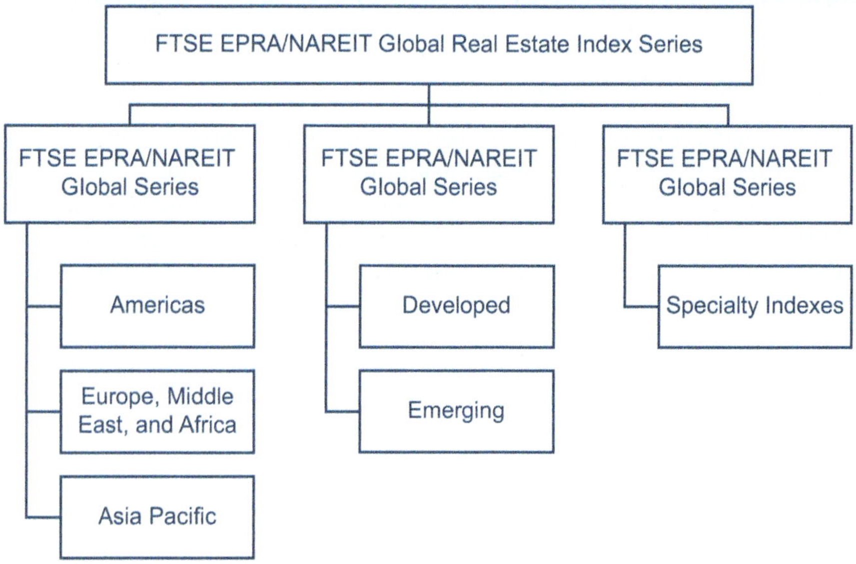

Source: FTSE International, "FTSE EPRA/NAREIT Global & Global Ex US Indices" Factsheet 2009). "FTSE®" is a trade mark of the London Stock Exchange Plc, "NAREIT®" is a trade mark of the National Association of Real Estate Investment Trusts ("NAREIT") and "EPRA®" is a trade mark of the European Public Real Estate Association ("EPRA") and all are used by FTSE International Limited ("FTSE") under license.

7.3 Hedge Fund Indexes

Hedge fund indexes reflect the returns on hedge funds. **Hedge funds** are private investment vehicles that typically use leverage and long and short investment strategies.

A number of research organizations maintain databases of hedge fund returns and summarize these returns into indexes. These database indexes are designed to represent the performance of the hedge funds on a very broad global level (hedge funds in general) or the strategy level. Most of these indexes are equal weighted and represent the performance of the hedge funds within a particular database.

Most research organizations rely on the voluntary cooperation of hedge funds to compile performance data. As unregulated entities, however, hedge funds are not required to report their performance to any party other than their investors. Therefore, each hedge fund decides to which database(s) it will report its performance. As a result, rather than index providers determining the constituents, the constituents determine the index.

Frequently, a hedge fund reports its performance to only one database. The result is little overlap of funds covered by the different indexes. With little overlap between their constituents, different global hedge fund indexes may reflect very different performance for the hedge fund industry over the same period of time.

Another consequence of the voluntary performance reporting is the potential for survivorship bias and, therefore, inaccurate performance representation. This means that hedge funds with poor performance may be less likely to report their performance to the database or may stop reporting to the database, so their returns may be excluded when measuring the return of the index. As a result, the index may not accurately reflect actual hedge fund performance so much as the performance of hedge funds that are performing well.

REPRESENTATIVE INDEXES WORLDWIDE

As indicated in this reading, the choice of indexes to meet the needs of investors is extensive. Investors using security market indexes must be careful in their selection of the index or indexes most appropriate for their needs. The following table illustrates the variety of indexes reflecting different asset classes, markets, and weighting methods.

Index	Representing	Number of Securities	Weighting Method	Comments
Dow Jones Industrial Average	US blue chip companies	30	Price	The oldest and most widely known US equity index. *Wall Street Journal* editors choose 30 stocks from among large, mature blue-chip companies.
Nikkei Stock Average	Japanese blue chip companies	225	Modified price	Known as the Nikkei 225 and originally formulated by Dow Jones & Company. Because of extreme variation in price levels of component securities, some high-priced shares are weighted as a fraction of share price.
TOPIX	All companies listed on the Tokyo Stock Exchange First Section	Varies	Float-adjusted market cap	Represents about 93 percent of the market value of all Japanese equities. Contains a large number of very small, illiquid stocks, making exact replication difficult.
MSCI All Country World Index	Stocks of 23 developed and 24 emerging markets	Varies	Free-float-adjusted market cap	Composed of companies representative of the market structure of developed and emerging market countries in the Americas, Europe/Middle East, and Asia/Pacific regions. Price return and total return versions available in both USD and local currencies.
S&P Developed Ex-US BMI Energy Sector Index	Energy sector of developed global markets outside the United States	Varies	Float-adjusted market cap	Serves as a model portfolio for the SPDR® S&P Energy Sector Exchange-Traded Fund (ETF).
Bloomberg Barclays Global Aggregate Bond Index	Investment-grade bonds in the North American, European, and Asian markets	Varies	Market cap	Formerly known as Lehman Brothers Global Aggregate Bond Index.

(continued)

Index	Representing	Number of Securities	Weighting Method	Comments
Markit iBoxx Euro High-Yield Bond Indexes	Sub-investment-grade euro-denominated corporate bonds	Varies	Market cap and variations	Rebalanced monthly. Represents tradable part of market. Price and total return versions available with such analytical values as yield, duration, modified duration, and convexity. Provides platform for research and structured products.
FTSE EPRA/NAREIT Global Real Estate Index	Real estate securities in the North American, European, and Asian markets	Varies	Float-adjusted market cap	The stocks of REITs that constitute the index trade on public stock exchanges and may be constituents of equity market indexes.
HFRX Global Hedge Fund Index	Overall composition of the HFR database	Varies	Asset weighted	Comprises all eligible hedge fund strategies. Examples include convertible arbitrage, distressed securities, market neutral, event driven, macro, and relative value arbitrage. Constituent strategies are asset weighted on the basis of asset distribution within the hedge fund industry.
HFRX Equal Weighted Strategies EUR Index	Overall composition of the HFR database	Varies	Equal weighted	Denominated in euros and is constructed from the same strategies as the HFRX Global Hedge Fund Index.
Morningstar Style Indexes	US stocks classified by market cap and value/growth orientation	Varies	Float-adjusted market cap	The nine indexes defined by combinations of market cap (large, mid, and small) and value/growth orientation (value, core, growth) have mutually exclusive constituents and are exhaustive with respect to the Morningstar US Market Index. Each is a model portfolio for one of the iShares Morningstar ETFs.

SUMMARY

This reading explains and illustrates the construction, management, and uses of security market indexes. It also discusses various types of indexes. Security market indexes are invaluable tools for investors, who can select from among thousands of indexes representing a variety of security markets, market segments, and asset classes. These indexes range from those representing the global market for major asset classes to those representing alternative investments in specific geographic markets. To benefit from the use of security market indexes, investors must understand their construction and determine whether the selected index is appropriate for their purposes. Frequently, an index that is well suited for one purpose may not be well suited for other purposes. Users of indexes must be familiar with how various indexes are constructed in order to select the index or indexes most appropriate for their needs.

Among the key points made in this reading are the following:

- Security market indexes are intended to measure the values of different target markets (security markets, market segments, or asset classes).
- The constituent securities selected for inclusion in the security market index are intended to represent the target market.
- A price return index reflects only the prices of the constituent securities.
- A total return index reflects not only the prices of the constituent securities but also the reinvestment of all income received since the inception of the index.
- Methods used to weight the constituents of an index range from the very simple, such as price and equal weightings, to the more complex, such as market-capitalization and fundamental weightings.
- Choices in index construction—in particular, the choice of weighting method—affect index valuation and returns.
- Index management includes 1) periodic rebalancing to ensure that the index maintains appropriate weightings and 2) reconstitution to ensure the index represents the desired target market.
- Rebalancing and reconstitution create turnover in an index. Reconstitution can dramatically affect prices of current and prospective constituents.
- Indexes serve a variety of purposes. They gauge market sentiment and serve as benchmarks for actively managed portfolios. They act as proxies for measuring systematic risk and risk-adjusted performance. They also serve as proxies for asset classes in asset allocation models and as model portfolios for investment products.
- Investors can choose from security market indexes representing various asset classes, including equity, fixed-income, commodity, real estate, and hedge fund indexes.
- Within most asset classes, index providers offer a wide variety of indexes, ranging from broad market indexes to highly specialized indexes based on the issuer's geographic region, economic development group, or economic sector or other factors.
- Proper use of security market indexes depends on understanding their construction and management.

PRACTICE PROBLEMS

1 A security market index represents the:

A risk of a security market.

B security market as a whole.

C security market, market segment, or asset class.

2 Security market indexes are:

A constructed and managed like a portfolio of securities.

B simple interchangeable tools for measuring the returns of different asset classes.

C valued on a regular basis using the actual market prices of the constituent securities.

3 When creating a security market index, an index provider must first determine the:

A target market.

B appropriate weighting method.

C number of constituent securities.

4 One month after inception, the price return version and total return version of a single index (consisting of identical securities and weights) will be equal if:

A market prices have not changed.

B capital gains are offset by capital losses.

C the securities do not pay dividends or interest.

5 The values of a price return index and a total return index consisting of identical equal-weighted dividend-paying equities will be equal:

A only at inception.

B at inception and on rebalancing dates.

C at inception and on reconstitution dates.

6 An analyst gathers the following information for an equal-weighted index comprised of assets Able, Baker, and Charlie:

Security	Beginning of Period Price (€)	End of Period Price (€)	Total Dividends (€)
Able	10.00	12.00	0.75
Baker	20.00	19.00	1.00
Charlie	30.00	30.00	2.00

The price return of the index is:

A 1.7%.

B 5.0%.

C 11.4%.

7 An analyst gathers the following information for an equal-weighted index comprised of assets Able, Baker, and Charlie:

Security	Beginning of Period Price (€)	End of Period Price (€)	Total Dividends (€)
Able	10.00	12.00	0.75
Baker	20.00	19.00	1.00
Charlie	30.00	30.00	2.00

The total return of the index is:

A 5.0%.

B 7.9%.

C 11.4%.

8 An analyst gathers the following information for a price-weighted index comprised of securities ABC, DEF, and GHI:

Security	Beginning of Period Price (£)	End of Period Price (£)	Total Dividends (£)
ABC	25.00	27.00	1.00
DEF	35.00	25.00	1.50
GHI	15.00	16.00	1.00

The price return of the index is:

A −4.6%.

B −9.3%.

C −13.9%.

9 An analyst gathers the following information for a market-capitalization-weighted index comprised of securities MNO, QRS, and XYZ:

Security	Beginning of Period Price (¥)	End of Period Price (¥)	Dividends per Share (¥)	Shares Outstanding
MNO	2,500	2,700	100	5,000
QRS	3,500	2,500	150	7,500
XYZ	1,500	1,600	100	10,000

The price return of the index is:

A −9.33%.

B −10.23%.

C −13.90%.

10 An analyst gathers the following information for a market-capitalization-weighted index comprised of securities MNO, QRS, and XYZ:

Security	Beginning of Period Price (¥)	End of Period Price (¥)	Dividends Per Share (¥)	Shares Outstanding
MNO	2,500	2,700	100	5,000
QRS	3,500	2,500	150	7,500
XYZ	1,500	1,600	100	10,000

The total return of the index is:

A 1.04%.

B −5.35%.

C −10.23%.

11 When creating a security market index, the target market:

A determines the investment universe.

B is usually a broadly defined asset class.

C determines the number of securities to be included in the index.

12 An analyst gathers the following data for a price-weighted index:

	Beginning of Period		End of Period	
Security	**Price (€)**	**Shares Outstanding**	**Price (€)**	**Shares Outstanding**
A	20.00	300	22.00	300
B	50.00	300	48.00	300
C	26.00	2,000	30.00	2,000

The price return of the index over the period is:

A 4.2%.

B 7.1%.

C 21.4%.

13 An analyst gathers the following data for a value-weighted index:

	Beginning of Period		End of Period	
Security	**Price (£)**	**Shares Outstanding**	**Price (£)**	**Shares Outstanding**
A	20.00	300	22.00	300
B	50.00	300	48.00	300
C	26.00	2,000	30.00	2,000

The return on the value-weighted index over the period is:

A 7.1%.

B 11.0%.

C 21.4%.

14 An analyst gathers the following data for an equally-weighted index:

	Beginning of Period		End of Period	
Security	**Price (¥)**	**Shares Outstanding**	**Price (¥)**	**Shares Outstanding**
A	20.00	300	22.00	300
B	50.00	300	48.00	300
C	26.00	2,000	30.00	2,000

The return on the index over the period is:

A 4.2%.

B 6.8%.

C 7.1%.

15 Which of the following index weighting methods requires an adjustment to the divisor after a stock split?

A Price weighting.

B Fundamental weighting.

C Market-capitalization weighting.

16 If the price return of an equal-weighted index exceeds that of a market-capitalization-weighted index comprised of the same securities, the *most likely* explanation is:

A stock splits.

B dividend distributions.

C outperformance of small-market-capitalization stocks.

17 A float-adjusted market-capitalization-weighted index weights each of its constituent securities by its price and:

A its trading volume.

B the number of its shares outstanding.

C the number of its shares available to the investing public.

18 Which of the following index weighting methods is most likely subject to a value tilt?

A Equal weighting.

B Fundamental weighting.

C Market-capitalization weighting.

19 Rebalancing an index is the process of periodically adjusting the constituent:

A securities' weights to optimize investment performance.

B securities to maintain consistency with the target market.

C securities' weights to maintain consistency with the index's weighting method.

20 Which of the following index weighting methods requires the most frequent rebalancing?

A Price weighting.

B Equal weighting.

C Market-capitalization weighting.

21 Reconstitution of a security market index reduces:

A portfolio turnover.

B the need for rebalancing.

C the likelihood that the index includes securities that are not representative of the target market.

22 Security market indexes are used as:

A measures of investment returns.

B proxies to measure unsystematic risk.

C proxies for specific asset classes in asset allocation models.

23 Uses of market indexes do not include serving as a:

A measure of systemic risk.

B basis for new investment products.

C benchmark for evaluating portfolio performance.

24 Which of the following statements regarding sector indexes is *most* accurate? Sector indexes:

A track different economic sectors and cannot be aggregated to represent the equivalent of a broad market index.

B provide a means to determine whether an active investment manager is more successful at stock selection or sector allocation.

C apply a universally agreed upon sector classification system to identify the constituent securities of specific economic sectors, such as consumer goods, energy, finance, health care.

25 Which of the following is an example of a style index? An index based on:

A geography.

B economic sector.

C market capitalization.

26 Which of the following statements regarding fixed-income indexes is *most* accurate?

A Liquidity issues make it difficult for investors to easily replicate fixed-income indexes.

B Rebalancing and reconstitution are the only sources of turnover in fixed-income indexes.

C Fixed-income indexes representing the same target market hold similar numbers of bonds.

27 An aggregate fixed-income index:

A comprises corporate and asset-backed securities.

B represents the market of government-issued securities.

C can be subdivided by market or economic sector to create more narrowly defined indexes.

28 Fixed-income indexes are *least likely* constructed on the basis of:

A maturity.

B type of issuer.

C coupon frequency.

29 Commodity index values are based on:

A futures contract prices.

B the market price of the specific commodity.

C the average market price of a basket of similar commodities.

30 Which of the following statements is *most* accurate?

A Commodity indexes all share similar weighting methods.

B Commodity indexes containing the same underlying commodities offer similar returns.

C The performance of commodity indexes can be quite different from that of the underlying commodities.

31 Which of the following is *not* a real estate index category?

A Appraisal index.

B Initial sales index.

C Repeat sales index.

32 A unique feature of hedge fund indexes is that they:

A are frequently equal weighted.

B are determined by the constituents of the index.

C reflect the value of private rather than public investments.

33 The returns of hedge fund indexes are *most likely*:

A biased upward.

B biased downward.

C similar across different index providers.

34 In comparison to equity indexes, the constituent securities of fixed-income indexes are:

A more liquid.

B easier to price.

C drawn from a larger investment universe.

SOLUTIONS

1 C is correct. A security market index represents the value of a given security market, market segment, or asset class.

2 A is correct. Security market indexes are constructed and managed like a portfolio of securities.

3 A is correct. The first decision is identifying the target market that the index is intended to represent because the target market determines the investment universe and the securities available for inclusion in the index.

4 C is correct. The difference between a price return index and a total return index consisting of identical securities and weights is the income generated over time by the underlying securities. If the securities in the index do not generate income, both indexes will be identical in value.

5 A is correct. At inception, the values of the price return and total return versions of an index are equal.

6 B is correct. The price return is the sum of the weighted returns of each security. The return of Able is 20 percent [(12 – 10)/10]; of Baker is –5 percent [(19 – 20)/20]; and of Charlie is 0 percent [(30 – 30)/30]. The price return index assigns a weight of 1/3 to each asset; therefore, the price return is 1/3 × [20% + (–5%) + 0%] = 5%.

7 C is correct. The total return of an index is calculated on the basis of the change in price of the underlying securities plus the sum of income received or the sum of the weighted total returns of each security. The total return of Able is 27.5 percent; of Baker is 0 percent; and of Charlie is 6.7 percent:

Able: (12 – 10 + 0.75)/10 = 27.5%

Baker: (19 – 20 + 1)/20 = 0%

Charlie: (30 – 30 + 2)/30 = 6.7%

An equal-weighted index applies the same weight (1/3) to each security's return; therefore, the total return = 1/3 × (27.5% + 0% + 6.7%) = 11.4%.

8 B is correct. The price return of the price-weighted index is the percentage change in price of the index: (68 – 75)/75 = –9.33%.

Security	Beginning of Period Price (£)	End of Period Price (£)
ABC	25.00	27.00
DEF	35.00	25.00
GHI	15.00	16.00
TOTAL	75.00	68.00

9 B is correct. The price return of the index is (48,250,000 – 53,750,000)/53,750,000 = –10.23%.

Security	Beginning of Period Price (¥)	Shares Outstanding	Beginning of Period Value (¥)	End of Period Price (¥)	End of Period Value (¥)
MNO	2,500	5,000	12,500,000	2,700	13,500,000
QRS	3,500	7,500	26,250,000	2,500	18,750,000

Security	Beginning of Period Price (¥)	Shares Outstanding	Beginning of Period Value (¥)	End of Period Price (¥)	End of Period Value (¥)
XYZ	1,500	10,000	15,000,000	1,600	16,000,000
Total			53,750,000		48,250,000

10 B is correct. The total return of the market-capitalization-weighted index is calculated below:

Security	Beginning of Period Value (¥)	End of Period Value (¥)	Total Dividends (¥)	Total Return (%)
MNO	12,500,000	13,500,000	500,000	12.00
QRS	26,250,000	18,750,000	1,125,000	–24.29
XYZ	15,000,000	16,000,000	1,000,000	13.33
Total	53,750,000	48,250,000	2,625,000	–5.35

11 A is correct. The target market determines the investment universe and the securities available for inclusion in the index.

12 A is correct. The sum of prices at the beginning of the period is 96; the sum at the end of the period is 100. Regardless of the divisor, the price return is 100/96 – 1 = 0.042 or 4.2 percent.

13 B is correct. It is the percentage change in the market value over the period:

Market value at beginning of period: (20 × 300) + (50 × 300) + (26 × 2,000) = 73,000

Market value at end of period: (22 × 300) + (48 × 300) + (30 × 2,000) = 81,000

Percentage change is 81,000/73,000 – 1 = 0.1096 or 11.0 percent with rounding.

14 C is correct. With an equal-weighted index, the same amount is invested in each security. Assuming $1,000 is invested in each of the three stocks, the index value is $3,000 at the beginning of the period and the following number of shares is purchased for each stock:

Security A: 50 shares

Security B: 20 shares

Security C: 38.46 shares.

Using the prices at the beginning of the period for each security, the index value at the end of the period is $3,213.8: ($22 × 50) + ($48 × 20) + ($30 × 38.46). The price return is $3,213.8/$3,000 – 1 = 7.1%.

15 A is correct. In the price weighting method, the divisor must be adjusted so the index value immediately after the split is the same as the index value immediately prior to the split.

16 C is correct. The main source of return differences arises from outperformance of small-cap securities or underperformance of large-cap securities. In an equal-weighted index, securities that constitute the largest fraction of the market are underrepresented and securities that constitute only a small fraction of the market are overrepresented. Thus, higher equal-weighted index returns will occur if the smaller-cap equities outperform the larger-cap equities.

17 C is correct. "Float" is the number of shares available for public trading.

18 B is correct. Fundamental weighting leads to indexes that have a value tilt.

19 C is correct. Rebalancing refers to adjusting the weights of constituent securities in an index to maintain consistency with the index's weighting method.

20 B is correct. Changing market prices will cause weights that were initially equal to become unequal, thus requiring rebalancing.

21 C is correct. Reconstitution is the process by which index providers review the constituent securities, re-apply the initial criteria for inclusion in the index, and select which securities to retain, remove, or add. Constituent securities that no longer meet the criteria are replaced with securities that do. Thus, reconstitution reduces the likelihood that the index includes securities that are not representative of the target market.

22 C is correct. Security market indexes play a critical role as proxies for asset classes in asset allocation models.

23 A is correct. Security market indexes are used as proxies for measuring market or systematic risk, not as measures of systemic risk.

24 B is correct. Sector indexes provide a means to determine whether a portfolio manager is more successful at stock selection or sector allocation.

25 C is correct. Style indexes represent groups of securities classified according to market capitalization, value, growth, or a combination of these characteristics.

26 A is correct. The large number of fixed-income securities—combined with the lack of liquidity of some securities—makes it costly and difficult for investors to replicate fixed-income indexes.

27 C is correct. An aggregate fixed-income index can be subdivided by market sector (government, government agency, collateralized, corporate), style (maturity, credit quality), economic sector, or some other characteristic to create more narrowly defined indexes.

28 C is correct. Coupon frequency is not a dimension on which fixed-income indexes are based.

29 A is correct. Commodity indexes consist of futures contracts on one or more commodities.

30 C is correct. The performance of commodity indexes can be quite different from that of the underlying commodities because the indexes consist of futures contracts on the commodities rather than the actual commodities.

31 B is correct. It is not a real estate index category.

32 B is correct. Hedge funds are not required to report their performance to any party other than their investors. Therefore, each hedge fund decides to which database(s) it will report its performance. Thus, for a hedge fund index, constituents determine the index rather than index providers determining the constituents.

33 A is correct. Voluntary performance reporting may lead to survivorship bias, and poorer performing hedge funds will be less likely to report their performance.

34 C is correct. The fixed-income market has more issuers and securities than the equity market.

READING

38

Market Efficiency

by Sean Cleary, PhD, CFA, Howard J. Atkinson, CIMA, ICD.D, CFA, and Pamela Peterson Drake, PhD, CFA

Sean Cleary, PhD, CFA, is at Queen's University (Canada). Howard J. Atkinson, CIMA, ICD.D, CFA, is at Horizons ETF Management (Canada) Inc. (Canada). Pamela Peterson Drake, PhD, CFA, is at James Madison University (USA).

LEARNING OUTCOMES

Mastery	*The candidate should be able to:*
☐	a. describe market efficiency and related concepts, including their importance to investment practitioners;
☐	b. distinguish between market value and intrinsic value;
☐	c. explain factors that affect a market's efficiency;
☐	d. contrast weak-form, semi-strong-form, and strong-form market efficiency;
☐	e. explain the implications of each form of market efficiency for fundamental analysis, technical analysis, and the choice between active and passive portfolio management;
☐	f. describe market anomalies;
☐	g. describe behavioral finance and its potential relevance to understanding market anomalies.

INTRODUCTION

1

Market efficiency concerns the extent to which market prices incorporate available information. If market prices do not fully incorporate information, then opportunities may exist to make a profit from the gathering and processing of information. The subject of market efficiency is, therefore, of great interest to investment managers, as illustrated in Example 1.

EXAMPLE 1

Market Efficiency and Active Manager Selection

The chief investment officer (CIO) of a major university endowment fund has listed eight steps in the active manager selection process that can be applied both to traditional investments (e.g., common equity and fixed-income securities) and to alternative investments (e.g., private equity, hedge funds, and real assets). The first step specified is the evaluation of market opportunity:

> What is the opportunity and why is it there? To answer this question, we start by studying capital markets and the types of managers operating within those markets. We identify market inefficiencies and try to understand their causes, such as regulatory structures or behavioral biases. We can rule out many broad groups of managers and strategies by simply determining that the degree of market inefficiency necessary to support a strategy is implausible. Importantly, we consider the past history of active returns meaningless unless we understand why markets will allow those active returns to continue into the future.[1]

The CIO's description underscores the importance of not assuming that past active returns that might be found in a historical dataset will repeat themselves in the future. **Active returns** refer to returns earned by strategies that do *not* assume that all information is fully reflected in market prices.

Governments and market regulators also care about the extent to which market prices incorporate information. Efficient markets imply informative prices—prices that accurately reflect available information about fundamental values. In market-based economies, market prices help determine which companies (and which projects) obtain capital. If these prices do not efficiently incorporate information about a company's prospects, then it is possible that funds will be misdirected. By contrast, prices that are informative help direct scarce resources and funds available for investment to their highest-valued uses.[2] Informative prices thus promote economic growth. The efficiency of a country's capital markets (in which businesses raise financing) is an important characteristic of a well-functioning financial system.

The remainder of this reading is organized as follows. Section 2 provides specifics on how the efficiency of an asset market is described and discusses the factors affecting (i.e., contributing to and impeding) market efficiency. Section 3 presents an influential three-way classification of the efficiency of security markets and discusses its implications for fundamental analysis, technical analysis, and portfolio management. Section 4 presents several market anomalies (apparent market inefficiencies that have received enough attention to be individually identified and named) and describes how these anomalies relate to investment strategies. Section 5 introduces behavioral finance and how that field of study relates to market efficiency. A summary concludes the reading.

1 The CIO is Christopher J. Brightman, CFA, of the University of Virginia Investment Management Company, as reported in Yau, Schneeweis, Robinson, and Weiss (2007, pp. 481–482).

2 This concept is known as allocative efficiency.

THE CONCEPT OF MARKET EFFICIENCY

2

2.1 The Description of Efficient Markets

An **informationally efficient market** (an **efficient market**) is a market in which asset prices reflect new information quickly and rationally. An efficient market is thus a market in which asset prices reflect all past and present information.[3]

In this section we expand on this definition by clarifying the time frame required for an asset's price to incorporate information as well as describing the elements of information releases assumed under market efficiency. We discuss the difference between market value and intrinsic value and illustrate how inefficiencies or discrepancies between these values can provide profitable opportunities for active investment. As financial markets are generally not considered being either completely efficient or inefficient, but rather falling within a range between the two extremes, we describe a number of factors that contribute to and impede the degree of efficiency of a financial market. Finally, we conclude our overview of market efficiency by illustrating how the costs incurred by traders in identifying and exploiting possible market inefficiencies affect how we interpret market efficiency.

Investment managers and analysts, as noted, are interested in market efficiency because the extent to which a market is efficient affects how many profitable trading opportunities (market inefficiencies) exist. Consistent, superior, risk-adjusted returns (net of all expenses) are not achievable in an efficient market.[4] In an efficient market, a **passive investment** strategy (i.e., buying and holding a broad market portfolio) that does not seek superior risk-adjusted returns can be preferred to an **active investment** strategy because of lower costs (for example, transaction and information-seeking costs). By contrast, in a very inefficient market, opportunities may exist for an active investment strategy to achieve superior risk-adjusted returns (net of all expenses in executing the strategy) as compared with a passive investment strategy. In inefficient markets, an active investment strategy may outperform a passive investment strategy on a risk-adjusted basis. Understanding the characteristics of an efficient market and being able to evaluate the efficiency of a particular market are important topics for investment analysts and portfolio managers.

An efficient market is a market in which asset prices reflect information quickly. But what is the time frame of "quickly"? Trades are the mechanism by which information can be incorporated into asset transaction prices. The time needed to execute trades to exploit an inefficiency may provide a baseline for judging speed of adjustment.[5] The time frame for an asset's price to incorporate information must be at least as long as the shortest time a trader needs to execute a transaction in the asset. In certain markets, such as foreign exchange and developed equity markets, market efficiency relative to certain types of information has been studied using time frames as short as one minute or less. If the time frame of price adjustment allows many traders to earn profits with little risk, then the market is relatively inefficient. These considerations lead to the observation that market efficiency can be viewed as falling on a continuum.

3 This definition is convenient for making several instructional points. The definition that most simply explains the sense of the word *efficient* in this context can be found in Fama (1976): "An efficient capital market is a market that is efficient in processing information" (p. 134).

4 The technical term for *superior* in this context is *positive abnormal* in the sense of higher than expected given the asset's risk (as measured, according to capital market theory, by the asset's contribution to the risk of a well-diversified portfolio).

5 Although the original theory of market efficiency does not quantify this speed, the basic idea is that it is sufficiently swift to make it impossible to consistently earn abnormal profits. Chordia, Roll, and Subrahmanyam (2005) suggest that the adjustment to information on the New York Stock Exchange (NYSE) is between 5 and 60 minutes.

Finally, an important point is that in an efficient market, prices should be expected to react only to the elements of information releases that are not anticipated fully by investors—that is, to the "unexpected" or "surprise" element of such releases. Investors process the unexpected information and revise expectations (for example, about an asset's future cash flows, risk, or required rate of return) accordingly. The revised expectations enter or get incorporated in the asset price through trades in the asset. Market participants who process the news and believe that at the current market price an asset does not offer sufficient compensation for its perceived risk will tend to sell it or even sell it short. Market participants with opposite views should be buyers. In this way the market establishes the price that balances the various opinions after expectations are revised.

EXAMPLE 2

Price Reaction to the Default on a Bond Issue

Suppose that a speculative-grade bond issuer announces, just before bond markets open, that it will default on an upcoming interest payment. In the announcement, the issuer confirms various reports made in the financial media in the period leading up to the announcement. Prior to the issuer's announcement, the financial news media reported the following: 1) suppliers of the company were making deliveries only for cash payment, reducing the company's liquidity; 2) the issuer's financial condition had probably deteriorated to the point that it lacked the cash to meet an upcoming interest payment; and 3) although public capital markets were closed to the company, it was negotiating with a bank for a private loan that would permit it to meet its interest payment and continue operations for at least nine months. If the issuer defaults on the bond, the consensus opinion of analysts is that bondholders will recover approximately \$0.36 to \$0.38 per dollar face value.

1. If the market for the bond is efficient, the bond's market price is *most likely* to fully reflect the bond's value after default:
   - **A** in the period leading up to the announcement.
   - **B** in the first trade prices after the market opens on the announcement day.
   - **C** when the issuer actually misses the payment on the interest payment date.
2. If the market for the bond is efficient, the piece of information that bond investors *most likely* focus on in the issuer's announcement is that the issuer had:
   - **A** failed in its negotiations for a bank loan.
   - **B** lacked the cash to meet the upcoming interest payment.
   - **C** been required to make cash payments for supplier deliveries.

Solution to 1:

B is correct. The announcement removed any uncertainty about default. In the period leading up to the announcement, the bond's market price incorporated a probability of default, but the price would not have fully reflected the bond's value after default. The possibility that a bank loan might permit the company to avoid default was not eliminated until the announcement.

Solution to 2:

A is correct. The failure of the loan negotiations first becomes known in this announcement. The failure implies default.

2.2 Market Value versus Intrinsic Value

Market value is the price at which an asset can currently be bought or sold. **Intrinsic value** (sometimes called **fundamental value**) is, broadly speaking, the value that would be placed on it by investors if they had a complete understanding of the asset's investment characteristics.[6] For a bond, for example, such information would include its interest (coupon) rate, principal value, the timing of its interest and principal payments, the other terms of the bond contract (indenture), a precise understanding of its default risk, the liquidity of its market, and other issue-specific items. In addition, market variables such as the term structure of interest rates and the size of various market premiums applying to the issue (for default risk, etc.) would enter into a discounted cash flow estimate of the bond's intrinsic value (discounted cash flow models are often used for such estimates). The word *estimate* is used because in practice, intrinsic value can be estimated but is not known for certain.

If investors believe a market is highly *efficient*, they will usually accept market prices as accurately reflecting intrinsic values. Discrepancies between market price and intrinsic value are the basis for profitable active investment. Active investors seek to own assets selling below perceived intrinsic value in the marketplace and to sell or sell short assets selling above perceived intrinsic value.

If investors believe an asset market is relatively *inefficient*, they may try to develop an independent estimate of intrinsic value. The challenge for investors and analysts is estimating an asset's intrinsic value. Numerous theories and models, including the dividend discount model, can be used to estimate an asset's intrinsic value, but they all require some form of judgment regarding the size, timing, and riskiness of the future cash flows associated with the asset. The more complex an asset's future cash flows, the more difficult it is to estimate its intrinsic value. These complexities and the estimates of an asset's market value are reflected in the market through the buying and selling of assets. The market value of an asset represents the intersection of supply and demand—the point that is low enough to induce at least one investor to buy while being high enough to induce at least one investor to sell. Because information relevant to valuation flows continually to investors, estimates of intrinsic value change, and hence, market values change.

EXAMPLE 3

Intrinsic Value

1 An analyst estimates that a security's intrinsic value is lower than its market value. The security appears to be:

  A undervalued.

  B fairly valued.

  C overvalued.

2 A market in which assets' market values are, on average, equal to or nearly equal to intrinsic values is *best described* as a market that is attractive for:

6 Intrinsic value is often defined as the present value of all expected future cash flows of the asset.

A active investment.

B passive investment.

C both active and passive investment.

3 Suppose that the future cash flows of an asset are accurately estimated. The asset trades in a market that you believe is efficient based on most evidence, but your estimate of the asset's intrinsic value exceeds the asset's market value by a moderate amount. The *most likely* conclusion is that you have:

A overestimated the asset's risk.

B underestimated the asset's risk.

C identified a market inefficiency.

Solution to 1:

C is correct. The market is valuing the asset at more than its true worth.

Solution to 2:

B is correct because an active investment is not expected to earn superior risk-adjusted returns if the market is efficient. The additional costs of active investment are not justified in such a market.

Solution to 3:

B is correct. If risk is underestimated, the discount rate being applied to find the present value of the expected cash flows (estimated intrinsic value) will be too low and the intrinsic value estimate will be too high.

2.3 Factors Contributing to and Impeding a Market's Efficiency

For markets to be efficient, prices should adjust quickly and rationally to the release of new information. In other words, prices of assets in an efficient market should "fully reflect" all information. Financial markets, however, are generally not classified at the two extremes as either completely inefficient or completely efficient but, rather, as exhibiting various degrees of efficiency. In other words, market efficiency should be viewed as falling on a continuum between extremes of completely efficient, at one end, and completely inefficient, at the other. Asset prices in a highly efficient market, by definition, reflect information more quickly and more accurately than in a less-efficient market. These degrees of efficiency also vary through time, across geographical markets, and by type of market. A number of factors contribute to and impede the degree of efficiency in a financial market.

2.3.1 *Market Participants*

One of the most critical factors contributing to the degree of efficiency in a market is the number of market participants. Consider the following example that illustrates the relationship between the number of market participants and market efficiency.

EXAMPLE 4

Illustration of Market Efficiency

Assume that the shares of a small market capitalization (cap) company trade on a public stock exchange. Because of its size, it is not considered "blue-chip" and not many professional investors follow the activities of the company.[7] A small-cap fund analyst reports that the most recent annual operating performance of the company has been surprisingly good, considering the recent slump in its industry. The company's share price, however, has been slow to react to the positive financial results because the company is not being recommended by the majority of research analysts. This mispricing implies that the market for this company's shares is less than fully efficient. The small-cap fund analyst recognizes the opportunity and immediately recommends the purchase of the company's shares. The share price gradually increases as more investors purchase the shares once the news of the mispricing spreads through the market. As a result, it takes a few days for the share price to fully reflect the information.

Six months later, the company reports another solid set of interim financial results. But because the previous mispricing and subsequent profit opportunities have become known in the market, the number of analysts following the company's shares has increased substantially. As a result, as soon as unexpected information about the positive interim results are released to the public, a large number of buy orders quickly drive up the stock price, thereby making the market for these shares more efficient than before.

A large number of investors (individual and institutional) follow the major financial markets closely on a daily basis, and if mispricings exist in these markets, as illustrated by the example, investors will act so that these mispricings disappear quickly. Besides the number of investors, the number of financial analysts who follow or analyze a security or asset should be positively related to market efficiency. The number of market participants and resulting trading activity can vary significantly through time. A lack of trading activity can cause or accentuate other market imperfections that impede market efficiency. In fact, in many of these markets, trading in many of the listed stocks is restricted for foreigners. By nature, this limitation reduces the number of market participants, restricts the potential for trading activity, and hence reduces market efficiency.

EXAMPLE 5

Factors Affecting Market Efficiency

The expected effect on market efficiency of opening a securities market to trading by foreigners would *most likely* be to:

A decrease market efficiency.

B leave market efficiency unchanged.

C increase market efficiency.

7 A "blue-chip" share is one from a well-recognized company that is considered to be high quality but low risk. This term generally refers to a company that has a long history of earnings and paying dividends.

Solution:

C is correct. The opening of markets as described should increase market efficiency by increasing the number of market participants.

2.3.2 *Information Availability and Financial Disclosure*

Information availability (e.g., an active financial news media) and financial disclosure should promote market efficiency. Information regarding trading activity and traded companies in such markets as the New York Stock Exchange, the London Stock Exchange, and the Tokyo Stock Exchange is readily available. Many investors and analysts participate in these markets, and analyst coverage of listed companies is typically substantial. As a result, these markets are quite efficient. In contrast, trading activity and material information availability may be lacking in smaller securities markets, such as those operating in some emerging markets.

Similarly, significant differences may exist in the efficiency of different types of markets. For example, many securities trade primarily or exclusively in dealer or over-the-counter (OTC) markets, including bonds, money market instruments, currencies, mortgage-backed securities, swaps, and forward contracts. The information provided by the dealers that serve as market makers for these markets can vary significantly in quality and quantity, both through time and across different product markets.

Treating all market participants fairly is critical for the integrity of the market and explains why regulators place such an emphasis on "fair, orderly, and efficient markets."[8] A key element of this fairness is that all investors have access to the information necessary to value securities that trade in the market. Rules and regulations that promote fairness and efficiency in a market include those pertaining to the disclosure of information and illegal insider trading.

For example, US Securities and Exchange Commission's (SEC's) Regulation FD (Fair Disclosure) requires that if security issuers provide nonpublic information to some market professionals or investors, they must also disclose this information to the public.[9] This requirement helps provide equal and fair opportunities, which is important in encouraging participation in the market. A related issue deals with illegal insider trading. The SEC's rules, along with court cases, define illegal insider trading as trading in securities by market participants who are considered insiders "while in possession of material, nonpublic information about the security."[10] Although these rules cannot guarantee that some participants will not have an advantage over others and that insiders will not trade on the basis of inside information, the civil and criminal penalties associated with breaking these rules are intended to discourage illegal insider trading and promote fairness. In the European Union, insider trading laws are generally enshrined in legislation and enforced by regulatory and judicial authorities.[11]

---

8 "The Investor's Advocate: How the SEC Protects Investors, Maintains Market Integrity, and Facilitates Capital Formation," US Securities and Exchange Commission (www.sec.gov/about/whatwedo.shtml).

9 Regulation FD, "Selective Disclosure and Insider Trading," 17 CFR Parts 240, 243, and 249, effective 23 October 2000.

10 Although not the focus of this particular reading, it is important to note that a party is considered an insider not only when the individual is a corporate insider, such as an officer or director, but also when the individual is aware that the information is nonpublic information [Securities and Exchange Commission, Rules 10b5-1 ("Trading on the Basis of Material Nonpublic Information in Insider Trading Cases") and Rule 10b5-2 "Duties of Trust or Confidence in Misappropriation Insider Trading Cases")].

11 See the European Union's Market Abuse Regulation (Regulation (EU) no. 596/2014 of the European Parliament and of the Council of 16 April 2014 on market abuse) and Directive for Criminal Sanctions for Market Abuse (Directive 2014/57/EU of the European Parliament and of the Council of 16 April 2014 on criminal sanctions for market abuse).

2.3.3 *Limits to Trading*

Arbitrage is a set of transactions that produces riskless profits. Arbitrageurs are traders who engage in such trades to benefit from pricing discrepancies (inefficiencies) in markets. Such trading activity contributes to market efficiency. For example, if an asset is traded in two markets but at different prices, the actions of buying the asset in the market in which it is underpriced and selling the asset in the market in which it is overpriced will eventually bring these two prices together. The presence of these arbitrageurs helps pricing discrepancies disappear quickly. Obviously, market efficiency is impeded by any limitation on arbitrage resulting from operating inefficiencies, such as difficulties in executing trades in a timely manner, prohibitively high trading costs, and a lack of transparency in market prices.

Some market experts argue that restrictions on short selling limit arbitrage trading, which impedes market efficiency. **Short selling** is the transaction whereby an investor sells shares that he or she does not own by borrowing them from a broker and agreeing to replace them at a future date. Short selling allows investors to sell securities they believe to be overvalued, much in the same way they can buy those they believe to be undervalued. In theory, such activities promote more efficient pricing. Regulators and others, however, have argued that short selling may exaggerate downward market movements, leading to crashes in affected securities. In contrast, some researchers report evidence indicating that when investors are unable to borrow securities, that is to short the security, or when costs to borrow shares are high, market prices may deviate from intrinsic values.[12] Furthermore, research suggests that short selling is helpful in price discovery (that is, it facilitates supply and demand in determining prices).[13]

2.4 Transaction Costs and Information-Acquisition Costs

The costs incurred by traders in identifying and exploiting possible market inefficiencies affect the interpretation of market efficiency. The two types of costs to consider are transaction costs and information-acquisition costs.

- *Transaction costs*: Practically, transaction costs are incurred in trading to exploit any perceived market inefficiency. Thus, "efficient" should be viewed as efficient within the bounds of transaction costs. For example, consider a violation of the principle that two identical assets should sell for the same price in different markets. Such a violation can be considered to be a rather simple possible exception to market efficiency because prices appear to be inconsistently processing information. To exploit the violation, a trader could arbitrage by simultaneously shorting the asset in the higher-price market and buying the asset in the lower-price market. If the price discrepancy between the two markets is smaller than the transaction costs involved in the arbitrage for the lowest cost traders, the arbitrage will not occur, and both prices are in effect efficient within the bounds of arbitrage. These bounds of arbitrage are relatively narrow in highly liquid markets, such as the market for US Treasury bills, but could be wide in illiquid markets.
- *Information-acquisition costs:* Practically, expenses are always associated with gathering and analyzing information. New information is incorporated in transaction prices by traders placing trades based on their analysis of information. Active investors who place trades based on information they have gathered and analyzed play a key role in market prices adjusting to reflect new information. The classic view of market efficiency is that active investors incur information

12 See Deng, Mortal, and Gupta (2017) and references therein."
13 See Bris, Goetzmann, and Zhu (2009).

acquisition costs but that money is wasted because prices already reflect all relevant information. This view of efficiency is very strict in the sense of viewing a market as inefficient if active investing can recapture any part of the costs, such as research costs and active asset selection. Grossman and Stiglitz (1980) argue that prices must offer a return to information acquisition; in equilibrium, if markets are efficient, returns net of such expenses are just fair returns for the risk incurred. The modern perspective views a market as inefficient if, after deducting such costs, active investing can earn superior returns. Gross of expenses, a return should accrue to information acquisition in an efficient market.

In summary, a modern perspective calls for the investor to consider transaction costs and information-acquisition costs when evaluating the efficiency of a market. A price discrepancy must be sufficiently large to leave the investor with a profit (adjusted for risk) after taking account of the transaction costs and information-acquisition costs to reach the conclusion that the discrepancy may represent a market inefficiency. Prices may somewhat less than fully reflect available information without there being a true market opportunity for active investors.

3 FORMS OF MARKET EFFICIENCY

Eugene Fama developed a framework for describing the degree to which markets are efficient.[14] In his efficient market hypothesis, markets are efficient when prices reflect *all* relevant information at any point in time. This means that the market prices observed for securities, for example, reflect the information available at the time.

In his framework, Fama defines three forms of efficiency: weak, semi-strong, and strong. Each form is defined with respect to the available information that is reflected in prices.

	Market Prices Reflect:		
Forms of Market Efficiency	**Past Market Data**	**Public Information**	**Private Information**
Weak form of market efficiency	✓		
Semi-strong form of market efficiency	✓	✓	
Strong form of market efficiency	✓	✓	✓

A finding that investors can consistently earn **abnormal returns** by trading on the basis of information is evidence contrary to market efficiency. In general, abnormal returns are returns in excess of those expected given a security's risk and the market's return. In other words, abnormal return equals actual return less expected return.

14 Fama (1970).

3.1 Weak Form

In the **weak-form efficient market hypothesis**, security prices fully reflect *all past market data*, which refers to all historical price and trading volume information. If markets are weak-form efficient, past trading data are already reflected in current prices and investors cannot predict future price changes by extrapolating prices or patterns of prices from the past.[15]

Tests of whether securities markets are weak-form efficient require looking at patterns of prices. One approach is to see whether there is any serial correlation in security returns, which would imply a predictable pattern.[16] Although there is some weak correlation in daily security returns, there is not enough correlation to make this a profitable trading rule after considering transaction costs.

An alternative approach to test weak-form efficiency is to examine specific trading rules that attempt to exploit historical trading data. If any such trading rule consistently generates abnormal risk-adjusted returns after trading costs, this evidence will contradict weak-form efficiency. This approach is commonly associated with **technical analysis**, which involves the analysis of historical trading information (primarily pricing and volume data) in an attempt to identify recurring patterns in the trading data that can be used to guide investment decisions. Many technical analysts, also referred to as "technicians," argue that many movements in stock prices are based, in large part, on psychology. Many technicians attempt to predict how market participants will behave, based on analyses of past behavior, and then trade on those predictions. Technicians often argue that simple statistical tests of trading rules are not conclusive because they are not applied to the more sophisticated trading strategies that can be used and that the research excludes the technician's subjective judgment. Thus, it is difficult to definitively refute this assertion because there are an unlimited number of possible technical trading rules.

Can technical analysts profit from trading on past trends? Overall, the evidence indicates that investors cannot consistently earn abnormal profits using past prices or other technical analysis strategies in developed markets.[17] Some evidence suggests, however, that there are opportunities to profit on technical analysis in countries with developing markets, including Hungary, Bangladesh, and Turkey, among others.[18]

3.2 Semi-Strong Form

In a **semi-strong-form efficient market**, prices reflect all publicly known and available information. Publicly available information includes financial statement data (such as earnings, dividends, corporate investments, changes in management, etc.) and financial market data (such as closing prices, shares traded, etc.). Therefore, the semi-strong form of market efficiency encompasses the weak form. In other words, if a market is semi-strong efficient, then it must also be weak-form efficient. A market that quickly incorporates all publicly available information into its prices is semi-strong efficient.

In a semi-strong market, efforts to analyze publicly available information are futile. That is, analyzing earnings announcements of companies to identify underpriced or overpriced securities is pointless because the prices of these securities already reflect all publicly available information. If markets are semi-strong efficient, no single investor has access to information that is not already available to other market participants,

---

15 Market efficiency should not be confused with the random walk hypothesis, in which price changes over time are independent of one another. A random walk model is one of many alternative expected return generating models. Market efficiency does not require that returns follow a random walk.

16 Serial correlation is a statistical measure of the degree to which the returns in one period are related to the returns in another period.

17 Bessembinder and Chan (1998) and Fifield, Power, and Sinclair (2005).

18 Fifield, Power, and Sinclair (2005), Chen and Li (2006), and Mobarek, Mollah, and Bhuyan (2008).

and as a consequence, no single investor can gain an advantage in predicting future security prices. In a semi-strong efficient market, prices adjust quickly and accurately to new information. Suppose a company announces earnings that are higher than expected. In a semi-strong efficient market, investors would not be able to act on this announcement and earn abnormal returns.

A common empirical test of investors' reaction to information releases is the event study. Suppose a researcher wants to test whether investors react to the announcement that the company is paying a special dividend. The researcher identifies a sample period and then those companies that paid a special dividend in the period and the date of the announcement. Then, for each company's stock, the researcher calculates the expected return on the share for the event date. This expected return may be based on many different models, including the capital asset pricing model, a simple market model, or a market index return. The researcher calculates the excess return as the difference between the actual return and the expected return. Once the researcher has calculated the event's excess return for each share, statistical tests are conducted to see whether the abnormal returns are statistically different from zero. The process of an event study is outlined in Exhibit 1.

Exhibit 1 The Event Study Process

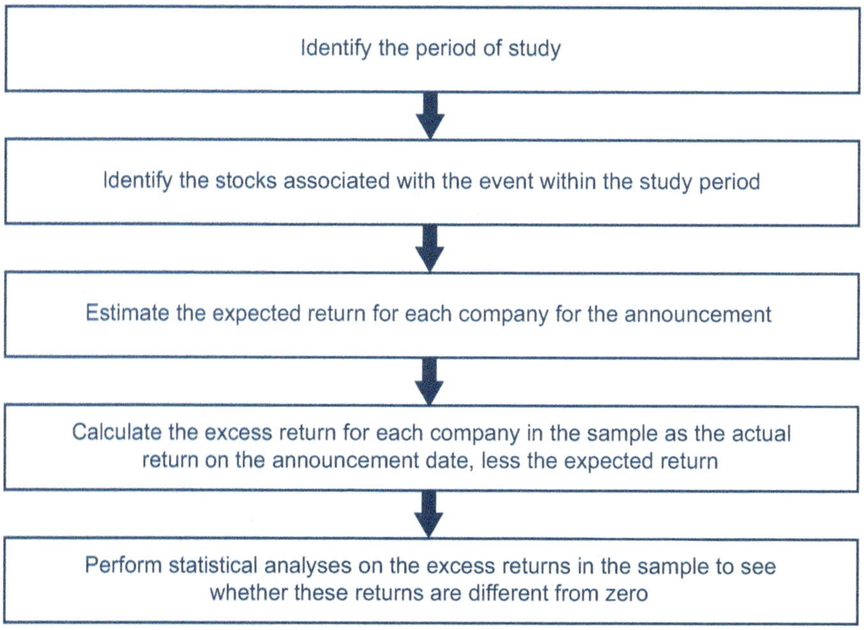

How do event studies relate to efficient markets? In a semi-strong efficient market, share prices react quickly and accurately to public information. Therefore, if the information is good news, such as better-than-expected earnings, one would expect the company's shares to increase immediately at the time of the announcement; if it is bad news, one would expect a swift, negative reaction. If actual returns exceed what is expected in absence of the announcement and these returns are confined to the announcement period, then they are consistent with the idea that market prices react quickly to new information. In other words, the finding of excess returns at the time of the announcement does not necessarily indicate market inefficiency. In contrast, the finding of consistent excess returns following the announcement would suggest a trading opportunity. Trading on the basis of the announcement—that is, once the announcement is made—would not, on average, yield abnormal returns.

EXAMPLE 6

Information Arrival and Market Reaction

Consider an example of a news item and its effect on a share's price. The following events related to Tesla, Inc. in August of 2018:

1 August 2018	After the market closes, Tesla, Inc., publicly reports that there was a smaller-than expected cash burn for the most recent quarter.
2 August 2018	Elon Musk, Chairman and CEO of Tesla, Inc., notifies Tesla's board of directors that he wants to take the company private. This is not public information at this point.
7 August 2018	Before the market opens, the *Financial Times* reports that a Saudi fund has a $2 billion investment in Tesla.
	During market trading, Musk announces on Twitter "Am considering taking Tesla private at $420. Funding secured." [Twitter, Elon Musk @elonmusk, 9:48 a.m., 7 August 2018]
24 August 2018	After the market closed, Musk announces that he no longer intends on taking Tesla private.

Exhibit 2 Price of Tesla, Inc. Stock: 31 July 2018–31 August 2018

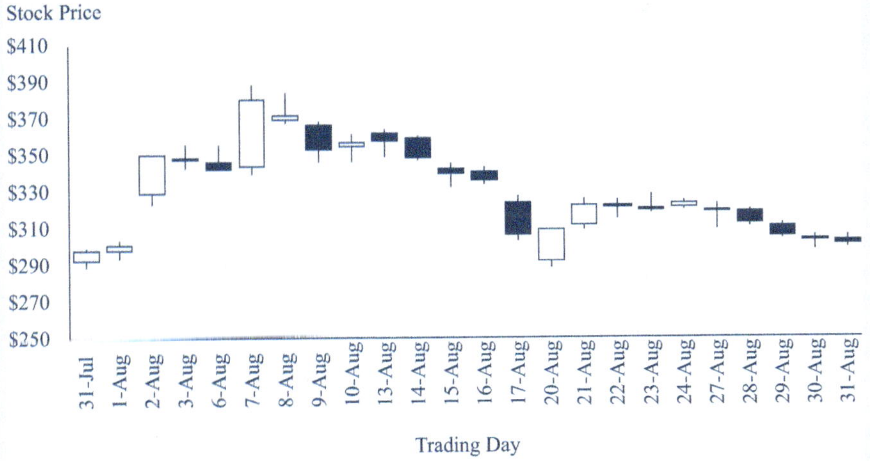

Note: Open-High-Low-Close graph of Tesla's stock price, with white rectangles indicating upward movement in the day and black rectangles indicating downward movement during the day.
Source of data: Yahoo! Finance.

Is the fact that the price of Tesla moves up immediately on the day after the Q2 earnings (the first day of trading with this information) indicative of efficiency regarding information? Most likely.

Does the fact that the price of Tesla moves up but does not reach $420 on the day the going-private Twitter announcement is made mean that investors underreacted? Not necessarily. There was confusion and uncertainty about the going-private transaction at the time, so the price did not close in on the proposed $420 per share for going private.

Does the fact that the market price of the stock declined well before the issue of going-private was laid to rest by Musk mean that the market is inefficient? Not necessarily. There were numerous analyses, discussions, and other news regarding the likelihood of the transaction, all of which was incorporated in the price of the stock before the going-private transaction was dismissed by Musk.

Researchers have examined many different company-specific information events, including stock splits, dividend changes, and merger announcements, as well as economy-wide events, such as regulation changes and tax rate changes. The results of most research are consistent with the view that developed securities markets might be semi-strong efficient. But some evidence suggests that the markets in developing countries may not be semi-strong efficient.[19]

3.3 Strong Form

In a **strong-form efficient market**, security prices fully reflect both public and private information. A market that is strong-form efficient is, by definition, also semi-strong- and weak-form efficient. In the case of a strong-form efficient market, insiders would not be able to earn abnormal returns from trading on the basis of private information. A strong-form efficient market also means that prices reflect all private information, which means that prices reflect everything that the management of a company knows about the financial condition of the company that has not been publicly released. However, this is not likely because of the strong prohibitions against insider trading that are found in most countries. If a market is strong-form efficient, those with insider information cannot earn abnormal returns.

Researchers test whether a market is strong-form efficient by testing whether investors can earn abnormal profits by trading on nonpublic information. The results of these tests are consistent with the view that securities markets are not strong-form efficient; many studies have found that abnormal profits can be earned when nonpublic information is used.[20]

3.4 Implications of the Efficient Market Hypothesis

The implications of efficient markets to investment managers and analysts are important because they affect the value of securities and how these securities are managed. Several implications can be drawn from the evidence on efficient markets for developed markets:

- Securities markets are weak-form efficient, and therefore, investors cannot earn abnormal returns by trading on the basis of past trends in price.
- Securities markets are semi-strong efficient, and therefore, analysts who collect and analyze information must consider whether that information is already reflected in security prices and how any new information affects a security's value.[21]
- Securities markets are not strong-form efficient because securities laws are intended to prevent exploitation of private information.

19 See Gan, Lee, Hwa, and Zhang (2005) and Raja, Sudhahar, and Selvam (2009).

20 Evidence that finds that markets are not strong-form efficient include Jaffe (1974) and Rozeff and Zaman (1988).

21 In the case of the Intel example, this implication would mean estimating how the actual filing of the lawsuit and the company's reaction to the lawsuit affect the value of Intel, while keeping in mind that the expectation of a lawsuit was already impounded in Intel's stock price.

3.4.1 *Fundamental Analysis*

Fundamental analysis is the examination of publicly available information and the formulation of forecasts to estimate the intrinsic value of assets. Fundamental analysis involves the estimation of an asset's value using company data, such as earnings and sales forecasts, and risk estimates as well as industry and economic data, such as economic growth, inflation, and interest rates. Buy and sell decisions depend on whether the current market price is less than or greater than the estimated intrinsic value.

The semi-strong form of market efficiency says that all available public information is reflected in current prices. So, what good is fundamental analysis? Fundamental analysis is necessary in a well-functioning market because this analysis helps the market participants understand the value implications of information. In other words, fundamental analysis facilitates a semi-strong efficient market by disseminating value-relevant information. And, although fundamental analysis requires costly information, this analysis can be profitable in terms of generating abnormal returns if the analyst creates a comparative advantage with respect to this information.[22]

3.4.2 *Technical Analysis*

Investors using **technical analysis** attempt to profit by looking at patterns of prices and trading volume. Although some price patterns persist, exploiting these patterns may be too costly and, hence, would not produce abnormal returns.

Consider a situation in which a pattern of prices exists. With so many investors examining prices, this pattern will be detected. If profitable, exploiting this pattern will eventually affect prices such that this pattern will no longer exist; it will be arbitraged away. In other words, by detecting and exploiting patterns in prices, technical analysts assist markets in maintaining weak-form efficiency. Does this mean that technical analysts cannot earn abnormal profits? Not necessarily, because there may be a possibility of earning abnormal profits from a pricing inefficiency. But would it be possible to earn abnormal returns on a consistent basis from exploiting such a pattern? No, because the actions of market participants will arbitrage this opportunity quickly, and the inefficiency will no longer exist.

3.4.3 *Portfolio Management*

If securities markets are weak-form and semi-strong-form efficient, the implication is that active trading, whether attempting to exploit price patterns or public information, is not likely to generate abnormal returns. In other words, portfolio managers cannot beat the market on a consistent basis, so therefore, passive portfolio management should outperform active portfolio management. Researchers have observed that mutual funds do not, on average, outperform the market on a risk-adjusted basis.[23] Mutual funds perform, on average, similar to the market before considering fees and expenses and perform worse than the market, on average, once fees and expenses are considered. Even if a mutual fund is not actively managed, there are costs to managing these funds, which reduces net returns.

So, what good are portfolio managers? The role of a portfolio manager is not necessarily to beat the market but, rather, to establish and manage a portfolio consistent with the portfolio's objectives, with appropriate diversification and asset allocation, while taking into consideration the risk preferences and tax situation of the investor.

---

22 Brealey (1983).

23 See Malkiel (1995). One of the challenges to evaluating mutual fund performance is that the researcher must control for survivorship bias.

4 MARKET PRICING ANOMALIES

Although considerable evidence shows that markets are efficient, researchers have identified a number of apparent market inefficiencies or anomalies. These market anomalies, if persistent, are exceptions to the notion of market efficiency. Researchers conclude that a **market anomaly** may be present if a change in the price of an asset or security cannot directly be linked to current relevant information known in the market or to the release of new information into the market.

The validity of any evidence supporting the potential existence of a market inefficiency or anomaly must be *consistent* over reasonably long periods. Otherwise, a detected market anomaly may largely be an artifact of the sample period chosen. In the widespread search for discovering profitable anomalies, many findings could simply be the product of a process called **data mining**, also known as **data snooping**. In generally accepted research practice, an initial hypothesis is developed which is based on economic rationale. Tests are then conducted on objectively selected data to either confirm or reject the original hypothesis. However, with data mining the process is typically reversed: data are examined with the intent to develop a hypothesis, instead of developing a hypothesis first. This is done by analyzing data in various manners, and even utilizing different empirical approaches until you find support for a desired result, in this case a profitable anomaly.

Can researchers look back on data and find a trading strategy that would have yielded abnormal returns? Absolutely. Enough data snooping often can detect a trading strategy that would have worked in the past by chance alone. But in an efficient market, such a strategy is unlikely to generate abnormal returns on a consistent basis in the future. Also, although identified anomalies may appear to produce excess returns, it is generally difficult to profitably exploit the anomalies after accounting for risk, trading costs, and so on.

Several well-known anomalies are listed in Exhibit 3. This list is by no means exhaustive, but it provides information on the breadth of the anomalies. A few of these anomalies are discussed in more detail in the following sections. The anomalies are placed into categories based on the research method that identified the anomaly. Time-series anomalies were identified using time series of data. Cross-sectional anomalies were identified based on analyzing a cross section of companies that differ on some key characteristics. Other anomalies were identified by a variety of means, including event studies.

Exhibit 3 Sampling of Observed Pricing Anomalies

Time Series	Cross-Sectional	Other
January effect	Size effect	Closed-end fund discount
Day-of-the-week effect	Value effect	Earnings surprise
Weekend effect	Book-to-market ratios	Initial public offerings
Turn-of-the-month effect	P/E ratio effect	Distressed securities effect
Holiday effect	Value Line enigma	Stock splits
Time-of-day effect		Super Bowl
Momentum		
Overreaction		

4.1 Time-Series Anomalies

Two of the major categories of time-series anomalies that have been documented are 1) calendar anomalies and 2) momentum and overreaction anomalies.

4.1.1 *Calendar Anomalies*

In the 1980s, a number of researchers reported that stock market returns in January were significantly higher compared to the rest of the months of the year, with most of the abnormal returns reported during the first five trading days in January. Since its first documentation in the 1980s, this pattern, known as the **January effect**, has been observed in most equity markets around the world. This anomaly is also known as the **turn-of-the-year effect**, or even often referred to as the "small firm in January effect" because it is most frequently observed for the returns of small market capitalization stocks.[24]

The January effect contradicts the efficient market hypothesis because excess returns in January are not attributed to any new and relevant information or news. A number of reasons have been suggested for this anomaly, including tax-loss selling. Researchers have speculated that, in order to reduce their tax liabilities, investors sell their "loser" securities in December for the purpose of creating capital losses, which can then be used to offset any capital gains. A related explanation is that these losers tend to be small-cap stocks with high volatility.[25] This increased supply of equities in December depresses their prices, and then these shares are bought in early January at relatively attractive prices. This demand then drives their prices up again. Overall, the evidence indicates that tax-loss selling may account for a portion of January abnormal returns, but it does not explain all of it.

Another possible explanation for the anomaly is so-called "window dressing", a practice in which portfolio managers sell their riskier securities prior to 31 December. The explanation is as follows: many portfolio managers prepare the annual reports of their portfolio holdings as of 31 December. Selling riskier securities is an attempt to make their portfolios appear less risky. After 31 December, a portfolio manager would then simply purchase riskier securities in an attempt to earn higher returns. However, similar to the tax-loss selling hypothesis, the research evidence in support of the window dressing hypothesis explains some, but not all, of the anomaly.

Recent evidence for both stock and bond returns suggests that the January effect is not persistent and, therefore, is not a pricing anomaly. Once an appropriate adjustment for risk is made, the January "effect" does not produce abnormal returns.[26]

Several other calendar effects, including the day-of-the-week and the weekend effects,[27] have been found. These anomalies are summarized in Exhibit 4.[28] But like the size effect, which will be described later, most of these anomalies have been eliminated over time. One view is that the anomalies have been exploited such that the effect has been arbitraged away. Another view, however, is that increasingly sophisticated statistical methodologies fail to detect pricing inefficiencies.

---

24 There is also evidence of a January effect in bond returns that is more prevalent in high-yield corporate bonds, similar to the small-company effect for stocks.

25 See Roll (1983).

26 See, for example, Kim (2006).

27 For a discussion of several of these anomalous patterns, see Jacobs and Levy (1988).

28 The weekend effect consists of a pattern of returns around the weekend: abnormal positive returns on Fridays followed by abnormally negative returns on Mondays. This is a day-of-the-week effect that specifically links Friday and Monday returns. It is interesting to note that in 2009, the weekend effect in the United States was inverted, with 80 percent of the gains from March 2009 onward coming from the first trading day of the week.

Exhibit 4 Calendar-Based Anomalies

Anomaly	Observation
Turn-of-the-month effect	Returns tend to be higher on the last trading day of the month and the first three trading days of the next month.
Day-of-the-week effect	The average Monday return is negative and lower than the average returns for the other four days, which are all positive.
Weekend effect	Returns on weekends tend to be lower than returns on weekdays.
Holiday effect	Returns on stocks in the day prior to market holidays tend to be higher than other days.

4.1.2 *Momentum and Overreaction Anomalies*

Momentum anomalies relate to short-term share price patterns. One of the earliest studies to identify this type of anomaly was conducted by Werner DeBondt and Richard Thaler, who argued that investors overreact to the release of unexpected public information.[29] Therefore, stock prices will be inflated (depressed) for those companies releasing good (bad) information. This anomaly has become known as the overreaction effect. Using the overreaction effect, they proposed a strategy that involved buying "loser" portfolios and selling "winner" portfolios. They defined stocks as winners or losers based on their total returns over the previous three- to five-year period. They found that in a subsequent period, the loser portfolios outperformed the market, while the winner portfolios underperformed the market. Similar patterns have been documented in many, but not all, global stock markets as well as in bond markets. One criticism is that the observed anomaly may be the result of statistical problems in the analysis.

A contradiction to weak-form efficiency occurs when securities that have experienced high returns in the short term tend to continue to generate higher returns in subsequent periods.[30] Empirical support for the existence of momentum in stock returns in most stock markets around the world is well documented. If investors can trade on the basis of momentum and earn abnormal profits, then this anomaly contradicts the weak form of the efficient market hypothesis because it represents a pattern in prices that can be exploited by simply using historical price information.[31]

Researchers have argued that the existence of momentum is rational and not contrary to market efficiency because it is plausible that there are shocks to the expected growth rates of cash flows to shareholders and that these shocks induce a serial correlation that is rational and short lived.[32] In other words, having stocks with some degree of momentum in their security returns may not imply irrationality but, rather, may reflect prices adjusting to a shock in growth rates.

---

29 DeBondt and Thaler (1985).

30 Notice that this pattern lies in sharp contrast to DeBondt and Thaler's reversal pattern that is displayed over longer periods of time. In theory, the two patterns could be related. In other words, it is feasible that prices are bid up extremely high, perhaps too high, in the short term for companies that are doing well. In the longer term (three-to-five years), the prices of these short-term winners correct themselves and they do poorly.

31 Jegadeesh and Titman (2001).

32 Johnson (2002).

4.2 Cross-Sectional Anomalies

Two of the most researched cross-sectional anomalies in financial markets are the size effect and the value effect.

4.2.1 *Size Effect*

The size effect results from the observation that equities of small-cap companies tend to outperform equities of large-cap companies on a risk-adjusted basis. Many researchers documented a small-company effect soon after the initial research was published in 1981. This effect, however, was not apparent in subsequent studies.[33] Part of the reason that the size effect was not confirmed by subsequent studies may be because of the fact that if it were truly an anomaly, investors acting on this effect would reduce any potential returns. But some of the explanation may simply be that the effect as originally observed was a chance outcome and, therefore, not actually an inefficiency.

4.2.2 *Value Effect*

A number of global empirical studies have shown that value stocks, which are generally referred to as stocks that have below-average price-to-earnings (P/E) and market-to-book (M/B) ratios, and above-average dividend yields, have consistently outperformed growth stocks over long periods of time.[34] If the effect persists, the value stock anomaly contradicts semi-strong market efficiency because all the information used to categorize stocks in this manner is publicly available.

Fama and French developed a three-factor model to predict stock returns.[35] In addition to the use of market returns as specified by the capital asset pricing model (CAPM), the Fama and French model also includes the size of the company as measured by the market value of its equity and the company's book value of equity divided by its market value of equity, which is a value measure. The Fama and French model captures risk dimensions related to stock returns that the CAPM model does not consider. Fama and French find that when they apply the three-factor model instead of the CAPM, the value stock anomaly disappears.

4.3 Other Anomalies

A number of additional anomalies has been documented in the financial markets, including the existence of closed-end investment fund discounts, price reactions to the release of earnings information, returns of initial public offerings, and the predictability of returns based on prior information.

4.3.1 *Closed-End Investment Fund Discounts*

A closed-end investment fund issues a fixed number of shares at inception and does not sell any additional shares after the initial offering. Therefore, the fund capitalization is fixed unless a secondary public offering is made. The shares of closed-end funds trade on stock markets like any other shares in the equity market (i.e., their prices are determined by supply and demand).

---

33 Although a large number of studies documents a small-company effect, these studies are concentrated in a period similar to that of the original research and, therefore, use a similar data set. The key to whether something is a true anomaly is persistence in out-of-sample tests. Fama and French (2008) document that the size effect is apparent only in microcap stocks but not in small- and large-cap stocks and these microcap stocks may have a significant influence in studies that document a size effect.

34 For example, see Capaul, Rowley, and Sharpe (1993) and Fama and French (1998).

35 Fama and French (1995).

Theoretically, these shares should trade at a price approximately equal to their net asset value (NAV) per share, which is simply the total market value of the fund's security holdings less any liabilities divided by the number of shares outstanding. An abundance of research, however, has documented that, on average, closed-end funds trade at a discount from NAV. Most studies have documented average discounts in the 4–10 percent range, although individual funds have traded at discounts exceeding 50 percent and others have traded at large premiums.[36]

The closed-end fund discount presents a puzzle because conceptually, an investor could purchase all the shares in the fund, liquidate the fund, and end up making a profit. Some researchers have suggested that these discounts are attributed to management fees or expectations of the managers' performance, but these explanations are not supported by the evidence.[37] An alternative explanation for the discount is that tax liabilities are associated with unrealized capital gains and losses that exist prior to when the investor bought the shares, and hence, the investor does not have complete control over the timing of the realization of gains and losses.[38] Although the evidence supports this hypothesis to a certain extent, the tax effect is not large enough to explain the entire discount. Finally, it has often been argued that the discounts exist because of liquidity problems and errors in calculating NAV. The illiquidity explanation is plausible if shares are recorded at the same price as more liquid, publicly traded stocks; some evidence supports this assertion. But as with tax reasons, liquidity issues explain only a portion of the discount effect.

Can these discounts be exploited to earn abnormal returns if transaction costs are taken into account? No. First, the transaction costs involved in exploiting the discount—buying all the shares and liquidating the fund—would eliminate any profit.[39] Second, these discounts tend to revert to zero over time. Hence, a strategy to trade on the basis of these discounts would not likely be profitable.[40]

4.3.2 *Earnings Surprise*

Although most event studies have supported semi-strong market efficiency, some researchers have provided evidence that questions semi-strong market efficiency. One of these studies relates to the extensively examined adjustment of stock prices to earnings announcements.[41] The unexpected part of the earnings announcement, or **earnings surprise**, is the portion of earnings that is unanticipated by investors and, according to the efficient market hypothesis, merits a price adjustment. Positive (negative) surprises should cause appropriate and rapid price increases (decreases). Several studies have been conducted using data from numerous markets around the world. Most of the results indicate that earnings surprises are reflected quickly in stock prices, but the adjustment process is not always efficient. In particular, although a substantial adjustment occurs prior to and at the announcement date, an adjustment also occurs after the announcement.[42]

As a result of these slow price adjustments, companies that display the largest positive earnings surprises subsequently display superior stock return performance, whereas poor subsequent performance is displayed by companies with low or negative

36 See Dimson and Minio-Kozerski (1999) for a review of this literature.

37 See Lee, Sheifer, and Thaler (1990).

38 The return to owners of closed-end fund shares has three parts: 1) the price appreciation or depreciation of the shares themselves, 2) the dividends earned and distributed to owners by the fund, and 3) the capital gains and losses earned by the fund that are distributed by the fund. The explanation of the anomalous pricing has to do with the timing of the distribution of capital gains.

39 See, for example, the study by Pontiff (1996), which shows how the cost of arbitraging these discounts eliminates the profit.

40 See Pontiff (1995).

41 See Jones, Rendleman, and Latané (1984).

42 Not surprisingly, it is often argued that this slow reaction contributes to a momentum pattern.

earnings surprises.[43] This finding implies that investors could earn abnormal returns using publicly available information by buying stocks of companies that had positive earnings surprises and selling those with negative surprises.

Although there is support for abnormal returns associated with earnings surprises, and some support for such returns beyond the announcement period, there is also evidence indicating that these observed abnormal returns are an artifact of studies that do not sufficiently control for transaction costs and risk.[44]

4.3.3 *Initial Public Offerings (IPOs)*

When a company offers shares of its stock to the public for the first time, it does so through an initial public offering (or IPO). This offering involves working with an investment bank that helps price and market the newly issued shares. After the offering is complete, the new shares trade on a stock market for the first time. Given the risk that investment bankers face in trying to sell a new issue for which the true price is unknown, it is perhaps not surprising to find that, on average, the initial selling price is set too low and that the price increases dramatically on the first trading day. The percentage difference between the issue price and the closing price at the end of the first day of trading is often referred to as the degree of underpricing.

The evidence suggests that, on average, investors who are able to buy the shares of an IPO at their offering price may be able to earn abnormal profits. For example, during the internet bubble of 1995–2000, many IPOs ended their first day of trading up by more than 100 percent. Such performance, however, is not always the case. Sometimes the issues are priced too high, which means that share prices drop on their first day of trading. In addition, the evidence also suggests that investors buying after the initial offering are not able to earn abnormal profits because prices adjust quickly to the "true" values, which supports semi-strong market efficiency. In fact, the subsequent long-term performance of IPOs is generally found to be below average. Taken together, the IPO underpricing and the subsequent poor performance suggests that the markets are overly optimistic initially (i.e., investors overreact).

Some researchers have examined closely why IPOs may appear to have anomalous returns. Because of the small size of the IPO companies and the method of equally weighting the samples, what appears to be an anomaly may simply be an artifact of the methodology.[45]

4.3.4 *Predictability of Returns Based on Prior Information*

A number of researchers have documented that equity returns are related to prior information on such factors as interest rates, inflation rates, stock volatility, and dividend yields.[46] But finding that equity returns are affected by changes in economic fundamentals is not evidence of market inefficiency and would not result in abnormal trading returns.[47]

43 A similar pattern has been documented in the corporate bond market, where bond prices react too slowly to new company earnings announcements as well as to changes in company debt ratings.

44 See Brown (1997) for a summary of evidence supporting the existence of this anomaly. See Zarowin (1989) for evidence regarding the role of size in explaining abnormal returns to surprises; Alexander, Goff, and Peterson (1989) for evidence regarding transaction costs and unexpected earnings strategies; and Kim and Kim (2003) for evidence indicating that the anomalous returns can be explained by risk factors.

45 See Brav, Geczy, and Gompers (1995).

46 See, for example, Fama and Schwert (1977) and Fama and French (1988).

47 See Fama and French (2008).

Furthermore, the relationship between stock returns and the prior information is not consistent over time. For example, in one study, the relationship between stock prices and dividend yields changed from positive to negative in different periods.[48] Hence, a trading strategy based on dividend yields would not yield consistent abnormal returns.

4.4 Implications for Investment Strategies

Although it is interesting to consider the anomalies just described, attempting to benefit from them in practice is not easy. In fact, most researchers conclude that observed anomalies are not violations of market efficiency but, rather, are the result of statistical methodologies used to detect the anomalies. As a result, if the methodologies are corrected, most of these anomalies disappear.[49] Another point to consider is that in an efficient market, overreactions may occur, but then so do under-reactions.[50] Therefore, on average, the markets are efficient. In other words, investors face challenges when they attempt to translate statistical anomalies into economic profits. Consider the following quote regarding anomalies from the *Economist* ("Frontiers of Finance Survey," 9 October 1993):

> Many can be explained away. When transactions costs are taken into account, the fact that stock prices tend to over-react to news, falling back the day after good news and bouncing up the day after bad news, proves unexploitable: price reversals are always within the bid-ask spread. Others such as the small-firm effect, work for a few years and then fail for a few years. Others prove to be merely proxies for the reward for risk taking. Many have disappeared since (and because) attention has been drawn to them.

It is difficult to envision entrusting your retirement savings to a manager whose strategy is based on buying securities on Mondays, which tends to have negative returns on average, and selling them on Fridays. For one thing, the negative Monday returns are merely an average, so on any given week, they could be positive. In addition, such a strategy would generate large trading costs. Even more importantly, investors would likely be uncomfortable investing their funds in a strategy that has no compelling underlying economic rationale.

5 BEHAVIORAL FINANCE

Behavioral finance examines investor behavior to understand how people make decisions, individually and collectively. Behavioral finance does not assume that people consider all available information in decision-making and act rationally by maximizing utility within budget constraints and updating expectations consistent with Bayes' formula. The resulting behaviors may affect what is observed in the financial markets.

In a broader sense, behavioral finance attempts to explain why individuals make the decisions that they do, whether these decisions are rational or irrational. The focus of much of the work in this area is on the behavioral biases that affect investment decisions. The behavior of individuals, in particular their behavioral biases, has been offered as a possible explanation for a number of pricing anomalies.

---

48 Schwert (2003, Chapter 15).
49 Fama (1998).
50 This point is made by Fama (1998).

Most asset-pricing models assume that markets are rational and that the intrinsic value of a security reflects this rationality. But market efficiency and asset-pricing models do not require that each individual is rational—rather, only that the market is rational. If individuals deviate from rationality, other individuals are assumed to observe this deviation and respond accordingly. These responses move the market toward efficiency. If this does not occur in practice, it may be possible to explain some market anomalies referencing observed behaviors and behavioral biases.

5.1 Loss Aversion

In most financial models, the assumption is that investors are risk averse. **Risk aversion** refers to the tendency of people to dislike risk and to require higher expected returns to compensate for exposure to additional risk. Behavioral finance allows for the possibility that the dissatisfaction resulting from a loss exceeds the satisfaction resulting from a gain of the same magnitude. **Loss aversion** refers to the tendency of people to dislike losses more than they like comparable gains. This results in a strong preference for avoiding losses as opposed to achieving gains.[51] Some argue that behavioral theories of loss aversion can explain observed overreaction in markets. If loss aversion is more important than risk aversion, researchers should observe that investors overreact.[52] Although loss aversion can explain the overreaction anomaly, evidence also suggests that under reaction is just as prevalent as overreaction, which counters these arguments.

5.2 Herding

Herding behavior has been advanced as a possible explanation of under reaction and overreaction in financial markets. **Herding** occurs when investors trade on the same side of the market in the same securities, or when investors ignore their own private information and/or analysis and act as other investors do. Herding is clustered trading that may or may not be based on information.[53] Herding may result in under- or over-reaction to information depending upon the direction of the herd.

5.3 Overconfidence

A behavioral bias offered to explain pricing anomalies is overconfidence. If investors are overconfident, they overestimate their ability to process and interpret information about a security. Overconfident investors may not process information appropriately, and if there is a sufficient number of these investors, stocks will be mispriced.[54] But most researchers argue that this mispricing is temporary, with prices correcting eventually. If it takes a sufficiently long time for prices to become correctly priced and the mispricing is predictable, it may be possible for investors to earn abnormal profits.

Evidence has suggested that overconfidence results in mispricing for US, UK, German, French, and Japanese markets.[55] This overconfidence, however, is predominantly in higher-growth companies, whose prices react slowly to new information.[56]

---

51 See DeBondt and Thaler (1985) and Tversky and Kahneman (1981).

52 See Fama (1998).

53 The term used when there is herding without information is "spurious herding."

54 Another aspect to overconfidence is that investors who are overconfident in their ability to select investments and manage a portfolio tend to use less diversification, investing in what is most familiar. Therefore, investor behavior may affect investment results—returns and risk—without implications for the efficiency of markets.

55 Scott, Stumpp, and Xu (2003) and Boujelbene Abbes, Boujelbene, and Bouri (2009).

56 Scott, Stumpp, and Xu (2003).

5.4 Information Cascades

An application of behavioral theories to markets and pricing focuses on the role of personal learning in markets. Personal learning is what investors learn by observing outcomes of trades and what they learn from "conversations"—ideas shared among investors about specific assets and the markets.[57] Social interaction and the resultant contagion is important in pricing and may explain such phenomena as price changes without accompanying news and mistakes in valuation.

Biases that investors possess can lead to herding behavior or information cascades. Herding and information cascades are related but not identical concepts. An **information cascade** is the transmission of information from those participants who act first and whose decisions influence the decisions of others. Those who are acting on the choices of others may be ignoring their own preferences in favor of imitating the choices of others. In particular, information cascades may occur with respect to the release of accounting information because accounting information may be difficult to interpret and may be noisy. For example, the release of earnings is difficult to interpret because it is necessary to understand how the number was arrived at and noisy because it is uncertain what the current earnings imply about future earnings.

Information cascades may result in serial correlation of stock returns, which is consistent with overreaction anomalies. Do information cascades result in correct pricing? Some argue that if a cascade is leading toward an incorrect value, this cascade is "fragile" and will be corrected because investors will ultimately give more weight to public information or the trading of a recognized informed trader.[58] Information cascades, although documented in markets, do not necessarily mean that investors can exploit knowledge of them as profitable trading opportunities.

Are information cascades rational? If the informed traders act first and uninformed traders imitate the informed traders, this behavior is consistent with rationality. The imitation trading by the uninformed traders may help the market incorporate relevant information and improve market efficiency.[59] However, the imitation trading may lead to an overreaction to information. The empirical evidence indicates that information cascades are greater for a stock when the information quality regarding the company is poor.[60] Information cascades may enhance the information available to investors.

5.5 Other Behavioral Biases

Other behavioral biases that have been put forth to explain observed investor behavior include the following:

- **representativeness**—investors assess new information and probabilities of outcomes based on similarity to the current state or to a familiar classification;
- **mental accounting**—investors keep track of the gains and losses for different investments in separate mental accounts and treat those accounts differently;
- **conservatism**—investors tend to be slow to react to new information and continue to maintain their prior views or forecasts; and
- **narrow framing**—investors focus on issues in isolation and respond to the issues based on how the issues are posed.[61]

57 Hirshleifer and Teoh (2009).

58 Avery and Zemsky (1999).

59 Another alternative is that the uninformed traders are the majority of the market participants and the imitators are imitating not because they agree with the actions of the majority but because they are looking to act on the actions of the uninformed traders.

60 Avery and Zemsky (1999) and Bikhchandani, Hirshleifer, and Welch (1992).

61 For a review of these behavioral issues, see Hirshleifer (2001).

The basic idea behind behavioral finance is that investors are humans and, therefore, imperfect. These observed less than rational behaviors may help explain observed pricing anomalies. The beliefs investors have about a given asset's value may not be homogeneous. But an issue, which is controversial, is whether these insights can help someone identify and exploit any mispricing. In other words, can investors use knowledge of behavioral biases to predict how asset prices will be affected and act based on the predictions to earn abnormal profits?

5.6 Behavioral Finance and Investors

Behavior biases can affect all market participants, from the novice investor to the most experienced investment manager. An understanding of behavioral finance can help market participants recognize their own and others' behavioral biases. As a result of this recognition, they may be able to respond and make improved decisions, individually and collectively.

5.7 Behavioral Finance and Efficient Markets

The use of behavioral finance to explain observed pricing is an important part of the understanding of how markets function and how prices are determined. Whether there is a behavioral explanation for market anomalies remains a debate. Pricing anomalies are continually being uncovered, and then statistical and behavioral explanations are offered to explain these anomalies.

On the one hand, if investors must be rational for efficient markets to exist, then all the imperfections of human investors suggest that markets cannot be efficient. On the other hand, if all that is required for markets to be efficient is that investors cannot consistently beat the market on a risk-adjusted basis, then the evidence does support market efficiency.

SUMMARY

This reading has provided an overview of the theory and evidence regarding market efficiency and has discussed the different forms of market efficiency as well as the implications for fundamental analysis, technical analysis, and portfolio management. The general conclusion drawn from the efficient market hypothesis is that it is not possible to beat the market on a consistent basis by generating returns in excess of those expected for the level of risk of the investment.

Additional key points include the following:

- The efficiency of a market is affected by the number of market participants and depth of analyst coverage, information availability, and limits to trading.
- There are three forms of efficient markets, each based on what is considered to be the information used in determining asset prices. In the weak form, asset prices fully reflect all market data, which refers to all past price and trading volume information. In the semi-strong form, asset prices reflect all publicly known and available information. In the strong form, asset prices fully reflect all information, which includes both public and private information.
- Intrinsic value refers to the true value of an asset, whereas market value refers to the price at which an asset can be bought or sold. When markets are efficient, the two should be the same or very close. But when markets are not efficient, the two can diverge significantly.

- Most empirical evidence supports the idea that securities markets in developed countries are semi-strong-form efficient; however, empirical evidence does not support the strong form of the efficient market hypothesis.
- A number of anomalies have been documented that contradict the notion of market efficiency, including the size anomaly, the January anomaly, and the winners–losers anomalies. In most cases, however, contradictory evidence both supports and refutes the anomaly.
- Behavioral finance uses human psychology, such as behavioral biases, in an attempt to explain investment decisions. Whereas behavioral finance is helpful in understanding observed decisions, a market can still be considered efficient even if market participants exhibit seemingly irrational behaviors, such as herding.

REFERENCES

Alexander, John C., Delbert Goff, and Pamela P. Peterson. 1989. "Profitability of a Trading Strategy Based on Unexpected Earnings." *Financial Analysts Journal*, vol. 45, no. 4:65–71.

Avery, Christopher, and Peter Zemsky. 1998. "Multi-Dimensional Uncertainty and Herding in Financial Markets." *American Economic Review*, vol. 88, no. 4:724–748.

Bessembinder, Hendrik, and Kalok Chan. 1998. "Market Efficiency and the Returns to Technical Analysis." *Financial Management*, vol. 27, no. 2:5–17.

Bikhchandani, Sushil, David Hirshleifer, and Ivo Welch. 1992. "A Theory of Fads, Fashion, Custom, and Cultural Change as Informational Cascades." *Journal of Political Economy*, vol. 100, no. 5:992–1026.

Bouljelbene Abbes, Mouna, Younes Boujelbene, and Abdelfettah Bouri. 2009. "Overconfidence Bias: Explanation of Market Anomalies French Market Case." *Journal of Applied Economic Sciences*, vol. 4, no. 1:12–25.

Brav, Alon, Christopher Geczy, and Paul A. Gompers. 1995. "The Long-Run Underperformance of Seasoned Equity Offerings Revisited." Working paper, Harvard University.

Brealey, Richard. 1983. "Can Professional Investors Beat the Market?" *An Introduction to Risk and Return from Common Stocks*, 2nd edition. Cambridge, MA: MIT Press.

Bris, Arturo, William N. Goetzmann, and Ning Zhu. 2009. "Efficiency and the Bear: Short Sales and Markets around the World." *Journal of Finance*, vol. 62, no. 3:1029–1079.

Brown, Laurence D. 1997. "Earning Surprise Research: Synthesis and Perspectives." *Financial Analysts Journal*, vol. 53, no. 2:13–19.

Capaul, Carlo, Ian Rowley, and William Sharpe. 1993. "International Value and Growth Stock Returns." *Financial Analysts Journal*, vol. 49:27–36.

Chen, Kong-Jun, and Xiao-Ming Li. 2006. "Is Technical Analysis Useful for Stock Traders in China? Evidence from the Szse Component A-Share Index." *Pacific Economic Review*, vol. 11, no. 4:477–488.

Chordia, Tarun, Richard Roll, and Avanidhar Subrahmanyam. 2005. "Evidence on the Speed of Convergence to Market Efficiency." *Journal of Financial Economics*, vol. 76, no. 2:271–292.

DeBondt, Werner, and Richard Thaler. 1985. "Does the Stock Market Overreact?" *Journal of Finance*, vol. 40, no. 3:793–808.

Deng, Xiaohu, Sandra Mortal, and Vishal Gupta. 2017. "The Real Effects of Short Selling Constraints: Cross-Country Evidence." Working paper.

Dimson, Elroy, and Carolina Minio-Kozerski. 1999. "Closed-End Funds: A Survey." *Financial Markets, Institutions & Instruments*, vol. 8, no. 2:1–41.

Fama, Eugene F. 1970. "Efficient Capital Markets: A Review of Theory and Empirical Work." *Journal of Finance*, vol. 25, no. 2:383–417.

Fama, Eugene F. 1976. *Foundations of Finance*. New York: Basic Books.

Fama, Eugene F. 1998. "Market Efficiency, Long-Term Returns, and Behavioral Finance." *Journal of Financial Economics*, vol. 50, no. 3:283–306.

Fama, Eugene F., and G. William Schwert. 1977. "Asset Returns and Inflation." *Journal of Financial Economics*, vol. 5, no. 2:115–146.

Fama, Eugene F., and Kenneth R. French. 1988. "Dividend Yields and Expected Stock Returns." *Journal of Financial Economics*, vol. 22, no. 1:3–25.

Fama, Eugene F., and Kenneth R. French. 1995. "Size and Book-to-Market Factors in Earnings and Returns." *Journal of Finance*, vol. 50, no. 1:131–155.

Fama, Eugene F., and Kenneth R. French. 1998. "Value versus Growth: The International Evidence." *Journal of Finance*, vol. 53:1975–1999.

Fama, Eugene F., and Kenneth R. French. 2008. "Dissecting Anomalies." *Journal of Finance*, vol. 63, no. 4:1653–1678.

Fifield, Suzanne, David Power, and C. Donald Sinclair. 2005. "An Analysis of Trading Strategies in Eleven European Stock Markets." *European Journal of Finance*, vol. 11, no. 6:531–548.

Gan, Christopher, Minsoo Lee, Au Yong Hue Hwa, and Jun Zhang. 2005. "Revisiting Share Market Efficiency: Evidence from the New Zealand, Australia, US and Japan Stock Indices." *American Journal of Applied Sciences*, vol. 2, no. 5:996–1002.

Grossman, Sanford J., and Joseph E. Stiglitz. 1980. "On the Impossibility of Informationally Efficient Markets." *American Economic Review*, vol. 70, no. 3:393–408.

Hirshleifer, David. 2001. "Investor Psychology and Asset Pricing." *Journal of Finance*, vol. 56, no. 4:1533–1597.

Hirshleifer, David, and Siew Hong Teoh. 2009. "Thought and Behavior Contagion in Capital Markets." In *Handbook of Financial Markets: Dynamics and Evolution*. Edited by Klaus Reiner Schenk-Hoppe and Thorstein Hens. Amsterdam: North Holland.

Jacobs, Bruce I., and Kenneth N. Levy. 1988. "Calendar Anomalies: Abnormal Returns at Calendar Turning Points." *Financial Analysts Journal*, vol. 44, no. 6:28–39.

Jaffe, Jeffrey. 1974. "Special Information and Insider Trading." *Journal of Business*, vol. 47, no. 3:410–428.

Jegadeesh, Narayan, and Sheridan Titman. 2001. "Profitability of Momentum Strategies: An Evaluation of Alternative Explanations." *Journal of Finance*, vol. 56:699–720.

Johnson, Timothy C. 2002. "Rational Momentum Effects." *Journal of Finance*, vol. 57, no. 2:585–608.

Jones, Charles P., Richard J. Rendleman, and Henry. A. Latané. 1984. "Stock Returns and SUEs during the 1970's." *Journal of Portfolio Management*, vol. 10:18–22.

Kim, Donchoi, and Myungsun Kim. 2003. "A Multifactor Explanation of Post-Earnings Announcement Drift." *Journal of Financial and Quantitative Analysis*, vol. 38, no. 2:383–398.

Kim, Dongcheol. 2006. "On the Information Uncertainty Risk and the January Effect." *Journal of Business*, vol. 79, no. 4:2127–2162.

Lee, Charles M.C., Andrei Sheifer, and Richard H. Thaler. 1990. "Anomalies: Closed-End Mutual Funds." *Journal of Economic Perspectives*, vol. 4, no. 4:153–164.

Malkiel, Burton G. 1995. "Returns from Investing in Equity Mutual Funds 1971 to 1991." *Journal of Finance*, vol. 50:549–572.

Mobarek, Asma, A. Sabur Mollah, and Rafiqul Bhuyan. 2008. "Market Efficiency in Emerging Stock Market." *Journal of Emerging Market Finance*, vol. 7, no. 1:17–41.

Pontiff, Jeffrey. 1995. "Closed-End Fund Premia and Returns: Implications for Financial Market Equilibrium." *Journal of Financial Economics*, vol. 37:341–370.

Pontiff, Jeffrey. 1996. "Costly Arbitrage: Evidence from Closed-End Funds." *Quarterly Journal of Economics*, vol. 111, no. 4:1135–1151.

Raja, M., J. Clement Sudhahar, and M. Selvam. 2009. "Testing the Semi-Strong Form Efficiency of Indian Stock Market with Respect to Information Content of Stock Split Announcement—A Study of IT Industry." *International Research Journal of Finance and Economics*, vol. 25:7–20.

Roll, Richard. 1983. "On Computing Mean Returns and the Small Firm Premium." *Journal of Financial Economics*, vol. 12:371–386.

Rozeff, Michael S., and Mir A. Zaman. 1988. "Market Efficiency and Insider Trading: New Evidence." *Journal of Business*, vol. 61:25–44.

Schwert, G. William. 2003. "Anomalies and Market Efficiency." *Handbook of the Economics of Finance*. Edited by George M. Constantinides, M. Harris, and Rene Stulz. Amsterdam: Elsevier Science, B. V.

Scott, James, Margaret Stumpp, and Peter Xu. 2003. "Overconfidence Bias in International Stock Prices." *Journal of Portfolio Management*, vol. 29, no. 2:80–89.

Tversky, Amos, and Daniel Kahneman. 1981. "The Framing of Decisions and the Psychology of Choice." *Science*, vol. 211, no. 30:453–458.

Yau, Jot, Thomas Schneeweis, Thomas Robinson, and Lisa Weiss. 2007. "Alternative Investments Portfolio Management." *Managing Investment Portfolios: A Dynamic Process*. Hoboken, NJ: John Wiley & Sons.

Zarowin, P. 1989. "Does the Stock Market Overreact to Corporate Earnings Information?" *Journal of Finance*, vol. 44:1385–1399.

PRACTICE PROBLEMS

1 In an efficient market, the change in a company's share price is *most likely* the result of:

A insiders' private information.

B the previous day's change in stock price.

C new information coming into the market.

2 Regulation that restricts some investors from participating in a market will *most likely*:

A impede market efficiency.

B not affect market efficiency.

C contribute to market efficiency.

3 With respect to efficient market theory, when a market allows short selling, the efficiency of the market is *most likely* to:

A increase.

B decrease.

C remain the same.

4 Which of the following regulations will *most likely* contribute to market efficiency? Regulatory restrictions on:

A short selling.

B foreign traders.

C insiders trading with nonpublic information.

5 Which of the following market regulations will *most likely* impede market efficiency?

A Restricting traders' ability to short sell.

B Allowing unrestricted foreign investor trading.

C Penalizing investors who trade with nonpublic information.

6 If markets are efficient, the difference between the intrinsic value and market value of a company's security is:

A negative.

B zero.

C positive.

7 The intrinsic value of an undervalued asset is:

A less than the asset's market value.

B greater than the asset's market value.

C the value at which the asset can currently be bought or sold.

8 The market value of an undervalued asset is:

A greater than the asset's intrinsic value.

B the value at which the asset can currently be bought or sold.

C equal to the present value of all the asset's expected cash flows.

9 With respect to the efficient market hypothesis, if security prices reflect *only* past prices and trading volume information, then the market is:

A weak-form efficient.

B strong-form efficient.

C semi-strong-form efficient.

10 Which one of the following statements *best* describes the semi-strong form of market efficiency?

A Empirical tests examine the historical patterns in security prices.

B Security prices reflect all publicly known and available information.

C Semi-strong-form efficient markets are not necessarily weak-form efficient.

11 If markets are semi-strong efficient, standard fundamental analysis will yield abnormal trading profits that are:

A negative.

B equal to zero.

C positive.

12 If prices reflect all public and private information, the market is *best* described as:

A weak-form efficient.

B strong-form efficient.

C semi-strong-form efficient.

13 If markets are semi-strong-form efficient, then passive portfolio management strategies are *most likely* to:

A earn abnormal returns.

B outperform active trading strategies.

C underperform active trading strategies.

14 If a market is semi-strong-form efficient, the risk-adjusted returns of a passively managed portfolio relative to an actively managed portfolio are *most likely*:

A lower.

B higher.

C the same.

15 Technical analysts assume that markets are:

A weak-form efficient.

B weak-form inefficient.

C semi-strong-form efficient.

16 Fundamental analysts assume that markets are:

A weak-form inefficient.

B semi-strong-form efficient.

C semi-strong-form inefficient.

17 If a market is weak-form efficient but semi-strong-form inefficient, then which of the following types of portfolio management is *most likely* to produce abnormal returns?

A Passive portfolio management.

B Active portfolio management based on technical analysis.

C Active portfolio management based on fundamental analysis.

18 An increase in the time between when an order to trade a security is placed and when the order is executed *most likely* indicates that market efficiency has:

A decreased.

B remained the same.

C increased.

19 With respect to efficient markets, a company whose share price reacts gradually to the public release of its annual report *most likely* indicates that the market where the company trades is:

A semi-strong-form efficient.

B subject to behavioral biases.

C receiving additional information about the company.

20 Which of the following is *least likely* to explain the January effect anomaly?

A Tax-loss selling.

B Release of new information in January.

C Window dressing of portfolio holdings.

21 If a researcher conducting empirical tests of a trading strategy using time series of returns finds statistically significant abnormal returns, then the researcher has *most likely* found:

A a market anomaly.

B evidence of market inefficiency.

C a strategy to produce future abnormal returns.

22 Which of the following market anomalies is inconsistent with weak-form market efficiency?

A Earnings surprise.

B Momentum pattern.

C Closed-end fund discount.

23 Researchers have found that value stocks have consistently outperformed growth stocks. An investor wishing to exploit the value effect should purchase the stock of companies with above-average:

A dividend yields.

B market-to-book ratios.

C price-to-earnings ratios.

24 With respect to rational and irrational investment decisions, the efficient market hypothesis requires:

A only that the market is rational.

B that all investors make rational decisions.

C that some investors make irrational decisions.

25 Observed overreactions in markets can be explained by an investor's degree of:

A risk aversion.

B loss aversion.

C confidence in the market.

26 Like traditional finance models, the behavioral theory of loss aversion assumes that investors dislike risk; however, the dislike of risk in behavioral theory is assumed to be:

A leptokurtic.

B symmetrical.

C asymmetrical.

SOLUTIONS

1 C is correct. Today's price change is independent of the one from yesterday, and in an efficient market, investors will react to new, independent information as it is made public.

2 A is correct. Reducing the number of market participants can accentuate market imperfections and impede market efficiency (e.g., restrictions on foreign investor trading).

3 A is correct. According to theory, reducing the restrictions on trading will allow for more arbitrage trading, thereby promoting more efficient pricing. Although regulators argue that short selling exaggerates downward price movements, empirical research indicates that short selling is helpful in price discovery.

4 C is correct. Regulation to restrict unfair use of nonpublic information encourages greater participation in the market, which increases market efficiency. Regulators (e.g., US SEC) discourage illegal insider trading by issuing penalties to violators of their insider trading rules.

5 A is correct. Restricting short selling will reduce arbitrage trading, which promotes market efficiency. Permitting foreign investor trading increases market participation, which makes markets more efficient. Penalizing insider trading encourages greater market participation, which increases market efficiency.

6 B is correct. A security's intrinsic value and market value should be equal when markets are efficient.

7 B is correct. The intrinsic value of an undervalued asset is greater than the market value of the asset, where the market value is the transaction price at which an asset can be currently bought or sold.

8 B is correct. The market value is the transaction price at which an asset can be currently bought or sold.

9 A is correct. The weak-form efficient market hypothesis is defined as a market where security prices fully reflect all market data, which refers to all past price and trading volume information.

10 B is correct. In semi-strong-form efficient markets, security prices reflect all publicly available information.

11 B is correct. If all public information should already be reflected in the market price, then the abnormal trading profit will be equal to zero when fundamental analysis is used.

12 B is correct. The strong-form efficient market hypothesis assumes all information, public or private, has already been reflected in the prices.

13 B is correct. Costs associated with active trading strategies would be difficult to recover; thus, such active trading strategies would have difficulty outperforming passive strategies on a consistent after-cost basis.

14 B is correct. In a semi-strong-form efficient market, passive portfolio strategies should outperform active portfolio strategies on a risk-adjusted basis.

15 B is correct. Technical analysts use past prices and volume to predict future prices, which is inconsistent with the weakest form of market efficiency (i.e., weak-form market efficiency). Weak-form market efficiency states that investors cannot earn abnormal returns by trading on the basis of past trends in price and volume.

16 C is correct. Fundamental analysts use publicly available information to estimate a security's intrinsic value to determine if the security is mispriced, which is inconsistent with the semi-strong form of market efficiency. Semi-strong-form market efficiency states that investors cannot earn abnormal returns by trading based on publicly available information.

17 C is correct. If markets are not semi-strong-form efficient, then fundamental analysts are able to use publicly available information to estimate a security's intrinsic value and identify misvalued securities. Technical analysis is not able to earn abnormal returns if markets are weak-form efficient. Passive portfolio managers outperform fundamental analysis if markets are semi-strong-form efficient.

18 A is correct. Operating inefficiencies reduce market efficiency.

19 C is correct. If markets are efficient, the information from the annual report is reflected in the stock prices; therefore, the gradual changes must be from the release of additional information.

20 B is correct. The excess returns in January are not attributed to any new information or news; however, research has found that part of the seasonal pattern can be explained by tax-loss selling and portfolio window dressing.

21 A is correct. Finding significant abnormal returns does not necessarily indicate that markets are inefficient or that abnormal returns can be realized by applying the strategy to future time periods. Abnormal returns are considered market anomalies because they may be the result of the model used to estimate the expected returns or may be the result of underestimating transaction costs or other expenses associated with implementing the strategy, rather than because of market inefficiency.

22 B is correct. Trading based on historical momentum indicates that price patterns exist and can be exploited by using historical price information. A momentum trading strategy that produces abnormal returns contradicts the weak form of the efficient market hypothesis, which states that investors cannot earn abnormal returns on the basis of past trends in prices.

23 A is correct. Higher than average dividend yield is a characteristic of a value stock, along with low price-to-earnings and low market-to-book ratios. Growth stocks are characterized by low dividend yields and high price-to-earnings and high market-to-book ratios.

24 A is correct. The efficient market hypothesis and asset-pricing models only require that the market is rational. Behavioral finance is used to explain *some* of the market anomalies as irrational decisions.

25 B is correct. Behavioral theories of loss aversion can explain observed overreaction in markets, such that investors dislike losses more than comparable gains (i.e., risk is not symmetrical).

26 C is correct. Behavioral theories of loss aversion allow for the possibility that the dislike for risk is not symmetrical, which allows for loss aversion to explain observed overreaction in markets such that investors dislike losses more than they like comparable gains.

EQUITY INVESTMENTS

STUDY SESSION 13

Equity Investments (2)

This study session focuses on the characteristics, analysis, and valuation of equity securities. Various equity types including public and private equities are described. The various industry classification approaches for global equities and useful frameworks for conducting industry and individual company analysis are presented. Coverage of the three main equity valuation approaches (present value, multiplier, and asset based) conclude the session.

READING ASSIGNMENTS

Reading 39	Overview of Equity Securities by Ryan C. Fuhrmann, CFA, and Asjeet S. Lamba, PhD, CFA
Reading 40	Introduction to Industry and Company Analysis by Patrick W. Dorsey, CFA, Anthony M. Fiore, CFA, and Ian Rossa O'Reilly, CFA
Reading 41	Equity Valuation: Concepts and Basic Tools by John J. Nagorniak, CFA, and Stephen E. Wilcox, PhD, CFA

READING

39

Overview of Equity Securities

by Ryan C. Fuhrmann, CFA, and Asjeet S. Lamba, PhD, CFA

Ryan C. Fuhrmann, CFA, is at Fuhrmann Capital LLC (USA). Asjeet S. Lamba, PhD, CFA, is at the University of Melbourne (Australia).

LEARNING OUTCOMES

Mastery	The candidate should be able to:
☐	a. describe characteristics of types of equity securities;
☐	b. describe differences in voting rights and other ownership characteristics among different equity classes;
☐	c. distinguish between public and private equity securities;
☐	d. describe methods for investing in non-domestic equity securities;
☐	e. compare the risk and return characteristics of different types of equity securities;
☐	f. explain the role of equity securities in the financing of a company's assets;
☐	g. distinguish between the market value and book value of equity securities;
☐	h. compare a company's cost of equity, its (accounting) return on equity, and investors' required rates of return.

INTRODUCTION

1

Equity securities represent ownership claims on a company's net assets. As an asset class, equity plays a fundamental role in investment analysis and portfolio management because it represents a significant portion of many individual and institutional investment portfolios.

The study of equity securities is important for many reasons. First, the decision on how much of a client's portfolio to allocate to equities affects the risk and return characteristics of the entire portfolio. Second, different types of equity securities have different ownership claims on a company's net assets, which affect their risk and return characteristics in different ways. Finally, variations in the features of equity securities are reflected in their market prices, so it is important to understand the valuation implications of these features.

This reading provides an overview of equity securities and their different features and establishes the background required to analyze and value equity securities in a global context. It addresses the following questions:

- What distinguishes common shares from preference shares, and what purposes do these securities serve in financing a company's operations?
- What are convertible preference shares, and why are they often used to raise equity for unseasoned or highly risky companies?
- What are private equity securities, and how do they differ from public equity securities?
- What are depository receipts and their various types, and what is the rationale for investing in them?
- What are the risk factors involved in investing in equity securities?
- How do equity securities create company value?
- What is the relationship between a company's cost of equity, its return on equity, and investors' required rate of return?

The remainder of this reading is organized as follows. Section 2 provides an overview of global equity markets and their historical performance. Section 3 examines the different types and characteristics of equity securities, and Section 4 outlines the differences between public and private equity securities. Section 5 provides an overview of the various types of equity securities listed and traded in global markets. Section 6 discusses the risk and return characteristics of equity securities. Section 7 examines the role of equity securities in creating company value and the relationship between a company's cost of equity, its return on equity, and investors' required rate of return. The final section summarizes the reading.

2 EQUITY SECURITIES IN GLOBAL FINANCIAL MARKETS

This section highlights the relative importance and performance of equity securities as an asset class. We examine the total market capitalization and trading volume of global equity markets and the prevalence of equity ownership across various geographic regions. We also examine historical returns on equities and compare them to the returns on government bonds and bills.

Exhibit 1 summarizes the contributions of selected countries and geographic regions to global gross domestic product (GDP) and global equity market capitalization. Analysts may examine the relationship between equity market capitalization and GDP as a rough indicator of whether the global equity market (or a specific country's or region's equity market) is under, over, or fairly valued, particularly compared to its long-run average.

Exhibit 1 illustrates the significant value that investors attach to publicly traded equities relative to the sum of goods and services produced globally every year. It shows the continued significance, and the potential over-representation, of US equity markets relative to their contribution to global GDP. That is, while US equity markets contribute around 51 percent to the total capitalization of global equity markets, their contribution to the global GDP is only around 25 percent. Following the stock market turmoil in 2008, however, the market capitalization to GDP ratio of the United States fell to 59 percent, which is significantly lower than its long-run average of 79 percent.

As equity markets outside the United States develop and become increasingly global, their total capitalization levels are expected to grow closer to their respective world GDP contributions. Therefore, it is important to understand and analyze equity securities from a global perspective.

Exhibit 1 Country and Regional Contributions to Global GDP and Equity Market Capitalization (2017)

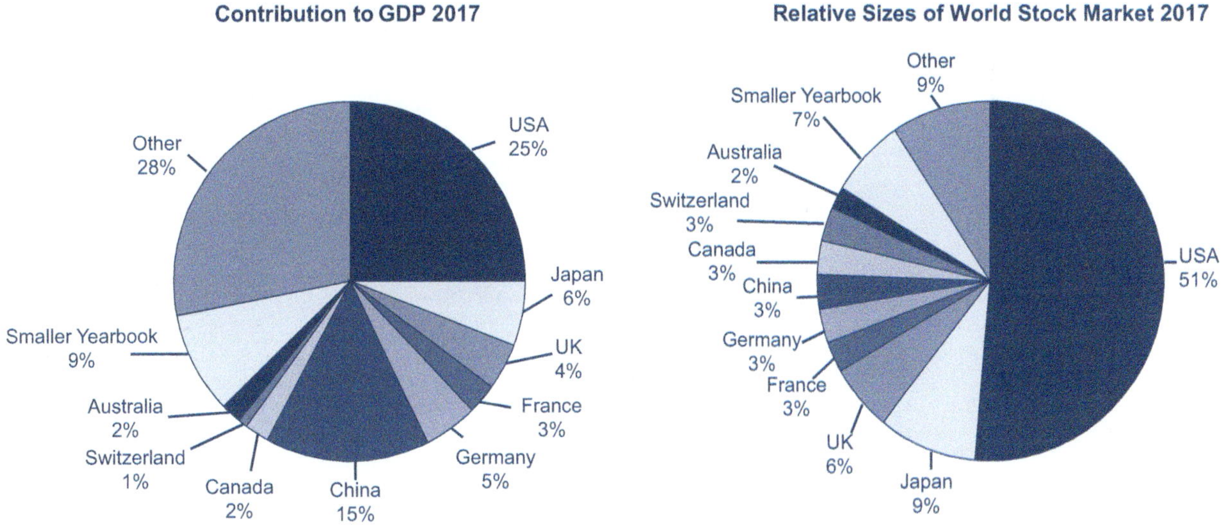

Source: The WorldBank Databank *2017*, and Dimson, Marsh, and Staunton (2018).

Exhibit 2 lists the top 10 equity markets at the end of 2017 based on total market capitalization (in billions of US dollars), trading volume, and the number of listed companies.[1] Note that the rankings differ based on the criteria used. For example, the top three markets based on total market capitalization are the NYSE Euronext (US), NASDAQ OMX, and the Japan Exchange Group; however, the top three markets based on total US dollar trading volume are the Nasdaq OMX, NYSE Euronext (US), and the Shenzhen Stock Exchange, respectively.[2]

Exhibit 2 Equity Markets Ranked by Total Market Capitalization at the End of 2017 (Billions of US Dollars)

Rank	Name of Market	Total US Dollar Market Capitalization	Total US Dollar Trading Volume	Number of Listed Companies
1	NYSE Euronext (US)	$22,081.4	$16,140.1	2,286
2	NASDAQ OMX	$10,039.4	$33,407.1	2,949
3	Japan Exchange Group[a]	$6,220.0	$6,612.1	3,604

(continued)

1 The market capitalization of an individual stock is computed as the share price multiplied by the number of shares outstanding. The total market capitalization of an equity market is the sum of the market capitalizations of each individual stock listed on that market. Similarly, the total trading volume of an equity market is computed by value weighting the total trading volume of each individual stock listed on that market. Total dollar trading volume is computed as the average share price multiplied by the number of shares traded.
2 NASDAQ is the acronym for the National Association of Securities Dealers Automated Quotations.

Exhibit 2 (Continued)

Rank	Name of Market	Total US Dollar Market Capitalization	Total US Dollar Trading Volume	Number of Listed Companies
4	Shanghai Stock Exchange	$5,084.4	$7,589.3	1,396
5	Euronext[b]	$4,393.0	$1,981.6	1,255
6	Hong Kong Exchanges	$4,350.5	$1,958.8	2,118
7	Shenzhen Stock Exchanges	$3,617.9	$9,219.7	2,089
8	National Stock Exchange of India	$2,351.5	$1,013.3	1,897
9	BSE Limited[c]	$2,331.6	$183.0	5,616
10	Deutsche Börse	$2,262.2	$1,497.9	499

Notes:

[a] Japan Exchange Group is the merged entity containing the Tokyo Stock Exchange and Osaka Securities Exchange.

[b] From 2001, includes Netherlands, France, England, Belgium, and Portugal.

[c] Bombay Stock Exchange.

Source: Adapted from the *World Federation of Exchanges 2017 Report* (see http://www.world-exchanges.org). Note that market capitalization by company is calculated by multiplying its stock price by the number of shares outstanding. The market's overall capitalization is the aggregate of the market capitalizations of all companies traded on that market. The number of listed companies includes both domestic and foreign companies whose shares trade on these markets.

Exhibit 3 compares the *real* (or inflation-adjusted) compounded returns on government bonds, government bills, and equity securities in 21 countries plus the world index ("Wld"), the world ex-US ("WxU"), and Europe ("Eur") during the 118 years 1900–2017.[3] In real terms, government bonds and bills have essentially kept pace with the inflation rate, earning annualized real returns of less than 2 percent in most countries.[4] By comparison, real returns in equity markets have generally been around 3.5 percent per year in most markets—with a world average return of around 5.2 percent and a world average return excluding the United States just under 5 percent. During this period, South Africa and Australia were the best performing markets followed by the United States, New Zealand, and Sweden.

3 The real return for a security is approximated by taking the nominal return and subtracting the observed inflation rate in that country.

4 The exceptions are Austria, Belgium, Finland, France, Germany, Portugal, and Italy—where the average real returns on government bonds and/or bills have been negative. In general, that performance reflects the very high inflation rates in these countries during the World War years.

Exhibit 3 Real Returns on Global Equity Securities, Bonds, and Bills During 1900–2017

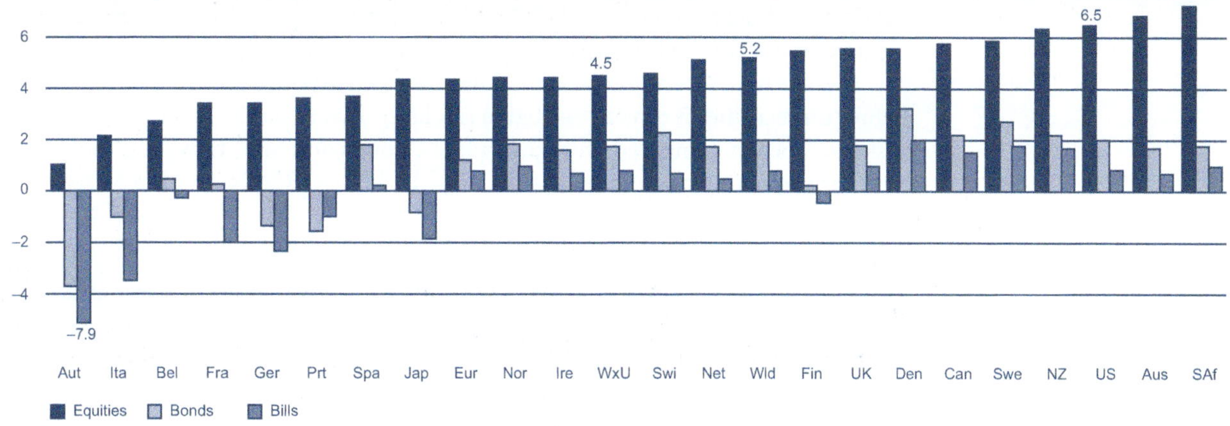

Source: Dimson, Marsh, and Staunton (2018).

Exhibit 4 shows the annualized real returns on major asset classes for the world index over 1900–2017.

Exhibit 4 Annualized Real Returns on Asset Classes for the World Index, 1900–2017

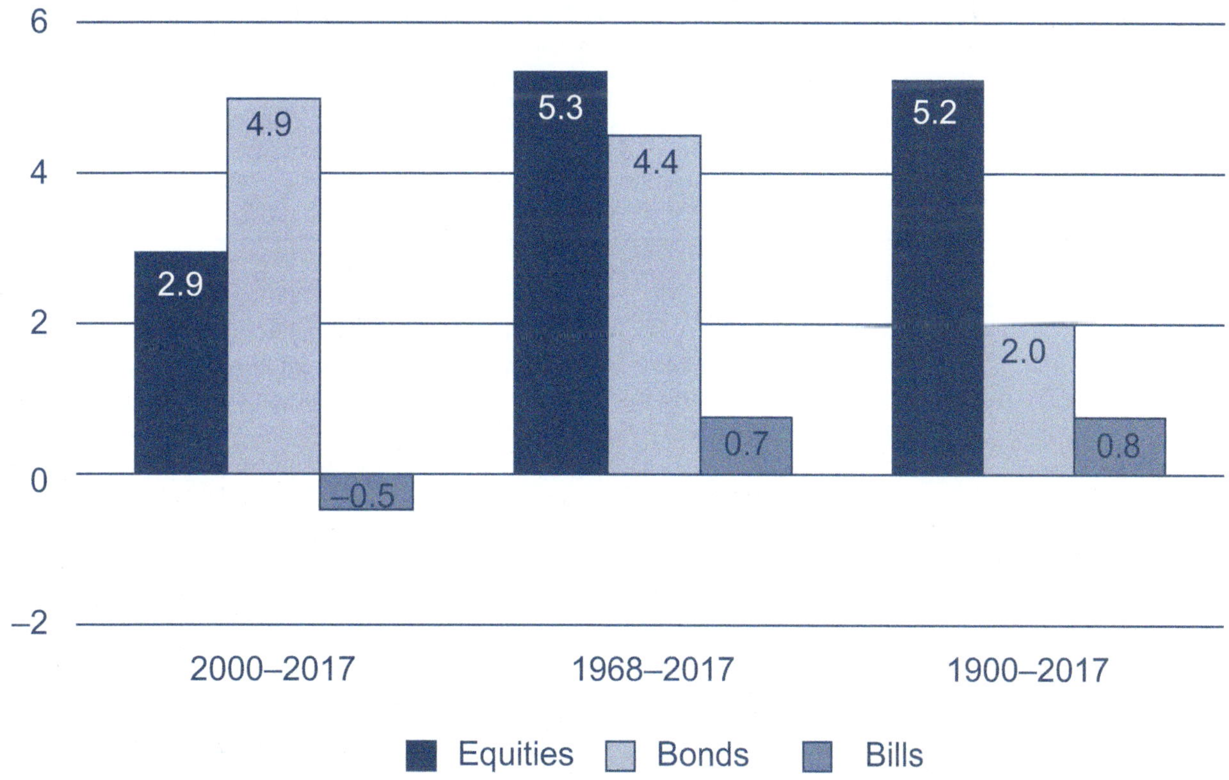

Source: Dimson, Marsh, and Staunton (2018).

The volatility in asset market returns is further highlighted in Exhibit 5, which shows the annualized risk premia for equity relative to bonds (EP Bonds), and equity relative to treasury bills (EP Bills). Maturity premium for government bond returns relative to treasury bill returns (Mat Prem) is also shown.

These observations and historical data are consistent with the concept that the return on securities is directly related to risk level. That is, equity securities have higher risk levels when compared with government bonds and bills, they earn higher rates of return to compensate investors for these higher risk levels, and they also tend to be more volatile over time.

Exhibit 5 Annualized Real Returns on Asset Classes and Risk Premiums for the World Index since 1900–2017

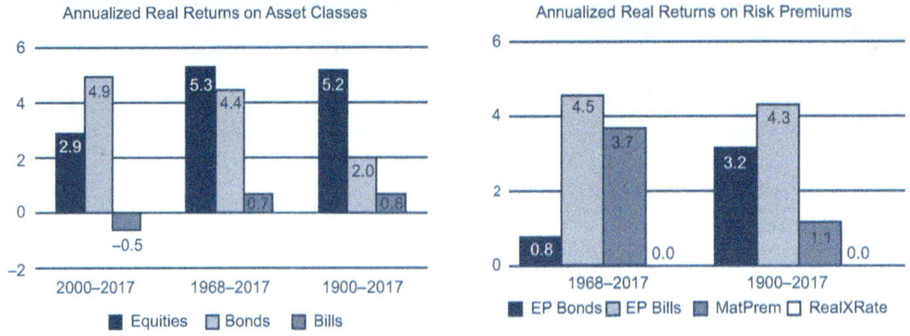

Notes: Equities are total returns, including reinvested dividend income. Bonds are total return, including reinvested coupons, on long-term government bonds. Bills denotes the total return, including any income, from Treasury bills. All returns are adjusted for inflation and are expressed as geometric mean returns. EP bonds denotes the equity risk premium relative to long-term government bonds. EP Bills denotes the equity premium relative to Treasury bills. MatPrem denotes the maturity premium for government bond returns relative to bill returns. RealXRate denotes the real (inflation-adjusted) change in the exchange rate against the US dollar.
Source: Dimson, Marsh, and Staunton (2018).

Given the high risk levels associated with equity securities, it is reasonable to expect that investors' tolerance for risk will tend to differ across equity markets. This is illustrated in Exhibit 6, which shows the results of a series of studies conducted by the Australian Securities Exchange on international differences in equity ownership. During the 2004–2014 period, equity ownership as a percentage of the population was lowest in South Korea (averaging 9.0 percent), followed by Germany (14.5 percent) and Sweden (17.7 percent). In contrast, Australia and New Zealand had the highest equity ownership as a percentage of the population (averaging more than 20 percent). In addition, there has been a relative decline in share ownership in several countries over recent years, which is not surprising given the recent overall uncertainty in global economies and the volatility in equity markets that this uncertainty has created.

Exhibit 6 International Comparisons of Stock Ownership: 2004–2014[5]

	2004	2006	2008	2010	2012	2014
Australia – Direct/ Indirect	55%	46%	41%	43%	38%	36%
South Korea – Shares	8	7	10	10	10	N/A
Germany – Shares/ Funds	16	16	14	13	15	13
Sweden – Shares	22	20	18	17	15	14
United Kingdom – Shares/Funds	22	20	18	N/A	17	N/A
New Zealand – Direct	23	26	N/A	22	23	26

Source: Adapted from the *2014 Australian Share Ownership Study* conducted by the Australian Securities Exchange (see http://www.asx.com.au). For Australia and the United States, the data pertain to direct and indirect ownership in equity markets; for other countries, the data pertain to direct ownership in shares and share funds. Data not available in specific years are shown as "N/A."

An important implication from the above discussion is that equity securities represent a key asset class for global investors because of their unique return and risk characteristics. We next examine the various types of equity securities traded on global markets and their salient characteristics.

TYPES AND CHARACTERISTICS OF EQUITY SECURITIES

3

Companies finance their operations by issuing either debt or equity securities. A key difference between these securities is that debt is a liability of the issuing company, whereas equity is not. This means that when a company issues debt, it is contractually obligated to repay the amount it borrows (i.e., the principal or face value of the debt) at a specified future date. The cost of using these funds is called interest, which the company is contractually obligated to pay until the debt matures or is retired.

When the company issues equity securities, it is not contractually obligated to repay the amount it receives from shareholders, nor is it contractually obligated to make periodic payments to shareholders for the use of their funds. Instead, shareholders have a claim on the company's assets after all liabilities have been paid. Because of this residual claim, equity shareholders are considered to be owners of the company. Investors who purchase equity securities are seeking total return (i.e., capital or price appreciation and dividend income), whereas investors who purchase debt securities (and hold until maturity) are seeking interest income. As a result, equity investors expect the company's management to act in their best interest by making operating decisions that will maximize the market price of their shares (i.e., shareholder wealth).

5 The percentages reported in the exhibit are based on samples of the adult population in each country who own equity securities either directly or indirectly through investment or retirement funds. For example, 36 percent of the adult population of Australia in 2014 (approximately 6.5 million people) owned equity securities either directly or indirectly. As noted in the study, it is not appropriate to make absolute comparisons across countries given the differences in methodology, sampling, timing, and definitions that have been used in different countries. However, trends across different countries can be identified.

In addition to common shares (also known as ordinary shares or common stock), companies may also issue preference shares (also known as preferred stock), the other type of equity security. The following sections discuss the different types and characteristics of common and preference securities.

3.1 Common Shares

Common shares represent an ownership interest in a company and are the predominant type of equity security. As a result, investors share in the operating performance of the company, participate in the governance process through voting rights, and have a claim on the company's net assets in the case of liquidation. Companies may choose to pay out some, or all, of their net income in the form of cash dividends to common shareholders, but they are not contractually obligated to do so.[6]

Voting rights provide shareholders with the opportunity to participate in major corporate governance decisions, including the election of its board of directors, the decision to merge with or take over another company, and the selection of outside auditors. Shareholder voting generally takes place during a company's annual meeting. As a result of geographic limitations and the large number of shareholders, it is often not feasible for shareholders to attend the annual meeting in person. For this reason, shareholders may **vote by proxy**, which allows a designated party—such as another shareholder, a shareholder representative, or management—to vote on the shareholders' behalf.

Regular shareholder voting, where each share represents one vote, is referred to as **statutory voting**. Although it is the common method of voting, it is not always the most appropriate one to use to elect a board of directors. To better serve shareholders who own a small number of shares, **cumulative voting** is often used. Cumulative voting allows shareholders to direct their total voting rights to specific candidates, as opposed to having to allocate their voting rights evenly among all candidates. Total voting rights are based on the number of shares owned multiplied by the number of board directors being elected. For example, under cumulative voting, if four board directors are to be elected, a shareholder who owns 100 shares is entitled to 400 votes and can either cast all 400 votes in favor of a single candidate or spread them across the candidates in any proportion. In contrast, under statutory voting, a shareholder would be able to cast only a maximum of 100 votes for each candidate.

The key benefit to cumulative voting is that it allows shareholders with a small number of shares to apply all of their votes to one candidate, thus providing the opportunity for a higher level of representation on the board than would be allowed under statutory voting.

Exhibit 7 describes the rights of Viacom Corporation's shareholders. In this case, a dual-share arrangement allows the founding chairman and his family to control more than 70 percent of the voting rights through the ownership of Class A shares. This arrangement gives them the ability to exert control over the board of director election process, corporate decision making, and other important aspects of managing the company. A cumulative voting arrangement for any minority shareholders of Class A shares would improve their board representation.

6 It is also possible for companies to pay more than the current period's net income as dividends. Such payout policies are, however, generally not sustainable in the long run.

Exhibit 7 Share Class Arrangements at Viacom Corporation[7]

Viacom has two classes of common stock: Class A, which is the voting stock, and Class B, which is the non-voting stock. There is no difference between the two classes except for voting rights; they generally trade within a close price range of each other. There are, however, far more shares of Class B outstanding, so most of the trading occurs in that class.

- **Voting Rights**—Holders of Class A common stock are entitled to one vote per share. Holders of Class B common stock do not have any voting rights, except as required by Delaware law. Generally, all matters to be voted on by Viacom stockholders must be approved by a majority of the aggregate voting power of the shares of Class A common stock present in person or represented by proxy, except as required by Delaware law.
- **Dividends**—Stockholders of Class A common stock and Class B common stock will share ratably in any cash dividend declared by the Board of Directors, subject to any preferential rights of any outstanding preferred stock. Viacom does not currently pay a cash dividend, and any decision to pay a cash dividend in the future will be at the discretion of the Board of Directors and will depend on many factors.
- **Conversion**—So long as there are 5,000 shares of Class A common stock outstanding, each share of Class A common stock will be convertible at the option of the holder of such share into one share of Class B common stock.
- **Liquidation Rights**—In the event of liquidation, dissolution, or winding-up of Viacom, all stockholders of common stock, regardless of class, will be entitled to share ratably in any assets available for distributions to stockholders of shares of Viacom common stock subject to the preferential rights of any outstanding preferred stock.
- **Split, Subdivision, or Combination**—In the event of a split, subdivision, or combination of the outstanding shares of Class A common stock or Class B common stock, the outstanding shares of the other class of common stock will be divided proportionally.
- **Preemptive Rights**—Shares of Class A common stock and Class B common stock do not entitle a stockholder to any preemptive rights enabling a stockholder to subscribe for or receive shares of stock of any class or any other securities convertible into shares of stock of any class of Viacom.

As seen in Exhibit 7, companies can issue different classes of common shares (Class A and Class B shares), with each class offering different ownership rights.[8] For example, as shown in Exhibit 8, the Ford Motor Company has Class A shares ("Common Stock"), which are owned by the investing public. It also has Class B shares, which are owned only by the Ford family. The exhibit contains an excerpt from Ford's *2017 Annual Report* (p. 144). Class A shareholders have 60 percent voting rights, whereas Class B shareholders have 40 percent. In the case of liquidation, however, Class B shareholders will not only receive the first US$0.50 per share that is available for

7 This information has been adapted from Viacom's investor relations website and its 10-K filing with the US Securities and Exchange Commission; see www.viacom.com.

8 In some countries, including the United States, companies can issue different classes of shares, with Class A shares being the most common. The role and function of different classes of shares is described in more detail in Exhibit 8.

distribution (as will Class A shareholders), but they will also receive the next US$1.00 per share that is available for distribution before Class A shareholders receive anything else. Thus, Class B shareholders have an opportunity to receive a larger proportion of distributions upon liquidation than do Class A shareholders.[9]

Exhibit 8 Share Class Arrangements at Ford Motor Company[10]

NOTE 21. CAPITAL STOCK AND AMOUNTS PER SHARE

All general voting power is vested in the holders of Common Stock and Class B Stock. Holders of our Common Stock have 60% of the general voting power and holders of our Class B Stock are entitled to such number of votes per share as will give them the remaining 40%. Shares of Common Stock and Class B Stock share equally in dividends when and as paid, with stock dividends payable in shares of stock of the class held.

If liquidated, each share of Common Stock is entitled to the first $0.50 available for distribution to holders of Common Stock and Class B Stock, each share of Class B Stock is entitled to the next $1.00 so available, each share of Common Stock is entitled to the next $0.50 so available, and each share of Common and Class B Stock is entitled to an equal amount thereafter.

3.2 Preference Shares

Preference shares (or preferred stock) rank above common shares with respect to the payment of dividends and the distribution of the company's net assets upon liquidation.[11] However, preference shareholders generally do not share in the operating performance of the company and do not have any voting rights, unless explicitly allowed for at issuance. Preference shares have characteristics of both debt securities and common shares. Similar to the interest payments on debt securities, the dividends on preference shares are fixed and are generally higher than the dividends on common shares. However, unlike interest payments, preference dividends are not contractual obligations of the company. Similar to common shares, preference shares can be perpetual (i.e., no fixed maturity date), can pay dividends indefinitely, and can be callable or putable.

Exhibit 9 provides an example of callable preference shares issued by the GDL Fund to raise capital to redeem the remaining outstanding Series B Preferred shares. In this case, the purchaser of the shares will receive an ongoing dividend from the GDL Fund. If the GDL Fund chooses to buy back the shares, it must do so at the $50 a share liquidation preference price. The purchasers of the shares also have the right to put back the shares to GDL at the $50 a share price.

9 For example, if US$2.00 per share is available for distribution, the Common Stock (Class A) shareholders will receive US$0.50 per share, while the Class B shareholders will receive US$1.50 per share. However, if there is US$3.50 per share available for distribution, the Common Stock shareholders will receive a total of US$1.50 per share and the Class B shareholders will receive a total of US$2.00 per share.

10 Extracted from Ford Motor Company's *2017 Annual Report* (http://s22.q4cdn.com/857684434/files/doc_financials/2017/annual/Final-Annual-Report-2017.pdf).

11 Preference shares have a lower priority than debt in the case of liquidation. That is, debt holders have a higher claim on a firm's assets in the event of liquidation and will receive what is owed to them first, followed by preference shareholders and then common shareholders.

Exhibit 9 Callable Stock offering by the GDL Fund[12]

RYE, NY—March 26, 2018—The GDL Fund (NYSE:GDL) (the "Fund") is pleased to announce the completion of a rights offering (the "Offering") in which the Fund issued 2,624,025 Series C Cumulative Puttable and Callable Preferred Shares (the "Series C Preferred"), totaling $131,201,250. Pursuant to the Offering, the Fund issued one non-transferable right (a "Right") for each outstanding Series B Cumulative Puttable and Callable Preferred Share (the "Series B Preferred") of the Fund to Series B Preferred shareholders of record as of February 14, 2018. Holders of Rights were entitled to purchase the Series C Preferred with any combination of cash or surrender of the Series B Preferred at liquidation preference. Therefore, one Right plus $50.00, or one Right plus one share of Series B Preferred with a liquidation value of $50.00 per share, was required to purchase each share of the Series C Preferred. The Offering expired at 5:00 PM Eastern Time on March 20, 2018.

Dividends on preference shares can be cumulative, non-cumulative, participating, non-participating, or some combination thereof (i.e., cumulative participating, cumulative non-participating, non-cumulative participating, non-cumulative non-participating).

Dividends on **cumulative preference shares** accrue so that if the company decides not to pay a dividend in one or more periods, the unpaid dividends accrue and must be paid in full before dividends on common shares can be paid. In contrast, **non-cumulative preference shares** have no such provision. This means that any dividends that are not paid in the current or subsequent periods are forfeited permanently and are not accrued over time to be paid at a later date. However, the company is still not permitted to pay any dividends to common shareholders in the current period unless preferred dividends have been paid first.

Participating preference shares entitle the shareholders to receive the standard preferred dividend plus the opportunity to receive an additional dividend if the company's profits exceed a pre-specified level. In addition, participating preference shares can also contain provisions that entitle shareholders to an additional distribution of the company's assets upon liquidation, above the par (or face) value of the preference shares. **Non-participating preference shares** do not allow shareholders to share in the profits of the company. Instead, shareholders are entitled to receive only a fixed dividend payment and the par value of the shares in the event of liquidation. The use of participating preference shares is much more common for smaller, riskier companies where the possibility of future liquidation is more of a concern to investors.

Preference shares can also be convertible. **Convertible preference shares** entitle shareholders to convert their shares into a specified number of common shares. This conversion ratio is determined at issuance. Convertible preference shares have the following advantages:

- They allow investors to earn a higher dividend than if they invested in the company's common shares.
- They allow investors the opportunity to share in the profits of the company.
- They allow investors to benefit from a rise in the price of the common shares through the conversion option.
- Their price is less volatile than the underlying common shares because the dividend payments are known and more stable.

12 https://www.businesswire.com/news/home/20180326005609/en/GDL-Fund-Successfully-Completes-Offering-Issues-131

As a result, the use of convertible preference shares is a popular financing option in venture capital and private equity transactions in which the issuing companies are considered to be of higher risk and when it may be years before the issuing company "goes public" (i.e., issues common shares to the public).

Exhibit 10 provides examples of the types and characteristics of preference shares as issued by Tsakos Energy Navigation Ltd (TNP.PRE).

Exhibit 10 Examples of Preference Shares Issued by TEN Ltd[13]

Athens, Greece, June 21, 2018—TEN Ltd. ("TEN") (NYSE: TNP), a leading diversified crude, product and LNG tanker operator, today announced the pricing of its public offering of its Series F Fixed-to-Floating Rate Cumulative Redeemable Perpetual Preferred Shares, par value $1.00 per share, liquidation preference $25.00 per share ("Series F Preferred Shares"). TEN will issue 5,400,000 Series F Preferred Shares at a price to the public of $25.00 per share. Dividends will be payable on the Series F Preferred Shares to July 30, 2028 at a fixed rate equal to 9.50% per annum and from July 30, 2028, if not redeemed, at a floating rate. In connection with the offering, TEN has granted the underwriters a 30-day option to purchase 810,000 additional Series F Preferred Shares, which, if exercised in full, would result in total gross proceeds of $155,250,000. TEN intends to use the net proceeds from the offering for general corporate purposes, which may include making vessel acquisitions and/or strategic investments and preferred share redemptions. Following the offering, TEN intends to file an application to list the Series F Preferred Shares on the New York Stock Exchange. The offering is expected to close on or about June 28, 2018.

4 PRIVATE VERSUS PUBLIC EQUITY SECURITIES

Our discussion so far has focused on equity securities that are issued and traded in public markets and on exchanges. Equity securities can also be issued and traded in private equity markets. **Private equity securities** are issued primarily to institutional investors via non-public offerings, such as private placements. Because they are not listed on public exchanges, there is no active secondary market for these securities. As a result, private equity securities do not have "market determined" quoted prices, are highly illiquid, and require negotiations between investors in order to be traded. In addition, financial statements and other important information needed to determine the fair value of private equity securities may be difficult to obtain because the issuing companies are typically not required by regulatory authorities to publish this information.

There are three primary types of private equity investments: venture capital, leveraged buyouts, and private investment in public equity (or PIPE). **Venture capital** investments provide "seed" or start-up capital, early-stage financing, or mezzanine financing to companies that are in the early stages of development and require additional capital for expansion. These funds are then used to finance the company's product development and growth. Venture capitalists range from family and friends to wealthy individuals and private equity funds. Because the equity securities issued to venture capitalists are not publicly traded, they generally require a commitment of funds for a relatively long period of time; the opportunity to "exit" the investment is typically

13 https://www.tenn.gr/wp-content/uploads/2018/06/tenn062118.pdf

within 3 to 10 years from the initial start-up. The exit return earned by these private equity investors is based on the price that the securities can be sold for if and when the start-up company first goes public, either via an **initial public offering** (IPO) on the stock market or by being sold to other investors.

A **leveraged buyout** (LBO) occurs when a group of investors (such as the company's management or a private equity partnership) uses a large amount of debt to purchase all of the outstanding common shares of a publicly traded company. In cases where the group of investors acquiring the company is primarily comprised of the company's existing management, the transaction is referred to as a **management buyout** (MBO). After the shares are purchased, they cease to trade on an exchange and the investor group takes full control of the company. In other words, the company is taken "private" or has been privatized. Companies that are candidates for these types of transactions generally have large amounts of undervalued assets (which can be sold to reduce debt) and generate high levels of cash flows (which are used to make interest and principal payments on the debt). The ultimate objective of a buyout (LBO or MBO) is to restructure the acquired company and later take it "public" again by issuing new shares to the public in the primary market.

The third type of private investment is a **private investment in public equity**, or PIPE.[14] This type of investment is generally sought by a public company that is in need of additional capital quickly and is willing to sell a sizeable ownership position to a private investor or investor group. For example, a company may require a large investment of new equity funds in a short period of time because it has significant expansion opportunities, is facing high levels of indebtedness, or is experiencing a rapid deterioration in its operations. Depending on how urgent the need is and the size of the capital requirement, the private investor may be able to purchase shares in the company at a significant discount to the publicly-quoted market price. Exhibit 11 contains a recent PIPE transaction for the health care company TapImmune, which also included the proposed merger with Maker Therapeutics.

Exhibit 11 Example of a PIPE Transaction[15]

JACKSONVILLE, Florida, June 8, 2018—TapImmune Inc. (NASDAQ: TPIV), a clinical-stage immuno-oncology company, today announced that it has entered into security purchase agreements with certain institutional and accredited investors in connection with a private placement of its equity securities. The private placement will be led by New Enterprise Associates (NEA) with participation from Aisling Capital and Perceptive Advisors, among other new and existing investors. The private placement is expected to be completed concurrently with the closing of the proposed merger between TapImmune Inc. and Marker Therapeutics, Inc., which was previously announced on May 15, 2018.

Upon closing the private placement, TapImmune will issue 17,500,000 shares of its common stock at a price of $4.00 per share. The aggregate offering size, before deducting the placement agent fees and other offering expenses, is expected to be $70 million. Additionally, TapImmune will issue warrants to purchase 13,125,000 shares of TapImmune common stock at an exercise price of $5.00 per share that will be exercisable for a period of five years from the date of issuance. The closing of the transaction, which is subject to the closing of the

(continued)

14 The term PIPE is widely used in the United States and is also used internationally, including in emerging markets.

15 https://tapimmune.com/2018/06/tapimmune-announces-pricing-of-70-million-private-placement/

Exhibit 11 (Continued)

merger with Marker, the approval by TapImmune's stockholders as required by NASDAQ Stock Market Rules, and other customary closing conditions, is anticipated to occur by the end of the third quarter of 2018.

While the global private equity market is relatively small in comparison to the global public equity market, it has experienced considerable growth over the past three decades. According to a study of the private equity market sponsored by the *World Economic Forum* and spanning the period 1970–2007, approximately US$3.6 trillion in debt and equity were acquired in leveraged buyouts. Of this amount, approximately 75 percent or US$2.7 trillion worth of transactions occurred during 2001–2007.[16] This pace continued with a further US$2.9 trillion in transactions occurring during 2008-2017.[17] While the US and the UK markets were the focus of most private equity investments during the 1980s and 1990s, private equity investments outside of these markets have grown substantially in recent years. In addition, the number of companies operating under private equity ownership has also grown. For example, during the mid-1990s, fewer than 2,000 companies were under LBO ownership compared to more than 20,000 companies that were under LBO ownership globally at the beginning of 2017. The holding period for private equity investments has also increased during this time period from 3 to 5 years (1980s and 1990s) to approximately 10 years.[18]

The move to longer holding periods has given private equity investors the opportunity to more effectively and patiently address any underlying operational issues facing the company and to better manage it for long-term value creation. Because of the longer holding periods, more private equity firms are issuing convertible preference shares because they provide investors with greater total return potential through their dividend payments and the ability to convert their shares into common shares during an IPO.

In operating a publicly traded company, management often feels pressured to focus on short-term results[19] (e.g., meeting quarterly sales and earnings targets from analysts biased toward near-term price performance) instead of operating the company to obtain long-term sustainable revenue and earnings growth. By "going private," management can adopt a more long-term focus and can eliminate certain costs that are necessary to operate a publicly traded company—such as the cost of meeting regulatory and stock exchange filing requirements, the cost of maintaining investor relations departments to communicate with shareholders and the media, and the cost of holding quarterly analyst conference calls.

As described above, public equity markets are much larger than private equity networks and allow companies more opportunities to raise capital that is subsequently actively traded in secondary markets. By operating under public scrutiny, companies are incentivized to be more open in terms of corporate governance and executive compensation to ensure that they are acting for the benefit of shareholders. In fact, some studies have shown that private equity firms score lower in terms of corporate governance effectiveness, which may be attributed to the fact that shareholders, analysts, and other stakeholders are able to influence management when corporate governance and other policies are public.

16 Stromberg (2008).
17 https://www.statista.com/statistics/270195/global-private-equity-deal-value/
18 See, for example, Bailey, Wirth, and Zapol (2005).
19 See, for example, Graham, Harvey, and Rajgopal (2005).

INVESTING IN NON-DOMESTIC EQUITY SECURITIES

5

Technological innovations and the growth of electronic information exchanges (electronic trading networks, the internet, etc.) have accelerated the integration and growth of global financial markets. As detailed previously, global capital markets have expanded at a much more rapid rate than global GDP in recent years; both primary and secondary international markets have benefited from the enhanced ability to rapidly and openly exchange information. Increased integration of equity markets has made it easier and less expensive for companies to raise capital and to expand their shareholder base beyond their local market. Integration has also made it easier for investors to invest in companies that are located outside of their domestic markets. This has enabled investors to further diversify and improve the risk and return characteristics of their portfolios by adding a class of assets with lower correlations to local country assets.

One barrier to investing globally is that many countries still impose "foreign restrictions" on individuals and companies from other countries that want to invest in their domestic companies. There are three primary reasons for these restrictions. The first is to limit the amount of control that foreign investors can exert on domestic companies. For example, some countries prevent foreign investors from acquiring a majority interest in domestic companies. The second is to give domestic investors the opportunity to own shares in the foreign companies that are conducting business in their country. For example, the Swedish home furnishings retailer IKEA abandoned efforts to invest in parts of the Asia/Pacific region because local governments did not want IKEA to maintain complete ownership of its stores. The third reason is to reduce the volatility of capital flows into and out of domestic equity markets. For example, one of the main consequences of the Asian Financial Crisis in 1997–98 was the large outflow of capital from such emerging market countries as Thailand, Indonesia, and South Korea. These outflows led to dramatic declines in the equity markets of these countries and significant currency devaluations and resulted in many governments placing restrictions on capital flows. Today, many of these same markets have built up currency reserves to better withstand capital outflows inherent in economic contractions and periods of financial market turmoil.

Studies have shown that reducing restrictions on foreign ownership has led to improved equity market performance over the long term.[20] Although restrictions vary widely, more countries are allowing increasing levels of foreign ownership. For example, Australia has sought tax reforms as a means to encourage international demand for its managed funds in order to increase its role as an international financial center.

Over the past two decades, three trends have emerged: a) an increasing number of companies have issued shares in markets outside of their home country; b) the number of companies whose shares are traded in markets outside of their home has increased; and c) an increasing number of companies are dual listed, which means that their shares are simultaneously issued and traded in two or more markets. Companies located in emerging markets have particularly benefited from these trends because they no longer have to be concerned with capital constraints or lack of liquidity in their domestic markets. These companies have found it easier to raise capital in the markets of developed countries because these markets generally have higher levels of liquidity and more stringent financial reporting requirements and accounting standards. Being listed on an international exchange has a number of benefits. It can increase

20 See, for example, Henry and Chari (2004).

investor awareness about the company's products and services, enhance the liquidity of the company's shares, and increase corporate transparency because of the additional market exposure and the need to meet a greater number of filing requirements.

Technological advancements have made it easier for investors to trade shares in foreign markets. The German insurance company Allianz SE recently delisted its shares from the NYSE and certain European markets because international investors increasingly traded its shares on the Frankfurt Stock Exchange. Exhibit 12 illustrates the extent to which the institutional shareholder base at BASF, a large German chemical corporation, has become increasingly global in nature.

Exhibit 12 Example of Increased Globalization of Share Ownership[21]

BASF is one of the largest publicly owned companies with over 500,000 shareholders and a high free float. An analysis of the shareholder structure carried out in March 2018 showed that, at 21% of share capital, the United States and Canada made up the largest regional group of institutional investors. Institutional investors from Germany made up 12%. Shareholders from United Kingdom and Ireland held 12% of BASF shares, while a further 17% are held by institutional investors from the rest of Europe. Around 28% of the company's share capital is held by private investors, most of whom are resident in Germany.

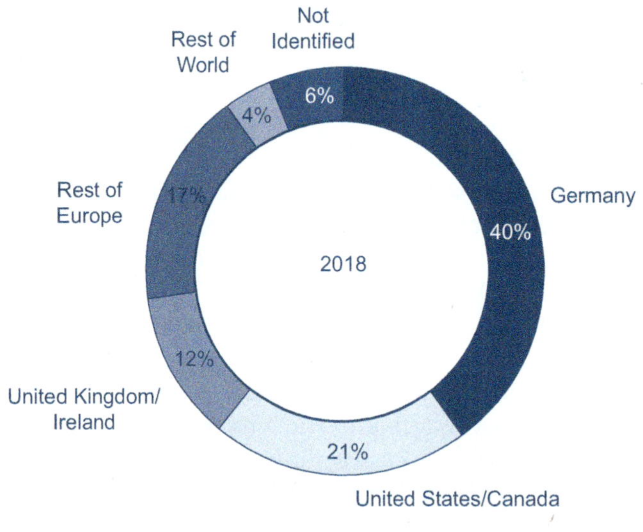

5.1 Direct Investing

Investors can use a variety of methods to invest in the equity of companies outside of their local market. The most obvious is to buy and sell securities directly in foreign markets. However, this means that all transactions—including the purchase and sale of shares, dividend payments, and capital gains—are in the company's, not the investor's, domestic currency. In addition, investors must be familiar with the trading, clearing, and settlement regulations and procedures of that market. Investing directly often results in less transparency and more volatility because audited financial information may not be provided on a regular basis and the market may be less liquid. Alternatively, investors can use such securities as depository receipts and global registered shares, which represent the equity of international companies and are traded on local exchanges

21 Adapted from BASF's investor relations website (www.basf.com). **Free float** refers to the extent that shares are readily and freely tradable in the secondary market.

and in the local currencies. With these securities, investors have to worry less about currency conversions (price quotations and dividend payments are in the investor's local currency), unfamiliar market practices, and differences in accounting standards. The sections that follow discuss various securities that investors can invest in outside of their home market.

5.2 Depository Receipts

A **depository receipt**[22] (DR) is a security that trades like an ordinary share on a local exchange and represents an economic interest in a foreign company. It allows the publicly listed shares of a foreign company to be traded on an exchange outside its domestic market. A depository receipt is created when the equity shares of a foreign company are deposited in a bank (i.e., the depository) in the country on whose exchange the shares will trade. The depository then issues receipts that represent the shares that were deposited. The number of receipts issued and the price of each DR is based on a ratio, which specifies the number of depository receipts to the underlying shares. Consequently, a DR may represent one share of the underlying stock, many shares of the underlying stock, or a fractional share of the underlying stock. The price of each DR will be affected by factors that affect the price of the underlying shares, such as company fundamentals, market conditions, analysts' recommendations, and exchange rate movements. In addition, any short-term valuation discrepancies between shares traded on multiple exchanges represent a quick arbitrage profit opportunity for astute traders to exploit. The responsibilities of the **depository bank** that issues the receipts include acting as custodian and as a registrar. This entails handling dividend payments, other taxable events, stock splits, and serving as the transfer agent for the foreign company whose securities the DR represents. The Bank of New York Mellon is the largest depository bank; however, Deutsche Bank, JPMorgan, and Citibank also offer depository services.[23]

A DR can be **sponsored** or **unsponsored**. A sponsored DR is when the foreign company whose shares are held by the depository has a direct involvement in the issuance of the receipts. Investors in sponsored DRs have the same rights as the direct owners of the common shares (e.g., the right to vote and the right to receive dividends). In contrast, with an unsponsored DR, the underlying foreign company has no involvement with the issuance of the receipts. Instead, the depository purchases the foreign company's shares in its domestic market and then issues the receipts through brokerage firms in the depository's local market. In this case, the depository bank, not the investors in the DR, retains the voting rights. Sponsored DRs are generally subject to greater reporting requirements than unsponsored DRs. In the United States, for example, sponsored DRs must be registered (meet the reporting requirements) with the US Securities and Exchange Commission (SEC). Exhibit 13 contains an example of a sponsored DR issued by Alibaba in September 2014.

Exhibit 13 Sponsored Depository Receipts[24]

NEW YORK—(BUSINESS WIRE)—Citi today announced that Alibaba Group Holding Limited ("Alibaba Group") has appointed Citi's Issuer Services business, acting through Citibank, N.A., as the depositary bank for its American Depositary

(continued)

22 Note that the spellings *depositary* and *depository* are used interchangeably in financial markets. In this reading, we use the spelling *depository* throughout.

23 Boubakri, Cosset, and Samet (2010).

24 https://www.businesswire.com/news/home/20140924005984/en/Citi-Appointed-Depositary-Bank-Alibaba-Group-Holding

Exhibit 13 (Continued)

Receipt ("ADR") program. Alibaba Group's ADRs, which began trading on September 19, 2014, represent the largest Depositary Receipt program in initial public offering market history.

Alibaba Group's ADR program was established through a $25.03 billion initial public offering of 368,122,000 American Depositary Shares ("ADSs"), representing ordinary shares of Alibaba Group, which was priced at $68 per ADS on September 18, 2014. The IPO ranks as the largest in history. The ADRs are listed on the New York Stock Exchange (the "NYSE") under the trading symbol BABA. Each ADS represents one ordinary share of the Company. In its role as depositary bank, Citibank will hold the underlying ordinary shares through its local custodian and issue ADSs representing such shares. Alibaba Group's ADSs trade on the NYSE in ADR form.

There are two types of depository receipts: Global depository receipts (GDRs) and American depository receipts (ADRs), which are described below.

5.2.1 *Global Depository Receipts*

A **global depository receipt** (GDR) is issued outside of the company's home country and outside of the United States. The depository bank that issues GDRs is generally located (or has branches) in the countries on whose exchanges the shares are traded. A key advantage of GDRs is that they are not subject to the foreign ownership and capital flow restrictions that may be imposed by the issuing company's home country because they are sold outside of that country. The issuing company selects the exchange where the GDR is to be traded based on such factors as investors' familiarity with the company or the existence of a large international investor base. The London and Luxembourg exchanges were the first ones to trade GDRs. Some other stock exchanges trading GDRs are the Dubai International Financial Exchange and the Singapore Stock Exchange. Currently, the London and Luxembourg exchanges are where most GDRs are traded because they can be issued in a more timely manner and at a lower cost. Regardless of the exchange they are traded on, the majority of GDRs are denominated in US dollars, although the number of GDRs denominated in pound sterling and euros is increasing. Note that although GDRs cannot be listed on US exchanges, they can be privately placed with institutional investors based in the United States.

5.2.2 *American Depository Receipts*

An **American depository receipt** (ADR) is a US dollar-denominated security that trades like a common share on US exchanges. First created in 1927, ADRs are the oldest type of depository receipts and are currently the most commonly traded depository receipts. They enable foreign companies to raise capital from US investors. Note that an ADR is one form of a GDR; however, not all GDRs are ADRs because GDRs cannot be publicly traded in the United States. The term **American depository share** (ADS) is often used in tandem with the term ADR. A depository share is a security that is actually traded in the issuing company's domestic market. That is, while American depository receipts are the certificates that are traded on US markets, American depository shares are the underlying shares on which these receipts are based.

There are four primary types of ADRs, with each type having different levels of corporate governance and filing requirements. Level I Sponsored ADRs trade in the over-the-counter (OTC) market and do not require full registration with the Securities and Exchange Commission (SEC). Level II and Level III Sponsored ADRs can trade on the New York Stock Exchange (NYSE), NASDAQ, and American Stock Exchange (AMEX). Level II and III ADRs allow companies to raise capital and make acquisitions using these securities. However, the issuing companies must fulfill all SEC requirements.

The fourth type of ADR, an SEC Rule 144A or a Regulation S depository receipt, does not require SEC registration. Instead, foreign companies are able to raise capital by privately placing these depository receipts with qualified institutional investors or to offshore non-US investors. Exhibit 14 summarizes the main features of ADRs.

Exhibit 14 Summary of the Main Features of American Depository Receipts

	Level I (Unlisted)	Level II (Listed)	Level III (Listed)	Rule 144A (Unlisted)
Objectives	Develop and broaden US investor base with existing shares	Develop and broaden US investor base with existing shares	Develop and broaden US investor base with existing/new shares	Access qualified institutional buyers (QIBs)
Raising capital on US markets?	No	No	Yes, through public offerings	Yes, through private placements to QIBs
SEC registration	Form F-6	Form F-6	Forms F-1 and F-6	None
Trading	Over the counter (OTC)	NYSE, NASDAQ, or AMEX	NYSE, NASDAQ, or AMEX	Private offerings, resales, and trading through automated linkages such as PORTAL
Listing fees	Low	High	High	Low
Size and earnings requirements	None	Yes	Yes	None

Source: Adapted from Boubakri, Cosset, and Samet (2010): Table 1.

More than 2,000 DRs, from over 80 countries, currently trade on US exchanges. Based on current statistics, the total market value of DRs issued and traded is estimated at approximately US$2 trillion, or 15 percent of the total dollar value of equities traded in US markets.[25]

5.2.3 *Global Registered Share*

A **global registered share** (GRS) is a common share that is traded on different stock exchanges around the world in different currencies. Currency conversions are not needed to purchase or sell them, because identical shares are quoted and traded in different currencies. Thus, the same share purchased on the Swiss exchange in Swiss francs can be sold on the Tokyo exchange for Japanese yen. As a result, GRSs offer more flexibility than depository receipts because the shares represent an actual ownership interest in the company that can be traded anywhere and currency conversions are not needed to purchase or sell them. GRSs were created and issued by Daimler Chrysler in 1998 and by UBS AG in 2011.

25 *JPMorgan Depositary Receipt Guide* (2005):4.

5.2.4 *Basket of Listed Depository Receipts*

Another type of global security is a **basket of listed depository receipts** (BLDR), which is an exchange-traded fund (ETF) that represents a portfolio of depository receipts. An ETF is a security that tracks an index but trades like an individual share on an exchange. An equity-ETF is a security that contains a portfolio of equities that tracks an index. It trades throughout the day and can be bought, sold, or sold short, just like an individual share. Like ordinary shares, ETFs can also be purchased on margin and used in hedging or arbitrage strategies. The BLDR is a specific class of ETF security that consists of an underlying portfolio of DRs and is designed to track the price performance of an underlying DR index. For example, the Invesco BLDRS Asia 50 ADR Index Fund is a capitalization-weighted ETF designed to track the performance of 50 Asian market-based ADRs.

6 RISK AND RETURN CHARACTERISTICS OF EQUITY SECURITIES

Different types of equity securities have different ownership claims on a company's net assets. The type of equity security and its features affect its risk and return characteristics. The following sections discuss the different return and risk characteristics of equity securities.

6.1 Return Characteristics of Equity Securities

There are two main sources of equity securities' total return: price change (or capital gain) and dividend income. The price change represents the difference between the purchase price (P_{t-1}) and the sale price (P_t) of a share at the end of time $t - 1$ and t, respectively. Cash or stock dividends (D_t) represent distributions that the company makes to its shareholders during period t. Therefore, an equity security's total return is calculated as:

$$\text{Total return, } R_t = (P_t - P_{t-1} + D_t)/P_{t-1} \quad (1)$$

For non-dividend-paying stocks, the total return consists of price appreciation only. Companies that are in the early stages of their life cycle generally do not pay dividends because earnings and cash flows are reinvested to finance the company's growth. In contrast, companies that are in the mature phase of their life cycle may not have as many profitable growth opportunities; therefore, excess cash flows are often returned to investors via the payment of regular dividends or through share repurchases.

For investors who purchase depository receipts or foreign shares directly, there is a third source of return: **foreign exchange gains (or losses)**. Foreign exchange gains arise because of the change in the exchange rate between the investor's currency and the currency that the foreign shares are denominated in. For example, US investors who purchase the ADRs of a Japanese company will earn an additional return if the yen appreciates relative to the US dollar. Conversely, these investors will earn a lower total return if the yen depreciates relative to the US dollar. For example, if the total return for a Japanese company was 10 percent in Japan and the yen depreciated by 10 percent against the US dollar, the total return of the ADR would be (approximately) 0 percent. If the yen had instead appreciated by 10 percent against the US dollar, the total return of the ADR would be (approximately) 20 percent.

Investors that only consider price appreciation overlook an important source of return: the compounding that results from reinvested dividends. Reinvested dividends are cash dividends that the investor receives and uses to purchase additional shares.

As Exhibit 15 shows, in the long run total returns on equity securities are dramatically influenced by the compounding effect of reinvested dividends. Between 1900 and 2016, US$1 invested in US equities in 1900 would have grown in *real* terms to US$1,402 with dividends reinvested, but to just US$11.9 when taking only the price appreciation or capital gain into account. This corresponds to a real compounded return of 6.4 percent per year with dividends reinvested, versus only 2.1 percent per year without dividends reinvested. The comparable ending real wealth for bonds and bills are US$9.8 and US$2.60, respectively. These ending real wealth figures correspond to annualized real compounded returns of 2.0 percent on bonds and 0.8 percent on bills.

Exhibit 15 Impact of Reinvested Dividends on Cumulative Real Returns in the US and UK Equity Market: 1900–2016

Source: Dimson, Marsh, and Staunton (2017). This chart is updated annually and can be found at http://publications.credit-suisse.com/index.cfm/publikationen-shop/research-institute/.

6.2 Risk of Equity Securities

The risk of any security is based on the uncertainty of its future cash flows. The greater the uncertainty of its future cash flows, the greater the risk and the more variable or volatile the security's price. As discussed above, an equity security's total return is determined by its price change and dividends. Therefore, the risk of an equity security can be defined as the uncertainty of its expected (or future) total return. Risk is most often measured by calculating the standard deviation of the equity's expected total return.

A variety of different methods can be used to estimate an equity's expected total return and risk. One method uses the equity's average historical return and the standard deviation of this return as proxies for its expected future return and risk. Another method involves estimating a range of future returns over a specified period of time, assigning probabilities to those returns, and then calculating an expected return and a standard deviation of return based on this information.

The type of equity security, as well as its characteristics, affects the uncertainty of its future cash flows and therefore its risk. In general, preference shares are less risky than common shares for three main reasons:

1 Dividends on preference shares are known and fixed, and they account for a large portion of the preference shares' total return. Therefore, there is less uncertainty about future cash flows.
2 Preference shareholders receive dividends and other distributions before common shareholders.
3 The amount preference shareholders will receive if the company is liquidated is known and fixed as the par (or face) value of their shares. However, there is no guarantee that investors will receive that amount if the company experiences financial difficulty.

With common shares, however, a larger portion of shareholders' total return (or all of their total return for non-dividend shares) is based on future price appreciation and future dividends are unknown. If the company is liquidated, common shareholders will receive whatever amount (if any) is remaining after the company's creditors and preference shareholders have been paid. In summary, because the uncertainty surrounding the total return of preference shares is less than common shares, preference shares have lower risk and lower expected return than common shares.

It is important to note that some preference shares and common shares can be riskier than others because of their associated characteristics. For example, from an investor's point of view, putable common or preference shares are less risky than their callable or non-callable counterparts because they give the investor the option to sell the shares to the issuer at a pre-determined price. This pre-determined price establishes a minimum price that investors will receive and reduces the uncertainty associated with the security's future cash flow. As a result, putable shares generally pay a lower dividend than non-putable shares.

Because the major source of total return for preference shares is dividend income, the primary risk affecting all preference shares is the uncertainty of future dividend payments. Regardless of the preference shares' features (callable, putable, cumulative, etc.), the greater the uncertainty surrounding the issuer's ability to pay dividends, the greater risk. Because the ability of a company to pay dividends is based on its future cash flows and net income, investors try to estimate these amounts by examining past trends or forecasting future amounts. The more earnings and the greater amount of cash flow that the company has had, or is expected to have, the lower the uncertainty and risk associated with its ability to pay future dividends.

Callable common or preference shares are riskier than their non-callable counterparts because the issuer has the option to redeem the shares at a pre-determined price. Because the call price limits investors' potential future total return, callable shares generally pay a higher dividend to compensate investors for the risk that the shares could be called in the future. Similarly, putable preference shares have lower risk than non-putable preference shares. Cumulative preference shares have lower risk than non-cumulative preference shares because the cumulative feature gives investors the right to receive any unpaid dividends before any dividends can be paid to common shareholders.

EQUITY SECURITIES AND COMPANY VALUE

7

Companies issue equity securities on primary markets to raise capital and increase liquidity. This additional liquidity also provides the corporation an additional "currency" (its equity), which it can use to make acquisitions and provide stock option-based incentives to employees. The primary goal of raising capital is to finance the company's revenue-generating activities in order to increase its net income and maximize the wealth of its shareholders. In most cases, the capital that is raised is used to finance the purchase of long-lived assets, capital expansion projects, research and development, the entry into new product or geographic regions, and the acquisition of other companies. Alternatively, a company may be forced to raise capital to ensure that it continues to operate as a going concern. In these cases, capital is raised to fulfill regulatory requirements, improve capital adequacy ratios, or to ensure that debt covenants are met.

The ultimate goal of management is to increase the book value (shareholders' equity on a company's balance sheet) of the company and maximize the market value of its equity. Although management actions can directly affect the book value of the company (by increasing net income or by selling or purchasing its own shares), they can only indirectly affect the market value of its equity. The book value of a company's equity—the difference between its total assets and total liabilities—increases when the company retains its net income. The more net income that is earned and retained, the greater the company's book value of equity. Because management's decisions directly influence a company's net income, they also directly influence its book value of equity.

The market value of the company's equity, however, reflects the collective and differing expectations of investors concerning the amount, timing, and uncertainty of the company's future cash flows. Rarely will book value and market value be equal. Although management may be accomplishing its objective of increasing the company's book value, this increase may not be reflected in the market value of the company's equity because it does not affect investors' expectations about the company's future cash flows. A key measure that investors use to evaluate the effectiveness of management in increasing the company's book value is the accounting return on equity.

7.1 Accounting Return on Equity

Return on equity (ROE) is the primary measure that equity investors use to determine whether the management of a company is effectively and efficiently using the capital they have provided to generate profits. It measures the total amount of net income available to common shareholders generated by the total equity capital invested in the company. It is computed as net income available to ordinary shareholders (i.e., after preferred dividends have been deducted) divided by the average total book value of equity (BVE). That is:

$$\text{ROE}_t = \frac{\text{NI}_t}{\text{Average BVE}_t} = \frac{\text{NI}_t}{(\text{BVE}_t + \text{BVE}_{t-1})/2} \tag{2}$$

where NI_t is the net income in year t and the average book value of equity is computed as the book values at the beginning and end of year t divided by 2. Return on equity assumes that the net income produced in the current year is generated by the equity existing at the beginning of the year and any new equity that was invested during the year. Note that some formulas only use shareholders' equity at the beginning of year t

(that is, the end of year $t - 1$) in the denominator. This assumes that only the equity existing at the beginning of the year was used to generate the company's net income during the year. That is:

$$ROE_t = \frac{NI_t}{BVE_{t-1}} \quad (3)$$

Both formulas are appropriate to use as long as they are applied consistently. For example, using beginning of the year book value is appropriate when book values are relatively stable over time or when computing ROE for a company annually over a period of time. Average book value is more appropriate if a company experiences more volatile year-end book values or if the industry convention is to use average book values in calculating ROE.

One caveat to be aware of when computing and analyzing ROE is that net income and the book value of equity are directly affected by management's choice of accounting methods, such as those relating to depreciation (straight line versus accelerated methods) or inventories (first in, first out versus weighted average cost). Different accounting methods can make it difficult to compare the return on equity of companies even if they operate in the same industry. It may also be difficult to compare the ROE of the same company over time if its accounting methods have changed during that time.

Exhibit 16 contains information on the net income and total book value of shareholders' equity for three **blue chip** (widely held large market capitalization companies that are considered financially sound and are leaders in their respective industry or local stock market) pharmaceutical companies: Pfizer, Novartis AG, and GlaxoSmithKline. The data are for their financial years ending December 2015 through December 2017.[26]

Exhibit 16 Net Income and Book Value of Equity for Pfizer, Novartis AG, and GlaxoSmithKline (in Thousands of US Dollars)

	Financial Year Ending		
	31 Dec 2015	**31 Dec 2016**	**31 Dec 2017**
Pfizer			
Net income	$6,960,000	$7,215,000	$21,308,000
Total stockholders' equity	$64,998,000	$59,840,000	$71,287,000
Novartis AG			
Net income	$17,783,000	$6,712,000	$7,703,000
Total stockholders' equity	$77,122,000	$74,891,000	$74,227,000
GlaxoSmithKline			
Net income	$12,420,000	$1,126,000	$2,070,700
Total stockholders' equity	$113,092,500	$6,127,800	$4,715,800

Using the average book value of equity, the return on equity for Pfizer for the years ending December 2016 and 2017 can be calculated as:

26 Pfizer uses US GAAP to prepare its financial statements; Novartis and GlaxoSmithKline use International Financial Reporting Standards. Therefore, it would be inappropriate to compare the ROE of Pfizer to that of Novartis or GlaxoSmithKline.

Return on equity for the year ending December 2016

$$ROE_{2016} = \frac{NI_{2016}}{(BVE_{2015} + BVE_{2016})/2} = \frac{7{,}215{,}000}{(64{,}998{,}000 + 59{,}840{,}000)/2} = 11.6\%$$

Return on equity for the year ending December 2017

$$ROE_{2017} = \frac{NI_{2017}}{(BVE_{2016} + BVE_{2017})/2} = \frac{21{,}308{,}000}{(59{,}840{,}000 + 71{,}287{,}000)/2} = 32.5\%$$

Exhibit 17 summarizes the return on equity for Novartis and GlaxoSmithKline in addition to Pfizer for 2016 and 2017.

Exhibit 17 Return on Equity for Pfizer, Novartis AG, and GlaxoSmithKline

	31 Dec 2016 (%)	31 Dec 2017 (%)
Pfizer	11.6	32.5
Novartis AG	8.8	10.3
GlaxoSmithKline	11.7	38.2

In the case of Pfizer, the ROE of 32.5 percent in 2017 indicates that the company was able to generate a return (profit) of US$0.325 on every US$1.00 of capital invested by shareholders. GlaxoSmithKline almost tripled its return on equity over this period, from 11.7 percent to 38.2 percent. Novartis's ROE remained relatively unchanged.

ROE can increase if net income increases at a faster rate than shareholders' equity or if net income decreases at a slower rate than shareholders' equity. In the case of GlaxoSmithKline, ROE almost tripled between 2016 and 2017 due to its net income almost doubling during the period and due to its average shareholder's fund decreasing by almost 45 percent during the period. Stated differently, in 2017 compared to 2016, GlaxoSmithKline was significantly more effective in using its equity capital to generate profits. In the case of Pfizer, its ROE increased dramatically from 11.6 percent to 32.5 percent in 2017 versus 2016 even though its average shareholder equity increased by around 5 percent due to a nearly tripling of net income during the period.

An important question to ask is whether an increasing ROE is always good. The short answer is, "it depends." One reason ROE can increase is if net income decreases at a slower rate than shareholders' equity, which is not a positive sign. In addition, ROE can increase if the company issues debt and then uses the proceeds to repurchase some of its outstanding shares. This action will increase the company's leverage and make its equity riskier. Therefore, it is important to examine the source of changes in the company's net income *and* shareholders' equity over time. The DuPont formula, which is discussed in a separate reading, can be used to analyze the sources of changes in a company's ROE.

The book value of a company's equity reflects the historical operating and financing decisions of its management. The market value of the company's equity reflects these decisions as well as investors' collective assessment and expectations about the company's future cash flows generated by its positive net present value investment opportunities. If investors believe that the company has a large number of these future cash flow-generating investment opportunities, the market value of the company's equity will exceed its book value. Exhibit 18 shows the market price per share, the total number of shares outstanding, and the total book value of shareholders' equity for

Pfizer, Novartis AG, and GlaxoSmithKline at the end of December 2017. This exhibit also shows the total market value of equity (or market capitalization) computed as the number of shares outstanding multiplied by the market price per share.

Exhibit 18 Market Information for Pfizer, Novartis AG, and GlaxoSmithKline (in Thousands of US Dollars except market price)

	Pfizer	Novartis AG	GlaxoSmithKline
Market price	$35.74	$90.99	$18.39
Total shares outstanding	5,952,900	2,317,500	4,892,200
Total shareholders' equity	$71,287,000	$74,227,000	$4,715,800
Total market value of equity	$212,756,646	$210,869,325	$89,967,558

Note that in Exhibit 18, the total market value of equity for Pfizer is computed as:

Market value of equity = Market price per share × Shares outstanding

Market value of equity = US$35.74 × 5,952,900 = US$212,756,646.

The book value of equity per share for Pfizer can be computed as:

Book value of equity per share = Total shareholders' equity/Shares outstanding

Book value of equity per share = US$71,287,000/5,952,900 = US$11.98.

A useful ratio to compute is a company's price-to-book ratio, which is also referred to as the market-to-book ratio. This ratio provides an indication of investors' expectations about a company's future investment and cash flow-generating opportunities. The larger the price-to-book ratio (i.e., the greater the divergence between market value per share and book value per share), the more favorably investors will view the company's future investment opportunities. For Pfizer the price-to-book ratio is:

Price-to-book ratio = Market price per share/Book value of equity per share

Price-to-book ratio = US$35.74/US$11.98= 2.98

Exhibit 19 contains the market price per share, book value of equity per share, and price-to-book ratios for Novartis and GlaxoSmithKline in addition to Pfizer.

Exhibit 19 Pfizer, Novartis AG, and GlaxoSmithKline

	Pfizer	Novartis AG	GlaxoSmithKline
Market price per share	$35.74	$90.99	$18.39
Book value of equity per share	$11.98	$32.03	$0.96
Price-to-book ratio	2.98	2.84	19.16

The market price per share of all three companies exceeds their respective book values, so their price-to-book ratios are all greater than 1.00. However, there are significant differences in the sizes of their price-to-book ratios. GlaxoSmithKline has the largest price-to-book ratio, while the price-to-book ratios of Pfizer and Novartis are similar to each other. This suggests that investors believe that GlaxoSmithKline has substantially higher future growth opportunities than either Pfizer or Novartis.

It is not appropriate to compare the price-to-book ratios of companies in different industries because their price-to-book ratios also reflect investors' outlook for the industry. Companies in high growth industries, such as technology, will generally have higher price-to-book ratios than companies in slower growth (i.e., mature) industries, such as heavy equipment. Therefore, it is more appropriate to compare the price-to-book ratios of companies in the same industry. A company with relatively high growth opportunities compared to its industry peers would likely have a higher price-to-book ratio than the average price-to-book ratio of the industry.

Book value and return on equity are useful in helping analysts determine value but can be limited as a primary means to estimate a company's true or intrinsic value, which is the present value of its future projected cash flows. In Exhibit 20, Warren Buffett, one of the most successful investors in the world and CEO of Berkshire Hathaway, provides an explanation of the differences between the book value of a company and its intrinsic value in a letter to shareholders. As discussed above, market value reflects the collective and differing expectations of investors concerning the amount, timing, and uncertainty of a company's future cash flows. A company's intrinsic value can only be estimated because it is impossible to predict the amount and timing of its future cash flows. However, astute investors—such as Buffett—have been able to profit from discrepancies between their estimates of a company's intrinsic value and the market value of its equity.

Exhibit 20 Book Value versus Intrinsic Value[27]

We regularly report our per-share book value, an easily calculable number, though one of limited use. Just as regularly, we tell you that what counts is intrinsic value, a number that is impossible to pinpoint but essential to estimate.

For example, in 1964, we could state with certitude that Berkshire's per-share book value was $19.46. However, that figure considerably overstated the stock's intrinsic value since all of the company's resources were tied up in a sub-profitable textile business. Our textile assets had neither going-concern nor liquidation values equal to their carrying values. In 1964, then, anyone inquiring into the soundness of Berkshire's balance sheet might well have deserved the answer once offered up by a Hollywood mogul of dubious reputation: "Don't worry, the liabilities are solid."

Today, Berkshire's situation has reversed: Many of the businesses we control are worth far more than their carrying value. (Those we don't control, such as Coca-Cola or Gillette, are carried at current market values.) We continue to give you book value figures, however, because they serve as a rough, understated, tracking measure for Berkshire's intrinsic value.

We define intrinsic value as the discounted value of the cash that can be taken out of a business during its remaining life. Anyone calculating intrinsic value necessarily comes up with a highly subjective figure that will change both as estimates of future cash flows are revised and as interest rates move. Despite its fuzziness, however, intrinsic value is all-important and is the only logical way to evaluate the relative attractiveness of investments and businesses.

To see how historical input (book value) and future output (intrinsic value) can diverge, let's look at another form of investment, a college education. Think of the education's cost as its "book value." If it is to be accurate, the cost should include the earnings that were foregone by the student because he chose college rather than a job.

(continued)

27 Extracts from Berkshire Hathaway's *2008 Annual Report* (www.berkshirehathaway.com).

Exhibit 20 (Continued)

For this exercise, we will ignore the important non-economic benefits of an education and focus strictly on its economic value. First, we must estimate the earnings that the graduate will receive over his lifetime and subtract from that figure an estimate of what he would have earned had he lacked his education. That gives us an excess earnings figure, which must then be discounted, at an appropriate interest rate, back to graduation day. The dollar result equals the intrinsic economic value of the education.

7.2 The Cost of Equity and Investors' Required Rates of Return

When companies issue debt (or borrow from a bank) or equity securities, there is a cost associated with the capital that is raised. In order to maximize profitability and shareholder wealth, companies attempt to raise capital efficiently so as to minimize these costs.

When a company issues debt, the cost it incurs for the use of these funds is called the cost of debt. The cost of debt is relatively easy to estimate because it reflects the periodic interest (or coupon) rate that the company is contractually obligated to pay to its bondholders (lenders). When a company raises capital by issuing equity, the cost it incurs is called the cost of equity. Unlike debt, however, the company is not contractually obligated to make any payments to its shareholders for the use of their funds. As a result, the cost of equity is more difficult to estimate.

Investors require a return on the funds they provide to the company. This return is called the investor's minimum required rate of return. When investors purchase the company's debt securities, their minimum required rate of return is the periodic rate of interest they charge the company for the use of their funds. Because all of the bondholders receive the same periodic rate of interest, their required rate of return is the same. Therefore, the company's cost of debt and the investors' minimum required rate of return on the debt are the same.

When investors purchase the company's equity securities, their minimum required rate of return is based on the future cash flows they expect to receive. Because these future cash flows are both uncertain and unknown, the investors' minimum required rate of return must be estimated. In addition, the minimum required return may differ across investors based on their expectations about the company's future cash flows. As a result, the company's cost of equity may be different from the investors' minimum required rate of return on equity.[28] Because companies try to raise capital at the lowest possible cost, the company's cost of equity is often used as a proxy for the investors' *minimum* required rate of return.

In other words, the cost of equity can be thought of as the minimum expected rate of return that a company must offer its investors to purchase its shares in the primary market and to maintain its share price in the secondary market. If this expected rate of return is not maintained in the secondary market, then the share price will adjust so that it meets the minimum required rate of return demanded by investors. For example, if investors require a higher rate of return on equity than the company's cost of equity, they would sell their shares and invest their funds elsewhere resulting in a decline in the company's share price. As the share price declined, the cost of equity would increase to reach the higher rate of return that investors require.

28 Another important factor that can cause a firm's cost of equity to differ from investors' required rate of return on equity is the flotation cost associated with equity

Two models commonly used to estimate a company's cost of equity (or investors' minimum required rate of return) are the dividend discount model (DDM) and the capital asset pricing model (CAPM). These models are discussed in detail in other curriculum readings.

The cost of debt (after tax) and the cost of equity (i.e., the minimum required rates of return on debt and equity) are integral components of the capital budgeting process because they are used to estimate a company's weighted average cost of capital (WACC). Capital budgeting is the decision-making process that companies use to evaluate potential long-term investments. The WACC represents the minimum required rate of return that the company must earn on its long-term investments to satisfy all providers of capital. The company then chooses among those long-term investments with expected returns that are greater than its WACC.

SUMMARY

Equity securities play a fundamental role in investment analysis and portfolio management. The importance of this asset class continues to grow on a global scale because of the need for equity capital in developed and emerging markets, technological innovation, and the growing sophistication of electronic information exchange. Given their absolute return potential and ability to impact the risk and return characteristics of portfolios, equity securities are of importance to both individual and institutional investors.

This reading introduces equity securities and provides an overview of global equity markets. A detailed analysis of their historical performance shows that equity securities have offered average real annual returns superior to government bills and bonds, which have provided average real annual returns that have only kept pace with inflation. The different types and characteristics of common and preference equity securities are examined, and the primary differences between public and private equity securities are outlined. An overview of the various types of equity securities listed and traded in global markets is provided, including a discussion of their risk and return characteristics. Finally, the role of equity securities in creating company value is examined as well as the relationship between a company's cost of equity, its accounting return on equity, investors' required rate of return, and the company's intrinsic value.

We conclude with a summary of the key components of this reading:

- Common shares represent an ownership interest in a company and give investors a claim on its operating performance, the opportunity to participate in the corporate decision-making process, and a claim on the company's net assets in the case of liquidation.
- Callable common shares give the issuer the right to buy back the shares from shareholders at a price determined when the shares are originally issued.
- Putable common shares give shareholders the right to sell the shares back to the issuer at a price specified when the shares are originally issued.
- Preference shares are a form of equity in which payments made to preference shareholders take precedence over any payments made to common stockholders.
- Cumulative preference shares are preference shares on which dividend payments are accrued so that any payments omitted by the company must be paid before another dividend can be paid to common shareholders. Non-cumulative

preference shares have no such provisions, implying that the dividend payments are at the company's discretion and are thus similar to payments made to common shareholders.

- Participating preference shares allow investors to receive the standard preferred dividend plus the opportunity to receive a share of corporate profits above a pre-specified amount. Non-participating preference shares allow investors to simply receive the initial investment plus any accrued dividends in the event of liquidation.
- Callable and putable preference shares provide issuers and investors with the same rights and obligations as their common share counterparts.
- Private equity securities are issued primarily to institutional investors in private placements and do not trade in secondary equity markets. There are three types of private equity investments: venture capital, leveraged buyouts, and private investments in public equity (PIPE).
- The objective of private equity investing is to increase the ability of the company's management to focus on its operating activities for long-term value creation. The strategy is to take the "private" company "public" after certain profit and other benchmarks have been met.
- Depository receipts are securities that trade like ordinary shares on a local exchange but which represent an economic interest in a foreign company. They allow the publicly listed shares of foreign companies to be traded on an exchange outside their domestic market.
- American depository receipts are US dollar-denominated securities trading much like standard US securities on US markets. Global depository receipts are similar to ADRs but contain certain restrictions in terms of their ability to be resold among investors.
- Underlying characteristics of equity securities can greatly affect their risk and return.
- A company's accounting return on equity is the total return that it earns on shareholders' book equity.
- A company's cost of equity is the minimum rate of return that stockholders require the company to pay them for investing in its equity.

REFERENCES

Bailey, Elizabeth, Meg Wirth, and David Zapol. 2005. "Venture Capital and Global Health." *Financing Global Health Ventures*, Discussion Paper (September 2005): http://www.commonscapital.com/downloads/Venture_Capital_and_Global_Health.pdf

Boubakri, Narjess, Jean-Claude Cosset, and Anis Samet. 2010. "The Choice of ADRs." *Journal of Banking and Finance*, vol. 34, no. 9:2077–2095.

Dimson, Elroy, Paul Marsh, and Mike Staunton. 2018. *Credit Suisse Global Investment Returns Sourcebook 2017*. Credit Suisse Research Institute.

Dimson, Elroy, Paul Marsh, and Mike Staunton. 2018. *Credit Suisse Global Investment Returns Yearbook 2018*. Credit Suisse Research Institute.

Graham, John R., Campbell R. Harvey, and Shiva Rajgopal. 2005. "The Economic Implications of Corporate Financial Reporting." *Journal of Accounting and Economics*, vol. 40, no. 1–3:3–73.

Henry, Peter Blair, and Anusha Chari. 2004. "Risk Sharing and Asset Prices: Evidence from a Natural Experiment." *Journal of Finance*, vol. 59, no. 3:1295–1324.

Strömberg, Per. 2008. "The New Demography of Private Equity." The *Global Economic Impact of Private Equity Report 2008*, World Economic Forum.

PRACTICE PROBLEMS

1 Which of the following is *not* a characteristic of common equity?

A It represents an ownership interest in the company.

B Shareholders participate in the decision-making process.

C The company is obligated to make periodic dividend payments.

2 The type of equity voting right that grants one vote for each share of equity owned is referred to as:

A proxy voting.

B statutory voting.

C cumulative voting.

3 All of the following are characteristics of preference shares *except*:

A They are either callable or putable.

B They generally do not have voting rights.

C They do not share in the operating performance of the company.

4 Participating preference shares entitle shareholders to:

A participate in the decision-making process of the company.

B convert their shares into a specified number of common shares.

C receive an additional dividend if the company's profits exceed a pre-determined level.

5 Which of the following statements about private equity securities is *incorrect*?

A They cannot be sold on secondary markets.

B They have market-determined quoted prices.

C They are primarily issued to institutional investors.

6 Venture capital investments:

A can be publicly traded.

B do not require a long-term commitment of funds.

C provide mezzanine financing to early-stage companies.

7 Which of the following statements *most accurately* describes one difference between private and public equity firms?

A Private equity firms are focused more on short-term results than public firms.

B Private equity firms' regulatory and investor relations operations are less costly than those of public firms.

C Private equity firms are incentivized to be more open with investors about governance and compensation than public firms.

8 Emerging markets have benefited from recent trends in international markets. Which of the following has *not* been a benefit of these trends?

A Emerging market companies do not have to worry about a lack of liquidity in their home equity markets.

B Emerging market companies have found it easier to raise capital in the markets of developed countries.

C Emerging market companies have benefited from the stability of foreign exchange markets.

9 When investing in unsponsored depository receipts, the voting rights to the shares in the trust belong to:

A the depository bank.

B the investors in the depository receipts.

C the issuer of the shares held in the trust.

10 With respect to Level III sponsored ADRs, which of the following is *least likely* to be accurate? They:

A have low listing fees.

B are traded on the NYSE, NASDAQ, and AMEX.

C are used to raise equity capital in US markets.

11 A basket of listed depository receipts, or an exchange-traded fund, would *most likely* be used for:

A gaining exposure to a single equity.

B hedging exposure to a single equity.

C gaining exposure to multiple equities.

12 Calculate the total return on a share of equity using the following data:

Purchase price: $50

Sale price: $42

Dividend paid during holding period: $2

A –12.0%

B –14.3%

C –16.0%

13 If a US-based investor purchases a euro-denominated ETF and the euro subsequently depreciates in value relative to the dollar, the investor will have a total return that is:

A lower than the ETF's total return.

B higher than the ETF's total return.

C the same as the ETF's total return.

14 Which of the following is *incorrect* about the risk of an equity security? The risk of an equity security is:

A based on the uncertainty of its cash flows.

B based on the uncertainty of its future price.

C measured using the standard deviation of its dividends.

15 From an investor's point of view, which of the following equity securities is the *least* risky?

A Putable preference shares.

B Callable preference shares.

C Non-callable preference shares.

16 Which of the following is *least likely* to be a reason for a company to issue equity securities on the primary market?

A To raise capital.

B To increase liquidity.

C To increase return on equity.

17 Which of the following is *not* a primary goal of raising equity capital?

A To finance the purchase of long-lived assets.

B To finance the company's revenue-generating activities.

C To ensure that the company continues as a going concern.

18 Which of the following statements is *most accurate* in describing a company's book value?

A Book value increases when a company retains its net income.

B Book value is usually equal to the company's market value.

C The ultimate goal of management is to maximize book value.

19 Calculate the book value of a company using the following information:

Number of shares outstanding	100,000
Price per share	€52
Total assets	€12,000,000
Total liabilities	€7,500,000
Net Income	€2,000,000

A €4,500,000.

B €5,200,000.

C €6,500,000.

20 Which of the following statements is *least accurate* in describing a company's market value?

A Management's decisions do not influence the company's market value.

B Increases in book value may not be reflected in the company's market value.

C Market value reflects the collective and differing expectations of investors.

21 Calculate the return on equity (ROE) of a stable company using the following data:

Total sales	£2,500,000
Net income	£2,000,000
Beginning of year total assets	£50,000,000
Beginning of year total liabilities	£35,000,000
Number of shares outstanding at the end of the year	1,000,000
Price per share at the end of the year	£20

A 10.0%.

B 13.3%.

C 16.7%.

22 Holding all other factors constant, which of the following situations will *most likely* lead to an increase in a company's return on equity?

A The market price of the company's shares increases.

B Net income increases at a slower rate than shareholders' equity.

C The company issues debt to repurchase outstanding shares of equity.

23 Which of the following measures is the *most difficult* to estimate?

A The cost of debt.

B The cost of equity.

C Investors' required rate of return on debt.

24 A company's cost of equity is often used as a proxy for investors':

A average required rate of return.

B minimum required rate of return.

C maximum required rate of return.

SOLUTIONS

1 C is correct. The company is not obligated to make dividend payments. It is at the discretion of the company whether or not it chooses to pay dividends.

2 B is correct. Statutory voting is the type of equity voting right that grants one vote per share owned.

3 A is correct. Preference shares do not have to be either callable or putable.

4 C is correct. Participating preference shares entitle shareholders to receive an additional dividend if the company's profits exceed a pre-determined level.

5 B is correct. Private equity securities do not have market-determined quoted prices.

6 C is correct. Venture capital investments can be used to provide mezzanine financing to companies in their early stage of development.

7 B is correct. Regulatory and investor relations costs are lower for private equity firms than for public firms. There are no stock exchange, regulatory, or shareholder involvements with private equity, whereas for public firms these costs can be high.

8 C is correct. The trends in emerging markets have not led to the stability of foreign exchange markets.

9 A is correct. In an unsponsored DR, the depository bank owns the voting rights to the shares. The bank purchases the shares, places them into a trust, and then sells shares in the trust—not the underlying shares—in other markets.

10 A is correct. The listing fees on Level III sponsored ADRs are high.

11 C is correct. An ETF is used to gain exposure to a basket of securities (equity, fixed income, commodity futures, etc.).

12 A is correct. The formula states $R_t = (P_t - P_{t-1} + D_t)/P_{t-1}$. Therefore, total return = (42 – 50 + 2)/50 = –12.0%.

13 A is correct. The depreciated value of the euro will create an additional loss in the form of currency return that is lower than the ETF's return.

14 C is correct. Some equity securities do not pay dividends, and therefore the standard deviation of dividends cannot be used to measure the risk of all equity securities.

15 A is correct. Putable shares, whether common or preference, give the investor the option to sell the shares back to the issuer at a pre-determined price. This pre-determined price creates a floor for the share's price that reduces the uncertainty of future cash flows for the investor (i.e., lowers risk relative to the other two types of shares listed).

16 C is correct. Issuing shares in the primary (and secondary) market *reduces* a company's return on equity because it increases the total amount of equity capital invested in the company (i.e., the denominator in the ROE formula).

17 C is correct. Capital is raised to ensure the company's existence only when it is required. It is not a typical goal of raising capital.

18 A is correct. A company's book value increases when a company retains its net income.

19 A is correct. The book value of the company is equal to total assets minus total liabilities, which is €12,000,000 – €7,500,000 = €4,500,000.

20 A is correct. A company's market value is affected by management's decisions. Management's decisions can directly affect the company's *book* value, which can then affect its market value.

21 B is correct. A company's ROE is calculated as (NI_t/BVE_{t-1}). The BVE_{t-1} is equal to the beginning total assets minus the beginning total liabilities, which equals £50,000,000 – £35,000,000 = £15,000,000. Therefore, ROE = £2,000,000/£15,000,000 = 13.3%.

22 C is correct. A company's ROE will increase if it issues debt to repurchase outstanding shares of equity.

23 B is correct. The cost of equity is not easily determined. It is dependent on investors' required rate of return on equity, which reflects the different risk levels of investors and their expectations about the company's future cash flows.

24 B is correct. Companies try to raise funds at the lowest possible cost. Therefore, cost of equity is used as a proxy for the minimum required rate of return.

READING

40

Introduction to Industry and Company Analysis

by Patrick W. Dorsey, CFA, Anthony M. Fiore, CFA, and Ian Rossa O'Reilly, CFA

Patrick W. Dorsey, CFA, is at Dorsey Asset Management (USA). Anthony M. Fiore, CFA, is at Silvercrest Asset Management (USA). Ian Rossa O'Reilly, CFA (Canada).

LEARNING OUTCOMES

Mastery	*The candidate should be able to:*
☐	a. explain uses of industry analysis and the relation of industry analysis to company analysis;
☐	b. compare methods by which companies can be grouped, current industry classification systems, and classify a company, given a description of its activities and the classification system;
☐	c. explain the factors that affect the sensitivity of a company to the business cycle and the uses and limitations of industry and company descriptors such as "growth," "defensive," and "cyclical";
☐	d. explain how a company's industry classification can be used to identify a potential "peer group" for equity valuation;
☐	e. describe the elements that need to be covered in a thorough industry analysis;
☐	f. describe the principles of strategic analysis of an industry;
☐	g. explain the effects of barriers to entry, industry concentration, industry capacity, and market share stability on pricing power and price competition;
☐	h. describe industry life cycle models, classify an industry as to life cycle stage, and describe limitations of the life-cycle concept in forecasting industry performance;
☐	i. compare characteristics of representative industries from the various economic sectors;
☐	j. describe macroeconomic, technological, demographic, governmental, and social influences on industry growth, profitability, and risk;
☐	k. describe the elements that should be covered in a thorough company analysis.

1 INTRODUCTION

Industry analysis is the analysis of a specific branch of manufacturing, service, or trade. Understanding the industry in which a company operates provides an essential framework for the analysis of the individual company—that is, **company analysis**. Equity analysis and credit analysis are often conducted by analysts who concentrate on one or several industries, which results in synergies and efficiencies in gathering and interpreting information.

Among the questions we address in this reading are the following:

- What are the similarities and differences among industry classification systems?
- How does an analyst go about choosing a peer group of companies?
- What are the key factors to consider when analyzing an industry?
- What advantages are enjoyed by companies in strategically well-positioned industries?

After discussing the uses of industry analysis in the next section, Sections 3 and 4 discuss, respectively, approaches to identifying similar companies and industry classification systems. Section 5 covers the description and analysis of industries. Also, Section 5, which includes an introduction to competitive analysis, provides a background to Section 6, which introduces company analysis. The reading ends with a summary, and practice problems follow the text.

2 USES OF INDUSTRY ANALYSIS

Industry analysis is useful in a number of investment applications that make use of fundamental analysis. Its uses include the following:

- *Understanding a company's business and business environment.* Industry analysis is often a critical early step in stock selection and valuation because it provides insights into the issuer's growth opportunities, competitive dynamics, and business risks. For a credit analyst, industry analysis provides insights into the appropriateness of a company's use of debt financing and into its ability to meet its promised payments during economic contractions.
- *Identifying active equity investment opportunities.* Investors taking a top-down investing approach use industry analysis to identify industries with positive, neutral, or negative outlooks for profitability and growth. Generally, investors will then overweight, market weight, or underweight those industries (as appropriate to their outlooks) relative to the investor's benchmark if the investor judges that the industry's perceived prospects are not fully incorporated in market prices. Apart from security selection, some investors attempt to outperform their benchmarks by industry or sector rotation—that is, timing investments in industries in relation to an analysis of industry fundamentals and/or business-cycle conditions (technical analysis may also play a role in such strategies). Several studies have underscored the importance of industry analysis by suggesting that the industry factor in stock returns is at least as important as the country factor (e.g., Cavaglia, Diermeier, Moroz, and De Zordo, 2004). In

addition, industry membership has been found to account for about 20 percent of the variability of a company's profitability in the United States (McGahan and Porter 1995).

- *Portfolio performance attribution.* Performance attribution, which addresses the sources of a portfolio's returns, usually in relation to the portfolio's benchmark, includes industry or sector selection. Industry classification schemes play a role in such performance attribution.

Later in this reading we explore the considerations involved in understanding a company's business and business environment. The next section addresses how companies may be grouped into industries.

APPROACHES TO IDENTIFYING SIMILAR COMPANIES 3

Industry classification attempts to place companies into groups on the basis of commonalities. In the following sections, we discuss the three major approaches to industry classification:

- products and/or services supplied;
- business-cycle sensitivities; and
- statistical similarities.

3.1 Products and/or Services Supplied

Modern classification schemes are most commonly based on grouping companies by similar products and/or services. According to this perspective, an **industry** is defined as a group of companies offering similar products and/or services. For example, major companies in the global heavy truck industry include Volvo, Daimler AG, Paccar, and Navistar, all of which make large commercial vehicles for the on-highway truck market. Similarly, some of the large players in the global automobile industry are Toyota, General Motors, Volkswagen, Ford, Honda, Nissan, PSA Peugeot Citroën, and Hyundai, all of which produce light vehicles that are close substitutes for one another.

Industry classification schemes typically provide multiple levels of aggregation. The term **sector** is often used to refer to a group of related industries. The health care sector, for example, consists of a number of related industries, including the pharmaceutical, biotechnology, medical device, medical supply, hospital, and managed care industries.

These classification schemes typically place a company in an industry on the basis of a determination of its principal business activity. A company's **principal business activity** is the source from which the company derives a majority of its revenues and/or earnings. For example, companies that derive a majority of their revenues from the sale of pharmaceuticals include Novartis AG, Pfizer Inc., Roche Holding AG, GSK plc, and Sanofi S.A., all of which could be grouped together as part of the global pharmaceutical industry. Companies that engage in more than one significant business activity usually report the revenues (and, in many cases, operating profits) of the different business segments in their financial statements.[1]

Examples of classification systems based on products and/or services include the commercial classification systems that will be discussed later, namely, the Global Industry Classification Standard (GICS), Russell Global Sectors (RGS), and Industry

1 For more information, see International Financial Reporting Standard (IFRS) 8: Operating Segments. In IFRS 8, *business segments* are called *operating segments*.

Classification Benchmark. In addition to grouping companies by product and/or service, some of the major classification systems, including GICS and RGS, group consumer-related companies into cyclical and non-cyclical categories depending on the company's sensitivity to the business cycle. The next section addresses how companies can be categorized on the basis of economic sensitivity.

3.2 Business-Cycle Sensitivities

Companies are sometimes grouped on the basis of their relative sensitivity to the business cycle. This method often results in two broad groupings of companies—cyclical and non-cyclical.

A **cyclical** company is one whose profits are strongly correlated with the strength of the overall economy. Such companies experience wider-than-average fluctuations in demand—high demand during periods of economic expansion and low demand during periods of economic contraction—and/or are subject to greater-than-average profit variability related to high operating leverage (i.e., high fixed costs). Concerning demand, cyclical products and services are often relatively expensive and/or represent purchases that can be delayed if necessary (e.g., because of declining disposable income). Examples of cyclical industries are autos, housing, basic materials, industrials, and technology. A **non-cyclical** company is one whose performance is largely independent of the business cycle. Non-cyclical companies produce goods or services for which demand remains relatively stable throughout the business cycle. Examples of non-cyclical industries are food and beverage, household and personal care products, health care, and utilities.

Although the classification systems we will discuss do not label their categories as cyclical or non-cyclical, certain sectors tend to experience greater economic sensitivity than others. Sectors that tend to exhibit a relatively high degree of economic sensitivity include consumer discretionary, energy, financials, industrials, technology, and materials. In contrast, sectors that exhibit relatively less economic sensitivity include consumer staples, health care, telecommunications, and utilities.

EXAMPLE 1

Descriptions Related to the Cyclical/Noncyclical Distinction

Analysts commonly encounter a number of labels related to the cyclical/non-cyclical distinction. For example, non-cyclical industries have sometimes been sorted into defensive (or stable) versus growth. Defensive industries and companies are those whose revenues and profits are least affected by fluctuations in overall economic activity. These industries/companies tend to produce staple consumer goods (e.g., bread), to provide basic services (grocery stores, drug stores, fast food outlets), or to have their rates and revenues determined by contracts or government regulation (e.g., cost-of-service, rate-of-return regulated public utilities). Growth industries would include industries with specific demand dynamics that are so strong that they override the significance of broad economic or other external factors and generate growth regardless of overall economic conditions, although their rates of growth may slow during an economic downturn.[2]

2 Sometimes the "growth" label is attached to countries or regions in which economic growth is so strong that the fluctuations in local economic activity do not produce an actual decline in economic output, merely variation from high to low rates of real growth (e.g., China, India).

The usefulness of industry and company labels such as cyclical, growth, and defensive is limited. Cyclical industries as well as growth industries often have growth companies within them. A cyclical industry itself, although exposed to the effects of fluctuations in overall economic activity, may grow at an above-average rate for periods spanning multiple business cycles. The label "**growth cyclical**" is sometimes used to describe companies that are growing rapidly on a long-term basis but that still experience above-average fluctuation in their revenues and profits over the course of a business cycle.

Furthermore, when fluctuations in economic activity are large, as in the deep recession of 2008–2009, few companies escape the effects of the cyclical weakness in overall economic activity.

The defensive label is also problematic. Industries may include both companies that are growth and companies that are defensive in character, making the choice between a "growth" and a "defensive" label difficult. Moreover, "defensive" cannot be understood as necessarily being descriptive of investment characteristics. Food supermarkets, for example, would typically be described as defensive but can be subject to profit-damaging price wars. So-called defensive industries/companies may sometimes face industry dynamics that make them far from defensive in the sense of preserving shareholders' capital.

One limitation of the cyclical/non-cyclical classification is that business-cycle sensitivity is a continuous spectrum rather than an "either/or" issue, so placement of companies in one of the two major groups is somewhat arbitrary. The impact of severe recessions usually reaches all parts of the economy, so non-cyclical is better understood as a relative term.

Another limitation of a business-cycle classification for global investing is that different countries and regions of the world frequently progress through the various stages of the business cycle at different times. While one region of the world may be experiencing economic expansion, other regions or countries may be in recession, which complicates the application of a business-cycle approach to industry analysis. For example, a jewelry retailer (i.e., a cyclical company) that is selling domestically into a weak economy will exhibit markedly different fundamental performance relative to a jewelry company operating in an environment where demand is robust. Comparing these two companies—that is, similar companies that are currently exposed to different demand environments—could suggest investment opportunities. Combining fundamental data from such companies, however, to establish industry benchmark values would be misleading.

3.3 Statistical Similarities

Statistical approaches to grouping companies are typically based on the correlations of past securities' returns. For example, using the technique known as cluster analysis, companies are separated (on the basis of historical correlations of stock returns) into groups *in which* correlations are relatively high but *between which* correlations are relatively low. This method of aggregation often results in non-intuitive groups of companies, and the composition of the groups may vary significantly by time period and region of the world. Moreover, statistical approaches rely on historical data, but analysts have no guarantee that past correlation values will continue in the future. In addition, such approaches carry the inherent dangers of all statistical methods, namely, 1) falsely indicating a relationship that arose because of chance or 2) falsely excluding a relationship that actually is significant.

4 INDUSTRY CLASSIFICATION SYSTEMS

A well-designed classification system often serves as a useful starting point for industry analysis. It allows analysts to compare industry trends and relative valuations among companies in a group. Classification systems that take a global perspective enable portfolio managers and research analysts to make global comparisons of companies in the same industry. For example, given the global nature of the automobile industry, a thorough analysis of the industry would include auto companies from many different countries and regions of the world.

4.1 Commercial Industry Classification Systems

Major index providers, including Standard & Poor's, MSCI, Russell Investments, Dow Jones, and FTSE, classify companies in their equity indexes into industry groupings. Most classification schemes used by these index providers contain multiple levels of classification that start at the broadest level with a general sector grouping, then, in several further steps, subdivide or disaggregate the sectors into more "granular" (i.e., more narrowly defined) sub-industry groups.

4.1.1 *Global Industry Classification Standard*

GICS was jointly developed by Standard & Poor's and MSCI, two of the largest providers of global equity indexes, in 1999. As the name implies, GICS was designed to facilitate global comparisons of industries, and it classifies companies in both developed and developing economies. Each company is assigned to a sub-industry according to its principal business activity. Each sub-industry belongs to a particular industry; each industry belongs to an industry group; and each group belongs to a sector. In June 2018, the GICS classification structure comprised four levels of detail consisting of 157 sub-industries, 68 industries, 24 industry groups, and 11 sectors. The composition of GICS has historically been adjusted over time to reflect changes in the global equity markets.

4.1.2 *Russell Global Sectors*

The RGS classification system uses a three-tier structure to classify companies globally on the basis of the products or services a company produces. In June 2018, the RGS classification system consisted of 9 sectors, 33 subsectors, and 157 industries. Besides the number of tiers, another difference between the RGS and GICS classification systems is that the RGS system contains nine sectors, whereas GICS consists of eleven. For example, the RGS system does not provide a separate sector for telecommunication service companies. Many companies that GICS classifies as "Telecommunication Services," including China Mobile Ltd., AT&T, and Telefonica, are assigned by RGS to its more broadly defined "Utilities" sector.

4.1.3 *Industry Classification Benchmark*

The Industry Classification Benchmark (ICB), which was jointly developed by Dow Jones and FTSE, uses a four-tier structure to categorize companies globally on the basis of the source from which a company derives the majority of its revenue. In June 2018, the ICB classification system consisted of 10 industries, 19 supersectors, 41 sectors, and 114 subsectors. Although the ICB is similar to GICS in the number of tiers and the method by which companies are assigned to particular groups, the two systems use significantly different nomenclature. For example, whereas GICS uses the term "sector" to describe its broadest grouping of companies, ICB uses the term "industry." Another difference between the two systems is that ICB distinguishes between consumer goods and consumer services companies, whereas both GICS and the RGS systems group consumer products companies and consumer services companies together into sectors on the basis of economic sensitivity. These stylistic distinctions tend to be less obvious at the more granular levels of the different hierarchies.

Despite these subtle differences, the three commercial classification systems use common methodologies for assigning companies to groups. Also, the broadest level of grouping for all three systems is quite similar. Specifically, GICS, the RGS, and the ICB each identify 9 to 11 broad groupings below which all other categories reside. Next, we describe sectors that are fairly representative of how the broadest level of industry classification is viewed by GICS, RGS, and ICB.

4.1.4 *Description of Representative Sectors*

Basic Materials and Processing: companies engaged in the production of building materials, chemicals, paper and forest products, containers and packaging, and metal, mineral, and mining companies.

Consumer Discretionary: companies that derive a majority of revenue from the sale of consumer-related products or services for which demand tends to exhibit a relatively high degree of economic sensitivity. Examples of business activities that frequently fall into this category are automotive, apparel, hotel, and restaurant businesses.

Consumer Staples: consumer-related companies whose business tends to exhibit less economic sensitivity than other companies; for example, manufacturers of food, beverage, tobacco, and personal care products.

Energy: companies whose primary line of business involves the exploration, production, or refining of natural resources used to produce energy; companies that derive a majority of revenue from the sale of equipment or through the provision of services to energy companies would also fall into this category.

Financial Services: companies whose primary line of business involves banking, finance, insurance, real estate, asset management, and/or brokerage services.

Health Care: manufacturers of pharmaceutical and biotech products, medical devices, health care equipment, and medical supplies and providers of health care services.

Industrial/Producer Durables: manufacturers of capital goods and providers of commercial services; for example, business activities would include heavy machinery and equipment manufacture, aerospace and defense, transportation services, and commercial services and supplies.

Real Estate: companies engaged in development and operation of real estate. This includes companies offering real estate related services as well as equity real estate investment trusts (REITs).

Technology: companies involved in the manufacture or sale of computers, software, semiconductors, and communications equipment; other business activities that frequently fall into this category are electronic entertainment, internet services, and technology consulting and services.

Telecommunications: companies that provide fixed-line and wireless communication services; some vendors prefer to combine telecommunication and utility companies together into a single "utilities" category.

Utilities: electric, gas, and water utilities; telecommunication companies are sometimes included in this category.

To classify a company accurately in a particular classification scheme requires definitions of the classification categories, a statement about the criteria used in classification, and detailed information about the subject company. Example 2 introduces an exercise in such classification. In addressing the question, the reader can make use of the widely applicable sector descriptions just given and familiarity with available business products and services.

EXAMPLE 2

Classifying Companies into Industries

The text defines 11 representative sectors, repeated here in Exhibit 1. Suppose the classification system is based on the criterion of a company's principal business activity as judged primarily by source of revenue.

Exhibit 1 Eleven Sectors

Sector
Basic Materials and Processing
Consumer Discretionary
Consumer Staples
Energy
Financial Services
Health Care
Industrial/Producer Durables
Real Estate
Technology
Telecommunications
Utilities

Based on the information given, determine an appropriate industry membership for each of the following hypothetical companies:

0 An operator of shopping malls
1 A natural gas transporter and marketer
2 A manufacturer of heavy construction equipment
3 A provider of regional telephone services
4 A semiconductor company
5 A manufacturer of medical devices
6 A chain of supermarkets
7 A manufacturer of chemicals and plastics
8 A manufacturer of automobiles
9 An investment management company
10 A manufacturer of luxury leather goods
11 A regulated supplier of electricity
12 A provider of wireless broadband services
13 A manufacturer of soaps and detergents

14 A software development company

15 An insurer

16 A regulated provider of water/wastewater services

17 A petroleum (oil) service company

18 A manufacturer of pharmaceuticals

19 A provider of rail transportation services

20 A metals mining company

21 A developer of residential housing

Solution:

Sector	Company Number
Basic Materials and Processing	7, 20
Consumer Discretionary	8, 10
Consumer Staples	6, 13
Energy	1, 17
Financial Services	9, 15
Health Care	5, 18
Industrial/Producer Durables	2, 19
Real Estate	0, 21
Technology	4, 14
Telecommunications	3, 12
Utilities	11, 16

Example 3 reviews some major concepts in industry classification.

EXAMPLE 3

Industry Classification Schemes

1 The GICS classification system classifies companies on the basis of a company's primary business activity as measured primarily by:

  A assets.

  B income.

  C revenue.

2 Which of the following is *least likely* to be accurately described as a cyclical company? A(n):

  A automobile manufacturer.

  B producer of breakfast cereals.

  C apparel company producing the newest trendy clothes for teenage girls.

3 Which of the following is the *most accurate* statement? A statistical approach to grouping companies into industries:

  A is based on historical correlations of the securities' returns.

B frequently produces industry groups whose composition is similar worldwide.

C emphasizes the descriptive statistics of industries consisting of companies producing similar products and/or services.

Solution to 1:

C is correct.

Solution to 2:

B is correct. A producer of staple foods such as cereals is a classic example of a non-cyclical company. Demand for automobiles is cyclical—that is, relatively high during economic expansions and relatively low during economic contractions. Also, demand for teenage fashions is likely to be more sensitive to the business cycle than demand for standard food items such as breakfast cereals. When budgets have been reduced, families may try to avoid expensive clothing or extend the life of existing wardrobes.

Solution to 3:

A is correct.

4.2 Governmental Industry Classification Systems

A number of classification systems in use by various governmental agencies today organize statistical data according to type of industrial or economic activity. A common goal of each government classification system is to facilitate the comparison of data—both over time and among countries that use the same system. Continuity of the data is critical to the measurement and evaluation of economic performance over time.

4.2.1 *International Standard Industrial Classification of All Economic Activities*

The International Standard Industrial Classification of All Economic Activities (ISIC) was adopted by the United Nations in 1948 to address the need for international comparability of economic statistics. ISIC classifies entities into various categories on the basis of the principal type of economic activity the entity performs. ISIC is organized into 11 categories, 21 sections, 88 divisions, 233 groups, and more than 400 classes. According to the United Nations, a majority of the countries around the world have either used ISIC as their national activity classification system or have developed national classifications derived from ISIC. Some of the organizations currently using the ISIC are the UN and its specialized agencies, the International Monetary Fund, the World Bank, and other international bodies.

4.2.2 *Statistical Classification of Economic Activities in the European Community*

Often regarded as the European version of ISIC, Statistical Classification of Economic Activities in the European Community (NACE) is the classification of economic activities that correspond to ISIC at the European level. Similar to ISIC, NACE classification is organized according to economic activity. NACE is composed of four levels—namely, sections (identified by alphabetical letters A through U), divisions (identified by two-digit numerical codes 01 through 99), groups (identified by three-digit numerical codes 01.1 through 99.0), and classes (identified by four-digit numerical codes 01.11 through 99.00).

4.2.3 *Australian and New Zealand Standard Industrial Classification*

The Australian and New Zealand Standard Industrial Classification (ANZSIC) was jointly developed by the Australian Bureau of Statistics and Statistics New Zealand in 1993 to facilitate the comparison of industry statistics of the two countries and comparisons with the rest of the world. International comparability was achieved by aligning ANZSIC with the international standards used by ISIC. ANZSIC has a structure comprising five levels—namely, divisions (the broadest level), subdivisions, groups, classes, and at the most granular level, subclasses (New Zealand only).

4.2.4 *North American Industry Classification System*

Jointly developed by the United States, Canada, and Mexico, the North American Industry Classification System (NAICS) replaced the Standard Industrial Classification (SIC) system in 1997. NAICS distinguishes between establishments and enterprises. NAICS classifies establishments into industries according to the primary business activity of the establishment. In the NAICS system, an *establishment* is defined as "a single physical location where business is conducted or where services or industrial operations are performed" (e.g., factory, store, hotel, movie theater, farm, office). An *enterprise* may consist of more than one location performing the same or different types of economic activities. Each establishment of that enterprise is assigned a NAICS code on the basis of its own primary business activity.[3]

NAICS uses a two-digit through six-digit code to structure its categories into five levels of detail. The greater the number of digits in the code, the more narrowly defined the category. The five levels of categories, from broadest to narrowest, are sector (signified by the first two digits of the code), subsector (third digit of the code), industry group (fourth digit), NAICS industry (fifth digit), and national industry (sixth digit). The five-digit code is the level of greatest amount of comparability among countries; a six-digit code provides for more country-specific detail.

Although differences exist, the structures of ISIC, NACE, ANZSIC, and NAICS are similar enough that many of the categories from each of the different classification systems are compatible with one another. The US Census Bureau has published tables showing how the various categories of the classification systems relate to one another.[4]

4.3 Strengths and Weaknesses of Current Systems

Unlike commercial classification systems, most government systems do not disclose information about a specific business or company, so an analyst cannot know all of the constituents of a particular category. For example, in the United States, federal law prohibits the Census Bureau from disclosing individual company activities, so, their NAICS and SIC codes are unknown.

Most government and commercial classification systems are reviewed and, if necessary, updated from time to time. Generally, commercial classification systems are adjusted more frequently than government classification systems, which may be updated only every five years or so. NAICS, for example, is reviewed for potential revisions every five years.

Government classification systems generally do not distinguish between small and large businesses, between for-profit and not-for-profit organizations, or between public and private companies. Many commercial classification systems have the ability to distinguish between large and small companies by virtue of association with a particular equity index, and these systems include only for-profit and publicly traded organizations.

3 For more information, see www.census.gov/eos/www/naics/faqs/faqs.html#q2.

4 For more information, see www.census.gov/eos/www/naics/concordances/concordances.html.

Another limitation of current systems is that the narrowest classification unit assigned to a company generally cannot be assumed to be its peer group for the purposes of detailed fundamental comparisons or valuation. A **peer group** is a group of companies engaged in similar business activities whose economics and valuation are influenced by closely related factors. Comparisons of a company in relation to a well-defined peer group can provide valuable insights into the company's performance and its relative valuation.

4.4 Constructing a Peer Group

The construction of a peer group is a subjective process; the result often differs significantly from even the most narrowly defined categories given by the commercial classification systems. However, commercial classification systems do provide a starting point for the construction of a relevant peer group because, by using such systems, an analyst can quickly discover the public companies operating in the chosen industry.

In fact, one approach to constructing a peer group is to start by identifying other companies operating in the same industry. Analysts who subscribe to one or more of the commercial classification systems that were discussed in Section 4.1 can quickly generate a list of other companies in the industry in which the company operates according to that particular service provider's definition of the industry. An analyst can then investigate the business activities of these companies and make adjustments as necessary to ensure that the businesses truly are comparable. The following lists of suggested steps and questions are given as practical aids to analysts in identifying peer companies.

Steps in constructing a preliminary list of peer companies

- Examine commercial classification systems, if available to the analyst. These systems often provide a useful starting point for identifying companies operating in the same industry.
- Review the subject company's annual report for a discussion of the competitive environment. Companies frequently cite specific competitors.
- Review competitors' annual reports to identify other potential comparable companies.
- Review industry trade publications to identify comparable companies.
- Confirm that each comparable company derives a significant portion of its revenue and operating profit from a business activity similar to the primary business of the subject company.

Questions that may improve the list of peer companies

- What proportion of revenue and operating profit is derived from business activities similar to those of the subject company? In general, a higher percentage results in a more meaningful comparison.

- Does a potential peer company face a demand environment similar to that of the subject company? For example, a comparison of growth rates, margins, and valuations may be of limited value when comparing companies that are exposed to different stages of the business cycle. (As mentioned, such differences may be the result of conducting business in geographically different markets.)
- Does a potential company have a finance subsidiary? Some companies operate a finance division to facilitate the sale of their products (e.g., Caterpillar Inc. and John Deere). To make a meaningful comparison of companies, the analyst should make adjustments to the financial statements to lessen the impact that the finance subsidiaries have on the various financial metrics being compared.

Example 4 illustrates the process of identifying a peer group of companies and shows some of the practical hurdles to determining a peer group.

EXAMPLE 4

An Analyst Researches the Peer Group of Brink's

Suppose that an analyst needs to identify the peer group of companies for Brink's for use in the valuation section of a company report. The Brink's Company (Brink's) is a provider of logistics and security solutions. Brink's operates through nine segments: US, France, Mexico, Brazil, Canada, Latin America, EMEA, Asia, and Payment Services. The analyst starts by looking at Brink's industry classification according to GICS. As previously discussed, the most narrowly defined category that GICS uses is the sub-industry level, and in June 2018, Brink's was in the GICS sub-industry called Security & Alarm Services, together with the companies listed here:

GICS Sector: Industrials
- GICS Industry Group: Commercial and Professional Services
  - GICS Industry: Commercial Services and Supplies
    - GICS Sub-Industry: Security and Alarm Services
      - Brink's, Inc.
      - AMN Healthcare Services, Inc.
      - Corecivic Inc.
      - Healthcare Services Group, Inc.
      - Korn/Ferry International
      - UniFirst Group
      - TriNet Group Inc.
      - Insperity Inc.
      - BEST Inc. (ADR)
      - Maximus, Inc.
      - ASGN Inc.
      - ManpowerGroup Inc.
      - Genpact Limited

After looking over the list of companies, the analyst quickly realizes that some adjustments need to be made to the list to end up with a peer group of companies that are comparable to Brink's. For example, Brink's has little in common with the talent management (executive search) services of Korn/Ferry

International. In fact, after careful inspection, the analyst concludes that none of the other companies included in the GICS sub-industry are particularly good "comparables" for Brink's.

Next, the analyst reviews the latest annual report for Brink's to find management statements concerning its competitors. On page 6 of Brink's 2017 10-K, in the section titled "Industry Trends and Competition," is a list of other companies with comparable business activities: "Brink's competes with large multinational, regional and smaller companies throughout the world. Our largest multinational competitors are G4S plc (UK); Loomis AB (Sweden); Prosegur Compania de Seguridad, S.A (Spain); and Garda World Security Corporation (Canada)." The analyst notes that G4S, Loomis, and Prosegur Compania de Seguridad S.A are all publicly held security services companies and are likely candidates for inclusion in the peer group for Brink's. Garda World Security Corporation is privately held, so the analyst excludes it from the peer group; up-to-date, detailed fundamental data are not available for it.

Just as the analyst reviewed the latest annual report for Brink's to identify additional potential comparables, the analyst should also scan the annual reports of the other companies listed to see if other comparables exist. In checking these three companies' annual reports, the analyst finds no additional specific competitors cited by the three companies.

The analyst decides that Brink's peer group consists of G4S plc (UK); Loomis AB (Sweden); Prosegur Compania de Seguridad, S.A (Spain).

In connection with this discussion, note that International Financial Reporting Standards and US GAAP require companies to disclose financial information about their operating segments (subject to certain qualifications). Such disclosures provide analysts with operational and financial information that can be helpful in peer-group determination.

Although companies with limited lines of business may neatly be categorized into a single peer group, companies with multiple divisions may be included in more than one category. For example, Belgium-based Anheuser-Busch InBev primarily makes and sells various brands of beer. It can easily be grouped together with other beverage companies (the theme park business constitutes a relatively immaterial part of total revenue). However, US-based Hewlett-Packard Company (HP), a global provider of technology and software solutions, might reasonably be included in more than one category. Investors interested in the personal computer (PC) industry, for example, would probably include HP in their peer group, but investors constructing a peer group of providers of information technology services would probably include HP in that group also.

In summary, analysts must distinguish between a company's industry—as defined by one or more of the various classification systems—and its peer group. A company's peer group should consist of companies with similar business activities whose economic activity depends on similar drivers of demand and similar factors related to cost structure and access to financial capital. In practice, these necessities frequently result in a smaller group (even a different group) of companies than the most narrowly defined categories used by the common commercial classification systems. Example 5 illustrates various aspects of developing and using peer groups.

EXAMPLE 5

The Semiconductor Industry: Business-Cycle Sensitivity and Peer-Group Determination

The GICS semiconductor and semiconductor equipment industry (453010) has two sub-industries—the semiconductor equipment sub-industry (45301010) and the semiconductors sub-industry (45301020). Members of the semiconductor equipment sub-industry include equipment suppliers such as Lam Research Corporation and ASML Holdings NV; the semiconductors sub-industry includes integrated circuit manufacturers Intel Corporation and Taiwan Semiconductor Manufacturing Company (TSMC) Ltd.

Lam Research is a leading supplier of wafer fabrication equipment and services to the world's semiconductor industry. Lam also offers wafer-cleaning equipment that is used after many of the individual steps required to manufacture a finished wafer. Often, the technical advances that Lam introduces in its wafer-etching and wafer-cleaning products are also available as upgrades to its installed base. This benefit provides customers with a cost-effective way to extend the performance and capabilities of their existing wafer fabrication lines.

ASML describes itself as the world's leading provider of lithography systems (etching and printing on wafers) for the semiconductor industry. ASML manufactures complex machines that are critical to the production of integrated circuits or microchips. ASML designs, develops, integrates, markets, and services these advanced systems, which help chip makers reduce the size and increase the functionality of microchips and consumer electronic equipment. The machines are costly and thus represent a substantial capital investment for a purchaser.

Based on revenue, Intel is the world's largest semiconductor chip maker and has the dominant share of microprocessors for the personal computer market. Intel has made significant investments in research and development (R&D) to introduce and produce new chips for new applications.

Established in 1987, Taiwan Semiconductor Manufacturing (TSMC) is the world's largest dedicated semiconductor foundries (semiconductor fabrication plants that execute the designs of other companies). TSMC describes itself as offering cutting-edge process technologies, pioneering design services, manufacturing efficiency, and product quality. The company's revenues represented more than 50 percent of the dedicated foundry segment in the semiconductor industry.

The questions that follow take the perspective of a recession similar to that of early 2009, when many economies around the world were in a recession. Based only on the information given, answer the following questions:

1 If the weak economy, similar to that of early 2009 were to recover within the next 12–18 months, which of the two sub-industries of the semiconductor and semiconductor equipment industry would most likely be the first to experience a positive improvement in business?

2 Explain whether Intel and TSMC should be considered members of the same peer group.

3 Explain whether Lam Research and ASML should be considered members of the same peer group.

Solution to 1:

In the most likely scenario, improvement in the business of the equipment makers (Lam and ASML) would lag that of semiconductor companies (Intel and TSM). Because of the weak economy, excess manufacturing capacity should be available to meet increased demand for integrated circuits in the near term without additional equipment, which is a major capital investment. When semiconductor manufacturers believe the longer-term outlook has improved, they should begin to place orders for additional equipment.

Solution to 2:

Intel and TSMC are not likely to be considered comparable members of the same peer group because they have different sets of customers and different business models. Intel designs and produces its own proprietary semiconductors for direct sale to customers, such as personal computer makers. TSMC provides design and production services to a diverse group of integrated circuit suppliers that generally do not have their own in-house manufacturing capabilities. Standard & Poor's does not group Intel and TSMC in the same peer group; Intel was in the Semiconductors, Logic, Larger Companies group and TSMC was in the Semiconductors, Foundry Services group.

Solution to 3:

Both Lam Research and ASML are leading companies that design and manufacture equipment to produce semiconductor chips. The companies are comparable because they both depend on the same economic factors that drive demand for their products. Their major customers are the semiconductor chip companies. Standard & Poor's grouped both companies in the same peer group—Semiconductor Equipment, Larger Front End.

The next section addresses fundamental skills in describing and analyzing an industry.

5 DESCRIBING AND ANALYZING AN INDUSTRY

In their work, analysts study statistical relationships between industry trends and a range of economic and business variables. Analysts use economic, industry, and business publications and internet resources as sources of information. They also seek information from industry associations, from the individual subject companies they are analyzing, and from these companies' competitors, suppliers, and customers. An analyst with a superior knowledge about an industry's characteristics, conditions, and trends has a competitive edge in evaluating the investment merits of the companies in the industry.

Analysts attempt to develop practical, reliable industry forecasts by using various approaches to forecasting. They often estimate a range of projections for a variable reflecting various possible scenarios. Analysts may seek to compare their projections with the projections of other analysts, partly to study differences in methodology and conclusions but also to identify differences between their forecasts and consensus forecasts. These latter differences are extremely important for uncovering investment opportunities because, to be the basis for superior investment performance, the forecast for a value-relevant variable must be both correct and sufficiently different from the consensus reflected in the price of publicly traded securities. Note that, although some information on analysts' revenue projections, EPS estimates, and ratings are accessible in some markets, analysts may have limited access to details about other analysts' work and assumptions because such details are kept confidential for competitive reasons.

Investment managers and analysts also examine industry performance 1) in relation to other industries to identify industries with superior/inferior returns and 2) over time to determine the degree of consistency, stability, and risk in the returns in the industry over time. The objective of this analysis is to identify industries that offer the highest potential for investment returns on a risk-adjusted basis. The investment time horizon can be either long or short, as is the case for a rotation strategy in which portfolios are rotated into the industry groups that are expected to benefit from the next stage in the business cycle.

Often, analysts examine **strategic groups** (groups sharing distinct business models or catering to specific market segments in an industry) almost as separate industries within industries. Criteria for selecting a strategic group might include the complexity of the product or service, its mode of delivery, and "barriers to entry." For example, charter airlines form a strategic group among "airlines" that is quite distinct from scheduled airlines; full-service hotels form a strategic group that is separate from limited-service or budget hotels; and companies that sell proprietary drugs (which are protected by patents) would be in a separate group from companies that sell generic drugs (which do not have patent protection) partly because the two groups pursue different strategies and use different business models.

Analysts often consider and classify industries according to industry **life-cycle stage**. The analyst determines whether an industry is in the embryonic, growth, shakeout, mature, or declining stage of the industry life cycle. During the stages of the life cycle of a product or industry, its position on the experience curve is often analyzed. The **experience curve** shows direct cost per unit of good or service produced or delivered as a typically declining function of cumulative output. The curve declines 1) because as the utilization of capital equipment increases, fixed costs (administration, overhead, advertising, etc.) are spread over a larger number of units of production, 2) because of improvements in labor efficiency and management of facilities, and 3) because of advances in production methods and product design. Examples exist in virtually all industries, but the experience curve is especially important in industries with high fixed overhead costs and/or repetitive production operations, such as electronics and appliance, automobile, and aircraft manufacturing. The industry life cycle is discussed in depth later in this reading.

Exhibit 2 provides a framework designed to help analysts check that they have considered the range of forces that may affect the evolution of an industry. It shows, at the macro level, macroeconomic, demographic, governmental, social, and technological influences affecting the industry. It then depicts how an industry is affected by the forces driving industry competition (threat of new entrants, substitution threats, customer and supplier bargaining forces), the competitive forces in the industry, life-cycle issues, business-cycle considerations, and position of the industry on the experience curve. Exhibit 2 summarizes and brings together pictorially topics and concepts discussed in this section.

Exhibit 2 A Framework for Industry Analysis

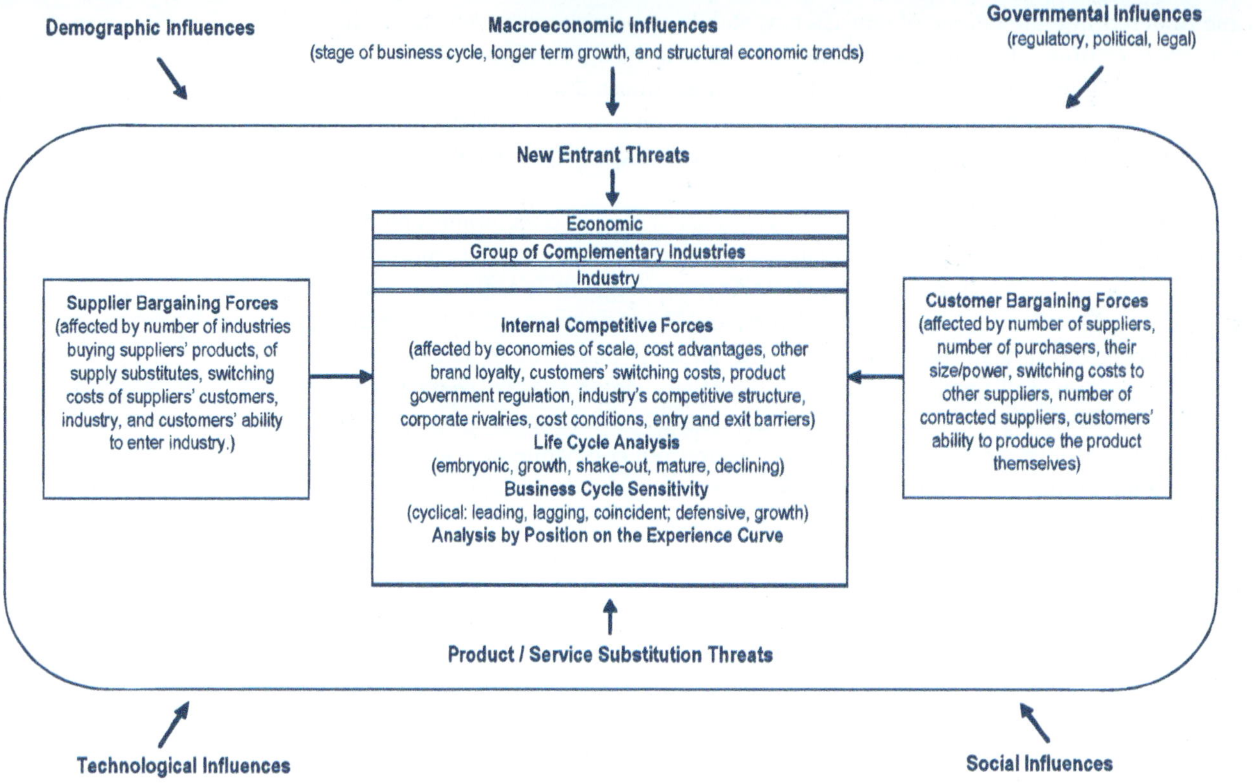

5.1 Principles of Strategic Analysis

When analyzing an industry, the analyst must recognize that the economic fundamentals can vary markedly among industries. Some industries are highly competitive, with most players struggling to earn adequate returns on capital, whereas other industries have attractive characteristics that allow almost all industry participants to generate healthy profits. Exhibit 3 makes this point graphically. It shows the average spread between return on invested capital (ROIC) and the cost of capital for 11 industries from 2014 through 2018.[5] Industries earning positive spreads appear to be earning **economic profits**, in the sense that they are achieving returns on investment above the opportunity cost of funds. This result should create value—that is, should increase the wealth of the investors, who are the providers of capital. In contrast, industries that are realizing negative spreads are destroying value. As can be seen, some industries struggled to generate positive economic returns (i.e., to create value) even during this period of synchronized global growth, while other industries did very well in earning such returns.

5 Return on invested capital can be defined as net operating profit after tax divided by the sum of common and preferred equity, long-term debt, and minority interests.

Exhibit 3 Some Industries Create Value, Others Destroy It: Average Industry ROIC Minus WACC, 2014–2018

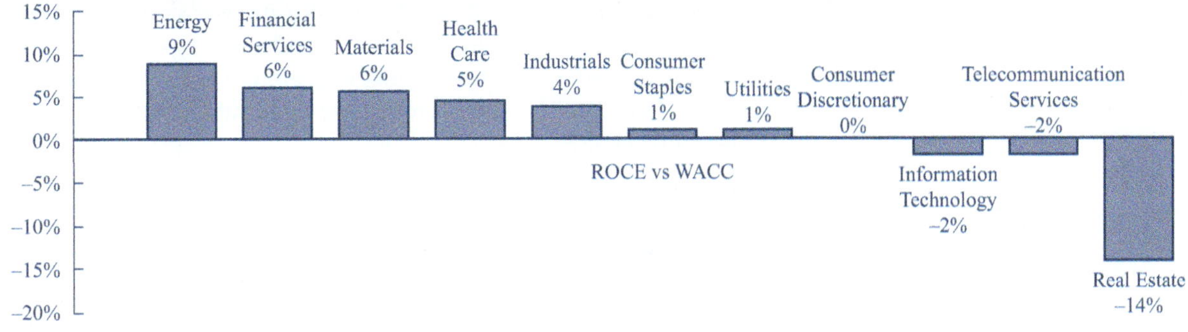

Source: Capital IQ.

Differing competitive environments are often tied to the structural attributes of an industry, which is one reason industry analysis is a vital complement to company analysis. To thoroughly analyze a company itself, the analyst needs to understand the context in which the company operates. Needless to say, industry analysis must be forward looking. Many of the industries in Exhibit 3 were very different 10 or 15 years ago and would have been placed differently with respect to value creation; many will look very different 10 or 15 years from now. As analysts examine the competitive structure of an industry, they should always be thinking about what attributes could change in the future.

Analysis of the competitive environment with an emphasis on the implications of the environment for corporate strategy is known as **strategic analysis**. Michael Porter's "five forces" framework is the classic starting point for strategic analysis;[6] although it was originally aimed more at internal managers of businesses than at external security analysts, the framework is useful to both.[7]

Porter (2008) identified the following five determinants of the intensity of competition in an industry:

- The **threat of entry** to the industry, which depends on barriers to entry, or how difficult it would be for new competitors to enter the industry. Industries that are easy to enter will generally be more competitive than industries with high barriers to entry.
- The **power of suppliers**, which may be able to raise prices or restrict the supply of key inputs to a company. For example, workers at a heavily unionized company may have greater bargaining power as suppliers of labor than workers at a comparable non-unionized company. Suppliers of scarce or limited parts or elements often possess significant pricing power.
- The **power of buyers**, which can affect the intensity of competition by exerting influence on suppliers regarding prices (and possibly other factors such as product quality). For example, auto parts companies generally sell to a small number of auto manufacturers, which allows those customers, the auto manufacturers, to be tough negotiators when it comes to setting prices.

6 See Porter (2008).

7 What aspects of a company are important may be different for internal and external analysts. Whether information about competitive positions is accurately reflected in market prices, for example, would be relatively more important to external analysts.

- The **threat of substitutes**, which can negatively affect demand if customers choose other ways of satisfying their needs. For example, consumers may trade down from premium beers to discount brands during recessions. Low-priced brands may be close substitutes for premium brands, which, when consumer budgets are constrained, reduces the ability of premium brands to maintain or increase prices. Substitutes do not have to be similar but can satisfy a need with a very different product.
- The **rivalry among existing competitors**, which is a function of the industry's competitive structure. Industries that are fragmented among many small competitors, have high fixed costs, provide undifferentiated (commodity-like) products, or have high exit barriers usually experience more intense rivalry than industries without these characteristics.

Although all five of these forces merit attention, the first and fifth are particularly recommended as a first focus for analysis. The two factors are broadly applicable because all companies have competitors and must worry about new entrants to their industries. Also, in investigating these two forces, the analyst may become familiar in detail with an industry's incumbents and potential entrants, and all these companies' relative competitive prospects.

Addressing the following questions should help the analyst evaluate the threat of new entrants and the level of competition in an industry and thereby provide an effective base for describing and analyzing the industry:

- What are the barriers to entry? Is it difficult or easy for a new competitor to challenge incumbents? Relatively high (low) barriers to entry imply that the threat of new entrants is relatively low (high).
- How concentrated is the industry? Do a small number of companies control a relatively large share of the market, or does the industry have many players, each with a small market share?
- What are capacity levels? That is, based on existing investment, how much of the goods or services can be delivered in a given time frame? Does the industry suffer chronic over- or under-capacity, or do supply and demand tend to come into balance reasonably quickly in the industry?
- How stable are market shares? Do companies tend to rapidly gain or lose share, or is the industry stable?
- Where is the industry in its life cycle? Does it have meaningful growth prospects, or is demand stagnant/declining?
- How important is price to the customer's purchase decision?

The answers to these questions are elements of any thorough industry analysis.

5.1.1 *Barriers to Entry*

When a company is earning economic profits, the chances that it will be able to sustain them through time are greater, all else being equal, if the industry has high barriers to entry. The ease with which new competitors can challenge incumbents is often an important factor in determining the competitive landscape of an industry. If new competitors can easily enter the industry, the industry is likely to be highly competitive because high returns on invested capital will quickly be competed away by new entrants eager to grab their share of economic profits. As a result, industries with low barriers to entry often have little pricing power because price increases that raise companies' returns on capital will eventually attract new competitors to the industry.

If incumbents are protected by barriers to entry, the threat of new entrants is lower, and incumbents may enjoy a more benign competitive environment. Often, these barriers to entry can lead to greater pricing power, because potential competitors would find it difficult to enter the industry and undercut incumbents' prices. Of course, high barriers to entry do not guarantee pricing power, because incumbents may compete fiercely among each other.

A classic example of an industry with low barriers to entry is restaurants. Anyone with a modest amount of capital and some culinary skill can open a restaurant, and popular restaurants quickly attract competition. As a result, the industry is very competitive, and many restaurants fail in their first few years of business.

At the other end of the spectrum of barriers to entry are the global credit card networks such as MasterCard and Visa, both of which often post operating margins greater than 30 percent. Such high profits should attract competition, but the barriers to entry are extremely high. Capital costs are one hurdle; also, building a massive data-processing network would not be cheap. Imagine for a moment that a venture capitalist was willing to fund the construction of a network that would replicate the physical infrastructure of the incumbents—the new card-processing company would have to convince millions of consumers to use the new card and convince thousands of merchants to accept the card. Consumers would not want to use a card that merchants did not accept, and merchants would not want to accept a card that few consumers carried. This problem would be difficult to solve, which is why the barriers to entering this industry are quite high. The barriers help preserve the profitability of the incumbent players.

One way of understanding barriers to entry is simply by thinking about what it would take for new players to compete in an industry. How much money would they need to spend? What kind of intellectual capital would they need to acquire? How easy would it be to attract enough customers to become successful?

Another way to investigate the issue is by looking at historical data. How often have new companies tried to enter the industry? Is a list of industry participants today markedly different from what it was five or ten years ago? These kinds of data can be very helpful because the information is based on the real-world experience of many entrepreneurs and businesses making capital allocation decisions. If an industry has seen a flood of new entrants over the past several years, odds are good that the barriers are low; conversely, if the same ten companies that dominate an industry today dominated it ten years ago, barriers to entry are probably fairly high.

Do not confuse barriers to *entry*, however, with barriers to *success*. In some industries, entering may be easy but becoming successful enough to threaten the incumbents might be quite hard. For example, in the United States, starting a mutual fund requires a capital investment of perhaps US$150,000—not much of a barrier to an industry with historically high returns on capital. But once one has started a mutual fund, how does the company gather assets? Financial intermediaries are unlikely to sell a mutual fund with no track record. So, the fund may need to incur operational losses for a few years until it has established a good track record. Even with a track record, the fund will be competing in a crowded marketplace against companies with massive advertising budgets and well-paid salespeople. In this industry, good distribution can be even more valuable than good performance. So, although entering the asset management industry may be relatively easy, succeeding is another thing altogether.

Also, high barriers to entry do not automatically lead to good pricing power and attractive industry economics. Consider the cases of auto making, commercial aircraft manufacturing, and refining industries. Starting up a new company in any of these industries would be tremendously difficult. Aside from the massive capital costs, there would be significant other barriers to entry: A new automaker would need manufacturing expertise and a dealer network; an aircraft manufacturer would need a tremendous amount of intellectual capital; and a refiner would need process expertise and regulatory approvals.

Yet, all of these industries are quite competitive, with limited or nonexistent pricing power, and few industry participants reliably generate returns on capital in excess of their costs of capital. Among the reasons for this seeming paradox of high barriers to entry plus poor pricing power, two stand out.

- First, price is a large component of the customer's purchase decision when buying from these companies in these industries. In some cases, the reason is that the companies (e.g., refiners) sell a commodity; in some cases, the product is expensive but has easily available substitutes. For example, most airlines choose between purchasing Boeing and Airbus airplanes not on brand but on cost-related considerations: Airlines need to transport people and cargo at the lowest possible cost per mile because the airlines have limited ability to pass along higher costs to customers. That consideration makes price a huge component of their purchase decision. Most airlines purchase whichever plane is the most cost efficient at any point in time. The result is that the Boeing Company and Airbus have limited ability to price their planes at a level that generates good returns on invested capital.[8]
- Second, these industries all have high barriers to exit, which means they are prone to overcapacity. A refinery or automobile plant cannot be used for anything other than, respectively, refining oil or producing cars, which makes it hard to redeploy the capital elsewhere and exit the industry if conditions become unprofitable. This barrier gives owners of these types of assets a strong incentive to attempt to keep those loss-making plants operating, which, of course, prolongs conditions of overcapacity.

A final consideration when analyzing barriers to entry is that they can change over time. Years ago, a potential new entrant to the semiconductor industry would have needed the capital and expertise to build a "fab" (the industry term for a semiconductor fabrication facility). Chip fabs are hugely expensive and technologically complex, which deterred potential new entrants. Starting in the mid-1990s, however, the outsourcing of chip making to contract semiconductor manufacturers became feasible, which meant that designers of chips could challenge the manufacturers without the need to build their own plants. As a result, the industry became much more fragmented through the late 1990s and into the first decade of the 21st century.

So, in general, high barriers to entry can lead to better pricing and less competitive industry conditions, but important exceptions are worth bearing in mind.

5.1.2 *Industry Concentration*

Much like industries with barriers to entry, industries that are concentrated among a relatively small number of players often experience relatively less price competition. Again, there are important exceptions, so the reader should not automatically assume that concentrated industries always have pricing power or that fragmented industries do not.

An analysis of industry concentration should start with market share: What percentage of the market does each of the largest players have, and how large are those shares relative to each other and relative to the remainder of the market? Often, the *relative* market shares of competitors matter as much as their *absolute* market shares.

8 Neither company's commercial aircraft segment has reliably generated returns on capital comfortably in excess of the company's cost of capital for many years. Boeing's returns on capital have been respectable overall, but the company's military segment is much more profitable than its commercial aircraft segment.

For example, the global market for long-haul commercial aircraft is extremely concentrated—only Boeing and Airbus manufacture these types of planes. The two companies have roughly similar market shares, however, and control essentially the entire market. Because neither enjoys a scale advantage relative to its competitor and because any business gained by one is lost by the other, competition tends to be fierce.

This situation contrasts with the market for home improvement products in the United States, which is dominated by Home Depot and Lowe's. These two companies have 11 percent and 7 percent market share, respectively, which doesn't sound very large. However, the next largest competitor has only 2 percent of the market, and most market participants are tiny with miniscule market shares. Both Home Depot and Lowe's have historically posted high returns on invested capital, in part because they could profitably grow by targeting smaller competitors rather than engaging in fierce competition with each other.

Fragmented industries tend to be highly price competitive for several reasons. First, the large number of companies makes coordination difficult because there are too many competitors for each industry member to monitor effectively. Second, each player has such a small piece of the market that even a small gain in market share can make a meaningful difference to its fortunes, which increases the incentive of each company to undercut prices and attempt to steal share. Finally, the large number of players encourages industry members to think of themselves individualistically rather than as members of a larger group, which can lead to fierce competitive behavior.

In concentrated industries, in contrast, each player can relatively easily keep track of what its competitors are doing, which makes tacit coordination much more feasible. Also, leading industry members are large, which means they have more to lose—and proportionately less to gain—by destructive price behavior. Large companies are also more tied to the fortunes of the industry as a whole, making them more likely to consider the long-run effects of a price war on overall industry economics.

As with barriers to entry, the level of industry concentration is a guideline rather than a hard and fast rule when thinking about the level of pricing power in an industry. For example, Exhibit 4 shows a rough classification of industries compiled by Morningstar after asking its equity analysts whether industries were characterized by strong or weak pricing power and whether those industries were concentrated or fragmented. Examples of companies in industries are included in parentheses. In the upper right quadrant ("concentrated with weak pricing power"), those industries that are capital intensive and/or sell commodity-like products are shown in boldface.

Exhibit 4 A Two-Factor Analysis of Industries

Concentrated with Strong Pricing Power	Concentrated with Weak Pricing Power
Soft Drinks (Coca-Cola Co., PepsiCo)	**Commercial Aircraft (Boeing, Airbus)**
Orthopedic Devices (Zimmer, Smith & Nephew)	**Automobiles (General Motors, Toyota, Daimler)**
Laboratory Services (Quest Diagnostics, LabCorp)	**Memory (DRAM & Flash Product, Samsung, Hynix)**
Biotech (Amgen, Genzyme)	**Semiconductor Equipment (Applied Materials, Tokyo Electron)**
Pharmaceuticals (Merck & Co., Novartis)	Generic Drugs (Teva Pharmaceutical Industries, Sandoz)
Microprocessors (Intel, Advanced Micro Devices)	Consumer Electronics (Sony Electronics, Koninklijke Philips Electronics)
Industrial Gases (Praxair, Air Products and Chemicals)	PCs (Dell, Acer, Lenovo)
Enterprise Storage (EMC)	Printers/Office Machines (HP, Lexmark)
Enterprise Networking (Cisco Systems)	**Refiners (Valero, Marathon Oil)**
Integrated Shippers (UPS, FedEx, DHL International)	**Major Integrated Oil (BP, ExxonMobil)**
US Railroads (Burlington Northern)	Equity Exchanges (NYSE, Deutsche Börse Group)
US Defense (General Dynamics)	
Heavy Construction Equipment (Caterpillar, Komatsu)	
Seaborne Iron Ore (Vale, Rio Tinto)	
Confections (Cadbury, Mars/Wrigley)	
Credit Card Networks (MasterCard, Visa)	
Custody & Asset Administration (BNY Mellon, State Street)	
Investment Banking /Mergers &Acquisitions (Goldman Sachs, UBS)	
Futures Exchanges (Chicago Mercantile Exchange, Intercontinental Exchange)	
Canadian Banking (RBC Bank, TD Bank)	
Australian Banking	
Tobacco (Philip Morris, British American Tobacco)	
Alcoholic Beverages (Diageo, Pernod Ricard)	

Fragmented with Strong Pricing Power	Fragmented with Weak Pricing Power
Asset Management (BlackRock, Fidelity)	Consumer Packaged Goods (Procter & Gamble, Unilever)
For-Profit Education (Apollo Group, DeVry University)	Retail (Walmart, Carrefour Group)
Analog Chips (Texas Instruments, STMicroelectronics)	Marine Transportation (Maersk Line, Frontline)
Industrial Distribution (Fastenal, W.W. Grainger)	Solar Panels
Propane Distribution (AmeriGas, Ferrellgas)	Homebuilding
Private Banking (Northern Trust, Credit Suisse)	Airlines
	Mining (metals)
	Chemicals
	Engineering & Construction
	Metal Service Centers
	Commercial Printing
	Restaurants
	Radio Broadcasting
	Oil Services
	Life Insurance
	Reinsurance
	Exploration & Production (E&P)
	US Banking
	Specialty Finance
	Property/Casualty Insurance
	Household and Personal Products

Source: Morningstar Equity Research.

The industries in the top right quadrant defy the "concentration is good for pricing" guideline. We discussed the commercial aircraft manufacturing example in the preceding section, but many other industries are dominated by a small number of players yet have difficult competitive environments and limited pricing power.

When we examine these concentrated-yet-competitive industries, a clear theme emerges: Many industries in this quadrant (the boldface ones) are highly capital intensive and sell commodity-like products. As we saw in the discussion of exit barriers, capital-intensive industries can be prone to overcapacity, which mitigates the benefits of industry concentration. Also, if the industry sells a commodity product that is difficult—or impossible—to differentiate, the incentive to compete on price increases because a lower price frequently results in greater market share.[9]

The computer memory market is a perfect example of a concentrated-yet-competitive industry. Dynamic random access memory (DRAM) is widely used in PCs, and the industry is concentrated, with about three-quarters of global market share held by the top four companies. The industry is also highly capital intensive; a new fab costs upwards of US$3 billion. But one DRAM chip is much like another, and players in this market have a huge economic incentive to capture market share because of the large scale economies involved in running a semiconductor manufacturing plant. As a result, price competition tends to be extremely fierce and industry concentration is essentially a moot point in the face of these other competitive dynamics.

The global soft drink market is also highly concentrated, of course, but capital requirements are relatively low and industry participants sell a differentiated product. Pepsi and Coca-Cola do not own their own bottling facilities, so a drop in market share does not affect them as much as it would a memory-chip maker. Moreover, although memory-chip companies are assured of gaining market share and increasing sales volumes by cutting prices, a sizable proportion of consumers would not switch from Pepsi to Coke (or vice-versa) even if one cost much less than the other.

Generally, industry concentration is a good indicator that an industry has pricing power and rational competition, but other factors may override the importance of concentration. Industry fragmentation is a much stronger signal that the industry is competitive with limited pricing power. Notice how few fragmented industries are in the bottom left quadrant in Exhibit 4.

The industry characteristics discussed here are guidelines meant to steer the analyst in a particular direction, not rules that should cause the analyst to ignore other relevant analytical factors.

5.1.3 *Industry Capacity*

The effect on pricing of industry capacity (the maximum amount of a good or service that can be supplied in a given time period) is clear: Tight, or limited, capacity gives participants more pricing power as demand for the product or service exceeds supply, whereas overcapacity leads to price cutting and a very competitive environment as excess supply chases demand. An analyst should think about not only current capacity conditions but future changes in capacity levels. How quickly can companies in the industry adjust to fluctuations in demand? How flexible is the industry in bringing supply and demand into balance? What will be the effect of that process on industry pricing power or on industry margins?

Generally, capacity is fixed in the short term and variable in the long term because capacity can be increased—e.g., new factories can be built—if time is sufficient. What is considered "sufficient" time—and, therefore, the duration of the short term,

9 There are a small number of concentrated and rational commodity industries, such as potash (a type of fertilizer) and seaborne iron ore. What sets these industries apart is that they are *hyper*-concentrated: The top two players control 60 percent of the global potash market, and the top three players control two-thirds of the global market for seaborne iron ore.

in which capacity cannot be increased—may vary dramatically among industries. Sometimes, adding capacity takes years to complete, as in the case of the construction of a "greenfield" (new) manufacturing plant for pharmaceuticals or for paper, which is complex and subject to regulatory requirements (e.g., relating to the plant's waste). In other situations, capacity may be added or reduced relatively quickly, as is the case with service industries, such as advertising. In cyclical markets, such as commercial paper and paperboard, capacity conditions can change rapidly. Strong demand in the early stages of an economic recovery can result in the addition of supply. Given the long lead times to build manufacturing plants, new supply may reach the market just as demand slows, rapidly changing capacity conditions from tight to loose. Such considerations underscore the importance of forecasting long-term industry demand in evaluating industry investments in capacity.

One of the more dramatic examples of this process in recent years occurred in the market for maritime dry-bulk shipping during the commodity boom of 2003–2008. Rapid industrialization in China—combined with synchronized global economic growth—increased demand for cargo ships that could transport iron ore, coal, grains, and other high-volume/low-value commodities. Given that the supply of cargo ships could not be increased very quickly (because ships take time to build and large commercial shipyards typically have multi-year backlogs), shippers naturally raised prices to take advantage of the tight global cargo capacity. In fact, the price to charter the largest type of dry-bulk vessel—a Capesize-class ship too big to fit through the Panama Canal—increased more than fivefold in only a year, from approximately US$30,000 per day in early 2006 to almost US$160,000 per day by late 2007.

As one would expect, orders for new dry-bulk carriers skyrocketed during this period as the industry scrambled to add shipping capacity to take advantage of seemingly insatiable demand and very favorable pricing. In early 2006, the number of dry-bulk carriers on order from shipyards represented approximately 20 percent of the worldwide fleet. By late 2008, the number of bulk ships on order represented almost 70 percent of the global bulk fleet.[10] Of course, the prospect of this additional capacity, combined with a dramatic slump in aggregate global demand for commodities, caused a massive decline in shipping rates. Capesize charter rates plummeted from the US$160,000/day high of late 2007 to a low of under US$10,000 per day just one year later.

In this example, the conditions of tight supply that were driving strong dry-bulk pricing were quite clear, and these high prices drove attractive returns on capital—and share-price performance—for dry-bulk-shipping companies. However, the careful analyst would have looked at future additions to supply in the form of new ships on order and would have forecasted that the tight supply conditions were not sustainable and thus that the pricing power of dry-bulk shippers was short-lived. These predictions are, in fact, precisely what occurred.

Note that capacity need not be physical. After Hurricane Katrina caused enormous damage to the southeastern United States in 2005, reinsurance rates quickly spiked as customers sought to increase their financial protection from future hurricanes. However, these high reinsurance rates enticed a flood of fresh capital into the reinsurance market, and a number of new reinsurance companies were founded, which brought rates back down.

Generally, if new capacity is physical—for example, an auto manufacturing plant or a massive cargo ship—it will take longer for new capacity to come on line to meet an increase in demand, resulting in a longer period of tight conditions. Unfortunately,

10 From "RS Platou Monthly" (November 2008): www.platou.com/loadfileservlet/loadfiledb?id=1228989312093PUBLISHER&key=1228989321421.

capacity additions frequently overshoot long-run demand, and because physical capital is often hard to re-deploy, industries reliant on physical capacity may get stuck in conditions of excess capacity and diminished pricing power for an extended period.

Financial and human capital, in contrast, can be quickly shifted to new uses. In the reinsurance example, for instance, financial capital was quick to enter the reinsurance market and take advantage of tight capacity conditions, but if too much capital had entered the market, some portion of that capital could easily have left to seek higher returns elsewhere. Money can be used for many things, but massive bulk cargo vessels are not useful for much more than transporting heavy goods across oceans.

5.1.4 *Market Share Stability*

Examining the stability of industry market shares over time is similar to thinking about barriers to entry and the frequency with which new players enter an industry. In fact, barriers to entry and the frequency of new product introductions, together with such factors as product differentiation—all affect market shares. Stable market shares typically indicate less competitive industries; unstable market shares often indicate highly competitive industries that have limited pricing power.

A comparison of two non-commodity markets in the health care sector illustrates this point. Over the past decade, the orthopedic device industry—mainly artificial hips and knees—has been a relatively stable global oligopoly. As Exhibit 5 indicates, five companies control about 75 percent of the worldwide market, and the market shares of those companies have changed by only small amounts over the past several years.

Exhibit 5 Market Share Stability in Global Orthopedic Devices (Entries Are Market Share)

Worldwide Knee/Hip Market Share	2014 (%)	2015 (%)	2016 (%)	2017 (%)
Stryker	32.0	31.5	31.0	31.8
Zimmer Biomet	15.4	19.0	21.0	20.0
Smith & Nephew	15.3	14.7	12.8	12.2
Hologic	8.4	8.6	7.7	7.8
Integer	2.3	2.5	3.8	3.7

Source: Company reports and Capital IQ estimates.

In contrast, although the US market for stents—small metal mesh devices used to prop open blocked arteries—is also controlled by a handful of companies, market shares recently have gone from being very stable to being marked by rapid change. Johnson & Johnson, which together with Boston Scientific, dominated the US stent market for many years, went from having about half the market in 2007 to having only 15 percent in early 2009, and exited the market in 2011; over the same period, Abbott Laboratories increased its market share from zero to around 30 percent. The reason for this change was the launch of new stents by Abbott and Medtronic, which took market share from Johnson & Johnson and Boston Scientific's established stents, leading Johnson & Johnson, which created the device, to exit the market due to slumping sales and market share that reflected an inability of the company to keep more innovative competitors out of the market.[11]

11 https://www.wsj.com/articles/SB10001424052702304186404576387420811221538.

Orthopedic device companies have experienced more stability in their market shares for two reasons. First, artificial hips and knees are complicated to implant, and each manufacturer's products are slightly different. As a result, orthopedic surgeons become proficient at using one or several companies' devices and may be reluctant to incur the time and cost of learning how to implant products from a competing company. The second reason is the relatively slow pace of innovation in the orthopedic device industry, which tends to be evolutionary rather than revolutionary, making the benefit of switching among product lines relatively low. In addition, the number of orthopedic device companies has remained fairly static over many years.

In contrast, the US stent market has experienced rapid shifts in market shares because of several factors. First, interventional cardiologists seem to be more open than orthopedic surgeons to implanting stents from different manufacturers; that tendency may reflect lower switching costs for stents relative to orthopedic devices. More importantly, however, the pace of innovation in the stent market has become quite rapid, giving cardiologists added incentive to switch to newer stents, with potentially better patient outcomes, as they became available.

Low switching costs plus a relatively high benefit from switching caused market shares to change quickly in the stent market. High switching costs for orthopedic devices coupled with slow innovation resulted in a lower benefit from switching, which led to greater market share stability in orthopedic devices.

5.1.5 *Industry Life Cycle*

An industry's life-cycle position often has a large impact on its competitive dynamics, making this position an important component of the strategic analysis of an industry.

5.1.5.1 Description of an Industry Life-Cycle Model Industries, like individual companies, tend to evolve over time, and usually experience significant changes in the rate of growth and levels of profitability along the way. Just as an investment in an individual company requires careful monitoring, industry analysis is a continuous process to identify changes that may be occurring or be likely to occur. A useful framework for analyzing the evolution of an industry is an industry life-cycle model, which identifies the sequential stages that an industry typically goes through. The five stages of an industry life-cycle model are embryonic, growth, shakeout, mature, and decline. Each stage is characterized by different opportunities and threats.[12] Exhibit 6 shows the model as a curve illustrating the level and growth rate of demand at each stage.

12 Much of the discussion that follows regarding life-cycle stages owes a debt to the discussion in Hill and Jones (2008).

Exhibit 6 An Industry Life-Cycle Model

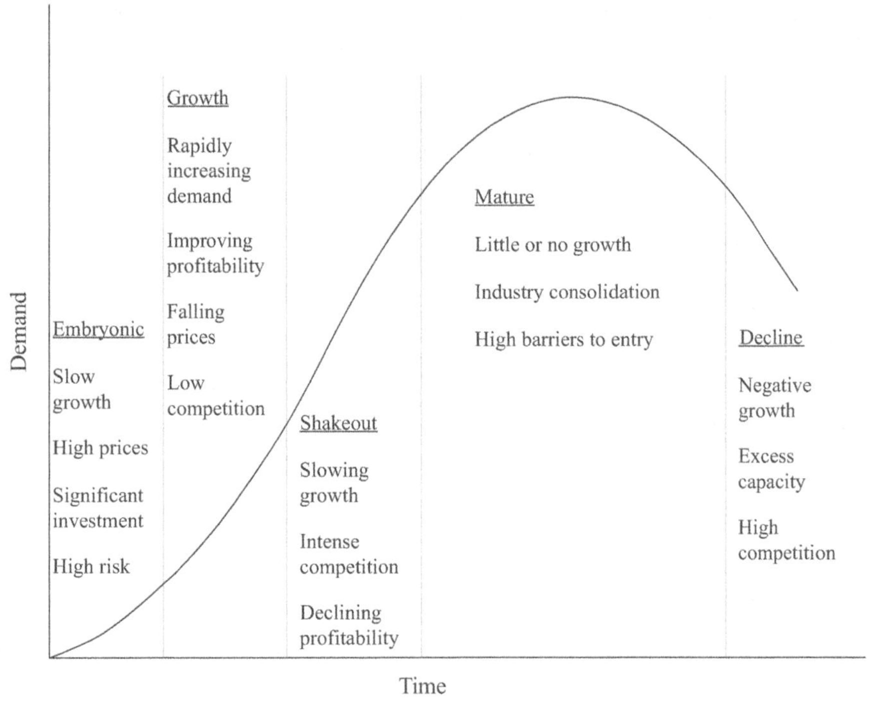

Source: Based on Figure 2.4 in Hill and Jones (2008).

Embryonic An embryonic industry is one that is just beginning to develop. For example, in the 1960s, the global semiconductor industry was in the embryonic stage (it has grown to become a US$463.4 billion industry in 2018)[13] and in the early 1980s, the global mobile phone industry was in the embryonic stage (it now produces and sells more than a billion handsets annually). Characteristics of the embryonic stage include slow growth and high prices because customers tend to be unfamiliar with the industry's product and volumes are not yet sufficient to achieve meaningful economies of scale. Increasing product awareness and developing distribution channels are key strategic initiatives of companies during this stage. Substantial investment is generally required, and the risk of failure is high. A majority of start-up companies do not succeed.

Growth A growth industry tends to be characterized by rapidly increasing demand, improving profitability, falling prices, and relativity low competition among companies in the industry. Demand is fueled by new customers entering the market, and prices fall as economies of scale are achieved and as distribution channels develop. The threat of new competitors entering the industry is usually highest during the growth stage, when barriers to entry are relatively low. Competition tends to be relatively limited, however, because rapidly expanding demand provides companies with an opportunity to grow without needing to capture market share from competitors. Industry profitability improves as volumes rise and economies of scale are attained.

Shakeout The shakeout stage is usually characterized by slowing growth, intense competition, and declining profitability. During the shakeout stage, demand approaches market saturation levels because few new customers are left to enter the market.

13 Semiconductor Industry Association Factsheet: www.sia-online.org/cs/industry_resources/industry_fact_sheet.

Competition is intense as growth becomes increasingly dependent on market share gains. Excess industry capacity begins to develop as the rate at which companies continue to invest exceeds the overall growth of industry demand. In an effort to boost volumes to fill excess capacity, companies often cut prices, so industry profitability begins to decline. During the shakeout stage, companies increasingly focus on reducing their cost structure (restructuring) and building brand loyalty. Marginal companies may fail or merge with others.

Mature Characteristics of a mature industry include little or no growth, industry consolidation, and relatively high barriers to entry. Industry growth tends to be limited to replacement demand and population expansion because the market at this stage is completely saturated. As a result of the shakeout, mature industries often consolidate and become oligopolies. The surviving companies tend to have brand loyalty and relatively efficient cost structures, both of which are significant barriers to entry. During periods of stable demand, companies in mature industries tend to recognize their interdependence and try to avoid price wars. Periodic price wars do occur, however, most notably during periods of declining demand (such as during economic downturns). Companies with superior products or services are likely to gain market share and experience above-industry-average growth and profitability.

Decline During the decline stage, industry growth turns negative, excess capacity develops, and competition increases. Industry demand at this stage may decline for a variety of reasons, including technological substitution (for example, the newspaper industry has been declining for years as more people turn to the internet and 24-hour cable news networks for information), social changes, and global competition (for example, low-cost foreign manufacturers pushing the US textile industry into decline). As demand falls, excess capacity in the industry forms and companies respond by cutting prices, which often leads to price wars. The weaker companies often exit the industry at this point, merge, or redeploy capital into different products and services.

When overall demand for an industry's products or services is declining, the opportunity for individual companies to earn above-average returns on invested capital tends to be less than when demand is stable or increasing, because of price cutting and higher per-unit costs as production is cut back. Example 6 deals with industry life cycles.

EXAMPLE 6

Industry Growth and Company Growth

US shipments of prefabricated housing (precut, modular housing) declined sharply in 1999–2004 as the abundant availability of low-cost mortgage financing and other factors led individuals to purchase site-built housing. In 1998, however, some forecasts had projected that prefabricated housing would gain market share at the expense of site-built housing. What would have been the probable impact on market share of a typical company in the prefabricated housing industry under the 1998 optimistic forecast and under actual conditions?

Solution:

Increasing industry demand as forecasted in 1998 would have given companies in the prefabricated housing industry the opportunity to grow without taking market share from one another, mitigating the intensity of competition in this industry. Under actual industry circumstances of declining demand and a shrinking market, in contrast, revenue growth for a prefabricated housing company could happen only through market share gains from its competitors.

5.1.5.2 Using an Industry Life-Cycle Model In general, new industries tend to be more competitive (with lots of players entering and exiting) than mature industries, which often have stable competitive environments and players that are more interested in protecting what they have than in gaining lots of market share. However, as industries move from maturity to decline, competitive pressures may increase again as industry participants perceive a zero-sum environment and fight over pieces of an ever-shrinking pie.

An important point for the analyst to think about is whether a company is "acting its age" relative to where its industry sits in the life cycle. Companies in growth industries should be building customer loyalty as they introduce consumers to new products or services, building scale, and reinvesting heavily in their operations to capitalize on increasing demand. They are probably not focusing strongly on internal efficiency. These companies are rather like young adults, who are reinvesting their human and financial capital with the goal of becoming more successful in life. Growth companies typically reinvest their cash flows in new products and product platforms rather than returning cash flows to shareholders because these companies still have many opportunities to deploy their capital to make positive returns. Although this analogy to the human life cycle is a helpful way to think about the model, the analyst should also be aware that the analogy is not exact in detail. Long-established companies sometimes find a way to accelerate growth through innovation or by expansion into new markets. Humans cannot really move back to the days of youth. So, a more precise formulation may be "acting its stage" rather than acting its age.

Companies in mature industries are likely to be pursuing replacement demand rather than new buyers and are probably focused on extending successful product lines rather than introducing revolutionary new products. They are also probably focusing on cost rationalization and efficiency gains rather than on taking lots of market share. Importantly, these companies have fewer growth opportunities than in the previous stage, and thus more limited avenues for profitably reinvesting capital, but they often have strong cash flows. Given their strong cash flows and relatively limited reinvestment opportunities, such companies should be, according to a common perspective, returning capital to shareholders via share repurchases or dividends. These companies are rather like middle-aged adults who are harvesting the fruits of their success earlier in life.

What can be a concern is a middle-aged company acting like a young, growth company and pouring capital into projects with low ROIC prospects in an effort to pursue size for its own sake. Many companies have a difficult time managing the transition from growth to maturity, and their returns on capital—and shareholder returns—may suffer until management decides to allocate capital in a manner more appropriate to the company's life-cycle stage.

For example, three large European retailers—Tesco, Carrefour SA, and Ahold—all went through the transition to maturity in the second decade of the 21st century. At various times between 2015 and 2018, these companies realized that their size and industry dominance meant that the days of double-digit growth that was driven largely by new store (domestic and international) openings were a thing of the past. All three firms reallocated capital away from opening new stores to other areas—namely, an increased digital presence (Carrefour teaming up with Google), merging with competitors to reduce pricing pressure (Ahold's merger with Belgium's Delhaize), and introduction of discount chains in order to retain/win market against discount retailers such as Lidl and Walmart (all three). As a result, returns on capital for each improved, as did shareholder returns.

5.1.5.3 Limitations of Industry Life-Cycle Analysis Although models can provide a useful framework for thinking about an industry, the evolution of an industry does not always follow a predictable pattern. Various external factors may significantly affect the shape of the pattern, causing some stages to be longer or shorter than expected and, in certain cases, causing some stages to be skipped altogether.

Technological changes may cause an industry to experience an abrupt shift from growth to decline, thus skipping the shakeout and mature stages. For example, transistors replaced vacuum tubes in the 1960s at a time when the vacuum tube industry was still in its growth stage; word processors replaced typewriters in the 1980s; and today the movie rental industry is experiencing rapid change as consumers increasingly turn to on-demand services such as downloading movies from the internet or through their cable providers.

Regulatory changes can also have a profound impact on the structure of an industry. A prime example is the deregulation of the US telecommunications industry in the 1990s, which transformed a monopolistic industry into an intensely competitive one. AT&T was broken into regional service providers, and many new long-distance telephone service entrants, such as Sprint, emerged. The result was a wider range of product and service offerings and lower consumer prices. Changes in government reimbursement rates for health care products and services may (and have) affected the profitability of companies in the health care industry globally.

Social changes also have the ability to affect the profile of an industry. The casual dining industry has benefited over the past 30 years from the increase in the number of dual-income families, who often have more income but less time to cook meals to eat at home.

Demographics also play an important role. As the Baby Boom generation ages, for instance, industry demand for health care services is likely to increase.

Thus, life-cycle models tend to be most useful for analyzing industries during periods of relative stability. They are less practical when the industry may be experiencing rapid change because of external or other special circumstances.

Another limiting factor of models is that not all companies in an industry experience similar performances. The key objective for the analyst is to identify the potential winners while avoiding potential losers. Highly profitable companies can exist in competitive industries with below-average profitability—and vice versa. For example, Nokia has historically been able to use its scale to generate levels of profitability that are well above average despite operating in a highly competitive industry. In contrast, despite the historically above-average growth and profitability of the software industry, countless examples exist of software companies that failed to ever generate a profit and eventually went out of business.

EXAMPLE 7

Industry Life Cycle

1 An industry experiencing slow growth and high prices is best characterized as being in the:

  A mature stage.

  B shakeout stage.

  C embryonic stage.

2 Which of the following statements about the industry life-cycle model is *least* accurate?

  A The model is more appropriately used during a period of rapid change than during a period of relative stability.

B External factors may cause some stages of the model to be longer or shorter than expected, and in certain cases, a stage may be skipped entirely.

C Not all companies in an industry will experience similar performance, and very profitable companies can exist in an industry with below-average profitability.

Solution to 1:

C is correct. Both slow growth and high prices are associated with the embryonic stage. High price is not a characteristic of the mature or shakeout stages.

Solution to 2:

A is correct. The statement is the least accurate. The model is best used during a period of relative stability rather than during a period of rapid change.

5.1.6 *Price Competition*

A highly useful tool for analyzing an industry is attempting to think like a customer of the industry. Whatever factor most influences customer purchase decisions is likely to also be the focus of competitive rivalry in the industry. In general, industries for which price is a large factor in customer purchase decisions tend to be more competitive than industries in which customers value other attributes more highly.

Although this depiction may sound like the description of a commodity industry versus a non-commodity industry, it is, in fact, a bit more subtle. Commercial aircraft and passenger cars are certainly more differentiated than lumps of coal or gallons of gasoline, but price nonetheless weighs heavily in the purchase decisions of buyers of aircraft and cars, because fairly good substitutes are easily available. If Airbus charges too much for an A320, an airline can buy a Boeing 737.[14] If BMW's price for a four-door luxury sedan rises too high, customers can switch to a Mercedes or other luxury brand with similar features. Similar switching can be expected as a result of a unilateral price increase in the case of most industries in the "Weak Pricing Power" column of Exhibit 4.

Contrast these industries with asset management, one of a handful of industries that is both fragmented and characterized by strong pricing power. Despite the well-documented impact of fees on future investment returns, the vast majority of asset management customers do not make decisions on the basis of price. Instead, asset management customers focus on historical returns, which allow this highly fragmented industry to maintain strong pricing power. Granted, the index fund arena is very price competitive, because any index fund is a perfect substitute for another fund tracking the same benchmark. But the active management segment of the industry has generally been able to price its products in an implicitly cooperative fashion that enables most players to generate consistently high returns on capital, presumably because price is not uppermost in the mind of a prospective mutual fund investor.

Returning to a more capital-intensive industry, consider heavy-equipment manufacturers, such as Caterpillar, JCB, and Komatsu. A large wheel loader or combine harvester requires a large capital outlay, so price certainly plays a part in the buyers' decisions. However, other factors are important enough to customers to allow these companies a small amount of pricing power. Construction equipment is typically used as a complement to other gear on a large project, which means that downtime for

14 A small amount of "path dependence" characterizes the airline industry, in that an airline with a large fleet of a particular Airbus model will be marginally more likely to stick with that model for a new purchase than it will be to buy a Boeing, but the aircraft manufacturers' ability to exploit this likelihood is minimal.

repairs increases costs because, for example, hourly laborers must wait for a bulldozer to be fixed. Broken equipment is also expensive for agricultural users, who may have only a few days in which to harvest a season's crop. Because of the importance to users of their products' reliability and their large service networks—which are important "differentiators" or factors bestowing a competitive advantage—Caterpillar, Komatsu, and Deere have historically been able to price their equipment at levels that have generated solid returns on invested capital.

5.1.7 *Industry Comparison*

To illustrate how these elements might be applied, Exhibit 7 uses the factors discussed in this reading to examine three industries.

Exhibit 7 Elements of a Strategic Analysis for Three Industries

	Branded Pharmaceuticals	Oil Services	Confections/Candy
Major Companies	Pfizer, Novartis, Merck, GSK plc	Schlumberger, Baker Hughes, Halliburton	Hershey, Mars/Wrigley, Nestle
Barriers to Entry	*Very High*: Substantial financial and intellectual capital required to compete effectively. A potential new entrant would need to create a sizable R&D operation, a global distribution network, and large-scale manufacturing capacity.	*Medium*: Technological expertise is required, but high level of innovation allows niche companies to enter the industry and compete in specific areas.	*Very High*: Low financial or technological hurdles, but new players would lack the established brands that drive consumer purchase decisions.
Level of Concentration	*Concentrated*: A small number of companies control the bulk of the global market for branded drugs. Recent mergers have increased level of concentration.	*Fragmented*: Although only a small number of companies provide a full range of services, many smaller players compete effectively in specific areas. Service arms of national oil companies may control significant market share in their own countries, and some product lines are concentrated in the mature US market.	*Very Concentrated*: Top four companies have a large proportion of global market share. Recent mergers have increased level of concentration.
Impact of Industry Capacity	*NA*: Pharmaceutical pricing is primarily determined by patent protection and regulatory issues, including government approvals of drugs and of manufacturing facilities. Manufacturing capacity is of little importance.	*Medium/High*: Demand can fluctuate quickly depending on commodity prices, and industry players often find themselves with too few (or too many) employees on the payroll.	*NA*: Pricing is driven primarily by brand strength. Manufacturing capacity has little effect.
Industry Stability	*Stable*: The branded pharmaceutical market is dominated by major companies and consolidation via mega-mergers. Market shares shift quickly, however, as new drugs are approved and gain acceptance or lose patent protection.	*Unstable*: Market shares may shift frequently depending on technology offerings and demand levels.	*Very Stable*: Market shares change glacially.

Exhibit 7 (Continued)

	Branded Pharmaceuticals	Oil Services	Confections/Candy
Life Cycle	*Mature*: Overall demand does not change greatly from year to year.	*Mature*: Demand does fluctuate with energy prices, but normalized revenue growth is only mid-single digits.	*Very Mature*: Growth is driven by population trends and pricing.
Price Competition	*Low/Medium*: In the United States, price is a minimal factor because of consumer- and provider-driven, de-regulated health care system. Price is a larger part of the decision process in single-payer systems, where efficacy hurdles are higher.	*High*: Price is a major factor in purchasers' decisions. Some companies have modest pricing power because of a wide range of services or best-in-class technology, but primary customers (major oil companies) can usually substitute with in-house services if prices are too high. Also, innovation tends to diffuse quickly throughout the industry.	*Low*: A lack of private-label competition keeps pricing stable among established players, and brand/familiarity plays a much larger role in consumer purchase decisions than price.
Demographic Influences	*Positive*: Populations of developed markets are aging, which slightly increases demand.	*NA*	*NA*
Government & Regulatory Influences	*Very High*: All drugs must be approved for sale by national safety regulators. Patent regimes may differ among countries. Also, health care is heavily regulated in most countries.	*Medium*: Regulatory frameworks can affect energy demand at the margin. Also, governments play an important role in allocating exploration opportunities to E&P companies, which can indirectly affect the amount of work flowing down to service companies.	*Low*: Industry is not regulated, but childhood obesity concerns in developed markets are a low-level potential threat. Also, high-growth emerging markets may block entry of established players into their markets, possibly limiting growth.
Social Influences	*NA*	*NA*	*NA*
Technological Influences	*Medium/High*: Biologic (large-molecule) drugs are pushing new therapeutic boundaries, and many large pharmaceutical companies have a relatively small presence in biotech.	*Medium/High*: Industry is reasonably innovative, and players must re-invest in R&D to remain competitive. Temporary competitive advantages are possible via commercialization of new processes or exploitation of accumulated expertise.	*Very Low*: Innovation does not play a major role in the industry.
Growth vs. Defensive vs. Cyclical	*Defensive*: Demand for most health care services does not fluctuate with the economic cycle, but demand is not strong enough to be considered "growth."	*Cyclical*: Demand is highly variable and depends on oil prices, exploration budgets, and the economic cycle.	*Defensive*: Demand for candy and gum is extremely stable.

Note: "*NA*" in this exhibit stands for "not applicable."

Example 8 reviews some of the information presented in Exhibit 7.

EXAMPLE 8

External Influences

1 Which of the following industries is *most* affected by government regulation?

   A Oil services.

   B Pharmaceuticals.

   C Confections and candy.

2 Which of the following industries is *least* affected by technological innovation?

   A Oil services.

   B Pharmaceuticals.

   C Confections and candy.

3 Which of the following statements about industry characteristics is *least* accurate?

   A Manufacturing capacity has little effect on pricing in the confections/candy industry.

   B The branded pharmaceutical industry is considered to be defensive rather than a growth industry.

   C With respect to the worldwide market, the oil services industry has a high level of concentration with a limited number of service providers.

Solution to 1:

B is correct. Exhibit 7 states that the pharmaceutical industry has high amount of government and regulatory influences.

Solution to 2:

C is correct. Exhibit 7 states that innovation does not play a large role in the candy industry.

Solution to 3:

C is correct; it is a false statement. From a worldwide perspective, the industry is considered fragmented. Although a small number of companies provide the full range of services, competition by many smaller players occurs in niche areas. In addition, national oil service companies control significant market share in their home countries.

5.2 External Influences on Industry Growth, Profitability, and Risk

External factors affecting an industry's growth include macroeconomic, technological, demographic, governmental, and social influences.

5.2.1 *Macroeconomic Influences*

Trends in overall economic activity generally have significant effects on the demand for an industry's products or services. These trends can be cyclical (i.e., related to the changes in economic activity caused by the business cycle) or structural (i.e., related to enduring changes in the composition or magnitude of economic activity). Among the economic variables that usually affect an industry's revenues and profits are the following:

- gross domestic product or the measure of the value of goods and services produced by an economy, either in current or constant currency (inflation-adjusted) terms;
- interest rates, which represent the cost of debt to consumers and businesses and are important ingredients in financial institutions' revenues and costs;
- the availability of credit, which affects business and consumer spending and financial solvency; and
- inflation, which reflects the changes in prices of goods and services and influences costs, interest rates, and consumer and business confidence.

5.2.2 *Technological Influences*

New technologies create new or improved products that can radically change an industry and can also change how other industries that use the products conduct their operations.

The computer hardware industry provides one of the best examples of how technological change can affect industries. The 1958 invention of the microchip (also known as an "integrated circuit," which is effectively a computer etched on a sliver of silicon) enabled the computer hardware industry to eventually create a new market of personal computing for the general public and radically extended the use of computers in business, government, and educational institutions.

Moore's law states that the number of transistors that can be inexpensively placed on an integrated circuit doubles approximately every two years. Several other measures of digital technology have improved at exponential rates related to Moore's law, including the size, cost, density and speed of components. As a result of these trends, the computer hardware industry encroached upon and, in time, came to dominate the fields of hardware for word processing and many forms of electronic communication and home entertainment. The computing industry's integrated circuit innovation increased economies of scale and erected large barriers to new entrants because the capital costs of innovation and production became very high. Intel capitalized on both factors which allowed it to garner an industry market leadership position and to become the dominant supplier of the PC industry's highest value component (the microprocessor). Thus, Intel became dominant because of its cost advantage, brand power, and access to capital.

Along the way, the computer hardware industry was supported and greatly assisted by the complementary industries of computer software and telecommunications (particularly in regard to development of the internet); also important were other industries—entertainment (television, movies, games), retailing, and the print media. Ever more powerful integrated circuits and advances in wireless technology, as well as the convergence of media, which the internet and new wireless technology have facilitated, continue to reshape the uses and the roles of PC hardware in business and personal life. In the middle of the 20th century, few people in the world would have imagined they would ever have any use for a home computer. Today, the estimate is that about 1.6 billion people, or almost a quarter of the world's population, have access to connected computing. For the United States, the estimate is at least 76 percent of the population; it is much less in emerging and underdeveloped countries. More than 5 billion mobile cellular telephone subscriptions exist in the world today,[15] and the

15 See https://venturebeat.com/2017/06/13/5-billion-people-now-have-a-mobile-phone-connection-according-to-gsma-data/.

advances of mobile telephony appear poised to increase this figure dramatically in the years ahead as mobile phone and computer hardware technologies merge to provide new hand-held computing and communication capabilities.

Another example of the effects of technology on an industry is the impact of digital imaging technology on the photographic film industry. Digital imaging uses an electronic image sensor to record an image as electronic data rather than as chemical changes on film. This difference allows a much greater degree of image processing and transmission than in film photography. Since their invention in 1981, digital cameras have become extremely popular and now widely outsell traditional film cameras (although many professional photographers continue to use film for esthetic reasons for certain applications). Digital cameras include such features as video and audio recording. The effects of this major change in photographic technology have caused film and camera manufacturers—including Kodak, Fujifilm, Nikon Corporation, and Ricoh—to completely restructure and redesign their products to adapt to the new technology's appeal to consumers. The introduction of "smart" mobile phones with inbuilt, high resolution pixel quality cameras, which are similar in resolution quality to some of the traditional film and camera products, has significantly reduced the market for the traditional photographic manufacturers, and has introduced a further layer of fierce competition to the industry.

5.2.3 *Demographic Influences*

Changes in population size, in the distributions of age and gender, and in other demographic characteristics may have significant effects on economic growth and on the amounts and types of goods and services consumed.

The effects of demographics on industries are well exemplified by the impact of the post–World War II Baby Boom in North America on demand for goods and services. Born between 1946 and 1964, this bulge of 76 million people in the North American population has influenced the composition of numerous products and services it needs in its passage from the cradle through childhood, adolescence, early adulthood, middle age, and into retirement. The teenage pop culture of the late 1950s and 1960s and all the products (records, movies, clothes, and fashions associated with it), the surge in demand for housing in the 1970s and 1980s, and the increasing demand for retirement-oriented investment products in the 1990s and early 2000s are all examples of the range of industries affected by this demographic bulge working its way through age categories of the population.

Another example of the effects of demographics on industries is the impact of an aging population in Japan, which has one of the highest percentages of elderly residents (26 percent over the age of 65) and a very low birth rate. Japan's ministry of health estimates that by 2055, the percentage of the population over 65 will rise to 40 percent and the total population will fall by 25 percent. These demographic changes are expected by some observers to have negative effects on the overall economy because, essentially, they imply a declining workforce. However, some sectors of the economy stand to benefit from these trends—for example, the health care industry.

EXAMPLE 9

Historical Example: The Post–World War II Baby Boom and Its Effects on the US Housing Industry

In the United States, Canada, and Australia, the end of World War II marked the beginning of a sustained period of elevated birth rates per thousand in the population. This rise reflected the relief from the hardships of the Great Depression of the 1930s and WWII, increased levels of immigration (immigrants tend to be younger and hence more fertile than average) and a protracted period of postwar economic prosperity. The rate of births in the United States rose from 18.7 per thousand in 1935 and 20.4 per thousand in 1945 to 24.1 per thousand in 1950 and a peak of more than 25.0 per thousand in 1955–1957. Twenty years later, when the babies born during the period 1946–1964 entered adulthood, the housing industry experienced a surge in demand that led to a period of high sales of new homes. The rate of new housing starts in this period rose from 20.1 per thousand of population in 1966 to a peak of 35.3 per thousand in 1972 and remained elevated, except during the economic recession of 1974–1975, until the end of the 1970s.

Another demographic effect on the housing industry arising from the post-WWII Baby Boom came from the children of the Baby Boom generation (the so-called Echo Boomers). The Echo Boomers started to enter their most fertile years in the late 1970s and caused an increase in the number of births per thousand from a post-WWII low of 14.8 in 1975 to a peak of 16.7 in 1990. The Echo Boomers did not have as large an effect on housing demand 20 years later as their parents had had, but there was still a significant increase in new housing starts from 13.7 per thousand in 1995 to a high of 18.8 per thousand in 2005; easily available mortgage financing contributed to the increase.

5.2.4 *Governmental Influences*

Governmental influence on industries' revenues and profits is pervasive and important. In setting tax rates and rules for corporations and individuals, governments affect profits and incomes, which in turn, affect corporate and personal spending. Governments are also major purchasers of goods and services from a range of industries.

Example 10 illustrates the sudden shifts in wealth that can occur when governments step in to support or quash a securities market innovation. In the example, an **income trust** refers to a type of equity ownership vehicle established as a trust issuing ownership shares known as units. Income trusts became extremely popular among income-oriented investors in Canada in the late 1990s and early 2000s because under then-current regulation, such trusts could avoid taxation on income distributed to unit-holders (investors)—that is, avoid double taxation (once at the corporate level and once at the investor level). As Example 10 describes, the tax advantage that regulations permitted was eventually removed.

EXAMPLE 10

Historical Example: The Effects of Tax Increases on Income Trusts in Canada

On 31 October 2006, in an effort to halt the rapid growth of income trust structures in the Canadian stock market, Canada's Minister of Finance James Flaherty announced that these tax-exempt flow-through entities would in the future be taxable on the income, with exemptions only for passive rent-collecting real estate investment trusts. A five-year hiatus was established for existing trusts to adapt. He stated that the government needed to clamp down on trusts because too many companies were converting to the high-yield securities, primarily to save taxes. The S&P/TSX Capped Income Trust Index declined 12 percent on the day after the announcement, wiping out C$24 billion in market value.

Often, governments exert their influence indirectly by empowering other regulatory or self-regulatory organizations (e.g., stock exchanges, medical associations, utility rate setters, and other regulatory commissions) to govern the affairs of an industry. By setting the terms of entry into various sectors, such as financial services and health care, and the rules that companies and individuals must adhere to in these fields, governments control the supply, quality, and nature of many products and services and the public's access to them. For example, in the financial industry, the acceptance of savings deposits from and the issuance of securities to the investing public are usually tightly controlled by governments and their agencies. This control is imposed through rules designed to protect investors from fraudulent operators and to ensure that investors receive adequate disclosure about the nature and risks of their investments. Another example is that medical patients in most developed countries are treated by doctors who are trained according to standards set by medical associations acting as self-regulatory organizations empowered under government laws. In addition, the medications that patients receive must be approved by government agencies. In a somewhat different vein, users of tobacco products purchase items for which the marketing and sales taxes are heavily controlled by governments in most developed countries and for which warnings to consumers about the dangers of smoking are mandated by governments. In the case of industries that supply branches of government, such as the military, public works, and law enforcement departments, government contracts directly affect the revenues and profits of the suppliers.

EXAMPLE 11

The Effects of Purchases by Government-Related Entities on the Aerospace Industry

The aerospace, construction, and firearms industries are prime examples of industries for which governments are major customers and whose revenues and profits are significantly—in some cases, predominantly—affected by their sales to governments. An example is the Airbus (formerly the European Aeronautic Defence and Space Company [EADS]), a global leader in aerospace, defense, and related services with head offices in Paris and Ottobrunn, Germany. In 2017, Airbus generated revenues of €66.8 billion and employed an international workforce of about 130,000. Besides being a leading manufacturer of commercial aircraft, the Group also includes Airbus Military, providing tanker, transport, and mission aircraft; Eurocopter, the world's largest helicopter supplier; and EADS Astrium, the European leader in space programs, including Ariane and Galileo. Its Defence & Security Division is a provider of comprehensive systems solutions and makes Airbus the major partner in the Eurofighter consortium and a stakeholder in missile systems provider MBDA. On 11 February 2018, Airbus shares rose 11.7 percent after Emirates Airlines, a Dubai based airline owned by the Dubai government,[16] signed a contract for up to 36 additional A380s aircraft at a cost of as much as US$16 billion.

16 Emirates Airlines is owned by the Investment Corporation of Dubai (ICD) a SWF sponsored by the Dubai Government. https://archive.is/20130103040416/http://www.gulfnews.com/business/Aviation/10271373.html.

5.2.5 *Social Influences*

Societal changes involving how people work, spend their money, enjoy their leisure time, and conduct other aspects of their lives can have significant effects on the sales of various industries.

Tobacco consumption in the United Kingdom provides a good example of the effects of social influences on an industry. Although the role of government in curbing tobacco advertising, legislating health warnings on the purchases of tobacco products, and banning smoking in public places (such as restaurants, bars, public houses, and transportation vehicles) probably has been the most powerful apparent instrument of changes in tobacco consumption, the forces underlying that change have really been social in nature—namely, increasing consciousness on the part of the population of the damage to the health of tobacco users and those in their vicinity from smoking, the increasing cost to individuals and governments of the chronic illnesses caused by tobacco consumption, and the accompanying shift in public perception of smokers from socially correct to socially incorrect—even inconsiderate or reckless. As a result of these changes in society's views of smoking, cigarette consumption in the United Kingdom declined from 102.5 billion cigarettes in 1990 to less than 40.0 billion in 2017, placing downward pressure on tobacco companies' unit sales.

EXAMPLE 12

The Effects on Various Industries of More Women Entering the Workforce

In 1870, women accounted for only 15 percent of the workforce in the United States outside the home. By 1950, after two world wars and the Great Depression, this figure had risen to 30 percent (it had been even higher temporarily during WWII because of high levels of war-mandated production) and by 2017, to 46 percent. Based on economic reasoning, identify four industries that should have benefitted from the social change that saw women shift from their most frequent historical roles in Western society as full-time homemakers to becoming more frequently full-time participants in the workforce.

Solution:

Industries include the following:

1 The restaurant business. The restaurant business stands to benefit from an increased demand given that women, because of their work responsibilities, may not have the time and energy to prepare meals. Restaurant industry growth was actually high in this period: From accounting for only 25 percent of every food dollar in the United States in 1950, the restaurant industry today consumes more than 44 percent of every food dollar, with 45 percent of current industry revenues arising from a category of restaurant that did not exist in 1950, namely, fast food.

2 Manufacturers of work clothing for women.

3 Home and child care services.

4 Automobile manufacturers. Extra vehicles became necessary to transport two members of the family to work, for instance, and children to school or day care.

5 Housing for the aging. With increasing workforce participation by women, aged family members requiring care or supervision became increasingly unable to rely on non-working female family members to provide care in their homes.

EXAMPLE 13

The Airline Industry: A Case Study of Many Influences

The global airline industry exemplifies many of the concepts and influences we have discussed.

Life-Cycle Stage

The industry can be described as having some mature characteristics because average annual growth in global passenger traffic has remained relatively stable at 5.5 percent in the 2000s and early 2010s (compared with 4.7 percent in the 1990s). Some market segments in the industry, however, are still in their growth phase—notably, the markets of the Middle East and Asia, which are expected to grow at 7.0 percent compared with projected North American growth of 4.2 percent over the next 20 years.

Sensitivity to Business Cycle

The airline industry is a cyclical industry; global economic activity produces swings in revenues and, especially, profitability, because of the industry's high fixed costs and operating leverage. In 2009, for example, global passenger traffic declined by approximately 3.5 percent and airlines lost close to US$11.0 billion, which was down from a global industry profit of US$12.9 billion in 2007. The industry tends to respond early to upward and downward moves in economic cycles; depending on the region, air travel changes at 1.5 times to 2.0 times GDP growth. It is highly regulated, with governments and airport authorities playing a large role in allocating routes and airport slots. Government agencies and the International Airline Transport Association set rules for aircraft and flight safety. Airline customers tend to have low brand loyalty (except at the extremes of high and low prices and service); leisure travelers focus mainly on price, and business travelers focus mostly on schedules and service. Product and service differentiation at particular price points is low because aircraft, cabin configuration, and catering tend to be quite similar in most cases. For leisure travelers, the price competition is intense and is led by low-cost discount carriers, including Southwest Airlines in the United States, Ryanair in Europe, and Air Asia in Asia. For business travelers, the major scheduled airlines and a few service-quality specialists, such as Singapore Airlines, are the main contenders. Fuel costs (typically more than 25 percent of total costs and highly volatile) and labor costs (around 10 percent of total costs) have been the focus of management cost-reduction efforts. The airline industry is highly unionized, and labor strife has frequently been a source of costly disruptions to the industry. Technology has always played a major role in the airline industry, from its origins with small propeller-driven planes through the advent of the jet age to the drive for greater fuel efficiency since the oil price increases of the 1970s. Technology also poses a threat to the growth of business air travel in the form of improved telecommunications—notably, videoconferencing and webcasting. Arguably, the airline industry has been a great force in shaping demography by permitting difficult-to-access geographical areas to be settled with large populations. At the same time, large numbers of post-WWII Baby Boomers have been a factor in generating the growth in demand for air travel in the past half-century. In recent years, social issues have started to play a role in the airline industry; carbon emissions, for example, have come under scrutiny by environmentalists and governments.

COMPANY ANALYSIS

6

Company analysis includes an analysis of the company's financial position, products and/or services, and **competitive strategy** (its plans for responding to the threats and opportunities presented by the external environment). Company analysis takes place after the analyst has gained an understanding of a company's external environment—the macroeconomic, demographic, governmental, technological, and social forces influencing the industry's competitive structure. The analyst should seek to determine whether the strategy is primarily defensive or offensive in its nature and how the company intends to implement the strategy.

Porter identifies two chief competitive strategies: a low-cost strategy (cost leadership) and a product/service differentiation strategy.

In a low-cost strategy, companies strive to become the low-cost producers and to gain market share by offering their products and services at lower prices than their competition while still making a profit margin sufficient to generate a superior rate of return based on the higher revenues achieved. Low-cost strategies may be pursued defensively to protect market positions and returns or offensively to gain market share and increase returns. Pricing also can be defensive (when the competitive environment is one of low rivalry) or aggressive (when rivalry is intense). In the case of intense rivalry, pricing may even become predatory—that is, aimed at rapidly driving competitors out of business at the expense of near-term profitability. The hope in such a strategy is that having achieved a larger market share, the company can later increase prices to generate higher returns than before. For example, the predatory strategy has been alleged by some analysts to have been followed by major airlines trying to protect lucrative routes from discount airlines. Although laws concerning anti-competitive practices often prohibit predatory pricing to gain market share, in most cases, it is difficult to accurately ascribe the costs of products or services with sufficient precision to demonstrate that predatory pricing (as opposed to intense but fair price competition) is occurring. Companies seeking to follow low-cost strategies must have tight cost controls, efficient operating and reporting systems, and appropriate managerial incentives. In addition, they must commit themselves to painstaking scrutiny of production systems and their labor forces and to low-cost designs and product distribution. They must be able to invest in productivity-improving capital equipment and to finance that investment at a low cost of capital.

In differentiation strategies, companies attempt to establish themselves as the suppliers or producers of products and services that are unique either in quality, type, or means of distribution. To be successful, their price premiums must be above their costs of differentiation and the differentiation must be appealing to customers and sustainable over time. Corporate managers who successfully pursue differentiation strategies tend to have strong market research teams to identify and match customer needs with product development and marketing. Such a strategy puts a premium on employing creative and inventive people.

6.1 Elements That Should be Covered in a Company Analysis

A thorough company analysis, particularly as presented in a research report, should

- provide an overview of the company (corporate profile), including a basic understanding of its businesses, investment activities, corporate governance, and perceived strengths and weaknesses;
- explain relevant industry characteristics;
- analyze the demand for the company's products and services;
- analyze the supply of products and services, which includes an analysis of costs;
- explain the company's pricing environment; and
- present and interpret relevant financial ratios, including comparisons over time and comparisons with competitors.

Company analysis often includes forecasting the company's financial statements, particularly when the purpose of the analysis is to use a discounted cash flow method to value the company's common equity.

Exhibit 8 provides a checklist of points to cover in a company analysis. The list may need to be adapted to serve the needs of a particular company analysis and is not exhaustive.

Exhibit 8 A Checklist for Company Analysis

Corporate Profile

- Identity of company's major products and services, current position in industry, and history
- Composition of sales
- Product life-cycle stages/experience curve effects[17]
- Research & development activities
- Past and planned capital expenditures
- Board structure, composition, electoral system, anti-takeover provisions, and other corporate governance issues
- Management strengths, weaknesses, compensation, turnover, and corporate culture
- Benefits, retirement plans, and their influence on shareholder value
- Labor relations
- Insider ownership levels and changes
- Legal actions and the company's state of preparedness
- Other special strengths or weaknesses

Industry Characteristics

- Stage in its life cycle
- Business-cycle sensitivity or economic characteristics

17 A *product life cycle* relates to stages in the sales of a product. *Experience curve effects* refer to the tendency for the cost of producing a good or service to decline with cumulative output.

Exhibit 8 (Continued)

- Typical product life cycles in the industry (short and marked by technological obsolescence or long, such as pharmaceuticals protected by patents)
- Brand loyalty, customer switching costs, and intensity of competition
- Entry and exit barriers
- Industry supplier considerations (concentration of sources, ability to switch suppliers or enter suppliers' business)
- Number of companies in the industry and whether it is, as determined by market shares, fragmented or concentrated
- Opportunity to differentiate product/service and relative product/service price, cost, and quality advantages/disadvantages
- Technologies used
- Government regulation
- State and history of labor relations
- Other industry problems/opportunities

Analysis of Demand for Products/Services

- Sources of demand
- Product differentiation
- Past record, sensitivities, and correlations with social, demographic, economic, and other variables
- Outlook—short, medium, and long term, including new product and business opportunities

Analysis of Supply of Products/Services

- Sources (concentration, competition, and substitutes)
- Industry capacity outlook—short, medium, and long term
- Company's capacity and cost structure
- Import/export considerations
- Proprietary products or trademarks

Analysis of Pricing

- Past relationships among demand, supply, and prices
- Significance of raw material and labor costs and the outlook for their cost and availability
- Outlook for selling prices, demand, and profitability based on current and anticipated future trends

Financial Ratios and Measures

(in multi-year spreadsheets with historical and forecast data)

I. **Activity ratios**, measuring how efficiently a company performs such functions as the collection of receivables and inventory management:
   - Days of sales outstanding (DSO)
   - Days of inventory on hand (DOH)

(continued)

Exhibit 8 (Continued)

- Days of payables outstanding (DPO)

II. **Liquidity ratios**, measuring a company's ability to meet its short-term obligations:

- Current ratio
- Quick ratio
- Cash ratio
- Cash conversion cycle (DOH + DSO – DPO)

III. **Solvency ratios**, measuring a company's ability to meet its debt obligations. (In the following, "net debt" is the amount of interest-bearing liabilities after subtracting cash and cash equivalents.)

- Net debt to EBITDA (earnings before interest, taxes, depreciation, and amortization)
- Net debt to capital
- Debt to assets
- Debt to capital (at book and market values)
- Financial leverage ratio (Average total assets/Average total equity)
- Cash flow to debt
- Interest coverage ratio
- Off-balance-sheet liabilities and contingent liabilities
- Non-arm's-length financial dealings

IV. **Profitability ratios**, measuring a company's ability to generate profitable sales from its resources (assets).

- Gross profit margin
- Operating profit margin
- Pretax profit margin
- Net profit margin
- Return on invested capital or ROIC (Net operating profits after tax/ Average invested capital)
- Return on assets or ROA (Net income/ Average total assets)
- Return on equity or ROE (Net income/Average total equity)

V. **Financial Statistics and Related Considerations**, quantities and facts about a company's finances that an analyst should understand.

- Growth rate of net sales
- Growth rate of gross profit
- EBITDA
- Net income
- Operating cash flow
- EPS
- Operating cash flow per share
- Operating cash flow in relation to maintenance and total capital expenditures
- Expected rate of return on retained cash flow
- Debt maturities and ability of company to refinance and/or repay debt

Exhibit 8 (Continued)

- Dividend payout ratio (Common dividends/Net income available to common shareholders)
- Off-balance-sheet liabilities and contingent liabilities
- Non-arm's-length financial dealings

To evaluate a company's performance, the key measures presented in Exhibit 8 should be compared over time and between companies (particularly peer companies). The following formula can be used to analyze how and why a company's ROE differs from that of other companies or its own ROE in other periods by tracing the differences to changes in its profit margin, the productivity of its assets, or its financial leverage:

ROE = (Net profit margin: Net earnings/Net sales) × (Asset turnover: Net sales/ Average total assets) × (Financial leverage: Average total assets/ Average common equity)

The financial statements of a company over time provide numerous insights into the effects of industry conditions on its performance and the success or failure of its strategies. They also provide a framework for forecasting the company's operating performance when given the analyst's assumptions for numerous variables in the future. The financial ratios listed in Exhibit 8 are applicable to a wide range of companies and industries, but other statistics and ratios are often also used.

6.2 Spreadsheet Modeling

Spreadsheet modeling of financial statements to analyze and forecast revenues, operating and net income, and cash flows has become one of the most widely used tools in company analysis. Although spreadsheet models are a valuable tool for understanding past financial performance and forecasting future performance, the complexity of such models can at times be a problem. Because modeling requires the analyst to predict and input numerous items in financial statements, there is a risk of errors—either in assumptions made or in formulas in the model—which can compound, leading to erroneous forecasts. Yet, those forecasts may seem precise because of the sheer complexity of the model. The result is often a false sense of understanding and security on the part of those who rely on the models. To guard against this, before or after a model is completed, a "reality check" of the model is useful.

Such testing for reasonableness can be done by, first, asking what the few most important changes in income statement items are likely to be from last year to this year and the next year and, second, attempting to quantify the effects of these significant changes or "swing factors" on the bottom line. If an analyst cannot summarize in a few points what factors are realistically expected to change income from year to year and is not convinced that these assumptions are correct, then he or she does not really understand the output of the computer modeling efforts. In general, financial models should be in a format that matches the company's reporting of its financial results or supplementary disclosures or that can be accurately derived from these reports. Otherwise, there will be no natural reality check when the company issues its financial results and the analyst will not be able to compare his or her estimates with actual reported results.

SUMMARY

In this reading, we have provided an overview of industry analysis and illustrated approaches that are widely used by analysts to examine an industry.

- Company analysis and industry analysis are closely interrelated. Company and industry analysis together can provide insight into sources of industry revenue growth and competitors' market shares and thus the future of an individual company's top-line growth and bottom-line profitability.
- Industry analysis is useful for:
  - understanding a company's business and business environment;
  - identifying active equity investment opportunities;
  - formulating an industry or sector rotation strategy; and
  - portfolio performance attribution.
- The three main approaches to classifying companies are:
  - products and/or services supplied;
  - business-cycle sensitivities; and
  - statistical similarities.
- Commercial industry classification systems include:
  - Global Industry Classification Standard;
  - Russell Global Sectors; and
  - Industry Classification Benchmark.
- Governmental industry classification systems include:
  - International Standard Industrial Classification of All Economic Activities;
  - Statistical Classification of Economic Activities in the European Community;
  - Australian and New Zealand Standard Industrial Classification; and
  - North American Industry Classification System.
- A limitation of current classification systems is that the narrowest classification unit assigned to a company generally cannot be assumed to constitute its peer group for the purposes of detailed fundamental comparisons or valuation.
- A peer group is a group of companies engaged in similar business activities whose economics and valuation are influenced by closely related factors.
- Steps in constructing a preliminary list of peer companies:
  - Examine commercial classification systems if available. These systems often provide a useful starting point for identifying companies operating in the same industry.
  - Review the subject company's annual report for a discussion of the competitive environment. Companies frequently cite specific competitors.
  - Review competitors' annual reports to identify other potential comparables.
  - Review industry trade publications to identify additional peer companies.
  - Confirm that each comparable or peer company derives a significant portion of its revenue and operating profit from a similar business activity as the subject company.

- Not all industries are created equal. Some are highly competitive, with many companies struggling to earn returns in excess of their cost of capital, and other industries have attractive characteristics that enable a majority of industry participants to generate healthy profits.
- Differing competitive environments are determined by the structural attributes of the industry. For this important reason, industry analysis is a vital complement to company analysis. The analyst needs to understand the context in which a company operates to fully understand the opportunities and threats that a company faces.
- The framework for strategic analysis known as "Porter's five forces" can provide a useful starting point. Porter maintains that the profitability of companies in an industry is determined by five forces: 1) The threat of new entrants, which in turn is determined by economies of scale, brand loyalty, absolute cost advantages, customer switching costs, and government regulation; 2) the bargaining power of suppliers, which is a function of the feasibility of product substitution, the concentration of the buyer and supplier groups, and switching costs and entry costs in each case; 3) the bargaining power of buyers, which is a function of switching costs among customers and the ability of customers to produce their own product; 4) the threat of substitutes; and 5) the intensity of rivalry among existing competitors, which in turn is a function of industry competitive structure, demand conditions, cost conditions, and the height of exit barriers.
- The concept of barriers to entry refers to the ease with which new competitors can challenge incumbents and can be an important factor in determining the competitive environment of an industry. If new competitors can easily enter the industry, the industry is likely to be highly competitive because incumbents that attempt to raise prices will be undercut by newcomers. As a result, industries with low barriers to entry tend to have low pricing power. Conversely, if incumbents are protected by barriers to entry, they may enjoy a more benign competitive environment that gives them greater pricing power over their customers because they do not have to worry about being undercut by upstarts.
- Industry concentration is often, although not always, a sign that an industry may have pricing power and rational competition. Industry fragmentation is a much stronger signal, however, that the industry is competitive and pricing power is limited.
- The effect of industry capacity on pricing is clear: Tight capacity gives participants more pricing power because demand for products or services exceeds supply; overcapacity leads to price cutting and a highly competitive environment as excess supply chases demand. The analyst should think about not only current capacity conditions but also future changes in capacity levels—how long it takes for supply and demand to come into balance and what effect that process has on industry pricing power and returns.
- Examining the market share stability of an industry over time is similar to thinking about barriers to entry and the frequency with which new players enter an industry. Stable market shares typically indicate less competitive industries, whereas unstable market shares often indicate highly competitive industries with limited pricing power.
- An industry's position in its life cycle often has a large impact on its competitive dynamics, so it is important to keep this positioning in mind when performing strategic analysis of an industry. Industries, like individual companies, tend to evolve over time and usually experience significant changes in the rate of growth and levels of profitability along the way. Just as an investment in an

individual company requires careful monitoring, industry analysis is a continuous process that must be repeated over time to identify changes that may be occurring.

- A useful framework for analyzing the evolution of an industry is an industry life-cycle model, which identifies the sequential stages that an industry typically goes through. The five stages of an industry life cycle according to the Hill and Jones model are:
  - embryonic;
  - growth;
  - shakeout;
  - mature; and
  - decline.
- Price competition and thinking like a customer are important factors that are often overlooked when analyzing an industry. Whatever factors most influence customer purchasing decisions are also likely to be the focus of competitive rivalry in the industry. Broadly, industries for which price is a large factor in customer purchase decisions tend to be more competitive than industries in which customers value other attributes more highly.
- External influences on industry growth, profitability, and risk include:
  - technology;
  - demographics;
  - government; and
  - social factors.
- Company analysis takes place after the analyst has gained an understanding of the company's external environment and includes answering questions about how the company will respond to the threats and opportunities presented by the external environment. This intended response is the individual company's competitive strategy. The analyst should seek to determine whether the strategy is primarily defensive or offensive in its nature and how the company intends to implement it.
- Porter identifies two chief competitive strategies:
  - A low-cost strategy (cost leadership) is one in which companies strive to become the low-cost producers and to gain market share by offering their products and services at lower prices than their competition while still making a profit margin sufficient to generate a superior rate of return based on the higher revenues achieved.
  - A product/service differentiation strategy is one in which companies attempt to establish themselves as the suppliers or producers of products and services that are unique either in quality, type, or means of distribution. To be successful, the companies' price premiums must be above their costs of differentiation and the differentiation must be appealing to customers and sustainable over time.
- A checklist for company analysis includes a thorough investigation of:
  - corporate profile;
  - industry characteristics;
  - demand for products/services;
  - supply of products/services;
  - pricing; and

- financial ratios.

- Spreadsheet modeling of financial statements to analyze and forecast revenues, operating and net income, and cash flows has become one of the most widely used tools in company analysis. Spreadsheet modeling can be used to quantify the effects of the changes in certain swing factors on the various financial statements. The analyst should be aware that the output of the model will depend significantly on the assumptions that are made.

REFERENCES

Cavaglia, Stefano, Jeffrey Diermeier, Vadim Moroz, and Sonia De Zordo. 2004. "Investing in Global Equities." *Journal of Portfolio Management*, vol. 30, no. 3:88–94.

Hill, Charles, and Gareth Jones. 2008. "External Analysis: The Identification of Opportunities and Threats." *Strategic Management: An Integrated Approach*. Boston, MA: Houghton Mifflin Co.

McGahan, Anita M., and Michael E. Porter. 1997. "How Much Does Industry Matter, Really?" *Strategic Management Journal*, vol. 18, no. No. S1:15–30.

Porter, Michael E. 2008. "The Five Competitive Forces That Shape Strategy." *Harvard Business Review*, vol. 86, no. 1:78–93.

PRACTICE PROBLEMS

1 Which of the following is *least likely* to involve industry analysis?

A Sector rotation strategy.

B Top-down fundamental investing.

C Tactical asset allocation strategy.

2 A sector rotation strategy involves investing in a sector by:

A making regular investments in it.

B investing in a pre-selected group of sectors on a rotating basis.

C timing investment to take advantage of business-cycle conditions.

3 Which of the following information about a company would *most likely* depend on an industry analysis? The company's:

A dividend policy.

B competitive environment.

C trends in corporate expenses.

4 Which industry classification system uses a three-tier classification system?

A Russell Global Sectors.

B Industry Classification Benchmark.

C Global Industry Classification Standard.

5 In which sector would a manufacturer of personal care products be classified?

A Health care.

B Consumer staples.

C Consumer discretionary.

6 A automotive manufacturer is *most likely* classified in which of the following industry sectors?

A Consumer staples

B Industrial durables

C Consumer discretionary

7 Which of the following statements about commercial and government industry classification systems is *most* accurate?

A Many commercial classification systems include private for-profit companies.

B Both commercial and government classification systems exclude not-for-profit companies.

C Commercial classification systems are generally updated more frequently than government classification systems.

8 Which of the following is *not* a limitation of the cyclical/non-cyclical descriptive approach to classifying companies?

A A cyclical company may have a growth component in it.

B Business-cycle sensitivity is a discrete phenomenon rather than a continuous spectrum.

C A global company can experience economic expansion in one part of the world while experiencing recession in another part.

9 A cyclical company is *most likely* to:

A have low operating leverage.

B sell relatively inexpensive products.

C experience wider-than-average fluctuations in demand.

10 A company that is sensitive to the business cycle would *most likely*:

A not have growth opportunities.

B experience below-average fluctuation in demand.

C sell products that the customer can purchase at a later date if necessary.

11 Which of the following factors would *most likely* be a limitation of applying business-cycle analysis to global industry analysis?

A Some industries are relatively insensitive to the business cycle.

B Correlations of security returns between different world markets are relatively low.

C One region or country of the world may experience recession while another region experiences expansion.

12 Which of the following statements about peer groups is *most* accurate?

A Constructing a peer group for a company follows a standardized process.

B Commercial industry classification systems often provide a starting point for constructing a peer group.

C A peer group is generally composed of all the companies in the most narrowly defined category used by the commercial industry classification system.

13 With regard to forming a company's peer group, which of the following statements is *not* correct?

A Comments from the management of the company about competitors are generally not used when selecting the peer group.

B The higher the proportion of revenue and operating profit of the peer company derived from business activities similar to the subject company, the more meaningful the comparison.

C Comparing the company's performance measures with those for a potential peer-group company is of limited value when the companies are exposed to different stages of the business cycle.

14 When selecting companies for inclusion in a peer group, a company operating in three different business segments would:

A be in only one peer group.

B possibly be in more than one peer group.

C not be included in any peer group.

15 An industry that *most likely* has both high barriers to entry and high barriers to exit is the:

A restaurant industry.

B advertising industry.

C automobile industry.

16 Which factor is *most likely* associated with stable market share?

A Low switching costs.

B Low barriers to entry.

C Slow pace of product innovation.

17 Which of the following companies *most likely* has the greatest ability to quickly increase its capacity?

A Restaurant.

B Steel producer.

C Legal services provider.

18 A population that is rapidly aging would *most likely* cause the growth rate of the industry producing eye glasses and contact lenses to:

A decrease.

B increase.

C not change.

19 If over a long period of time a country's average level of educational accomplishment increases, this development would *most likely* lead to the country's amount of income spent on consumer discretionary goods to:

A decrease.

B increase.

C not change.

20 If the technology for an industry involves high fixed capital investment, then one way to seek higher profit growth is by pursuing:

A economies of scale.

B diseconomies of scale.

C removal of features that differentiate the product or service provided.

21 Which of the following life-cycle phases is typically characterized by high prices?

A Mature.

B Growth.

C Embryonic.

22 In which of the following life-cycle phases are price wars *most likely* to be absent?

A Mature.

B Decline.

C Growth.

23 When graphically depicting the life-cycle model for an industry as a curve, the variables on the axes are:

A price and time.

B demand and time.

C demand and stage of the life cycle.

24 Industry consolidation and high barriers to entry *most likely* characterize which life-cycle stage?

A Mature

B Growth

C Embryonic

25 Which of the following is *most likely* a characteristic of a concentrated industry?

A Infrequent, tacit coordination.

B Difficulty in monitoring other industry members.

C Industry members attempting to avoid competition on price.

26 Which of the following industry characteristics is generally *least likely* to produce high returns on capital?

- **A** High barriers to entry
- **B** High degree of concentration
- **C** Short lead time to build new plants

27 An industry with high barriers to entry and weak pricing power *most likely* has:

- **A** high barriers to exit.
- **B** stable market shares.
- **C** significant numbers of issued patents.

28 Economic value is created for an industry's shareholders when the industry earns a return:

- **A** below the cost of capital.
- **B** equal to the cost of capital.
- **C** above the cost of capital.

29 Which of the following industries is *most likely* to be characterized as concentrated with strong pricing power?

- **A** Asset management.
- **B** Alcoholic beverages.
- **C** Household and personal products.

30 With respect to competitive strategy, a company with a successful cost leadership strategy is *most likely* characterized by:

- **A** a low cost of capital.
- **B** reduced market share.
- **C** the ability to offer products at higher prices than competitors.

31 When conducting a company analysis, the analysis of demand for a company's product is *least likely* to consider the:

- **A** company's cost structure.
- **B** motivations of the customer base.
- **C** product's differentiating characteristics.

32 Which of the following statements about company analysis is *most* accurate?

- **A** The complexity of spreadsheet modeling ensures precise forecasts of financial statements.
- **B** The interpretation of financial ratios should focus on comparing the company's results over time but not with competitors.
- **C** The corporate profile would include a description of the company's business, investment activities, governance, and strengths and weaknesses.

SOLUTIONS

1 C is correct. Tactical asset allocation involves timing investments in asset classes and does not make use of industry analysis.

2 C is correct. A sector rotation strategy is conducted by investors wishing to time investment in industries through an analysis of fundamentals and/or business-cycle conditions.

3 B is correct. Determination of a company's competitive environment depends on understanding its industry.

4 A is correct. The Russell system uses three tiers, whereas the other two systems are based on four tiers or levels.

5 B is correct. Personal care products are classified as consumer staples in the "Description of Representative Sectors."

6 C is correct. Automotive manufacturers are classified as consumer discretionary. Consumer discretionary companies derive a majority of revenue from the sale of consumer-related products for which demand tends to exhibit a high degree of economic sensitivity—that is, high demand during periods of economic expansion and low demand during periods of contraction.

7 C is correct. Commercial systems are generally updated more frequently than government systems, and include only publicly traded for-profit companies.

8 B is correct. Business-cycle sensitivity falls on a continuum and is not a discrete "either–or" phenomenon.

9 C is correct. Cyclical companies are sensitive to the business cycle, with low product demand during periods of economic contraction and high product demand during periods of economic expansion. They, therefore, experience wider-than-average fluctuations in product demand.

10 C is correct. Customers' flexibility as to when they purchase the product makes the product more sensitive to the business cycle.

11 C is correct. Varying conditions of recession or expansion around the world would affect the comparisons of companies with sales in different regions of the world.

12 B is correct. Constructing a peer group is a subjective process, and a logical starting point is to begin with a commercially available classification system. This system will identify a group of companies that may have properties comparable to the business activity of interest.

13 A is correct because it is a false statement. Reviewing the annual report to find management's discussion about the competitive environment and specific competitors is a suggested step in the process of constructing a peer group.

14 B is correct. The company could be in more than one peer group depending on the demand drivers for the business segments, although the multiple business segments may make it difficult to classify the company.

15 C is correct. For the automobile industry, the high capital requirements and other elements mentioned in the reading provide high barriers to entry, and recognition that auto factories are generally only of use for manufacturing cars implies a high barrier to exit.

16 C is correct. A slow pace of product innovation often means that customers prefer to stay with suppliers they know, implying stable market shares.

17 C is correct. Capacity increases in providing legal services would not involve several factors that would be important to the other two industries, including the need for substantial fixed capital investments or, in the case of a restaurant, outfitting rental or purchased space. These requirements would tend to slow down, respectively, steel production and restaurant expansion.

18 B is correct. Vision typically deteriorates at advanced ages. An increased number of older adults implies more eyewear products will be purchased.

19 B is correct. As their educational level increases, workers are able to perform more skilled tasks, earn higher wages, and as a result, have more income left for discretionary expenditures.

20 A is correct. Seeking economies of scale would tend to reduce per-unit costs and increase profit.

21 C is correct. The embryonic stage is characterized by slow growth and high prices.

22 C is correct. The growth phase is not likely to experience price wars because expanding industry demand provides companies the opportunity to grow even without increasing market share. When industry growth is stagnant, companies may only be able to grow by increasing market share, e.g., by engaging in price competition.

23 B is correct. The industry life-cycle model shows how demand evolves through time as an industry passes from the embryonic stage through the stage of decline.

24 A is correct. Industry consolidation and relatively high barriers to entry are two characteristics of a mature-stage industry.

25 C is correct. The relatively few members of the industry generally try to avoid price competition.

26 C is correct. With short lead times, industry capacity can be rapidly increased to satisfy demand, but it may also lead to overcapacity and lower profits.

27 A is correct. An industry that has high barriers to entry generally requires substantial physical capital and/or financial investment. With weak pricing power in the industry, finding a buyer for excess capacity (i.e., to exit the industry) may be difficult.

28 C is correct. Economic profit is earned and value created for shareholders when the company earns returns above the company's cost of capital.

29 B is correct. As displayed in Exhibit 4, the alcoholic beverage industry is concentrated and possesses strong pricing power.

30 A is correct. Companies with low cost strategies must be able to invest in productivity-improving equipment and finance that investment at a low cost of capital. Market share and pricing depend on whether the strategy is pursued defensively or offensively.

31 A is correct. The cost structure is an appropriate element when analyzing the supply of the product, but analysis of demand relies on the product's differentiating characteristics and the customers' needs and wants.

32 C is correct. The corporate profile would provide an understanding of these elements.

READING

41

Equity Valuation: Concepts and Basic Tools

by John J. Nagorniak, CFA, and Stephen E. Wilcox, PhD, CFA

John J. Nagorniak, CFA (USA). Stephen E. Wilcox, PhD, CFA, is at Minnesota State University, Mankato (USA).

LEARNING OUTCOMES

Mastery	*The candidate should be able to:*
☐	a. evaluate whether a security, given its current market price and a value estimate, is overvalued, fairly valued, or undervalued by the market;
☐	b. describe major categories of equity valuation models;
☐	c. describe regular cash dividends, extra dividends, stock dividends, stock splits, reverse stock splits, and share repurchases;
☐	d. describe dividend payment chronology;
☐	e. explain the rationale for using present value models to value equity and describe the dividend discount and free-cash-flow-to-equity models;
☐	f. calculate the intrinsic value of a non-callable, non-convertible preferred stock;
☐	g. calculate and interpret the intrinsic value of an equity security based on the Gordon (constant) growth dividend discount model or a two-stage dividend discount model, as appropriate;
☐	h. identify characteristics of companies for which the constant growth or a multistage dividend discount model is appropriate;
☐	i. explain the rationale for using price multiples to value equity, how the price to earnings multiple relates to fundamentals, and the use of multiples based on comparables;
☐	j. calculate and interpret the following multiples: price to earnings, price to an estimate of operating cash flow, price to sales, and price to book value;

(continued)

LEARNING OUTCOMES

Mastery	*The candidate should be able to:*
☐	k. describe enterprise value multiples and their use in estimating equity value;
☐	l. describe asset-based valuation models and their use in estimating equity value;
☐	m. explain advantages and disadvantages of each category of valuation model.

1 INTRODUCTION

Analysts gather and process information to make investment decisions, including buy and sell recommendations. What information is gathered and how it is processed depend on the analyst and the purpose of the analysis. Technical analysis uses such information as stock price and trading volume as the basis for investment decisions. Fundamental analysis uses information about the economy, industry, and company as the basis for investment decisions. Examples of fundamentals are unemployment rates, gross domestic product (GDP) growth, industry growth, and quality of and growth in company earnings. Whereas technical analysts use information to predict price movements and base investment decisions on the direction of predicted change in prices, fundamental analysts use information to estimate the value of a security and to compare the estimated value to the market price and then base investment decisions on that comparison.

This reading introduces equity valuation models used to estimate the **intrinsic value** (synonym: **fundamental value**) of a security; intrinsic value is based on an analysis of investment fundamentals and characteristics. The fundamentals to be considered depend on the analyst's approach to valuation. In a top-down approach, an analyst examines the economic environment, identifies sectors that are expected to prosper in that environment, and analyzes securities of companies from previously identified attractive sectors. In a bottom-up approach, an analyst typically follows an industry or industries and forecasts fundamentals for the companies in those industries in order to determine valuation. Whatever the approach, an analyst who estimates the intrinsic value of an equity security is implicitly questioning the accuracy of the market price as an estimate of value. Valuation is particularly important in active equity portfolio management, which aims to improve on the return–risk trade-off of a portfolio's benchmark by identifying mispriced securities.

This reading is organized as follows. Section 2 discusses the implications of differences between estimated value and market price. Section 3 introduces three major categories of valuation model. Section 4 presents an overview of present value models with a focus on the dividend discount model. Section 5 describes and examines the use of multiples in valuation. Section 6 explains asset-based valuation and demonstrates how these models can be used to estimate value. Section 7 states conclusions and summarizes the reading.

ESTIMATED VALUE AND MARKET PRICE

2

By comparing estimates of value and market price, an analyst can arrive at one of three conclusions: The security is *undervalued*, *overvalued*, or *fairly valued* in the marketplace. For example, if the market price of an asset is $10 and the analyst estimates intrinsic value at $10, a logical conclusion is that the security is fairly valued. If the security is selling for $20, the security would be considered overvalued. If the security is selling for $5, the security would be considered undervalued. Basically, by estimating value, the analyst is assuming that the market price is not necessarily the best estimate of intrinsic value. If the estimated value exceeds the market price, the analyst infers the security is *undervalued*. If the estimated value equals the market price, the analyst infers the security is *fairly valued*. If the estimated value is less than the market price, the analyst infers the security is *overvalued*.

In practice, the conclusion is not so straightforward. Analysts must cope with uncertainties related to model appropriateness and the correct value of inputs. An analyst's final conclusion depends not only on the comparison of the estimated value and the market price but also on the analyst's confidence in the estimated value (i.e., in the model selected and the inputs used in it). One can envision a spectrum running from relatively high confidence in the valuation model *and* the inputs to relatively low confidence in the valuation model *and/or* the inputs. When confidence is relatively low, the analyst might demand a substantial divergence between his or her own value estimate and the market price before acting on an apparent mispricing. For instance, if the estimate of intrinsic value is $10 and the market price is $10.05, the analyst might reasonably conclude that the security is fairly valued and that the 1/2 of 1 percent market price difference from the estimated value is within the analyst's confidence interval.

Confidence in the convergence of the market price to the intrinsic value over the investment time horizon relevant to the objectives of the portfolio must also be taken into account before an analyst acts on an apparent mispricing or makes a buy, sell, or hold recommendation: The ability to benefit from identifying a mispriced security depends on the market price converging to the estimated intrinsic value.

In seeking to identify mispricing and attractive investments, analysts are treating market prices with skepticism, but they are also treating market prices with respect. For example, an analyst who finds that many securities examined appear to be overvalued will typically recheck models and inputs before acting on a conclusion of overvaluation. Analysts also often recognize and factor into recommendations that different market segments—such as securities closely followed by analysts versus securities relatively neglected by analysts—may differ in how common or persistent mispricing is. Mispricing may be more likely in securities neglected by analysts.

EXAMPLE 1

Valuation and Analyst Response

1 An analyst finds that all the securities analyzed have estimated values higher than their market prices. The securities all appear to be:

A overvalued.

B undervalued.

C fairly valued.

2 An analyst finds that nearly all companies in a market segment have common shares which are trading at market prices above the analyst's estimate of the shares' values. This market segment is widely followed by analysts. Which of the following statements describes the analyst's *most appropriate* first action?

A Issue a sell recommendation for each share issue.

B Issue a buy recommendation for each share issue.

C Reexamine the models and inputs used for the valuations.

3 An analyst, using a number of models and a range of inputs, estimates a security's value to be between ¥250 and ¥270. The security is trading at ¥265. The security appears to be:

A overvalued.

B undervalued.

C fairly valued.

Solution to 1:

B is correct. The estimated intrinsic value for each security is greater than the market price. The securities all appear to be undervalued in the market. Note, however, that the analyst may wish to reexamine the model and inputs to check that the conclusion is valid.

Solution to 2:

C is correct. It seems improbable that all the share issues analyzed are overvalued, as indicated by market prices in excess of estimated value—particularly because the market segment is widely followed by analysts. Thus, the analyst will not issue a sell recommendation for each issue. The analyst will *most appropriately* reexamine the models and inputs prior to issuing any recommendations. A buy recommendation is not an appropriate response to an overvalued security.

Solution to 3:

C is correct. The security's market price of ¥265 is within the range estimated by the analyst. The security appears to be fairly valued.

Analysts often use a variety of models and inputs to achieve greater confidence in their estimates of intrinsic value. The use of more than one model and a range of inputs also helps the analyst understand the sensitivity of value estimates to different models and inputs.

3 MAJOR CATEGORIES OF EQUITY VALUATION MODELS

Three major categories of equity valuation models are as follows:

- **Present value models** (synonym: **discounted cash flow models**). These models estimate the intrinsic value of a security as the present value of the future benefits expected to be received from the security. In present value models, benefits are often defined in terms of cash expected to be distributed to shareholders (**dividend discount models**) or in terms of cash flows available to be distributed to shareholders after meeting capital expenditure and working capital needs (**free-cash-flow-to-equity models**). Many models fall within this category, ranging from the relatively simple to the very complex. In Section 4, we discuss in detail two of the simpler models, the Gordon (constant) growth model and the two-stage dividend discount models.

- **Multiplier models** (synonym: **market multiple models**). These models are based chiefly on share price multiples or enterprise value multiples. The former model estimates intrinsic value of a common share from a price multiple for some fundamental variable, such as revenues, earnings, cash flows, or book value. Examples of the multiples include price to earnings (P/E, share price divided by earnings per share) and price to sales (P/S, share price divided by sales per share). The fundamental variable may be stated on a forward basis (e.g., forecasted EPS for the next year) or a trailing basis (e.g., EPS for the past year), as long as the usage is consistent across companies being examined. Price multiples are also used to compare relative values. The use of the ratio of share price to EPS—that is, the P/E multiple—to judge relative value is an example of this approach to equity valuation.

  Enterprise value (EV) multiples have the form (Enterprise value)/(Value of a fundamental variable). Two possible choices for the denominator are earnings before interest, taxes, depreciation, and amortization (EBITDA) and total revenue. Enterprise value, the numerator, is a measure of a company's total market value from which cash and short-term investments have been subtracted (because an acquirer could use those assets to pay for acquiring the company). An estimate of common share value can be calculated indirectly from the EV multiple; the value of liabilities and preferred shares can be subtracted from the EV to arrive at the value of common equity.

- **Asset-based valuation models**. These models estimate intrinsic value of a common share from the estimated value of the assets of a corporation minus the estimated value of its liabilities and preferred shares. The estimated market value of the assets is often determined by making adjustments to the **book value** (synonym: **carrying value**) of assets and liabilities. The theory underlying the asset-based approach is that the value of a business is equal to the sum of the value of the business's assets.

As already mentioned, many analysts use more than one type of model to estimate value. Analysts recognize that each model is a simplification of the real world and that there are uncertainties related to model appropriateness and the inputs to the models. The choice of model(s) will depend on the availability of information to input into the model(s) and the analyst's confidence in the information and in the appropriateness of the model(s).

EXAMPLE 2

Categories of Equity Valuation Models

1 An analyst is estimating the intrinsic value of a new company. The analyst has one year of financial statements for the company and has calculated the average values of a variety of price multiples for the industry in which the company operates. The analyst plans to use at least one model from each of the three categories of valuation models. The analyst is *least likely* to rely on the estimate(s) from the:

A multiplier model(s).

B present value model(s).

C asset-based valuation model(s).

2 Based on a company's EPS of €1.35, an analyst estimates the intrinsic value of a security to be €16.60. Which type of model is the analyst *most likely* to be using to estimate intrinsic value?

A Multiplier model.

B Present value model.

C Asset-based valuation model.

Solution to 1:

B is correct. Because the company has only one year of data available, the analyst is *least likely* to be confident in the inputs for a present value model. The values on the balance sheet, even before adjustment, are likely to be close to market values because the assets are all relatively new. The multiplier models are based on average multiples from the industry.

Solution to 2:

A is correct. The analyst is using a multiplier model based on the P/E multiple. The P/E multiple used was 16.60/1.35 = 12.3.

As you begin the study of specific equity valuation models in the next section, you must bear in mind that any model of value is, by necessity, a simplification of the real world. Never forget this simple fact! You may encounter models much more complicated than the ones discussed here, but even those models will be simplifications of reality.

4 PRESENT VALUE MODELS: THE DIVIDEND DISCOUNT MODEL

Present value models follow a fundamental tenet of economics which states that individuals defer consumption—that is, they invest—for the future benefits expected. Individuals and companies make an investment because they expect thereby to earn a rate of return over the investment period. Logically, the value of an investment should be equal to the present value of the expected future benefits. For common shares, an analyst can equate benefits to the cash flows to be generated by the investment. The simplest present value model of equity valuation is the dividend discount model (DDM), which specifies cash flows from a common stock investment to be dividends.

The next section describes aspects of dividends that users of dividend discount models should understand.

4.1 Dividends: Background for the Dividend Discount Model

Generally, there are two sources of return from investing in equities: (1) cash dividends received by an investor over his or her holding period and (2) the change in the market price of equities over that holding period.

A **dividend** is a distribution paid to shareholders based on the number of shares owned, and a cash dividend is a cash distribution made to a company's shareholders. Cash dividends are typically paid out regularly at known intervals; such dividends are known as regular cash dividends. By contrast, an **extra dividend** or **special dividend** is a dividend paid by a company that does not pay dividends on a regular schedule or a dividend that supplements regular cash dividends with an extra payment. Companies in cyclical industries and companies undergoing corporate and/or financial restructuring are among those observed to use extra dividends.[1]

The payment of dividends is not a legal obligation: dividends must be declared (i.e., authorized) by a company's board of directors; in some jurisdictions, they must also be approved by shareholders. Regular cash dividends are customarily declared and paid out quarterly in the United States and Canada; semiannually in Europe and Japan; and annually in some other countries, including China.

Dividend discount models address discounting expected cash dividends. A **stock dividend** (also known as a **bonus issue of shares**) is a type of dividend in which a company distributes additional shares of its common stock (typically, 2%–10% of the shares then outstanding) to shareholders instead of cash. A stock dividend divides the "pie" (the market value of shareholders' equity) into smaller pieces without affecting the value of the pie or any shareholder's proportional ownership in the company. Thus, stock dividends are not relevant for valuation. Stock splits and reverse stock splits are similar to stock dividends in that they have no economic effect on the company or shareholders. A **stock split** involves an increase in the number of shares outstanding with a consequent decrease in share price. An example of a stock split is a two-for-one stock split in which each shareholder is issued an additional share for each share currently owned. A **reverse stock split** involves a reduction in the number of shares outstanding with a corresponding increase in share price. In a one-for-two reverse stock split, each shareholder would receive one new share for every two old shares held, thereby reducing the number of shares outstanding by half.

In contrast to stock dividends and stock splits, share repurchases are an alternative to cash dividend payments. A **share repurchase** (or **buyback**) is a transaction in which a company uses cash to buy back its own shares. Shares that have been repurchased are not considered for dividends, voting, or computing earnings per share. A share repurchase is viewed as equivalent to the payment of cash dividends of equal value in terms of the effect on shareholders' wealth, all other things being equal. Company managements have expressed several key reasons for engaging in share repurchases—namely, (1) signaling a belief that their shares are undervalued (or, more generally, to support share prices), (2) flexibility in the amount and timing of distributing cash to shareholders, (3) tax efficiency in markets where tax rates on dividends exceed tax rates on capital gains, and (4) the ability to absorb increases in outstanding shares because of the exercise of employee stock options.

The payout of regular cash dividends to common shareholders follows a fairly standard chronology that is set in motion once the company's board of directors votes to pay the dividend. First is the **declaration date**, the day that the company issues a statement declaring a specific dividend. Next comes the **ex-dividend date** (or ex-date), the first date that a share trades without (i.e., "ex") the dividend. This is followed closely (one or two business days later) by the **holder-of-record date** (also called the owner-of-record date, shareholder-of-record date, record date, date of record, or date of book closure), the date that a shareholder listed on the company's books will be deemed to have ownership of the shares for purposes of receiving the upcoming dividend; the amount of time between the ex-date and the holder-of-record date is linked to the trade settlement cycle in force. The final milestone is the **payment date** (or **payable date**), which is the day that the company actually mails out (or electronically transfers) a dividend payment to shareholders.

---

1 Another type of dividend is a liquidating dividend, which is a return of capital rather than a distribution from earnings or retained earnings. Liquidating dividends are used when a company goes out of business and distributes its net assets, sells a portion of its business for cash and distributes the sale's proceeds, or pays a dividend that exceeds its accumulated retained earnings.

EXAMPLE 3

Total S.A. Dividend Payment Time Line

On 26 May 2017, Total S.A., one of the world's largest integrated energy companies, declared an annual dividend of €2.48 per share, payable on a quarterly basis. The first quarterly dividend of €2.48/4 = €0.62 was payable on 12 October 2017. The holder-of-record date was 26 September, and the ex-dividend date was 25 September. A timeline for the upcoming Total S.A. quarterly dividend is shown in Exhibit 1.

Exhibit 1 Timeline for Total S.A. Quarterly Dividend

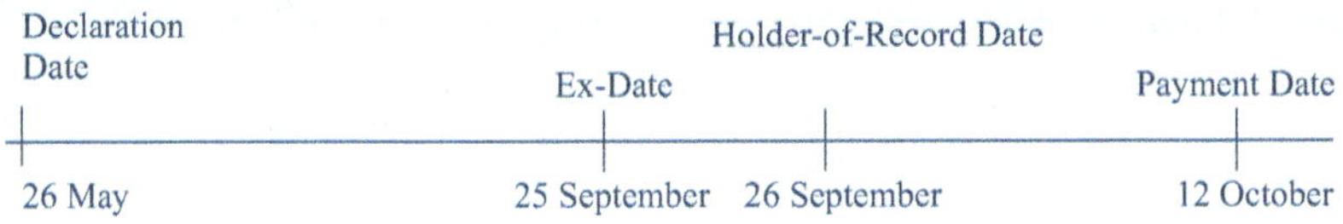

Source: Total S.A. website: www.total.com.

Because buyers of a company's shares on the ex-dividend date are no longer eligible to receive the upcoming dividend, all else being equal, on that day the company's share price immediately decreases by the amount of the foregone dividend. Exhibit 2 illustrates the decrease in share price that occurs for a hypothetical company that has declared a $1.00 per share dividend as trading begins on its ex-dividend date.

Exhibit 2 Stock Price Change for Hypothetical Company on Ex-Dividend Date

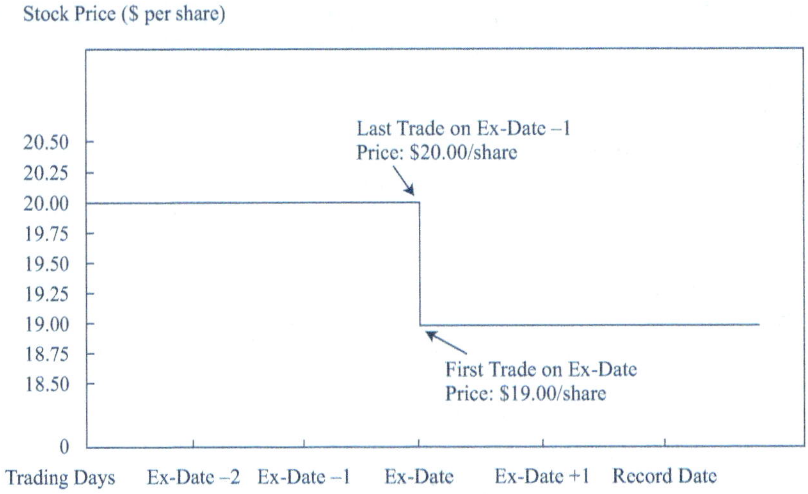

Note: Assumes dividend declared is $1 per share and convention for stock trade settlement is $T + 3$.

4.2 The Dividend Discount Model: Description

If the issuing company is assumed to be a going concern, the intrinsic value of a share is the present value of expected future dividends. If a constant required rate of return is also assumed, then the DDM expression for the intrinsic value of a share is Equation 1:

$$V_0 = \sum_{t=1}^{\infty} \frac{D_t}{(1+r)^t} \quad (1)$$

where

V_0 = value of a share of stock today, at $t = 0$

D_t = expected dividend in year t, assumed to be paid at the end of the year

r = required rate of return on the stock

At the shareholder level, cash received from a common stock investment includes any dividends received and the proceeds when shares are sold. If an investor intends to buy and hold a share for one year, the value of the share today is the present value of two cash flows—namely, the expected dividend *plus* the expected selling price in one year:

$$V_0 = \frac{D_1 + P_1}{(1+r)^1} = \frac{D_1}{(1+r)^1} + \frac{P_1}{(1+r)^1} \quad (2)$$

where P_1 = the expected price per share at $t = 1$.

To estimate the expected selling price, P_1, the analyst could estimate the price another investor with a one-year holding period would pay for the share in one year. If V_0 is based on D_1 and P_1, it follows that P_1 could be estimated from D_2 and P_2:

$$P_1 = \frac{D_2 + P_2}{(1+r)}$$

Substituting the right side of this equation for P_1 in Equation 2 results in V_0 estimated as

$$V_0 = \frac{D_1}{(1+r)} + \frac{D_2 + P_2}{(1+r)^2} = \frac{D_1}{(1+r)} + \frac{D_2}{(1+r)^2} + \frac{P_2}{(1+r)^2}$$

Repeating this process, we find the value for n holding periods is the present value of the expected dividends for the n periods plus the present value of the expected price in n periods:

$$V_0 = \frac{D_1}{(1+r)^1} + \cdots + \frac{D_n}{(1+r)^n} + \frac{P_n}{(1+r)^n}$$

Using summation notation to represent the present value of the n expected dividends, we arrive at the general expression for an n-period holding period or investment horizon:

$$V_0 = \sum_{t=1}^{n} \frac{D_t}{(1+r)^t} + \frac{P_n}{(1+r)^n} \quad (3)$$

The expected value of a share at the end of the investment horizon—in effect, the expected selling price—is often referred to as the **terminal stock value** (or **terminal value**).

EXAMPLE 4

Estimating Share Value for a Three-Year Investment Horizon

For the next three years, the annual dividends of a stock are expected to be €2.00, €2.10, and €2.20. The stock price is expected to be €20.00 at the end of three years. If the required rate of return on the shares is 10 percent, what is the estimated value of a share?

Solution:

The present values of the expected future cash flows can be written as follows:

$$V_0 = \frac{2.00}{(1.10)^1} + \frac{2.10}{(1.10)^2} + \frac{2.20}{(1.10)^3} + \frac{20.00}{(1.10)^3}$$

Calculating and summing these present values gives an estimated share value of V_0 = 1.818 + 1.736 + 1.653 + 15.026 = €20.23.

The three dividends have a total present value of €5.207, and the terminal stock value has a present value of €15.026, for a total estimated value of €20.23.

Extending the holding period into the indefinite future, we can say that a stock's estimated value is the present value of all expected future dividends as shown in Equation 1.

Consideration of an indefinite future is valid because businesses established as corporations are generally set up to operate indefinitely. This general form of the DDM applies even in the case in which the investor has a finite investment horizon. For that investor, stock value today depends *directly* on the dividends the investor expects to receive before the stock is sold and depends *indirectly* on the expected dividends for periods subsequent to that sale, because those expected future dividends determine the expected selling price. Thus, the general expression given by Equation 1 holds irrespective of the investor's holding period.

In practice, many analysts prefer to use a free-cash-flow-to-equity (FCFE) valuation model. These analysts assume that dividend-paying *capacity* should be reflected in the cash flow estimates rather than *expected dividends.* FCFE is a measure of dividend-paying capacity. Analysts may also use FCFE valuation models for a non-dividend-paying stock. To use a DDM, the analyst needs to predict the timing and amount of the first dividend and all the dividends or dividend growth thereafter. Making these predictions for non-dividend-paying stock accurately is typically difficult, so in such cases, analysts often resort to FCFE models.

The calculation of FCFE starts with the calculation of cash flow from operations (CFO). CFO is simply defined as net income plus non-cash expenses minus investment in working capital. FCFE is a measure of cash flow generated in a period that is available for distribution to common shareholders. What does "available for distribution" mean? The entire CFO is *not* available for distribution; the portion of the CFO needed for fixed capital investment (FCInv) during the period to maintain the value of the company as a going concern is *not* viewed as available for distribution to common shareholders. Net amounts borrowed (borrowings minus repayments) are considered to be available for distribution to common shareholders. Thus, FCFE can be expressed as

$$\text{FCFE} = \text{CFO} - \text{FCInv} + \text{Net borrowing} \quad (4)$$

The information needed to calculate historical FCFE is available from a company's statement of cash flows and financial disclosures. Frequently, under the assumption that management is acting in the interest of maintaining the value of the company as a going concern, reported capital expenditure is taken to represent FCInv. Analysts must make projections of financials to forecast future FCFE. Valuation obtained by using FCFE involves discounting expected future FCFE by the required rate of return on equity; the expression parallels Equation 1:

$$V_0 = \sum_{t=1}^{\infty} \frac{\text{FCFE}_t}{(1+r)^t}$$

EXAMPLE 5

Present Value Models

1 An investor expects a share to pay dividends of \$3.00 and \$3.15 at the end of Years 1 and 2, respectively. At the end of the second year, the investor expects the shares to trade at \$40.00. The required rate of return on the shares is 8 percent. If the investor's forecasts are accurate and the market price of the shares is currently \$30, the *most likely* conclusion is that the shares are:

- **A** overvalued.
- **B** undervalued.
- **C** fairly valued.

2 Two investors with different holding periods but the same expectations and required rate of return for a company are estimating the intrinsic value of a common share of the company. The investor with the shorter holding period will *most likely* estimate a:

- **A** lower intrinsic value.
- **B** higher intrinsic value.
- **C** similar intrinsic value.

3 An equity valuation model that focuses on expected dividends rather than the capacity to pay dividends is the:

- **A** dividend discount model.
- **B** free cash flow to equity model.
- **C** cash flow return on investment model.

Solution to 1:

B is correct.

$$V_0 = \frac{3.00}{(1.08)^1} + \frac{3.15}{(1.08)^2} + \frac{40.00}{(1.08)^2} = 39.77$$

The value estimate of \$39.77 exceeds the market price of \$30, so the conclusion is that the shares are undervalued.

Solution to 2:

C is correct. The intrinsic value of a security is independent of the investor's holding period.

Solution to 3:

A is correct. Dividend discount models focus on expected dividends.

How is the required rate of return for use in present value models estimated? To estimate the required rate of return on a share, analysts frequently use the capital asset pricing model (CAPM):

$$\begin{aligned} \text{Required rate of return on share } i &= \text{Current expected risk} \\ &\quad -\text{free rate of return} \\ &\quad + \text{Beta}_i\left[\text{Market (equity) risk premium}\right] \end{aligned} \tag{5}$$

Equation 5 states that the required rate of return on a share is the sum of the current expected risk-free rate plus a risk premium that equals the product of the stock's beta (a measure of non-diversifiable risk) and the market risk premium (the expected return of the market in excess of the risk-free return, where in practice, the "market" is often represented by a broad stock market index). However, even if analysts agree that the CAPM is an appropriate model, their inputs into the CAPM may differ. Thus, there is no uniquely correct answer to the question: What is the required rate of return?

Other common methods for estimating the required rate of return for the stock of a company include adding a risk premium that is based on economic judgments, rather than the CAPM, to an appropriate risk-free rate (usually a government bond) and adding a risk premium to the yield on the company's bonds. Good business and economic judgment is paramount in estimating the required rate of return. In many investment firms, required rates of return are determined by firm policy.

4.3 Preferred Stock Valuation

General dividend discount models are relatively easy to apply to preferred shares. In its simplest form, **preferred stock** is a form of equity (generally, non-voting) that has priority over common stock in the receipt of dividends and on the issuer's assets in the event of a company's liquidation. It may have a stated maturity date at which time payment of the stock's par (face) value is made or it may be perpetual with no maturity date; additionally, it may be callable or convertible.

For a non-callable, non-convertible perpetual preferred share paying a level dividend D and assuming a constant required rate of return over time, Equation 1 reduces to the formula for the present value of a perpetuity. Its value is:

$$V_0 = \frac{D_0}{r} \tag{6}$$

For example, a \$100 par value non-callable perpetual preferred stock offers an annual dividend of \$5.50. If its required rate of return is 6 percent, the value estimate would be \$5.50/0.06 = \$91.67.

For a non-callable, non-convertible preferred stock with maturity at time n, the estimated intrinsic value can be estimated by using Equation 3 but using the preferred stock's par value, F, instead of P_n:

$$V_0 = \sum_{t=1}^{n} \frac{D_t}{(1+r)^t} + \frac{F}{(1+r)^n} \tag{7}$$

When Equation 7 is used, the most precise approach is to use values for n, r, and D that reflect the payment schedule of the dividends. This method is similar to the practice of fixed-income analysts in valuing a bond. For example, a non-convertible preferred stock with a par value of £20.00, maturity in six years, a nominal required rate of return of 8.20 percent, and semiannual dividends of £2.00 would be valued by using an n of 12, an r of 4.10 percent, a D of £2.00, and an F of £20.00. The result would be an estimated value of £31.01. Assuming payments are annual rather than semiannual (i.e., assuming that n = 6, r = 8.20 percent, and D = £4.00) would result in an estimated value of £30.84.

Preferred stock issues are frequently callable (redeemable) by the issuer at some point prior to maturity, often at par value or at prices in excess of par value that decline to par value as the maturity date approaches. Such call options tend to reduce the value of a preferred issue to an investor because the option to redeem will be exercised by the issuer when it is in the issuer's favor and ignored when it is not. For example, if an issuer can redeem shares at par value that would otherwise trade (on the basis of dividends, maturity, and required rate of return) above par value, the issuer has motivation to redeem the shares.

Preferred stock issues can also include a retraction option that enables the holder of the preferred stock to sell the shares back to the issuer prior to maturity on prespecified terms. Essentially, the holder of the shares has a put option. Such put options tend to increase the value of a preferred issue to an investor because the option to retract will be exercised by the investor when it is in the investor's favor and ignored when it is not. Although the precise valuation of issues with such embedded options is beyond the scope of this reading, Example 6 includes a case in which Equation 7 can be used to approximate the value of a callable, retractable preferred share.

EXAMPLE 6

Preferred Share Valuation: Two Cases

Case 1: Non-callable, Non-convertible, Perpetual Preferred Shares

The following facts concerning the Union Electric Company 4.75 percent perpetual preferred shares are as follows:

- Issuer: Union Electric Co. (owned by Ameren)
- Par value: US$100
- Dividend: US$4.75 per year
- Maturity: perpetual
- Embedded options: none
- Credit rating: Moody's Investors Service/Standard & Poor's Ba1/BB
- Required rate of return on Ba1/BB rated preferred shares as of valuation date: 7.5 percent.

A Estimate the intrinsic value of this preferred share.

B Explain whether the intrinsic value of this issue would be higher or lower if the issue were callable (with all other facts remaining unchanged).

Solution to 1A:

Basing the discount rate on the required rate of return on Ba1/BB rated preferred shares of 7.5 percent gives an intrinsic value estimate of US$4.75/0.075 = US$63.33.

Solution to 1B:

The intrinsic value would be lower if the issue were callable. The option to redeem or call the issue is valuable to the issuer because the call will be exercised when doing so is in the issuer's interest. The intrinsic value of the shares to the investor will typically be lower if the issue is callable. In this case, because the intrinsic value without the call is much less than the par value, the issuer would be unlikely to redeem the issue if it were callable; thus, callability would reduce intrinsic value, but only slightly.

Case 2: Retractable Term Preferred Shares

Retractable term preferred shares are a type of preferred share that has been previously issued by Canadian companies, and have now began to be offered by companies in other jurisdictions, including Japan. This type of issue specifies a "retraction date" when the preferred shareholders have the option to sell back their shares to the issuer at par value (i.e., the shares are "retractable" or "putable" at that date).[2] At predetermined dates prior to the retraction date, the issuer has the option to redeem the preferred issue at predetermined prices (which are always at or above par value).

An example of a retractable term preferred share currently outstanding is TMC (Toyota Motor Corporation), First Series Model AA class shares, with a 0.5 percent dividend rate, increasing by 0.5 percent every year until 2020 and thereafter, becoming fixed at 2.5 percent. TMC is leading global automobile manufacturer, with headquarters in Japan and global operations. The issue is in Japanese Yen. The shares have a ¥10,598 par value and pay a semiannual dividend of ¥26.5 [= (0.5 percent × ¥10,598)/2] on 31 March 2016. The annual dividend is expected to increase to ¥132.5 [= (2.5 percent × ¥10,598)/2] on 31 March 2020 and beyond. As of 31 December 2017 the company carried ratings from Moody's and Standard & Poor's of Aa3 and AA–, respectively. Thus, the shares are viewed by Moody's and Standard & Poor's as having "adequate" credit quality, qualified by "Aa3 and AA–," which means relatively high quality within that group. Beginning from 2 April 2021, the shares are redeemable at the option of TMC at ¥10,598 (par value). The retraction date is the last day of March, June, September, and December of each year, starting from 1 September 2020, with the shares retractable at par value. The Series AA shares have voting rights and may exercise their voting rights and other rights held by holders of common shares of TMC in the same manner. The Series AA shares were issued at a 20% premium to the common shares price in 2015, and since then the share price has decreased to ¥7,243 as at 31 December 2017, and with a current required rate of 3.05 per year (1.525 percent semiannual). Because the issue's market price is so far below the prices at which TMC could redeem or call the issue, redemption is considered to be unlikely by TMC, whereas the retraction option for the Series AA holders appears to have a significant value since they will potentially be able to put back the shares to TMC at approximately 45 percent over the current market value (¥10,598 compared to ¥7,243).

A Assume that the issue will be retracted in December 2020; the holders of the shares will put the shares to the company in December 2020. Based on the information given, estimate the intrinsic value of a share.

Solution to 2A:

An intrinsic value estimate of a share of this preferred issue is ¥10,279.

Expected semiannual dividends:

Year ended March 31, 2018: ¥79.5 [= (1.5 percent × ¥10,598)/2]

Year ended March 31, 2019: ¥106 [= (2.0 percent × ¥10,598)/2]

Year ended March 31, 2020: ¥132.5 [= (2.5 percent × ¥10,598)/2]

2 "Retraction" refers to this option, which is a put option. The terminology is not completely settled: The type of share being called "retractable term preferred" is also known as "hard retractable preferred," with "hard" referring to payment in cash rather than common shares at the retraction date.

$$V_0 = \left[\frac{¥79.5}{1.01525} + \frac{¥79.5}{1.01525^2} + \frac{¥106}{1.01525^3} + \frac{¥106}{1.01525^4} + \frac{¥132.5}{1.01525^5} + \frac{¥132.5}{1.01525^6} + \frac{¥10{,}598}{1.01525^6}\right]$$
$$\approx ¥10{,}279$$

The difference between the current market price of ¥7,243 and the intrinsic value of ¥10,279 is the implied value of retractable option given to the holders of the Series AA shares.

4.4 The Gordon Growth Model

A rather obvious problem when one is trying to implement Equation 1 for common equity is that it requires the analyst to estimate an infinite series of expected dividends. To simplify this process, analysts frequently make assumptions about how dividends will grow or change over time. The Gordon (constant) growth model (Gordon, 1962) is a simple and well-recognized DDM. The model assumes dividends grow indefinitely at a constant rate.

Because of its assumption of a constant growth rate, the Gordon growth model is particularly appropriate for valuing the equity of dividend-paying companies that are relatively insensitive to the business cycle and in a mature growth phase. Examples might include an electric utility serving a slowly growing area or a producer of a staple food product (e.g., bread). A history of increasing the dividend at a stable growth rate is another practical criterion if the analyst believes that pattern will hold in the future.

With a constant growth assumption, Equation 1 can be written as Equation 8, where g is the constant growth rate:

$$V_0 = \sum_{t=1}^{\infty} \frac{D_0(1+g)^t}{(1+r)^t} = D_0\left[\frac{(1+g)}{(1+r)} + \frac{(1+g)^2}{(1+r)^2} + \ldots + \frac{(1+g)^\infty}{(1+r)^\infty}\right] \tag{8}$$

If required return r is assumed to be strictly greater than growth rate g, then the square-bracketed term in Equation 8 is an infinite geometric series and sums to $[(1 + g)/(r - g)]$. Substituting into Equation 8 produces the Gordon growth model as presented in Equation 9:

$$V_0 = \frac{D_0(1+g)}{r-g} = \frac{D_1}{r-g} \tag{9}$$

For an illustration of the expression, suppose the current (most recent) annual dividend on a share is €5.00 and dividends are expected to grow at 4 percent per year. The required rate of return on equity is 8 percent. The Gordon growth model estimate of intrinsic value is, therefore, €5.00(1.04)/(0.08 – 0.04) = €5.20/0.04 = €130 per share. Note that the numerator is D_1 not D_0. (Using the wrong numerator is a common error.)

The Gordon growth model estimates intrinsic value as the present value of a growing perpetuity. If the growth rate, g, is assumed to be zero, Equation 8 reduces to the expression for the present value of a perpetuity, given earlier as Equation 6.

In estimating a long-term growth rate, analysts use a variety of methods, including assessing the growth in dividends or earnings over time, using the industry median growth rate, and using the relationship shown in Equation 10 to estimate the sustainable growth rate:

$$g = b \times \text{ROE} \tag{10}$$

where

g = dividend growth rate

b = earnings retention rate = (1 – Dividend payout ratio)

ROE = return on equity

Example 7 illustrates the application of the Gordon growth model to the shares of a large industrial manufacturing company. The analyst believes it will continue to grow at a rate that it achieved in the previous three years and remain stable in the future. The example asks how much the dividend growth assumption adds to the intrinsic value estimate. The question is relevant to valuation because if the amount is high on a percentage basis, a large part of the value of the share depends on the realization of the growth estimate. One can answer the question by subtracting from the intrinsic value estimate determined by Equation 9 the value determined by Equation 6, which assumes no dividend growth.[3]

EXAMPLE 7

Applying the Gordon Growth Model

Siemens AG operates in the capital goods and technology space. It is involved in the engineering, manufacturing, automation, power, and transportation sectors. It operates globally and is one of the largest companies in the sectors in which it operates. It is a substantial employer in both its original, domestic German market, as well as dozens of countries around the world. Selected financial information for Siemens appears in Exhibit 3.

Exhibit 3 Selected Financial Information for Siemens AG

Year	2017	2016	2015	2014	2013
EPS	€7.45	€6.74	€8.85	€6.37	€5.08
DPS	€3.7	€3.6	€3.5	€3.3	€3.0
Payout ratio	50%	53%	40%	52%	59%
ROE	15.6%	15.9%	22.3%	18.2%	14.6%
Share price (XETRA - Frankfurt)	€119.2	€104.2	€79.94	€94.37	€89.06

Note: DPS stands for "dividends per share."
Source: Morningstar, www.siemens.com.

The analyst estimates the growth rate to be approximately 5.4 percent based on the dividend growth rate over the period 2013 to 2017 [$3(1 + g)^4 = 3.7$, so $g = 5.4\%$]. To verify that the estimated growth rate of 5.4 percent is feasible in the future, the analyst also uses the average of Siemens's retention rate and ROE for the previous five years ($g \approx 0.49 \times 17.3\% \approx 8.5\%$) to estimate the sustainable growth rate.

Using a number of approaches, including adding a risk premium to a long-term German government bond and using the CAPM, the analyst estimates a required return of 7.5 percent. The most recent dividend of €3.70 is used for D_0.

1 Use the Gordon growth model to estimate Siemens's intrinsic value.

2 How much does the dividend growth assumption add to the intrinsic value estimate?

3 A related concept, the present value of growth opportunities (PVGO), is discussed in more advanced readings.

3 Based on the estimated intrinsic value, is a share of Siemens undervalued, overvalued, or fairly valued?

4 What is the intrinsic value if the growth rate estimate is lowered to 4.4 percent?

5 What is the intrinsic value if the growth rate estimate is lowered to 4.4 percent and the required rate of return estimate is increased to 8.5 percent?

Solution to 1:

$$V_0 = \frac{€3.70(1 + 0.054)}{0.075 - 0.054} = €184.20$$

Solution to 2:

$$€184.20 - \frac{€3.70}{0.075} = €134.87$$

Solution to 3:

A share of Siemens appears to be undervalued. The analyst, before making a recommendation, might consider how realistic the estimated inputs are and check the sensitivity of the estimated value to changes in the inputs.

Solution to 4:

$$V_0 = \frac{€3.70(1 + 0.044)}{0.075 - 0.044} = €124.61$$

Solution to 5:

$$V_0 = \frac{€3.70(1 + 0.044)}{0.085 - 0.044} = €94.21$$

The Gordon growth model estimate of intrinsic value is extremely sensitive to the choice of required rate of return r and growth rate g. It is possible that the growth rate assumption and the required return assumption used initially were too high. Worldwide economic growth is typically in the low single digits, which may mean that a large company such as Siemens may struggle to grow dividends at 5.4 percent into perpetuity. Exhibit 4 presents a further sensitivity analysis of Siemens's intrinsic value to the required return and growth estimates.

Exhibit 4 Sensitivity Analysis of the Intrinsic-Value Estimate for Siemens AG

	g = 2.5%	g = 3.5%	g = 4.5%	g = 5.5%	g = 6.5%
r = 6%	€108.4	€153.2	€257.8	€780.7	—
r = 7%	€84.3	€109.4	€154.7	€260.2	€788.1
r = 8%	€69.0	€85.1	€110.5	€156.1	€262.7
r = 9%	€58.3	€69.6	€85.9	€111.5	€157.6
r = 10%	€50.6	€58.9	€70.3	€86.7	€112.6

Note that no value is shown when the growth rate exceeds the required rate of return. The Gordon growth model assumes that the growth rate cannot be greater than the required rate of return.

The assumptions of the Gordon model are as follows:

- Dividends are the correct metric to use for valuation purposes.
- The dividend growth rate is forever: It is perpetual and never changes.
- The required rate of return is also constant over time.
- The dividend growth rate is strictly less than the required rate of return.

An analyst might be dissatisfied with these assumptions for many reasons. The equities being examined might not currently pay a dividend. The Gordon assumptions might be too simplistic to reflect the characteristics of the companies being evaluated. Some alternatives to using the Gordon model are as follows:

- Use a more robust DDM that allows for varying patterns of growth.
- Use a cash flow measure other than dividends for valuation purposes.
- Use some other approach (such as a multiplier method) to valuation.

Applying a DDM is difficult if the company being analyzed is not currently paying a dividend. A company may not be paying a dividend if 1) the investment opportunities the company has are all so attractive that the retention and reinvestment of funds is preferable, from a return perspective, to the distribution of a dividend to shareholders or 2) the company is in such shaky financial condition that it cannot afford to pay a dividend. An analyst might still use a DDM to value such companies by assuming that dividends will begin at some future point in time. The analyst might further assume that constant growth occurs after that date and use the Gordon growth model for valuation. Extrapolating from no current dividend, however, generally yields highly uncertain forecasts. Analysts typically choose to use one or more of the alternatives instead of or as a supplement to the Gordon growth model.

EXAMPLE 8

Gordon Growth Model in the Case of No Current Dividend

A company does not currently pay a dividend but is expected to begin to do so in five years (at $t = 5$). The first dividend is expected to be \$4.00 and to be received five years from today. That dividend is expected to grow at 6 percent into perpetuity. The required return is 10 percent. What is the estimated current intrinsic value?

Solution:

The analyst can value the share in two pieces:

1 The analyst uses the Gordon growth model to estimate the value at $t = 5$; in the model, the year-ahead dividend is \$4(1.06). Then the analyst finds the present value of this value as of $t = 0$.

2 The analyst finds the present value of the \$4 dividend not "counted" in the estimate in Piece 1 (which values dividends from $t = 6$ onward). Note that the statement of the problem implies that D_0, D_1, D_2, D_3, and D_4 are zero.

Piece 1: The value of this piece is \$65.818:

$$V_n = \frac{D_n(1+g)}{r-g} = \frac{D_{n+1}}{r-g}$$

$$V_5 = \frac{\$4(1+0.06)}{0.10-0.06} = \frac{\$4.24}{0.04} = \$106$$

$$V_0 = \frac{\$106}{(1+0.10)^5} = \$65.818$$

Piece 2: The value of this piece is \$2.484:

$$V_0 = \frac{\$4}{(1+0.10)^5} = \$2.484$$

The sum of the two pieces is \$65.818 + \$2.484 = \$68.30.

Alternatively, the analyst could value the share at $t = 4$, the point at which dividends are expected to be paid in the following year and from which point they are expected to grow at a constant rate.

$$V_4 = \frac{\$4.00}{0.10-0.06} = \frac{\$4.00}{0.04} = \$100$$

$$V_0 = \frac{\$100}{(1+0.10)^4} = \$68.30$$

The next section addresses the application of the DDM with more flexible assumptions as to the dividend growth rate.

4.5 Multistage Dividend Discount Models

Multistage growth models are often used to model rapidly growing companies. The *two-stage DDM* assumes that at some point the company will begin to pay dividends that grow at a constant rate, but prior to that time the company will pay dividends that are growing at a higher rate than can be sustained in the long run. That is, the company is assumed to experience an initial, finite period of high growth, perhaps prior to the entry of competitors, followed by an infinite period of sustainable growth. The two-stage DDM thus makes use of two growth rates: a high growth rate for an initial, finite period followed by a lower, sustainable growth rate into perpetuity. The Gordon growth model is used to estimate a terminal value at time n that reflects the present value at time n of the dividends received during the sustainable growth period.

Equation 11 will be used here as the starting point for a two-stage valuation model. The two-stage valuation model is similar to Example 8 except that instead of assuming zero dividends for the initial period, the analyst assumes that dividends will exhibit a high rate of growth during the initial period. Equation 11 values the dividends over the short-term period of high growth and the terminal value at the end of the period of high growth. The short-term growth rate, g_S, lasts for n years. The intrinsic value per share in year n, V_n, represents the year n value of the dividends received during the sustainable growth period or the terminal value at time n. V_n can be estimated by using the Gordon growth model as shown in Equation 12, where g_L is the long-term or sustainable growth rate. The dividend in year n + 1, D_{n+1}, can be determined by using Equation 13:

$$V_0 = \sum_{t=1}^{n} \frac{D_0(1+g_S)^t}{(1+r)^t} + \frac{V_n}{(1+r)^n} \quad (11)$$

$$V_n = \frac{D_{n+1}}{r - g_L} \quad (12)$$

$$D_{n+1} = D_0(1 + g_S)^n(1 + g_L) \quad (13)$$

EXAMPLE 9

Applying the Two-Stage Dividend Discount Model

The current dividend, D_0, is \$5.00. Growth is expected to be 10 percent a year for three years and then 5 percent thereafter. The required rate of return is 15 percent. Estimate the intrinsic value.

Solution:

$$D_1 = \$5.00(1 + 0.10) = \$5.50$$

$$D_2 = \$5.00(1 + 0.10)^2 = \$6.05$$

$$D_3 = \$5.00(1 + 0.10)^3 = \$6.655$$

$$D_4 = \$5.00(1 + 0.10)^3(1 + 0.05) = \$6.98775$$

$$V_3 = \frac{\$6.98775}{0.15 - 0.05} = \$69.8775$$

$$V_0 = \frac{\$5.50}{(1 + 0.15)} + \frac{\$6.05}{(1 + 0.15)^2} + \frac{\$6.655}{(1 + 0.15)^3} + \frac{\$69.8775}{(1 + 0.15)^3} \approx \$59.68$$

The DDM can be extended to as many stages as deemed appropriate. For most publicly traded companies (that is, companies beyond the start-up stage), practitioners assume growth will ultimately fall into three stages: 1) growth, 2) transition, and 3) maturity. This assumption supports the use of a *three-stage DDM*, which makes use of three growth rates: a high growth rate for an initial finite period, followed by a lower growth rate for a finite second period, followed by a lower, sustainable growth rate into perpetuity.

One can make the case that a three-stage DDM would be most appropriate for a fairly young company, one that is just entering the growth phase. The two-stage DDM would be appropriate to estimate the value of an older company that has already moved through its growth phase and is currently in the transition phase (a period with a higher growth rate than the sustainable growth rate) prior to moving to the maturity phase (the period with a lower, sustainable growth rate).

However, the choice of a two-stage DDM need not rely solely on the age of a company. Long-established companies sometimes manage to restart above-average growth through, for example, innovation, expansion to new markets, or acquisitions. Or a company's long-run growth rate may be interrupted by a period of subnormal performance. If growth is expected to moderate (in the first case) or improve (in the second case) toward some long-term growth rate, a two-stage DDM may be appropriate. Thus, we chose a two-stage DDM to value International Business Machines Corporation in Example 10.

EXAMPLE 10

Two-Stage Dividend Discount Model: International Business Machines Corporation

International Business Machines Corporation (IBM) is a US based leading technology company. IBM was founded in 1911, initially as a company that manufactured machinery for sale and lease, ranging from commercial scales and industrial time recorders, meat and cheese slicers, to punched cards. IBM introduced the personal computer in 1981; however, by the 1990s, it began to suffer losses in its core computer manufacturing business and by the 2000s, it had begun to diversify into business consulting, which was finalized in 2005 when it sold its personal computer business to Chinese company Lenovo. IBM now operates through five segments: Cognitive Solutions, Global Business Services (GBS), Technology Services & Cloud Platforms, Systems, and Global Financing. The Cognitive Solutions segment delivers a spectrum of capabilities from descriptive, predictive, and prescriptive analytics to cognitive systems. Cognitive Solutions includes Watson, a cognitive computing platform that has the ability to interact in natural language, process big data, and learn from interactions with people and computers. The GBS segment provides clients with consulting, application management services, and global process services. The Technology Services & Cloud Platforms segment provides information technology infrastructure services. The Systems segment provides clients with infrastructure technologies. The Global Financing segment includes client financing, commercial financing, and remanufacturing and remarketing.

The 30 July 2018 *Value Line* report on IBM appears in Exhibit 5. IBM has increased its dividends every year over the past 15 years. Information from *Value Line* shows that the dividend growth is around 17.0 percent for the past 10 years, 13.5 percent for the past 5 years, and estimated to be 4.5 percent for 2015 to 2023. After a period of growth through acquisition and merger, the pattern suggests that IBM may be transitioning to a mature growth phase.

The two-stage DDM is arguably a good choice for valuing IBM because the company appears to be transitioning from a high-growth phase (note the 13.5 percent dividend growth for the past 5 years) to a lower-growth phase (note the forecast of 4.5 percent dividend growth to 2015–2023).

The CAPM can be used to estimate the required return, r, for IBM. The *Value Line* report (in the top left corner) estimates beta to be 0.95. Using the yield of about 2.0 percent on 10-year US Treasury notes as a proxy for the risk-free rate and assuming an equity risk premium of 5.0 percent, we find the estimate for r would be 6.75 percent [2.0% + 0.95(5.0%)].

To estimate the intrinsic value at the end of 2018, we use the 2018 dividend of US$6.21 from the *Value Line* report. The dividend is assumed to grow at a rate of 5.0 percent for one year and then 2.33 percent thereafter. The growth rate assumption for the first stage is consistent with the *Value Line* forecast for the 2018 and 2019 dividends. Our assumption of a 2.33 percent perpetual growth rate produces an 8-year growth rate assumption near 4.5%,[4] which is consistent with the *Value Line* forecast of 4.5 percent growth from 2015–2022. Thus:

$$D_{2019} = \text{US\$}6.21(1 + 0.05) = \text{US\$}6.5205$$

$$D_{2020} = \text{US\$}6.21(1 + 0.05)(1 + 0.0233) = \text{US\$}6.6724$$

$$D_{2021} = \text{US\$}6.21(1 + 0.05)(1 + 0.0233)^2 = \text{US\$}6.8279$$

4 The exact geometric average annual growth rate for 2015–2023 can be determined as $[(1 + 0.10)(1 + 0.0727)(1 + 0.0525)(1 + 0.499)(1 + 0.022)(1 + 0.022)(1 + 0.022)(1 + 0.022)]^{1/8} - 1 = 4.5\%$.

$$V_{2020} = \frac{\text{US\$6.8279}}{0.0675 - 0.0233} = \text{US\$154.4774}$$

$$V_{2018} = \frac{\text{US\$6.5205}}{(1 + 0.0675)} + \frac{\text{US\$6.6724}}{(1 + 0.0675)^2} + \frac{\text{US\$154.4774}}{(1 + 0.0675)^2} \approx \text{US\$147.523}$$

Given a recent price of US$148.56, as noted at the top left corner of the *Value Line* report, the intrinsic-value estimate of US$147.523 suggests that IBM is approximately fairly valued.

Exhibit 5 *Value Line* Report on IBM

INT'L BUS. MACH. NYSE-IBM | RECENT PRICE 148.56 | P/E RATIO 12.8 (Trailing: 12.2; Median: 12.0) | RELATIVE P/E RATIO 0.70 | DIV'D YLD 4.3% | VALUE LINE

TIMELINESS 3 Raised 12/7/18
SAFETY 1 Raised 4/15/05
TECHNICAL 5 Lowered 9/28/18
BETA .95 (1.00 = Market)

High:	121.5	130.9	132.9	147.5	194.9	211.8	215.9	199.2	176.3	170.0	182.8	171.1
Low:	88.8	69.5	81.8	116.0	146.6	177.3	172.6	150.5	131.6	116.9	139.1	137.5

Target Price Range 2021 2022 2023

LEGENDS
—— 11.5 x "Cash Flow" p sh
.... Relative Price Strength
Options: Yes
Shaded area indicates recession

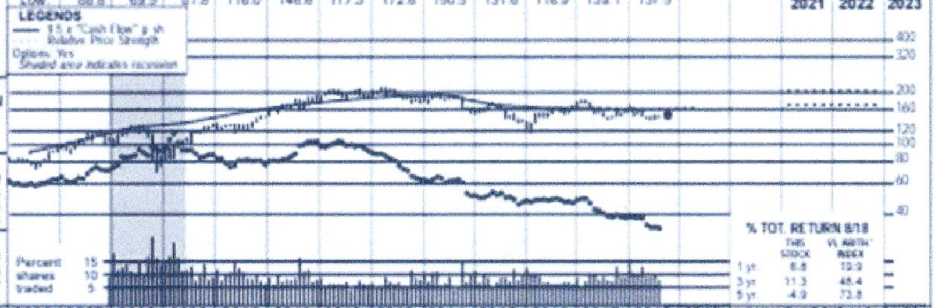

2021-23 PROJECTIONS

	Price	Gain	Ann'l Total Return
High	205	(+40%)	12%
Low	170	(+15%)	8%

Insider Decisions

	N	D	J	F	M	A	M	J	J
to Buy	0	0	0	0	0	0	0	0	0
Options	0	4	1	9	0	0	0	9	0
to Sell	0	0	0	2	0	0	0	0	0

Institutional Decisions

	4Q2017	1Q2018	2Q2018
to Buy	821	937	823
to Sell	718	828	912
Hld's(000)	516405	517270	510324

Percent shares traded 15 10 5

% TOT. RETURN 8/18

	THIS STOCK	VL ARITH.* INDEX
1 yr.	8.8	13.9
3 yr.	11.3	48.4
5 yr.	-4.9	73.8

2002	2003	2004	2005	2006	2007	2008	2009	2010	2011	2012	2013	2014	2015	2016	2017	2018	2019	© VALUE LINE PUB. LLC	21-23
47.14	52.60	58.52	57.90	60.89	71.31	77.39	73.36	81.33	91.92	93.53	94.61	93.68	84.64	84.49	85.82	90.00	92.95	Revenues per sh	100.00
6.53	7.27	8.24	8.71	9.56	11.28	13.28	14.11	16.01	17.77	19.04	20.07	20.44	17.83	17.19	17.13	16.85	17.25	"Cash Flow" per sh	19.20
3.95	4.34	5.05	5.22	6.01	7.18	8.93	10.01	11.52	13.06	14.37	14.94	16.59	13.60	12.39	12.04	11.60	11.85	Earnings per sh A	13.00
.59	.63	.70	.78	1.10	1.50	1.90	2.15	2.50	2.90	3.30	3.70	4.25	5.00	5.50	5.90	6.21	6.52	Div'ds Decl'd per sh B ■	7.15
2.76	2.59	2.65	2.44	2.90	3.34	3.11	2.64	3.41	3.53	3.65	3.93	4.22	3.71	3.77	3.50	4.00	4.00	Cap'l Spending per sh	5.00
13.23	16.44	18.06	21.03	18.92	20.55	10.06E	17.43	18.87	17.40	16.88	21.62	11.98	14.77	19.29	19.08	22.60	25.25	Book Value per sh D	38.20
1722.4	1694.5	1645.6	1574.0	1506.5	1385.2	1339.1	1305.3	1228.0	1163.2	1117.4	1054.4	990.52	965.73	945.87	922.18	900.0	880.0	Common Shs Outst'g C	850.0
21.4	19.8	18.0	16.1	13.9	14.8	12.3	10.9	11.4	13.1	13.7	13.0	11.7	11.4	12.1	13.1	Bold figures are Value Line estimates		Avg Ann'l P/E Ratio	14.5
1.17	1.12	.95	.86	.75	.79	.74	.73	.73	.82	.87	.73	.62	.57	.64	.65			Relative P/E Ratio	.80
.7%	.7%	.8%	.9%	1.3%	1.4%	1.7%	2.0%	1.9%	1.7%	1.7%	1.9%	2.3%	3.2%	3.7%	3.7%			Avg Ann'l Div'd Yield	3.8%

CAPITAL STRUCTURE as of 6/30/18

Total Debt $45497 mill. **Due in 5 Yrs** $29841 mill.
LT Debt $37851 mill. **LT Interest** $715 mill.
(LT interest earned: 16.9x; total interest coverage: 9.9x) (67% of Cap'l)

Pension Assets-12/17 $93.6 bill. **Oblig.** $106.5 bill.

Pfd Stock None
Common Stock 912,768,189 shs.

MARKET CAP $136 billion (Large Cap)

2008	2009	2010	2011	2012	2013	2014	2015	2016	2017	2018	2019		21-23
103630	95758	99870	106916	104507	99751	92793	81741	79919	79139	81000	81800	Revenues ($mill)	85000
20.6%	23.0%	23.0%	23.5%	25.1%	24.3%	24.0%	23.9%	19.8%	19.0%	20.5%	21.0%	Operating Margin	21.5%
5450.0	4994.0	4831.0	4815.0	4676.0	4678.0	4492.0	3855.0	4381.0	4541.0	4500	4550	Depreciation ($mill)	5200
12334	13425	14833	15855	16604	16483	15751	13364	11881	11258	10650	10650	Net Profit ($mill)	11100
26.2%	26.0%	24.8%	24.5%	24.2%	15.6%	21.2%	18.2%	3.6%	1.2%	7.0%	13.0%	Income Tax Rate	13.0%
11.9%	14.0%	14.9%	14.8%	15.9%	16.5%	17.0%	16.3%	14.9%	14.2%	13.1%	13.0%	Net Profit Margin	13.1%
6569.0	12933	7554.0	8805.0	5808.0	11196	9822.0	8235.0	7613.0	12372	11000	11500	Working Cap'l ($mill)	13000
22689	21932	21846	22857	24088	32856	35073	33428	34655	39837	37500	40000	Long-Term Debt ($mill)	55000
13465E	22755	23172	20236	18860	22792	11868	14262	18246	17594	20325	22225	Shr. Equity ($mill) D	32450
35.8%	31.2%	33.8%	37.6%	39.5%	30.4%	34.6%	28.4%	23.4%	18.1%	19.0%	17.5%	Return on Total Cap'l	13.5%
91.6%	59.0%	64.0%	78.4%	88.0%	72.3%	132.7%	93.7%	65.1%	64.0%	52.5%	48.0%	Return on Shr. Equity	34.0%
72.4%	46.4%	50.3%	61.2%	68.0%	54.5%	96.8%	58.4%	36.3%	32.6%	24.0%	21.5%	Retained to Com Eq	15.5%
21%	21%	21%	22%	23%	25%	27%	37%	44%	49%	54%	55%	All Div'ds to Net Prof	55%

CURRENT POSITION ($MILL.)	2016	2017	6/30/18
Cash Assets	8527	12580	11926
Receivables	29245	31630	28340
Inventory (Avg Cst)	1553	1583	1742
Other	4563	3942	4787
Current Assets	43888	49735	46795
Accts Payable	6209	6451	5518
Debt Due	7513	6987	7646
Other	22553	23925	22278
Current Liab.	36275	37363	35442

ANNUAL RATES of change (per sh)	Past 10 Yrs.	Past 5 Yrs.	Est'd '15-'17 to '21-'23
Revenues	3.0%	-1.0%	2.5%
"Cash Flow"	6.0%	-.5%	1.5%
Earnings	7.5%	-.5%	.5%
Dividends	17.0%	13.5%	4.5%
Book Value	-1.5%	--	13.5%

Cal-endar	QUARTERLY REVENUES ($ mill.) Mar.31	Jun.30	Sep.30	Dec.31	Full Year
2015	19590	20813	19280	22059	81741
2016	18684	20238	19226	21771	79919
2017	18155	19289	19153	22542	79139
2018	19072	20003	19315	22610	81000
2019	19200	19900	19600	23100	81800

Cal-endar	EARNINGS PER SHARE A Mar.31	Jun.30	Sep.30	Dec.31	Full Year
2015	2.44	3.58	3.02	4.59	13.60
2016	2.09	2.61	2.98	4.73	12.39
2017	1.85	2.48	2.92	4.79	12.04
2018	1.81	2.61	2.70	4.48	11.60
2019	1.85	2.65	2.75	4.60	11.85

Cal-endar	QUARTERLY DIVIDENDS PAID B ■ Mar.31	Jun.30	Sep.30	Dec.31	Full Year
2014	.95	1.10	1.10	1.10	4.25
2015	1.10	1.30	1.30	1.30	5.00
2016	1.30	1.40	1.40	1.40	5.50
2017	1.40	1.50	1.50	1.50	5.90
2018	1.50	1.57	1.57		

BUSINESS: International Business Machines Corporation is a worldwide supplier of technology and business services, software, and systems hardware. 2017 revenue breakdown: Technology Services & Cloud Platforms, 43%; Global Business Services, 21%; Systems, 10%; Cognitive Solutions, 23%; Financing & Other, 3%. Geographic mix: Americas region, 48% of revenue; EMEA, 31%; Asia, 21%. R&D, 7.3% of '17 revenue. '17 depreciation rate: 14.0%. About 380,000 employees. Officers & directors control less than 1% of stock; The Vanguard Group, 6.88%; BlackRock, 6.2%; State Street, 5.6% (3/18 proxy). Chairman, Pres. & CEO: Virginia M. Rometty. Inc.: NY. Address: New Orchard Road, Armonk, NY 10504. Tel.: 914-499-1900. Internet: www.ibm.com.

The renewed growth in International Business Machines' revenues in the past three quarters was a positive development, but the top-line momentum looks likely to slow. Revenues in the last nine months benefited from a favorable currency situation as well as the introduction of the z14 mainframe computer in September, 2017 and rollout of the POWER9 system in 2018. But management expected currency to shift from a tailwind to a headwind in the back half of this year. Moreover, revenues generated by new systems usually moderate after a period of initial good reception (although IBM indicated that z14 adoption is tracking ahead of prior systems). The top-line comparison in the final period of 2018 may be especially tough.

On an encouraging note, however, strategic market revenues (from cloud computing, analytics, and information security) have risen at a mid-teens pace in the past year. The as-a-service business is growing nicely. And services signings, a forerunner of the services revenues, rose 6% in the June term, auguring well for revenues farther down the road.

The company expects expense reductions from initiatives undertaken earlier in 2018 to ramp up in the second half. These measures included implementing new ways of working and shifting the expense mix to more variable (rather than fixed) costs. Although spending on growth initiatives is likely to remain high, services margins should expand.

Management still looks to report earnings per share of at least $11.60 in 2018. This includes an estimated $2.20 a share of acquisition/retirement costs. Full-year results in 2018 are likely to be held back by a higher tax rate, even excluding the $5.5 billion charge recorded in late 2017 associated with tax reform in the U.S. At present, we tentatively expect IBM to make slight share-net progress in 2019, supported by modest revenue growth, the expense-reduction initiatives, and stock repurchases.

IBM's dividend yield is more than double the *Value Line* median. But the stock is ranked only 3 (Average) for Timeliness. Too, long-term investors may need to be very patient.

Theresa Brophy *September 28, 2018*

(A) Based on diluted shs. Excl. gains (losses) from discontinued operations: '03, ($0.02); '04, $0.01); '05, ($0.02); '06, $0.06; '14, ($3.66). In '17, excludes $5.90 charge related to tax reform. Quarters may not sum due to change in shs. Next earnings report mid-October. (B) Dividends historically paid in early March, June, September, and December. ■ Dividend reinvestment plan available. (C) In millions. (D) Incl. intangibles. As of 6/30/18, $39.8 billion, $43.63/sh. (E) In '08, incl. $15.2 bil. retirement benefit plan loss.

Company's Financial Strength	A++
Stock's Price Stability	90
Price Growth Persistence	15
Earnings Predictability	90

5 MULTIPLIER MODELS

The term **price multiple** refers to a ratio that compares the share price with some sort of monetary flow or value to allow evaluation of the relative worth of a company's stock. Some practitioners use price ratios as a screening mechanism. If the ratio falls below a specified value, the shares are identified as candidates for purchase, and if the ratio exceeds a specified value, the shares are identified as candidates for sale. Many practitioners use ratios when examining a group or sector of stocks and consider the shares for which the ratio is relatively low to be attractively valued securities.

Price multiples that are used by security analysts include the following:

- Price-to-earnings ratio (P/E). This measure is the ratio of the stock price to earnings per share. P/E is arguably the price multiple most frequently cited by the media and used by analysts and investors (Block 1999). The seminal works of McWilliams (1966), Miller and Widmann (1966), Nicholson (1968), Dreman (1977), and Basu (1977) presented evidence of a return advantage to low-P/E stocks.
- Price-to-book ratio (P/B). The ratio of the stock price to book value per share. Considerable evidence suggests that P/B multiples are inversely related to future rates of return (Fama and French 1995).
- Price-to-sales ratio (P/S). This measure is the ratio of stock price to sales per share. O'Shaughnessy (2005) provided evidence that a low P/S multiple is the most useful multiple for predicting future returns.
- Price-to-cash-flow ratio (P/CF). This measure is the ratio of stock price to some per-share measure of cash flow. The measures of cash flow include free cash flow (FCF) and operating cash flow (OCF).

A common criticism of all of these multiples is that they do not consider the future. This criticism is true if the multiple is calculated from trailing or current values of the divisor. Practitioners seek to counter this criticism by a variety of techniques, including forecasting fundamental values (the divisors) one or more years into the future. The resulting forward (leading or prospective) price multiples may differ markedly from the trailing price multiples. In the absence of an explicit forecast of fundamental values, the analyst is making an implicit forecast of the future when implementing such models. The choice of price multiple—trailing or forward—should be used consistently for companies being compared.

Besides the traditional price multiples used in valuation, just presented, analysts need to know how to calculate and interpret other ratios. Such ratios include those used to analyze business performance and financial condition based on data reported in financial statements. In addition, many industries have specialized measures of business performance that analysts covering those industries should be familiar with. In analyzing cable television companies, for example, the ratio of total market value of the company to the total number of subscribers is commonly used. Another common measure is revenue per subscriber. In the oil industry, a commonly cited ratio is proved reserves per common share. Industry-specific or sector-specific ratios such as these can be used to understand the key business variables in an industry or sector as well as to highlight attractively valued securities.

5.1 Relationships among Price Multiples, Present Value Models, and Fundamentals

Price multiples are frequently used independently of present value models. One price multiple valuation approach, the method of comparables, does not involve cash flow forecasts or discounting to present value. A price multiple is often related to fundamentals through a discounted cash flow model, however, such as the Gordon growth model. Understanding such connections can deepen the analyst's appreciation of the factors that affect the value of a multiple and often can help explain reasons for differences in multiples that do not involve mispricing. The expressions that are developed can be interpreted as the *justified value* of a multiple—that is, the value justified by (based on) fundamentals or a set of cash flow predictions. These expressions are an alternative way of presenting intrinsic-value estimates.

As an example, using the Gordon growth model identified previously in Equation 9 and assuming that price equals intrinsic value ($P_0 = V_0$), we can restate Equation 9 as follows:

$$P_0 = \frac{D_1}{r - g} \tag{9.1}$$

To arrive at the model for the justified forward P/E given in Equation 14, we divide both sides of Equation 9.1 by a forecast for next year's earnings, E_1. In Equation 14, the dividend payout ratio, p, is the ratio of dividends to earnings:

$$\frac{P_0}{E_1} = \frac{D_1/E_1}{r - g} = \frac{p}{r - g} \tag{14}$$

Equation 14 indicates that the P/E is inversely related to the required rate of return and positively related to the growth rate; that is, as the required rate of return increases, the P/E declines, and as the growth rate increases, the P/E increases. The P/E and the payout ratio appear to be positively related. This relationship may not be true, however, because a higher payout ratio may imply a slower growth rate as a result of the company retaining a lower proportion of earnings for reinvestment. This phenomenon is referred to as the dividend displacement of earnings.

EXAMPLE 11

Value Estimate Based on Fundamentals

Petroleo Brasileiro SA, commonly known as Petrobras, was once labeled "the most expensive oil company" by Bloomberg.com. Data for Petrobras and the oil industry, including the trailing twelve-month (TTM) P/E and payout ratios, appear below.

	Petrobras	Industry
P/E ratio (TTM)	39.61	13.0
Return on assets (TTM) (%)	3. 0	3.2
EPS 3-year growth rate (%)	NM	66.00
EPS (MRQ) vs. Qtr. 1 yr. ago (% change)	138.96	−12.0

Note: NM stands for non-quantifiable. Petrobras EPS has decreased from a loss of BRL 1.14 per share to a profit of BRL 0.16 per share in the most recent period. MRQ stands for "most recent quarter."
Source: Reuters.

Explain how the information shown supports a higher P/E for Petrobras than for the industry.

Solution:

The data support a higher P/E for Petrobras because its return on assets and (MRQ) EPS growth rate exceed those of the industry. Equation 14 implies a positive relationship between the payout ratio and the P/E multiple. Petrobras has had a negative EPS for the period 2014 to 2017, and has paid no dividend during that period. A higher payout ratio supports a higher P/E. Furthermore, to the extent that higher EPS growth implies a high growth rate in dividends, the high EPS growth rate supports a high P/E. The higher P/E ratio is due to an improvement in the underlying financial performance of the company and the expected higher growth potential of the stock compared to the median firms in the industry.

EXAMPLE 12

Determining Justified Forward P/E

Heinrich Gladisch, CFA, is estimating the justified forward P/E for Nestlé, one of the world's leading nutrition and health companies. Gladisch notes that sales for 2017 were SFr89.78 billion (US$90.3 billion) and that net income was SFr7.18 billion (US$7.25 billion). He organizes the data for EPS, dividends per share, and the dividend payout ratio for the years 2013–2017 in the following table:

	2013	2014	2015	2016	2017
Earnings per share	SFr3.24	SFr4.54	SFr2.90	SFr2.76	SFr2.32
Year over year % change		44.6%	−36.1%	−4.8%	−15.9%
Dividend per share	SFr2.15	SFr2.2	SFr2.25	SFr2.3	SFr2.35
Year over year % change		2.3%	2.3%	2.2%	2.2%
Dividend payout ratio	68.5%	48.5%	77.6%	83.3%	99.2%

Gladisch calculates that ROE averaged 15.5 percent in the period 2013–2017 but was below that level at 11.7 percent in 2017. In that year, however, Nestlé's reported net income included a large nonrecurring component. The company reported 2017 "underlying earnings," which it defined as net income "from continuing operations before impairments, restructuring costs, results on disposals and significant one-off items," to be SFr2.93, giving an adjusted 14.8% ROE. Predicting increasing improvement in Nestlé's profit margins from growth in its product markets, Gladisch estimates a long-run ROE of 21.5 percent.

Gladisch decides that the dividend payout ratios of the 2013–2016 period—averaging 67.7 percent—are more representative of Nestlé's future payout ratio than is the high 2017 dividend payout ratio (when based on reported earnings). The dividend payout ratio in 2017 was higher because management apparently based the 2017 dividend on the components of net income that were expected to continue into the future. But basing a dividend on net income including non-recurring items creates the potential need to increase dividends in the future. Rounding up the 2013–2017 average, Gladisch settles on an estimate of 68 percent for the dividend payout ratio for use in calculating a justified forward P/E using Equation 14.

Gladisch's firm estimates that the required rate of return for Nestlé's shares is 9 percent per year. Gladisch also finds the following data at the opposite ends of the spectrum of external research analyst forecasts:

	2018E	2019E
Most optimistic analyst forecast:		
EPS	SFr3.99	SFr4.33
Year over year % change	71.9%	8.5%
P/E (based on a target price of SFr105)	26.3	24.2
Least optimistic analyst forecast:		
EPS	SFr3.52	SFr3.59
Year over year % change	51.7%	2.0%
P/E (based on a target price of SFr68)	19.3	18.9

1 Based only on information and estimates developed by Gladisch and his firm, estimate Nestlé's justified forward P/E.

2 Compare and contrast the justified forward P/E estimate from Question 1 to the estimates from each end of the spectrum of external research analysts forecasts.

Solution to 1:

The estimate of the justified forward P/E is 32.38. The dividend growth rate can be estimated by using Equation 10 as (1 – Dividend payout ratio) × ROE = (1 – 0.68) × 0.21.5 = 0.069, or 6.9 percent. Therefore,

$$\frac{P_0}{E_1} = \frac{\text{Payout}}{r - g} = \frac{0.68}{0.09 - 0.069} = 32.38$$

Solution to 2:

The estimated justified forward P/E of 32.38 is higher than the justified 2018 P/E estimates of 26.3 and 19.3 of the two analysts. Using a required rate of return of 9.5 percent rather than 9 percent results in a justified forward P/E estimate of 26.2 = 0.68/(0.095 – 0.069). Using an ROE of 16.5 percent (the average ROE of the 2013–2016 period) rather than 21.5 percent results in a justified forward P/E estimate of 18.4 = 0.68/[0.09 – (0.32)(0.165)] = 0.68/(0.09 – 0.053). The justified forward P/E is very sensitive to changes in the inputs.

Justified forward P/E estimates can be sensitive to small changes in assumptions. Therefore, analysts can benefit from carrying out a sensitivity analysis, as shown in Exhibit 6, which is based on Example 12. Exhibit 6 shows how the justified forward P/E varies with changes in the estimates for the dividend payout ratio (columns) and return on equity. The dividend growth rate (rows) changes because of changes in the retention rate (1 – Payout rate) and ROE. Recall g = ROE times retention rate.

Exhibit 6 Estimates for Nestlé's Justified Forward P/E (Required Rate of Return = 9 Percent)

Constant Dividend Growth Rate (%)	Dividend Payout Ratio				
	55%	60%	65%	70%	75%
4.0	11.0	12.0	13.0	14.0	15.0
4.5	12.2	13.3	14.4	15.6	16.7
5.0	13.8	15.0	16.3	17.5	18.8
5.5	15.7	17.1	18.6	20.0	21.4
6.0	18.3	20.0	21.7	23.3	25.0
6.5	22.0	24.0	26.0	28.0	30.0
7.0	27.5	30.0	32.5	35.0	37.5
7.5	36.7	40.0	43.3	46.7	50.0

5.2 The Method of Comparables

The method of comparables is the most widely used approach for analysts reporting valuation judgments on the basis of price multiples. This method essentially compares relative values estimated using multiples or the relative values of multiples. The economic rationale underlying the method of comparables is the **law of one price**: Identical assets should sell for the same price. The methodology involves using a price multiple to evaluate whether an asset is fairly valued, undervalued, or overvalued in relation to a benchmark value of the multiple. Choices for the benchmark multiple include the multiple of a closely matched individual stock or the average or median value of the multiple for the stock's industry. Some analysts perform trend or time-series analyses and use past or average values of a price multiple as a benchmark.

Identifying individual companies or even an industry as the "comparable" may present a challenge. Many large corporations operate in several lines of business, so the scale and scope of their operations can vary significantly. When identifying comparables (sometimes referred to as "comps"), the analyst should be careful to identify companies that are most similar according to a number of dimensions. These dimensions include (but are not limited to) overall size, product lines, and growth rate. The type of analysis shown in Section 5.1 relating multiples to fundamentals is a productive way to identify the fundamental variables that should be taken into account in identifying comparables.

EXAMPLE 13

Method of Comparables (1)

As noted previously, P/E is a price multiple frequently used by analysts. Using P/E in the method of comparables can be problematic, however, as a result of business cycle effects on EPS. An alternative valuation tool that is useful during periods of economic slowdown or extraordinary growth is the P/S multiple. Although sales will decline during a recession and increase during a period of economic growth, the change in sales will be less than the change in earnings in percentage terms because earnings are heavily influenced by fixed operating and financing costs (operating and financial leverage).

The following data provide the P/S for most of the major automobile manufacturers as at December 2017:

Company	P/S
Peugeot	0.28
Ford Motor	0.33
General Motors	0.36
Nissan Motor	0.38
Honda Motor	0.46
Tata Motors	0.49
Daimler	0.55
BMW	0.57
Toyota Motor	0.80

Sources: Morningstar and company websites.

Based on the data presented, which stock appears to be undervalued when compared with the others?

Solution:

The P/S analysis suggests that Peugeot shares offer the best value. An analyst must be alert for a range of potential explanations of apparently low or high multiples when performing comparables analysis, rather than just assuming a relative mispricing.

EXAMPLE 14

Method of Comparables (2)

Incorporated in the Netherlands, Airbus is active in the aerospace and defense industry. It is a dominant aerospace company in Europe. Its largest business, Airbus Commercial Aircraft, is a manufacturing company with bases in several European countries and accounts for the majority of Airbus SE profits. Airbus and its primary competitor, Boeing, control most of the global commercial airplane industry.

Comparisons are frequently made between Airbus and Boeing. As noted in Exhibit 7, the companies are broadly similar in size as measured by total revenues. Converting total forecast revenues from euros to US dollars using the average exchange rate for 2017 of US$1.13/€ results in a value of $75.5 billion for Airbus's total revenues. Thus, total revenues for Boeing are expected to be about a fifth higher than those for Boeing.

The companies do differ, however, in several important areas. Airbus derives a greater share of its revenue from commercial aircraft production than does Boeing, and the order backlog for Airbus is much higher than that for Boeing. Converting the Airbus order backlog from euros to US dollars using the quarter-end rate for September 2017 of $1.1813/€ results in a value of $1.12 billion for Airbus's order backlog. Thus, the order backlog for Airbus is more than twice as high as the backlog for Boeing.[5]

5 Exchange rate data are available from FRED (Federal Reserve Economic Data) at http://research.stlouisfed.org/fred2/. Each company uses slightly different methodology for calculating order backlog.

Exhibit 7 Data for EADS and Boeing

	Airbus	Boeing
Total revenues (billions, 2017)	€66.8	$92.2
Annual revenue growth (2015–2017 average)	1.8%	−2.1%
Percent of revenues from commercial aircraft	75%	69%
Order backlog (billions)	€945	$474
Share price, 12/Dec/17	€86.96	$283.73
EPS (basic)	€3.33	$10.18
DPS	€1.48	$5.7
Dividend payout ratio	44%	56%
P/E ratio	26.1	27.9

Note: 2017 forecast data and YTD average exchange rate as of 12 December 2017. Order backlog as of 30 September 2017.
Sources: Company websites: www.airbus.com and www.boeing.com, *Financial Times*.

What data shown in Exhibit 7 support a higher P/E for Boeing than for Airbus?

Solution:

Recall from Equation 14 and the discussion that followed it that P/E is directly related to the payout ratio and the dividend growth rate. The P/E is inversely related to the required rate of return. The only data presented in Exhibit 7 that support a higher P/E for Boeing is the company's higher dividend payout ratio (expected at 56 percent versus 44 percent for Airbus).

The following implicitly supports a higher P/E for Airbus: Airbus has higher revenue growth (as reported for 2016 and expected for 2017) and a higher backlog of orders, suggesting that it may have a higher future growth rate.

EXAMPLE 15

Method of Comparables (3)

Canon Inc. is a leading worldwide manufacturer of business machines, cameras, and optical products. Canon was founded in 1937 as a camera manufacturer and is incorporated in Tokyo. The corporate philosophy of Canon is *kyosei* or "living and working together for the common good." The following data can be used to determine a P/E for Canon over the time period 2013–2017. Analyze the P/E of Canon over time and discuss the valuation of Canon.

Year	Price (a)	EPS (b)	P/E (a) ÷ (b)
2013	¥3,330	¥200.8	16.6
2014	¥3,840.5	¥229.0	16.8
2015	¥3,675	¥201.7	18.2

Year	Price (a)	EPS (b)	P/E (a) ÷ (b)
2016	¥3,295	¥138	23.9
2017	¥4,200	¥222.88	18.8

Sources: EPS, year-end prices, and P/E data are from Capital IQ and the *Financial Times*.

Solution:

Trend analysis of Canon's P/E reveals a peak of 23.9 at the end of 2016. The 2013 P/E of 16.6 is the lowest of the five years reported. This finding suggests that Canon's share price may be fairly price as of year-end 2017. A bearish case for Canon's stock can be made if an analyst believes that P/E will return to its historical low (16.6 over this five-year period) or be lower. Such a bearish prediction requires that a decrease in P/E not be offset by an increase in EPS. A bullish case can be made if the analyst believes the stock deserves re-rating and an even higher than trend P/E.

5.3 Illustration of a Valuation Based on Price Multiples

Telefónica S.A., a world leader in the telecommunication sector, provides communication, information, and entertainment products and services in Europe, Africa, and Latin America. It has operated in its home country of Spain since 1924, but as of 2017, more than 75 percent of its business was outside its home market.

Deutsche Telekom AG provides network access, communication services, and value-added services via fixed and mobile networks. It generates more than half of its revenues outside its home country, Germany.

Exhibit 8 provides comparable data for these two communication giants for 2015–2017.

Exhibit 8 Data for Telefónica and Deutsche Telekom

	Telefónica			Deutsche Telekom		
	2017	2016	2015	2017	2016	2015
(1) Total assets (€ billions)	115.0	123.6	120.3	141.3	148.5	143.9
Asset growth	−6.9%	2.7%	—	-4.9%	3.2%	—
(2) Net revenues (€ billions)	52.0	52.0	54.9	77.3	75.2	71.3
Revenue growth	0%	-5.2%	—	2.8%	5.5%	—
(3) Net cash flow from operating activities (€ billions)	13.8	13.3	13.6	17.2	15.5	15.0
Cash flow growth	3.4%	-2.0%	—	11.0%	3.3%	—
(4) Book value of common shareholders' equity (€ billions)	16.9	18.2	15.8	42.5	38.8	38.2
Debt ratio: 1 − [(4) ÷ (1)]	85.3%	85.3%	86.9%	70.0%	73.9%	73.5%
(5) Net profit (€ billions)	2.9	2.1	0.4	3.5	2.7	3.3
Earnings growth	38.1%	425.0%	—	29.6%	−18.2%	—
(6) Weighted average number of shares outstanding (millions)	5,122.9	4,896.6	4,833.6	4,740.2	4,654.9	4,584.8

(continued)

Exhibit 8 (Continued)

	Telefónica			Deutsche Telekom		
	2017	2016	2015	2017	2016	2015
(7) Price per share (€)	7.93	9.52	9.13	13.42	16.21	15.44
Price-to-revenue ratio (P/R):						
(7) ÷ [(2) ÷ (6)]	0.8	0.9	0.8	0.8	1.0	1.0
P/CF:						
(7) ÷ [(3) ÷ (6)]	2.9	3.5	3.2	3.7	4.9	4.7
P/B:						
(7) ÷ [(4) ÷ (6)]	2.4	2.6	2.8	1.5	1.9	1.9
P/E:						
(7) ÷ [(5) ÷ (6)]	14.0	22.2	110.3	18.2	27.9	21.5

Sources: Company websites: www.telefonica.es and www.deutschetelekom.com.

Time-series analysis of all price multiples in Exhibit 8 suggests that both companies are currently attractively valued. For example, the 2017 price-to-revenue ratio (P/R) of 0.78 for Telefónica is below the 2015–2017 average for this ratio of approximately 0.83. The 2017 P/CF of 3.7 for Deutsche Telekom is below the 2015–2017 average for this ratio of approximately 4.4.

A comparative analysis produces somewhat mixed results. The 2017 values for Deutsche Telekom for the P/R, P/CF, P/E multiples are higher than those for Telefónica. This result suggests that Telefónica is attractively valued when compared with Deutsche Telekom. The 2017 P/B for Telefónica, however, is higher than for Deutsche Telekom.

An analyst investigating these contradictory results would look for information not reported in Exhibit 8. For example, the earnings before interest, taxes, depreciation, and amortization (EBITDA) for Telefónica was €16.4 billion in 2017. The EBITDA value for Deutsche Telekom was €20.7 billion in 2017. The 2017 price-to-EBITDA ratio for Telefónica is [(7.93 × 5,123)/16,400] or [7.92/(16,400/5,123] = 2.5, whereas the 2017 price-to-EBITDA ratio for Deutsche Telekom is 3.1. Thus, the higher P/E for Deutsche Telekom can-not be explained by higher depreciation charges, higher interest costs, and/or a greater tax burden, but appears to be due to a better quality of earnings

In summary, the major advantage of using price multiples is that they allow for relative comparisons, both cross-sectional (versus the market or another comparable) and in time series. The approach can be especially beneficial for analysts who are assigned to a particular industry or sector and need to identify the expected best performing stocks within that sector. Price multiples are popular with investors because the multiples can be calculated easily and many multiples are readily available from financial websites and newspapers.

Caution is necessary. A stock may be relatively undervalued when compared with its benchmarks but overvalued when compared with an estimate of intrinsic value as determined by one of the discounted cash flow methodologies. Furthermore, differences in reporting rules among different markets and in chosen accounting methods can result in revenues, earnings, book values, and cash flows that are not easily comparable. These differences can, in turn, result in multiples that are not easily comparable. Finally, the multiples for cyclical companies may be highly influenced by current economic conditions.

5.4 Enterprise Value

An alternative to estimating the value of equity is to estimate the value of the enterprise. Enterprise value is most frequently determined as market capitalization plus market value of preferred stock plus market value of debt minus cash and investments (cash equivalents and short-term investments). Enterprise value is often viewed as the cost of a takeover: In the event of a buyout, the acquiring company assumes the acquired company's debt but also receives its cash. Enterprise value is most useful when comparing companies with significant differences in capital structure.

Enterprise value (EV) multiples are widely used in Europe, with EV/EBITDA arguably the most common. EBITDA is a proxy for operating cash flow because it excludes depreciation and amortization. EBITDA may include other non-cash expenses, however, and non-cash revenues. EBITDA can be viewed as a source of funds to pay interest, dividends, and taxes. Because EBITDA is calculated prior to payment to any of the company's financial stakeholders, using it to estimate enterprise value is logically appropriate.

Using enterprise value instead of market capitalization to determine a multiple can be useful to analysts. Even where the P/E is problematic because of negative earnings, the EV/EBITDA multiple can generally be computed because EBITDA is usually positive. An alternative to using EBITDA in EV multiples is to use operating income.

In practice, analysts may have difficulty accurately assessing enterprise value if they do not have access to market quotations for the company's debt. When current market quotations are not available, bond values may be estimated from current quotations for bonds with similar maturity, sector, and credit characteristics. Substituting the book value of debt for the market value of debt provides only a rough estimate of the debt's market value. This is because market interest rates change and investors' perception of the issuer's credit risk may have changed since the debt was issued.

EXAMPLE 16

Estimating the Market Value of Debt and Enterprise Value

Cameco Corporation is one of the world's largest uranium producers; it accounts for 16 percent of world production from its mines in Canada and the United States. Cameco estimates it has about 458 million kilograms of proven and probable reserves and holds premier land positions in the world's most promising areas for new uranium discoveries in Canada and Australia. Cameco is also a leading provider of processing services required to produce fuel for nuclear power plants. It generates 1,000 megawatts of electricity through a partnership in North America's largest nuclear generating station located in Ontario, Canada.

For simplicity of exposition in this example, we will present share counts in thousands and all dollar amounts in thousands of Canadian dollars. In 2017, Cameco had 395,793 shares outstanding. Its 2017 year-end share price was $14.11. Therefore, Cameco's 2017 year-end market capitalization was $5,584,640.

In its 2017 Annual Report (available at www.cameco.com), Cameco reported total debt and other liabilities of $2,919,100. The company presented the following schedule for long-term debt payments:

Year	Payment
2018	$69,000
2019 and 2020	610,000

(continued)

Year	Payment
2021 and 2022	482,000
Thereafter	744,000
Total	$1,905,000

Cameco's longest maturity debt matures in 2042. We will assume that the amounts paid in 2019 and 2020, and in 2021 and 2022, will be paid equally during the two years. The "thereafter" period includes two debenture tranches, the first one maturing in 2024 for a total value of $620,000 and the second tranche maturing in 2042 for the remaining $124,000. A yield curve for zero-coupon Canadian government securities was available from the Bank of Canada. The yield-curve data and assumed risk premiums in Exhibit 9 were used to estimate the market value of Cameco's long-term debt:

Exhibit 9 Estimated Market Value

Year	Yield on Zero-Coupon Government Security (%)	Assumed Risk Premium (%)	Discount Rate (%)	Book Value	Market Value
2018	0.89	0.50	1.39	$69,000	$68,054
2019	1.11	1.00	2.11	$305,000	$292,525
2020	1.39	1.50	2.89	$305,000	$280,014
2021	1.65	2.00	3.65	$241,000	$208,804
2022	1.88	2.50	4.38	$241,000	$194,505
2023	2.10	3.00	5.10	$0	$0
2024	2.30	3.50	5.80	$620,000	$417,823
2025	2.50	4.00	6.50	$0	$0
...	...	...	...	$...	$...
2042	2.92	5.00	7.92	$124,000	$18,445
				$1,905,000	$1,480,170

Note from Exhibit 9 that the book value of long-term debt is $1,905,000 and its estimated market value is $1,480,170. The book value of total debt and liabilities of $2,919,100 minus the book value of long-term debt of $1,905,000 is $1,014,100. If we assume that the market value of that remaining debt is equal to its book value of $1,014,100 an estimate of the market value of total debt and liabilities is that amount plus the estimated market value of long-term debt of $1,480,170 or $2,494,270.

At the end of 2017, Cameco had cash and equivalents of $591,600. Enterprise value can be estimated as the $5,584,640 market value of stock plus the $2,494,270 market value of debt minus the $591,600 cash and equivalents, or $7,487,310. Cameco's 2017 EBITDA was $606,000; an estimate of EV/EBITDA is, therefore, $7,487,310 divided by $606,000, or 12.4.

EXAMPLE 17

EV/Operating Income

Exhibit 10 presents data for twelve major mining companies. Based only on the information in Exhibit 10, which two mining companies seem to be the *most* undervalued?

Exhibit 10 Data for Twelve Major Mining Companies

Company	EV (US$ millions)	Operating Income (OI) (US$ millions)	EV/OI
BHP Billiton	119,712.3	11,753	10.19
Rio Tinto	93,856.1	6,471	14.5
Vale	82,051.2	6,366	12.89
Glencore	80,772.0	–549	–147.13
Southern Copper	37,817.0	1,564	24.18
Freeport-McMoRan	33,452.0	–2,766	–12.09
Anglo American	32,870.3	2,562	12.83
Norilsk Nickel	22,483.0	3,377	6.66
Coal India	21,652.1	1,382	15.67
Barrick Gold	21,549.8	2,424	8.89
Newmont Mining	20,683.0	–65	–318.20
Goldcorp	12,986.7	369	35.19

Source: www.miningfeeds.com, Morningstar.

Solution:

Norilsk Nickel and Barrick Gold have the lowest EV/OI and thus appear to be the *most* undervalued or favorably priced on the basis of the EV/OI. Note the negative ratio for Glencore, Freeport-McMoRan, and Newmont Mining. Negative ratios are difficult to interpret, so other means are used to evaluate companies with negative ratios.

ASSET-BASED VALUATION 6

An asset-based valuation of a company uses estimates of the market or fair value of the company's assets and liabilities. Thus, asset-based valuations work well for companies that do not have a high proportion of intangible or "off the books" assets and that do have a high proportion of current assets and current liabilities. The analyst may be able to value these companies' assets and liabilities in a reasonable fashion by starting with balance sheet items. For most companies, however, balance sheet values are different from market (fair) values, and the market (fair) values can be difficult to determine.

Asset-based valuation models are frequently used together with multiplier models to value private companies. As public companies increase reporting or disclosure of fair values, asset-based valuation may be increasingly used to supplement present value and multiplier models of valuation. Important facts that the practitioner should realize are as follows:

- Companies with assets that do not have easily determinable market (fair) values—such as those with significant property, plant, and equipment—are very difficult to analyze using asset valuation methods.
- Asset and liability fair values can be very different from the values at which they are carried on the balance sheet of a company.
- Some assets that are "intangible" are shown on the books of the company. Other intangible assets, such as the value from synergies or the value of a good business reputation, may not be shown on the books. Because asset-based valuation may not consider some intangibles, it can give a "floor" value for a situation involving a significant amount of intangibles. When a company has significant intangibles, the analyst should prefer a forward-looking cash flow valuation.
- Asset values may be more difficult to estimate in a hyper-inflationary environment.

We begin by discussing asset-based valuation for hypothetical nonpublic companies and then move on to a public company example. Analysts should consider the difficulties and rewards of using asset-based valuation for companies that are suited to this measure. Owners of small privately held businesses are familiar with valuations arrived at by valuing the assets of the company and then subtracting any relevant liabilities.

EXAMPLE 18

An Asset-Based Valuation of a Family-Owned Laundry

A family owns a laundry and the real estate on which the laundry stands. The real estate is collateral for an outstanding loan of $100,000. How can asset-based valuation be used to value this business?

Solution:

The analyst should get at least two market appraisals for the real estate (building and land) and estimate the cost to extinguish the $100,000 loan. This information would provide estimated values for everything except the laundry as a going concern. That is, the analyst has market values for the building and land and the loan but needs to value the laundry business. The analyst can value the assets of the laundry: the equipment and inventory. The equipment can be valued at depreciated value, inflation-adjusted depreciated value, or replacement cost. Replacement cost in this case means the amount that would have to be spent to buy equivalent used machines. This amount is the market value of the used machines. The analyst will recognize that any intangible value of the laundry (prime location, clever marketing, etc.) is being excluded, which will result in an inaccurate asset-based valuation.

Example 18 shows some of the subtleties present in applying asset-based valuation to determine company value. It also shows how asset-based valuation does not deal with intangibles. Example 19 emphasizes this point.

EXAMPLE 19

An Asset-Based Valuation of a Restaurant

The business being valued is a restaurant that serves breakfast and lunch. The owner/proprietor wants to sell the business and retire. The restaurant space is rented, not owned. This particular restaurant is hugely popular because of the proprietor's cooking skills and secret recipes. How can the analyst value this business?

Solution:

Because of the intangibles, setting a value on this business is challenging. A multiple of income or revenue might be considered. But even those approaches overlook the fact that the proprietor may not be selling his secret recipes and, furthermore, does not intend to continue cooking. Some (or all) of the intangible assets may vanish when the business is sold. Asset-based valuation for this restaurant would begin with estimating the value of the restaurant equipment and inventory and subtracting the value of any liabilities. This approach will provide only a good baseline, however, for a minimum valuation.

For public companies, the assets will typically be so extensive that a piece-by-piece analysis will be impossible, and the transition from book value to market value is a nontrivial task. The asset-based valuation approach is most applicable when the market value of the corporate assets is readily determinable and the intangible assets, which are typically difficult to value, are a relatively small proportion of corporate assets. Asset-based valuation has also been applied to financial companies, natural resource companies, and formerly going-concerns that are being liquidated. Even for other types of companies, however, asset-based valuation of tangible assets may provide a baseline for a minimal valuation.

EXAMPLE 20

An Asset-Based Valuation of an Airline

Consider the value of an airline company that has few routes, high labor and other operating costs, has stopped paying dividends, and is losing millions of dollars each year. Using most valuation approaches, the company will have a negative value. Why might an asset-based valuation approach be appropriate for use by one of the company's competitors that is considering acquisition of this airline?

Solution:

The airline's routes, landing rights, leases of airport facilities, and ground equipment and airplanes may have substantial value to a competitor. An asset-based approach to valuing this company would value the company's assets separately and aside from the money-losing business in which they are presently being utilized.

Analysts recognizing the uncertainties related to model appropriateness and the inputs to the models frequently use more than one model or type of model in valuation to increase their confidence in their estimates of intrinsic value. The choice of models will depend on the availability of information to put into the models. Example 21 illustrates the use of three valuation methods.

EXAMPLE 21

A Simple Example of the Use of Three Major Equity Valuation Models

Company data for dividend per share (DPS), earnings per share (EPS), share price, and price-to-earnings ratio (P/E) for the most recent five years are presented in Exhibit 11. In addition, estimates (indicated by an "E" after the amount) of DPS and EPS for the next five years are shown. The valuation date is at the end of Year 5. The company has 1,000 shares outstanding.

Exhibit 11 Company DPS, EPS, Share Price, and P/E Data

Year	DPS	EPS	Share Price	TTM P/E
10	$3.10E	$5.20E	—	—
9	$2.91E	$4.85E	—	—
8	$2.79E	$4.65E	—	—
7	$2.65E	$4.37E	—	—
6	$2.55E	$4.30E	—	—
5	$2.43	$4.00	$50.80	12.7
4	$2.32	$3.90	$51.48	13.2
3	$2.19	$3.65	$59.86	16.4
2	$2.14	$3.60	$54.72	15.2
1	$2.00	$3.30	$46.20	14.0

The company's balance sheet at the end of Year 5 is given in Exhibit 12.

Exhibit 12 Balance Sheet as of End of Year 5

Cash	$ 5,000
Accounts receivable	15,000
Inventories	30,000
Net fixed assets	50,000
Total assets	$100,000
Accounts payable	$ 3,000
Notes payable	17,000
Term loans	25,000
Common shareholders' equity	55,000
Total liabilities and equity	$100,000

1 Using a Gordon growth model, estimate intrinsic value. Use a discount rate of 10 percent and an estimate of growth based on growth in dividends over the next five years.

2 Using a multiplier approach, estimate intrinsic value. Assume that a reasonable estimate of P/E is the average trailing twelve-month (TTM) P/E ratio over Years 1 through 4.

3 Using an asset-based valuation approach, estimate value per share from adjusted book values. Assume that the market values of accounts receivable and inventories are as reported, the market value of net fixed assets is 110 percent of reported book value, and the reported book values of liabilities reflect their market values.

Solution to 1:

$D_5 (1 + g)^5 = D_{10} 2.43(1 + g)^5 = 3.10$

$g \approx 5.0\%$

Estimate of value = V_5 = 2.55/(0.10 – 0.05) = \$51.00

Solution to 2:

Average P/E = (14.0 + 15.2 + 16.4 + 13.2)/4 = 14.7

Estimate of value = \$4.00 × 14.7 = \$58.80

Solution to 3:

Market value of assets = 5,000 + 15,000 + 30,000 + 1.1(50,000) = \$105,000

Market value of liabilities = \$3,000 + 17,000 + 25,000 = \$45,000

Adjusted book value = \$105,000 – 45,000 = \$60,000

Estimated value (adjusted book value per share) = \$60,000 ÷ 1,000 shares = \$60.00

Given the current share price of \$50.80, the multiplier and the asset-based valuation approaches indicate that the stock is undervalued. Given the intrinsic value estimated using the Gordon growth model, the analyst is likely to conclude that the stock is fairly priced. The analyst might examine the assumptions in the multiplier and the asset-based valuation approaches to determine why their estimated values differ from the estimated value provided by the Gordon growth model and the market price.

SUMMARY

The equity valuation models used to estimate intrinsic value—present value models, multiplier models, and asset-based valuation—are widely used and serve an important purpose. The valuation models presented here are a foundation on which to base analysis and research but must be applied wisely. Valuation is not simply a numerical analysis. The choice of model and the derivation of inputs require skill and judgment.

When valuing a company or group of companies, the analyst wants to choose a valuation model that is appropriate for the information available to be used as inputs. The available data will, in most instances, restrict the choice of model and influence the way it is used. Complex models exist that may improve on the simple valuation models described in this reading; but before using those models and assuming that complexity increases accuracy, the analyst would do well to consider the "law of parsimony:" A model should be kept as simple as possible in light of the available inputs. Valuation is a fallible discipline, and any method will result in an inaccurate forecast at some time. The goal is to minimize the inaccuracy of the forecast.

Among the points made in this reading are the following:

- An analyst estimating intrinsic value is implicitly questioning the market's estimate of value.
- If the estimated value exceeds the market price, the analyst infers the security is *undervalued*. If the estimated value equals the market price, the analyst infers the security is *fairly valued*. If the estimated value is less than the market price, the analyst infers the security is *overvalued*. Because of the uncertainties involved in valuation, an analyst may require that value estimates differ markedly from market price before concluding that a misvaluation exists.
- Analysts often use more than one valuation model because of concerns about the applicability of any particular model and the variability in estimates that result from changes in inputs.
- Three major categories of equity valuation models are present value, multiplier, and asset-based valuation models.
- Present value models estimate value as the present value of expected future benefits.
- Multiplier models estimate intrinsic value based on a multiple of some fundamental variable.
- Asset-based valuation models estimate value based on the estimated value of assets and liabilities.
- The choice of model will depend upon the availability of information to input into the model and the analyst's confidence in both the information and the appropriateness of the model.
- Companies distribute cash to shareholders using dividend payments and share repurchases.
- Regular cash dividends are a key input to dividend valuation models.
- Key dates in dividend chronology are the declaration date, ex-dividend date, holder-of-record date, and payment date.
- In the dividend discount model, value is estimated as the present value of expected future dividends.
- In the free cash flow to equity model, value is estimated as the present value of expected future free cash flow to equity.
- The Gordon growth model, a simple DDM, estimates value as $D_1/(r - g)$.
- The two stage dividend discount model estimates value as the sum of the present values of dividends over a short-term period of high growth and the present value of the terminal value at the end of the period of high growth. The terminal value is estimated using the Gordon growth model.
- The choice of dividend model is based upon the patterns assumed with respect to future dividends.
- Multiplier models typically use multiples of the form: P/ measure of fundamental variable or EV/ measure of fundamental variable.
- Multiples can be based upon fundamentals or comparables.
- Asset-based valuations models estimate value of equity as the value of the assets less the value of liabilities.

REFERENCES

Basu, S. 1977. "Investment Performance of Common Stocks in Relation to Their Price-Earnings Ratios: A Test of the Efficient Market Hypothesis." *Journal of Finance*, vol. 32, no. 3:663–682.

Block, S. 1999. "A Study of Financial Analysts: Practice and Theory." *Financial Analysts Journal*, vol. 55, no. 4:86–95.

Dreman, D. 1977. *Psychology of the Stock Market*. New York: AMACOM.

Fama, E., and K. French. 1995. "Size and Book-to-Market Factors in Earnings and Returns." *Journal of Finance*, vol. 50, no. 1:131–155.

McWilliams, J. 1966. "Prices, Earnings and P-E Ratios." *Financial Analysts Journal*, vol. 22, no. 3:137.

Miller, P., and E. Widmann. 1966. "Price Performance Outlook for High & Low P/E Stocks." *1966 Stock & Bond Issue, Commercial & Financial Chronicle*: 26–28.

Nicholson, S. 1968. "Price Ratios in Relation to Investment Results." *Financial Analysts Journal*, vol. 24, no. 1:105–109.

O'Shaughnessy, J. 2005. *What Works on Wall Street*. New York: McGraw-Hill.

PRACTICE PROBLEMS

1 An analyst estimates the intrinsic value of a stock to be in the range of €17.85 to €21.45. The current market price of the stock is €24.35. This stock is *most likely*:

A overvalued.

B undervalued.

C fairly valued.

2 An analyst determines the intrinsic value of an equity security to be equal to $55. If the current price is $47, the equity is *most likely*:

A undervalued.

B fairly valued.

C overvalued.

3 In asset-based valuation models, the intrinsic value of a common share of stock is based on the:

A estimated market value of the company's assets.

B estimated market value of the company's assets plus liabilities.

C estimated market value of the company's assets minus liabilities.

4 Which of the following is *most likely* used in a present value model?

A Enterprise value.

B Price to free cash flow.

C Free cash flow to equity.

5 Book value is *least likely* to be considered when using:

A a multiplier model.

B an asset-based valuation model.

C a present value model.

6 An analyst is attempting to calculate the intrinsic value of a company and has gathered the following company data: EBITDA, total market value, and market value of cash and short-term investments, liabilities, and preferred shares. The analyst is *least likely* to use:

A a multiplier model.

B a discounted cash flow model.

C an asset-based valuation model.

7 An analyst who bases the calculation of intrinsic value on dividend-paying capacity rather than expected dividends will *most likely* use the:

A dividend discount model.

B free cash flow to equity model.

C cash flow from operations model.

8 An investor expects to purchase shares of common stock today and sell them after two years. The investor has estimated dividends for the next two years, D_1 and D_2, and the selling price of the stock two years from now, P_2. According to the dividend discount model, the intrinsic value of the stock today is the present value of:

A next year's dividend, D_1.

B future expected dividends, D_1 and D_2.

C future expected dividends and price—D_1, D_2 and P_2.

9 In the free cash flow to equity (FCFE) model, the intrinsic value of a share of stock is calculated as:

A the present value of future expected FCFE.

B the present value of future expected FCFE plus net borrowing.

C the present value of future expected FCFE minus fixed capital investment.

10 With respect to present value models, which of the following statements is *most accurate*?

A Present value models can be used only if a stock pays a dividend.

B Present value models can be used only if a stock pays a dividend or is expected to pay a dividend.

C Present value models can be used for stocks that currently pay a dividend, are expected to pay a dividend, or are not expected to pay a dividend.

11 A Canadian life insurance company has an issue of 4.80 percent, $25 par value, perpetual, non-convertible, non-callable preferred shares outstanding. The required rate of return on similar issues is 4.49 percent. The intrinsic value of a preferred share is *closest to*:

A $25.00.

B $26.75.

C $28.50.

12 Two analysts estimating the value of a non-convertible, non-callable, perpetual preferred stock with a constant dividend arrive at different estimated values. The *most likely* reason for the difference is that the analysts used different:

A time horizons.

B required rates of return.

C estimated dividend growth rates.

13 The Beasley Corporation has just paid a dividend of $1.75 per share. If the required rate of return is 12.3 percent per year and dividends are expected to grow indefinitely at a constant rate of 9.2 percent per year, the intrinsic value of Beasley Corporation stock is *closest* to:

A $15.54.

B $56.45.

C $61.65.

14 An investor is considering the purchase of a common stock with a $2.00 annual dividend. The dividend is expected to grow at a rate of 4 percent annually. If the investor's required rate of return is 7 percent, the intrinsic value of the stock is *closest* to:

A $50.00.

B $66.67.

C $69.33.

15 An analyst gathers or estimates the following information about a stock:

Current price per share	€22.56
Current annual dividend per share	€1.60
Annual dividend growth rate for Years 1–4	9.00%
Annual dividend growth rate for Years 5+	4.00%
Required rate of return	12%

Based on a dividend discount model, the stock is *most likely*:

A undervalued.

B fairly valued.

C overvalued.

16 An analyst is attempting to value shares of the Dominion Company. The company has just paid a dividend of $0.58 per share. Dividends are expected to grow by 20 percent next year and 15 percent the year after that. From the third year onward, dividends are expected to grow at 5.6 percent per year indefinitely. If the required rate of return is 8.3 percent, the intrinsic value of the stock is *closest* to:

A $26.00.

B $27.00.

C $28.00.

17 Hideki Corporation has just paid a dividend of ¥450 per share. Annual dividends are expected to grow at the rate of 4 percent per year over the next four years. At the end of four years, shares of Hideki Corporation are expected to sell for ¥9000. If the required rate of return is 12 percent, the intrinsic value of a share of Hideki Corporation is *closest* to:

A ¥5,850.

B ¥7,220.

C ¥7,670.

18 The Gordon growth model can be used to value dividend-paying companies that are:

A expected to grow very fast.

B in a mature phase of growth.

C very sensitive to the business cycle.

19 The best model to use when valuing a young dividend-paying company that is just entering the growth phase is *most likely* the:

A Gordon growth model.

B two-stage dividend discount model.

C three-stage dividend discount model.

20 An equity analyst has been asked to estimate the intrinsic value of the common stock of Omega Corporation, a leading manufacturer of automobile seats. Omega is in a mature industry, and both its earnings and dividends are expected to grow at a rate of 3 percent annually. Which of the following is *most likely* to be the best model for determining the intrinsic value of an Omega share?

A Gordon growth model.

B Free cash flow to equity model.

C Multistage dividend discount model.

21 A price earnings ratio that is derived from the Gordon growth model is inversely related to the:

A growth rate.

B dividend payout ratio.

C required rate of return.

22 The primary difference between P/E multiples based on comparables and P/E multiples based on fundamentals is that fundamentals-based P/Es take into account:

A future expectations.

B the law of one price.

C historical information.

23 An analyst makes the following statement: "Use of P/E and other multiples for analysis is not effective because the multiples are based on historical data and because not all companies have positive accounting earnings." The analyst's statement is *most likely*:

A inaccurate with respect to both historical data and earnings.

B accurate with respect to historical data and inaccurate with respect to earnings.

C inaccurate with respect to historical data and accurate with respect to earnings.

24 An analyst has prepared a table of the average trailing twelve-month price-to-earning (P/E), price-to-cash flow (P/CF), and price-to-sales (P/S) for the Tanaka Corporation for the years 2014 to 2017.

Year	P/E	P/CF	P/S
2014	4.9	5.4	1.2
2015	6.1	8.6	1.5
2016	8.3	7.3	1.9
2017	9.2	7.9	2.3

As of the date of the valuation in 2018, the trailing twelve-month P/E, P/CF, and P/S are, respectively, 9.2, 8.0, and 2.5. Based on the information provided, the analyst may reasonably conclude that Tanaka shares are *most likely*:

A overvalued.

B undervalued.

C fairly valued.

25 An analyst has gathered the following information for the Oudin Corporation:

Expected earnings per share = €5.70

Expected dividends per share = €2.70

Dividends are expected to grow at 2.75 percent per year indefinitely

The required rate of return is 8.35 percent

Based on the information provided, the price/earnings multiple for Oudin is *closest* to:

A 5.7.

B 8.5.

C 9.4.

26 An analyst gathers the following information about two companies:

	Alpha Corp.	Delta Co.
Current price per share	\$57.32	\$18.93
Last year's EPS	\$3.82	\$1.35
Current year's estimated EPS	\$4.75	\$1.40

Which of the following statements is *most accurate*?

A Delta has the higher trailing P/E multiple and lower current estimated P/E multiple.

B Alpha has the higher trailing P/E multiple and lower current estimated P/E multiple.

C Alpha has the higher trailing P/E multiple and higher current estimated P/E multiple.

27 An analyst gathers the following information about similar companies in the banking sector:

	First Bank	Prime Bank	Pioneer Trust
P/B	1.10	0.60	0.60
P/E	8.40	11.10	8.30

Which of the companies is *most likely* to be undervalued?

A First Bank.

B Prime Bank.

C Pioneer Trust.

28 The market value of equity for a company can be calculated as enterprise value:

A minus market value of debt, preferred stock, and short-term investments.

B plus market value of debt and preferred stock minus short-term investments.

C minus market value of debt and preferred stock plus short-term investments.

29 Which of the following statements regarding the calculation of the enterprise value multiple is *most likely* correct?

A Operating income may be used instead of EBITDA.

B EBITDA may not be used if company earnings are negative.

C Book value of debt may be used instead of market value of debt.

30 An analyst has determined that the appropriate EV/EBITDA for Rainbow Company is 10.2. The analyst has also collected the following forecasted information for Rainbow Company:

EBITDA = \$22,000,000

Market value of debt = \$56,000,000

Cash = \$1,500,000

The value of equity for Rainbow Company is *closest* to:

A \$169 million.

B \$224 million.

C \$281 million.

31 Enterprise value is most often determined as market capitalization of common equity and preferred stock minus the value of cash equivalents plus the:

A book value of debt.

B market value of debt.

C market value of long-term debt.

32 Asset-based valuation models are best suited to companies where the capital structure does not have a high proportion of:

A debt.

B intangible assets.

C current assets and liabilities.

33 Which of the following is *most likely* a reason for using asset-based valuation?

A The analyst is valuing a privately held company.

B The company has a relatively high level of intangible assets.

C The market values of assets and liabilities are different from the balance sheet values.

34 A disadvantage of the EV method for valuing equity is that the following information may be difficult to obtain:

A Operating income.

B Market value of debt.

C Market value of equity.

35 Which type of equity valuation model is *most likely* to be preferable when one is comparing similar companies?

A A multiplier model.

B A present value model.

C An asset-based valuation model.

36 Which of the following is *most likely* considered a weakness of present value models?

A Present value models cannot be used for companies that do not pay dividends.

B Small changes in model assumptions and inputs can result in large changes in the computed intrinsic value of the security.

C The value of the security depends on the investor's holding period; thus, comparing valuations of different companies for different investors is difficult.

SOLUTIONS

1 A is correct. The current market price of the stock exceeds the upper bound of the analyst's estimate of the intrinsic value of the stock.

2 A is correct. The market price is less than the estimated intrinsic, or fundamental, value.

3 C is correct. Asset-based valuation models calculate the intrinsic value of equity by subtracting liabilities from the market value of assets.

4 C is correct. FCFE can be used in a form of present value, or discounted cash flow, model. Both EV and price to free cash flow are forms of multiplier models.

5 C is correct. Multiplier valuation models (in the form of P/B) and asset-based valuation models (in the form of adjustments to book value) use book value, whereas present value models typically discount future expected cash flows.

6 B is correct. To use a discounted cash flow model, the analyst will require FCFE or dividend data. In addition, the analyst will need data to calculate an appropriate discount rate.

7 B is correct. The FCFE model assumes that dividend-paying capacity is reflected in FCFE.

8 C is correct. According to the dividend discount model, the intrinsic value of a stock today is the present value of all future dividends. In this case, the intrinsic value is the present value of D_1, D_2, and P_2. Note that P_2 is the present value at Period 2 of all future dividends from Period 3 to infinity.

9 A is correct. In the FCFE model, the intrinsic value of stock is calculated by discounting expected future FCFE to present value. No further adjustments are required.

10 C is correct. Dividend discount models can be used for a stock that pays a current dividend or a stock that is expected to pay a dividend. FCFE can be used for both of those stocks and for stocks that do not, or are not expected to, pay dividends in the near future. Both of these models are forms of present value models.

11 B is correct. The expected annual dividend is 4.80% × \$25 = \$1.20. The value of a preferred share is \$1.20/0.0449 = \$26.73.

12 B is correct. The required rate of return, r, can vary widely depending on the inputs and is not unique. A preferred stock with a constant dividend would not have a growth rate to estimate, and the investor's time horizon would have no effect on the calculation of intrinsic value.

13 C is correct. $P_0 = D_1/(r - g) = 1.75(1.092)/(0.123 - 0.092) = \$61.65$.

14 C is correct. According to the Gordon growth model, $V_0 = D_1/(r - g)$. In this case, $D_1 = \$2.00 \times 1.04 = \$2.08$, so $V_0 = \$2.08/(0.07 - 0.04) = \$69.3333 = \$69.33$.

15 A is correct. The current price of €22.56 is less than the intrinsic value (V_0) of €24.64; therefore, the stock appears to be currently undervalued. According to the two-stage dividend discount model:

$$V_0 = \sum_{t=1}^{n} \frac{D_0(1+g_S)^t}{(1+r)^t} + \frac{V_n}{(1+r)^n} \text{ and } V_n = \frac{D_{n+1}}{r - g_L}$$

$$D_{n+1} = D_0(1 + g_S)^n(1 + g_L)$$
$$D_1 = €1.60 \times 1.09 = €1.744$$

$$D_2 = €1.60 \times (1.09)^2 = €1.901$$
$$D_3 = €1.60 \times (1.09)^3 = €2.072$$
$$D_4 = €1.60 \times (1.09)^4 = €2.259$$
$$D_5 = [€1.60 \times (1.09)^4](1.04) = €2.349$$
$$V_4 = €2.349/(0.12 - 0.04) = €29.363$$
$$V_0 = \frac{1.744}{(1.12)^1} + \frac{1.901}{(1.12)^2} + \frac{2.072}{(1.12)^3} + \frac{2.259}{(1.12)^4} + \frac{29.363}{(1.12)^4}$$
$$= 1.557 + 1.515 + 1.475 + 1.436 + 18.661$$
$$= €24.64 \text{ (which is greater than the current price of €22.56)}$$

16 C is correct.

$$V_0 = \frac{D_1}{(1+r)} + \frac{D_2}{(1+r)^2} + \frac{P_2}{(1+r)^2}$$
$$= \frac{0.70}{(1.083)} + \frac{0.80}{(1.083)^2} + \frac{31.29}{(1.083)^2}$$
$$= \$28.01$$

Note that $D_1 = 0.58(1.20) = 0.70$, $D_2 = 0.58(1.20)(1.15) = 0.80$, and $P_2 = D_3/(k - g) = 0.80(1.056)/(0.083 - 0.056) = 31.29$

17 B is correct.

$$V_0 = \frac{D_1}{(1+r)} + \frac{D_2}{(1+r)^2} + \frac{D_3}{(1+r)^3} + \frac{D_4}{(1+r)^4} + \frac{P_4}{(1+r)^4}$$
$$= \frac{468}{(1.12)} + \frac{486.72}{(1.12)^2} + \frac{506.19}{(1.12)^3} + \frac{526.44}{(1.12)^4} + \frac{9000}{(1.12)^4}$$
$$= ¥7,220$$

18 B is correct. The Gordon growth model (also known as the constant growth model) can be used to value dividend-paying companies in a mature phase of growth. A stable dividend growth rate is often a plausible assumption for such companies.

19 C is correct. The Gordon growth model is best suited to valuing mature companies. The two-stage model is best for companies that are transitioning from a growth stage to a mature stage. The three-stage model is appropriate for young companies just entering the growth phase.

20 A is correct. The company is a mature company with a steadily growing dividend rate. The two-stage (or multistage) model is unnecessary because the dividend growth rate is expected to remain stable. Although an FCFE model could be used, that model is more often chosen for companies that currently pay no dividends.

21 C is correct. The justified forward P/E is calculated as follows:

$$\frac{P_0}{E_1} = \frac{\dfrac{D_1}{E_1}}{r - g}$$

P/E is inversely related to the required rate of return, r, and directly related to the growth rate, g, and the dividend payout ratio, D/E.

22 A is correct. Multiples based on comparables are grounded in the law of one price and take into account historical multiple values. In contrast, P/E multiples based on fundamentals can be based on the Gordon growth model, which takes into account future expected dividends.

23 A is correct. The statement is inaccurate in both respects. Although multiples can be calculated from historical data, forecasted values can be used as well. For companies without accounting earnings, several other multiples can be used. These multiples are often specific to a company's industry or sector and include price-to-sales and price-to-cash flow.

24 A is correct. Tanaka shares are most likely overvalued. As the table below shows, all the 2018 multiples are currently above their 2014–2017 averages.

Year	P/E	P/CF	P/R
2014	4.9	5.4	1.2
2015	6.1	8.6	1.5
2016	8.3	7.3	1.9
2017	9.2	7.9	2.3
Average	7.1	7.3	1.7

25 B is correct.

$$\frac{P_0}{E_1} = \frac{\frac{D_1}{E_1}}{r - g} = \frac{\frac{2.7}{5.7}}{0.0835 - 0.0275} = 8.5$$

26 B is correct. P/E = Current price/EPS, and Estimated P/E = Current price/Estimated EPS.

Alpha P/E = \$57.32/\$3.82 = 15.01

Alpha estimated P/E = \$57.32/4.75 = 12.07

Delta P/E = \$18.93/\$1.35 = 14.02

Delta estimated P/E = \$18.93/\$1.40 = 13.52

27 C is correct. Relative to the others, Pioneer Trust has the lowest P/E multiple and the P/B multiple is tied for the lowest with Prime Bank. Given the law of one price, similar companies should trade at similar P/B and P/E levels. Thus, based on the information presented, Pioneer is most likely to be undervalued.

28 C is correct. Enterprise value is calculated as the market value of equity plus the market value of debt and preferred stock minus short-term investments. Therefore, the market value of equity is enterprise value minus the market value of debt and preferred stock plus short-term investments.

29 A is correct. Operating income may be used in place of EBITDA when calculating the enterprise value multiple. EBITDA may be used when company earnings are negative because EBITDA is usually positive. The book value of debt cannot be used in place of market value of debt.

30 A is correct.

$$EV = 10.2 \times 22{,}000{,}000 = \$224{,}400{,}000$$

$$\begin{aligned}\text{Equity value} &= EV - \text{Debt} + \text{Cash} \\ &= 224{,}400{,}000 - 56{,}000{,}000 + 1{,}500{,}000 \\ &= \$169{,}900{,}000\end{aligned}$$

31 B is correct. The market value of debt must be calculated and taken out of the enterprise value. Enterprise value, sometimes known as the cost of a takeover, is the cost of the purchase of the company, which would include the assumption of the company's debts at market value.

32 B is correct. Intangible assets are hard to value. Therefore, asset-based valuation models work best for companies that do not have a high proportion of intangible assets.

33 A is correct. Asset-based valuations are most often used when an analyst is valuing private enterprises. Both B and C are considerations in asset-based valuations but are more likely to be reasons to avoid that valuation model rather than reasons to use it.

34 B is correct. According to the reading, analysts may have not have access to market quotations for company debt.

35 A is correct. Although all models can be used to compare various companies, multiplier models have the advantage of reducing varying fundamental data points into a format that allows direct comparisons. As long as the analyst applies the data in a consistent manner for all the companies, this approach provides useful comparative data.

36 B is correct. Very small changes in inputs, such as required rate of return or dividend growth rate, can result in large changes to the valuation model output. Some present value models, such as FCFE models, can be used to value companies without dividends. Also, the intrinsic value of a security is independent of the investor's holding period.

Glossary

A priori probability A probability based on logical analysis rather than on observation or personal judgment.

Abnormal return The amount by which a security's actual return differs from its expected return, given the security's risk and the market's return.

Absolute advantage A country's ability to produce a good or service at a lower absolute cost than its trading partner.

Absolute dispersion The amount of variability present without comparison to any reference point or benchmark.

Absolute frequency The number of observations in a given interval (for grouped data).

Accelerated book build An offering of securities by an investment bank acting as principal that is accomplished in only one or two days.

Accelerated methods Depreciation methods that allocate a relatively large proportion of the cost of an asset to the early years of the asset's useful life.

Accounting costs Monetary value of economic resources used in performing an activity. These can be explicit, out-of-pocket, current payments, or an allocation of historical payments (depreciation) for resources. They do not include implicit opportunity costs.

Accounting profit Income as reported on the income statement, in accordance with prevailing accounting standards, before the provisions for income tax expense. Also called *income before taxes* or *pretax income*.

Accounts payable Amounts that a business owes to its vendors for goods and services that were purchased from them but which have not yet been paid.

Accounts receivable turnover Ratio of sales on credit to the average balance in accounts receivable.

Accrued expenses Liabilities related to expenses that have been incurred but not yet paid as of the end of an accounting period—an example of an accrued expense is rent that has been incurred but not yet paid, resulting in a liability "rent payable." Also called *accrued liabilities*.

Accrued interest Interest earned but not yet paid.

Acid-test ratio A stringent measure of liquidity that indicates a company's ability to satisfy current liabilities with its most liquid assets, calculated as (cash + short-term marketable investments + receivables) divided by current liabilities.

Acquisition method A method of accounting for a business combination where the acquirer is required to measure each identifiable asset and liability at fair value. This method was the result of a joint project of the IASB and FASB aiming at convergence in standards for the accounting of business combinations.

Action lag Delay from policy decisions to implementation.

Active investment An approach to investing in which the investor seeks to outperform a given benchmark.

Active return The return on a portfolio minus the return on the portfolio's benchmark.

Active strategy In reference to short-term cash management, an investment strategy characterized by monitoring and attempting to capitalize on market conditions to optimize the risk and return relationship of short-term investments.

Activity ratios Ratios that measure how efficiently a company performs day-to-day tasks, such as the collection of receivables and management of inventory. Also called *asset utilization ratios* or *operating efficiency ratios*.

Add-on rates Bank certificates of deposit, repos, and indexes such as Libor and Euribor are quoted on an add-on rate basis (bond equivalent yield basis).

Addition rule for probabilities A principle stating that the probability that *A* or *B* occurs (both occur) equals the probability that *A* occurs, plus the probability that *B* occurs, minus the probability that both *A* and *B* occur.

Agency bonds See *quasi-government bond*.

Agency RMBS In the United States, securities backed by residential mortgage loans and guaranteed by a federal agency or guaranteed by either of the two GSEs (Fannie Mae and Freddie Mac).

Aggregate demand The quantity of goods and services that households, businesses, government, and foreign customers want to buy at any given level of prices.

Aggregate demand curve Inverse relationship between the price level and real output.

Aggregate income The value of all the payments earned by the suppliers of factors used in the production of goods and services.

Aggregate output The value of all the goods and services produced in a specified period of time.

Aggregate supply The quantity of goods and services producers are willing to supply at any given level of price.

Aggregate supply curve The level of domestic output that companies will produce at each price level.

Aging schedule A breakdown of accounts into categories of days outstanding.

All-or-nothing (AON) orders An order that includes the instruction to trade only if the trade fills the entire quantity (size) specified.

Allocationally efficient A characteristic of a market, a financial system, or an economy that promotes the allocation of resources to their highest value uses.

Alternative data Non-traditional data types generated by the use of electronic devices, social media, satellite and sensor networks, and company exhaust.

Alternative investment markets Market for investments other than traditional securities investments (i.e., traditional common and preferred shares and traditional fixed income instruments). The term usually encompasses direct and indirect investment in real estate (including timberland and farmland) and commodities (including precious metals); hedge funds, private equity, and other investments requiring specialized due diligence.

Alternative trading systems Trading venues that function like exchanges but that do not exercise regulatory authority over their subscribers except with respect to the conduct of the subscribers' trading in their trading systems. Also called *electronic communications networks* or *multilateral trading facilities*.

American depository receipt A US dollar-denominated security that trades like a common share on US exchanges.

American depository share The underlying shares on which American depository receipts are based. They trade in the issuing company's domestic market.

American-style Type of option contract that can be exercised at any time up to the option's expiration date.

Amortisation The process of allocating the cost of intangible long-term assets having a finite useful life to accounting periods; the allocation of the amount of a bond premium or discount to the periods remaining until bond maturity.

Amortised cost The historical cost (initially recognised cost) of an asset, adjusted for amortisation and impairment.

Amortizing bond Bond with a payment schedule that calls for periodic payments of interest and repayments of principal.

Amortizing loan Loan with a payment schedule that calls for periodic payments of interest and repayments of principal.

Annual percentage rate The cost of borrowing expressed as a yearly rate.

Annuity A finite set of level sequential cash flows.

Annuity due An annuity having a first cash flow that is paid immediately.

Anticipation stock Excess inventory that is held in anticipation of increased demand, often because of seasonal patterns of demand.

Antidilutive With reference to a transaction or a security, one that would increase earnings per share (EPS) or result in EPS higher than the company's basic EPS—antidilutive securities are not included in the calculation of diluted EPS.

Arbitrage 1) The simultaneous purchase of an undervalued asset or portfolio and sale of an overvalued but equivalent asset or portfolio, in order to obtain a riskless profit on the price differential. Taking advantage of a market inefficiency in a risk-free manner. 2) The condition in a financial market in which equivalent assets or combinations of assets sell for two different prices, creating an opportunity to profit at no risk with no commitment of money. In a well-functioning financial market, few arbitrage opportunities are possible. 3) A risk-free operation that earns an expected positive net profit but requires no net investment of money.

Arbitrage-free pricing The overall process of pricing derivatives by arbitrage and risk neutrality. Also called the *principle of no arbitrage.*

Arbitrageurs Traders who engage in arbitrage. See *arbitrage.*

Arithmetic mean The sum of the observations divided by the number of observations.

Arms index A flow of funds indicator applied to a broad stock market index to measure the relative extent to which money is moving into or out of rising and declining stocks.

Artificial intelligence Computer systems that exhibit cognitive and decision-making ability comparable (or superior) to that of humans.

Asian call option A European-style option with a value at maturity equal to the difference between the stock price at maturity and the average stock price during the life of the option, or $0, whichever is greater.

Ask The price at which a dealer or trader is willing to sell an asset, typically qualified by a maximum quantity (ask size). See *offer.*

Ask size The maximum quantity of an asset that pertains to a specific ask price from a trader. For example, if the ask for a share issue is $30 for a size of 1,000 shares, the trader is offering to sell at $30 up to 1,000 shares.

Asset allocation The process of determining how investment funds should be distributed among asset classes.

Asset-backed securities A type of bond issued by a legal entity called a *special purpose entity* (SPE) on a collection of assets that the SPE owns. Also, securities backed by receivables and loans other than mortgages.

Asset-based loan A loan that is secured with company assets.

Asset-based valuation models Valuation based on estimates of the market value of a company's assets.

Asset beta The unlevered beta; reflects the business risk of the assets; the asset's systematic risk.

Asset class A group of assets that have similar characteristics, attributes, and risk/return relationships.

Asset swap Converts the periodic fixed coupon of a specific bond to a Libor plus or minus a spread.

Asset utilization ratios Ratios that measure how efficiently a company performs day-to-day tasks, such as the collection of receivables and management of inventory.

Assets Resources controlled by an enterprise as a result of past events and from which future economic benefits to the enterprise are expected to flow.

Assignment of accounts receivable The use of accounts receivable as collateral for a loan.

At the money An option in which the underlying's price equals the exercise price.

Auction A type of bond issuing mechanism often used for sovereign bonds that involves bidding.

Autarkic price The price of a good or service in an autarkic economy.

Autarky A state in which a country does not trade with other countries.

Automated Clearing House (ACH) An electronic payment network available to businesses, individuals, and financial institutions in the United States, US Territories, and Canada.

Automatic stabilizer A countercyclical factor that automatically comes into play as an economy slows and unemployment rises.

Available-for-sale Under US GAAP, debt securities not classified as either held-to-maturity or held-for-trading securities. The investor is willing to sell but not actively planning to sell. In general, available-for-sale debt securities are reported at fair value on the balance sheet, with unrealized gains included as a component of other comprehensive income.

Average accounting rate of return (ARR) Over the life of a project, the AAR can be defined as the average net income divided by the average book value.

Average fixed cost Total fixed cost divided by quantity produced.

Average life See *weighted average life.*

Average product Measures the productivity of inputs on average and is calculated by dividing total product by the total number of units for a given input that is used to generate that output.

Average revenue Total revenue divided by quantity sold.

Average total cost Total cost divided by quantity produced.

Average variable cost Total variable cost divided by quantity produced.

Back simulation Another term for the historical method of estimating VaR. This term is somewhat misleading in that the method involves not a *simulation* of the past but rather what *actually happened* in the past, sometimes adjusted to reflect the fact that a different portfolio may have existed in the past than is planned for the future.

Back-testing With reference to portfolio strategies, the application of a strategy's portfolio selection rules to historical data to assess what would have been the strategy's historical performance.

Backup lines of credit A type of credit enhancement provided by a bank to an issuer of commercial paper to ensure that the issuer will have access to sufficient liquidity to repay maturing commercial paper if issuing new paper is not a viable option.

Balance of payments A double-entry bookkeeping system that summarizes a country's economic transactions with the rest of the world for a particular period of time, typically a calendar quarter or year.

Balance of trade deficit When the domestic economy is spending more on foreign goods and services than foreign economies are spending on domestic goods and services.

Balance sheet The financial statement that presents an entity's current financial position by disclosing resources the entity controls (its assets) and the claims on those resources (its liabilities and equity claims), as of a particular point in time (the date of the balance sheet). Also called *statement of financial position* or *statement of financial condition.*

Balance sheet ratios Financial ratios involving balance sheet items only.

Balanced With respect to a government budget, one in which spending and revenues (taxes) are equal.

Balloon payment Large payment required at maturity to retire a bond's outstanding principal amount.

Bar chart A price chart with four bits of data for each time interval—the high, low, opening, and closing prices. A vertical line connects the high and low. A cross-hatch left indicates the opening price and a cross-hatch right indicates the close.

Barter economy An economy where economic agents as house-holds, corporations, and governments "pay" for goods and services with another good or service.

Base rates The reference rate on which a bank bases lending rates to all other customers.

Basic EPS Net earnings available to common shareholders (i.e., net income minus preferred dividends) divided by the weighted average number of common shares outstanding.

Basis point Used in stating yield spreads, one basis point equals one-hundredth of a percentage point, or 0.01%.

Basket of listed depository receipts An exchange-traded fund (ETF) that represents a portfolio of depository receipts.

Bearer bonds Bonds for which ownership is not recorded; only the clearing system knows who the bond owner is.

Behavioral finance A field of finance that examines the psychological variables that affect and often distort the investment decision making of investors, analysts, and portfolio managers.

Behind the market Said of prices specified in orders that are worse than the best current price; e.g., for a limit buy order, a limit price below the best bid.

Benchmark A comparison portfolio; a point of reference or comparison.

Benchmark issue The latest sovereign bond issue for a given maturity. It serves as a benchmark against which to compare bonds that have the same features but that are issued by another type of issuer.

Benchmark rate Typically the yield-to-maturity on a government bond having the same, or close to the same, time-to-maturity.

Benchmark spread The yield spread over a specific benchmark, usually measured in basis points.

Bernoulli random variable A random variable having the outcomes 0 and 1.

Bernoulli trial An experiment that can produce one of two outcomes.

Best bid The highest bid in the market.

Best effort offering An offering of a security using an investment bank in which the investment bank, as agent for the issuer, promises to use its best efforts to sell the offering but does not guarantee that a specific amount will be sold.

Best-in-class An ESG implementation approach that seeks to identify the most favorable companies in an industry based on ESG considerations.

Best offer The lowest offer (ask price) in the market.

Beta A measure of the sensitivity of a given investment or portfolio to movements in the overall market.

Bid The price at which a dealer or trader is willing to buy an asset, typically qualified by a maximum quantity.

Bid–ask spread The difference between the prices at which dealers will buy from a customer (bid) and sell to a customer (offer or ask). It is often used as an indicator of liquidity.

Bid–offer spread The difference between the prices at which dealers will buy from a customer (bid) and sell to a customer (offer or ask). It is often used as an indicator of liquidity.

Bid size The maximum quantity of an asset that pertains to a specific bid price from a trader.

Big Data The vast amount of data being generated by industry, governments, individuals, and electronic devices that arises from both traditional and non-traditional data sources.

Bilateral loan A loan from a single lender to a single borrower.

Binomial model A model for pricing options in which the underlying price can move to only one of two possible new prices.

Binomial random variable The number of successes in n Bernoulli trials for which the probability of success is constant for all trials and the trials are independent.

Binomial tree The graphical representation of a model of asset price dynamics in which, at each period, the asset moves up with probability p or down with probability $(1 - p)$.

Bitcoin A cryptocurrency using blockchain technology that was created in 2009.

Block brokers A broker (agent) that provides brokerage services for large-size trades.

Blockchain A type of digital ledger in which information is recorded sequentially and then linked together and secured using cryptographic methods.

Blue chip Widely held large market capitalization companies that are considered financially sound and are leaders in their respective industry or local stock market.

Bollinger Bands A price-based technical analysis indicator consisting of a moving average plus a higher line representing the moving average plus a set number of standard deviations from average price (for the same number of periods as used to calculate the moving average) and a lower line that is a moving average minus the same number of standard deviations.

Bond Contractual agreement between the issuer and the bondholders.

Bond equivalent yield A calculation of yield that is annualized using the ratio of 365 to the number of days to maturity. Bond equivalent yield allows for the restatement and comparison of securities with different compounding periods.

Bond indenture The governing legal credit agreement, typically incorporated by reference in the prospectus. Also called *trust deed.*

Bond market vigilantes Bond market participants who might reduce their demand for long-term bonds, thus pushing up their yields.

Bond yield plus risk premium approach An estimate of the cost of common equity that is produced by summing the before-tax cost of debt and a risk premium that captures the additional yield on a company's stock relative to its bonds. The additional yield is often estimated using historical spreads between bond yields and stock yields.

Bonus issue of shares A type of dividend in which a company distributes additional shares of its common stock to shareholders instead of cash.

Book building Investment bankers' process of compiling a "book" or list of indications of interest to buy part of an offering.

Book value The net amount shown for an asset or liability on the balance sheet; book value may also refer to the company's excess of total assets over total liabilities. Also called *carrying value.*

Boom An expansionary phase characterized by economic growth "testing the limits" of the economy.

Bottom-up analysis An investment selection approach that focuses on company-specific circumstances rather than emphasizing economic cycles or industry analysis.

Break point In the context of the weighted average cost of capital (WACC), a break point is the amount of capital at which the cost of one or more of the sources of capital changes, leading to a change in the WACC.

Breakeven point The number of units produced and sold at which the company's net income is zero (Revenues = Total cost); in the case of perfect competition, the quantity at which price, average revenue, and marginal revenue equal average total cost.

Bridge financing Interim financing that provides funds until permanent financing can be arranged.

Broad money Encompasses narrow money plus the entire range of liquid assets that can be used to make purchases.

Broker 1) An agent who executes orders to buy or sell securities on behalf of a client in exchange for a commission. 2) See *futures commission merchants.*

Broker–dealer A financial intermediary (often a company) that may function as a principal (dealer) or as an agent (broker) depending on the type of trade.

Brokered market A market in which brokers arrange trades among their clients.

Budget surplus/deficit The difference between government revenue and expenditure for a stated fixed period of time.

Bullet bond Bond in which the principal repayment is made entirely at maturity.

Business risk The risk associated with operating earnings. Operating earnings are uncertain because total revenues and many of the expenditures contributed to produce those revenues are uncertain.

Buy-side firm An investment management company or other investor that uses the services of brokers or dealers (i.e., the client of the sell side firms).

Buyback A transaction in which a company buys back its own shares. Unlike stock dividends and stock splits, share repurchases use corporate cash.

Call An option that gives the holder the right to buy an underlying asset from another party at a fixed price over a specific period of time.

Call market A market in which trades occur only at a particular time and place (i.e., when the market is called).

Call money rate The interest rate that buyers pay for their margin loan.

Call option An option that gives the holder the right to buy an underlying asset from another party at a fixed price over a specific period of time.

Call protection The time during which the issuer of the bond is not allowed to exercise the call option.

Callable bond A bond containing an embedded call option that gives the issuer the right to buy the bond back from the investor at specified prices on pre-determined dates.

Candlestick chart A price chart with four bits of data for each time interval. A candle indicates the opening and closing price for the interval. The body of the candle is shaded if the opening price was higher than the closing price, and the body is clear if the opening price was lower than the closing price. Vertical lines known as wicks or shadows extend from the top and bottom of the candle to indicate the high and the low prices for the interval.

Cannibalization Cannibalization occurs when an investment takes customers and sales away from another part of the company.

Capacity The ability of the borrower to make its debt payments on time.

Capital account A component of the balance of payments account that measures transfers of capital.

Capital allocation line (CAL) A graph line that describes the combinations of expected return and standard deviation of return available to an investor from combining the optimal portfolio of risky assets with the risk-free asset.

Capital asset pricing model (CAPM) An equation describing the expected return on any asset (or portfolio) as a linear function of its beta relative to the market portfolio.

Capital budgeting The process that companies use for decision making on capital projects—those projects with a life of one year or more.

Capital consumption allowance A measure of the wear and tear (depreciation) of the capital stock that occurs in the production of goods and services.

Capital deepening investment Increases the stock of capital relative to labor.

Capital expenditure Expenditure on physical capital (fixed assets).

Capital lease See *finance lease.*

Capital market expectations An investor's expectations concerning the risk and return prospects of asset classes.

Capital market line (CML) The line with an intercept point equal to the risk-free rate that is tangent to the efficient frontier of risky assets; represents the efficient frontier when a risk-free asset is available for investment.

Capital market securities Securities with maturities at issuance longer than one year.

Capital markets Financial markets that trade securities of longer duration, such as bonds and equities.

Capital rationing A capital rationing environment assumes that the company has a fixed amount of funds to invest.

Capital restrictions Controls placed on foreigners' ability to own domestic assets and/or domestic residents' ability to own foreign assets.

Capital stock The accumulated amount of buildings, machinery, and equipment used to produce goods and services.

Capital structure The mix of debt and equity that a company uses to finance its business; a company's specific mixture of long-term financing.

Captive finance subsidiary A wholly-owned subsidiary of a company that is established to provide financing of the sales of the parent company.

Carry The net of the costs and benefits of holding, storing, or "carrying" an asset.

Carrying amount The amount at which an asset or liability is valued according to accounting principles.

Carrying value The net amount shown for an asset or liability on the balance sheet; book value may also refer to the company's excess of total assets over total liabilities. For a bond, the purchase price plus (or minus) the amortized amount of the discount (or premium).

Cartel Participants in collusive agreements that are made openly and formally.

Cash collateral account Form of external credit enhancement whereby the issuer immediately borrows the credit-enhancement amount and then invests that amount, usually in highly rated short-term commercial paper.

Cash conversion cycle A financial metric that measures the length of time required for a company to convert cash invested in its operations to cash received as a result of its operations; equal to days of inventory on hand + days of sales outstanding – number of days of payables. Also called *net operating cycle.*

Cash flow additivity principle The principle that dollar amounts indexed at the same point in time are additive.

Cash flow from operating activities The net amount of cash provided from operating activities.

Cash flow from operations The net amount of cash provided from operating activities.

Cash flow yield The internal rate of return on a series of cash flows.

Cash market securities Money market securities settled on a "same day" or "cash settlement" basis.

Cash markets See *spot markets.*

Cash prices See *spot prices.*

Cash-settled forwards See *non-deliverable forwards.*

CBOE Volatility Index A measure of near-term market volatility as conveyed by S&P 500 stock index option prices.

Central bank funds market The market in which deposit-taking banks that have an excess reserve with their national central bank can loan money to banks that need funds for maturities ranging from overnight to one year. Called the Federal or Fed funds market in the United States.

Central bank funds rates Interest rates at which central bank funds are bought (borrowed) and sold (lent) for maturities ranging from overnight to one year. Called Federal or Fed funds rates in the United States.

Central banks The dominant bank in a country, usually with official or semi-official governmental status.

Certificate of deposit An instrument that represents a specified amount of funds on deposit with a bank for a specified maturity and interest rate. CDs are issued in various denominations and can be negotiable or non-negotiable.

Change in polarity principle A tenet of technical analysis that once a support level is breached, it becomes a resistance level. The same holds true for resistance levels; once breached, they become support levels.

Change of control put A covenant giving bondholders the right to require the issuer to buy back their debt, often at par or at some small premium to par value, in the event that the borrower is acquired.

Character The quality of a debt issuer's management.

Classified balance sheet A balance sheet organized so as to group together the various assets and liabilities into subcategories (e.g., current and noncurrent).

Clawback A requirement that the general partner return any funds distributed as incentive fees until the limited partners have received back their initial investment and a percentage of the total profit.

Clearing The process by which the exchange verifies the execution of a transaction and records the participants' identities.

Clearing instructions Instructions that indicate how to arrange the final settlement ("clearing") of a trade.

Clearinghouse An entity associated with a futures market that acts as middleman between the contracting parties and guarantees to each party the performance of the other.

Closed economy An economy that does not trade with other countries; an *autarkic economy.*

Closed-end fund A mutual fund in which no new investment money is accepted. New investors invest by buying existing shares, and investors in the fund liquidate by selling their shares to other investors.

Code of ethics An established guide that communicates an organization's values and overall expectations regarding member behavior. A code of ethics serves as a general guide for how community members should act.

Coefficient of variation (CV) The ratio of a set of observations' standard deviation to the observations' mean value.

Coincident economic indicators Turning points that are usually close to those of the overall economy; they are believed to have value for identifying the economy's present state.

Collateral manager Buys and sells debt obligations for and from the CDO's portfolio of assets (i.e., the collateral) to generate sufficient cash flows to meet the obligations to the CDO bondholders.

Collateral trust bonds Bonds secured by securities such as common shares, other bonds, or other financial assets.

Collateralized bond obligations A structured asset-backed security that is collateralized by a pool of bonds.

Collateralized debt obligation Generic term used to describe a security backed by a diversified pool of one or more debt obligations.

Collateralized loan obligations A structured asset-backed security that is collateralized by a pool of loans.

Collateralized mortgage obligation A security created through the securitization of a pool of mortgage-related products (mortgage pass-through securities or pools of loans).

Collaterals Assets or financial guarantees underlying a debt obligation that are above and beyond the issuer's promise to pay.

Combination A listing in which the order of the listed items does not matter.

Commercial paper A short-term, negotiable, unsecured promissory note that represents a debt obligation of the issuer.

Committed capital The amount that the limited partners have agreed to provide to the private equity fund.

Committed lines of credit A bank commitment to extend credit up to a pre-specified amount; the commitment is considered a short-term liability and is usually in effect for 364 days (one day short of a full year).

Commodity swap A swap in which the underlying is a commodity such as oil, gold, or an agricultural product.

Common market Level of economic integration that incorporates all aspects of the customs union and extends it by allowing free movement of factors of production among members.

Common shares A type of security that represent an ownership interest in a company.

Common-size analysis The restatement of financial statement items using a common denominator or reference item that allows one to identify trends and major differences; an example is an income statement in which all items are expressed as a percent of revenue.

Common stock See *common shares.*

Company analysis Analysis of an individual company.

Comparable company A company that has similar business risk; usually in the same industry and preferably with a single line of business.

Comparative advantage A country's ability to produce a good or service at a lower relative cost, or opportunity cost, than its trading partner.

Competitive strategy A company's plans for responding to the threats and opportunities presented by the external environment.

Complements Goods that tend to be used together; technically, two goods whose cross-price elasticity of demand is negative.

Complete markets Informally, markets in which the variety of distinct securities traded is so broad that any desired payoff in a future state-of-the-world is achievable.

Component cost of capital The rate of return required by suppliers of capital for an individual source of a company's funding, such as debt or equity.

Compounding The process of accumulating interest on interest.

Comprehensive income The change in equity of a business enterprise during a period from nonowner sources; includes all changes in equity during a period except those resulting from investments by owners and distributions to owners; comprehensive income equals net income plus other comprehensive income.

Conditional expected value The expected value of a stated event given that another event has occurred.

Conditional probability The probability of an event given (conditioned on) another event.

Conditional variances The variance of one variable, given the outcome of another.

Consistent With reference to estimators, describes an estimator for which the probability of estimates close to the value of the population parameter increases as sample size increases.

Constant-yield price trajectory A graph that illustrates the change in the price of a fixed-income bond over time assuming no change in yield-to-maturity. The trajectory shows the "pull to par" effect on the price of a bond trading at a premium or a discount to par value.

Constituent securities With respect to an index, the individual securities within an index.

Consumer surplus The difference between the value that a consumer places on units purchased and the amount of money that was required to pay for them.

Contingency provision Clause in a legal document that allows for some action if a specific event or circumstance occurs.

Contingent claims Derivatives in which the payoffs occur if a specific event occurs; generally referred to as options.

Contingent convertible bonds Bonds that automatically convert into equity if a specific event or circumstance occurs, such as the issuer's equity capital falling below the minimum requirement set by the regulators. Also called *CoCos.*

Continuation patterns A type of pattern used in technical analysis to predict the resumption of a market trend that was in place prior to the formation of a pattern.

Continuous random variable A random variable for which the range of possible outcomes is the real line (all real numbers between $-\infty$ and $+\infty$ or some subset of the real line).

Continuous time Time thought of as advancing in extremely small increments.

Continuous trading market A market in which trades can be arranged and executed any time the market is open.

Continuously compounded return The natural logarithm of 1 plus the holding period return, or equivalently, the natural logarithm of the ending price over the beginning price.

Contra account An account that offsets another account.

Contract rate See *mortgage rate.*

Contraction The period of a business cycle after the peak and before the trough; often called a *recession* or, if exceptionally severe, called a *depression.*

Contraction risk The risk that when interest rates decline, the security will have a shorter maturity than was anticipated at the time of purchase because borrowers refinance at the new, lower interest rates.

Contractionary Tending to cause the real economy to contract.

Contractionary fiscal policy A fiscal policy that has the objective to make the real economy contract.

Contracts for differences See *non-deliverable forwards.*

Contribution margin The amount available for fixed costs and profit after paying variable costs; revenue minus variable costs.

Controlling shareholders A particular shareholder or block of shareholders holding a percentage of shares that gives them significant voting power.

Convenience yield A non-monetary advantage of holding an asset.

Conventional bond See *plain vanilla bond.*

Conventional cash flow A conventional cash flow pattern is one with an initial outflow followed by a series of inflows.

Convergence The tendency for differences in output per capita across countries to diminish over time; in technical analysis, a term that describes the case when an indicator moves in the same manner as the security being analyzed.

Conversion price For a convertible bond, the price per share at which the bond can be converted into shares.

Conversion ratio For a convertible bond, the number of common shares that each bond can be converted into.

Conversion value For a convertible bond, the current share price multiplied by the conversion ratio.

Convertible bond Bond that gives the bondholder the right to exchange the bond for a specified number of common shares in the issuing company.

Convertible preference shares A type of equity security that entitles shareholders to convert their shares into a specified number of common shares.

Convexity adjustment For a bond, one half of the annual or approximate convexity statistic multiplied by the change in the yield-to-maturity squared.

Core inflation The inflation rate calculated based on a price index of goods and services except food and energy.

Corporate governance The system of internal controls and procedures by which individual companies are managed.

Correlation A number between −1 and +1 that measures the comovement (linear association) between two random variables.

Correlation coefficient A number between −1 and +1 that measures the consistency or tendency for two investments to act in a similar way. It is used to determine the effect on portfolio risk when two assets are combined.

Cost averaging The periodic investment of a fixed amount of money.

Cost of capital The rate of return that suppliers of capital require as compensation for their contribution of capital.

Cost of carry See *carry.*

Cost of debt The cost of debt financing to a company, such as when it issues a bond or takes out a bank loan.

Cost of preferred stock The cost to a company of issuing preferred stock; the dividend yield that a company must commit to pay preferred stockholders.

Cost-push Type of inflation in which rising costs, usually wages, compel businesses to raise prices generally.

Cost structure The mix of a company's variable costs and fixed costs.

Counterparty risk The risk that the other party to a contract will fail to honor the terms of the contract.

Coupon rate The interest rate promised in a contract; this is the rate used to calculate the periodic interest payments.

Cournot assumption Assumption in which each firm determines its profit-maximizing production level assuming that the other firms' output will not change.

Covariance A measure of the co-movement (linear association) between two random variables.

Covariance matrix A matrix or square array whose entries are covariances; also known as a variance–covariance matrix.

Covenants The terms and conditions of lending agreements that the issuer must comply with; they specify the actions that an issuer is obligated to perform (affirmative covenant) or prohibited from performing (negative covenant).

Covered bond Debt obligation secured by a segregated pool of assets called the cover pool. The issuer must maintain the value of the cover pool. In the event of default, bondholders have recourse against both the issuer and the cover pool.

Credit analysis The evaluation of credit risk; the evaluation of the creditworthiness of a borrower or counterparty.

Credit curve A curve showing the relationship between time to maturity and yield spread for an issuer with comparable bonds of various maturities outstanding, usually upward sloping.

Credit default swap (CDS) A type of credit derivative in which one party, the credit protection buyer who is seeking credit protection against a third party, makes a series of regularly scheduled payments to the other party, the credit protection seller. The seller makes no payments until a credit event occurs.

Credit derivatives A contract in which one party has the right to claim a payment from another party in the event that a specific credit event occurs over the life of the contract.

Credit enhancements Provisions that may be used to reduce the credit risk of a bond issue.

Credit-linked coupon bond Bond for which the coupon changes when the bond's credit rating changes.

Credit-linked note (CLN) Fixed-income security in which the holder of the security has the right to withhold payment of the full amount due at maturity if a credit event occurs.

Credit migration risk The risk that a bond issuer's creditworthiness deteriorates, or migrates lower, leading investors to believe the risk of default is higher. Also called *downgrade risk.*

Credit risk The risk of loss caused by a counterparty's or debtor's failure to make a promised payment. Also called *default risk.*

Credit scoring model A statistical model used to classify borrowers according to creditworthiness.

Credit spread option An option on the yield spread on a bond.

Credit tranching A structure used to redistribute the credit risk associated with the collateral; a set of bond classes created to allow investors a choice in the amount of credit risk that they prefer to bear.

Credit-worthiness The perceived ability of the borrower to pay what is owed on the borrowing in a timely manner; it represents the ability of a company to withstand adverse impacts on its cash flows.

Cross-default provisions Provisions whereby events of default such as non-payment of interest on one bond trigger default on all outstanding debt; implies the same default probability for all issues.

Cross-price elasticity of demand The percentage change in quantity demanded for a given percentage change in the price of another good; the responsiveness of the demand for Product A that is associated with the change in price of Product B.

Cross-sectional analysis Analysis that involves comparisons across individuals in a group over a given time period or at a given point in time.

Cross-sectional data Observations over individual units at a point in time, as opposed to time-series data.

Crossing networks Trading systems that match buyers and sellers who are willing to trade at prices obtained from other markets.

Crowding out The thesis that government borrowing may divert private sector investment from taking place.

Cryptocurrency An electronic medium of exchange that lacks physical form.

Cryptography An algorithmic process to encrypt data, making the data unusable if received by unauthorized parties.

Cumulative distribution function A function giving the probability that a random variable is less than or equal to a specified value.

Cumulative preference shares Preference shares for which any dividends that are not paid accrue and must be paid in full before dividends on common shares can be paid.

Cumulative relative frequency For data grouped into intervals, the fraction of total observations that are less than the value of the upper limit of a stated interval.

Cumulative voting A voting process whereby each shareholder can accumulate and vote all his or her shares for a single candidate in an election, as opposed to having to allocate their voting rights evenly among all candidates.

Currencies Monies issued by national monetary authorities.

Currency option bonds Bonds that give the bondholder the right to choose the currency in which he or she wants to receive interest payments and principal repayments.

Currency swap A swap in which each party makes interest payments to the other in different currencies.

Current account A component of the balance of payments account that measures the flow of goods and services.

Current assets Assets that are expected to be consumed or converted into cash in the near future, typically one year or less. *Also called liquid assets.*

Current cost With reference to assets, the amount of cash or cash equivalents that would have to be paid to buy the same or an equivalent asset today; with reference to liabilities, the undiscounted amount of cash or cash equivalents that would be required to settle the obligation today.

Current government spending With respect to government expenditures, spending on goods and services that are provided on a regular, recurring basis including health, education, and defense.

Current liabilities Short-term obligations, such as accounts payable, wages payable, or accrued liabilities, that are expected to be settled in the near future, typically one year or less.

Current ratio A liquidity ratio calculated as current assets divided by current liabilities.

Current yield The sum of the coupon payments received over the year divided by the flat price; also called the *income* or *interest yield* or *running yield.*

Curve duration The sensitivity of the bond price (or the market value of a financial asset or liability) with respect to a benchmark yield curve.

Customs union Extends the free trade area (FTA) by not only allowing free movement of goods and services among members, but also creating a common trade policy against nonmembers.

CVaR Conditional VaR, a tail loss measure. The weighted average of all loss outcomes in the statistical distribution that exceed the VaR loss.

Cyclical See *cyclical companies.*

Cyclical companies Companies with sales and profits that regularly expand and contract with the business cycle or state of economy.

Daily settlement See *mark to market* and *marking to market.*

Dark pools Alternative trading systems that do not display the orders that their clients send to them.

Data mining The practice of determining a model by extensive searching through a dataset for statistically significant patterns. Also called *data snooping.*

Data science An interdisciplinary field that brings computer science, statistics, and other disciplines together to analyze and produce insights from Big Data.

Data snooping See *data mining.*

Day order An order that is good for the day on which it is submitted. If it has not been filled by the close of business, the order expires unfilled.

Day's sales outstanding Estimate of the average number of days it takes to collect on credit accounts.

Days in receivables Estimate of the average number of days it takes to collect on credit accounts.

Days of inventory on hand An activity ratio equal to the number of days in the period divided by inventory turnover over the period.

Dealers A financial intermediary that acts as a principal in trades.

Dealing securities Securities held by banks or other financial intermediaries for trading purposes.

Death cross A technical analysis term that describes a situation where a short-term moving average crosses from above a longer-term moving average to below it; this movement is considered bearish.

Debentures Type of bond that can be secured or unsecured.

Debt incurrence test A financial covenant made in conjunction with existing debt that restricts a company's ability to incur additional debt at the same seniority based on one or more financial tests or conditions.

Debt-rating approach A method for estimating a company's before-tax cost of debt based upon the yield on comparably rated bonds for maturities that closely match that of the company's existing debt.

Debt-to-assets ratio A solvency ratio calculated as total debt divided by total assets.

Debt-to-capital ratio A solvency ratio calculated as total debt divided by total debt plus total shareholders' equity.

Debt-to-equity ratio A solvency ratio calculated as total debt divided by total shareholders' equity.

Declaration date The day that the corporation issues a statement declaring a specific dividend.

Decreasing returns to scale When a production process leads to increases in output that are proportionately smaller than the increase in inputs.

Deductible temporary differences Temporary differences that result in a reduction of or deduction from taxable income in a future period when the balance sheet item is recovered or settled.

Deep learning Machine learning using neural networks with many hidden layers.

Deep learning nets Machine learning using neural networks with many hidden layers.

Default probability The probability that a borrower defaults or fails to meet its obligation to make full and timely payments of principal and interest, according to the terms of the debt security. Also called *default risk.*

Default risk The probability that a borrower defaults or fails to meet its obligation to make full and timely payments of principal and interest, according to the terms of the debt security. Also called *default probability.*

Default risk premium An extra return that compensates investors for the possibility that the borrower will fail to make a promised payment at the contracted time and in the contracted amount.

Defensive companies Companies with sales and profits that have little sensitivity to the business cycle or state of the economy.

Defensive interval ratio A liquidity ratio that estimates the number of days that an entity could meet cash needs from liquid assets; calculated as (cash + short-term marketable investments + receivables) divided by daily cash expenditures.

Deferred coupon bond Bond that pays no coupons for its first few years but then pays a higher coupon than it otherwise normally would for the remainder of its life. Also called *split coupon bond.*

Deferred income A liability account for money that has been collected for goods or services that have not yet been delivered; payment received in advance of providing a good or service.

Deferred revenue A liability account for money that has been collected for goods or services that have not yet been delivered; payment received in advance of providing a good or service.

Deferred tax assets A balance sheet asset that arises when an excess amount is paid for income taxes relative to accounting profit. The taxable income is higher than accounting profit and income tax payable exceeds tax expense. The company expects to recover the difference during the course of future operations when tax expense exceeds income tax payable.

Deferred tax liabilities A balance sheet liability that arises when a deficit amount is paid for income taxes relative to accounting profit. The taxable income is less than the accounting profit and income tax payable is less than tax expense. The company expects to eliminate the liability over the course of future operations when income tax payable exceeds tax expense.

Defined benefit pension plans Plans in which the company promises to pay a certain annual amount (defined benefit) to the employee after retirement. The company bears the investment risk of the plan assets.

Defined contribution pension plans Individual accounts to which an employee and typically the employer makes contributions during their working years and expect to draw on the accumulated funds at retirement. The employee bears the investment and inflation risk of the plan assets.

Deflation Negative inflation.

Degree of confidence The probability that a confidence interval includes the unknown population parameter.

Degree of financial leverage (DFL) The ratio of the percentage change in net income to the percentage change in operating income; the sensitivity of the cash flows available to owners when operating income changes.

Degree of operating leverage (DOL) The ratio of the percentage change in operating income to the percentage change in units sold; the sensitivity of operating income to changes in units sold.

Degree of total leverage The ratio of the percentage change in net income to the percentage change in units sold; the sensitivity of the cash flows to owners to changes in the number of units produced and sold.

Degrees of freedom (df) The number of independent observations used.

Delta The sensitivity of the derivative price to a small change in the value of the underlying asset.

Demand curve Graph of the inverse demand function. A graph showing the demand relation, either the highest quantity willingly purchased at each price or the highest price willingly paid for each quantity.

Demand function A relationship that expresses the quantity demanded of a good or service as a function of own-price and possibly other variables.

Demand-pull Type of inflation in which increasing demand raises prices generally, which then are reflected in a business's costs as workers demand wage hikes to catch up with the rising cost of living.

Demand shock A typically unexpected disturbance to demand, such as an unexpected interruption in trade or transportation.

Dependent With reference to events, the property that the probability of one event occurring depends on (is related to) the occurrence of another event.

Depository bank A bank that raises funds from depositors and other investors and lends it to borrowers.

Depository institutions Commercial banks, savings and loan banks, credit unions, and similar institutions that raise funds from depositors and other investors and lend it to borrowers.

Depository receipt A security that trades like an ordinary share on a local exchange and represents an economic interest in a foreign company.

Depreciation The process of systematically allocating the cost of long-lived (tangible) assets to the periods during which the assets are expected to provide economic benefits.

Depression See *contraction.*

Derivative pricing rule A pricing rule used by crossing networks in which a price is taken (derived) from the price that is current in the asset's primary market.

Derivatives A financial instrument whose value depends on the value of some underlying asset or factor (e.g., a stock price, an interest rate, or exchange rate).

Descriptive statistics The study of how data can be summarized effectively.

Development capital Minority equity investments in more mature companies that are seeking capital to expand or restructure operations, enter new markets, or finance major acquisitions.

Diffuse prior The assumption of equal prior probabilities.

Diffusion index Reflects the proportion of the index's components that are moving in a pattern consistent with the overall index.

Diluted EPS The EPS that would result if all dilutive securities were converted into common shares.

Diluted shares The number of shares that would be outstanding if all potentially dilutive claims on common shares (e.g., convertible debt, convertible preferred stock, and employee stock options) were exercised.

Diminishing balance method An accelerated depreciation method, i.e., one that allocates a relatively large proportion of the cost of an asset to the early years of the asset's useful life.

Diminishing marginal productivity Describes a state in which each additional unit of input produces less output than previously.

Direct debit program An arrangement whereby a customer authorizes a debit to a demand account; typically used by companies to collect routine payments for services.

Direct financing leases Under US GAAP, a type of finance lease, from a lessor perspective, where the present value of the lease payments (lease receivable) equals the carrying value of the leased asset. No selling profit is recognized at lease inception. The revenues earned by the lessor are financing in nature.

Direct format With reference to the cash flow statement, a format for the presentation of the statement in which cash flow from operating activities is shown as operating cash receipts less operating cash disbursements. Also called *direct method.*

Direct method See *direct format.*

Direct taxes Taxes levied directly on income, wealth, and corporate profits.

Direct write-off method An approach to recognizing credit losses on customer receivables in which the company waits until such time as a customer has defaulted and only then recognizes the loss.

Disbursement float The amount of time between check issuance and a check's clearing back against the company's account.

Discount To reduce the value of a future payment in allowance for how far away it is in time; to calculate the present value of some future amount. Also, the amount by which an instrument is priced below its face (par) value.

Discount interest A procedure for determining the interest on a loan or bond in which the interest is deducted from the face value in advance.

Discount margin See *required margin.*

Discount rates In general, the interest rate used to calculate a present value. In the money market, however, discount rate is a specific type of quoted rate.

Discounted cash flow models Valuation models that estimate the intrinsic value of a security as the present value of the future benefits expected to be received from the security.

Discounted payback period the number of years it takes for the cumulative discounted cash flows from a project to equal the original investment.

Discouraged worker A person who has stopped looking for a job or has given up seeking employment.

Discrete random variable A random variable that can take on at most a countable number of possible values.

Discriminatory pricing rule A pricing rule used in continuous markets in which the limit price of the order or quote that first arrived determines the trade price.

Diseconomies of scale Increase in cost per unit resulting from increased production.

Dispersion The variability around the central tendency.

Display size The size of an order displayed to public view.

Distressed investing Investing in securities of companies in financial difficulty. Private equity funds that specialize in distressed investing typically buy the debt of mature companies in financial difficulty.

Distributed ledger A type of database that may be shared among entities in a network.

Distributed ledger technology Technology based on a distributed ledger.

Divergence In technical analysis, a term that describes the case when an indicator moves differently from the security being analyzed.

Diversification ratio The ratio of the standard deviation of an equally weighted portfolio to the standard deviation of a randomly selected security.

Dividend A distribution paid to shareholders based on the number of shares owned.

Dividend discount model (DDM) A present value model that estimates the intrinsic value of an equity share based on the present value of its expected future dividends.

Dividend discount model based approach An approach for estimating a country's equity risk premium. The market rate of return is estimated as the sum of the dividend yield and the growth rate in dividends for a market index. Subtracting the risk-free rate of return from the estimated market return produces an estimate for the equity risk premium.

Dividend payout ratio The ratio of cash dividends paid to earnings for a period.

Divisor A number (denominator) used to determine the value of a price return index. It is initially chosen at the inception of an index and subsequently adjusted by the index provider, as necessary, to avoid changes in the index value that are unrelated to changes in the prices of its constituent securities.

Domestic content provisions Stipulate that some percentage of the value added or components used in production should be of domestic origin.

Double bottoms In technical analysis, a reversal pattern that is formed when the price reaches a low, rebounds, and then sells off back to the first low level; used to predict a change from a downtrend to an uptrend.

Double coincidence of wants A prerequisite to barter trades, in particular that both economic agents in the transaction want what the other is selling.

Double declining balance depreciation An accelerated depreciation method that involves depreciating the asset at double the straight-line rate. This rate is multiplied by the book value of the asset at the beginning of the period (a declining balance) to calculate depreciation expense.

Double top In technical analysis, a reversal pattern that is formed when an uptrend reverses twice at roughly the same high price level; used to predict a change from an uptrend to a downtrend.

Down transition probability The probability that an asset's value moves down in a model of asset price dynamics.

Downgrade risk The risk that a bond issuer's creditworthiness deteriorates, or migrates lower, leading investors to believe the risk of default is higher. Also called *credit migration risk.*

Drag on liquidity When receipts lag, creating pressure from the decreased available funds.

Drawdown A percentage peak-to-trough reduction in net asset value.

Dual-currency bonds Bonds that make coupon payments in one currency and pay the par value at maturity in another currency.

DuPont analysis An approach to decomposing return on investment, e.g., return on equity, as the product of other financial ratios.

Duration A measure of the approximate sensitivity of a security to a change in interest rates (i.e., a measure of interest rate risk).

Duration gap A bond's Macaulay duration minus the investment horizon.

Dutch Book theorem A result in probability theory stating that inconsistent probabilities create profit opportunities.

Early repayment option See *prepayment option.*

Earnings per share The amount of income earned during a period per share of common stock.

Earnings surprise The portion of a company's earnings that is unanticipated by investors and, according to the efficient market hypothesis, merits a price adjustment.

Economic costs All the remuneration needed to keep a productive resource in its current employment or to acquire the resource for productive use; the sum of total accounting costs and implicit opportunity costs.

Economic indicator A variable that provides information on the state of the overall economy.

Economic loss The amount by which accounting profit is less than normal profit.

Economic order quantity–reorder point (EOQ–ROP) An approach to managing inventory based on expected demand and the predictability of demand; the ordering point for new inventory is determined based on the costs of ordering and carrying inventory, such that the total cost associated with inventory is minimized.

Economic profit Equal to accounting profit less the implicit opportunity costs not included in total accounting costs; the difference between total revenue (TR) and total cost (TC). Also called *abnormal profit* or *supernormal profit*.

Economic stabilization Reduction of the magnitude of economic fluctuations.

Economic union Incorporates all aspects of a common market and in addition requires common economic institutions and coordination of economic policies among members.

Economies of scale Reduction in cost per unit resulting from increased production.

Effective annual rate The amount by which a unit of currency will grow in a year with interest on interest included.

Effective convexity A *curve convexity* statistic that measures the secondary effect of a change in a benchmark yield curve on a bond's price.

Effective duration The sensitivity of a bond's price to a change in a benchmark yield curve.

Effective interest rate The borrowing rate or market rate that a company incurs at the time of issuance of a bond.

Efficient market A market in which asset prices reflect new information quickly and rationally.

Elastic Said of a good or service when the magnitude of elasticity is greater than one.

Elasticity The percentage change in one variable for a percentage change in another variable; a general measure of how sensitive one variable is to a change in the value of another variable.

Elasticity of demand A measure of the sensitivity of quantity demanded to a change in a product's own price: $\%\Delta Q^D/\%\Delta P$.

Elasticity of supply A measure of the sensitivity of quantity supplied to a change in price: $\%\Delta Q^S/\%\Delta P$.

Electronic communications networks See *alternative trading systems*.

Electronic funds transfer (EFT) The use of computer networks to conduct financial transactions electronically.

Elliott wave theory A technical analysis theory that claims that the market follows regular, repeated waves or cycles.

Embedded option Contingency provisions that provide the issuer or the bondholders the right, but not the obligation, to take action. These options are not part of the security and cannot be traded separately.

Empirical probability The probability of an event estimated as a relative frequency of occurrence.

Employed The number of people with a job.

Engagement/active ownership An ESG investment style that uses shareholder power to influence corporate behavior through direct corporate engagement (i.e., communicating with senior management and/or boards of companies), filing or co-filing shareholder proposals, and proxy voting that is directed by ESG guidelines.

Enterprise risk management An overall assessment of a company's risk position. A centralized approach to risk management sometimes called firmwide risk management.

Enterprise value A measure of a company's total market value from which the value of cash and short-term investments have been subtracted.

Equal weighting An index weighting method in which an equal weight is assigned to each constituent security at inception.

Equipment trust certificates Bonds secured by specific types of equipment or physical assets.

Equity Assets less liabilities; the residual interest in the assets after subtracting the liabilities.

Equity risk premium The expected return on equities minus the risk-free rate; the premium that investors demand for investing in equities.

Equity swap A swap transaction in which at least one cash flow is tied to the return to an equity portfolio position, often an equity index.

ESG An acronym that encompasses environmental, social and governance.

ESG integration The integration of qualitative and quantitative environmental, social, and governance factors into traditional security and industry analysis; also known as *ESG incorporation*.

ESG investing The consideration of environmental, social, and governance factors in the investment process.

Estimate The particular value calculated from sample observations using an estimator.

Estimation With reference to statistical inference, the subdivision dealing with estimating the value of a population parameter.

Estimator An estimation formula; the formula used to compute the sample mean and other sample statistics are examples of estimators.

Ethical principles Beliefs regarding what is good, acceptable, or obligatory behavior and what is bad, unacceptable, or forbidden behavior.

Ethics The study of moral principles or of making good choices. Ethics encompasses a set of moral principles and rules of conduct that provide guidance for our behavior.

Eurobonds Type of bond issued internationally, outside the jurisdiction of the country in whose currency the bond is denominated.

European option An option that can only be exercised on its expiration date.

European-style Said of an option contract that can only be exercised on the option's expiration date.

Event Any outcome or specified set of outcomes of a random variable.

Ex-dividend date The first date that a share trades without (i.e., "ex") the dividend.

Excess kurtosis Degree of kurtosis (fatness of tails) in excess of the kurtosis of the normal distribution.

Exchanges Places where traders can meet to arrange their trades.

Exclusionary screening An ESG implementation approach that excludes certain sectors or companies that deviate from an investor's accepted standards. Also called *negative screening* or *norms-based screening*.

Execution instructions Instructions that indicate how to fill an order.

Exercise The process of using an option to buy or sell the underlying.

Exercise price The fixed price at which an option holder can buy or sell the underlying. Also called *strike price, striking price*, or *strike*.

Exercise value The value obtained if an option is exercised based on current conditions. Also known as *intrinsic value*.

Exhaustive Covering or containing all possible outcomes.

Expansion The period of a business cycle after its lowest point and before its highest point.

Expansionary Tending to cause the real economy to grow.

Expansionary fiscal policy Fiscal policy aimed at achieving real economic growth.

Expected inflation The level of inflation that economic agents expect in the future.

Expected loss Default probability times Loss severity given default.

Expected value The probability-weighted average of the possible outcomes of a random variable.

Expenses Outflows of economic resources or increases in liabilities that result in decreases in equity (other than decreases because of distributions to owners); reductions in net assets associated with the creation of revenues.

Experience curve A curve that shows the direct cost per unit of good or service produced or delivered as a typically declining function of cumulative output.

Export subsidy Paid by the government to the firm when it exports a unit of a good that is being subsidized.

Exports Goods and services that an economy sells to other countries.

Extension risk The risk that when interest rates rise, fewer prepayments will occur because homeowners are reluctant to give up the benefits of a contractual interest rate that now looks low. As a result, the security becomes longer in maturity than anticipated at the time of purchase.

Externality An effect of a market transaction that is borne by parties other than those who transacted.

Extra dividend A dividend paid by a company that does not pay dividends on a regular schedule, or a dividend that supplements regular cash dividends with an extra payment.

Extreme value theory A branch of statistics that focuses primarily on extreme outcomes.

Face value The amount of cash payable by a company to the bondholders when the bonds mature; the promised payment at maturity separate from any coupon payment.

Factor A common or underlying element with which several variables are correlated.

Fair value The amount at which an asset could be exchanged, or a liability settled, between knowledgeable, willing parties in an arm's-length transaction; the price that would be received to sell an asset or paid to transfer a liability in an orderly transaction between market participants.

Fed funds rate The US interbank lending rate on overnight borrowings of reserves.

Federal funds rate The US interbank lending rate on overnight borrowings of reserves.

Fiat money Money that is not convertible into any other commodity.

Fibonacci sequence A sequence of numbers starting with 0 and 1, and then each subsequent number in the sequence is the sum of the two preceding numbers. In Elliott Wave Theory, it is believed that market waves follow patterns that are the ratios of the numbers in the Fibonacci sequence.

Fiduciary call A combination of a European call and a risk-free bond that matures on the option expiration day and has a face value equal to the exercise price of the call.

FIFO method The first in, first out, method of accounting for inventory, which matches sales against the costs of items of inventory in the order in which they were placed in inventory.

Fill or kill See *immediate or cancel order*.

Finance lease From the lessee perspective, under US GAAP, a type of lease which is more akin to the purchase of an asset by the lessee. From the lessor perspective, under IFRS, a lease which "transfers substantially all the risks and rewards incidental to ownership of an underlying asset."

Financial account A component of the balance of payments account that records investment flows.

Financial flexibility The ability to react and adapt to financial adversity and opportunities.

Financial leverage The extent to which a company can effect, through the use of debt, a proportional change in the return on common equity that is greater than a given proportional change in operating income; also, short for the financial leverage ratio.

Financial leverage ratio A measure of financial leverage calculated as average total assets divided by average total equity.

Financial risk The risk that environmental, social, or governance risk factors will result in significant costs or other losses to a company and its shareholders; the risk arising from a company's obligation to meet required payments under its financing agreements.

Financing activities Activities related to obtaining or repaying capital to be used in the business (e.g., equity and long-term debt).

Fintech Technological innovation in the design and delivery of financial services and products in the financial industry.

Firm commitment offering See *underwritten offering*.

First-degree price discrimination Where a monopolist is able to charge each customer the highest price the customer is willing to pay.

First lien debt Debt secured by a pledge of certain assets that could include buildings, but may also include property and equipment, licenses, patents, brands, etc.

First mortgage debt Debt secured by a pledge of a specific property.

Fiscal multiplier The ratio of a change in national income to a change in government spending.

Fiscal policy The use of taxes and government spending to affect the level of aggregate expenditures.

Fisher effect The thesis that the real rate of interest in an economy is stable over time so that changes in nominal interest rates are the result of changes in expected inflation.

Fisher index The geometric mean of the Laspeyres index.

Fixed charge coverage A solvency ratio measuring the number of times interest and lease payments are covered by operating income, calculated as (EBIT + lease payments) divided by (interest payments + lease payments).

Fixed costs Costs that remain at the same level regardless of a company's level of production and sales.

Fixed-for-floating interest rate swap An interest rate swap in which one party pays a fixed rate and the other pays a floating rate, with both sets of payments in the same currency. Also called *plain vanilla swap* or *vanilla swap*.

Fixed rate perpetual preferred stock Nonconvertible, noncallable preferred stock that has a fixed dividend rate and no maturity date.

Flags A technical analysis continuation pattern formed by parallel trendlines, typically over a short period.

Flat price The full price of a bond minus the accrued interest; also called the *quoted* or *clean* price.

Float In the context of customer receipts, the amount of money that is in transit between payments made by customers and the funds that are usable by the company.

Float-adjusted market-capitalization weighting An index weighting method in which the weight assigned to each constituent security is determined by adjusting its market capitalization for its market float.

Float factor An estimate of the average number of days it takes deposited checks to clear; average daily float divided by average daily deposit.

Floaters See *floating-rate notes*.

Floating-rate notes A note on which interest payments are not fixed, but instead vary from period to period depending on the current level of a reference interest rate.

Flotation cost Fees charged to companies by investment bankers and other costs associated with raising new capital.

Foreclosure Allows the lender to take possession of a mortgaged property if the borrower defaults and then sell it to recover funds.

Foreign currency reserves Holding by the central bank of non-domestic currency deposits and non-domestic bonds.

Foreign direct investment Direct investment by a firm in one country (the source country) in productive assets in a foreign country (the host country).

Foreign exchange gains (or losses) Gains (or losses) that occur when the exchange rate changes between the investor's currency and the currency that foreign securities are denominated in.

Foreign portfolio investment Shorter-term investment by individuals, firms, and institutional investors (e.g., pension funds) in foreign financial instruments such as foreign stocks and foreign government bonds.

Forward commitments Class of derivatives that provides the ability to lock in a price to transact in the future at a previously agreed-upon price.

Forward contract An agreement between two parties in which one party, the buyer, agrees to buy from the other party, the seller, an underlying asset at a later date for a price established at the start of the contract.

Forward curve A series of forward rates, each having the same timeframe.

Forward market For future delivery, beyond the usual settlement time period in the cash market.

Forward price The fixed price or rate at which the transaction scheduled to occur at the expiration of a forward contract will take place. This price is agreed on at the initiation date of the contract.

Forward rate The interest rate on a bond or money market instrument traded in a forward market. A forward rate can be interpreted as an incremental, or marginal, return for extending the time-to-maturity for an additional time period.

Forward rate agreements A forward contract calling for one party to make a fixed interest payment and the other to make an interest payment at a rate to be determined at the contract expiration.

Fractile A value at or below which a stated fraction of the data lies.

Fractional reserve banking Banking in which reserves constitute a fraction of deposits.

Free cash flow The actual cash that would be available to the company's investors after making all investments necessary to maintain the company as an ongoing enterprise (also referred to as free cash flow to the firm); the internally generated funds that can be distributed to the company's investors (e.g., shareholders and bondholders) without impairing the value of the company.

Free cash flow to equity (FCFE) The cash flow available to a company's common shareholders after all operating expenses, interest, and principal payments have been made, and necessary investments in working and fixed capital have been made.

Free-cash-flow-to-equity models Valuation models based on discounting expected future free cash flow to equity.

Free cash flow to the firm (FCFF) The cash flow available to the company's suppliers of capital after all operating expenses have been paid and necessary investments in working capital and fixed capital have been made.

Free float The number of shares that are readily and freely tradable in the secondary market.

Free trade When there are no government restrictions on a country's ability to trade.

Free trade areas One of the most prevalent forms of regional integration, in which all barriers to the flow of goods and services among members have been eliminated.

Frequency distribution A tabular display of data summarized into a relatively small number of intervals.

Frequency polygon A graph of a frequency distribution obtained by drawing straight lines joining successive points representing the class frequencies.

Full integration An ESG investment style that focuses on the explicit inclusion of ESG factors into the traditional financial analysis of individual stocks for the purpose of valuation (e.g., as inputs into cash flow forecasts and/or cost-of-capital estimates).

Full price The price of a security with accrued interest; also called the *invoice* or *dirty* price.

Fundamental analysis The examination of publicly available information and the formulation of forecasts to estimate the intrinsic value of assets.

Fundamental value The underlying or true value of an asset based on an analysis of its qualitative and quantitative characteristics. Also called *intrinsic value*.

Fundamental weighting An index weighting method in which the weight assigned to each constituent security is based on its underlying company's size. It attempts to address the disadvantages of market-capitalization weighting by using measures that are independent of the constituent security's price.

Funds of hedge funds Funds that hold a portfolio of hedge funds, more commonly shortened to *funds of funds*.

Future value (FV) The amount to which a payment or series of payments will grow by a stated future date.

Futures contract A variation of a forward contract that has essentially the same basic definition but with some additional features, such as a clearinghouse guarantee against credit losses, a daily settlement of gains and losses, and an organized electronic or floor trading facility.

Futures price The agreed-upon price of a futures contract.

FX swap The combination of a spot and a forward FX transaction.

G-spread The yield spread in basis points over an actual or interpolated government bond.

Gains Asset inflows not directly related to the ordinary activities of the business.

Game theory The set of tools decision makers use to incorporate responses by rival decision makers into their strategies.

Gamma A numerical measure of how sensitive an option's delta (the sensitivity of the derivative's price) is to a change in the value of the underlying.

GDP deflator A gauge of prices and inflation that measures the aggregate changes in prices across the overall economy.

General partner The partner that runs the business and ultimately bears unlimited liability for the business's debts and obligations.

Geometric mean A measure of central tendency computed by taking the *n*th root of the product of *n* non-negative values.

Giffen goods Goods that are consumed more as the price of the good rises because it is a very inferior good whose income effect overwhelms its substitution effect when price changes.

Gilts Bonds issued by the UK government.

Giro system An electronic payment system used widely in Europe and Japan.

Global depository receipt A depository receipt that is issued outside of the company's home country and outside of the United States.

Global minimum-variance portfolio The portfolio on the minimum-variance frontier with the smallest variance of return.

Global registered share A common share that is traded on different stock exchanges around the world in different currencies.

Gold standard With respect to a currency, if a currency is on the gold standard a given amount can be converted into a prespecified amount of gold.

Golden cross A technical analysis term that describes a situation where a short-term moving average crosses from below a longer-term moving average to above it; this movement is considered bullish.

Good-on-close An execution instruction specifying that an order can only be filled at the close of trading. Also called *market on close.*

Good-on-open An execution instruction specifying that an order can only be filled at the opening of trading.

Good-till-cancelled order An order specifying that it is valid until the entity placing the order has cancelled it (or, commonly, until some specified amount of time such as 60 days has elapsed, whichever comes sooner).

Goodwill An intangible asset that represents the excess of the purchase price of an acquired company over the value of the net assets acquired.

Government equivalent yield A yield that restates a yield-to-maturity based on 30/360 day-count to one based on actual/actual.

Green bonds A bond used in green finance whereby the proceeds are earmarked towards environmental-related products.

Green finance A type of finance that addresses environmental concerns while achieving economic growth.

Grey market The forward market for bonds about to be issued. Also called "when issued" market.

Gross domestic product The market value of all final goods and services produced within the economy in a given period of time (output definition) or, equivalently, the aggregate income earned by all households, all companies, and the government within the economy in a given period of time (income definition).

Gross margin Sales minus the cost of sales (i.e., the cost of goods sold for a manufacturing company).

Gross profit Sales minus the cost of sales (i.e., the cost of goods sold for a manufacturing company).

Gross profit margin The ratio of gross profit to revenues.

Grouping by function With reference to the presentation of expenses in an income statement, the grouping together of expenses serving the same function, e.g. all items that are costs of goods sold.

Grouping by nature With reference to the presentation of expenses in an income statement, the grouping together of expenses by similar nature, e.g., all depreciation expenses.

Growth cyclical A term sometimes used to describe companies that are growing rapidly on a long-term basis but that still experience above-average fluctuation in their revenues and profits over the course of a business cycle.

Growth investors With reference to equity investors, investors who seek to invest in high-earnings-growth companies.

Guarantee certificate A type of structured financial instrument that provides investors capital protection. It combines a zero-coupon bond and a call option on some underlying asset.

Haircut See *repo margin*.

Harmonic mean A type of weighted mean computed by averaging the reciprocals of the observations, then taking the reciprocal of that average.

Head and shoulders pattern In technical analysis, a reversal pattern that is formed in three parts: a left shoulder, head, and right shoulder; used to predict a change from an uptrend to a downtrend.

Headline inflation The inflation rate calculated based on the price index that includes all goods and services in an economy.

Hedge funds Private investment vehicles that typically use leverage, derivatives, and long and short investment strategies.

Hedge portfolio A hypothetical combination of the derivative and its underlying that eliminates risk.

Held-to-maturity Debt (fixed-income) securities that a company intends to hold to maturity; these are presented at their original cost, updated for any amortisation of discounts or premiums.

Herding Clustered trading that may or may not be based on information.

Hidden order An order that is exposed not to the public but only to the brokers or exchanges that receive it.

High-frequency trading A form of algorithmic trading that makes use of vast quantities of data to execute trades on ultra-high-speed networks in fractions of a second.

High-water mark The highest value, net of fees, that a fund has reached in history. It reflects the highest cumulative return used to calculate an incentive fee.

Histogram A bar chart of data that have been grouped into a frequency distribution.

Historical cost In reference to assets, the amount paid to purchase an asset, including any costs of acquisition and/or preparation; with reference to liabilities, the amount of proceeds received in exchange in issuing the liability.

Historical equity risk premium approach An estimate of a country's equity risk premium that is based upon the historical averages of the risk-free rate and the rate of return on the market portfolio.

Historical simulation Another term for the historical method of estimating VaR. This term is somewhat misleading in that the method involves not a *simulation* of the past but rather what *actually happened* in the past, sometimes adjusted to reflect the fact that a different portfolio may have existed in the past than is planned for the future.

Holder-of-record date The date that a shareholder listed on the corporation's books will be deemed to have ownership of the shares for purposes of receiving an upcoming dividend.

Holding period return The return that an investor earns during a specified holding period; a synonym for total return.

Homogeneity of expectations The assumption that all investors have the same economic expectations and thus have the same expectations of prices, cash flows, and other investment characteristics.

Horizon yield The internal rate of return between the total return (the sum of reinvested coupon payments and the sale price or redemption amount) and the purchase price of the bond.

Horizontal analysis Common-size analysis that involves comparing a specific financial statement with that statement in prior or future time periods; also, cross-sectional analysis of one company with another.

Horizontal demand schedule Implies that at a given price, the response in the quantity demanded is infinite.

Hostile takeover An attempt by one entity to acquire a company without the consent of the company's management.

Household A person or a group of people living in the same residence, taken as a basic unit in economic analysis.

Human capital The accumulated knowledge and skill that workers acquire from education, training, or life experience and the corresponding present value of future earnings to be generated by said skilled individual.

Hurdle rate The rate of return that must be met for a project to be accepted.

Hypothesis With reference to statistical inference, a statement about one or more populations.

Hypothesis testing With reference to statistical inference, the subdivision dealing with the testing of hypotheses about one or more populations.

I-spread The yield spread of a specific bond over the standard swap rate in that currency of the same tenor.

Iceberg order An order in which the display size is less than the order's full size.

If-converted method A method for accounting for the effect of convertible securities on earnings per share (EPS) that specifies what EPS would have been if the convertible securities had been converted at the beginning of the period, taking account of the effects of conversion on net income and the weighted average number of shares outstanding.

Immediate or cancel order An order that is valid only upon receipt by the broker or exchange. If such an order cannot be filled in part or in whole upon receipt, it cancels immediately. Also called *fill or kill*.

Impact lag The lag associated with the result of actions affecting the economy with delay.

Implicit price deflator for GDP A gauge of prices and inflation that measures the aggregate changes in prices across the overall economy.

Implied forward rates Calculated from spot rates, an implied forward rate is a break-even reinvestment rate that links the return on an investment in a shorter-term zero-coupon bond to the return on an investment in a longer-term zero-coupon bond.

Implied volatility The volatility that option traders use to price an option, implied by the price of the option and a particular option-pricing model.

Import license Specifies the quantity of a good that can be imported into a country.

Imports Goods and services that a domestic economy (i.e., house-holds, firms, and government) purchases from other countries.

In the money Options that, if exercised, would result in the value received being worth more than the payment required to exercise.

Incentive fee Fees paid to the general partner from the limited partner(s) based on realized net profits.

Income Increases in economic benefits in the form of inflows or enhancements of assets, or decreases of liabilities that result in an increase in equity (other than increases resulting from contributions by owners).

Income elasticity of demand A measure of the responsiveness of demand to changes in income, defined as the percentage change in quantity demanded divided by the percentage change in income.

Income tax paid The actual amount paid for income taxes in the period; not a provision, but the actual cash outflow.

Income tax payable The income tax owed by the company on the basis of taxable income.

Income trust A type of equity ownership vehicle established as a trust issuing ownership shares known as units.

Increasing marginal returns When the marginal product of a resource increases as additional units of that input are employed.

Increasing returns to scale When a production process leads to increases in output that are proportionately larger than the increase in inputs.

Incremental cash flow The cash flow that is realized because of a decision; the changes or increments to cash flows resulting from a decision or action.

Indenture Legal contract that describes the form of a bond, the obligations of the issuer, and the rights of the bondholders. Also called the *trust deed*.

Independent With reference to events, the property that the occurrence of one event does not affect the probability of another event occurring.

Independent projects Independent projects are projects whose cash flows are independent of each other.

Independently and identically distributed (IID) With respect to random variables, the property of random variables that are independent of each other but follow the identical probability distribution.

Index-linked bond Bond for which coupon payments and/or principal repayment are linked to a specified index.

Index of Leading Economic Indicators A composite of economic variables used by analysts to predict future economic conditions.

Indexing An investment strategy in which an investor constructs a portfolio to mirror the performance of a specified index.

Indifference curve A curve representing all the combinations of two goods or attributes such that the consumer is entirely indifferent among them.

Indirect format With reference to cash flow statements, a format for the presentation of the statement which, in the operating cash flow section, begins with net income then shows additions and subtractions to arrive at operating cash flow. Also called *indirect method*.

Indirect method See *indirect format*.

Indirect taxes Taxes such as taxes on spending, as opposed to direct taxes.

Industry A group of companies offering similar products and/or services.

Industry analysis The analysis of a specific branch of manufacturing, service, or trade.

Inelastic Said of a good or service when the magnitude of elasticity is less than one. Insensitive to price changes.

Inferior goods A good whose consumption decreases as income increases.

Inflation The percentage increase in the general price level from one period to the next; a sustained rise in the overall level of prices in an economy.

Inflation-linked bond Type of index-linked bond that offers investors protection against inflation by linking the bond's coupon payments and/or the principal repayment to an index of consumer prices. Also called *linkers.*

Inflation premium An extra return that compensates investors for expected inflation.

Inflation rate The percentage change in a price index—that is, the speed of overall price level movements.

Inflation Reports A type of economic publication put out by many central banks.

Inflation uncertainty The degree to which economic agents view future rates of inflation as difficult to forecast.

Information cascade The transmission of information from those participants who act first and whose decisions influence the decisions of others.

Information-motivated traders Traders that trade to profit from information that they believe allows them to predict future prices.

Informationally efficient market A market in which asset prices reflect new information quickly and rationally.

Initial coin offering An unregulated process whereby companies raise capital by selling crypto tokens to investors in exchange for fiat money or another agreed-upon cryptocurrency.

Initial margin The amount that must be deposited in a clearinghouse account when entering into a futures contract.

Initial margin requirement The margin requirement on the first day of a transaction as well as on any day in which additional margin funds must be deposited.

Initial public offering (IPO) The first issuance of common shares to the public by a formerly private corporation.

Input productivity The amount of output produced by workers in a given period of time—for example, output per hour worked; measures the efficiency of labor.

Intangible assets Assets lacking physical substance, such as patents and trademarks.

Interbank market The market of loans and deposits between banks for maturities ranging from overnight to one year.

Interbank money market The market of loans and deposits between banks for maturities ranging from overnight to one year.

Interest Payment for lending funds.

Interest coverage A solvency ratio calculated as EBIT divided by interest payments.

Interest-only mortgage A loan in which no scheduled principal repayment is specified for a certain number of years.

Interest rate A rate of return that reflects the relationship between differently dated cash flows; a discount rate.

Interest rate swap A swap in which the underlying is an interest rate. Can be viewed as a currency swap in which both currencies are the same and can be created as a combination of currency swaps.

Intergenerational data mining A form of data mining that applies information developed by previous researchers using a dataset to guide current research using the same or a related dataset.

Intermarket analysis A field within technical analysis that combines analysis of major categories of securities—namely, equities, bonds, currencies, and commodities—to identify market trends and possible inflections in a trend.

Internal rate of return (IRR) The discount rate that makes net present value equal 0; the discount rate that makes the present value of an investment's costs (outflows) equal to the present value of the investment's benefits (inflows).

Internet of Things A network arrangement of structures and devices whereby the objects on the network are able to interact and share information.

Interpolated spread The yield spread of a specific bond over the standard swap rate in that currency of the same tenor.

Interquartile range The difference between the third and first quartiles of a dataset.

Interval With reference to grouped data, a set of values within which an observation falls.

Interval scale A measurement scale that not only ranks data but also gives assurance that the differences between scale values are equal.

Intrinsic value See *exercise value.*

Inventory blanket lien The use of inventory as collateral for a loan. Though the lender has claim to some or all of the company's inventory, the company may still sell or use the inventory in the ordinary course of business.

Inventory investment Net change in business inventory.

Inventory turnover An activity ratio calculated as cost of goods sold divided by average inventory.

Inverse demand function A restatement of the demand function in which price is stated as a function of quantity.

Inverse floater A type of leveraged structured financial instrument. The cash flows are adjusted periodically and move in the opposite direction of changes in the reference rate.

Investing activities Activities associated with the acquisition and disposal of property, plant, and equipment; intangible assets; other long-term assets; and both long-term and short-term investments in the equity and debt (bonds and loans) issued by other companies.

Investment banks Financial intermediaries that provide advice to their mostly corporate clients and help them arrange transactions such as initial and seasoned securities offerings.

Investment opportunity schedule A graphical depiction of a company's investment opportunities ordered from highest to lowest expected return. A company's optimal capital budget is found where the investment opportunity schedule intersects with the company's marginal cost of capital.

Investment policy statement (IPS) A written planning document that describes a client's investment objectives and risk tolerance over a relevant time horizon, along with constraints that apply to the client's portfolio.

Investment property Property used to earn rental income or capital appreciation (or both).

January effect Calendar anomaly that stock market returns in January are significantly higher compared to the rest of the months of the year, with most of the abnormal returns reported during the first five trading days in January. Also called *turn-of-the-year effect.*

Joint probability The probability of the joint occurrence of stated events.

Joint probability function A function giving the probability of joint occurrences of values of stated random variables.

Just-in-time (JIT) method Method of managing inventory that minimizes in-process inventory stocks.

Key rate duration A method of measuring the interest rate sensitivities of a fixed-income instrument or portfolio to shifts in key points along the yield curve.

Keynesians Economists who believe that fiscal policy can have powerful effects on aggregate demand, output, and employment when there is substantial spare capacity in an economy.

Kondratieff wave A 54-year long economic cycle postulated by Nikolai Kondratieff.

Kurtosis The statistical measure that indicates the combined weight of the tails of a distribution relative to the rest of the distribution.

Labor force The portion of the working age population (over the age of 16) that is employed or is available for work but not working (unemployed).

Labor productivity The quantity of goods and services (real GDP) that a worker can produce in one hour of work.

Laddering strategy A form of active strategy which entails scheduling maturities on a systematic basis within the investment portfolio such that investments are spread out equally over the term of the ladder.

Lagging economic indicators Turning points that take place later than those of the overall economy; they are believed to have value in identifying the economy's past condition.

Laspeyres index A price index created by holding the composition of the consumption basket constant.

Law of demand The principle that as the price of a good rises, buyers will choose to buy less of it, and as its price falls, they will buy more.

Law of diminishing marginal returns The observation that a variable factor's marginal product must eventually fall as more of it is added to a fixed amount of the other factors.

Law of diminishing returns The smallest output that a firm can produce such that its long run average costs are minimized.

Law of one price The condition in a financial market in which two equivalent financial instruments or combinations of financial instruments can sell for only one price. Equivalent to the principle that no arbitrage opportunities are possible.

Lead underwriter The lead investment bank in a syndicate of investment banks and broker–dealers involved in a securities underwriting.

Leading economic indicators Turning points that usually precede those of the overall economy; they are believed to have value for predicting the economy's future state, usually near-term.

Legal tender Something that must be accepted when offered in exchange for goods and services.

Lender of last resort An entity willing to lend money when no other entity is ready to do so.

Leptokurtic Describes a distribution that has fatter tails than a normal distribution.

Lessee The party obtaining the use of an asset through a lease.

Lessor The owner of an asset that grants the right to use the asset to another party.

Letter of credit Form of external credit enhancement whereby a financial institution provides the issuer with a credit line to reimburse any cash flow shortfalls from the assets backing the issue.

Level of significance The probability of a Type I error in testing a hypothesis.

Leverage In the context of corporate finance, leverage refers to the use of fixed costs within a company's cost structure. Fixed costs that are operating costs (such as depreciation or rent) create operating leverage. Fixed costs that are financial costs (such as interest expense) create financial leverage.

Leveraged buyout A transaction whereby the target company's management team converts the target to a privately held company by using heavy borrowing to finance the purchase of the target company's outstanding shares.

Liabilities Present obligations of an enterprise arising from past events, the settlement of which is expected to result in an outflow of resources embodying economic benefits; creditors' claims on the resources of a company.

Life-cycle stage The stage of the life cycle: embryonic, growth, shakeout, mature, declining.

LIFO layer liquidation With respect to the application of the LIFO inventory method, the liquidation of old, relatively low-priced inventory; happens when the volume of sales rises above the volume of recent purchases so that some sales are made from relatively old, low-priced inventory. Also called *LIFO liquidation.*

LIFO method The last in, first out, method of accounting for inventory, which matches sales against the costs of items of inventory in the reverse order the items were placed in inventory (i.e., inventory produced or acquired last are assumed to be sold first).

LIFO reserve The difference between the reported LIFO inventory carrying amount and the inventory amount that would have been reported if the FIFO method had been used (in other words, the FIFO inventory value less the LIFO inventory value).

Likelihood The probability of an observation, given a particular set of conditions.

Limit down A limit move in the futures market in which the price at which a transaction would be made is at or below the lower limit.

Limit order Instructions to a broker or exchange to obtain the best price immediately available when filling an order, but in no event accept a price higher than a specified (limit) price when buying or accept a price lower than a specified (limit) price when selling.

Limit order book The book or list of limit orders to buy and sell that pertains to a security.

Limit up A limit move in the futures market in which the price at which a transaction would be made is at or above the upper limit.

Limitations on liens Meant to put limits on how much secured debt an issuer can have.

Limited partners Partners with limited liability. Limited partnerships in hedge and private equity funds are typically restricted to investors who are expected to understand and to be able to assume the risks associated with the investments.

Line chart In technical analysis, a plot of price data, typically closing prices, with a line connecting the points.

Linear interpolation The estimation of an unknown value on the basis of two known values that bracket it, using a straight line between the two known values.

Linear scale A scale in which equal distances correspond to equal absolute amounts. Also called *arithmetic scale.*

Linker See *inflation-linked bond.*

Liquid market Said of a market in which traders can buy or sell with low total transaction costs when they want to trade.
Liquidation To sell the assets of a company, division, or subsidiary piecemeal, typically because of bankruptcy; the form of bankruptcy that allows for the orderly satisfaction of creditors' claims after which the company ceases to exist.
Liquidity The ability to purchase or sell an asset quickly and easily at a price close to fair market value. The ability to meet short-term obligations using assets that are the most readily converted into cash.
Liquidity premium An extra return that compensates investors for the risk of loss relative to an investment's fair value if the investment needs to be converted to cash quickly.
Liquidity ratios Financial ratios measuring the company's ability to meet its short-term obligations.
Liquidity risk The risk that a financial instrument cannot be purchased or sold without a significant concession in price due to the size of the market.
Liquidity trap A condition in which the demand for money becomes infinitely elastic (horizontal demand curve) so that injections of money into the economy will not lower interest rates or affect real activity.
Load fund A mutual fund in which, in addition to the annual fee, a percentage fee is charged to invest in the fund and/or for redemptions from the fund.
Loan-to-value ratio The ratio of a property's purchase price to the amount of its mortgage.
Lockbox system A payment system in which customer payments are mailed to a post office box and the banking institution retrieves and deposits these payments several times a day, enabling the company to have use of the fund sooner than in a centralized system in which customer payments are sent to the company.
Locked limit A condition in the futures markets in which a transaction cannot take place because the price would be beyond the limits.
Lockup period The minimum holding period before investors are allowed to make withdrawals or redeem shares from a fund.
Logarithmic scale A scale in which equal distances represent equal proportional changes in the underlying quantity.
London interbank offered rate (Libor) Collective name for multiple rates at which a select set of banks believe they could borrow unsecured funds from other banks in the London interbank market for different currencies and different borrowing periods ranging from overnight to one year.
Long The buyer of a derivative contract. Also refers to the position of owning a derivative.
Long-lived assets Assets that are expected to provide economic benefits over a future period of time, typically greater than one year. Also called *long-term assets.*
Long position A position in an asset or contract in which one owns the asset or has an exercisable right under the contract.
Long-run average total cost The curve describing average total cost when no costs are considered fixed.
Longitudinal data Observations on characteristic(s) of the same observational unit through time.
Look-ahead bias A bias caused by using information that was unavailable on the test date.
Loss aversion The tendency of people to dislike losses more than they like comparable gains.
Loss severity Portion of a bond's value (including unpaid interest) an investor loses in the event of default.
Losses Asset outflows not directly related to the ordinary activities of the business.
Lower bound The lowest possible value of an option.
M^2 A measure of what a portfolio would have returned if it had taken on the same total risk as the market index.
M^2 alpha Difference between the risk-adjusted performance of the portfolio and the performance of the benchmark.
Macaulay duration The approximate amount of time a bond would have to be held for the market discount rate at purchase to be realized if there is a single change in interest rate. It indicates the point in time when the coupon reinvestment and price effects of a change in yield-to- maturity offset each other.
Machine learning Computer based techniques that seek to extract knowledge from large amounts of data by "learning" from known examples and then generating structure or predictions. ML algorithms aim to "find the pattern, apply the pattern."
Macroeconomics The branch of economics that deals with aggregate economic quantities, such as national output and national income.
Maintenance covenants Covenants in bank loan agreements that require the borrower to satisfy certain financial ratio tests while the loan is outstanding.
Maintenance margin The minimum amount that is required by a futures clearinghouse to maintain a margin account and to protect against default. Participants whose margin balances drop below the required maintenance margin must replenish their accounts.
Maintenance margin requirement The margin requirement on any day other than the first day of a transaction.
Management buy-ins Leveraged buyout in which the current management team is being replaced and the acquiring team will be involved in managing the company.
Management buyout A leveraged buyout event in which a group of investors consisting primarily of the company's existing management purchase at least controlling interest in its outstanding shares. At the extreme, they may purchase all shares and take the company private.
Management fee A fee based on assets under management or committed capital, as applicable, also called a *base fee.*
Manufacturing resource planning (MRP) The incorporation of production planning into inventory management. A MRP analysis provides both a materials acquisition schedule and a production schedule.
Margin The amount of money that a trader deposits in a margin account. The term is derived from the stock market practice in which an investor borrows a portion of the money required to purchase a certain amount of stock. In futures markets, there is no borrowing so the margin is more of a down payment or performance bond.
Margin bond A cash deposit required by the clearinghouse from the participants to a contract to provide a credit guarantee. Also called a *performance bond.*
Margin call A request for the short to deposit additional funds to bring their balance up to the initial margin.
Margin loan Money borrowed from a broker to purchase securities.
Marginal cost The cost of producing an additional unit of a good.
Marginal probability The probability of an event *not* conditioned on another event.

Marginal product Measures the productivity of each unit of input and is calculated by taking the difference in total product from adding another unit of input (assuming other resource quantities are held constant).

Marginal propensity to consume The proportion of an additional unit of disposable income that is consumed or spent; the change in consumption for a small change in income.

Marginal propensity to save The proportion of an additional unit of disposable income that is saved (not spent).

Marginal revenue The change in total revenue divided by the change in quantity sold; simply, the additional revenue from selling one more unit.

Marginal value curve A curve describing the highest price consumers are willing to pay for each additional unit of a good.

Mark to market The revaluation of a financial asset or liability to its current market value or fair value.

Market anomaly Change in the price or return of a security that cannot directly be linked to current relevant information known in the market or to the release of new information into the market.

Market bid–ask spread The difference between the best bid and the best offer.

Market-capitalization weighting An index weighting method in which the weight assigned to each constituent security is determined by dividing its market capitalization by the total market capitalization (sum of the market capitalization) of all securities in the index. Also called *value weighting*.

Market discount rate The rate of return required by investors given the risk of the investment in a bond; also called the *required yield* or the *required rate of return*.

Market float The number of shares that are available to the investing public.

Market liquidity risk The risk that the price at which investors can actually transact—buying or selling—may differ from the price indicated in the market.

Market model A regression equation that specifies a linear relationship between the return on a security (or portfolio) and the return on a broad market index.

Market multiple models Valuation models based on share price multiples or enterprise value multiples.

Market-on-close An execution instruction specifying that an order can only be filled at the close of trading.

Market order Instructions to a broker or exchange to obtain the best price immediately available when filling an order.

Market-oriented investors With reference to equity investors, investors whose investment disciplines cannot be clearly categorized as value or growth.

Market rate of interest The rate demanded by purchasers of bonds, given the risks associated with future cash payment obligations of the particular bond issue.

Market risk The risk that arises from movements in interest rates, stock prices, exchange rates, and commodity prices.

Market value The price at which an asset or security can currently be bought or sold in an open market.

Marketable limit order A buy limit order in which the limit price is placed above the best offer, or a sell limit order in which the limit price is placed below the best bid. Such orders generally will partially or completely fill right away.

Markowitz efficient frontier The graph of the set of portfolios offering the maximum expected return for their level of risk (standard deviation of return).

Matching principle The accounting principle that expenses should be recognized in the same period in which the associated revenue is recognized.

Matching strategy An active investment strategy that includes intentional matching of the timing of cash outflows with investment maturities.

Matrix pricing Process of estimating the market discount rate and price of a bond based on the quoted or flat prices of more frequently traded comparable bonds.

Maturity premium An extra return that compensates investors for the increased sensitivity of the market value of debt to a change in market interest rates as maturity is extended.

Maturity structure A factor explaining the differences in yields on similar bonds; also called *term structure*.

Mean absolute deviation With reference to a sample, the mean of the absolute values of deviations from the sample mean.

Mean–variance analysis An approach to portfolio analysis using expected means, variances, and covariances of asset returns.

Measure of central tendency A quantitative measure that specifies where data are centered.

Measure of value A standard for measuring value; a function of money.

Measurement scales A scheme of measuring differences. The four types of measurement scales are nominal, ordinal, interval, and ratio.

Measures of location A quantitative measure that describes the location or distribution of data; includes not only measures of central tendency but also other measures such as percentiles.

Median The value of the middle item of a set of items that has been sorted into ascending or descending order; the 50th percentile.

Medium of exchange Any asset that can be used to purchase goods and services or to repay debts; a function of money.

Medium-term note A corporate bond offered continuously to investors by an agent of the issuer, designed to fill the funding gap between commercial paper and long-term bonds.

Menu costs A cost of inflation in which businesses constantly have to incur the costs of changing the advertised prices of their goods and services.

Mesokurtic Describes a distribution with kurtosis identical to that of the normal distribution.

Mezzanine financing Debt or preferred shares with a relationship to common equity resulting from a feature such as attached warrants or conversion options. Mezzanine financing is subordinate to both senior and high-yield debt but is senior to equity. It is referred to as "mezzanine" because of its location on the balance sheet.

Microeconomics The branch of economics that deals with markets and decision making of individual economic units, including consumers and businesses.

Minimum efficient scale The smallest output that a firm can produce such that its long-run average total cost is minimized.

Minimum-variance portfolio The portfolio with the minimum variance for each given level of expected return.

Minority shareholders A particular shareholder or block of shareholders holding a small proportion of a company's outstanding shares, resulting in a limited ability to exercise control in voting activities.

Minsky moment Named for Hyman Minksy: A point in a business cycle when, after individuals become overextended in borrowing to finance speculative investments, people start realizing that something is likely to go wrong and a panic ensues leading to asset sell-offs.

Mismatching strategy An active investment strategy whereby the timing of cash outflows is not matched with investment maturities.

Modal interval With reference to grouped data, the most frequently occurring interval.

Mode The most frequently occurring value in a set of observations.

Modern portfolio theory (MPT) The analysis of rational portfolio choices based on the efficient use of risk.

Modified duration A measure of the percentage price change of a bond given a change in its yield-to-maturity.

Momentum oscillators A graphical representation of market sentiment that is constructed from price data and calculated so that it oscillates either between a high and a low or around some number.

Monetarists Economists who believe that the rate of growth of the money supply is the primary determinant of the rate of inflation.

Monetary policy Actions taken by a nation's central bank to affect aggregate output and prices through changes in bank reserves, reserve requirements, or its target interest rate.

Monetary transmission mechanism The process whereby a central bank's interest rate gets transmitted through the economy and ultimately affects the rate of increase of prices.

Monetary union An economic union in which the members adopt a common currency.

Money A generally accepted medium of exchange and unit of account.

Money convexity For a bond, the annual or approximate convexity multiplied by the full price.

Money creation The process by which changes in bank reserves translate into changes in the money supply.

Money duration A measure of the price change in units of the currency in which the bond is denominated given a change in its yield-to-maturity.

Money market The market for short-term debt instruments (one-year maturity or less).

Money market securities Fixed-income securities with maturities at issuance of one year or less.

Money market yield A yield on a basis comparable to the quoted yield on an interest-bearing money market instrument that pays interest on a 360-day basis; the annualized holding period yield, assuming a 360-day year.

Money multiplier Describes how a change in reserves is expected to affect the money supply; in its simplest form, 1 divided by the reserve requirement.

Money neutrality The thesis that an increase in the money supply leads in the long-run to an increase in the price level, while leaving real variables like output and employment unaffected.

Money-weighted return The internal rate of return on a portfolio, taking account of all cash flows.

Moneyness The relationship between the price of the underlying and an option's exercise price.

Monopolistic competition Highly competitive form of imperfect competition; the competitive characteristic is a notably large number of firms, while the monopoly aspect is the result of product differentiation.

Monopoly In pure monopoly markets, there are no substitutes for the given product or service. There is a single seller, which exercises considerable power over pricing and output decisions.

Monte Carlo simulation An approach to estimating a probability distribution of outcomes to examine what might happen if particular risks are faced. This method is widely used in the sciences as well as in business to study a variety of problems.

Moral principles Beliefs regarding what is good, acceptable, or obligatory behavior and what is bad, unacceptable, or forbidden behavior.

Mortgage-backed securities Debt obligations that represent claims to the cash flows from pools of mortgage loans, most commonly on residential property.

Mortgage loan A loan secured by the collateral of some specified real estate property that obliges the borrower to make a predetermined series of payments to the lender.

Mortgage pass-through security A security created when one or more holders of mortgages form a pool of mortgages and sell shares or participation certificates in the pool.

Mortgage rate The interest rate on a mortgage loan; also called *contract rate* or *note rate*.

Moving average The average of the closing price of a security over a specified number of periods. With each new period, the average is recalculated.

Moving-average convergence/divergence oscillator (MACD) A momentum oscillator that is constructed based on the difference between short-term and long-term moving averages of a security's price.

Multi-factor model A model that explains a variable in terms of the values of a set of factors.

Multi-market indexes Comprised of indexes from different countries, designed to represent multiple security markets.

Multi-step format With respect to the format of the income statement, a format that presents a subtotal for gross profit (revenue minus cost of goods sold).

Multilateral trading facilities See *alternative trading systems*.

Multinational corporation A company operating in more than one country or having subsidiary firms in more than one country.

Multiplication rule for probabilities The rule that the joint probability of events A and B equals the probability of A given B times the probability of B.

Multiplier models Valuation models based on share price multiples or enterprise value multiples.

Multivariate distribution A probability distribution that specifies the probabilities for a group of related random variables.

Multivariate normal distribution A probability distribution for a group of random variables that is completely defined by the means and variances of the variables plus all the correlations between pairs of the variables.

Municipal bonds A type of non-sovereign bond issued by a state or local government in the United States. It very often (but not always) offers income tax exemptions.

Munis A type of non-sovereign bond issued by a state or local government in the United States. It very often (but not always) offers income tax exemptions.

Mutual fund A comingled investment pool in which investors in the fund each have a pro-rata claim on the income and value of the fund.

Mutually exclusive projects Mutually exclusive projects compete directly with each other. For example, if Projects A and B are mutually exclusive, you can choose A or B, but you cannot choose both.

***n* Factorial** For a positive integer *n*, the product of the first *n* positive integers; 0 factorial equals 1 by definition. *n* factorial is written as *n*!.

Narrow money The notes and coins in circulation in an economy, plus other very highly liquid deposits.

Nash equilibrium When two or more participants in a non-coop-erative game have no incentive to deviate from their respective equilibrium strategies given their opponent's strategies.

National income The income received by all factors of production used in the generation of final output. National income equals gross domestic product (or, in some countries, gross national product) minus the capital consumption allowance and a statistical discrepancy.

Natural language processing Computer programs developed to analyze and interpret human language.

Natural rate of unemployment Effective unemployment rate, below which pressure emerges in labor markets.

Negative screening An ESG investment style that focuses on the exclusion of certain sectors, companies, or practices in a fund or portfolio on the basis of specific ESG criteria.

Neo-Keynesians A group of dynamic general equilibrium models that assume slow-to-adjust prices and wages.

Net book value The remaining (undepreciated) balance of an asset's purchase cost. For liabilities, the face value of a bond minus any unamortized discount, or plus any unamortized premium.

Net exports The difference between the value of a country's exports and the value of its imports (i.e., value of exports minus imports).

Net income The difference between revenue and expenses; what remains after subtracting all expenses (including depreciation, interest, and taxes) from revenue.

Net operating cycle An estimate of the average time that elapses between paying suppliers for materials and collecting cash from the subsequent sale of goods produced.

Net present value (NPV) The present value of an investment's cash inflows (benefits) minus the present value of its cash outflows (costs).

Net profit margin An indicator of profitability, calculated as net income divided by revenue; indicates how much of each dollar of revenues is left after all costs and expenses. Also called *profit margin* or *return on sales.*

Net realisable value Estimated selling price in the ordinary course of business less the estimated costs necessary to make the sale.

Net revenue Revenue after adjustments (e.g., for estimated returns or for amounts unlikely to be collected).

Net tax rate The tax rate net of transfer payments.

Neural networks Computer programs based on how our own brains learn and process information.

Neutral rate of interest The rate of interest that neither spurs on nor slows down the underlying economy.

New classical macroeconomics An approach to macroeconomics that seeks the macroeconomic conclusions of individuals maximizing utility on the basis of rational expectations and companies maximizing profits.

New Keynesians A group of dynamic general equilibrium models that assume slow-to-adjust prices and wages.

No-load fund A mutual fund in which there is no fee for investing in the fund or for redeeming fund shares, although there is an annual fee based on a percentage of the fund's net asset value.

Node Each value on a binomial tree from which successive moves or outcomes branch.

Nominal GDP The value of goods and services measured at current prices.

Nominal rate A rate of interest based on the security's face value.

Nominal risk-free interest rate The sum of the real risk-free interest rate and the inflation premium.

Nominal scale A measurement scale that categorizes data but does not rank them.

Non-accelerating inflation rate of unemployment Effective unemployment rate, below which pressure emerges in labor markets.

Non-agency RMBS In the United States, securities issued by private entities that are not guaranteed by a federal agency or a GSE.

Non-cumulative preference shares Preference shares for which dividends that are not paid in the current or subsequent periods are forfeited permanently (instead of being accrued and paid at a later date).

Non-current assets Assets that are expected to benefit the company over an extended period of time (usually more than one year).

Non-current liabilities Obligations that broadly represent a probable sacrifice of economic benefits in periods generally greater than one year in the future.

Non-cyclical A company whose performance is largely independent of the business cycle.

Non-deliverable forwards Cash-settled forward contracts, used predominately with respect to foreign exchange forwards. Also called *contracts for differences.*

Non-financial risks Risks that arise from sources other than changes in the external financial markets, such as changes in accounting rules, legal environment, or tax rates.

Non-participating preference shares Preference shares that do not entitle shareholders to share in the profits of the company. Instead, shareholders are only entitled to receive a fixed dividend payment and the par value of the shares in the event of liquidation.

Non-recourse loan Loan in which the lender does not have a shortfall claim against the borrower, so the lender can look only to the property to recover the outstanding mortgage balance.

Non-renewable resources Finite resources that are depleted once they are consumed, such as oil and coal.

Non-sovereign bonds A bond issued by a government below the national level, such as a province, region, state, or city.

Non-sovereign government bonds A bond issued by a government below the national level, such as a province, region, state, or city.

Nonconventional cash flow In a nonconventional cash flow pattern, the initial outflow is not followed by inflows only, but the cash flows can flip from positive (inflows) to negative (outflows) again (or even change signs several times).

Nonparametric test A test that is not concerned with a parameter, or that makes minimal assumptions about the population from which a sample comes.

Nonsystematic risk Unique risk that is local or limited to a particular asset or industry that need not affect assets outside of that asset class.

Normal distribution A continuous, symmetric probability distribution that is completely described by its mean and its variance.

Normal goods Goods that are consumed in greater quantities as income increases.

Normal profit The level of accounting profit needed to just cover the implicit opportunity costs ignored in accounting costs.

Notching Ratings adjustment methodology where specific issues from the same borrower may be assigned different credit ratings.

Note rate See *mortgage rate.*

Notice period The length of time (typically 30–90 days) in advance that investors may be required to notify a fund of their intent to redeem some or all of their investment.

Notional principal An imputed principal amount.

Number of days of inventory An activity ratio equal to the number of days in a period divided by the inventory ratio for the period; an indication of the number of days a company ties up funds in inventory.

Number of days of payables An activity ratio equal to the number of days in a period divided by the payables turnover ratio for the period; an estimate of the average number of days it takes a company to pay its suppliers.

Number of days of receivables Estimate of the average number of days it takes to collect on credit accounts.

Objective probabilities Probabilities that generally do not vary from person to person; includes a priori and objective probabilities.

Off-the-run Seasoned government bonds are off-the-run securities; they are not the most recently issued or the most actively traded.

Offer The price at which a dealer or trader is willing to sell an asset, typically qualified by a maximum quantity (ask size).

Official interest rate An interest rate that a central bank sets and announces publicly; normally the rate at which it is willing to lend money to the commercial banks. Also called *official policy rate* or *policy rate.*

Official policy rate An interest rate that a central bank sets and announces publicly; normally the rate at which it is willing to lend money to the commercial banks.

Oligopoly Market structure with a relatively small number of firms supplying the market.

On-the-run The most recently issued and most actively traded sovereign securities.

One-sided hypothesis test A test in which the null hypothesis is rejected only if the evidence indicates that the population parameter is greater than (smaller than) θ_0. The alternative hypothesis also has one side.

One-tailed hypothesis test A test in which the null hypothesis is rejected only if the evidence indicates that the population parameter is greater than (smaller than) θ_0. The alternative hypothesis also has one side.

Open economy An economy that trades with other countries.

Open-end fund A mutual fund that accepts new investment money and issues additional shares at a value equal to the net asset value of the fund at the time of investment.

Open interest The number of outstanding contracts in a clearinghouse at any given time. The open interest figure changes daily as some parties open up new positions, while other parties offset their old positions.

Open market operations The purchase or sale of bonds by the national central bank to implement monetary policy. The bonds traded are usually sovereign bonds issued by the national government.

Operating activities Activities that are part of the day-to-day business functioning of an entity, such as selling inventory and providing services.

Operating breakeven The number of units produced and sold at which the company's operating profit is zero (revenues = operating costs).

Operating cash flow The net amount of cash provided from operating activities.

Operating cycle A measure of the time needed to convert raw materials into cash from a sale; it consists of the number of days of inventory and the number of days of receivables.

Operating efficiency ratios Ratios that measure how efficiently a company performs day-to-day tasks, such as the collection of receivables and management of inventory.

Operating lease An agreement allowing a lessee to use some asset for a period of time; essentially a rental.

Operating leverage The use of fixed costs in operations.

Operating profit A company's profits on its usual business activities before deducting taxes. Also called *operating income.*

Operating profit margin A profitability ratio calculated as operating income (i.e., income before interest and taxes) divided by revenue. Also called *operating margin.*

Operating risk The risk attributed to the operating cost structure, in particular the use of fixed costs in operations; the risk arising from the mix of fixed and variable costs; the risk that a company's operations may be severely affected by environmental, social, and governance risk factors.

Operational independence A bank's ability to execute monetary policy and set interest rates in the way it thought would best meet the inflation target.

Operational risk The risk that arises from inadequate or failed people, systems, and internal policies, procedures, and processes, as well as from external events that are beyond the control of the organization but that affect its operations.

Operationally efficient Said of a market, a financial system, or an economy that has relatively low transaction costs.

Opportunity cost The value that investors forgo by choosing a particular course of action; the value of something in its best alternative use.

Option A financial instrument that gives one party the right, but not the obligation, to buy or sell an underlying asset from or to another party at a fixed price over a specific period of time. Also referred to as *contingent claim* or *option contract.*

Option-adjusted price The value of the embedded option plus the flat price of the bond.

Option-adjusted spread OAS = Z-spread – Option value (in basis points per year).

Option-adjusted yield The required market discount rate whereby the price is adjusted for the value of the embedded option.

Option contract See *option.*

Option premium The amount of money a buyer pays and seller receives to engage in an option transaction.

Order A specification of what instrument to trade, how much to trade, and whether to buy or sell.

Order-driven markets A market (generally an auction market) that uses rules to arrange trades based on the orders that traders submit; in their pure form, such markets do not make use of dealers.

Order precedence hierarchy With respect to the execution of orders to trade, a set of rules that determines which orders execute before other orders.

Ordinal scale A measurement scale that sorts data into categories that are ordered (ranked) with respect to some characteristic.

Ordinary annuity An annuity with a first cash flow that is paid one period from the present.

Ordinary shares Equity shares that are subordinate to all other types of equity (e.g., preferred equity). Also called *common stock* or *common shares*.

Organized exchange A securities marketplace where buyers and seller can meet to arrange their trades.

Other comprehensive income Items of comprehensive income that are not reported on the income statement; comprehensive income minus net income.

Out-of-sample test A test of a strategy or model using a sample outside the time period on which the strategy or model was developed.

Out of the money Options that, if exercised, would require the payment of more money than the value received and therefore would not be currently exercised.

Outcome A possible value of a random variable.

Over-the-counter (OTC) markets A decentralized market where buy and sell orders initiated from various locations are matched through a communications network.

Overbought A market condition in which market sentiment is thought to be unsustainably bullish.

Overcollateralization Form of internal credit enhancement that refers to the process of posting more collateral than needed to obtain or secure financing.

Overfitting An undesirable result from fitting a model so closely to a dataset that it does not perform well on new data.

Overlay/portfolio tilt An ESG investment style that focuses on the use of certain investment strategies or products to change specific aggregate ESG characteristics of a fund or investment portfolio to a desired level (e.g., tilting an investment portfolio toward a desired carbon footprint).

Oversold A market condition in which market sentiment is thought to be unsustainably bearish.

Own price The price of a good or service itself (as opposed to the price of something else).

Own-price elasticity of demand The percentage change in quantity demanded for a percentage change in good's own price, holding all other things constant.

Owners' equity The excess of assets over liabilities; the residual interest of shareholders in the assets of an entity after deducting the entity's liabilities. Also called *shareholders' equity* or *shareholders' funds*.

Paasche index An index formula using the current composition of a basket of products.

Paired comparisons test A statistical test for differences based on paired observations drawn from samples that are dependent on each other.

Paired observations Observations that are dependent on each other.

Pairs arbitrage trade A trade in two closely related stocks involving the short sale of one and the purchase of the other.

Panel data Observations through time on a single characteristic of multiple observational units.

Par curve A sequence of yields-to-maturity such that each bond is priced at par value. The bonds are assumed to have the same currency, credit risk, liquidity, tax status, and annual yields stated for the same periodicity.

Par value The amount of principal on a bond.

Parallel shift A parallel yield curve shift implies that all rates change by the same amount in the same direction.

Parameter A descriptive measure computed from or used to describe a population of data, conventionally represented by Greek letters.

Parametric test Any test (or procedure) concerned with parameters or whose validity depends on assumptions concerning the population generating the sample.

Pari passu On an equal footing.

Partial duration See *key rate duration.*

Participating preference shares Preference shares that entitle shareholders to receive the standard preferred dividend plus the opportunity to receive an additional dividend if the company's profits exceed a pre-specified level.

Pass-through rate The coupon rate of a mortgage pass-through security.

Passive investment A buy and hold approach in which an investor does not make portfolio changes based on short-term expectations of changing market or security performance.

Passive strategy In reference to short-term cash management, it is an investment strategy characterized by simple decision rules for making daily investments.

Payable date The day that the company actually mails out (or electronically transfers) a dividend payment.

Payback period the number of years required to recover the original investment in a project. The payback is based on cash flows.

Payment date The day that the company actually mails out (or electronically transfers) a dividend payment.

Payments system The system for the transfer of money.

Peak The highest point of a business cycle.

Peer group A group of companies engaged in similar business activities whose economics and valuation are influenced by closely related factors.

Pennants A technical analysis continuation pattern formed by trendlines that converge to form a triangle, typically over a short period.

Per capita real GDP Real GDP divided by the size of the population, often used as a measure of the average standard of living in a country.

Per unit contribution margin The amount that each unit sold contributes to covering fixed costs—that is, the difference between the price per unit and the variable cost per unit.

Percentiles Quantiles that divide a distribution into 100 equal parts.

Perfect competition A market structure in which the individual firm has virtually no impact on market price, because it is assumed to be a very small seller among a very large number of firms selling essentially identical products.

Perfectly elastic When the quantity demanded or supplied of a given good is infinitely sensitive to a change in the value of a specified variable (e.g., price).

Perfectly inelastic When the quantity demanded or supplied of a given good is completely insensitive to a change in the value of a specified variable (e.g., price).

Performance bond See *margin bond.*

Performance evaluation The measurement and assessment of the outcomes of investment management decisions.

Performance fee Fees paid to the general partner from the limited partner(s) based on realized net profits.

Period costs Costs (e.g., executives' salaries) that cannot be directly matched with the timing of revenues and which are thus expensed immediately.

Periodicity The assumed number of periods in the year, typically matches the frequency of coupon payments.

Permanent differences Differences between tax and financial reporting of revenue (expenses) that will not be reversed at some future date. These result in a difference between the company's effective tax rate and statutory tax rate and do not result in a deferred tax item.

Permissioned networks Networks that are fully open only to select participants on a DLT network.

Permissionless networks Networks that are fully open to any user on a DLT network.

Permutation An ordered listing.

Perpetual bonds Bonds with no stated maturity date.

Perpetuity A perpetual annuity, or a set of never-ending level sequential cash flows, with the first cash flow occurring one period from now. A bond that does not mature.

Personal consumption expenditures All domestic personal consumption; the basis for a price index for such consumption called the PCE price index.

Personal disposable income Equal to personal income less personal taxes.

Personal income A broad measure of household income that includes all income received by households, whether earned or unearned; measures the ability of consumers to make purchases.

Plain vanilla bond Bond that makes periodic, fixed coupon payments during the bond's life and a lump-sum payment of principal at maturity. Also called *conventional bond.*

Platykurtic Describes a distribution that has relatively less weight in the tails than the normal distribution.

Point and figure chart A technical analysis chart that is constructed with columns of X's alternating with columns of O's such that the horizontal axis represents only the number of changes in price without reference to time or volume.

Point estimate A single numerical estimate of an unknown quantity, such as a population parameter.

Point of sale (POS) Systems that capture transaction data at the physical location in which the sale is made.

Policy rate An interest rate that a central bank sets and announces publicly; normally the rate at which it is willing to lend money to the commercial banks.

Population All members of a specified group.

Population mean The arithmetic mean value of a population; the arithmetic mean of all the observations or values in the population.

Population standard deviation A measure of dispersion relating to a population in the same unit of measurement as the observations, calculated as the positive square root of the population variance.

Population variance A measure of dispersion relating to a population, calculated as the mean of the squared deviations around the population mean.

Portfolio company In private equity, the company in which the private equity fund is investing.

Portfolio demand for money The demand to hold speculative money balances based on the potential opportunities or risks that are inherent in other financial instruments.

Portfolio planning The process of creating a plan for building a portfolio that is expected to satisfy a client's investment objectives.

Position The quantity of an asset that an entity owns or owes.

Positive screening An ESG investment style that focuses on the inclusion of certain sectors, companies, or practices in a fund or portfolio on the basis of specific minimum ESG criteria.

Posterior probability An updated probability that reflects or comes after new information.

Potential GDP The level of real GDP that can be produced at full employment; measures the productive capacity of the economy.

Power of a test The probability of correctly rejecting the null—that is, rejecting the null hypothesis when it is false.

Precautionary money balances Money held to provide a buffer against unforeseen events that might require money.

Precautionary stocks A level of inventory beyond anticipated needs that provides a cushion in the event that it takes longer to replenish inventory than expected or in the case of greater than expected demand.

Preference shares A type of equity interest which ranks above common shares with respect to the payment of dividends and the distribution of the company's net assets upon liquidation. They have characteristics of both debt and equity securities. Also called *preferred stock.*

Preferred stock See *preference shares.*

Premium In the case of bonds, premium refers to the amount by which a bond is priced above its face (par) value. In the case of an option, the amount paid for the option contract.

Prepaid expense A normal operating expense that has been paid in advance of when it is due.

Prepayment option Contractual provision that entitles the borrower to prepay all or part of the outstanding mortgage principal prior to the scheduled due date when the principal must be repaid. Also called *early repayment option.*

Prepayment penalty mortgages Mortgages that stipulate a monetary penalty if a borrower prepays within a certain time period after the mortgage is originated.

Prepayment risk The uncertainty that the timing of the actual cash flows will be different from the scheduled cash flows as set forth in the loan agreement due to the borrowers' ability to alter payments, usually to take advantage of interest rate movements.

Present value (PV) The present discounted value of future cash flows: For assets, the present discounted value of the future net cash inflows that the asset is expected to generate; for liabilities, the present discounted value of the future net cash outflows that are expected to be required to settle the liabilities.

Present value models Valuation models that estimate the intrinsic value of a security as the present value of the future benefits expected to be received from the security. Also called *discounted cash flow models.*

Pretax margin A profitability ratio calculated as earnings before taxes divided by revenue.

Price elasticity of demand Measures the percentage change in the quantity demanded, given a percentage change in the price of a given product.

Price index Represents the average prices of a basket of goods and services.

Price limits Limits imposed by a futures exchange on the price change that can occur from one day to the next.

Price multiple A ratio that compares the share price with some sort of monetary flow or value to allow evaluation of the relative worth of a company's stock.

Price priority The principle that the highest priced buy orders and the lowest priced sell orders execute first.

Price relative A ratio of an ending price over a beginning price; it is equal to 1 plus the holding period return on the asset.

Price return Measures *only* the price appreciation or percentage change in price of the securities in an index or portfolio.

Price return index An index that reflects *only* the price appreciation or percentage change in price of the constituent securities. Also called *price index*.

Price stability In economics, refers to an inflation rate that is low on average and not subject to wide fluctuation.

Price takers Producers that must accept whatever price the market dictates.

Price to book value A valuation ratio calculated as price per share divided by book value per share.

Price to cash flow A valuation ratio calculated as price per share divided by cash flow per share.

Price to earnings ratio (P/E ratio or P/E) The ratio of share price to earnings per share.

Price to sales A valuation ratio calculated as price per share divided by sales per share.

Price value of a basis point A version of money duration, it is an estimate of the change in the full price of a bond given a 1 basis point change in the yield-to-maturity.

Price weighting An index weighting method in which the weight assigned to each constituent security is determined by dividing its price by the sum of all the prices of the constituent securities.

Priced risk Risk for which investors demand compensation for bearing (e.g. equity risk, company-specific factors, macroeconomic factors).

Primary bond markets Markets in which issuers first sell bonds to investors to raise capital.

Primary capital markets (primary markets) The market where securities are first sold and the issuers receive the proceeds.

Primary dealers Financial institutions that are authorized to deal in new issues of sovereign bonds and that serve primarily as trading counterparties of the office responsible for issuing sovereign bonds.

Primary market The market where securities are first sold and the issuers receive the proceeds.

Prime brokers Brokers that provide services that commonly include custody, administration, lending, short borrowing, and trading.

Principal The amount of funds originally invested in a project or instrument; the face value to be paid at maturity.

Principal–agent relationship A relationship in which a principal hires an agent to perform a particular task or service; also known as an *agency relationship*.

Principal amount Amount that an issuer agrees to repay the debt holders on the maturity date.

Principal business activity The business activity from which a company derives a majority of its revenues and/or earnings.

Principal value Amount that an issuer agrees to repay the debt holders on the maturity date.

Principle of no arbitrage See *arbitrage-free pricing*.

Prior probabilities Probabilities reflecting beliefs prior to the arrival of new information.

Priority of claims Priority of payment, with the most senior or highest ranking debt having the first claim on the cash flows and assets of the issuer.

Private equity fund A hedge fund that seeks to buy, optimize, and ultimately sell portfolio companies to generate profits. See *venture capital fund*.

Private equity securities Securities that are not listed on public exchanges and have no active secondary market. They are issued primarily to institutional investors via non-public offerings, such as private placements.

Private investment in public equity (PIPE) An investment in the equity of a publicly traded firm that is made at a discount to the market value of the firm's shares.

Private placement Typically, a non-underwritten, unregistered offering of securities that are sold only to an investor or a small group of investors. It can be accomplished directly between the issuer and the investor(s) or through an investment bank.

Probability A number between 0 and 1 describing the chance that a stated event will occur.

Probability density function A function with non-negative values such that probability can be described by areas under the curve graphing the function.

Probability distribution A distribution that specifies the probabilities of a random variable's possible outcomes.

Probability function A function that specifies the probability that the random variable takes on a specific value.

Producer price index Reflects the price changes experienced by domestic producers in a country.

Production function Provides the quantitative link between the levels of output that the economy can produce and the inputs used in the production process.

Productivity The amount of output produced by workers in a given period of time—for example, output per hour worked; measures the efficiency of labor.

Profession An occupational group that has specific education, expert knowledge, and a framework of practice and behavior that underpins community trust, respect, and recognition.

Profit The return that owners of a company receive for the use of their capital and the assumption of financial risk when making their investments.

Profit and loss (P&L) statement A financial statement that provides information about a company's profitability over a stated period of time. Also called the *income statement*.

Profit margin An indicator of profitability, calculated as net income divided by revenue; indicates how much of each dollar of revenues is left after all costs and expenses.

Profitability index (PI) For a simple project, the PI is the present value of a project's future cash flows divided by the initial investment.

Profitability ratios Ratios that measure a company's ability to generate profitable sales from its resources (assets).

Project sequencing To defer the decision to invest in a future project until the outcome of some or all of a current project is known. Projects are sequenced through time, so that investing in a project creates the option to invest in future projects.

Promissory note A written promise to pay a certain amount of money on demand.

Property, plant, and equipment Tangible assets that are expected to be used for more than one period in either the production or supply of goods or services, or for administrative purposes.

Prospectus The document that describes the terms of a new bond issue and helps investors perform their analysis on the issue.

Protective put An option strategy in which a long position in an asset is combined with a long position in a put.

Proxy contest Corporate takeover mechanism in which shareholders are persuaded to vote for a group seeking a controlling position on a company's board of directors.

Proxy voting A process that enables shareholders who are unable to attend a meeting to authorize another individual to vote on their behalf.

Pseudo-random numbers Numbers produced by random number generators.

Public offer See *public offering*.

Public offering An offering of securities in which any member of the public may buy the securities. Also called *public offer*.

Pull on liquidity When disbursements are paid too quickly or trade credit availability is limited, requiring companies to expend funds before they receive funds from sales that could cover the liability.

Pure discount bonds See *zero-coupon bonds*.

Pure-play method A method for estimating the beta for a company or project; it requires using a comparable company's beta and adjusting it for financial leverage differences.

Put An option that gives the holder the right to sell an underlying asset to another party at a fixed price over a specific period of time.

Put–call–forward parity The relationship among puts, calls, and forward contracts.

Put–call parity An equation expressing the equivalence (parity) of a portfolio of a call and a bond with a portfolio of a put and the underlying, which leads to the relationship between put and call prices.

Put/call ratio A technical analysis indicator that evaluates market sentiment based upon the volume of put options traded divided by the volume of call options traded for a particular financial instrument.

Put option An option that gives the holder the right to sell an underlying asset to another party at a fixed price over a specific period of time.

Putable bonds Bonds that give the bondholder the right to sell the bond back to the issuer at a predetermined price on specified dates.

Quantile A value at or below which a stated fraction of the data lies. Also called *fractile*.

Quantitative easing An expansionary monetary policy based on aggressive open market purchase operations.

Quantity equation of exchange An expression that over a given period, the amount of money used to purchase all goods and services in an economy, $M \times V$, is equal to monetary value of this output, $P \times Y$.

Quantity theory of money Asserts that total spending (in money terms) is proportional to the quantity of money.

Quartiles Quantiles that divide a distribution into four equal parts.

Quasi-fixed cost A cost that stays the same over a range of production but can change to another constant level when production moves outside of that range.

Quasi-government bonds A bond issued by an entity that is either owned or sponsored by a national government. Also called *agency bond*.

Quick assets Assets that can be most readily converted to cash (e.g., cash, short-term marketable investments, receivables).

Quick ratio A stringent measure of liquidity that indicates a company's ability to satisfy current liabilities with its most liquid assets, calculated as (cash + short-term marketable investments + receivables) divided by current liabilities.

Quintiles Quantiles that divide a distribution into five equal parts.

Quota rents Profits that foreign producers can earn by raising the price of their goods higher than they would without a quota.

Quotas Government policies that restrict the quantity of a good that can be imported into a country, generally for a specified period of time.

Quote-driven market A market in which dealers acting as principals facilitate trading.

Quoted interest rate A quoted interest rate that does not account for compounding within the year. Also called *stated annual interest rate*.

Quoted margin The specified yield spread over the reference rate, used to compensate an investor for the difference in the credit risk of the issuer and that implied by the reference rate.

Random number An observation drawn from a uniform distribution.

Random number generator An algorithm that produces uniformly distributed random numbers between 0 and 1.

Random variable A quantity whose future outcomes are uncertain.

Range The difference between the maximum and minimum values in a dataset.

Ratio scales A measurement scale that has all the characteristics of interval measurement scales as well as a true zero point as the origin.

Real GDP The value of goods and services produced, measured at base year prices.

Real income Income adjusted for the effect of inflation on the purchasing power of money. Also known as the *purchasing power of income*. If income remains constant and a good's price falls, real income is said to rise, even though the number of monetary units (e.g., dollars) remains unchanged.

Real interest rate Nominal interest rate minus the expected rate of inflation.

Real risk-free interest rate The single-period interest rate for a completely risk-free security if no inflation were expected.

Realizable (settlement) value With reference to assets, the amount of cash or cash equivalents that could currently be obtained by selling the asset in an orderly disposal; with reference to liabilities, the undiscounted amount of cash or cash equivalents expected to be paid to satisfy the liabilities in the normal course of business.

Rebalancing Adjusting the weights of the constituent securities in an index.

Rebalancing policy The set of rules that guide the process of restoring a portfolio's asset class weights to those specified in the strategic asset allocation.

Recession A period during which real GDP decreases (i.e., negative growth) for at least two successive quarters, or a period of significant decline in total output, income, employment, and sales usually lasting from six months to a year.

Recognition lag The lag in government response to an economic problem resulting from the delay in confirming a change in the state of the economy.

Recourse loan Loan in which the lender has a claim against the borrower for any shortfall between the outstanding mortgage balance and the proceeds received from the sale of the property.

Redemption yield See *yield to maturity.*

Redemptions Withdrawals of funds by investors, as allowed by the notice period and other terms in the partnership agreement.

Refinancing rate A type of central bank policy rate.

Registered bonds Bonds for which ownership is recorded by either name or serial number.

Relative/best-in-class screening An ESG investment style that focuses on sectors, companies, or projects selected for ESG performance relative to industry peers.

Relative dispersion The amount of dispersion relative to a reference value or benchmark.

Relative frequency With reference to an interval of grouped data, the number of observations in the interval divided by the total number of observations in the sample.

Relative price The price of a specific good or service in comparison with those of other goods and services.

Relative strength analysis A comparison of the performance of one asset with the performance of another asset or a benchmark based on changes in the ratio of the securities' respective prices over time.

Relative strength index A technical analysis momentum oscillator that compares a security's gains with its losses over a set period.

Renewable resources Resources that can be replenished, such as a forest.

Rent Payment for the use of property.

Reorganization Agreements made by a company in bankruptcy under which a company's capital structure is altered and/or alternative arrangements are made for debt repayment; US Chapter 11 bankruptcy. The company emerges from bankruptcy as a going concern.

Replication The creation of an asset or portfolio from another asset, portfolio, and/or derivative.

Repo A form of collateralized loan involving the sale of a security with a simultaneous agreement by the seller to buy the same security back from the purchaser at an agreed-on price and future date. The party who sells the security at the inception of the repurchase agreement and buys it back at maturity is borrowing money from the other party, and the security sold and subsequently repurchased represents the collateral.

Repo margin The difference between the market value of the security used as collateral and the value of the loan. Also called *haircut.*

Repo rate The interest rate on a repurchase agreement.

Repurchase agreement A form of collateralized loan involving the sale of a security with a simultaneous agreement by the seller to buy the same security back from the purchaser at an agreed-on price and future date. The party who sells the security at the inception of the repurchase agreement and buys it back at maturity is borrowing money from the other party, and the security sold and subsequently repurchased represents the collateral.

Repurchase date The date when the party who sold the security at the inception of a repurchase agreement buys the security back from the cash lending counterparty.

Repurchase price The price at which the party who sold the security at the inception of the repurchase agreement buys the security back from the cash lending counterparty.

Required margin The yield spread over, or under, the reference rate such that an FRN is priced at par value on a rate reset date.

Required rate of return See *market discount rate.*

Required yield See *market discount rate.*

Required yield spread The difference between the yield-to-maturity on a new bond and the benchmark rate; additional compensation required by investors for the difference in risk and tax status of a bond relative to a government bond. Sometimes called the *spread over the benchmark.*

Reserve accounts Form of internal credit enhancement that relies on creating accounts and depositing in these accounts cash that can be used to absorb losses. Also called *reserve funds.*

Reserve funds See *reserve accounts.*

Reserve requirement The requirement for banks to hold reserves in proportion to the size of deposits.

Resistance In technical analysis, a price range in which selling activity is sufficient to stop the rise in the price of a security.

Responsible investing The practice of identifying companies that can efficiently manage their financial, environmental, and human capital resources to generate attractive long-term profitability; often synonymous with *sustainable investing.*

Restricted payments A bond covenant meant to protect creditors by limiting how much cash can be paid out to shareholders over time.

Retracement In technical analysis, a reversal in the movement of a security's price such that it is counter to the prevailing longerterm price trend.

Return-generating model A model that can provide an estimate of the expected return of a security given certain parameters and estimates of the values of the independent variables in the model.

Return on assets (ROA) A profitability ratio calculated as net income divided by average total assets; indicates a company's net profit generated per dollar invested in total assets.

Return on equity (ROE) A profitability ratio calculated as net income divided by average shareholders' equity.

Return on sales An indicator of profitability, calculated as net income divided by revenue; indicates how much of each dollar of revenues is left after all costs and expenses. Also referred to as *net profit margin.*

Return on total capital A profitability ratio calculated as EBIT divided by the sum of short- and long-term debt and equity.

Revaluation model Under IFRS, the process of valuing long-lived assets at fair value, rather than at cost less accumulated depreciation. Any resulting profit or loss is either reported on the income statement and/or through equity under revaluation surplus.

Revenue The amount charged for the delivery of goods or services in the ordinary activities of a business over a stated period; the inflows of economic resources to a company over a stated period.

Reversal patterns A type of pattern used in technical analysis to predict the end of a trend and a change in direction of the security's price.

Reverse repo A repurchase agreement viewed from the perspective of the cash lending counterparty.

Reverse repurchase agreement A repurchase agreement viewed from the perspective of the cash lending counterparty.

Reverse stock split A reduction in the number of shares outstanding with a corresponding increase in share price, but no change to the company's underlying fundamentals.

Revolving credit agreements The strongest form of short-term bank borrowing facilities; they are in effect for multiple years (e.g., 3–5 years) and may have optional medium-term loan features.

Rho The sensitivity of the option price to the risk-free rate.

Ricardian equivalence An economic theory that implies that it makes no difference whether a government finances a deficit by increasing taxes or issuing debt.

Risk Exposure to uncertainty. The chance of a loss or adverse outcome as a result of an action, inaction, or external event.

Risk averse The assumption that an investor will choose the least risky alternative.

Risk aversion The degree of an investor's inability and unwillingness to take risk.

Risk budgeting The establishment of objectives for individuals, groups, or divisions of an organization that takes into account the allocation of an acceptable level of risk.

Risk exposure The state of being exposed or vulnerable to a risk. The extent to which an organization is sensitive to underlying risks.

Risk factor/risk premium investing An ESG investment style that focuses on the inclusion of ESG information in the analysis of systematic risks as, for example, in smart beta and factor investment strategies (similar to size, value, momentum, and growth strategies).

Risk governance The top-down process and guidance that directs risk management activities to align with and support the overall enterprise.

Risk management The process of identifying the level of risk an organization wants, measuring the level of risk the organization currently has, taking actions that bring the actual level of risk to the desired level of risk, and monitoring the new actual level of risk so that it continues to be aligned with the desired level of risk.

Risk management framework The infrastructure, process, and analytics needed to support effective risk management in an organization.

Risk-neutral pricing Sometimes said of derivatives pricing, uses the fact that arbitrage opportunities guarantee that a risk-free portfolio consisting of the underlying and the derivative must earn the risk-free rate.

Risk-neutral probabilities Weights that are used to compute a binomial option price. They are the probabilities that would apply if a risk-neutral investor valued an option.

Risk premium An extra return expected by investors for bearing some specified risk.

Risk shifting Actions to change the distribution of risk outcomes.

Risk tolerance The amount of risk an investor is willing and able to bear to achieve an investment goal.

Risk transfer Actions to pass on a risk to another party, often, but not always, in the form of an insurance policy.

Robo-adviser A machine-based analytical tool or service that provides technology-driven investment solutions through online platforms.

Robust The quality of being relatively unaffected by a violation of assumptions.

Rule of 72 The principle that the approximate number of years necessary for an investment to double is 72 divided by the stated interest rate.

Running yield See *current yield*.

Safety-first rules Rules for portfolio selection that focus on the risk that portfolio value will fall below some minimum acceptable level over some time horizon.

Safety stock A level of inventory beyond anticipated needs that provides a cushion in the event that it takes longer to replenish inventory than expected or in the case of greater than expected demand.

Sales Generally, a synonym for revenue; "sales" is generally understood to refer to the sale of goods, whereas "revenue" is understood to include the sale of goods or services.

Sales risk Uncertainty with respect to the quantity of goods and services that a company is able to sell and the price it is able to achieve; the risk related to the uncertainty of revenues.

Sales-type leases Under US GAAP, a type of finance lease, from a lessor perspective, where the present value of the lease payments (lease receivable) exceeds the carrying value of the leased asset. The revenues earned by the lessor both a selling profit at inception and financing (interest) revenues.

Sample A subset of a population.

Sample excess kurtosis A sample measure of the degree of a distribution's kurtosis in excess of the normal distribution's kurtosis.

Sample kurtosis A sample measure of the degree of a distribution's peakedness.

Sample mean The sum of the sample observations, divided by the sample size.

Sample selection bias Bias introduced by systematically excluding some members of the population according to a particular attribute—for example, the bias introduced when data availability leads to certain observations being excluded from the analysis.

Sample skewness A sample measure of degree of asymmetry of a distribution.

Sample standard deviation The positive square root of the sample variance.

Sample statistic A quantity computed from or used to describe a sample.

Sample variance A sample measure of the degree of dispersion of a distribution, calculated by dividing the sum of the squared deviations from the sample mean by the sample size minus 1.

Sampling The process of obtaining a sample.

Sampling distribution The distribution of all distinct possible values that a statistic can assume when computed from samples of the same size randomly drawn from the same population.

Sampling error The difference between the observed value of a statistic and the quantity it is intended to estimate.

Sampling plan The set of rules used to select a sample.

Say on pay A process whereby shareholders may vote on executive remuneration (compensation) matters.

Say's law Named for French economist J.B. Say: All that is produced will be sold because supply creates its own demand.

Scatter plot A two-dimensional plot of pairs of observations on two data series.

Scenario analysis Analysis that shows the changes in key financial quantities that result from given (economic) events, such as the loss of customers, the loss of a supply source, or a catastrophic event; a risk management technique involving examination of the performance of a portfolio under specified situations. Closely related to stress testing.

Screening The application of a set of criteria to reduce a set of potential investments to a smaller set having certain desired characteristics.

Seasoned offering An offering in which an issuer sells additional units of a previously issued security.

Second-degree price discrimination When the monopolist charges different per-unit prices using the quantity purchased as an indicator of how highly the customer values the product.

Second lien A secured interest in the pledged assets that ranks below first lien debt in both collateral protection and priority of payment.

Secondary bond markets Markets in which existing bonds are traded among investors.

Secondary market The market where securities are traded among investors.

Secondary precedence rules Rules that determine how to rank orders placed at the same time.

Sector A group of related industries.

Sector indexes Indexes that represent and track different economic sectors—such as consumer goods, energy, finance, health care, and technology—on either a national, regional, or global basis.

Secured bonds Bonds secured by assets or financial guarantees pledged to ensure debt repayment in case of default.

Secured debt Debt in which the debtholder has a direct claim—a pledge from the issuer—on certain assets and their associated cash flows.

Securitization A process that involves moving assets into a special legal entity, which then uses the assets as guarantees to secure a bond issue.

Securitized assets Assets that are typically used to create asset-backed bonds; for example, when a bank securitizes a pool of loans, the loans are said to be securitized.

Security characteristic line A plot of the excess return of a security on the excess return of the market.

Security market index A portfolio of securities representing a given security market, market segment, or asset class.

Security market line (SML) The graph of the capital asset pricing model.

Security selection The process of selecting individual securities; typically, security selection has the objective of generating superior risk-adjusted returns relative to a portfolio's benchmark.

Self-investment limits With respect to investment limitations applying to pension plans, restrictions on the percentage of assets that can be invested in securities issued by the pension plan sponsor.

Sell-side firm A broker/dealer that sells securities and provides independent investment research and recommendations to their clients (i.e., buy-side firms).

Semi-strong-form efficient market A market in which security prices reflect all publicly known and available information.

Semiannual bond basis yield An annual rate having a periodicity of two; also known as a *semiannual bond equivalent yield*.

Semiannual bond equivalent yield See *semiannual bond basis yield*.

Semideviation The positive square root of semivariance (sometimes called *semistandard deviation*).

Semilogarithmic Describes a scale constructed so that equal intervals on the vertical scale represent equal rates of change, and equal intervals on the horizontal scale represent equal amounts of change.

Semivariance The average squared deviation below the mean.

Seniority ranking Priority of payment of various debt obligations.

Sensitivity analysis Analysis that shows the range of possible outcomes as specific assumptions are changed.

Separately managed account (SMA) An investment portfolio managed exclusively for the benefit of an individual or institution.

Serial maturity structure Structure for a bond issue in which the maturity dates are spread out during the bond's life; a stated number of bonds mature and are paid off each year before final maturity.

Settlement The process that occurs after a trade is completed, the securities are passed to the buyer, and payment is received by the seller.

Settlement date Date when the buyer makes cash payment and the seller delivers the security.

Settlement price The official price, designated by the clearinghouse, from which daily gains and losses will be determined and marked to market.

Share repurchase A transaction in which a company buys back its own shares. Unlike stock dividends and stock splits, share repurchases use corporate cash.

Shareholder activism Strategies used by shareholders to attempt to compel a company to act in a desired manner.

Shareholder engagement The process whereby companies engage with their shareholders.

Shareholders' equity Assets less liabilities; the residual interest in the assets after subtracting the liabilities.

Sharpe ratio The average return in excess of the risk-free rate divided by the standard deviation of return; a measure of the average excess return earned per unit of standard deviation of return.

Shelf registration Type of public offering that allows the issuer to file a single, all-encompassing offering circular that covers a series of bond issues.

Short The seller of an asset or derivative contract. Also refers to the position of being short an asset or derivative contract.

Short position A position in an asset or contract in which one has sold an asset one does not own, or in which a right under a contract can be exercised against oneself.

Short-run average total cost The curve describing average total cost when some costs are considered fixed.

Short selling A transaction in which borrowed securities are sold with the intention to repurchase them at a lower price at a later date and return them to the lender.

Shortfall risk The risk that portfolio value will fall below some minimum acceptable level over some time horizon.

Shutdown point The point at which average revenue is equal to the firm's average variable cost.

Simple interest The interest earned each period on the original investment; interest calculated on the principal only.

Simple random sample A subset of a larger population created in such a way that each element of the population has an equal probability of being selected to the subset.

Simple random sampling The procedure of drawing a sample to satisfy the definition of a simple random sample.

Simple yield The sum of the coupon payments plus the straight-line amortized share of the gain or loss, divided by the flat price.

Simulation Computer-generated sensitivity or scenario analysis that is based on probability models for the factors that drive outcomes.

Simulation trial A complete pass through the steps of a simulation.

Single-step format With respect to the format of the income statement, a format that does not subtotal for gross profit (revenue minus cost of goods sold).

Sinking fund arrangement Provision that reduces the credit risk of a bond issue by requiring the issuer to retire a portion of the bond's principal outstanding each year.

Situational influences External factors, such as environmental or cultural elements, that shape our behavior.

Skewed Not symmetrical.

Skewness A quantitative measure of skew (lack of symmetry); a synonym of skew.

Small country A country that is a price taker in the world market for a product and cannot influence the world market price.

Smart beta Involves the use of simple, transparent, rules-based strategies as a basis for investment decisions.

Smart contract A computer program that is designed to self-execute on the basis of pre-specified terms and conditions agreed to by parties to a contract.

Socially responsible investing An investment approach that excludes investments in companies or industries that deviate from an organization's beliefs and sometimes includes investments with favorable environmental or social profiles.

Solvency With respect to financial statement analysis, the ability of a company to fulfill its long-term obligations.

Solvency ratios Ratios that measure a company's ability to meet its long-term obligations.

Solvency risk The risk that an organization does not survive or succeed because it runs out of cash, even though it might otherwise be solvent.

Sovereign A bond issued by a national government.

Sovereign bond A bond issued by a national government.

Sovereign yield spread An estimate of the country spread (country equity premium) for a developing nation that is based on a comparison of bonds yields in country being analyzed and a developed country. The sovereign yield spread is the difference between a government bond yield in the country being analyzed, denominated in the currency of the developed country, and the Treasury bond yield on a similar maturity bond in the developed country.

Spearman rank correlation coefficient A measure of correlation applied to ranked data.

Special dividend A dividend paid by a company that does not pay dividends on a regular schedule, or a dividend that supplements regular cash dividends with an extra payment.

Special purpose entity A non-operating entity created to carry out a specified purpose, such as leasing assets or securitizing receivables; can be a corporation, partnership, trust, limited liability, or partnership formed to facilitate a specific type of business activity. Also called *special purpose vehicle* or *variable interest entity.*

Special purpose vehicle See *special purpose entity.*

Specific identification method An inventory accounting method that identifies which specific inventory items were sold and which remained in inventory to be carried over to later periods.

Speculative demand for money The demand to hold speculative money balances based on the potential opportunities or risks that are inherent in other financial instruments. Also called *portfolio demand for money.*

Speculative money balances Monies held in anticipation that other assets will decline in value.

Split coupon bond See *deferred coupon bond.*

Sponsored A type of depository receipt in which the foreign company whose shares are held by the depository has a direct involvement in the issuance of the receipts.

Spot curve A sequence of yields-to-maturity on zero-coupon bonds. Sometimes called *zero* or *strip curve* because coupon payments are "stripped" off of the bonds.

Spot markets Markets in which assets are traded for immediate delivery.

Spot prices The price of an asset for immediately delivery.

Spot rates A sequence of market discount rates that correspond to the cash flow dates; yields-to-maturity on zero-coupon bonds maturing at the date of each cash flow.

Spread In general, the difference in yield between different fixed income securities. Often used to refer to the difference between the yield-to-maturity and the benchmark.

Spread over the benchmark See *required yield spread.*

Spread risk Bond price risk arising from changes in the yield spread on credit-risky bonds; reflects changes in the market's assessment and/or pricing of credit migration (or downgrade) risk and market liquidity risk.

Spurious correlation A correlation that misleadingly points toward associations between variables.

Stackelberg model A prominent model of strategic decision making in which firms are assumed to make their decisions sequentially.

Stagflation When a high inflation rate is combined with a high level of unemployment and a slowdown of the economy.

Staggered boards Election process whereby directors are typically divided into multiple classes that are elected separately in consecutive years—that is, one class every year.

Stakeholder management The identification, prioritization, and understanding of the interests of stakeholder groups, and managing the company's relationships with these groups.

Stakeholders Individuals or groups of individuals who may be affected either directly or indirectly by a decision and thus have an interest, or stake, in the decision.

Standard deviation The positive square root of the variance; a measure of dispersion in the same units as the original data.

Standard normal distribution The normal density with mean (μ) equal to 0 and standard deviation (σ) equal to 1.

Standardizing A transformation that involves subtracting the mean and dividing the result by the standard deviation.

Standards of conduct Behaviors required by a group; established benchmarks that clarify or enhance a group's code of ethics.

Standing limit orders A limit order at a price below market and which therefore is waiting to trade.

Stated annual interest rate A quoted interest rate that does not account for compounding within the year. Also called *quoted interest rate.*

Statement of changes in equity (statement of owners' equity) A financial statement that reconciles the beginning-of-period and end-of-period balance sheet values of shareholders' equity; provides information about all factors affecting shareholders' equity. Also called *statement of owners' equity.*

Statement of financial condition The financial statement that presents an entity's current financial position by disclosing resources the entity controls (its assets) and the claims on those resources (its liabilities and equity claims), as of a particular point in time (the date of the balance sheet).

Statement of financial position The financial statement that presents an entity's current financial position by disclosing resources the entity controls (its assets) and the claims on those resources (its liabilities and equity claims), as of a particular point in time (the date of the balance sheet).

Statement of operations A financial statement that provides information about a company's profitability over a stated period of time.

Statistic A quantity computed from or used to describe a sample of data.

Statistical inference Making forecasts, estimates, or judgments about a larger group from a smaller group actually observed; using a sample statistic to infer the value of an unknown population parameter.

Statistically significant A result indicating that the null hypothesis can be rejected; with reference to an estimated regression coefficient, frequently understood to mean a result indicating that the corresponding population regression coefficient is different from 0.

Statutory voting A common method of voting where each share represents one vote.

Step-up coupon bond Bond for which the coupon, which may be fixed or floating, increases by specified margins at specified dates.

Stock dividend A type of dividend in which a company distributes additional shares of its common stock to shareholders instead of cash.

Stock-out losses Profits lost from not having sufficient inventory on hand to satisfy demand.

Stock split An increase in the number of shares outstanding with a consequent decrease in share price, but no change to the company's underlying fundamentals.

Stop-loss order See *stop order*.

Stop order An order in which a trader has specified a stop price condition. Also called *stop-loss order*.

Store of value The quality of tending to preserve value.

Store of wealth Goods that depend on the fact that they do not perish physically over time, and on the belief that others would always value the good.

Straight-line method A depreciation method that allocates evenly the cost of a long-lived asset less its estimated residual value over the estimated useful life of the asset.

Straight voting A shareholder voting process in which shareholders receive one vote for each share owned.

Strategic analysis Analysis of the competitive environment with an emphasis on the implications of the environment for corporate strategy.

Strategic asset allocation The set of exposures to IPS-permissible asset classes that is expected to achieve the client's long-term objectives given the client's investment constraints.

Strategic groups Groups sharing distinct business models or catering to specific market segments in an industry.

Street convention Yield measure that neglects weekends and holidays; the internal rate of return on cash flows assuming payments are made on the scheduled dates, even when the scheduled date falls on a weekend or holiday.

Stress testing A specific type of scenario analysis that estimates losses in rare and extremely unfavorable combinations of events or scenarios.

Strong-form efficient market A market in which security prices reflect all public and private information.

Structural (or cyclically adjusted) budget deficit The deficit that would exist if the economy was at full employment (or full potential output).

Structural subordination Arises in a holding company structure when the debt of operating subsidiaries is serviced by the cash flow and assets of the subsidiaries before funds can be passed to the holding company to service debt at the parent level.

Structured financial instruments Financial instruments that share the common attribute of repackaging risks. Structured financial instruments include asset-backed securities, collateralized debt obligations, and other structured financial instruments such as capital protected, yield enhancement, participation and leveraged instruments.

Subjective probability A probability drawing on personal or subjective judgment.

Subordinated debt A class of unsecured debt that ranks below a firm's senior unsecured obligations.

Subordination Form of internal credit enhancement that relies on creating more than one bond tranche and ordering the claim priorities for ownership or interest in an asset between the tranches. The ordering of the claim priorities is called a senior/subordinated structure, where the tranches of highest seniority are called senior followed by subordinated or junior tranches. Also called *credit tranching*.

Substitutes Said of two goods or services such that if the price of one increases the demand for the other tends to increase, holding all other things equal (e.g., butter and margarine).

Sunk cost A cost that has already been incurred.

Supervised learning A machine learning approach that makes use of labeled training data.

Supply shock A typically unexpected disturbance to supply.

Support In technical analysis, a price range in which buying activity is sufficient to stop the decline in the price of a security.

Support tranche A class or tranche in a CMO that protects the PAC tranche from prepayment risk.

Supranational bonds A bond issued by a supranational agency such as the World Bank.

Surety bond Form of external credit enhancement whereby a rated and regulated insurance company guarantees to reimburse bondholders for any losses incurred up to a maximum amount if the issuer defaults.

Survey approach An estimate of the equity risk premium that is based upon estimates provided by a panel of finance experts.

Survivorship bias The bias resulting from a test design that fails to account for companies that have gone bankrupt, merged, or are otherwise no longer reported in a database.

Sustainable growth rate The rate of dividend (and earnings) growth that can be sustained over time for a given level of return on equity, keeping the capital structure constant and without issuing additional common stock.

Sustainable investing The practice of identifying companies that can efficiently manage their financial, environmental, and human capital resources to generate attractive long-term profitability; often synonymous with *responsible investing*.

Sustainable rate of economic growth The rate of increase in the economy's productive capacity or potential GDP.

Swap contract An agreement between two parties to exchange a series of future cash flows.

Syndicated loans Loans from a group of lenders to a single borrower.

Syndicated offering A bond issue that is underwritten by a group of investment banks.

Systematic risk Risk that affects the entire market or economy; it cannot be avoided and is inherent in the overall market. Systematic risk is also known as non-diversifiable or market risk.

Systematic sampling A procedure of selecting every *k*th member until reaching a sample of the desired size. The sample that results from this procedure should be approximately random.

***t*-Test** A hypothesis test using a statistic (*t*-statistic) that follows a *t*-distribution.

Tactical asset allocation The decision to deliberately deviate from the strategic asset allocation in an attempt to add value based on forecasts of the near-term relative performance of asset classes.

Target balance A minimum level of cash to be held available—estimated in advance and adjusted for known funds transfers, seasonality, or other factors.

Target capital structure A company's chosen proportions of debt and equity.

Target independent A bank's ability to determine the definition of inflation that they target, the rate of inflation that they target, and the horizon over which the target is to be achieved.

Target semideviation The positive square root of target semivariance.

Target semivariance The average squared deviation below a target value.

Tariffs Taxes that a government levies on imported goods.

Tax base The amount at which an asset or liability is valued for tax purposes.

Tax expense An aggregate of an entity's income tax payable (or recoverable in the case of a tax benefit) and any changes in deferred tax assets and liabilities. It is essentially the income tax payable or recoverable if these had been determined based on accounting profit rather than taxable income.

Tax loss carry forward A taxable loss in the current period that may be used to reduce future taxable income.

Taxable income The portion of an entity's income that is subject to income taxes under the tax laws of its jurisdiction.

Taxable temporary differences Temporary differences that result in a taxable amount in a future period when determining the taxable profit as the balance sheet item is recovered or settled.

Technical analysis A form of security analysis that uses price and volume data, which is often displayed graphically, in decision making.

Technology The process a company uses to transform inputs into outputs.

Tender offer Corporate takeover mechanism which involves shareholders selling their interests directly to the group seeking to gain control.

Tenor The time-to-maturity for a bond or derivative contract. Also called *term to maturity*.

Term maturity structure Structure for a bond issue in which the bond's notional principal is paid off in a lump sum at maturity.

Term structure See *maturity structure*.

Term structure of credit spreads The relationship between the spreads over the "risk-free" (or benchmark) rates and times-to-maturity.

Term structure of yield volatility The relationship between the volatility of bond yields-to-maturity and times-to-maturity.

Terminal stock value The expected value of a share at the end of the investment horizon—in effect, the expected selling price. Also called *terminal value*.

Terminal value The expected value of a share at the end of the investment horizon—in effect, the expected selling price.

Terms of trade The ratio of the price of exports to the price of imports, representing those prices by export and import price indexes, respectively.

Text analytics The use of computer programs to analyze and derive meaning from typically large, unstructured text- or voice-based datasets.

Thematic investment An ESG investing style that focuses on investing in themes or assets specifically relating to ESG factors, such as clean energy, green technology, or sustainable agriculture.

Third-degree price discrimination When the monopolist segregates customers into groups based on demographic or other characteristics and offers different pricing to each group.

Time-period bias The possibility that when we use a time-series sample, our statistical conclusion may be sensitive to the starting and ending dates of the sample.

Time-series data Observations of a variable over time.

Time tranching The creation of classes or tranches in an ABS/MBS that possess different (expected) maturities.

Time value The difference between the market price of the option and its intrinsic value.

Time value decay Said of an option when, at expiration, no time value remains and the option is worth only its exercise value.

Time value of money The principles governing equivalence relationships between cash flows with different dates.

Time-weighted rate of return The compound rate of growth of one unit of currency invested in a portfolio during a stated measurement period; a measure of investment performance that is not sensitive to the timing and amount of withdrawals or additions to the portfolio.

Tokenization The process of representing ownership rights to physical assets on a blockchain or distributed ledger.

Top-down analysis An investment selection approach that begins with consideration of macroeconomic conditions and then evaluates markets and industries based upon such conditions.

Total comprehensive income The change in equity during a period resulting from transaction and other events, other than those changes resulting from transactions with owners in their capacity as owners.

Total cost The summation of all costs, for which costs are classified as fixed or variable.

Total factor productivity A scale factor that reflects the portion of growth that is not accounted for by explicit factor inputs (e.g. capital and labor).

Total fixed cost The summation of all expenses that do not change as the level of production varies.

Total invested capital The sum of market value of common equity, book value of preferred equity, and face value of debt.

Total probability rule A rule explaining the unconditional probability of an event in terms of probabilities of the event conditional on mutually exclusive and exhaustive scenarios.

Total probability rule for expected value A rule explaining the expected value of a random variable in terms of expected values of the random variable conditional on mutually exclusive and exhaustive scenarios.

Total return Measures the price appreciation, or percentage change in price of the securities in an index or portfolio, plus any income received over the period.

Total return index An index that reflects the price appreciation or percentage change in price of the constituent securities plus any income received since inception.

Total return swap A swap in which one party agrees to pay the total return on a security. Often used as a credit derivative, in which the underlying is a bond.

Total variable cost The summation of all variable expenses.

Tracking error The standard deviation of the differences between a portfolio's returns and its benchmark's returns; a synonym of active risk.

Tracking risk The standard deviation of the differences between a portfolio's returns and its benchmarks returns. Also called *tracking error.*

Trade creation When regional integration results in the replacement of higher cost domestic production by lower cost imports from other members.

Trade credit A spontaneous form of credit in which a purchaser of the goods or service is financing its purchase by delaying the date on which payment is made.

Trade diversion When regional integration results in lower-cost imports from non-member countries being replaced with higher-cost imports from members.

Trade payables Amounts that a business owes to its vendors for goods and services that were purchased from them but which have not yet been paid.

Trade protection Government policies that impose restrictions on trade, such as tariffs and quotas.

Trade surplus (deficit) When the value of exports is greater (less) than the value of imports.

Trading securities Under US GAAP, a category of debt securities held by a company with the intent to trade them. Also called *held-for-trading securities.*

Traditional investment markets Markets for traditional investments, which include all publicly traded debts and equities and shares in pooled investment vehicles that hold publicly traded debts and/or equities.

Transactions money balances Money balances that are held to finance transactions.

Transactions motive In the context of inventory management, the need for inventory as part of the routine production–sales cycle.

Transfer payments Welfare payments made through the social security system that exist to provide a basic minimum level of income for low-income households.

Transparency Said of something (e.g., a market) in which information is fully disclosed to the public and/or regulators.

Treasury Inflation-Protected Securities A bond issued by the United States Treasury Department that is designed to protect the investor from inflation by adjusting the principal of the bond for changes in inflation.

Treasury stock method A method for accounting for the effect of options (and warrants) on earnings per share (EPS) that specifies what EPS would have been if the options and warrants had been exercised and the company had used the proceeds to repurchase common stock.

Tree diagram A diagram with branches emanating from nodes representing either mutually exclusive chance events or mutually exclusive decisions.

Trend A long-term pattern of movement in a particular direction.

Treynor ratio A measure of risk-adjusted performance that relates a portfolio's excess returns to the portfolio's beta.

Triangle patterns In technical analysis, a continuation chart pattern that forms as the range between high and low prices narrows, visually forming a triangle.

Trimmed mean A mean computed after excluding a stated small percentage of the lowest and highest observations.

TRIN A flow of funds indicator applied to a broad stock market index to measure the relative extent to which money is moving into or out of rising and declining stocks.

Triple bottoms In technical analysis, a reversal pattern that is formed when the price forms three troughs at roughly the same price level; used to predict a change from a downtrend to an uptrend.

Triple tops In technical analysis, a reversal pattern that is formed when the price forms three peaks at roughly the same price level; used to predict a change from an uptrend to a downtrend.

Trough The lowest point of a business cycle.

True yield The internal rate of return on cash flows using the actual calendar including weekends and bank holidays.

Trust deed The governing legal credit agreement, typically incorporated by reference in the prospectus. Also called *bond indenture.*

Trust receipt arrangement The use of inventory as collateral for a loan. The inventory is segregated and held in trust, and the proceeds of any sale must be remitted to the lender immediately.

Turn-of-the-year effect Calendar anomaly that stock market returns in January are significantly higher compared to the rest of the months of the year, with most of the abnormal returns reported during the first five trading days in January.

Two-fund separation theorem The theory that all investors regardless of taste, risk preferences, and initial wealth will hold a combination of two portfolios or funds: a risk-free asset and an optimal portfolio of risky assets.

Two-sided hypothesis test A test in which the null hypothesis is rejected in favor of the alternative hypothesis if the evidence indicates that the population parameter is either smaller or larger than a hypothesized value.

Two-tailed hypothesis test A test in which the null hypothesis is rejected in favor of the alternative hypothesis if the evidence indicates that the population parameter is either smaller or larger than a hypothesized value.

Two-week repo rate The interest rate on a two-week repurchase agreement; may be used as a policy rate by a central bank.

Type I error The error of rejecting a true null hypothesis.

Type II error The error of not rejecting a false null hypothesis.

Unanticipated (unexpected) inflation The component of inflation that is a surprise.

Unconditional probability The probability of an event *not* conditioned on another event.

Underemployed A person who has a job but has the qualifications to work a significantly higher-paying job.

Underlying An asset that trades in a market in which buyers and sellers meet, decide on a price, and the seller then delivers the asset to the buyer and receives payment. The underlying is the asset or other derivative on which a particular derivative is based. The market for the underlying is also referred to as the *spot market*.

Underwriter A firm, usually an investment bank, that takes the risk of buying the newly issued securities from the issuer, and then reselling them to investors or to dealers, thus guaranteeing the sale of the securities at the offering price negotiated with the issuer.

Underwritten offering A type of securities issue mechanism in which the investment bank guarantees the sale of the securities at an offering price that is negotiated with the issuer. Also known as *firm commitment offering*.

Unearned revenue A liability account for money that has been collected for goods or services that have not yet been delivered; payment received in advance of providing a good or service. Also called *deferred revenue* or *deferred income*.

Unemployed People who are actively seeking employment but are currently without a job.

Unemployment rate The ratio of unemployed to the labor force.

Unexpected inflation The component of inflation that is a surprise.

Unit elastic An elasticity with a magnitude of negative one. Also called *unitary elastic*.

Unit labor cost The average labor cost to produce one unit of output.

Unit normal distribution The normal density with mean (μ) equal to 0 and standard deviation (σ) equal to 1.

Units-of-production method A depreciation method that allocates the cost of a long-lived asset based on actual usage during the period.

Univariate distribution A distribution that specifies the probabilities for a single random variable.

Universal owners Long-term investors, such as pension funds, that have significant assets invested in globally diversified portfolios.

Unlimited funds An unlimited funds environment assumes that the company can raise the funds it wants for all profitable projects simply by paying the required rate of return.

Unsecured debt Debt which gives the debtholder only a general claim on an issuer's assets and cash flow.

Unsponsored A type of depository receipt in which the foreign company whose shares are held by the depository has no involvement in the issuance of the receipts.

Unsupervised learning A machine learning approach that does not make use of labeled training data.

Up transition probability The probability that an asset's value moves up.

Validity instructions Instructions which indicate when the order may be filled.

Valuation allowance A reserve created against deferred tax assets, based on the likelihood of realizing the deferred tax assets in future accounting periods.

Valuation ratios Ratios that measure the quantity of an asset or flow (e.g., earnings) in relation to the price associated with a specified claim (e.g., a share or ownership of the enterprise).

Value at risk (VaR) A money measure of the minimum value of losses expected during a specified time period at a given level of probability.

Value investors With reference to equity investors, investors who are focused on paying a relatively low share price in relation to earnings or assets per share.

VaR See *value at risk*.

Variable costs Costs that fluctuate with the level of production and sales.

Variance The expected value (the probability-weighted average) of squared deviations from a random variable's expected value.

Variation margin Additional margin that must be deposited in an amount sufficient to bring the balance up to the initial margin requirement.

Veblen goods Goods that increase in desirability with increasing price.

Vega A measure of the sensitivity of an option's price to changes in the underlying's volatility.

Venture capital Investments that provide "seed" or startup capital, early-stage financing, or later-stage financing (including mezzanine-stage financing) to companies that are in early development stages and require additional capital for expansion or preparation for an initial public offering.

Venture capital fund A hedge fund that seeks to buy, optimize, and ultimately sell portfolio companies to generate profits. See *private equity fund*.

Vertical analysis Common-size analysis using only one reporting period or one base financial statement; for example, an income statement in which all items are stated as percentages of sales.

Vertical demand schedule Implies that some fixed quantity is demanded, regardless of price.

Volatility As used in option pricing, the standard deviation of the continuously compounded returns on the underlying asset.

Voluntarily unemployed A person voluntarily outside the labor force, such as a jobless worker refusing an available vacancy.

Voluntary export restraint A trade barrier under which the exporting country agrees to limit its exports of the good to its trading partners to a specific number of units.

Vote by proxy A mechanism that allows a designated party—such as another shareholder, a shareholder representative, or management—to vote on the shareholder's behalf.

Warehouse receipt arrangement The use of inventory as collateral for a loan; similar to a trust receipt arrangement except there is a third party (i.e., a warehouse company) that supervises the inventory.

Warrant Attached option that gives its holder the right to buy the underlying stock of the issuing company at a fixed exercise price until the expiration date.

Weak-form efficient market hypothesis The belief that security prices fully reflect all past market data, which refers to all historical price and volume trading information.

Wealth effect An increase (decrease) in household wealth increases (decreases) consumer spending out of a given level of current income.

Weighted average cost method An inventory accounting method that averages the total cost of available inventory items over the total units available for sale.

Weighted average cost of capital A weighted average of the aftertax required rates of return on a company's common stock, preferred stock, and long-term debt, where the weights are the fraction of each source of financing in the company's target capital structure.

Weighted average coupon rate Weighting the mortgage rate of each mortgage loan in the pool by the percentage of the mortgage outstanding relative to the outstanding amount of all the mortgages in the pool.

Weighted average life A measure that gives investors an indication of how long they can expect to hold the MBS before it is paid off; the convention-based average time to receipt of all principal repayments. Also called *average life*.

Weighted average maturity Weighting the remaining number of months to maturity for each mortgage loan in the pool by the amount of the outstanding mortgage balance.

Weighted mean An average in which each observation is weighted by an index of its relative importance.

Wholesale price index Reflects the price changes experienced by domestic producers in a country.

Winsorized mean A mean computed after assigning a stated percent of the lowest values equal to one specified low value, and a stated percent of the highest values equal to one specified high value.

Working capital The difference between current assets and current liabilities.

Working capital management The management of a company's short-term assets (such as inventory) and short-term liabilities (such as money owed to suppliers).

World price The price prevailing in the world market.

Yield The actual return on a debt security if it is held to maturity.

Yield duration The sensitivity of the bond price with respect to the bond's own yield-to-maturity.

Yield to maturity Annual return that an investor earns on a bond if the investor purchases the bond today and holds it until maturity. It is the discount rate that equates the present value of the bond's expected cash flows until maturity with the bond's price. Also called *yield-to-redemption* or *redemption yield*.

Yield to redemption See *yield to maturity*.

Yield-to-worst The lowest of the sequence of yields-to-call and the yield-to-maturity.

Zero-coupon bonds Bonds that do not pay interest during the bond's life. It is issued at a discount to par value and redeemed at par. Also called *pure discount bonds*.

Zero volatility spread (Z-spread) Calculates a constant yield spread over a government (or interest rate swap) spot curve.